nos Amis
TEACHER'S EDITION

french 1

HARCOURT BRACE JOVANOVICH, PUBLISHERS

Orlando   New York   Chicago   San Diego   Atlanta   Dallas

Printed in the United States of America

ISBN 0-15-381840-9

® *Registered Trademark, Harcourt Brace Jovanovich,*

PICTURE CREDITS FOR TEACHER'S MANUAL SECTION

PHOTO CREDITS All photos by Pierre Capretz except: Page T71 #4, Oscar Buitrago; T73, Patrick Courtault.

ART CREDITS Manny Haller, T62, T77, T81, T100-101, T110-111, T127, T132, T135, T137, T147, T157-158, T170. Don Crews, T64, T113, T117, T132, T161.

Contents

Introduction T1

Main Features of the Program T1

Internal Organization of the Units T4

How to Use This Program   T7

Scope and Sequence Chart

nos Amis

TEACHER'S EDITION

Introduction

This Harcourt Brace Jovanovich foreign language program is a completely new series, based in part on the A-LM® series, but greatly expanded in the areas of visuals, reading, and writing, and with a special emphasis on the foreign culture as seen in the daily lives of young people.

In creating this new program, we have incorporated suggestions from foreign language teachers in all parts of the country. We are grateful to you for talking and writing to us. We feel that, based on your suggestions and on what we have observed about general trends in foreign language teaching, we have produced a program that you and your students will profit from and enjoy.

Main Features of the Program

1. Versatile materials

Different students learn best in different ways. Some learn new material most easily when they are allowed to listen to it and repeat it. Others do best when they see it in writing. Still others respond best to visual experiences—filmstrips, photographs, and drawings. And some students need to be involved physically or emotionally with the material they are learning and to respond concretely and personally. Moreover, all students need variety in the learning experience; the same student may respond differently on different days.

Recognizing that learning styles differ, we have designed the materials of this program to be highly adaptable. You will be able to offer a variety of experiences in learning and using the foreign language, choosing materials that correspond to the learning needs of each student.

The various parts of the program are as follows:

• THE CORE PROGRAM, consisting of this Teacher's Edition, the student textbook, and the accompanying recordings. The core program is intended for every student. It provides practice in all four basic language skills: listening, speaking, reading, and writing. It also encourages cultural awareness through an abundance of photographs, drawings, realia, and cultural information.

Three strands or satellite programs accompany the core program and provide more practice in the basic language skills:

• THE LISTENING COMPREHENSION PROGRAM. This program is designed for students who want to become more proficient in listening and speaking. It consists of recordings and a student answer booklet, which is printed in the front section of the activity book (Cahier d'Activités). The complete script for the listening comprehension program appears in this Teacher's Edition, starting on page T59.

• THE READING PROGRAM. This program provides additional practice in reading and expands the students' vocabulary beyond that taught in the textbook. There are two readers. One is highly visual and primarily for fun. It supplements the core program, giving students additional reading practice on the themes of the textbook. The other reader provides more challenging reading selections and introduces new points of grammar, especially the grammar of the written language. It is intended for those students who want to go beyond the grammar in the textbook and who are ready for more difficult reading.

• THE WRITING PROGRAM. This program gives students additional practice in writing the foreign language. It consists of two workbooks: an activity book (Cahier d'Activités) and an exercise book (Cahier d'Exercices). The Cahier d'Activités includes many puzzles, games, drawings, and photographs. It gives students practice with vocabulary and structure in ways that are fun. The *Cahier d'Exercices* restates the grammar points taught in the textbook. Each grammar point is followed by extensive exercises for more practice.

In addition to the core program and the three strand programs, the series includes the following materials:

• A VISUAL SUPPORT PROGRAM, consisting of filmstrips and two kinds of posters, one set depicting specific vocabulary items, the other showing situations based on the unit themes. The filmstrips, one for each unit of the textbook, expand on the themes of the units, providing additional cultural insights and background through pictures and commentary. You can use them to introduce the theme of each unit and to provide extra practice in listening comprehension. The item posters are an excellent resource for practicing and recombining vocabulary and structure in class. The situation posters can be used to stimulate conversation on the theme of each unit.

• A TESTING PROGRAM. This consists of printed student tests, recorded listening tests, and a teacher's test manual.

2. Thematic units

There are 24 units in *Nos Amis,* the first textbook of this series. Each unit revolves around a theme — school, music, sports, going out, and so forth. The material presented on each theme is practical and useful; students will be able to make use of the vocabulary and cultural information if they ever travel or live in a French-speaking country. At the same time, the situations depicted in the units relate to students' everyday lives here and now. They will spend as much time talking about their own world as about that of the boys and girls in the book.

Because the theme for each unit is different and the material illustrating each theme so various, we have adopted a flexible design. No two units look alike. This variety, and the close correlation of form and content, should make the material fun to learn; we hope students will always be eager to find out what comes next.

In this textbook, *Nos Amis,* we show boys and girls between the ages of thirteen and sixteen. They appear individually, in groups, and with their parents or other adults, doing the things that young people everywhere do — studying, working, playing, spending time with family and friends. In choosing themes, we made sure that boys and girls were equally represented. Some units focus on boys only, some on girls only, and some are mixed. Both boys and girls are shown in active, interesting roles, sometimes doing things that contradict traditional stereotypes but that represent cultural reality nonetheless.

For a complete listing of unit themes, see the "Scope and Sequence Chart," which starts on page T172.

3. Culture as an integral part of the program

The culture — that is, the behavior, beliefs, and values — of the people in French-speaking countries is an integral part of the material of every unit. It can be seen in the experiences, attitudes, and surroundings of the young people in the book. As we prepared this series, we spent months abroad, finding and interviewing people, visiting schools and homes, and sharing many of the experiences that became the subject matter of the book. We collected books, magazines, and information about French-speaking young people and taped scenes and dialogs to use as a basis for the units. The extensive coverage of these experiences is what you find in this book and in the filmstrips. We feel that this personal experience "on location" has given the series a dimension of reality and cultural authenticity.

4. Local flavor

The young people in the series live in various areas of France, Canada, Martinique, Tunisia, Belgium, Switzerland, and the Ivory Coast. In using these materials students will become aware that French is spoken by a great many people belonging to very different cultures throughout the world.

5. Useful and interesting vocabulary

Many of you have asked us to introduce enough vocabulary to give the students choices when expressing themselves. You have also asked us to include words that students will enjoy learning and find useful. As we chose themes for the book, we kept these criteria in mind. Sometimes we introduced vocabulary items we thought students would enjoy using, even though these words don't necessarily appear on frequency lists.

Some of the units contain a certain amount of vocabulary for recognition only and not for active recall or manipulation on tests. This vocabulary is included as part of the cultural background material on the theme of a given unit, or as a colorful addition to the dialog or reading passage. The Word List at the end of each unit presents active vocabulary in boldface (heavy type), and recognition vocabulary in light-face, so that you and your students will know immediately which words are introduced for recognition only and which are for active recall.

For further discussion of vocabulary, see page T7.

6. Basic grammar in two levels

Because our previous foreign language program was based on the assumption that students would learn foreign languages over a period of four to six years, the basic grammar points could be spread over three levels of the earlier series. Now, however, at the urging of many teachers, we have condensed the presentation of basic grammar into two levels. In the first and second textbooks of this series, we present mainly the grammar of the spoken language; interested students can learn additional points of grammar, including some structures used mainly in writing, from the reading strand of the program.

7. Situational exercises and activities instead of mechanical drills

Mechanical exercises, like item-substitution drills, have not been included. Should teachers want to use such exercises, they can easily provide them at the initial stage of learning. Most exercises in this program elicit personal reactions from the students. Transformations are "motivated" — that is, the response is so natural that the exercise seems less one of grammatical manipulation than one of real conversational stimulus and response. The headings for these exercises usually suggest the situation in which the lines that follow could be said.

Almost every unit has one or two activity-related exercises or games that encourage students to review and practice while having fun. The game of Lotto in Unit 2, for example, is a device to have students practice numbers from 1 to 20, which were introduced in this unit. You can adapt the techniques of many of these games and activities to units other than the ones where they are first introduced.

8. Review units

Every sixth unit in the textbook is a review unit, in which the main grammar points of the previous five units are reviewed and summarized. These review units all have themes: using the telephone (Unit 6), writing a letter (Unit 12), writing a diary at summer camp (Unit 18), and watching television (Unit 24). Introduction of new grammar is held to a bare minimum in these units.

9. Coordination of strand materials with textbook; color-coding

Within each unit of the textbook, all material is numbered consecutively. Each dialog, narrative, grammar point, exercise, and activity has its own number. These numbers reappear in the strand materials for reference, to show exactly what item or items in the textbook unit are being practiced.

In the textbook these numbers are color-coded: orange for new material (dialog, narrative, grammar), blue for exercises, green for grammar review, and purple for all material that is optional (i.e., that should be done for fun or general interest, but that does not need to be studied intensively). Color-coding is also used in the grammar charts, in which new structures are highlighted in orange and review charts in green.

10. Cultural photo essays on the countries and the people

Following each review unit in the textbook, you will find a cultural photo essay of eight pages. These eight-page sections, called "French Throughout the World," "City Life," "Country Life," and "Festivals," give further insights into the life and surroundings of the people whose language your students are studying.

11. Photo essay: "Foreign Language and You"

In a sixteen-page pictorial essay at the front of the textbook, we give students a glimpse of what foreign language study can do for them in terms of their personal education and their eventual position in the job market. We expect this section to be a useful resource for answering the question many students ask: "Why should we study a foreign language?"

Internal Organization of the Units

As we mentioned earlier, no two units are exactly alike; therefore, we cannot give a typical lesson plan in detail. What follows is a rough outline of unit format, with a brief description of the different parts of a unit.

1. Average length

The average length of a unit is ten pages. Of these, the first page of many units is usually devoted to visual illustration of the unit theme—art work, graphics, photographs, and so forth—while the last page of each unit is taken up by the vocabulary list, leaving eight pages in between for the material of the unit. Each lesson is also enlivened by many photographs, drawings, and realia, which in many cases are part of the basic text.

2. Division of new material into sections

New material in each unit is divided into two, three, or four sections and presented one part at a time, with accompanying exercises. Dividing the lessons this way provides a natural pacing; students are presented with only a small amount to learn at one time. The word lists at the end of the units reflect these divisions. This manner of presentation allows for variety in the basic material and the exercises, and makes for easier teaching and learning.

3. Different forms of basic material

The basic material in each unit may take a variety of forms, depending on the theme and the structures being taught. At different points we have presented new material in the form of a dialog, a narrative, a letter, a diary entry, or a piece of realia, such as a newspaper article or a menu.

4. Questions on the basic material

Each piece of basic material is followed by a set of questions which the students must answer by rephrasing or recombining parts of the basic material. The aim of these questions is to have students practice new vocabulary and to check their comprehension.

5. Personalized questions

The content questions are followed by a set of personalized questions. They encourage the students to talk about themselves in the situation or setting described in the basic material — to say, for example, what books they read, what sports they like, what plans they have for their vacation. These questions should make the new material more relevant for your students and therefore easier for them to master.

6. Exercice oral (Pronunciation)

Each section of each lesson includes a pronunciation exercise with the heading "Exercice Oral." These are recorded exercises that help students pronounce the new material correctly by giving them short phrases and sentences to repeat. In the Exercice Oral, only active material is practiced. If a student has particular difficulty with certain sounds, you might assign the special pronunciation exercises that are part of the lessons of the listening comprehension program. For a listing of these exercises, see the Table of Contents for this Teacher's Edition, p. Tvii.

7. Presentation of grammar

Most of the time, new grammar is discussed in two sections: a grammar discovery exercise and a grammar generalization. The first part consists of sentences illustrating the new structure, followed by questions to the student. In studying the sample sentences and answering the questions, students should come to understand the grammatical principle involved.

These discovery sections have been recorded, and the recordings can serve as a model for your own grammar presentation in class. Students, too, will benefit from hearing the recorded presentations before practicing a point of grammar. The recorded discovery exercises will be especially useful to students who work well on their own or who are absent when the new grammar is introduced in class.

Following the grammar discovery sections is a generalization. Although it usually follows immediately after the discovery section, it should be read only after students have done the appropriate structure drills at least once in class. By treating new grammar in this sequence — discovery, application, and finally generalization — students should begin to realize that grammar "rules" derive from speech patterns rather than lead to them.

A more detailed discussion of the procedure for introducing new grammar is given on page T7, in the section of this Introduction called "How to Use This Program."

8. Structure drills

The structure drills which follow a grammar presentation provide practice in manipulating the new grammatical structure. Most of these drills appear in a two-column format, with the stimulus on the left side and the response on the right. Responses and suggestions for drill variations are indicated in the annotated part of this Teacher's Edition.

9. Exercises for fun

Almost every unit includes one or more activities in which students review vocabulary or structure while having fun. Activities may be guessing games, memory games, charades, sayings, songs, etc. The purpose of these exercises is to give students a chance to relax and play with the language. You can use them in many ways—as a review, a warm-up before class starts, or a way of filling a few extra minutes at the end of class. Most are versatile enough to be used with vocabulary and structures from other units in the book. We have made specific suggestions for variations in the annotated pages of this Teacher's Edition.

10. Exercice de compréhension (Listening)

Each unit contains at least one listening exercise. The script for each Exercice de Compréhension is printed, together with the discussion of the unit, in the section called "Teaching Suggestions for Each Unit," which starts on page T11. For more extensive listening practice, students should do the exercises in the listening comprehension program.

11. Exercice écrit (Writing) — Rédaction (Composition)

Most exercises in the textbook are presented as oral exercises, but can be used for writing practice as well. In addition, each unit has exercises designed specifically for writing. These exercises require one- or two-word answers in the early units; in later units they require complete sentences and, eventually, compositions. Additional writing practice is provided in the *Cahier d'Activités* and the *Cahier d'Exercices*. The composition-writing exercises in the *Cahier d'Exercices* should be especially helpful in preparing students for the writing assignments in the textbook.

12. Exercice de conversation (Conversation)

There is at least one Exercice de Conversation in each unit, usually toward the end of the lesson. The purpose is to get students to talk about the theme of the unit in the context of their own experiences. The conversation exercises allow room for a multitude of different responses, which may be simple or complex depending on the student's language skills. You will have to determine how much additional vocabulary and information to provide for individual students so that they can talk about their own experiences. As much as possible, have them rely on the structure and vocabulary they know already. In conjunction with these exercises, use the situation posters to stimulate conversation.

The readers supply additional information and related vocabulary which may be useful in preparing for these exercises. Students will also benefit from doing the appropriate listening and speaking exercises in the listening comprehension program before they do the conversation exercise for a given unit. After the conversation exercises have been done orally, they may be used as additional writing exercises.

13. Culture notes

Most of the units contain a culture note in English or French, expanding on aspects of the unit theme, clarifying points of cultural behavior, or giving background information about the people in the unit.

14. Optional cultural readings

Many units include a reading selection in French. These pieces give further insights into the unit theme, reinforcing vocabulary and often giving additional cultural information. The readings are optional; they are intended to enrich the program if time permits.

How to Use This Program

1. Presenting and practicing new material

The basic material of the program has different forms and purposes. The aim of a particular segment may be to model what to say in a situation—for example, buying food (Unit 8), being at a party (Unit 9), asking for flight information at an airport (Unit 19). It may be to introduce new grammar and vocabulary, as in the picture captions throughout the book. It may also be to give cultural information, as in "En Tunisie" (Unit 20), or to give practical tips on how to write a letter (Unit 12).

Before you introduce any piece of basic material, consult the list of learning objectives in the "Scope and Sequence Chart," which starts on page T172. These are functional objectives; that is, they have to do with practical tasks and experiences like reading a map, talking to a salesperson, planning a party, ordering food, or using the telephone. New material should be presented in ways that emphasize these functional objectives.

The following suggestions for presenting and practicing basic material can be adapted to your own classroom style, the learning needs of your students, the format of the material itself, and the time available. We do not, however, advocate rote memorization of dialogs and narrative passages. Students should be made to feel that they are using the language to respond naturally and spontaneously in real situations. The aim should be to make the language part of their personal experience. Also, since the dialogs and readings in this book are only samples of what a particular speaker might say or do in a given situation, they should not be taught as fixed and rigid sequences.

a. Establishing context

Since each unit is developed around a specific theme, it is essential to establish the context, so that the student can understand the new material more easily. There are several ways in which you can give information about the theme and situation of the material you are about to teach:
• State the gist of the passage in English.
• Show the unit filmstrip, pausing to identify important persons and objects that appear on the screen.
• Use the photographs in the text, magazine pictures, actual objects (realia), and your own imagination in acting out the situation with your students.
• Involve the students in finding and bringing to class specific items that may serve as "props."

b. Presenting the basic material

You might present the basic material as follows:
• Read the passage aloud, first with students' books closed and a second time with books open.
• Go on to both the factual and the personalized questions that follow the basic material. Do not emphasize pronunciation at this point. However, note the difficult words and phrases, and have the class practice them afterwards.

Of course, it is essential that students understand the meaning of the new material. The many illustrations in the book should help greatly in establishing meaning. Should all possible methods to help a student understand fail, a single word or expression in English will not significantly disrupt the pattern in French. Whole sentences in English, on the other hand, do break the pattern and should be used as little as possible.

c. Practicing the basic material

As a guide to the practice of pronunciation, the sample script of an Exercice Oral is printed in the "Recording Materials: Format and Samples" section, beginning on page T56. Use the recorded Exercice Oral for each unit, and correct students' pronunciation in class. Students should always practice words in meaningful groupings rather than as isolated sounds or nonsense phrases. Good pronunciation is important. Students should learn to speak in a way that will be understood by a native speaker.

Sound-letter correspondence is taught in the lessons of the listening comprehension program, with dictations of words containing critical sounds. You can, in addition, select passages, phrases, or vocabulary words for dictation whenever you feel the class would benefit.

As much as possible, take advantage of the diversity of materials in the series. Different students may need specific practice of different kinds. A student who needs help with a grammar point might be directed to the *Cahier d'Exercices*, to read the presentation on that point and do the exercises that follow. Another might benefit more from doing a puzzle or activity on that point in the *Cahier d'Activités*. Students who like to speak in French and listen to French should do the exercises in the listening comprehension program. Those who enjoy reading can do appropriate assignments in one of the two readers, while those who like writing and other paper-and-pencil activities can practice in either of the two workbooks. For additional vocabulary practice, use the vocabulary posters that accompany each unit, as well as the vocabulary exercises in the workbooks. To stimulate classroom conversation on unit themes, use the appropriate situation poster or filmstrip.

2. Presenting and practicing new grammar

The sequence for presenting new grammar might be more or less as follows:
• Start by listening to the recorded grammar discovery exercise, so that you can use it as a model for your classroom presentation.
• Present the new grammar to your class, using the discovery exercise printed in the book. Read the presentation aloud and ask the questions, helping students both to hear the new forms and to see how they are written.
• If you feel it is necessary, you may do a few quick item-substitution drills, especially when dealing with verb forms.
• For the time being, skip over the grammar generalization section, which is printed after the discovery exercise, and go immediately to the grammar exercises. After they have had a chance to use the grammar point by doing the exercises, your students will be ready to read and understand the generalization.

The exercises are designed to resemble conversations as much as possible. The heading is a leading sentence setting the scene for the conversation that follows. You might want to expand it. For example, before doing Number 24 in Unit 5, you could say, *"Les quatre amis sont chez Catherine et Philippe. Ils ont soif. Catherine leur demande : Qu'est-ce que vous voulez comme boisson?"* To keep students alert and to encourage them to speak clearly, you should call for individual rather than choral responses. Go through each exercise fairly rapidly. Words presenting a particular problem can be practiced afterwards.
• To reinforce and review the grammar point your students have been practicing, you should next have them listen to the recorded discovery exercise, either individually or as a class. They can also do the recorded grammar exercises, which are exactly the same as those printed in the textbook. The recorded grammar materials are a valuable variation on your classroom presentation. They stress the sounds of the forms and structures rather than the spelling. Encourage your students to do the recorded exercises twice, if they have trouble the first time. They can also come back to the same exercise later, for review.
• Finally, assign your students a reading of the generalization section for the grammar point they have been practicing, and then have them write the answers to one or more of the structure drills.

The item posters that accompany the program are useful as visual cues in grammar exercises. You can vary the exercises by using familiar vocabulary from other units when practicing new structures. For further practice of grammar, direct your students to the two workbooks.

3. Presenting and discussing culture

The kind of culture we introduce at this level of the program is not, primarily, a matter of statistics and facts; it is a matter of observation, experience, feeling, behavior, and attitude. It is the kind of culture that could best be taught through daily contact with life in a French-speaking community. Since such contact is not possible for most students, we have to rely on the kinds of experience available in the classroom — a variety of sensory stimuli, information, and lively discussion that allows students to express what they observe and feel, both about French culture and about their own.

Many different methods have been suggested for teaching culture to students in the classroom. In the first level of this series, we hope to instill cultural awareness by exposing students to all the different kinds of cultural expression contained in the materials — the authenticity of written and spoken words, a rich collection of photographs showing a cross-section of people and places, a multitude of "realia" (a menu, a page from a phone book, a recipe, etc.), and special culture notes in English. We also encourage students to "get acquainted" with a few French-speaking young people, so that they can develop a feel for the everyday life of people their own age in the foreign culture.

Throughout this Teacher's Edition we have noted additional cultural points that may interest you and your students or that clarify certain situations depicted in the units. The section titled "Teaching Suggestions for Each Unit," starting on page T11, provides more background information on the unit themes. Be sure you consult this section as you prepare to introduce each unit to your class, and include in your teaching as much of this information as you find helpful.

Sources for cultural awareness are present on almost every page of the textbook. They are especially concentrated, however, in the photo essays that follow each review unit. These photo essays are related in a general way to the material of the six preceding units, but you can use the photographs and accompanying text of each one at any point in the program. To help you in presenting the photo essays, we have included background information on the various topics, and some details about the specific photographs, as part of the section called "Teaching Suggestions for Each Unit," following the material on the four review units.

Because the cultural materials are inherent in the units of the program, many aspects of the foreign culture will come out naturally in the course of each lesson. Each unit is a starting point to explore the many cultural differences students should be aware of. When you are exploring them, your own attitude toward the people whose language your students are studying is very important. In all probability, your students will adopt whatever you project. Only if you arouse interest and enthusiasm, are they then ready to be receptive to this foreign people's value systems and behavior patterns.

Encourage your students to "personalize" the French-speaking cultures as they study and practice the themes and vocabulary of the units. Assign as many activities and projects as possible. Have students make a pain-bagnat (p. 85), write a grocery list (p. 88), plan a party (p. 95). Have them act out scenes that might take place in a French café (p. 49) or at a marketplace (p. 77). Play the games suggested in the book, and add whatever French games you like. (For additional suggestions, see the section called "Games and Classroom Phrases," beginning on page T53.) In playing games and doing projects, your students not only practice their speaking skills, but they also share in an experience that helps them learn about the particular country's culture in a direct and personal way.

4. Scheduling time to complete the program

The units in this textbook are of fairly uniform length (averaging about ten pages); but the length of time needed to teach each unit will vary according to the amount of vocabulary and the difficulty of the grammar being introduced. To some extent, you can control the time you spend on each unit by including or omitting the optional elements — games and cultural readings — and by using or not using the related satellite or strand materials. Some units, however, will simply take longer than others.

You may find it helpful to devise a schedule for the year, to use as a reference in planning the time you can afford to spend on any given unit. The following chart might serve as a basis for your timetable. Note that your schedule will vary according to the grade level of your students and the material you expect to cover in a year.

Units	Grade 7 Goal: 12 units	Grade 8 Goal: 12 units	Grade 9 Goal: 18 units	Grade 9 Goal: 24 units
	Finish by	*Finish by*	*Finish by*	*Finish by*
1–6	Middle of January	—	Middle of November	End of October
7–12	Middle of June	—	End of February	Middle of January
13–18	—	Middle of January	Middle of June	End of March
19–24	—	Middle of June	—	Middle of June

Teaching Suggestions for Each Unit

In this section each unit is discussed separately, with special comments on theme and culture, grammar, vocabulary, and classroom projects. Included with the teaching suggestions for each unit is the script for the Exercice de Compréhension (listening practice exercise) for that unit and the exercise answers that did not fit on the text pages. There is at least one Exercice de Compréhension for each unit.

Preceding the comments on Unit 1, and following those on Units 6, 12, 18, and 24, are comments and background information about the textbook's five photo essays. Detailed information about specific photographs is included.

PHOTO ESSAY Preceding Unit 1 — Pages F1–F16

FOREIGN LANGUAGE AND YOU

Through text and photographs we have tried to show a variety of ways that students can expect to use their foreign language skills, both for personal enjoyment and in their careers. The first part of the photo essay illustrates how knowing a foreign language can increase a person's appreciation of other people and other cultures and can make travel more fun and interesting. The remainder is devoted to career opportunities involving knowledge of a foreign language.

As you discuss this photo essay with your students, be sure they realize that the examples of careers shown here are only a few out of many different possibilities. In doing research for this photo essay, we spoke to employment agency personnel, who told us two things we thought students ought to hear. First, foreign language skills are a valuable asset in practically any profession, at any level. In other words, knowing a foreign language increases your chances of finding an interesting job in the field you like best. Second, it is essential to combine foreign language skills with training in a particular field — to specialize in something besides the language, and to apply the language to your area of specialization. Foreign language proficiency can be a tremendous asset when combined with professional training.

Page F2

(1), (3), (4), (5): The Charles-de-Gaulle Airport (also known as Roissy Airport) in Paris.

Page F3

(8), (9): French road signs. Note that the speed limits are in kilometers per hour.
(10): One of the many ''special deals'' offered by the *SNCF (Société Nationale des Chemins de Fer Français),* the French National Railroad.
(11): Toll booths on the *Autoroute des Laurentides,* the highway to the Laurentian Mountains, north of Montreal, Canada. (See map, page 151.)

Pages F4 – F5

(1): The *Château Frontenac* in Quebec City is a luxury hotel.

(2): Ornate sign of a famous restaurant in Colmar, Alsace. The restaurant takes its name from the stone animal heads that adorn its façade.

(3): A famous restaurant in picturesque old Quebec City.

(4): Paul Bocuse is the famous French chef who, along with a handful of other chefs, has created a "revolution" in French cuisine. He advocated *la nouvelle cuisine,* with lighter sauces and unorthodox food combinations.

(5): A boutique in Colmar, Alsace.

(6): A pharmacy in the Pyrenees.

(7): A typical street sign in France.

(8): In France, many stores still close for lunch, especially in the country or in small towns. One should always inquire about the hours of any particular store—especially dry cleaners.

(9): A bank in Fort-de-France, Martinique.

(10): A parking meter in Paris.

(11): A subway in Montreal, Canada.

Page F6 – F7

(1): The Winged Victory *(La Victoire de Samothrace),* in the Louvre Museum in Paris.

(2): The famous Hall of Mirrors. *(La Galerie des Glaces),* in Versailles Palace.

(3): Versailles Palace in the background—the statue is a personification of the River Rhône.

(4): Portrait of Napoleon from the *Musée National de la Maison Bonaparte,* in Ajaccio, Corsica.

(5): Signs of the *Centre National d'Art et de Culture Georges Pompidou,* better known as *Beaubourg.*

(8): The Cathedral of Chartres.

(9): The chapel in the Maeght Foundation, an indoor and outdoor museum of modern art, located in Aix-en-Provence, in the south of France.

Page F9

(3): The Michelin guides, published by the tire manufacturer of the same name, are much used by travelers. The hardbound, red guides list and rate all the hotels and restaurants in France. The softbound, green ones give historical background and geographical information about the various regions of France. Michelin also puts out guides for other countries. The guides are published in several languages.

Page F12

(1): Petit Clamart was the site of an attempt on General de Gaulle's life in the early 1960s. The attempt failed, but the event has since been fictionalized in a book titled *The Day of the Jackal* and a movie by the same name.

(2): Interpreters at the United Nations headquarters in New York.

(3): The fifth General Conference of Economic and Technical Cooperation of French-speaking countries in Abidjan, Ivory Coast.

Page F14

(3): The International Institute of Education organizes or sponsors academic exchange programs between foreign countries all over the world. It stands directly opposite the headquarters of the United Nations in New York.

Page F15

(1): A bowl from Charente.
(4): Nuit de Noël by the French painter Henri Matisse (1869-1954).

Page F16

The following companies are French and have factories and/or branches in the United States.
(1): L'Oréal is an important manufacturer of hair products.
(2): Allibert manufactures bathroom fixtures.
(3): Péchiney Ugine Kuhlmann is one of the world's leading steel manufacturers.
(4): Guerlain is a well-known manufacturer of perfumes.
There are many other French companies that have factories or branches in the United States—among them, Michelin, a tire manufacturer, and Moulinex, a manufacturer of small household electrical appliances.

1 NOS AMIS

Theme and Culture

The photographs on page 1 introduce six French-speaking young people who reappear often in the units of this textbook, **Nos Amis.**

Point out that the name *Jean* is a boy's name in French, corresponding to the English name *John.* Its feminine counterpart is *Jeanne,* corresponding to the English name *Joan.* French children are often given compound names. Boys' names are usually compounded with *Jean (Jean-Michel, Jean-Paul, Jean-Philippe),* and girls' names with *Marie (Marie-Christine, Marie-France, Marie-Hélène).* The family names *Dubois* and *Fort* are very common in France, like *Smith* or *Brown* in this country.

You may want to tell your students that French is spoken in some 40 countries around the world, by about 92 million people. Of these, 52 million are in France and 6 million in French-Canada. The photo essay after Unit 6, titled "French Throughout the World," deals with the subject of *francophonie.*

This is a good place to introduce words and gestures of meeting and greeting, such as *bonjour, salut, ça va?* and the typical French handshake (one shake up and one down, unlike the American handshake, which repeats the shake several times). You might mention that in France everyone shakes hands each time they meet or part. Another distinctively French gesture that you might like to mention is the use of the thumb to signal "one," instead of the index finger. In Unit 6, which deals with the telephone, more will be discussed about greetings and farewells.

Grammar

The main objective in this unit is to enable students to tell their own names and the names of their friends, to talk about how old they and their friends are, and to say where they and their friends live.

The verb *avoir* is formally introduced in Unit 3, and reflexive constructions in Unit 13. They appear in this unit in phrases and should be taught lexically, without discussing related forms. Plural subject pronouns are taught in Unit 2.

The important concept of gender is introduced in this unit. For English-speaking students, grammatical gender is a new idea and needs to be handled accordingly.

Vocabulary

You might mention some more boys' names: *Denis, Didier, Eric, Hervé, Pascal, Stéphane*. Other girls names include *Anne, Corinne, Elisabeth, Martine,* and *Sabine*.

Game

The map of France on page 8 lends itself to other exercises besides the conversation exercise given on page 9. For instance, you can use the map as the basis for a game of *Devinettes:* you say: *C'est un grand port sur la Garonne;* and students reply: *Bordeaux.*

Script of Listening Exercise 24

You will hear ten sentences, each containing a noun. For each sentence, you will have to decide whether the noun is masculine or feminine. For example, you hear: *J'habite dans un appartement.* You put your check mark in the row labeled Masculine, because the article preceding *appartement* is the masculine article *un.* Let's begin.

1. J'habite dans une grande maison. _____ *(une grande maison   feminine)*
2. J'habite près de la mer. _____ *(la mer   feminine)*
3. J'habite dans une île. _____ *(une île   feminine)*
4. C'est la ville où j'habite. _____ *(la ville   feminine)*
5. C'est un grand port. _____ *(un grand port   masculine)*
6. C'est à la Martinique. _____ *(la Martinique   feminine)*
7. C'est la capitale. _____ *(la capitale   feminine)*
8. C'est loin de la France. _____ *(la France   feminine)*
9. Comment s'appelle ce village? _____ *(ce village   masculine)*
10. Qui habite dans cette maison? _____ *(cette maison   feminine)*

Now check your answers. *Read each item again and give the correct answer.*

2   LES SPORTS

Theme and Culture

Young people in France today engage in sports much more than their parents did. The overwhelming favorite among team sports is soccer, which is played all over the country. Rugby follows closely, played especially in the southwest of France. Swimming has recently been increasing in popularity. Thousands of swimming pools have been built in the last few years, and swimming is even required for the *baccalauréat*. Other very popular sports are gymnastics, basketball, handball, volleyball—not to mention ice-skating, judo, karate, and sailing. Skiing is also popular. Until recently, almost all the ski resorts were in the Alps. Now more and more resorts are being built in the Pyrenees, which offer great possibilities for ski enthusiasts.

Among spectator sports, the most popular are soccer and rugby. The *Tour de France,* a bicycle race that takes place once a year, also creates great excitement and enthusiasm among spectators.

Grammar

The plural subject pronouns are introduced here. Students should practice addressing one classmate (*tu*), then two classmates (*vous*). Set up situations to help them address more than one student at a time. The formal singular address is introduced in Unit 4.

Vocabulary

Colors are introduced in this unit as nouns. Some of them reappear as adjectives in Unit 7.

Before doing Exercise 10, which requires personal answers, you might want to give your students vocabulary for some of the sports they engage in.

athletics	*faire de l'athlétisme*	mountain climbing	*faire de l'escalade*
boxing	*faire de la boxe*	motorcycling	*faire de la moto*
canoeing	*faire du canoë/canot*	roller-skating	*faire du patin à roulettes*
deep-sea diving	*faire de la plongée*	rowing	*faire de l'aviron*
fencing	*faire de l'escrime*	skateboard	*faire de la planchette*
gymnastics	*faire de la gymnastique*		*(de la planche à roulettes)*
ice-skating	*faire du patin à glace*	field hockey	*jouer au hockey sur gazon*
karate	*faire du karaté*		

These are more specific terms for the positions of players on a soccer field, if you should want to use them in discussing the playing field, Number 13.

right wingback	*arrière droit*	center midfielder	*demi centre*
stopper	*stopper* or *stoppant*	left midfielder	*demi gauche*
sweeper (behind stopper)	*arrière central (libero)*	right winger	*ailier droit*
left wingback	*arrière gauche*	center winger	*avant centre*
right midfielder	*demi droit*	left winger	*ailier gauche*

Script of Listening Exercise 31

Listen to the following sentences. For each one, decide whether the sentence refers to one person or more than one. For example, you hear: *Ils aiment le tennis.* You put your check mark in the row labeled "More than one" because the liaison sound between *ils* and *aiment—ils aiment—*tells you that *ils* is plural. Let's begin.

1. Il habite au Canada. _____ *(il habite   one person)*
2. Ils aiment le hockey. _____ *(ils aiment   more than one person)*
3. Elles habitent à Paris. _____ *(elles habitent   more than one person)*
4. Elle aime jouer au tennis. _____ *(elle aime   one person)*
5. Il aime la France. _____ *(il aime   one person)*
6. Ils habitent près de la mer. _____ *(ils habitent   more than one person)*
7. Elles aiment faire du vélo. _____ *(elles aiment   more than one person)*
8. Elle habite aux Etats-Unis. _____ *(elle habite   one person)*

Now check your answers. *Read each item again and give the correct answer.*

Answers to Exercise 8: Qu'est-ce qu'ils font? Qu'est-ce qu'elles font?

1. Ils font de la natation.   2. Elles font du judo.   3. Ils font du ski.

3 LES PASSE-TEMPS

Theme and Culture

Because of the demands of school, most French youngsters have little time left for leisure activities. They use what time they have for pursuing hobbies, listening to music, watching television, and playing board games or cards with friends and family.

These activities are not too different from those of American teenagers. Some of the board games are even the same. Chess and checkers, of course, do not change; but the Monopoly board shows streets, railroads, and famous places of Paris. French cards, as you can see in this unit, are also somewhat different.

Like Philippe and Catherine Lardan (brother and sister from Dieppe who appear again in Units 5, 7 and 9), a great many French teenagers have their own radios, record players and tape recorders, but they rarely have their own TV sets. There is usually one large TV set in the family living room which is used by the whole family.

Mopeds and motorcycles are the most common means of transportation for French teenagers. The only requirement for a moped rider is to wear a helmet.

Grammar

Although the use of *si* as an affirmative answer to a negative question seems simple enough, students are often confused by it. The *oui/si* distinction needs drilling in order to become automatic.

Games

• *Le jeu de loto* (page 3) can be played in this unit. Use numbers from 20 to 2,000.
• A modified form of the American card game "Go Fish" can be used to help students review the numbers from 1 to 10. The object of the game is to collect "books" of four cards with the same value, by asking other players for the cards you need. Deal five cards to each player, and put the remaining cards in a "pool" in the middle of the table. Starting with the player to the dealer's left, the players ask each other for cards of the same value as the cards they are holding. For example, a player with two sevens in his hand may ask any other player: *"Tu as des 7?"* If the player who is asked has any sevens, he or she must hand them over, saying: *"Oui, j'ai des 7."* If not, he or she must say: *"Non, je n'ai pas de 7. Tire une carte!"* Then the first player draws a card from the pool, and his or her turn is over—unless the requested card is drawn. As long as a player continues to get the cards that are requested, his or her turn continues. When a player answers, *"Non, tire une carte,"* it is that player's turn. The game ends when all the cards are sorted into books. The player with the most books wins.

Script of Listening Exercise 10

You will hear ten sentences. For each one, decide whether the noun is singular or plural. For example, you hear: *Elle a des disques.* You put your check mark in the row labeled "Plural" because *disques* is preceded by the plural article *des*. Let's begin.

1. Elle lit une revue. _____ (une revue   singular)
2. Il a un vélomoteur. _____ (un vélomoteur   singular)
3. Tu aimes ces disques? _____ (ces disques   plural)
4. Nous regardons un match. _____ (un match   singular)
5. C'est la radio de Catherine. _____ (la radio   singular)
6. Elle aime beaucoup cette revue. _____ (cette revue   singular)

7. Où sont les cassettes de Philippe? _____ (les cassettes   plural)
8. Il a des cassettes? _____ (des cassettes   plural)
9. C'est le vélomoteur de Philippe? _____ (le vélomoteur   singular)
10. Tu veux regarder ce match? _____ (ce match   singular)

Now check your answers. *Read each item again and give the correct answer.*

Script of Listening Exercise 26

Listen to the following ten statements, and decide whether each statement is affirmative or negative. For example, you hear: *Il n'habite pas à Paris.* You place your check mark in the row labeled *"Non"* because you heard the negative words *ne . . . pas.* Let's begin.

1. Il aime bricoler. _____ *(il aime   oui)*
2. Elle n'aime pas tricoter. _____ *(elle n'aime pas   non)*
3. Je n'ai pas d'appareil-photo. _____ *(je n'ai pas   non)*
4. Nous regardons la télévision. _____ *(nous regardons   oui)*
5. Je ne joue pas au rugby. _____ *(je ne joue pas   non)*
6. Ils font de la natation. _____ *(ils font   oui)*
7. Elles aiment beaucoup le ping-pong. _____ *(elles aiment   oui)*
8. C'est une amie. _____ *(c'est   oui)*
9. Il est photographe. _____ *(il est   oui)*
10. Elle n'a pas de vélomoteur. _____ *(elle n'a pas   non)*

Now check your answers. *Read each item again and give the correct answer.*

Answers to Writing Exercise 20

1. Oui, je suis collectionneur (-euse). / Non, je ne suis pas collectionneur (-euse).
2. Je collectionne les timbres (les petites voitures / les maquettes d'avion / les pièces de monnaie / les affiches / les coquillages / les disques / les livres).
3. Non, je n'ai pas de difficultés à en trouver. / Oui, j'ai des difficultés à en trouver.
4. Oui, je fais de la photo. / Non, je ne fais pas de photo.

4   L'ECOLE

Theme and Culture

French students attend a *CES (Collège d'Enseignement Secondaire)* from the age of 12 to the age of 16. They enter in *sixième* (about 7th grade) and leave in *troisième* (about 10th grade). At 16 (after 3e) some leave school and go to work. Others go to a *lycée* in order to go on to the university. French students have very little choice as to which courses they take. In *sixième,* however, they may choose one of several foreign languages, and in *quatrième* they choose a second. These choices fall within the basic framework of a distinction made in France between *les langues vivantes* (English, German, Spanish, Russian, etc.) and *les langues mortes* (Latin and classical Greek).

French students must devote a lot of time and energy to their school work. There is very little time left for extra-curricular activities. The expectations are high and competition stiff.

It is difficult to give a general description of the French school system. It is nationalized and firmly controlled throughout France. The curriculum is set by the Minister of Education. In the last decade there have been many changes, and more are coming. However, you may want to elaborate on the degree of importance given to education by the French—to gain the esteem of one's peers and to have an advantage in the job market, as well.

In recent years the system of letter grades (A, B, C, D, E) has been used in French schools along with the old system of number grades (1 to 20). In some schools, teacher comments *(appréciations)* are used instead of grades. National examinations, like the *baccalauréat,* still use the old grading system.

Grammar

Contractions with à and *de* require a great deal of practice. Use the layout of François' school on page 35 for some fast drilling.

Point out to your students that adjective agreement also occurs with first- and second-person subject pronouns. Variations of drills on this point have been suggested on the annotated pages of this teacher's edition.

The choice between *vous* and *tu* will need practice. Establish in a relaxed way the fact that students should use *vous* for yourself and the rest of the faculty and administration.

Vocabulary

The vocabulary in this unit includes groups of words that are useful on a day-to-day basis, especially for school: days of the week, telling time, school subjects, forms of address, directions, school supplies. All of these are easy to work into classroom conversation.

Games

Le jeu des adverbes (page 228) can become *le jeu des adjectifs:* one student chooses an adjective and acts it out. Others have to guess what the adjective is and say, *"Tu es amusant(e),"* for instance.

Script of Listening Exercise 40

You will hear ten sentences. For each sentence, decide whether the person talked about is a boy or a girl. All the names used, such as *Michel (Michèle),* can be either boys' names or girls' names. For example, you hear: *Michel est paresseux.* You put your check mark in the row labeled *Un garçon* because the masculine adjective *paresseux* refers to a boy. Let's begin.

1. Dominique est amusant. _____ *(amusant   un garçon)*
2. Danièle est intelligente. _____ *(intelligente   une fille)*
3. Michel est très distrait. _____ *(distrait   un garçon)*
4. Claude est ennuyeuse. _____ *(ennuyeuse   une fille)*
5. Michèle est très sérieuse. _____ *(sérieuse   une fille)*
6. Joël est paresseux. _____ *(paresseux   un garçon)*
7. Claude est distraite. _____ *(distraite   une fille)*
8. Noël est intelligent. _____ *(intelligent   un garçon)*
9. Gabrièle est amusante. _____ *(amusante   une fille)*
10. Dominique est sérieux. _____ *(sérieux   un garçon)*

Now check your answers. *Read each item again and give the correct answer.*

Answers to Exercise 41: Demandez à des camarades:

Vous parlez de François.
Oui, il est bon en français.
Oui, il est doué en latin.
Oui, il est intelligent.
Oui, il est paresseux.
Oui, il est doué pour les langues.
Oui, il est distrait.

Vous parlez de Florence.
Oui, elle est bonne en français.
Oui, elle est douée en latin.
Oui, elle est intelligente.
Oui, elle est paresseuse.
Oui, elle est douée pour les langues.
Oui, elle est distraite.

5 UNE SORTIE

Theme and Culture

In France boys and girls frequently go out together in groups, which are not necessarily made up of couples. A boy or girl may have a girlfriend or boyfriend within the group, but not necessarily. Catherine and her brother Philippe often go out with Catherine's friend Sylvie and with Philippe's friend Bernard. Bernard's brother Dominique often joins them, too.

French young people are very fond of movies—witness the many *ciné-clubs* and *cinémathèques*. They like all kinds of films, but seem especially to enjoy westerns and cartoons.

All *cafés* serve sandwiches. Some also serve hot dishes such as *croque-monsieur*—a hot sandwich, usually open-faced, with ham and melted cheese—hot dogs, and quiches. Whether the tip is included in the bill is indicated by the words *Service Compris,* or *Service non Compris* on the check.

The *2CV* (*Deux-Chevaux*—the car in the unit opener) is the cheapest, smallest, and most economical of French cars. The design of both inside and outside was inspired by the cockpits of early airplanes. Although the *2CV* is no longer made, these cars can still be seen all over France.

Since this unit mentions Dieppe, you might want to tell your students that pebbles from the beach at Dieppe are sealed into one of the pillars of the Verrazano Bridge in New York City. When the bridge was built, the pebbles were placed there in honor of Jean Ango, a rich shipowner from Dieppe who lived in the sixteenth century. The Italian explorer Verrazano made an expedition to America in one of Jean Ango's ships, in the course of which he is said to have entered what is now New York Harbor.

Grammar

One of the great difficulties in teaching French is the difference between the spoken and the written language. Question formation is a good example of this difference. In spoken French, the most common way of asking questions is to use intonation, even with information questions: *Tu vas où? Tu pars quand?* But, although this form of question is acceptable when it is spoken, it is not appropriate to the written language.

Vocabulary

Point out to your students the idiomatic expression with à: *un sandwich au camembert, une glace à la vanille.*

Project

If school policy allows it, have students bring in the necessary items to make sandwiches, as described in the culture note on page 49. Have them write out menus, listing the foods they have prepared, and then act out a *café* scene. Assign roles (waiter and diners): waiters can recommend foods, bring what is ordered, and write up checks; diners can order from the menu, ask for the check, and pay the waiter. Use real French money, if possible. (Obviously, if real sandwiches are involved, everyone should have a turn at being a "diner"!)

Script of Listening Exercise 41

In each sentence, determine whether the pronoun is singular or plural. For example, you hear: *Ils partent dans une heure.* You put your check mark in the row labeled "Plural" because the verb form *partent* indicates that the pronoun *ils* is plural. Let's begin.

1. Il ne finit pas avant 5 h. _____ *(il ne finit pas   singular)*
2. Ils choisissent un film. _____ *(ils choisissent   plural)*
3. Elle part avec Catherine. _____ *(elle part   singular)*
4. Ils sortent le mercredi après-midi. _____ *(ils sortent   plural)*
5. Ils finissent vers midi. _____ *(ils finissent   plural)*
6. Elle sort souvent. _____ *(elle sort   singular)*
7. Il choisit un journal. _____ *(il choisit   singular)*
8. Elles partent au cinéma. _____ *(elles partent   plural)*

Now check your answers. *Read each item again and give the correct answer.*

Answers to Writing Exercise 29

1. Ils ne veulent pas de Coca-Cola.
2. Je n'ai pas d'eau minérale.
3. Catherine n'aime pas le Schweppes.
4. Dominique ne mange pas de sandwich.
5. Vous n'avez pas de limonade?
6. Ils ne commandent pas de glaces.

6 AU TELEPHONE

Theme and Culture

P.T.T. is actually an acronym for *Postes, Télégraphes et Téléphones,* the former name of the French post office and telephone company. In 1959, the name was changed to *Postes et Télécommunications.* However, the new acronym *P. et T.* never caught on, and even the officials of the company still refer to it as *P.T.T.*

The French use the phone less freely than we do. It has been estimated that the average French person has 139 phone conversations per year, as compared to 227 for a German, 282 for an English person, and 955 for an American. This difference is not entirely because of the lack of phones in France. The French tend to use the phone sparingly, even when they have one at home.

Grammar

All articles are reviewed here, as are the contractions with *à* and *de.* You should be certain that your students have mastered all the liaison and elision forms.

The pluralization of adjectives is introduced here along with a review of adjective agreement.

Vocabulary

Practice in saying phone numbers is a good review of numbers.

To reinforce phone vocabulary, you may want to suggest topics of discussion for phone conversations, and have students pretend to call each other up. Speaking a foreign language on the phone is a difficult exercise in real life. You might simulate the reality of the situation by having students sit with their backs to each other or across the room, so they cannot see each other's gestures.

Game

Le jeu du téléphone, as described on page T53, is obviously the game to play in this unit.

Script of Listening Exercise 21

You will hear six fragments of telephone conversations. For each one, decide whether the person at the other end of the line—that is, the person being spoken to—is a boy or a girl. For example, you hear: *Allô oui, bonjour . . . C'est ça, je te téléphone pour les maths; tu es très intelligent.* You put your check mark in the row labeled *Un garçon* because the masculine adjective *intelligent* indicates that the person at the other end of the line is a boy. Let's begin.

1. Allô oui? . . . Tu ne peux pas être prêt à cinq heures? Et à six heures? . . . D'accord. Alors à six heures.
   _____ *(prêt   un garçon)*
2. Pourquoi est-ce que tu ne veux pas aller au cinéma ce soir? Oh, écoute, tu es vraiment trop paresseuse!
   _____ *(paresseuse   une fille)*
3. Tu veux aller au bowling? . . . Tu travailles . . . Mais tu peux finir après . . . Tu sais, je trouve que tu es trop sérieux! _____ *(sérieux   un garçon)*
4. Salut! Ça va? . . . Alors qu'est-ce qu'on fait? . . . Jouer aux échecs! Tu veux toujours jouer aux échecs! Tu es ennuyeuse avec tes échecs! _____ *(ennuyeuse   une fille)*
5. Dis donc, toi qui es bon en maths. Je n'arrive pas à faire le problème de maths. Je ne comprends pas la question. _____ *(bon   un garçon)*
6. Qu'est-ce que tu dis? . . . Mais non! On va au cinéma avec Michel et Alain. Tu es bien distrait aujourd'hui! _____ *(distrait   un garçon)*

Now check your answers. *Read each item again and give the correct answer.*

Answers to Writing Exercise 11

1. Il y a des téléphones ici?
2. Où sont les téléphones, s'il vous plaît?

3. Les cabines sont au fond du couloir.
4. Compose ces numéros.

PHOTO ESSAY Following Unit 6 — Plates 1–8

FRENCH THROUGHOUT THE WORLD

French is spoken in some forty countries in the world besides France. This photo essay gives glimpses of France and of these countries, all of which are very different from one another, and of the people who live there.

Plate 1

(1): Young child from Quebec City in Canada.
(2): Tunisian mother and daughter having tea.
(3): Teenagers from Quebec eating in a cafeteria.
(4): Young man from the Ivory Coast.
(5): Girl from Neuchâtel in Switzerland.
(6): Mother and child from Laos.
(7): Woman from Ouagadougou, the capital of Upper Volta.
(8): French mother and daughter playing chess.

Plates 4–5

France is often called *l'hexagone* because of its 6-sided shape; three of these sides are bounded by land and three by sea. France is roughly 550,000 sq. km (about 213,000 sq. mi.). In this relatively small area, many features of the European landscape can be found; the flat lands of the North, the rounded mountains that make up the Jura and the Vosges in the East, the high jagged peaks of the Alps, the Mediterranean coast of the Southeast, the long sandy beaches of the Atlantic Ocean in the Southwest. The climate varies from region to region, but the proximity of the sea in most areas makes it relatively mild. Of the total surface of the land, 31% is cultivated, 24% is pastures, 2.5% is vineyards, and 26% is woods or forests.

(1): Menton, on the Côte d'Azur near the Italian border, is considered to be the warmest resort on the Riviera. It is especially pleasant in winter.
(2): The inland part of Brittany, with its fields and woods, is in striking contrast to its ragged and rocky coastline. There are many dolmens and menhirs, vestiges of prehistoric times, in Brittany. Dolmens are thought to be tombs. The menhirs, which often weigh up to 380 tons, were erected between 3500 and 1800 B.C. They are thought to be remnants of religious monuments.
(3): The Gué-Péan is one of many châteaux in Touraine. It is a Renaissance château. "Renaissance" is the architectural style that prevailed in the Loire Valley for most châteaux built during the fifteenth and sixteenth centuries.
(4): A section of Colmar in Alsace, which is called "Little Venice" because of its canals.
(5): Vineyards in Provence, which produce many fine table wines, rosés in particular.
(6): In Camargue, *gardians* (the French equivalent of cowboys) watch herds of black bulls. The white horses they ride are raised in the region. Camargue is also noted for its wildlife; a botanical and zoological reserve is located there.

Plates 6–7

(1): Quebec City was founded in 1608 by the French explorer Samuel de Champlain. It is often considered the most European-like city in North America. The *Château Frontenac* was built in 1892. It is a luxury hotel.
(2): The Jacques Cartier River, which was named after the French navigator who took possession of Canada in 1534 in the name of the king of France, Francis I.
(3): Haiti ("Mountainous Country") is a republic in the western part of Hispaniola, an island in the West Indies. The eastern part of the island is the Dominican Republic. The island was discovered by Christopher Columbus in 1492, who gave it the name of Hispaniola. In 1697 the part now known as Haiti was ceded to the French by a treaty. The independent Republic of Haiti was created in 1844.
(4): A French protectorate for a long time, Vietnam was divided into North and South Vietnam in 1954. In 1976, at the end of a long military conflict, North and South Vietnam were united under a single government.
(5), (6): Belgium is a kingdom in western Europe. It borders France to the north. It has close to 10 million inhabitants, 33% of whom speak French and 56% Dutch (also called Flemish). Some German is also spoken

in Belgium. Liège is a very old city, which was fortified centuries ago. In addition to being an industrial center, it is an important cultural center in French-speaking Belgium. It is also the seat of a university. *(7), (8):* Switzerland borders France to the east. It has 6,400,000 inhabitants, 18% of whom speak French, 65% German, 12% Italian, and 1% Romansch. It is a federation of 25 cantons, which have complete control when it comes to local matters. The federal capital is Bern. Switzerland is a beautiful country with high mountains, green hills, and calm lakes. The Swiss are very proud of the beauty of their country; they have stringent laws protecting the natural resources — wildlife and landscape — from pollution and destruction.

Plate 8

France once held many territories throughout Africa. In Algeria and Morocco, French is still widely used, but Arabic is the official language and is replacing French as the language used in schools. In Tunisia, French and Arabic both have the status of official languages. Unit 20, which starts on page 203, is entirely devoted to Tunisia. Refer to the Teaching Suggestions for that unit for additional information on Tunisia and North Africa.

France no longer holds any territories in Africa, but most sub-Saharan states have chosen to retain strong economic and cultural ties with France. French is used in schools and universities for business and administrative affairs. For additional information on African countries, see *"Documentaire sur le Sénégal,"* page 250, and Plates 8 and 27 in the photo essays.

(1): Abidjan, capital of the Ivory Coast, has close to 300,000 inhabitants. It is an important industrial and cultural center in Ivory Coast and West Africa.

7 LA FAMILLE DE CATHERINE LARDAN

Theme and Culture

The contemporary French family is very different from what the French family used to be. New economic factors are responsible in large part for the many changes that have occurred. In the past two decades, France has become a truly modern country. The French have more leisure time than they used to have, which means that they not only go out more but also entertain more, thus opening up the family and the home to friends and business acquaintances. The days when the home was almost exclusively a family place are gone.

Nowadays about 40% of French women work outside the home, encouraged by government assistance in the form of day-care centers and revised pay scales and job opportunities. As a result, all members of the family, including the children, have to share in the household responsibilities. Children also have a great deal more freedom than parents allowed a generation ago: they go out at an earlier age and are free to choose their own friends.

Regardless of these changes, French families still tend to settle down in one area, close to relatives. Catherine's family is typical in this respect: her grandparents live in Luneray, as do several aunts and uncles and their children.

Grammar

The interference of English in the use of *son, sa,* and *ses* is usually great. Make sure your students understand that only the gender and number of the noun that *follows* determine whether *son, sa* or *ses* is to be used.

Vocabulary

We are teaching students to discuss professions, using the construction *Il est (médecin)/Elle est (médecin)*, rather than the construction *C'est un (médecin)/C'est une (femme médecin)*, which is more difficult to handle. Make sure that students do not use an indefinite article in the construction *Il est (médecin)*.

Here is an expanded list of professions, which will help in answering Exercise 20:

accounting executive	*expert comptable*
advertising executive	*chef de publicité*
business manager	*cadre commercial*
president (of a company)	*P.D.G. (Président-Directeur Général)*
computer analyst	*informaticien*
financial analyst	*analyste financier*
insurance manager	*assureur*
legal counsel	*conseiller juridique*
real-estate agent	*agent immobilier*
sales manager	*chef de ventes*
salesman (woman)	*représentant(e)*
stockbroker	*agent de change*

Although there is a word in French for housewife—*ménagère*—it is seldom used. Magazines often use the expression *femme au foyer*. Students can say *Elle tient la maison,* or *Elle élève ses enfants.* Part-time work is *travail à mi-temps*.

Project

Have your students draw and label their family trees, indicating the professions of the adults on it. You may want to supply them with the appropriate vocabulary on an individual basis.

Game

Le jeu des familles: Have students make a deck of cards that will consist of drawings illustrating professions: one card will have a drawing of a male lawyer, another of a female lawyer. You should end up with an even number of cards. You may also want to add more professions. Cards are then shuffled and distributed. Students have to put couples back together by asking others: "Tu as la femme qui est médecin? Tu as l'homme qui est fermier?" The winner is the first one to have nothing but couples in his hand.

Script of Listening Exercise 34

You will hear eight sentences. For each one, decide whether we are talking about Philippe or about Catherine and Philippe. For example, you hear: *Ils n'attendent jamais les autres!* You place your check mark in the row labeled *Catherine et Philippe* because you heard the plural verb form *attendent*. Let's begin.

1. Il n'entend pas ce que vous dites. _____ *(il n'entend pas   Philippe)*
2. Ils descendent en ville toutes les semaines. _____ *(ils descendent   Catherine et Philippe)*
3. Ils ne répondent jamais au téléphone. _____ *(ils ne répondent jamais   Catherine et Philippe)*
4. Il descend dans cinq minutes. _____ *(il descend   Philippe)*
5. Ils tondent la pelouse pour gagner de l'argent. _____ *(ils tondent   Catherine et Philippe)*
6. Il répond toujours à toutes les questions. _____ *(il répond   Philippe)*

7. La ligne est mauvaise: ils n'entendent rien. _____ *(ils n'entendent rien   Catherine et Philippe)*
8. Il n'attend pas Dominique? _____ *(il n'attend pas   Philippe)*

Now check your answers. *Read each item again and give the correct answer.*

8 BON APPETIT

Theme and Culture

Although the percentage of a family budget allowed for food is decreasing, it is still 25% of the total, in comparison with 22% for lodgings and upkeep, 18% for leisure activities, and less than 10% for clothing. French people care a great deal about the food they eat. They care about the quality of the food they buy as much as about the preparation. Everyday meals may be quite simple, but they include a variety of well-prepared dishes, and they are nutritionally well balanced. Sunday dinner (always called *déjeuner* in France) is often more elaborate. It is a favorite time to invite relatives and friends.

There are many large supermarkets all over France, but the small specialized shops as well as open-air markets survive. Most towns, and even cities, have an open-air market once or twice a week. In Nice, the *Marché aux Fleurs* is open every day except holidays. The Giulianis buy their fruits and vegetables there, but they go to a butcher shop for their meat, a dairy outlet for their dairy products, a fishmonger for their fish, and a bakery for their bread. Fortunately, all these shops are located in the same area as the *Marché aux Fleurs*. The Giulianis shop twice a week, except for their bread, which they buy fresh daily.

You may want to say a few words about *la haute cuisine* and how it is changing, too, to suit the tastes of modern French people. Students may be interested in seeing some of the guides that list and grade restaurants all over France and Europe.

Grammar

We chose to introduce indirect-object pronouns before direct-object pronouns to make the distinction between the concept of indirect and direct object clearer: all the sentences students manipulate also include a direct object in the form of a noun phrase. Direct-object pronouns are introduced in Unit 10.

Vocabulary

The expression *une livre* (also *une demi-livre, un quart de livre*) is used in shopping; but it is not a unit of measure in the metric system. Students should understand that *une livre* is heavier than a pound. Discourage them from converting into ounces. You may want to give rough equivalents: *un kilo*—two pounds, *un litre*—one quart, etc.

Project

If school policy allows, have students bring all necessary items to make some *pain-bagnat,* following the recipe given on page 85.

Game

Le jeu de l'odorat can be transformed into *Le jeu du toucher:* students are blindfolded and must identify items only by touch.

In order to give students more experience with the metric system, you may want to have them guess (in metric units, of course) the weight or capacity of familiar food items: a quart of milk, a loaf of bread, a pint of cream, etc. This exercise is also a good way to review numbers.

Script of Listening Exercise 41

Mme Giuliani is asking Jean-Marcel to do a few errands for her. Can you figure out which stores Jean-Marcel will have to go to? For example, you hear: *Il n'y a pas de lait! Il faut acheter du lait pour le petit déjeuner.* You check the row labeled *Chez le crémier,* because Jean-Marcel has to buy some milk. Let's begin.

1. Prends deux gâteaux seulement, un pour toi et un pour papa. _____ *(Jean-Marcel va aller chez le boulanger pour acheter deux gâteaux.)*
2. Il faut de la crème fraîche pour les carottes. Achète un petit pot. _____ *(Il va aller chez le crémier pour acheter un petit pot de crème fraîche.)*
3. Qu'est-ce que tu aimes mieux pour dimanche un rôti de bœuf ou un gigot? _____ *(Il va aller chez le boucher pour acheter un rôti de bœuf ou un gigot.)*
4. Ce soir, on va manger une omelette. Achète une douzaine d'œufs. _____ *(Il va aller chez le crémier pour acheter une douzaine d'œufs.)*
5. Nous n'avons pas de hors-d'œuvre pour le déjeuner. Prends donc un peu de pâté. _____ *(Il va aller chez le charcutier pour acheter du pâté.)*
6. N'achète pas de croissants. Une baguette, c'est tout. _____ *(Il va aller chez le boulanger pour acheter une baguette.)*
7. Je sais que tu n'aimes pas ça, mais prends quand même 150 g de rillettes. _____ *(Il va aller chez le charcutier pour acheter des rillettes.)*
8. S'il n'y a plus de côtelettes de porc, prends des côtelettes d'agneau. _____ *(Il va aller chez le boucher pour acheter des côtelettes de porc ou d'agneau.)*
9. Ne prends pas trop de jambon. Trois tranches c'est assez. _____ *(Il va aller chez le charcutier pour acheter trois tranches de jambon.)*
10. Un yaourt à la vanille pour moi et des yaourts aux fruits pour ton père et toi. _____ *(Il va aller chez le crémier pour acheter des yaourts.)*

Now check your answers. *Read each item again and give the correct answer.*

9 LA SURPRISE-PARTIE

Theme and Culture

Parties are very popular with young people in France, especially the kind Catherine, Philippe, and their friends give: they do not live in or near a big city and therefore do not have access to much entertainment. Parties often take place on Wednesday or Saturday afternoons, sometimes on Saturday night. The food may consist of appetizingly decorated, small, open sandwiches called *canapés;* potato chips and other "crunchy" snacks; cheese bits; miniature puffs with various salted fillings; miniature pastries; and fruit salads. The drinks include all sorts of sodas, fruit punches, and sometimes beer and wine. The host family often provides food and drinks. For more informal parties, everyone brings something.

French young people take great care with the way they dress. The party described in this unit is very informal; but even so, both girls and boys choose their clothing carefully. For instance, the girls are careful about coordinating jewelry, scarves, and sandals; and the boys, their socks, pants, and shirts.

You may want to mention, as an aside, that clothes are very expensive in France, even the casual ones like jeans. But they are well made and last a long time. French young people do not have many outfits, but they usually look well dressed wherever they go.

Grammar

In this unit, only the formation of the *passé composé* with *avoir* is introduced. Agreement of the past participle with a preceding direct object is treated in Units 10 and 14. The *passé composé* with *être* is introduced in Unit 11.

The use of *en* usually requires a great deal of practice. The use of *en* in negative constructions with the *passé composé* presents the added difficulty of pronunciation. Suggestions for drills on this specific point appear on the text page.

Vocabulary

The vocabulary covers a wide range of party activities and gives the appropriate expressions for asking for, giving, and taking food and drink, asking someone to dance, and so forth. Use the project below or a variation of it to help students practice the new words and phrases.

Project

Help the class to plan a French party (perhaps for after school). Prepare food and drinks, listen to music, sing French songs, play games. Use *Les Secrets d'une Bonne Surprise-Partie*, page 95, as a guide.

Game

The game of *Devinettes* often makes use of *en*. Have students ask riddles using *en*. For example, *On en boit au petit déjeuner. Qu'est-ce que c'est?* Answer: *Du café au lait.*

Script of Listening Exercise 20

You will hear ten sentences. For each one, decide whether we are talking about something that took place last night, *Hier soir,* or something that will take place in an hour, *Dans une heure.* For example, you hear: *Ils ont donné une surprise-partie.* You put your check mark in the row labeled *Hier soir,* because you heard a form of the verb *avoir, ils ont,* and not a form of the verb *aller.* Let's begin.

1. Ils ont invité leurs amis. _____ *(ils ont (avoir)   Hier soir)*
2. Ils ont acheté le pâté et le saucisson. _____ *(ils ont (avoir)   Hier soir)*
3. Ils vont préparer les sandwiches. _____ *(ils vont (aller)   Dans une heure)*
4. Ils vont balayer leur pièce. _____ *(ils vont (aller)   Dans une heure)*
5. Ils vont ranger leurs disques. _____ *(ils vont (aller)   Dans une heure)*
6. Il a réparé l'électrophone. _____ *(il a (avoir)   Hier soir)*
7. Elle a tout vérifié. _____ *(elle a (avoir)   Hier soir)*
8. On va écouter des disques. _____ *(on va (aller)   Dans une heure)*
9. On va manger les sandwiches. _____ *(on va (aller)   Dans une heure)*
10. On a discuté. _____ *(on a (avoir)   Hier soir)*

Now check your answers. *Read each item again and give the correct answer.*

Answers to Writing Exercise 19

Philippe et moi, nous avons donné une surprise-partie. Nous avons préparé les sandwiches. Nous avons rangé notre pièce. Nous avons réparé l'électrophone. Nous avons descendu les disques. Nous avons choisi nos vêtements.

10   VILLE D'AVRAY

Theme and Culture

Ville d'Avray is a typical small town in the suburb of Paris. It has 11,700 inhabitants, and the population is increasing because of the construction of new housing, in particular the *résidences,* the type of garden apartments that Christine and her family just moved into. *Résidences* are always surrounded by lawns and trees. They often have their own tennis courts and recreation facilities for children. Even in the suburbs, many people have to live in apartments and therefore welcome the concept of *résidence* as a step away from the large housing developments that have sprung up in and around cities. For example, it is estimated that in Paris and its suburbs, one out of five families lives in an apartment.

Although a lot of progress has been made in the last two decades, finding adequate housing at an affordable price is still a problem for many French families. According to a recent poll, 70% of French people would like to live in private houses. Only 50% do.

Grammar

In this unit we are introducing the agreement of past participles of verbs conjugated with *avoir* in the *passé composé.* This presentation is limited to direct-object pronouns, which always precede the verb. Agreement with nouns as preceding direct objects will be treated in Unit 14.

Vocabulary

The verb *connaître* is introduced in this unit. *Savoir* and the contrast between *connaître* and *savoir* will be treated in Unit 16.

Project

Have students draw a map of the town (or district, in a big city) where they live. Have them say how to go from their homes to school, to the library, to the post office, etc.

Game

Using the map on page 102, have one student tell which way he or she goes and have the others figure out where he or she ended up.

Script of Listening Exercise 40

You will hear eight sentences, each one followed by two items, A and B. Decide whether each sentence refers to item A or item B. For example, you hear: *Qui est-ce qui l'a pris?*   A   *mon électrophone;*

B ma grande affiche. The sentence contains the word *pris*, the masculine form of the past participle. So you check the row labeled A, because *électrophone* is a masculine word, corresponding to the masculine form *pris*. Let's begin.

1. C'est la tante de Christine qui l'a fait.
   A ce gâteau B cette tarte _____ *(qui l'a fait A, ce gâteau)*
2. Je ne l'ai pas comprise.
   A ce problème B cette question _____ *(ne l'ai pas comprise B, cette question)*
3. Qui est-ce qui l'a faite?
   A cette petite affiche B ce dessin _____ *(qui l'a faite A, cette petite affiche)*
4. Ce n'est pas moi qui l'ai prise.
   A ta cassette B ton disque _____ *(qui l'ai prise A, ta cassette)*
5. Où est-ce que je les ai mises?
   A mes bijoux B mes lunettes _____ *(je les ai mises B, mes lunettes)*
6. C'est toi qui l'a pris?
   A ma limonade B mon Cola-Cola _____ *(qui l'a pris B, mon Cola-Cola)*
7. Nous l'avons mis dans ta chambre.
   A ta revue B ton journal _____ *(l'avons mis B, ton journal)*
8. Tu l'as compris?
   A le deuxième exercice B la première question _____ *(l'as compris A, le deuxième exercice)*

Now check your answers. *Read each item again and give the correct answer.*

Answers to Exercise 24: C'est vous le guide!

1. On prend la rue de la Ronce, la rue de Versailles et la rue de Saint-Cloud.
2. On prend la rue Corot.
3. On prend l'avenue Gambetta.
4. On prend l'allée des Etangs, la rue de Versailles, la rue de la Ronce et la rue de la Prairie.
5. On prend la rue de la Prairie, la rue de Sèvres et la rue de Versailles.
6. On prend la rue de Versailles et la rue de la Ronce.

11 PARIS

Theme and Culture

Taking a ride on a *bateau-mouche* allows one to see many of Paris' historical sights, because many of these sights are on or near the river. The boats leave from the *Pont de l'Alma*. There are two routes: both go as far as the *Ile Saint-Louis* to the east, but to the west one goes only as far as the Eiffel Tower while the other goes on to the *Statue de la Liberté*, a small replica of Bartholdi's work. (The map on page 111 shows only the shorter route.) In the summer, boats leave every half hour. Lunch is served on the 1:00 p. m. boat (longer excursion), and dinner on the 8:30 p.m. one. In the winter, boats leave only three or four times a day.

This unit gives a glimpse of Paris in words and pictures. Many books are available on Paris, some of them lavishly illustrated. Encourage students to read about Paris, both as it is in modern times and as it was in history.

Grammar

Point out to students that verbs which can form their *passé composé* with either *être* or *avoir* have different meanings, depending on which auxiliary is used. The translations of the sentences in the chart on page 113 appear in the word list of this unit.

Vocabulary

The texts of the captions of all photographs in this unit are recognition material. They are for information only and are translated in a special "For Reference" section at the end of the unit. They should be gone over carefully, however, to establish the names of the monuments and landmarks and what they represent. These names are very useful for the games and special features of this unit.

Project

Have students build a Monopoly game, using the names of the streets and avenues on the map on page 117. Give them the names of four railroad stations in Paris: *Gare du Nord, Gare de l'Est, Gare de Lyon, Gare d'Austerlitz,* or *Gare Montparnasse.* Have them use some device to represent houses and apartment buildings. This game provides a good review of all the vocabulary introduced in Unit 10.

You might also assign an illustrated paper on Paris, which would give some history and background of some of the monuments. It could be modeled on this unit.

Games

The *Devinettes* game on page 115 can be expanded: using the map on page 111, one student can say, *"Je fais une promenade en bateau-mouche. Nous sommes au Pont des Invalides; nous allons vers* (give translation "toward") *le Pont Alexandre III. Le premier monument à gauche, qu'est-ce que c'est? Et le deuxième?"* The other students have to figure out what the monuments are. This is a good way to review ordinal numbers.

Script of Listening Exercise 27

You are going to hear sentences describing several Paris landmarks. For each sentence, decide which landmark is being described. For example, you hear: *On peut y voir le tombeau de Napoléon.* You put your check mark in the row labeled *Les Invalides.* Let's begin.

1. Cette cathédrale se dresse au cœur de Paris. _____ (Notre-Dame)
2. Cette grande église blanche est en haut de Montmarte. _____ (Le Sacré-Coeur)
3. Cet ancien palais royal est maintenant un grand musée. _____ (Le Louvre)
4. On y trouve de nombreuses expositions d'art moderne. _____ (Beaubourg)
5. Cet édifice domine les Champs-Elysées. _____ (L'Arc de Triomphe)
6. Il se dresse au milieu de la Place de la Concorde. _____ (L'Obélisque)
7. Ce musée abrite *La Joconde.* _____ (Le Louvre)
8. Il a été construit au milieu d'une place en forme d'étoile. _____ (L'Arc de Triomphe)

Now check your answers. *Read each item again and give the correct answer.*

Answers to Exercise 10: Les Sautelet ont visité la France.

Oui, nous avons passé une semaine à Nice.
Oui, elle a passé une semaine à Dieppe.
Oui, ils ont passé une semaine à Montargis.

Answers to Exercise 24: Suivez la piste!

Itinéraire Palais de Chaillot-Louvre: L'Avenue Kléber, L'Avenue des Champs-Elysées, la Rue Royale, le Boulevard des Capucines, l'Avenue de l'Opéra.

Itinéraire Tour Eiffel-Ile de la Cité: l'Avenue de la Bourdonnais et l'Avenue de Tourville, le Boulevard des Invalides, le Boulevard du Montparnasse et la Rue de Vaugirard, la Rue Médicis, le Boulevard Saint-Michel et le Pont Saint-Michel.

12   LA LETTRE

Theme and Culture

The French Post Office—les P.T.T. (see Teaching Suggestions for Unit 6)—is a large company that not only moves and distributes the mail but also operates the telephone and telegraph services. In addition, it offers a service of Boîtes Postales, abbreviated B.P. (P.O. Box), and of Poste Restante (General Delivery)—and it administers the Service des Chèques Postaux, a national banking service of checking accounts. It houses transaction counters for the Caisse Nationale d'Epargne, a national savings bank. And it publishes a calendar sold door-to-door at the beginning of each year. The proceeds of this sale go to the letter carriers.

French stamps usually make elaborate use of French art and are very beautiful. Those on page 122 are good examples and will probably interest the philatelists in your class.

Point out to your students that the French zip code comes before the name of the town or city. The first 2 numbers correspond to the number of the départment, the last 3 to the number of the delivering post office. There are from 30 to 250 post offices for each départment. In the case of Paris and Marseille, the last 2 numbers correspond to the number of the arrondissement.

Grammar

We have generally avoided introducing new grammar points in review units. Given the topic of this unit, however, it was necessary to introduce the verb écrire.

Project

Have students make a French calendar. Start the week with Monday; label the months; and, referring to a recent French calendar, write in the holidays, etc. If you can find a P.T.T. calendar, so much the better!

Script of Listening Exercise 23

You will hear nine sentences. For each one, decide whether we are talking about 1) something that is taking place now, En ce moment, 2) something that will take place in an hour, Dans une heure, or 3) something that took place last night, Hier soir. For example, you hear: J'ai écrit à mon cousin. You place your check mark in the row labeled Hier soir, because the words j'ai écrit refer to past time. Let's begin.

1. Jean-Marcel est allé à Monaco. _____ (est allé   Hier soir)
2. Il visite le musée océanographique. _____ (visite   En ce moment)
3. Jean-Marcel est sur la terrasse. _____ (est   En ce moment)
4. Il regarde les bateaux dans le port. _____ (regarde   En ce moment)
5. Les bateaux vont sortir du port. _____ (vont sortir   Dans une heure)

6. Jean-Marcel raconte sa visite à ses parents. _____ *(raconte   En ce moment)*
7. Il va écrire une lettre à ses cousins. _____ *(va écrire   Dans une heure)*
8. Il va mettre sa lettre à la poste. _____ *(va mettre   Dans une heure)*
9. Il a acheté des timbres. _____ *(a acheté   Hier soir)*

Now check your answers. *Read each item again and give the correct answer.*

Answers to Exercise 12: Lisez les dates suivantes:

4/7/1976	le quatre juillet mille neuf cent soixante-seize
29/2/1982	le vingt-neuf février mille neuf cent quatre-vingt deux
14/5/1960	le quatorze mai mille neuf cent soixante
24/9/1999	le vingt-quatre septembre mille neuf cent quatre-vingt dix-neuf
1/1/1980	le premier janvier mille neuf cent quatre-vingts
12/10/1492	le douze octobre mille quatre cent quatre-vingt douze

Answers to Writing Exercise 25

1. Je vais donner une surprise-partie et je t'invite.
2. Elle va avoir lieu le . . . à . . .
3. J'ai invité . . .
4. Mets ce que tu veux comme vêtements.

5. Quels disques est-ce que tu peux apporter?
6. J'attends ta réponse avec impatience.
7. Je te rappelle mon numéro de téléphone: . . .

PHOTO ESSAY Following Unit 12 — Plates 8–16

CITY LIFE

Most of the population of French-speaking countries lives in or around cities. The people from these cities all share certain experiences — the hectic pace of city life with its cultural opportunities and its excitement, along with its crowds and noise.

Plate 9

Façade of one of the towers at *La Défense* (Paris).

Plates 10–11

(1): The small window panes are very typical of Quebec houses.
(2): The red tiles are made of clay found in the south of France. The way they are laid out provides especially good insulation from the sun. Notice the Byzantine influence on the church steeple.
(4): Lyon is 20 centuries old. In Roman times, it was called Lugdunum. It is a large industrial center which produces steel and silk and artificial fabrics. Lyon and its surrounding areas are also famous for their cuisine.
(5): This square is named after Stanislas Leczinsky, father-in-law of King Louis XV.
(7): Neuchâtel is located on the lake of the same name. It is a charming, small city with houses of ocher color, surrounded by vineyards.
(9): Nice's location on the *Baie des Anges* has made it the capital of the *Côte d'Azur*. It has grown very rapidly in the last decade, ever since the expansion of its airport, the third largest in France.

(5): Juggler of firebrands in front of *Beaubourg,* in Paris.
(6): La Défense, Paris.
(7): The Luxembourg Garden in Paris.
(8): Exhibition, called *Salon de la Jeune Sculpture,* in the Champs-Elysées Gardens, in Paris.

13   LA JOURNEE DE VIVIANE

Theme and Culture

At the age of 16, young people have the choice of either staying in school or going to work. Many, like Viviane, choose to go to work. Until the age of 18, they are considered *enfants* under the labor laws: their employers must therefore abide by certain rules, such as the ones regulating the number of hours a week they work (a maximum of 40 for 16-year-olds). About 60% of young workers have only a *Certificat d'Etudes Primaires,* a diploma marking the end of elementary school.

Most young people who work live at home until they get married and often afterwards, for economic reasons. They usually contribute a large portion of their income to the family expenses.

Grammar

We have deliberately underplayed the "myself, yourself" equivalents of the reflexive pronouns, since most of the time they do not appear in the corresponding English constructions. In this unit we have also limited the constructions to the present tense and the imperative. Their use in the past tense is treated in Unit 15. Reflexive constructions are reviewed in Unit 18.

Since most English-speaking students find the concept of reflexive constructions new and strange, they may find it difficult to master their use. For that reason we have devoted most of the grammar work in the unit to this subject.

Make sure students understand that when *ne . . . personne* is used in the *passé composé, personne* does not behave like other negative words.

Vocabulary

The vocabulary in this unit is extremely useful everyday vocabulary that can be drilled in a number of ways and should be fun to work with.

Game

Le jeu des charades mimées could be played to elicit reflexive verbs. Make two teams of five students each. Give each student one reflexive verb to act out. The winning team will be the one that conveys the correct meanings of its five verbs in the shortest time.

Script of Listening Exercise 36

You will hear six brief statements, each one followed by two sentences, A and B. Decide which sentence makes more sense after the statement you heard. For example, you hear: *Viviane a faim. A   Elle me fait un sandwich; B   Elle se fait un sandwich.* If Viviane is hungry, she'll make a sandwich for herself, not for you. So you put your check mark in the row labeled B. Let's begin.

1. Mon réveil sonne.
   A Je me réveille.   B Viviane me réveille. _____ *(A, Je me réveille.)*
2. Viviane va sortir avec des amis.
   A Elle s'habille.   B Elle m'habille. _____ *(A, Elle s'habille.)*
3. Viviane a le téléphone.
   A Elle s'appelle Viviane.   B Je l'appelle souvent. _____ *(B, Je l'appelle souvent.)*
4. Mon chien a envie de sortir.
   A Je vais le promener.   B Je vais me promener. _____ *(A, Je vais le promener.)*
5. Viviane va de la Porte d'Orléans à la Concorde.
   A Elle se change.   B Elle change à Montparnasse. _____ *(B, Elle change à Montparnasse.)*
6. Viviane est épuisée!
   A Elle va la coucher.   B Elle va se coucher. _____ *(B, Elle va se coucher.)*

Now check your answers. *Read each item again and give the correct answer.*

Answers to Writing Exercise 20

1. Nous nous lavons et nous nous habillons en vingt minutes.
2. Pour le petit déjeuner, nous nous faisons du chocolat.
3. A huit heures, nous sommes prêts à partir à l'école.
4. Nous avons un trajet d'une heure pour nous rendre à l'école.
5. Nous prenons d'abord l'autobus, puis nous y allons à pied.

Answers to Exercise 21: Dans le métro.

1. Pour aller de la station Odéon à la station Trocadéro, on prend la ligne No 10, direction Porte d'Auteuil, on change à la station La Motte Picquet et on prend la ligne No 6, direction Charles de Gaulle Etoile, jusqu'à la station Trocadéro.
2. Pour aller de la station Trocadéro à la station Père-Lachaise, on prend la ligne No 9, direction Mairie de Montreuil, on change à la station République et on prend la ligne No 3, direction Gallieni, jusqu'à la station Père-Lachaise.

14   JAZZ A LUNERAY

Theme and Culture

Jazz in all its forms has always been very popular in France with people of all ages. The annual festival held in Antibes-Juan-les-Pins in August brings together many celebrities from the jazz world. On a smaller scale, Luneray has its own annual jazz festival. It is called the *Jam Potato* because it is held in a converted potato silo. The members of the *Canards à l'Orange* and their parents actively participate in the organizing of the festival.

As for pop music, young people in France often listen to the same popular music that we hear in the United States. Many records on the French Hit Parade are from the United States or Great Britain. Furthermore, many French singers of pop music translate American or English songs into French.

There is also a truly French kind of song, however, characterized by a particular style of singing and declamation. In France, songs have traditionally been thought of as vehicles for political and social messages, as well as for poetry of the more lyrical kind. Like singers in other countries, and like the troubadours, some French singers write their own words and music, thus expressing their personal perception of the world. Such singers—the late Jacques Brel, for example—appeal to people of all ages and social backgrounds.

Grammar

The interrogative adjectives and interrogative and demonstrative pronouns lend themselves well to quick-response exercises. Have students pick up items and ask questions, such as: *"Tu veux quel livre?"* Answer: *"Celui-là."* Question: *"Lequel?!"* Answer: *"Celui-là!!"* You can also use item posters to cue such an exchange.

Project

You may want to introduce your students to some French or Canadian singers. Since students may find it difficult to understand the words of songs in a foreign language, you may want to tell your students what the songs are about before you play them.

Vocabulary

Apart from the general music vocabulary, you may find the vocabulary related to tape recorders especially useful.

Script of Listening Exercise 18

You will hear five questions, each followed by the sound of a different musical instrument. Answer each question by checking the appropriate row, to indicate what instrument you heard. For example, you hear: *Qu'est-ce que c'est, de la batterie ou du trombone?* [sound of drums]. You check the box next to *batterie,* since the instrument you heard was the drums. Let's begin.

1. C'est du saxophone ou du violoncelle? [saxophone] _____ *(C'est du saxophone.)*
2. C'est du tuba ou de l'orgue? [organ] _____ *(C'est de l'orgue.)*
3. C'est du banjo ou du piano? [banjo] _____ *(C'est du banjo.)*
4. C'est de la guitare ou de la trompette? [trumpet] _____ *(C'est de la trompette.)*
5. C'est de la flûte ou du violon? [violin] _____ *(C'est du violon.)*

Now check your answers. *Read each item again and give the correct answer.*

Answers to Writing Exercise 13

1. Je viens d'entrer dans un groupe.
2. Nous venons de jouer dans toute la région.
3. Mon groupe vient d'aller à Luneray.
4. Nous venons de rencontrer les Canards.
5. Je viens d'entendre leur dernier disque.

Answers to Writing Exercise 25

1. Quel groupe est-ce qu'il a écouté?
2. Quelles chansons est-ce qu'ils ont chantées?
3. Quel air est-ce qu'ils ont répété?
4. Quels morceaux est-ce qu'ils ont choisis?

15 SKI AU QUEBEC

Theme and Culture

Skiing is the favorite sport of most young *Québécois*. The winter is long and there is lots of snow—ideal conditions for skiing. Many *Québécois* learn to ski when they are very young. They ski on weekends or even after school, since most places have night skiing. The other sport they like is ice-hockey for boys and a tamer version for girls, called *ballon-balai*.

Saint-Sauveur is one of the ski resorts closest to Montreal. Further north in the Laurentians is the famous resort of Mont-Tremblant. The mountain of the same name is the highest in the Laurentians. The area is a year-round operation and very beautiful at any time. Winter-sports enthusiasts come in winter and in spring; in summer and fall come the hikers, the anglers, and the campers. Most of the resorts also cater to the tourists' appetite for food: one can find many good restaurants and inns throughout the region.

This unit on Quebec takes us outside France for the first time (except for Units 1 and 3). You may want to indicate that French Canadians speak with an accent different from the French and use different words or expressions in some instances. No Canadianisms have been included in this unit, however. Point out that the French spoken by educated Canadians is slightly different from that spoken by educated French people, just as the English spoken by educated Americans is slightly different from that spoken by educated Britishers.

Grammar

We have chosen not to teach double object pronouns in Level One. Sentence sequences like *Elle s'est lavé les mains.—Elle se les est lavées* should therefore be avoided, especially since they present an additional problem of agreement.

Vocabulary

Try to make your students "think in Celsius." For example, you can link Celsius degrees to weather expressions: *Il fait 14, il fait bon*. Although perceived heat and cold are subjective matters, there is usually sufficient consensus in a given place on the "feel" of the temperature.

Projects

• Have students keep a daily record of the outside temperature in Celsius.
• The students might make a table using a Celsius scale from 45° to −40°. Make three columns next to the scale and label them *Eté*, *Printemps et Automne*, and *Hiver*. In each column the students should write a weather expression, such as, *Il fait très chaud. Il fait très froid*. For example, 20° in summer is mild; in spring and fall it is warm; and in winter it is very hot.

Script of Listening Exercise 32

You will hear six statements, each one followed by three possible questions: question A, question B, and question C. Decide which question is the correct one following each statement. For example, you hear: *Nous sommes allés dans une station des Laurentides.   A. Dans lequel? B. Dans laquelle? C. Dans lesquels?* You put your check mark in the row labeled B, because *une station* is feminine singular and requires the feminine singular form of the interrogative pronoun, which is *laquelle*. Let's begin.

1. Ces montagnes sont très belles.
   A Lequel?   B Laquelle?   C Lesquelles? _____ *(C, Lesquelles?)*
2. Prenons cette piste.
   A Lequel?   B Laquelle?   C Lesquels? _____ *(B, Laquelle?)*
3. Ils ont parlé à un moniteur.
   A Auquel?   B A laquelle?   C Duquel? _____ *(A, Auquel?)*
4. J'ai mal à la jambe.
   A Auquel?   B A laquelle?   C De laquelle? _____ *(B, A laquelle?)*
5. Denise et ses amis parlent d'un moniteur.
   A A laquelle?   B De laquelle?   C Duquel? _____ *(C, Duquel?)*
6. Ce vent vient des montagnes.
   A Desquelles?   B Auxquelles?   C Duquel? _____ *(A, Desquelles?)*

Now check your answers. *Read each item again and give the correct answer.*

16   UN VILLAGE DANS LES PYRENEES

Theme and Culture

In France, farmers make up about 12% of the population, but their number is diminishing. Work on a small French farm is hard. It is usually divided among all members of the family. The father and the older sons will work the fields, take care of the equipment, and, generally speaking, do the heavy work; the mother and the other children will take care of the animals, tend the vegetable garden, and prepare meals.

Although farming is very much mechanized nowadays, and farmers have formed cooperatives, many farmers find that they still cannot make an adequate living; so they move to the city, just as Monique's family did.

Grammar

In this unit we introduce only one use of the *imparfait,* the equivalent of "used to." In the next unit, we introduce other uses of the *imparfait* and also contrast the *imparfait* with the *passé composé.* The *imparfait* and the *passé composé* are reviewed in Unit 18.

The contrast between *connaître* and *savoir* is dealt with here. It can be practiced with common classroom situations, like talking about a map.

Vocabulary

The vocabulary in this unit is rather specific, since it deals with farm life, an experience not all students will have had. They will become familiar with what life is like in a small French village, and they may find similar situations in their own experiences—visiting grandparents in the country, for example, or having outings on weekends.

Game

You may want to expand on the *Devinettes* game on page 168.

Script of Listening Exercise 21

You will hear a series of animal sounds. For each one, decide which animal made the sound. For example, you hear: *Voilà le premier animal, Qu'est-ce que c'est?* [sheep bleating] You place the number 1 next to *un mouton,* because the sound was a sheep bleating. Let's begin.

Le deuxième animal, qu'est-ce que c'est? [pigeon cooing] _____ *(C'est un pigeon.)*
Le troisième animal, qu'est-ce que c'est? [dog barking] _____ *(C'est un chien.)*
Le quatrième animal, qu'est-ce que c'est? [hen cackling] _____ *(C'est une poule.)*
Le cinquième animal, qu'est-ce que c'est? [cat mewing] _____ *(C'est un chat.)*
Le sixième animal, qu'est-ce que c'est? [duck quacking] _____ *(C'est un canard.)*
Le septième animal, qu'est-ce que c'est? [pig grunting] _____ *(C'est un cochon.)*
Le huitième animal, qu'est-ce que c'est? [cow mooing] _____ *(C'est une vache.)*

Now check your answers. *Read each item again and give the correct answer.*

Script of Listening Exercise 32

You will hear ten sentences. For each one, decide whether we are talking about something that is taking place now, *maintenant,* or something that was taking place or used to take place in the past, *avant.* For example, you hear: *Nous habitions un petit village.* You place your check mark in the row labeled *Avant* because you hear the *imparfait* form *habitions.* Let's begin.

1. Nous habitons dans le même village. _____ *(habitons, présent   Maintenant)*
2. Nous allions à l'école ensemble. _____ *(allions, imparfait   Avant)*
3. Nous étions dans la même classe. _____ *(étions, imparfait   Avant)*
4. Nous avions les mêmes camarades. _____ *(avions, imparfait   Avant)*
5. Nous passons nos vacances ensemble. _____ *(passons, présent   Maintenant)*
6. Nous jouions dans les prés. _____ *(jouions, imparfait   Avant)*
7. Nous faisons nos devoirs. _____ *(faisons, présent   Maintenant)*
8. Nous sommes amis. _____ *(sommes, présent   Maintenant)*
9. Nous faisions des confitures. _____ *(faisions, imparfait   Avant)*
10. Nous visitons les Pyrénées. _____ *(visitons, présent   Maintenant)*

Now check your answers. *Read each item again and give the correct answer.*

Answers to Writing Exercise 10

1. Ils ont une nouvelle ferme.
2. Il y a un beau hangar.
3. Ils ont acheté un nouveau tracteur.
4. Ils ont gardé la vieille grange.
5. Il y a de beaux arbres à Ore.
6. Le vieux grenier n'a pas changé.

Answers to Writing Exercise 33

Il y a six ans, mes parents et moi, nous habitions Ore. Nous avions une grande ferme. Mon père cultivait nos champs de blé et de maïs. Ma mère s'occupait du jardin potager. Moi, je gardais nos moutons avec l'aide de mon chien César. Mon frère s'occupait des vaches. Nous aidions aussi nos parents à faire les foins. En général, c'était moi qui faisais la litière du cochon. J'aimais beaucoup les travaux de la ferme.

17 LA MARTINIQUE

Theme and Culture

Martinique is one of the *départements d'outre-mer,* which means that it is a part of France even though it is 3,000 miles from Europe. It has about 325,000 inhabitants, who speak French and a local dialect called *créole.* (The adjective *créole* applied to a person designates a white man or woman born in the Caribbean islands.)

Martinique was discovered by Christopher Columbus. The French landed there in 1635. On June 25 of that year, 550 people from Dieppe arrived and founded St-Pierre. Most of them left almost immediately for the neighboring island of Guadeloupe: Martinique had far too many snakes for their liking!

The first wife of Napoleon I, Joséphine Tascher de la Pagerie, was born in Martinique. The reading at the end of the unit tells the story of the eruption of Mount Pelée, on the 5th of August 1902, which killed 26,000 people and destroyed St-Pierre.

There are many books on the Caribbean Islands. Encourage students to read about the islands where French is spoken (Martinique, Guadeloupe, Haïti, St-Barthélemy, St-Martin, Dominique, Grenade, Grenadines, Ste-Lucie, St-Vincent).

Grammar

The distinction between *imparfait* and *passé composé* is, for most students, one of the most difficult points of grammar to master. The more often students are exposed to it, the more they will come to internalize the distinction. But it usually takes a lot of practice.

We have simplified the contrast between *passé composé* and *imparfait* to make it easier for the students. You may want to tell them, however, that the choice of the *imparfait* or the *passé composé* does not depend on when the action took place but on how the speaker chooses to describe the action or condition he is referring to. For example, both sentences are possible: *Nous allions au bord de la mer tous les ans,* and *Nous sommes allés au bord de la mer tous les ans.* In the first sentence, the speaker considers the duration of the action, and in the second, the speaker considers the action as being completed. The contrast between *passé composé* and *imparfait* is reviewed in the next unit.

Vocabulary

Many words in this unit are for recognition only. They are technical words relating largely to the sea and tropical islands. Students should enjoy learning about the sea fauna; some may want to use the words in projects.

Project

The project on page 184 can be expanded. Have students incorporate the vocabulary introduced in Numbers 17 and 18. Individual reading and research will help here, along with a study of photographs from the unit and elsewhere. Reviewing earlier photographs would also be a useful preparation.

Script of Listening Exercise 24

You will hear five brief dialogs. After each one, you will hear two brief statements, A and B. These statements are printed on the page in front of you. Decide which statement best describes the situation discussed in the dialog, and put your check mark in the appropriate row.

For example, you hear: (Danou parle à Doris.)

> DANOU Où étais-tu? Je te cherchais...
>
> DORIS J'étais derrière ce rocher. J'essayais d'attraper un poisson pour mon aquarium.

You hear and read: A. Doris essayait d'attraper un poisson pour son aquarium.

> B. Doris a attrapé un poisson pour son aquarium.

You put your check mark in the row labeled A, because statement A best describes the situation in the dialog. Let's begin.

1. (Anne, une amie de Danou, lui demande...)

ANNE Tu as déjà fait de l'exploration sous-marine?

DANOU J'en faisais tous les week-ends avant mon accident, mais maintenant je n'en fais plus.

A. Danou a fait de l'exploration sous-marine le week-end dernier.

B. Danou faisait de l' exploration sous-marine avant son accident. _____ (B)

2. (Doris parle à Daquin.)

DORIS Tu vas à la pêche tous les jours?

DAQUIN J'allais à la pêche tous les jours quand j'étais plus jeune. Maintenant j'y vais une fois par semaine.

A. Daquin n'est jamais allé à la pêche.

B. Daquin allait à la pêche tous les jours quand il était jeune. _____ (B)

3. (Mme Dubois parle à Danou.)

MME DUBOIS Tu as eu un accident?

> DANOU Oui, je poursuivais un beau poisson-clown avec une épuisette, quand une énorme vague m'a jeté contre un rocher plein d'oursins!

A. Danou poursuivait un poisson-clown quand il a eu un accident.

B. Danou a attrapé un poisson-clown et des oursins. _____ (A)

4. (M. Dubois parle à Doris.)

M. DUBOIS Où est-ce que vous êtes allés à la pêche avec Daquin?

> DORIS Nous sommes allés du côté de la Pointe du Diable. Il faisait très beau et nous avons attrapé beaucoup de langoustes.

A. Doris, Danou et Daquin sont allés pêcher la langouste du côté de la Pointe du Diable.

B. Doris est allée pêcher avec son père du côté de la Pointe du Diable. _____ (A)

5. (Paul, un ami de Doris, lui demande...)

PAUL Il y a des récifs du côté de la Pointe du Diable?

DORIS Oui, ils sont très beaux. Nous les avons explorés le week-end dernier. C'était fantastique!

A. Avant, il y avait des récifs de coraux de côté de la Pointe du Diable, mais maintenant il n'y en a plus.

B. Le week-end dernier, les Dubois ont exploré les récifs de coraux de la Pointe de Diable. _____ (B)

Now check your answers. *Read each item again and give the correct answer.*

Answers to Exercise 6: Regardez la carte des Antilles, page 174.

Et Haïti?	A l'est de la Jamaïque et à l'ouest de Porto-Rico.
Et Cuba?	Au sud de la Floride et au nord de la Jamaïque.
Et la Guadeloupe?	Au sud-est de Porto-Rico et au nord de la Martinique.
Et la Jamaïque?	Au sud de Cuba et à l'ouest d'Haïti.
Et Porto-Rico?	A l'est d'Haïti et au nord-ouest de la Guadeloupe.

Answers to Writing Exercise 23

Samedi dernier, comme il faisait beau et chaud, mon père a décidé de nous emmener faire de l'exploration sous-marine. Nous avons pris notre équipement, nous sommes allés au port, nous sommes montés sur notre bateau et nous sommes partis. Mais, comme nous arrivions près des récifs de coraux, le temps a commencé à changer et la mer est devenue mauvaise. Les vagues jetaient/ont jeté notre bateau vers les rochers . . . C'était très dangereux. Nous sommes partis le plus vite possible vers une petite baie qui n'était pas loin de là, pour attendre le beau temps.

18 FRANÇOIS A L'ECOLE DE VOILE

Theme and Culture

Young and old alike in France have taken an increasingly active interest in sailing. As a result, many sailing camps are run in the summer for young people as well as for adults; and because of their popularity, sessions (courses) are booked far in advance. The best-known of these camps is the *Centre Nautique des Glénans* in Brittany.

La Gracieuse is one of the camps operated by *Jeunesse et Marine,* an organization devoted to teaching sailing to young people. It is situated near Bordeaux on the *lac d'Hourtin* (18 km long and 4 km wide), which is also the training center of the *Marine Nationale,* the French Navy. The Navy helps *Jeunesse et Marine* by lending them boats, giving them food, and making available to them its health and rescue services. The camp is totally isolated in the middle of a dense pine forest. The closest road is 3 km away, and the camp is accessible only by a narrow, private path reserved for the Forest Rangers.

Grammar

Double object pronouns, as we said, are not included in Level One. This is why in reflexive constructions used in the *passé composé,* agreement of the past participle will be made only with a reflexive pronoun (*Elle s'est lavée*) or a direct object in an interrogative phrase (*Quelle boisson est-ce qu'elle s'est faite?*), and not with the direct-object pronouns *le, la,* and *les.*

Vocabulary

This unit provides enough vocabulary to allow students to recount their own camp experiences.

Projects

Have students plan what they would take if they went away to camp. You might also assign a journal or diary to be written, based on camp or vacation experiences.

Script of Listening Exercise 17

Listen to the following eight sentences. Each one refers to something but does not name it. For each sentence, figure out what is being referred to — a lake, a boat, a tent, or a beach — and check the appropriate row. For example, you hear: *On va peut-être le prendre cet après-midi s'il y a du vent.* You check the row labeled *Un bateau.* Let's begin.

1. Il a l'air calme maintenant, mais il faut faire attention aux tempêtes. _____ *(Un lac)*
2. Il a de belles voiles rouges. _____ *(Un bateau)*
3. Elle a presque 10 km de long! _____ *(Une plage)*
4. Il a un moteur qui ne marche jamais. _____ *(Un bateau)*
5. Elle est très belle, mais on ne peut pas s'y baigner parce que l'eau est trop froide. _____ *(Une plage)*
6. Il n'est pas prudent de s'en servir parce qu'il est trop vieux. _____ *(Un bateau)*
7. On peut le traverser en quelques heures. _____ *(Un lac)*
8. Elle n'est pas très grande, mais on a tout de même assez de place pour y mettre nos sacs de couchage. _____ *(Une tente)*

Now check your answers. *Read each item again and give the correct answer.*

Answers to Writing Exercise 16

2. Je me suis levé tôt. Tout le monde dormait encore. Je suis sorti de la tente. Il faisait beau. Ça sentait bon les pins. Les oiseaux chantaient. Je ne savais pas où aller. J'ai décidé de me promener au bord du lac. Il y avait déjà beaucoup de bateaux sur le lac. J'étais tout content à l'idée de faire un pique-nique l'après-midi.
3. Nous nous sommes levés tôt. Tout le monde dormait encore. Nous sommes sortis de la tente. Il faisait beau. Ça sentait bon les pins. Les oiseaux chantaient. Nous ne savions pas où aller. Nous avons décidé de nous promener au bord du lac. Il y avait déjà beaucoup de bateaux sur le lac. Nous étions tout contents à l'idée de faire un pique-nique l'après-midi.

PHOTO ESSAY Following Unit 18 — Plates 17–24

COUNTRY LIFE

Farming still forms the nucleus of rural life in France, Belgium, French Switzerland, and Quebec. Small and medium-sized farms dot the countryside or are grouped in villages and small towns. For the most part, these farms are worked with modern equipment, but they look very much as they did centuries ago. Everyday life for country people hasn't changed much, either. They now wear T-shirts and jeans, rather than the traditional dress of their region; but markets and fairs are still major events in their business and social life, and the rhythms of nature—the seasons, planting and harvest, floods and droughts—still influence their work and their welfare.

Plate 24

(1): Market in a small town in Switzerland.
(2): Rainy day in a market in a Normandy village.
(3): Farm products sold at a market in a village in Provence.
(4): Country fair in a small town in Switzerland. Notice that some farmers wear the traditional costume of the region of Neuchâtel.
(5): Cowbells in the French and Swiss Alps.

19 A L'AEROPORT

Theme and Culture

Youngsters in France, and in Europe generally, often have pen pals. Schools organize pen pal exchanges. And sometimes one can get a pen pal through a friend who already has one. After a few years of correspondence between two pen pals, their parents may agree to let them exchange visits. During the summer holidays, one student goes to stay with the family of the other for a month; then both return to the home of the first for a month. In the case of French and English pen pals, the French student usually makes the first trip, because French schools close for the summer before British schools.

Exchanges of visits between pen pals from different countries in Europe are fairly common and easy, because the distances between countries are small. From the age of thirteen on, European young people often travel to foreign countries by themselves. They have the great advantage of being able to immerse themselves from time to time in a foreign culture without crossing the ocean, or even going very far from home.

Grammar and Vocabulary

The grammar in this unit concerns itself mainly with the rules needed to handle a vocabulary of countries, nationalities, and languages. Students generally enjoy learning about different countries and languages. The map on page 197 introduces more countries, and you may want to tell your students the corresponding names of nationalities and languages.

The vocabulary of the airport can be practiced by role-playing various situations appropriate to airports.

Project

Help students to contact French or Canadian schools and request lists of French-speaking young people who would like to correspond with them.

Game

Le jeu du baccalauréat, described on page T53, is appropriate for this unit. You can choose several or all of the following categories: countries, nationalities, languages, cities, seas, or oceans. Tell students they can turn to the map on page 197 for help.

A good way of reviewing kilometers, as well as having students learn about distances in Europe, is to play a guessing game about the distances (in km, of course) between various European cities.

Script of Listening Exercise 30

You will hear eight brief groups of statements, each one addressed to either a man or a woman. In each group of statements, listen for the masculine or feminine form of an adjective. Decide who is being spoken to, and then check the appropriate row. For example, you hear: *Vous êtes canadienne? Mais vous avez un passeport américain.* You place your check mark in the row labeled *Une femme,* because the feminine adjective form *canadienne* tells you that the person being addressed is a woman. Let's begin.

1. Pardon . . . Klaus comment? Klaus Kröger? Vous êtes allemand? _____ *(allemand   Un homme)*
2. Vous êtes italienne? Mais vous habitez à Paris, non? _____ *(italienne   Une femme)*
3. Vous travaillez aux Etats-Unis? Mais vous n'êtes pas américain, vous? _____ *(américain   Un homme)*
4. Où est-ce que vous habitez? A Toronto? Vous êtes canadienne? _____ *(canadienne   Une femme)*

5. Vous êtes allemande? Mais vous êtes brune! Tous les allemands ne sont pas blonds, alors. _____
   (allemande, brune   Une femme)
6. Vous n'êtes pas anglais? Américain, alors . . . Non? _____ *(anglais, américain   Un homme)*
7. Vous préparez des spécialités françaises, et vous n'êtes pas français! _____ *(français   Un homme)*
8. Vous vous appelez Mercier, et vous êtes américaine? _____ *(américaine   Une femme)*

Now check your answers. *Read each item again and give the correct answer.*

20   EN TUNISIE

Theme and Culture

Tunisia's history began with the founding of Carthage in the ninth century B.C. (If you have students who study Latin or History, you may want to suggest that they look up the period of Carthaginian rule over the Mediterranean world, and also look up the Punic Wars.) French is spoken in Tunisia, because the country was a French protectorate from 1877 to 1956.

In modern Tunisian society, men and women lead quite separate lives—separate, but not necessarily unequal. Husbands and wives share equally in decisions concerning the life of the family, but in different ways. The inside world—the home—is primarily the woman's world; the outside world, primarily the man's. This distinction persists, even though women are becoming more educated and more in touch with the modern world. For example, although Nadia goes to the University of Tunis, she is expected also to be able to run a household, maintain a budget, and so forth. And Aziz often accompanies his father when he goes to visit male friends. His father wants him to learn about the world by listening to their conversation.

Many of the traditional customs in Tunisia are still respected, and the authority of parents is absolute. When it comes to marriage, parents usually choose their children's partners—for boys as well as for girls. This custom sometimes creates tensions today, especially in families whose children have studied abroad and become less tolerant of the old ways. A great many young Tunisians study in France.

The other side of the coin is that North Africa has had its influence on French life. Many French people who formerly lived in North Africa have returned to France, bringing with them a taste for North African foods. A fairly large population of North Africans also lives and works in France, with the result that foods like *couscous* and *merguez* (a kind of sausage) are easy to obtain. North African leather goods are common in French stores. And certain Arabic words have become part of the French language: for example, *le toubib* (doctor) and *le bled* (boondocks) are now heard in very informal spoken French.

Grammar

It is difficult for English-speakers to learn and remember which French verbs are followed immediately by the infinitive, and which take à or *de* plus the infinitive. Only intensive practice will help students learn to use these infinitive constructions correctly. You may find item substitution drills helpful in providing the needed practice.

Vocabulary

The vocabulary of sections 1 and 16 is for recognition only. The texts are translated in a special reference list at the end of the unit. Many of the words in this unit refer specifically to Tunisian items. You may want to tell your students that these words are all a part of the vocabulary of young people in France, who become acquainted with North African culture at an early age.

Project

Make a travel folder on Tunisia. Use the project on Martinique (page 184) as a guide.

Script of Listening Exercise 12

You will hear eight questions, each one followed by two answers, A and B. For each question, decide whether A or B is the correct answer. For example, you hear: *Qui est-ce qui marchande?*   *A   Le client; B   Le portefeuille.* You check the row labeled A, because the interrogative pronoun started with *qui*, indicating that the question referred to a person and not to a thing. Let's begin.

1. Qu'est-ce qu'on vend dans les souks?
   A   Des tapis.   B   Des marchands. _____ *(A, Des tapis.)*
2. Qui est-ce qui travaille ici?
   A   Un burnous.   B   Un tailleur. _____ *(B, Un tailleur.)*
3. Qu'est-ce qui t'intéresse?
   A   Le potier.   B   Les poteries. _____ *(B, Les poteries.)*
4. Qui est-ce que tu as vu dans les souks?
   A   Des poufs.   B   Des artisans. _____ *(B, Des artisans.)*
5. De qui est-ce que vous parlez?
   A   Des frères Slim   B   Des souks. _____ *(A, Des frères Slim.)*
6. De quoi est-ce que vous rêvez?
   A   De la Tunisie.   B   Des Tunisiens. _____ *(A, De la Tunisie.)*
7. Avec quoi est-ce qu'il travaille?
   A   Avec ses mains.   B   Avec ses cousins. _____ *(A, Avec ses mains.)*
8. Pour qui est-ce que tu achètes ce plateau?
   A   Pour servir le thé.   B   Pour ma mère. _____ *(B, Pour ma mère.)*

Now check your answers. *Read each item again and give the correct answer.*

Answers to Writing Exercise 24

1. Samir aime flâner dans les souks.
2. Il veut acheter quelque chose pour sa mère.
3. Il décide d'acheter un plateau en cuivre.
4. Samir s'amuse à marchander.
5. Le marchand lui demande de payer dix dinars.
6. Samir lui dit de garder son plateau en cuivre.
7. Le marchand commence à baisser son prix.
8. Samir continue à marchander.
9. A la fin, il réussit à acheter le plateau en cuivre pour cinq dinars.
10. Samir a hâte de montrer son achat à Aziz.

21   LA FÊTE FORAINE

Theme and Culture

Young people in France are very fond of fairs, amusement parks, and amusement arcades with their electronic games. They do not consider it childish to like such places. As a matter of fact, well into their teens, French young people still enjoy going to fairs, playing pranks, seeing cartoons at the movies, or just being slightly silly. It is very likely that Anna and Sylvie will come back with their new friends to the *Fête des Loges* before it moves to another location.

Grammar

The interference of English is very strong when it comes to the use of the future, especially after *quand*. Make sure students use the future after *quand* when the verb of the main clause is in the future.

Vocabulary

Some of the words and expressions used in this unit are slang. They are very typical of what young French people say in this type of situation. We have indicated such expressions in the annotations of the Teacher's Edition.

Game

To practice the future tense, and at the same time to review numbers and colors, you might have the students play a fortune-telling game, using *une salière* — a device made of folded paper, sometimes called a ''fortune-teller'' in English, with four open cones into which you put your thumbs and index fingers. Most American school children know how to fold a ''fortune-teller'' by the time they're in third or fourth grade. Ask your students if they still remember how to do it!

Once you have folded *la salière,* draw four different spots of color on the surface of the four cones, and write four different sentences about a person's future life underneath the color spots. For example: *Tu auras douze enfants; Tu habiteras en Suède,* and so forth. Now you are ready to play. The student holding the *salière* asks a friend to choose a number from one to ten. If the number is, for example, four, the fortune teller switches the opening of the *salière* four times, and shows it to the friend. The friend then chooses one of the two colors that are showing. Underneath the flap with the chosen color spot is the friend's ''fortune.''

The construction of *la salière* also allows for eight color spots and eight sentences, if four doesn't seem to be enough. Of course, if everyone in the class constructs *une salière* and writes future sentences, there will be plenty of variety in the available ''fortunes'' and, incidentally, in chances to practice the future tense.

Script of Listening Exercise 14

You will hear ten sentences. Decide whether each one is referring to something that took place in the past, *Jadis,* or to something that will take place in the future, *A l'avenir.* For example, you hear: *Vous habiterez dans une île des Caraïbes.* You put your check mark in the row labeled *A l'avenir,* because you heard the future form *habiterez.* Let's begin.

1. Nous montions sur tous les manèges. _____ *(montions, imparfait   Jadis)*
2. J'achèterai mon horoscope. _____ *(achèterai, future   A l'avenir)*
3. Vous rencontrerez un fakir. _____ *(rencontrerez, future   A l'avenir)*
4. Je gagnais toujours. _____ *(gagnais, imparfait   Jadis)*
5. Nous tenterons notre chance à la loterie. _____ *(tenterons, future   A l'avenir)*
6. J'avais souvent le mal de mer. _____ *(avais, imparfait   Jadis)*
7. Nous tentions notre chance au tir. _____ *(tentions, imparfait   Jadis)*
8. Je mangerai dans une rôtisserie. _____ *(mangerai, future   A l'avenir)*

9. Je faisais de longs voyages. _____ (faisais, imparfait   Jadis)
10. Je me reposerai après un tour de grande roue. _____ (reposerai, future   A l'avenir)

Now check your answers. *Read each item again and give the correct answer.*

22   GYMNASTIQUE ET ATHLETISME

Theme and Culture

The young people in this unit attend a public secondary school called *Ecole Secondaire Polyvalente Antoine-Brossard,* in Brossard, a suburb of Montreal. *Polyvalente* means that their school combines academic, commercial, and vocational programs. These young people are in *Secondaire 3,* the equivalent of the ninth grade. They started in *Secondaire 1,* the first grade in secondary school. They will stay at *Antoine-Brossard* for another two years. After graduation, they may choose to take a two-year academic program leading to the university, or to take a three-year program, after which they will go to work.

In the province of Quebec, sports are an important part of the school curriculum. Students practice gymnastics, track and field, and swimming every week during school hours. They usually practice other sports, like ice-hockey, for example, outside of school hours. At the end of every school year, schools compete with one another in championship meets, both district- and province-wide. Although these events are not co-ed, boys and girls often train together in preparation for these meets.

On the whole, young *Québécois* are very sports-minded and enthusiastic about the outdoors. In winter both alpine and cross-country skiing are very popular. So is ice-skating. When the snow has melted, young people from Quebec enjoy hiking in their beautiful countryside. The many rivers provide them with excellent opportunities for canoe trips, which can become real exploring expeditions.

Grammar

We have introduced only the formation of adverbs. The placement of adverbs will be dealt with in Level Two.

In this unit we introduce only superlative constructions that do not include a noun *(C'est la plus courageuse de la classe).* Superlative constructions including a noun *(C'est la fille la plus courageuse de la classe)* are included in the review of comparatives and superlatives of adjectives, in Unit 24.

Vocabulary

The vocabulary is specific to the topic of sports, but it also includes many words and expressions to allow for class discussion about other subjects important to students. This unit also teaches vocabulary related to parts of the body and body movement.

Project

Have students use a world record book for this project. Ask them to research items such as *Celui/Celle qui a sauté le plus haut,* for example. They should make a chart which says: *C'est* (name). *Il/Elle est* (nationality). *Il/Elle a sauté* (performance in metric measures) *en* (year). This project is a good review of adjectives of nationality and also a review of dates.

Have them keep records of games and sports activities at school so that they can turn them into short stories in French. In this way they can compare individuals and teams.

Script of Listening Exercise 38

You will hear ten pairs of statements. On the basis of the first statement in each pair, decide whether the second one is true *(vrai)* or false *(faux),* and place your check mark in the appropriate row. For example, you hear: *C'est Suzanne qui court le plus vite. Suzanne court plus vite que Louis.* You put your check mark in the row labeled *Vrai,* because the second statement agrees with the first. Let's begin.

1. C'est Louis qui lance le disque le plus loin. Louis est meilleur que Jean-Raymond au lancer du disque. _____ *(Vrai)*
2. C'est Hélène qui est la plus gracieuse. Ghislaine est plus gracieuse qu'Hélène. _____ *(Faux)*
3. C'est Jean-François qui saute le plus haut. Jean-Raymond saute moins haut que Jean-François. _____ *(Vrai)*
4. C'est Johanne qui gagne le plus souvent. Suzanne gagne moins souvent que Johanne. _____ *(Vrai)*
5. C'est Ghislaine qui est la plus jeune de la classe. Hélène est plus jeune que Ghislaine. _____ *(Faux)*
6. C'est Jean-Raymond qui est le plus drôle. Jean-François est aussi drôle que Jean-Raymond. _____ *(Faux)*
7. C'est Suzanne qui est la plus énergique. Johanne est aussi énergique que Suzanne. _____ *(Faux)*
8. C'est Louis qui est le plus fort. Daniel est moins fort que Louis. _____ *(Vrai)*
9. C'est Ghislaine qui est la plus paresseuse. Suzanne est plus paresseuse que Ghislaine. _____ *(Faux)*
10. C'est Jean-François qui est le plus sérieux. Jean-François est plus sérieux que Louis. _____ *(Vrai)*

Now check your answers. *Read each item again and give the correct answer.*

Answers to Writing Exercise 37

1. Hélène est la plus courageuse de la classe.
2. C'est Jean-François qui saute le plus haut.
3. Louis est le meilleur de la classe aux lancers.
4. C'est Johanne qui court le plus vite.
5. C'est Jean-Raymond qui est le moins bon à la course.
6. Ghislaine fera mieux la prochaine fois.
7. C'est Suzanne qui est la plus rapide de la classe.
8. C'est Louis qui lance le javelot le plus loin.
9. C'est Jean-François qui fait le moins bien ces exercices.
10. Johanne gagne le plus souvent.

23 POUR MAMAN

Theme and Culture

Belgium is a small country to the north of France which borders France, Luxembourg, the Netherlands, and the Federal Republic of Germany. (See map, page 197.) It is divided into nine provinces, among which is the Province of Liège where the Duponts live. Belgium is a parliamentary monarchy; the present king is Baudouin I, who came to the throne in 1951.

The 10 million inhabitants of Belgium belong to different cultural groups and speak different languages: about 56% of the population speak Dutch (a variant of which is called Flemish). 32% speak French, 11% are bilingual Dutch-French, and 0.7% speak German.

Liège is the capital of the Province of Liège. It is a very old city, situated on the river Meuse. It is and has always been an active cultural center for French-speaking Belgians, an important industrial center, and an important port because of the river. And just as in any modern city, shopping here is good, ranging from large department stores to a variety of boutiques.

The Dupont children lead a life very similar to that of young French people of the same age. Most of their time is taken up with school and school work, with few opportunities for play or leisure activities. Françoise attends a public secondary school, and Vincent a private Catholic one, but both have a long school day and lots of homework when they come home. As for the parents, M. Dupont is an engineer who works near home and Mme Dupont takes care of the home and family.

Grammar

Some English grammar books use the terms "possessive article" and "possessive pronoun" interchangeably. Possessive articles and possessive pronouns are distinctly different in French, however, and the distinction between them should be made clear.

Vocabulary

In addition to the items introduced in this unit, many items mentioned in preceding units may also be offered as presents. See especially the vocabulary from units 2, 3, 4, 9, and 14.

Projects

Have a contest to see who can draw the best or most original birthday card.

Have students plan a birthday party for someone in the class. Someone can try his or her hand at making a birthday cake from the recipe on page 247, among other things.

Game

The *Devinettes* game is easy to play in this unit: *On y met de l'argent. Qu'est-ce que c'est?* Answer: *Un portefeuille.*

Script of Listening Exercise 23

You will hear eight incomplete sentences, each one followed by two possible completions, A and B. Only one of the completions is grammatically correct. Decide which one completes the sentence correctly, and put a check mark in the appropriate row.

For example, you hear: *Nous lui donnerions un foulard rouge...   A   si elle aimait cette couleur; B   si elle aime cette couleur.* You place your check mark in row A. Let's begin.

1. Si ce chemisier ne lui va pas...
   A   elle pourra l'échanger.   B   elle pourrait l'échanger. _____ *(A, elle pourra l'échanger.)*
2. Si ce parfum ne coûtait pas si cher...
   A   nous en achèterons.   B   nous en achèterions. _____ *(B, nous en achèterions.)*
3. Téléphonez-moi...
   A   si vous ne pouviez pas venir.   B   si vous ne pouvez pas venir. _____ *(B, si vous ne pouvez pas venir.)*
4. Papa nous prêtera un peu d'argent...
   A   si nous n'en avions pas assez.   B   si nous n'en avons pas assez. _____ *(B, si nous n'en avons pas assez.)*

5. Nous irons au restaurant . . .
   A   si votre mère en a envie.   B   si votre mère en avait envie. _____ *(A, si votre mère en a envie.)*

6. Si vous vous dépêchez . . .
   A   nous serions à l'heure.   B   nous serons à l'heure. _____ *(B, nous serons à l'heure.)*

7. Si tu as de l'argent . . .
   A   donnes-en un peu à ton frère.   B   tu en donnerais un peu à ton frère. _____ *(A, donnes-en un peu à ton frère.)*

8. Nous partirons dans une heure . . .
   A   si tout le monde était prêt.   B   si tout le monde est prêt. _____ *(B, si tout le monde est prêt.)*

Now check your answers. *Read each item again and give the correct answer.*

24   LA TELEVISION

Theme and Culture

About 80% of French households have television sets. Every owner of a set (radio as well as television) has to register it and pay an annual tax. Failure to do so usually results in stiff penalties for the delinquent party. There are three channels, *TF (Télévision Française) 1, Antenne 2,* and *FR (France) 3,* all state-owned. *TF 1* and *Antenne 2* are national networks. FR 3 broadcasts on a national level only four hours a day. The rest of broadcasting time is taken up by regional programs or feature films.

Only *TF 1* and *Antenne 2* have advertisements, which run between programs. Advertising on French television is strictly regulated by the *Régie Française de Publicité.* For example, alcoholic beverages and tobacco products cannot be advertised on French television.

Grammar

Comparatives and superlatives of adjectives are reviewed in this unit. Superlative constructions including a noun are introduced. You can use the "advertisements" to review comparatives and superlatives.

Project

Have students draw up an imaginary television listing for one day. Use the one on page 255 as a guide. They may also be interested in finding some Canadian TV programs and recordings.

Using a world record book, have students draw up a list of records for fun, such as the weight of the world's biggest cat.

They may also be interested in doing their own TV documentary, similar to the one on Senegal in this unit.

Game

Have students make up advertisement copy which does not identify the product. Other students have to guess what kind of product is being described.

Script of Listening Exercise 12

You will hear ten sentences. For each one, decide whether the action will definitely take place, *C'est sûr*, or whether it would take place if something else happened, *Si ça arrivait*. For example, you hear: *Il achèterait un grand bateau à voiles.* You put your check mark in the row labeled *Si ça arrivait*, because the conditional form, *achèterait*, tells you the action is not definite. Let's begin.

1. Ils ne regarderaient jamais la télévision. _____ (*Si ça arrivait*)
2. Vous ne pourrez pas regarder cette émission. _____ (*C'est sûr*)
3. Nous regarderions le journal télévisé tous les jours. _____ (*Si ça arrivait*)
4. Tu irais au Sénégal. _____ (*Si ça arrivait*)
5. Ils feront le tour du monde. _____ (*C'est sûr*)
6. Ils ne sauront pas comment y aller. _____ (*C'est sûr*)
7. Nous viendrions l'année prochaine. _____ (*Si ça arrivait*)
8. Elle ne finira jamais. _____ (*C'est sûr*)
9. Tu feras mieux la prochaine fois. _____ (*C'est sûr*)
10. Il voyagerait tout le temps. _____ (*Si ça arrivait*)

Now check your answers. *Read each item again and give the correct answer.*

Answers to Exercise 16: Jouons aux publicités.

—Il est moins simple que celui-là.
—Oui, celui-là est plus simple.
—C'est le plus simple de tous.

—Elle est moins bonne que celle-là.
—Oui, celle-là est meilleure.
—C'est la meilleure de toutes.

—Il est moins amusant que celui-là.
—Oui, celui-là est plus amusant.
—C'est le plus amusant de tous.

—Elle est moins rapide que celle-là.
—Oui, celle-là est plus rapide.
—C'est la plus rapide de toutes.

—Elle est moins chère que celle-là.
—Oui, celle-là est plus chère.
—C'est la plus chère de toutes.

—Ils sont moins bons que ceux-là.
—Oui, ceux-là sont meilleurs.
—Ce sont les meilleurs de tous.

PHOTO ESSAY Following Unit 24 — Plates 25–32

FESTIVALS

Like people all over the world, French-speaking people love a good festival. They love the crowds, the music, the colors, the pageantry, the food, and above all they love to share with others their *joie de vivre* and their feelings of pride in their culture. French-speaking people have evolved their own special festivals, and this photo essay shows a few glimpses of some of the most typical ones.

Plate 26

(1): The *Garde Républicaine* circling the *Arc de Triomphe* before riding down the *Champs-Elysées*.
(2): Women soldiers from the Army, the Navy, and the Air Force.
(3): The band of the *Garde Républicaine*.
(4): The *Chasseurs Alpins* or Alpine troops parading with skiis.
(5): People watching the parade with the help of periscopes.

Plate 27

(1): A group of "elders."
(2): A group of boy scouts with Ivory Coast flags.
(3): Members of the Union of Ivory Coast Workers.
(4): A group of high-school students.
(5): Militant supporters of President Felix Houphouet-Boigny (whose picture decorates their shirts), leader of the country since its independence from France in 1960.

Plate 30

(3): The highlight of the festival is the shepherds singing their beautiful, ancient songs in *gascon,* the dialect spoken in the region of Bigorre.

Games and Classroom Phrases

Many of the games and activities included in **Nos Amis** can be used with vocabulary and structures from other units. The following is a list of these games and some suggestions on how to vary them.

• *Le jeu de loto* (page 3) can become a word game. Select twenty items from vocabulary posters. Have students draw a rectangle and divide it into twenty squares. Have them write at random the name of one item in each square. A silent "caller" holds up the vocabulary posters one at a time. The winner is the first one to fill in a horizontal line.

• *Chaîne de mots* (page 40) is used several times in **Nos Amis.** It can easily fit many situations.

• *Le jeu de l'odorat* (page 80) can easily be transformed into *Le jeu du toucher* or *Le jeu de l'ouïe.* Students are blindfolded and have to identify items by touching, or by hearing someone give clues.

• *Devinez qui c'est* (page 67) can become *Devinez ce que c'est.*

• *Charmante Rencontre* (page 95) can be turned into amusing writing exercises.

• *C'est vous le guide!* (page 103) can be reversed, as can any games involving maps. Instead of having students say which way they go, tell them which way you go and have them figure out where you end up.

• *Devinettes* (page 115) are used several times in the book. They can fit many situations.

• *Histoire en chaîne* (page 190) is especially good to encourage speaking in a group.

• *Le jeu des photos* (page 214) can be used throughout the program.

• *Le jeu des adverbes* (page 228) is one variant of the "acting out" type of game. Instead of adverbs, you may want to work with nouns, verbs, or adjectives. In that case, select topics such as places (swimming pool, restaurant), events (jazz concert, party), professions, types of movies, etc.

• *Le jeu des portraits chinois* (page 244) is a variant of the game called *Le jeu des portraits.* One student waits outside while the others select a person, an animal, an object, etc. The student comes back in and has to guess what was chosen by asking questions.

Here are other games that French-speaking young people often play:

• *Le téléphone:* a student thinks of a sentence and whispers it to his neighbor, who then whispers it to his neighbor, and so on around the room. The last person says aloud the sentence he or she heard, which is usually quite different from the original one. You may want to control the situation by suggesting sentences to start off with.

• *Le jeu du baccalauréat:* select several categories such as countries, cities, rivers. In a given time period, see who can find the greatest number of words related to the chosen categories beginning with a certain letter of the alphabet. Students should use the maps in the book to help them find words. An easier version of the same game is to choose a letter of the alphabet and try to find as many words as possible beginning with this letter.

• *Le pendu:* one student thinks of a word and writes on the blackboard the first letter and enough blank spaces to spell the rest. Then the other people in the class guess letters, one at a time. When they give a letter that occurs in the word, it is written in its place. When a wrong letter is given, the person at the blackboard starts to draw a gallows. With every wrong letter, he or she adds one line to the drawing. Unless the word is spelled out in time, the student will have drawn a person hanging from the gallows, and the hangman wins.

• *Mots en chaîne:* one student chooses a word and says it to his neighbor, who must find a word beginning with the last sound (syllable) of that word and say it to his or her neighbor, and so on around the room. For example, the first student says *"parents,"* the second says *"ranger,"* the third says *"géographie,"* the fourth says *"filet,"* etc.

Classroom phrases

In Unit 4, students will pick up a good deal of useful classroom vocabulary, to which you might add certain phrases that they should recognize when they hear them. Some common classroom instructions are given below, with their French equivalents.

Listen!	Ecoutez!
Repeat (after me).	Répétez (après moi).
Try it again. Say it again.	Essayez encore une fois.
Say that . . .	Dites que . . .
Answer.	Répondez.
Speak louder.	Parlez plus fort.
Get up.	Levez-vous.
Go to the blackboard.	Allez au tableau.
Write . . . on the blackboard.	Ecrivez . . . au tableau.
Erase.	Effacez.
Go back to your seat.	Retournez à votre place.
Sit down.	Asseyez-vous.
Quiet, please.	Un peu de silence, s'il vous plaît.
We're going to have a test.	Il va y avoir une interrogation écrite.
We're going to have a dictation.	Nous allons faire une dictée.
Give a piece of paper to everybody.	Distribuez une feuille de papier à tout le monde.
Take out a piece of paper.	Prenez une feuille de papier.
Let's begin.	Commençons.
Write in pencil/pen.	Ecrivez au crayon/à l'encre.
Have you finished?	Vous avez fini?
Give me the test papers.	Rendez-moi vos copies.
Be sure to hand in your homework on time.	Remettez vos devoirs à temps.
Write down the assignment.	Notez ce que vous avez comme devoir(s).
Pay attention.	Soyez attentif (-ive)(s).
Raise your hand.	Levez la main.
Open your book(s) to page . . .	Ouvrez votre (vos) livre(s) à la page . . .
Look at Exercise 8.	Regardez l'exercice numéro 8.
Ready?	Vous êtes prêt(e)(s)?
Turn the page.	Tournez la page.
Read . . . out loud	Lisez . . . à haute voix.
Wait.	Attendez.
Start.	Commencez.
Go on.	Continuez.
Stop.	Arrêtez-vous.
That's all.	C'est tout.
Get rid of your chewing gum.	Jetez votre chewing gum.
Put the . . . away.	Rangez le/la . . .
See me after class.	J'aimerais vous parler à la fin de l'heure.
That's right.	C'est ça.
That's wrong.	Ce n'est pas ça.
Good.	Bien.
Excellent.	Excellent.
That's better.	C'est mieux.
Perfect.	C'est parfait.

As you and your students do some of the projects suggested in the book, you may want to use French terms for various tools and supplies, some of which are listed below.

bulletin board	un tableau d'affichage
thumbtack	une punaise
paperclip	un trombone
stapler	une agrafeuse
staple	une agrafe
transparent tape	du papier collant
glue, paste	de la colle
cardboard, poster board	du carton
placard, sign	un écriteau
scissors	des ciseaux
felt-tip pen	un feutre
watercolor, poster paint	de la peinture
paintbrush	un pinceau
string	de la ficelle
wire	du fil de fer
hammer	un marteau
nail	un clou
pliers	des pinces
wastepaper basket	une corbeille à papier

Recorded Materials: Format and Samples

All recorded material throughout this program is signaled with a special "tape symbol." Basic material, grammar presentations, and drills are recorded for practice. Exercises for fun are also recorded to give students the correct pronunciation of new vocabulary, the pronunciation of proper names on maps, and the melodies of songs.

Basic Material

First, the students hear the basic material (dialog, narrative, etc.) in its entirety. They then hear it again, this time divided into fragments with pauses following each fragment. Then they repeat each fragment in the pause provided. In the beginning units, the students are asked to repeat the whole text. In the later units, where the basic material is usually longer, they hear the whole selection but are asked to repeat only selected fragments of the text, where new vocabulary and structures are introduced.

For example, let's take the beginning of Unit 5, page 46. The recorded material is as follows:

CHAPITRE 5   UNE SORTIE

In this unit, we are going to talk about going on an outing. Our friends Catherine and Philippe feel like going out, since it is Wednesday and there is no school. Unfortunately the nearest town, Dieppe, is some twenty miles away, a long way to bicycle to! Philippe calls his friend Dominique, whose brother has a car. It just happens that Dominique and his brother were going to Dieppe that afternoon. All four will go out together. Listen.

Numéro 1 — Qu'est-ce qu'on fait cet après-midi?

C'est mercredi, aujourd'hui. Philippe et Catherine Lardan n'ont pas classe. Ils sont chez eux, mais ils ne veulent pas rester à la maison toute la journée. Ils ont envie de sortir avec des amis. Philippe téléphone à son ami Dominique pour lui demander s'il est libre.

PHILIPPE	Qu'est-ce que tu fais cet après-midi?
DOMINIQUE	Je sors avec Bernard. On va à Dieppe.
PHILIPPE	Vous allez aux Ambassadeurs?
DOMINIQUE	Oui . . . Et après on pense aller au cinéma.
PHILIPPE	Est-ce qu'on peut venir avec vous? Il y a assez de place dans la voiture?
DOMINIQUE	Bien sûr! Quand est-ce qu'on passe vous prendre?
PHILIPPE	Quand vous voulez . . . Nous sommes prêts à partir!
DOMINIQUE	Ça tombe bien! Nous aussi. On est chez vous dans cinq minutes.

Now you will practice saying what you just heard. You will hear sentences or parts of sentences. You will hear each one twice, and you are to repeat it once in the pause provided. Let's start!

Qu'est-ce qu'on fait *(repeat)* . . .
cet après-midi *(repeat)* . . .
Qu'est-ce qu'on fait cet après-midi? *(repeat)* . . .
C'est mercredi, aujourd'hui. *(repeat)* . . .
Philippe et Catherine Lardan *(repeat)* . . .
Philippe et Catherine Lardan n'ont pas classe. *(repeat)* . . .
Ils sont chez eux. *(repeat)* . . .
Ils ne veulent pas *(repeat)* . . .
rester à la maison *(repeat)* . . .
Ils ne veulent pas rester à la maison *(repeat)* . . .
toute la journée. *(repeat)* . . .
Ils ont envie *(repeat)* . . .
Ils ont envie de sortir *(repeat)* . . .
Ils ont envie de sortir avec des amis. *(repeat)* . . .
Philippe téléphone à son ami Dominique *(repeat)* . . .
pour lui demander s'il est libre. *(repeat)* . . .
s'il est libre. *(repeat)* . . .
Qu'est-ce que tu fais cet après-midi? *(repeat)* . . .
Je sors avec Bernard. *(repeat)* . . .
On va à Dieppe. *(repeat)* . . .
Vous allez aux Ambassadeurs? *(repeat)* . . .
Oui. Et après *(repeat)* . . .
on pense aller au cinéma. *(repeat)* . . .
Est-ce qu'on peut venir avec vous? *(repeat)* . . .
Il y a assez de place *(repeat)* . . .
Il y a assez de place dans la voiture? *(repeat)* . . .
Bien sûr! *(repeat)* . . .
Quand est-ce qu'on passe *(repeat)* . . .
Quand est-ce qu'on passe vous prendre? *(repeat)* . . .
Quand vous voulez. *(repeat)* . . .
Nous sommes prêts *(repeat)* . . .
à partir *(repeat)* . . .
Nous sommes prêts à partir. *(repeat)* . . .
Ça tombe bien! Nous aussi. *(repeat)* . . .
On est chez vous *(repeat)* . . .
On est chez vous dans cinq minutes. *(repeat)* . . .

Numéro 4 — Exercice oral

In this exercise, you will be saying the sound (r). You will hear each sentence twice. "Ecoutez et répétez!"

Les trois amis sortent avec Bernard (r) . . .
Les garçons partent dans quatre minutes (r) . . .
On passe vous prendre dans un quart d'heure (r) . . .
Il ne peut pas venir; il n'est pas libre (r) . . .

Grammar Presentations

These recordings present only the oral grammar related to each structural point. You may tell your students that the oral grammar of French is usually simpler than the written grammar. With several variations, the basic format of the grammar presentation recordings is as follows: first, the students hear and repeat sentences containing examples of the structure being taught. They are then asked for answers to questions that will lead them to discover the grammatical point involved. Answers to these questions are given after a short pause provided for the students' response. For example, the recording of the grammar presentation on page 46 is as follows:

Numéro 5 — Verbs ending in [ir]

You have already learned a group of verbs — the verbs like *jouer* whose infinitive ends in [e]. You are going to learn another group of verbs. First, listen to the following sentences and repeat each one after the model.
Catherine veut partir. . . .
Philippe veut sortir. . . .
Now answer the following questions. Each question is followed by a short pause for your response. Listen to the verb at the end of each sentence: *Catherine veut partir. Philippe veut sortir.* What sound do they end in? . . . ([ir]) What forms of the verb are *partir* and *sortir?* . . . (The infinitives.) In this new class of verbs, all infinitives end in [ir]. Now listen to these sentences and repeat after the model.
Nous sortons. . . .
Vous sortez? . . .
Les amis sortent. . . .
What part of the verb stays the same in *sortons, sortez,* and *sortent?* . . . ([sɔrt]) What is the last consonant sound? . . . ([t])
Now listen to these sentences and repeat after the model.
Je sors. . . .
Tu sors? . . .
Catherine sort. . . .
Do the verbs in these sentences sound alike or different? . . . (Alike.) What consonant sound was present in the plural forms but is not present in the singular forms? . . . (The sound [t].) All verbs in this class drop a consonant sound in the singular form. This consonant sound is not always [t]. Later on, you will learn the verb *servir* — to serve — with a [v]-sound, and the verb *dormir* — to sleep — with an [m]-sound.

Structure drills

The structure drills have been recorded in a three-phase format: stimulus — pause for response — confirmation. Drill 7 on page 47 is recorded as follows:

Exercice No 7 — Les trois amis sortent avec Bernard

Since Bernard has a car, he is taking lots of people to Dieppe, including our three friends. You will hear a series of questions. Answer them according to the model. For example, you hear: *Qu'est-ce que tu fais cet après-midi?* You say: *Je sors avec Bernard.* Let's start.

Qu'est-ce que tu fais cet après-midi? (   ) *Je sors avec Bernard.*
Et vous deux? (   ) *Nous sortons avec Bernard.*
Et Dominique? (   ) *Il sort avec Bernard.*
Et Catherine et Philippe? (   ) *Ils sortent avec Bernard.*

Listening Comprehension Program

Prepared by Pierre J. Capretz

This strand of the series is intended to improve the students' listening and speaking skills. For each unit a variety of exercises is given. Some require students only to listen, some to give a minimal written response, and some to initiate their own spoken response using vocabulary and structures from the unit. Certain exercises require students to respond orally to a pictorial stimulus—a drawing or photograph. For most units there is also an exercise that will prepare students to do the Conversation Exercise for that unit of the textbook.

Because of the numerous problems that all beginners have with the interferences of the English and French sound-letter correspondence systems, an important section is devoted, in each unit, to the way French sounds are represented in writing.

Above each exercise or group of exercises is a statement of the specific learning objective, together with a numeral. These numerals are reference numbers, showing which items in the textbook unit are being practiced.

Answer forms for exercises requiring a written response, as well as all visual cues, are printed in the front section of the Activity Book.

This Listening Comprehension Program will be more useful to some students than to others. It is designed specifically for those who can profit from extra listening and speaking practice. Certain students will derive more benefit from the reading and writing strands of the series.

CHAPITRE 1

Pronunciation of the French [l] sound (2)

1. Speaking Exercise

Listen carefully to the following dialog. Watch in particular the [l]-sound, such as in *Je m'appelle, Michelle, elle.*

> —Comment t'appelles-tu?
> —Je m'appelle Michelle.
> —Et elle? Elle s'appelle Danièle?
> —Non, Isabelle.

You notice that the French word *elle,* for example, sounds quite different from, say, the English words "ale" or "ail." The vowel sound is different, but the consonant sound [l] is also quite different.

Listen to an American say the name Michelle: *(American voice)* "Michelle." Now listen to the way a French person says it. Watch the [l]-sound: *(French voice)* Michelle. Do you hear the difference? *(American voice)* "Michelle, mademoiselle." *(French voice)* Michelle, mademoiselle.

The American and French [l]-sounds are different because American and French speakers do not do the same things when they pronounce these sounds. The difference is essentially in the position of the tongue. American speakers tend to curve their tongue backwards. French speakers don't. In producing an American [l], the tip of the tongue touches the roof of the mouth at a higher point than that for a

T59

French [l]. When producing a French [l], French speakers press the tip of the tongue against the ridge at the base of the upper front teeth. Now try it. Listen carefully to the models, and imitate the French [l]-sound as closely as possible.

Je m'appelle Michelle.   Et elle?   Elle, elle s'appelle Danièle.

Practice with names and gender markers (2)

2. Listening Comprehension and Speaking Exercise

You see in front of you six pictures of young French people. Each picture is identified by a number, from 1 to 6. Under the six pictures you see a list of names. Those are the names of the six boys and girls represented. Try to guess the name of each one of the boys and girls. Of course, you have no way of knowing. So just guess, and let's see how lucky you are. But first, let's read together the list of names:

Arnaud   Caroline   David   Muriel   Sylvie   Viviane

All right! Now let's look at picture number 1. First, what is it a picture of? Is it a girl or a boy?
C'est une fille ou un garçon? (   ) *C'est un garçon.*
Do you know what his name is? It's David.
Comment s'appelle ce garçon? (   ) *Eh bien, il s'appelle David! Oui, David. Il s'appelle David.*
Write his name under the picture. If you are not sure of the spelling, check with the list of names in front of you. Make sure you write those names carefully because you will have to read them later.
Ecrivez: Numéro 1 — NOM: David.

Now look at picture number 2. Numéro 2.
Qu'est-ce que c'est? C'est un garçon ou une fille? (   ) *C'est une fille!*
Comment s'appelle-t-elle? Elle s'appelle (   ) *Muriel.*
Ecrivez: Numéro 2 — NOM: Muriel.

Voyons maintenant le numéro 3.
C'est un garçon ou une fille? (   ) *C'est un garçon.*
Comment s'appelle-t-il? Il s'appelle (   ) *Arnaud.*
Ecrivez: Numéro 3 — NOM: Arnaud.

Numéro 4.
Qu'est-ce que c'est? (   ) *C'est une fille.*
Comment est-ce qu'elle s'appelle? (   ) *Elle s'appelle Viviane.*
Ecrivez sous le numéro 4 — NOM: Viviane.

Numéro 5.
Qu'est-ce que c'est? (   ) *C'est une fille!*
Comment s'appelle-t-elle? Elle s'appelle (   ) *Caroline.*
Ecrivez sous le numéro 5 — NOM: Caroline.

Numéro 6.
Ça c'est . . . (   ) *C'est une fille.*
Et elle s'appelle (   ) *Elle s'appelle Sylvie!*
Ecrivez: Numéro 6 — NOM: Sylvie.

1. NOM: _____

AGE: _____ ans

2. NOM: _____

AGE: _____ ans

3. NOM: _____

AGE: _____ ans

4. NOM: _____

AGE: _____ ans

5. NOM: _____

AGE: _____ ans

6. NOM: _____

AGE: _____ ans

Arnaud   Caroline   David   Muriel   Sylvie   Viviane

Practice with speaking about age (8)

3. Listening Comprehension and Speaking Exercise

Look again at the pictures in Exercise 2, and be prepared to write in the blanks provided. The pictures represent six young French people. You have just found out what their names are. Now let's see if you can guess how old each one is. Make a good guess and tell us the age. Then we will tell you the real age, and you will write it in the space provided under the picture. Use figures. Let's begin.
Numéro 1. David. Quel âge a David? Devinez! (   ) *David a 10 ans! Il a 10 ans.*
Ecrivez: AGE: 10 ans.

Numéro 2. Muriel. Quel âge a Muriel? (   ) *Muriel a 6 ans.*
Ecrivez: AGE: 6 ans.

Numéro 3. Arnaud. Quel âge a-t-il? (   ) *Il a 11 ans.*
Ecrivez: AGE: 11 ans.

Numéro 4. Ça c'est Viviane. Quel âge a-t-elle? (   ) *16 ans! Elle a 16 ans.*
Ecrivez: AGE: 16 ans.

Numéro 5. Caroline. Quel âge a Caroline? (   ) *Elle a 14 ans.*
Ecrivez: AGE: 14 ans.

Numéro 6. Sylvie. Quel âge a Sylvie? (   ) *Elle a 15 ans.*
Ecrivez: AGE: 15 ans.

Now check your answers. The numbers under the photographs should read, from left to right: *10, 6, 11, 16, 14, 15.*

Using the pronouns il and elle (18)

4. Listening, Writing, and Speaking Exercise

You will hear twelve sentences. These same sentences, with a word missing from each, are printed in your Activity Book. Some sentences refer to a girl, others to a boy. The only way you can tell is by noticing whether *il* or *elle* is used. If *il* is used, the sentence refers to a boy. If *elle* is used, the sentence refers to a girl. Now listen carefully for the difference between *il* and *elle*, and complete each sentence by writing *il* or *elle*. The number of each sentence will be given in French. Let's begin.

1. Elle s'appelle Claude. _____ *(elle—fille)*
2. Il s'appelle Claude. _____ *(il—garçon)*
3. Comment s'appelle-t-il? _____ *(il—garçon)*
4. Comment s'appelle-t-elle? _____ *(elle—fille)*
5. Et elle? _____ *(elle—fille)*
6. Quel âge a-t-il? _____ *(il—garçon)*
7. Quel âge a-t-elle? _____ *(elle—fille)*
8. Elle a treize ans. _____ *(elle—fille)*
9. Il a douze ans. _____ *(il—garçon)*
10. Il habite au Canada. _____ *(il—garçon)*
11. Où est-il? _____ *(il—garçon)*
12. Où est-elle? _____ *(elle—fille)*

Now listen to the sentences again, and indicate whether the sentence refers to a girl or a boy by checking the proper column to the right. Let's begin.

Now check your answers. *(Read each sentence again, and after a brief pause, give the correct answer.)*

1. _____ s'appelle Claude.

2. _____ s'appelle Claude.

3. Comment s'appelle-t-_____?

4. Comment s'appelle-t-_____?

5. Et _____?

6. Quel âge a-t-_____?

7. Quel âge a-t-_____?

8. _____ a treize ans.

9. _____ a douze ans.

10. _____ habite au Canada.

11. Où est-_____?

12. Où est-_____?

fille (elle)	garçon (il)
1.	7.
2.	8.
3.	9.
4.	10.
5.	11.
6.	12.

5. Listening Exercise

In this exercise you will hear a group of French people describing where they live in France. Listen carefully to what they say, and then on the map in your Activity Book try to find where they live. Each time, after a short pause, the name of the town where each person lives will be given.

Dialog 1
—Moi, je m'appelle Vincent, j'habite en Provence, près de Marseille . . .
—Sur la mer?
—Non, pas sur la mer, sur un fleuve, sur le Rhône.
—(   ) Avignon?
—C'est ça!

Dialog 2
—Moi, je m'appelle Corinne. J'habite dans une ville près de Paris.
—Montargis?
—Non, mais c'est près de Montargis. C'est aussi près de Tours. C'est sur un fleuve . . . C'est sur la Loire. Vous trouvez?
—(   ) Orléans?
—C'est ça, Orléans. J'habite à Orléans.

Dialog 3
—Moi, je m'appelle Brigitte. J'habite dans une grande ville, près de la Belgique.
—Sur la mer?
—Non!
—Alors . . . c'est . . . (   ) *Lille?*
—Oui, c'est ça. J'habite à Lille.

Dialog 4
—Moi, je m'appelle Michel. J'habite en Alsace, près de l'Allemagne.
—. . . en Alsace . . . près de l'Allemagne . . . Voyons . . . (   ) *A Strasbourg?*
—Oui, j'habite à Strasbourg.

Dialog 5
—Moi, je m'appelle Marie-Christine. J'habite dans une ville, une petite ville; c'est aussi un port, et c'est près de l'Espagne.
—C'est sur la mer?
—Oui, c'est sur la mer.
—Sur la Méditerranée?
—Non . . . pas sur la Méditerranée.
—Alors . . . C'est . . . (   ) *Bayonne?*
—Oui, c'est ça! C'est Bayonne. J'habite à Bayonne.

Look at the map once again. The towns in which these people live are *Avignon, Orléans, Lille, Strasbourg, Bayonne.*

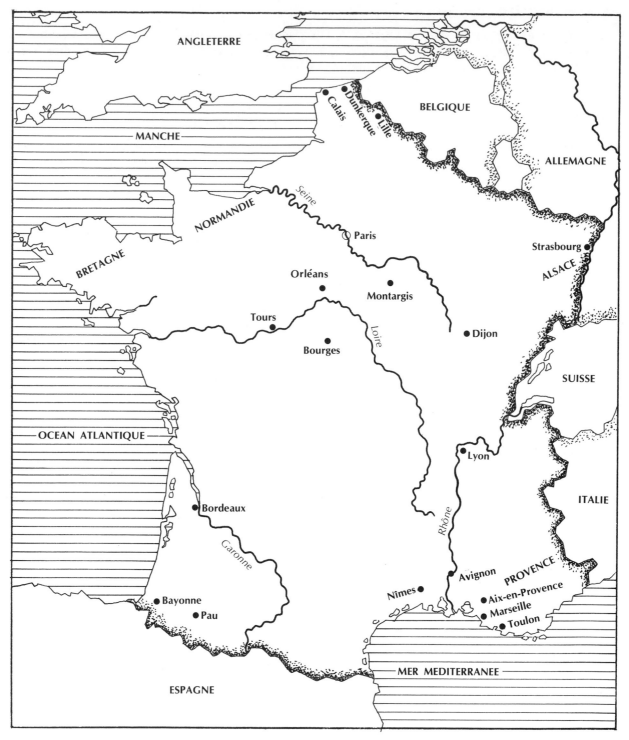

6. Pronunciation Exercise

By now you may have noticed that French and English do not sound alike. The most obvious reason is that the sounds which make up the two languages are different. There is, however, another reason — French and English have different rhythms.

Compare the rhythm of these two sentences.[1]
> **1.** *(American voice)* I līve in a smāll apārtment in Pāris.
> **2.** *(French voice)*   J'habite dans un petit appartement à Parī̄s.

In the English sentence you notice four well-marked beats. There are four syllables that stand out. All the others are said with much less energy; in fact, they tend to be slurred. Listen again to that sentence, and notice the four stresses on "live, small, -part-, Pa."

> *(American voice)* I līve in a smāll apārtment in Pāris.

Now listen how different the rhythm is in the French sentence. There are no obvious beats; syllables seem to be at the same level. *(French voice) J'habite dans un petit appartement à Paris.* If you listen carefully to the French, you may hear a slight stress at the very end. This slight stress falls on the very last syllable of the group of words — here, the last syllable in *Paris*. Listen. *(French voice) J'habite dans un petit appartement à Paris.* There is a slight stress on the *ris* of *Paris,* but on nothing else, and even that stress is not very well marked.

When Americans first try to speak French, they sometimes sound a little strange to French people, just because they don't get the right rhythm. They tend to place stress in several places within the sentence, whereas French people don't.

If you wish to get into the rhythm of French, you should say all syllables pretty much on the same level, except perhaps for a slight stress on the last syllable of a group of words. *(French voice) J'ai un petit appartement à Paris.* Now try to say it yourself.

> *(French voice)* J'ai un petit appartement à Paris.

Now let us compare the two words *(American voice)* "apartment" and *(French voice) appartement.* Whenever you hear "apartment" in English, there is a stress on the second syllable. *(American voice)* . . . "apartment. I have a small apartment. I have an apartment, an apartment in Paris."

The stress is always there on the English word "apartment," whereas in French there is no such stress. Listen. *(French voice)* . . . *appartement. J'ai un petit appartement. J'ai un appartement, un appartement à Paris.*

Now let's practice. Repeat each utterance you hear. Remember not to place any stress within the group of words, only slightly on the last syllable.

Denise habite au Canada.   au Canada   C'est un village.   C'est un petit village.
C'est un petit village au Canada.

Richard habite à Paris.   Il habite dans un petit appartement.   Il habite dans un petit
appartement à Paris.

Doris habite à la Martinique.   Elle habite dans une petite maison.   Elle habite dans
une petite maison à la Martinique.

---

[1] Stress is indicated by a short line printed above the stressed syllable.

7. Listening and Reading Exercise

If you look at some written French and read it aloud, what will come out of your mouth will certainly have very little resemblance to French speech. This is true because you very naturally tend to read French as if it were English. You assume that the letters or combinations of letters that you see represent the same sounds as in English. But they don't. The sounds of French are quite different from the sounds of English. Therefore, the letters you see necessarily represent different sounds.

Look, for example, at the word represented by the letters *v-i-l-l-a-g-e,* which is given as number 1 on the page in front of you.

1. village

This word exists both in English and in French, and it happens to be spelled the same way in both languages. Now compare the way it sounds in English: *(American voice)* "village"; and in French: *(French voice) village.* You see that the same combination of letters represents completely different sounds in the two languages.

First of all, the letter **a** represents a different sound in English from that in French. Listen. *(American voice)* "village"; *(French voice) village.* Repeat the French word: *village.*

The sounds represented by the letter **i** are quite different too. *(American voice)* "village"; *(French voice) village.* Now say the French word yourself: *village.*

Now listen to the English **g** as opposed to the French **g** in the following example. *(American voice)* "village"; *(French voice) village.* Now it's your turn: *village.*

If you listen very carefully you will notice that even the sounds represented by the letters **v** and **l** are not exactly the same. Listen. *(American voice)* "village"; *(French voice) village.* Try to say it the French way: *village.*

Even when you have more or less similar sounds in English and in French, they are often represented by different combinations of letters. Take the sound represented by the letter **i** in "I am fourteen." A similar sound does exist in French. There is, for example, a French word which sounds very much like the word "I" in English, but it is spelled "a-i-l." (It means "garlic," by the way.) So you see that two sounds which might be considered the same are not represented in the same way in the two languages. The letters used to represent the sounds of English and French in writing are the same—that is, the alphabet used in French is the same as the one used in English. As a rule, however, it represents different sounds. Here is how the French say the alphabet. Look at number 2.

2. A B C D E F G H I J K L M N O P Q R S T U V W X Y Z

The same combination of letters may represent a certain sound and meaning in English, while representing a completely different sound and meaning in French. Take for example the combination of letters **a-i-l.** We have just seen that in French, these three letters represent the sound [aj] and mean "garlic." Now an English reader, seeing those three letters, will pronounce them as "ail" and will take it to be a form of the verb "to ail," as in "an ailing mother" or "it ails me." A French reader will pronounce it in a totally different way and will think of garlic.

You must always remember that the combinations of letters you observe in written French do not represent English sounds. Little by little you will learn to guess which French sounds a given combination of letters may stand for, though you will never be absolutely sure until you have heard that particular word said by a speaker of French.

8. Reading and Speaking Exercise

Consonants at the end of words offer a good example of the differences between the French and English systems of sound-letter correspondence. For example, look at the combination of letters in number 1.

1. p-o-r-t

In English they represent the word "port," which is pronounced with consonant sound [t] at the end. In French they represent the word *port,* which has no [t]-sound at the end. For another example, look at the letters in number 2.

2. g-r-a-n-d

In English they represent the word "grand," said with a [d]-sound. In French they represent the word *grand,* said without a [d]-sound. This is quite general. Most consonants you see at the end of English words are pronounced, but most consonants you see at the end of French words are not.

Listen carefully to the following words. Do you hear any consonant at the end? Is the last sound a consonant sound?

Christian　　Jean　　garçon　　non　　Lyon　　Alain　　loin　　un

You noticed that there was no consonant [n]-sound at the end of these words. Yet all these words are spelled with an **n** at the end. Read each of these words aloud, making sure not to pronounce the **n** at the end. Look at number 3.

3. garçon　　Alain　　un　　Jean　　non　　loin　　Christian

Now listen to the following names. Do you hear any [d]-sound at the end?

Arnaud　　Bernard　　Richard

Though there is no [d] in the spoken word, there is a **d** in the written word. When you say these words, make sure you do not sound the final **d.** Try to imitate the voice as you look at the words in number 4.

4. Richard　　Bernard　　Arnaud

Now listen to these words. What is the last sound you hear in the names of these two cities?

Strasbourg　　Luxembourg

Say the names in 5.

5. Strasbourg　　Luxembourg

Listen to the way this word sounds: *vingt.* What is the last sound you hear? Is it a consonant sound? No, yet it is spelled with a **g** and **t** at the end. Look at number 6.

6. vingt

Listen again and repeat: *vingt.*

CHAPITRE 2

Recognizing subject pronouns (7)

1. Listening Comprehension Exercise

When talking about people, we do not always mention them by name. Yet we usually know whom we are talking about. Suppose we are talking about a girl, Catherine, and her brother, François. If I say *Elle aime le tennis,* do you know whom I am talking about? Of course you do! You know I am talking about the girl. Why? Simple: because *elle* represents a girl, not a boy. And if I say *Il aime le tennis,* you know I am talking about François, the boy, and not his sister, because *il* represents a boy and not a girl. You already know that. The only tricky part is to hear the difference between *il* and *elle*. Now suppose I say *Elles aiment le tennis*. Am I talking about a boy? a girl? several boys? several girls? several boys and girls? Listen again: *Elles aiment le tennis*. You know I am talking about several girls, because I said *Elles aiment le tennis*. You heard *elle* and not *il,* so you know it is feminine. Then you heard a /z/-sound, *elles aiment,* which tells you it is plural.

If I say *Ils aiment le tennis,* you know I am talking about more than one person. It could be two or more boys, one boy and one or more girls, or any number of boys plus any number of girls. Now, if I say *Elles jouent au tennis,* am I talking about one girl or several girls? Can you tell? No, you can't! It could be either. With a verb that begins with a vowel sound, like *aimer, habiter,* you can tell: *elles aiment le tennis, elles habitent à Paris.* But with most verbs that begin with a consonant, like *jouer, regarder, parler,* you can't tell.

Sometimes, though, you can tell, even with a verb that begins with a consonant. Listen to this, for example: *Elles font du tennis.* Am I talking about one girl or several girls? Several, of course! Because if I had been talking about a single girl, I would have said *Elle fait du tennis.* The verb would have sounded different—*fait* instead of *font.*

Of course, when you are listening to someone talk, it is important to know whom that person is talking about. Let's see whether you can figure it out. Look at the pictures in front of you. They represent the people we will be talking about. We will be talking about either Sylvie (one girl, picture 1), or Arnaud (one boy, picture 2), or Caroline and Christine (two girls, picture 3), or else Doris and her brother Danou (a girl and a boy, picture 4).

To the right of the pictures you see vertical columns, which correspond to the sentences you are about to hear. For each sentence you hear, check the row corresponding to the picture the sentence is about. For example, you hear the sentence: *Il habite à Montréal.* You heard *il habite,* so you know it is about one boy. You place your check mark opposite the picture of the only boy who is alone: Arnaud. Let's begin.

1. Il habite à Paris. _____ *(Who is it? Arnaud, of course, il habite. It's a boy, one boy.)*
2. Elle habite à Toulouse. _____ *(Elle habite, that's a girl, one girl. It must be Sylvie.)*
3. Elles habitent à Lyon. _____ *(Elles habitent, more than one girl: Caroline and Christine.)*
4. Il fait du cheval. _____ *(Il fait, one boy: Arnaud.)*
5. Elle aime beaucoup le tennis. _____ *(Elle aime, one girl: Sylvie.)*
6. Elles font du vélo. _____ *(Elles font, more than one girl: Caroline and Christine.)*
7. Elles aiment regarder les matchs de tennis à la télé. _____ *(Elles aiment, more than one girl: Caroline and Christine.)*
8. Elle aime beaucoup le rouge. _____ *(Elle aime, one girl: Sylvie.)*
9. Ils habitent dans un grand port. _____ *(Ils habitent, well . . . that's several people. One of them at least is a boy, so it must be Doris and her brother Danou.)*
10. Elles habitent dans une grande ville. _____ *(Elles habitent, more than one girl: Caroline and Christine.)*

Now check your answers. *Read each sentence again and give the correct answer.*

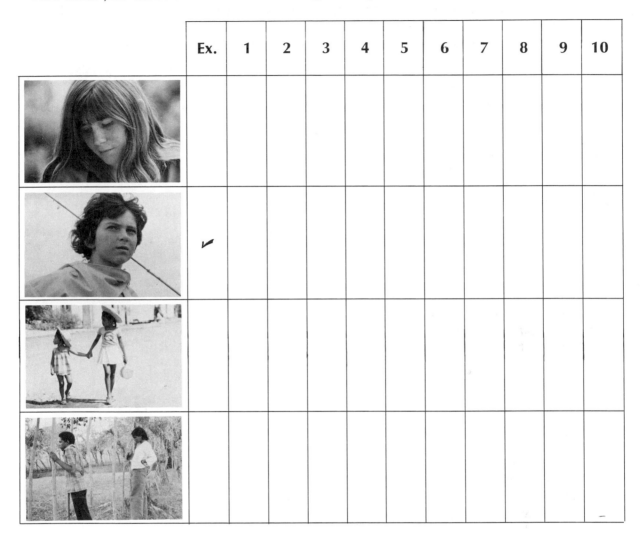

	Ex.	1	2	3	4	5	6	7	8	9	10
	✓										

Practice with the [y]-sound (15)

2. Pronunciation Exercise

Listen to the following words or phrases, and try to figure out what sound is in each one of them. *Le judo . . . Tu aimes ça? Et le rugby?* They all contain a very remarkable sound, the sound [y]. Here are a few more examples of utterances that all have this same sound. *Où habites-tu? Dans une ville? Aux Etats-Unis? A Luneray? A Luchon? Dans le Jura?* This [y]-sound does not exist in English, so you may have some difficulty in pronouncing it. We will have to practice. Listen to the [y]-sound in the following words, and repeat after the model.

Quel âge as-tu?   une balle   Luchon   le rugby   le judo

If you seem to have trouble producing [y], you may try this: start by saying [u] in a continuous way. (That should not be difficult because you have the sound [u] in such English words as "Sue" or "shoe.") Then, while still saying [u], shift gradually to [i]. As you go from [u] toward [i] you should hit the [y] sound. Listen again: [u] → [y]. Now you try it!

Repeat the following words and sentences:

Où habites-tu?	A Luchon?	Tu fais du judo?
Tu habites aux Etats-Unis?	Dans une île?	Tu joues au rugby?
Tu habites à Luneray?	Dans une maison?	Tu es gardien de but?

3. Reading Exercise

Listen to the voice as you look at the words in number 1. How is the sound [y] represented in these words?

1. tu   une   sur   judo

The sound [y] is represented by the letter **u.** Does the letter **u** always represent a [y]sound? Look at the words or phrases in number 2 as you listen to the way they sound.

2. où   elle joue   le jeu   un   quatre

Did you hear any [y]-sound in those words. No? Well, then, the letter **u** does not always represent the sound [y] in French! Sometimes it does and sometimes it doesn't. Can you tell when it does and when it doesn't? It isn't easy, but in most cases you can. Let's see if we can figure out some kind of system. Look at the words in number 3 as you listen.

3. la raquette   l'équipe   quelle balle
   qui   à la Martinique   quinze ans

Did you hear any [y]-sound? No! Yet each word has the letter **u** in it. What sound does it represent in the words above? Look at *qui* for example. How many sounds are in that word? Listen: *qui*. Two sounds: a consonant [k] and a vowel [i]. The consonant [k] is represented by the letter **q** and the vowel [i] by the letter **i.** And what about **u,** what sound does the letter **u** represent? None, really!

How can you tell whether the letter **u** in a word is silent or not? Look at the words in number 3 again. Do you notice something? Yes, in each of them the letter **u** comes right after the letter **q.** It is part of the spelling for the [k]-sound. The [k]-sound is represented by a combination of **q** and **u.**

Let's practice. In the following exercises we use many cognates—that is to say, French words that look like English words. Remember that although these words may look alike, they are not pronounced as in English. Some of them have different meanings, too. Now repeat the words in number 4 after the model.

4. quatre   question   Québec
   quart   quatorze   l'équipe

Remember when you see **u** after **q** in a French word, chances are that this **u** does not represent any sound. Now look at the words in number 5.

5. où   vous   elle joue
   rouge   couleur   beaucoup

It seems that the combination of letters **o-u** represents the sound [u], right? Let's practice. Read the words in number 6 after the model.

6. boutique   souvenir   soupe   cousin
   double   courage   boulevard   journal

Now read the words in number 7 after the model.

7. jeu   deux   dangereuse

Do you hear any [y]-sound? No! Here the letter **u** is used in combination with **e** to represent the sound [ø]. Let's see if you can read aloud the following French words in number 8.

8. au tennis   Arnaud   auto
   aussi   jaune   restaurant

You didn't hear any [y]-sound, did you? Here, the letter **u** is used in combination with the letter **a** to represent the sound [o].

Now look at the words in number 9 and listen to how they sound.

9. un   un demi   un avant

It seems that the letter combination **u-n** represents the nasal sound [œ̃]. Fine!

But what about these words? Look at the words in number 10.

10. une   uniforme   Etats-Unis   Luneray

In these words the **n** is followed by a vowel. That's the difference.

Practice with the vocabulary of the unit (23)

4. Listening Comprehension Exercise

You see six pictures on this page. You will hear six spoken items numbered from 1 to 6. Write down the number of each item you hear under the picture it corresponds to. Let's begin.

1. On a un filet, des balles, des raquettes! On va aller jouer!
2. C'est un peu dangereux, mais elle aime bien faire du cheval!
3. Nous faisons de la natation, c'est très amusant et c'est moins dangereux que le ski.
4. —Tu aimes ça?
   —Oui, c'est amusant, on a une bonne équipe.
   —Ce n'est pas dangereux?
   —Non, on a un ballon ovale, mais ce n'est pas le football américain!
5. Pour jouer, d'abord il faut de la glace, et puis il faut avoir une crosse et une rondelle.
6. Quand on a un vélo, c'est plus amusant d'aller faire un tour que de regarder la télé!

Now check your answers. The numbers next to the photographs should read, from left to right, *4, 6, 2, 5, 3, 1.*

Getting into the rhythm of French: syllabication (34)

5. Speaking Exercise

When you hear a French utterance, it sounds like an uninterrupted chain of sounds. Listen, for example, to this French question: *Qu'est-ce que tu fais?* It sounds as if it were a single, long word: *Qu'est-ce que tu fais?* Yet it is a full sentence. There are really six different words in it. But when it is said normally, it is said in one piece.

   Now suppose you didn't hear it well, and the speaker repeats it for you. This time, to make sure you hear it, he will not say it all at once but will break it up into small parts. He will say:

	1	2	3	4
1.	Qu'est-ce	que	tu	fais?
	c v c	c v	c v	c v

He will cut it up into 4 parts: Qu'est-ce—que—tu—fais? (That's number 1 in your Activity Book.) Each of these parts is called a syllable. As you can see, a syllable does not necessarily correspond to a word. A syllable is a sound unit. It is made up of a vowel sound, which may or may not be accompanied by one or more consonant sounds. In our example—*Qu'est-ce que tu fais?*—the first syllable, *Qu'est-ce,* is made up of a consonant sound, a vowel sound, and a consonant sound: **c-v-c** if we represent consonants by **c** and vowels by **v**.

   A syllable ending with a vowel sound is called an "open syllable." A syllable ending with a consonant sound is called a "closed syllable." In French, one tends to cut up the chain of sounds into open syllables as much as possible. The French word *télévision,* for example, is cut up into four open syllables: *té-lé-vi-sion.* In English, the first syllable is a closed syllable: "tel." Look at number 2.

		1	2	3	4
2.	*French*	té	lé	vi	sion
		cv	cv	cv	c v
	English	tel	e	vi	sion
		cvc	c	cv	c v c

   Syllables may be made up of parts of two different words. This is so whenever you have *élision* and *liaison.* Look at number 3. *Vous aimez ça?*

	Vous	ai	mez	ça?
3.	c v c v		c v	c v
	1 2		3	4

Syllable number 2 is made of the last part of the word *vous* and the first part of the word *aimez.* Now look at number 4.

	l'é	quipe
4.	c v	c v c
	1	2

The first syllable, *l'é,* is made up of the word *le* and part of the word *équipe.*

   Now practice saying the sentences in number 5. Pay special attention to *élisions* and *liaisons,* and follow the markings under each sentence. In the first sentence, for example, notice the marks between the first **v** and second **c** and between the second **v** and the third **c**. These marks tell you to say /nu-za-lɔ̃/. Now read each sentence aloud before you hear it on the recording.

		Nous	allons	faire	du	vélo.
5.	a.	c v c	v c v	c vc	cv	cv cv

	C'est	amusant!
b.	c v c	v c v c v

	Elle	parle	à	une	amie.
c.	v c	c v c c	v	v c	v c v

d. J'aime beaucoup les autres couleurs.

   c v c   c v c v   cvc   v cc   c v c v

e. Lambert aussi est dans l'équipe.

   c v c vc   v cv   v   c v   c vc vc

f. Vous aimez le tennis?

   c v c   v c v   cv   cv cvc

CHAPITRE 3

Comprehension of new vocabulary (1)

1. Listening Exercise

In this unit we talk about various things our friends like to do. Here are six statements that refer to leisure activities. Write the number of each statement next to the photograph to which it refers. Listen.

1. Il aime bricoler.
2. Elle aime tricoter.
3. Elles aiment discuter.

4. Il aime lire des revues.
5. Il aime écouter des disques.
6. Elles aiment regarder la télévision.

Now check your answers. The numbers next to the photographs should read, from left to right: *6, 4, 5, 3, 1, 2.*

*Aural discrimination [ø] ≠ [e] (ce ≠ ces); perception of number;
spelling of plural nouns (6)*

2. Listening and Writing Exercise

Suppose you are talking about new records, and someone says: *J'aime beaucoup ce disque.* Is that person speaking about one record or several? And if you hear: *J'aime beaucoup ces disques,* is that person speaking about one or several records? How can you tell that *ce disque* refers to only one record, but that *ces disques* refers to several records? What difference do you hear between *ce disque* and *ces disques* that enables you to tell? It's the difference between *ce* and *ces.* Ce indicates a singular, while *ces* indicates a plural. In the same way, if I ask: *C'est toi qui as le livre?,* you know I am talking about one book, while if I ask: *C'est toi qui as les livres?,* you know I am talking about several.

You remember that most nouns are written with an **s** at the end when they are plural. The **s** at the end of *livres* is written but is not heard. It is a written mark of the plural.

Part 1

In this exercise you will hear a number of sentences. Tell whether the noun in each of these sentences is singular or plural by filling in the proper spelling of the noun marker and the noun. Let's begin.

1. J'aime beaucoup ce disque.   *(Ce disque—singular. You didn't have to add anything.)*
2. J'aime beaucoup ces disques.   *(Ces disques—plural this time. You should have added an **s** to the end of ce and disque.)*
3. J'aime beaucoup ces livres.   *(Plural. There is an **s** on ces and livres.)*
4. J'aime beaucoup ce livre.   *(Singular. No **s**.)*
5. J'aime beaucoup ces garçons.   *(Plural. There is an **s** on ces and garçons.)*
6. J'aime beaucoup ce garçon.   *(Singular. No **s**.)*

Now check your answers. *Read each item again with the correct answer.*

1. J'aime beaucoup ce___ disque___.
2. J'aime beaucoup ce___ disque___.
3. J'aime beaucoup ce___ livre___.
4. J'aime beaucoup ce___ livre___.
5. J'aime beaucoup ce___ garçon___.
6. J'aime beaucoup ce___ garçon___.

Part 2

In this exercise you will have to decide whether the noun is singular or plural by hearing the difference between *cette,* the feminine singular form, and *ces,* the plural form. Fill in the blanks with the appropriate endings. Let's begin.

1. J'aime beaucoup cette revue.   *(Cette: singular. Write **-tte** for cette; nothing for revue.)*
2. J'aime beaucoup ces revues.   *(Ces: plural. Write **s** at the end of ces and at the end of revue.)*
3. J'aime beaucoup ces revues.   *(Plural. Write **s** on both.)*
4. J'aime beaucoup cette cassette.   *(Singular. Write **-tte** for cette; nothing for cassette.)*
5. J'aime beaucoup cette fille.   *(Singular. Write **-tte** for cette, nothing for fille.)*
6. J'aime beaucoup ces filles.   *(Plural. Write **s** at the end of ces and at the end of filles.)*

Now check your answers. *Read each item again with the correct answer.*

1. J'aime beaucoup ce___ revue___.
2. J'aime beaucoup ce___ revue___.
3. J'aime beaucoup ce___ revue___.
4. J'aime beaucoup ce___ cassette___.
5. J'aime beaucoup ce___ fille___.
6. J'aime beaucoup ce___ fille___.

3. Listening and Reading Exercise

Let's look at the words in column A. You see that in the words *les, des, ces,* the ending *-es* represents the sound [e]. Now look at column B. Here the ending *-es* does not represent the sound [e]. As a verb ending *(écoutes, aimes)*, as a plural noun ending *(timbres)*, or as a plural adjective ending *(extraordinaires)*, *-es* does not represent the sound [e].

A	B
les vélos	Qu'est-ce que tu écoutes?
des radios	Tu aimes ça?
ces photos	J'ai une collection de timbres
ces skis	Ils sont extraordinaires!

4. Reading and Speaking Exercise

Read each sentence aloud before you hear it. Let's begin.

1. Tu écoutes des disques?
2. Non, j'écoute des cassettes.

3. Tu aimes ces livres?
4. Tu collectionnes les coquillages.

5. Listening and Writing Exercise

Write down what you hear.

1. J'aime écouter des disques.
2. Catherine tricote. Toi aussi, tu tricotes?

3. Tu regardes des revues?
4. Tu aimes les livres?

To verify your spelling, see the answer key at the end of your *Activity Book.*

Getting into the rhythm of French: tonic stress and duration of syllables (13)

6. Listening and Speaking Exercise

As we said before, one way that spoken English differs from spoken French is that certain English words or parts of words are strongly stressed. In French, however, there is hardly any stress at all, except a slight one at the end of a group of words. This difference can be illustrated with the word *orange,* which you learned in Unit 2. This French word is also used in English, but it sounds quite different in the two languages, English: "orange"; French: *orange.* Notice the strong stress placed at the beginning of the word in English—"orange"—while there is no such stress in French: *orange.* Listen to the following words. Compare the English and French. Repeat the French.

English	*French*
collection	collection
photography	photographie
amusing	amusant
American	Américain
basket	basket
racket	raquette
radio	radio

So, in English you stress some parts of the words, some syllables. In French you don't (unless, of course, if you want to insist on something, or to attract attention to one word for some special reason).

When you stress a syllable in English, you not only make it sound louder, but you also tend to make it longer. Take "basket," for example. The first syllable sounds louder and longer than the second. In English, the tendency to make some syllables shorter than others is so great that some syllables tend to disappear altogether. Take, for example, the word "captain." It comes from the French *capitaine*. When you pronounce the French word, there are three parts, three syllables: *ca-pi-taine*. In English, the middle part became so short that it disappeared completely. The word is pronounced in only two parts—two syllables—"cap-tain."

Now we will practice with a few words. We will include a few English words that are used in French, and French words that are close to English words, so that you may better appreciate the difference in pronunciation. Remember to pronounce all the words in the French way: no stress (except perhaps a very slight one at the end) and all syllables equal.

Richard	Macbeth	MacDonald	télévision
capitaine	basket-ball	pénalité	électronique
américain	amusant	dangereux	

Recognition of numbers (29)

7. Listening Exercise

Sylvie, Philippe, Catherine, and Arnaud are playing a game. At the end of each set, each announces the number of points he or she has made. The one that has the highest score is the winner for that set. Listen to the scores for each set, and write them down on the score sheet. Use Arabic numerals. Let's begin.

	Sylvie	Philippe	Catherine	Arnaud	
First set	120	21	81	91	*(120)*
Second set	60	500	165	105	*(500)*
Third set	112	72	712	592	*(712)*
Fourth set	711	171	691	185	*(711)*
Fifth set	410	190	206	670	*(670)*
Sixth set	501	101	111	505	*(505)*

Now check your answers. *Read each number again, followed by its English equivalent.*

	1	2	3	4	5	6
Sylvie						
Philippe						
Catherine						
Arnaud						

Practicing new vocabulary in unit (31)

8. Listening Comprehension Exercise

In front of you are seven pictures. You will hear seven sentences, each of which refers to one of the pictures. You may not entirely understand every sentence. However, if you listen carefully, you should be able to guess which picture the sentence refers to. Indicate your choice by writing the number of each sentence under the appropriate picture. Here we go. Listen for the clues and do some quick thinking.

1. Je la regarde tous les jours.
2. Elle l'écoute de temps en temps.
3. C'est toujours elle qui gagne.
4. C'est toujours moi qui dois le réparer.

5. Il en a beaucoup mais il n'aime pas lire.
6. J'ai le 4 de pique et le 2 de carreau.
7. Elle les trouve sur la plage.

Now check your answers. The numbers next to the pictures should read, from left to right: *6, 3, 5, 7, 1, 2, 4.*

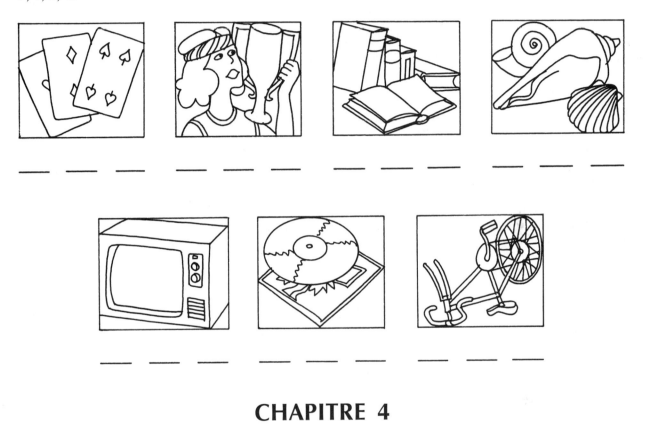

CHAPITRE 4

Telling Time (9)

1. Listening Exercise

In front of you are eight photographs identified by a number from 1 to 8. They represent various clocks in Paris. The first one is at la Conciergerie, one of the old historical buildings in the center of Paris. The second is in a *passage*, a kind of nineteenth-century mall. The next two clocks are at railroad stations, the gare du Nord and gare de Lyon. The fifth clock is in a secondary-school courtyard, the next one is in front of the Opéra, and so on. Before you do the exercise, look at the eight pictures and listen as we describe them in French.

Photo no. 1: Ça c'est l'horloge de la Conciergerie, à Paris, dans l'Ile de la Cité. C'est une très belle horloge, très vieille, très ancienne, très ornée.

Photo no. 2: Ça, c'est l'horloge du passage Jouffroy, Boulevard Montmartre.

Photo no. 3: Ça, c'est l'horloge de la gare du Nord. C'est l'horloge qui est sur la façade principale de la gare du Nord, rue de Dunkerque.

Photo no. 4: Ça c'est encore une horloge de gare. C'est l'horloge de la gare de Lyon, Boulevard Diderot.

Photo no. 5: Ça c'est l'horloge du lycée Jules Ferry, Boulevard de Clichy.

Photo no. 6: Et ça c'est l'horloge de la place de l'Opéra. C'est une horloge moderne, une horloge électrique.

Photo no. 7: Ça aussi c'est une horloge électrique moderne. C'est le même modèle. Mais celle-ci est rue Saint-Antoine.

Photo no. 8: Voilà encore une horloge très moderne. C'est l'horloge d'Hermès, un magasin très chic dans une rue très chic, la rue du Faubourg Saint-Honoré.

Now you will hear the times shown by the eight clocks, but in scrambled order. Each time you hear will be identified by a letter of the alphabet, from A to H. Write down each letter under the picture of the clock which marks that time. Let's begin.

A	midi	E	3 heures et demie
B	3 heures	F	3 heures et quart
C	3 heures moins 5	G	11 heures 10
D	3 heures 20	H	2 heures 10

Now check your answers. The letters under each clock read, from left to right: *E, F, G, C, A, D, B, H.*

1 Horloge de la _____ Conciergerie	2 Horloge du pas- _____ sage Jouffroy	3 Horloge de la _____ gare du Nord	4 Horloge de la _____ gare de Lyon
5 Horloge du lycée _____ Jules Ferry	6 Horloge de la _____ Place de l'Opéra	7 Horloge de la rue _____ Saint-Antoine	8 Horloge de _____ chez Hermès

2. Speaking Exercise

Now look again at the eight photographs of clocks, and answer the following questions, telling what time each clock says. The questions are not in the same order as the photographs, so you'll have to find the right clock each time. Ready? Let's begin.

1. Quelle heure est-il à l'horloge du lycée Jules Ferry? ( ) *midi*
2. Quelle heure est-il à l'horloge de la rue Saint-Antoine? ( ) *trois heures*
3. Quelle heure est-il à l'horloge du passage Jouffroy? ( ) *trois heures et quart*
4. Quelle heure est-il à l'horloge de la Conciergerie? ( ) *trois heures et demie*
5. Et à l'horloge de la gare de Lyon? ( ) *trois heures moins cinq*
6. Et à l'horloge de la Place de l'Opéra? ( ) *trois heures vingt*

3. Listening and Writing Exercise

You have in front of you a blank schedule form from a French school. Imagine you are a student in this French school. It is the first day of class, and your teacher is giving you your schedule for this trimester. For the sake of keeping the exercise short, you will be given the schedule for only three days. Write it down on the blank form provided. Be careful to write legibly, because you will have to refer to it later. To make things easier for you, we have listed the different subjects; in alphabetical order, just in case you forgot how to spell one of the words. Let's begin.

Lundi   de   8 à 9: mathématiques   —salle 26
                  9 à 10: gymnastique
              10 à 11: latin   —salle 26
              11 à 12: français   —salle 26
                2 à 3: histoire   —salle 3
                3 à 4: espagnol   —salle 8

Mardi   de   8 à 9: latin   —salle 26
                9 à 10: mathématiques —salle 26
              10 à 12: technologie   —salle 6
                2 à 3: dessin   —salle 1
                3 à 4: français   —salle 26
                4 à 5: anglais   —salle 9

Jeudi   de   8 à 9: géographie   —salle 32
                9 à 10: français   —salle 25
               10 à 11: latin   —salle 25
              11 à 12: espagnol   —salle 10
                3 à 4: anglais   —salle 8
                4 à 5: musique   —salle 2

anglais	français	histoire	musique
dessin	géographie	latin	technologie
espagnol	gymnastique	mathématiques	

EMPLOI DU TEMPS DU 2e TRIMESTRE

HORAIRE	LUNDI	HORAIRE	MARDI	HORAIRE	MERCREDI

HORAIRE	JEUDI	HORAIRE	VENDREDI	HORAIRE	SAMEDI

4. Listening and Speaking Exercise

Now you will be asked a number of questions about the schedule you have just written down for yourself. Answer as fast as you can. Try to understand the question right away, so that you can find the information and give the answer before it is given to you. Ready?

1. Qu'est-ce que tu as le lundi de 2 à 3? (   ) *Histoire.*
2. Et le mardi de 9 à 10? (   ) *Maths. Mathématiques.*
3. Quand est-ce que tu as technologie? (   ) *Le mardi de 10 à 12h.*
4. A quelle heure est-ce que tu finis le jeudi? (   ) *A 5 heures.*
5. Est-ce que tu peux aller jouer au basket le lundi à 4 heures et demie? (   ) *Oui.*
6. Est-ce que tu peux aller faire du cheval le lundi à 3 heures? (   ) *Non! J'ai espagnol.*
7. Dans quelle salle est-ce que tu as français le jeudi de 9 à 10 heures? (   ) *Dans la salle 25.*
8. Et où est-ce que tu as latin mardi de 8 à 9? (   ) *Dans la salle 26.*

Practice with the vocabulary of the unit (21)

5. Listening Comprehension Exercise

You will hear a series of sentences having to do with school. In front of you is another series of sentences. For each sentence you hear, pick the written sentence that would follow most logically. Indicate your choice by writing the number of the sentence you hear next to the written sentence it corresponds to. Let's begin.

1. Regardez vos devoirs. _____ *(Corrigez les fautes d'orthographe, 2.)*
2. C'est midi. _____ *(Allons au réfectoire, 4.)*
3. Qui est-ce qui veut répondre? _____ *(Levez la main, 1.)*
4. Ouvrez vos livres. _____ *(Regardez la photo à la page 24, 3.)*
5. Il n'y a pas cours aujourd'hui. _____ *(C'est mercredi, 5.)*

Now you will hear the correct response. *Read each item again and give the correct response.*

1. Levez la main. _____
2. Corrigez les fautes d'orthographe. _____
3. Regardez la photo à la page 24. _____
4. Allons au réfectoire. _____
5. C'est mercredi. _____

6. Listening Comprehension Exercise

Florence is a student. She is 13. As you hear her speak, she will be talking sometimes to Mlle Dubois, her English teacher, and sometimes to Françoise, a friend her own age who is in the same class. For each sentence you hear, try to figure out whether Florence is speaking to her friend Françoise or to her teacher. Then put a check mark in the appropriate column. Let's begin.

1. Tu as classe ce matin? _____ *(Françoise)*
2. Regardez! _____ *(Mlle Dubois)*
3. Corrige les fautes s'il te plaît! _____ *(Françoise)*
4. Tu parles bien anglais! _____ *(Françoise)*
5. Vous parlez aussi allemand? _____ *(Mlle Dubois)*
6. Quelle heure est-il s'il vous plaît? _____ *(Mlle Dubois)*
7. Vous avez cours tous les jours? _____ *(Mlle Dubois)*
8. Tu aimes mon dessin? _____ *(Françoise)*
9. Où est-ce que tu vas? _____ *(Françoise)*
10. Vous aimez les maths, vous? _____ *(Mlle Dubois)*

Now check your answers. *Read each item again, giving the correct answer.*

Florence parle à	1	2	3	4	5	6	7	8	9	10
Mlle Dubois, (le professeur d'anglais)										
Françoise (une amie de son âge)										

Practice with comprehension of new vocabulary (33)

7. Listening Exercise

You have in front of you eight pictures of school objects. For each picture, you will hear a statement. Write the number of each statement below the picture to which it refers. Listen.

1. François a une règle.
2. Arnaud n'a pas de cahier.
3. Tu as une boîte de couleurs?
4. Qui a un compas?

5. Je n'ai pas de crayon.
6. C'est la trousse de Catherine.

7. C'est le livre de Philippe.
8. Sylvie n'a pas de stylo.

Now check your answers. The numbers below the drawings should read from left to right: 6, 4, 1, 3, 5, 8, 2, 7.

Discrimination between masculine and feminine adjectives (39)

8. Listening Comprehension Exercise

You will hear a number of statements. Some will be about a girl; others about a boy. Try to find out whether each statement you hear is about a girl or a boy, and indicate your choice by putting a check mark in either the row marked _une fille_ or that marked _un garçon_. But be careful. The name won't give you a hint because each of these names could belong to either a boy or a girl. So, you will have to watch for some other clue—like the ending of an adjective, for example. Let's begin.

1. Claude est très intelligente! _____ (une fille)
2. Michel n'est pas très sérieux. _____ (un garçon)
3. Andrée est un peu distraite. _____ (une fille)
4. Claude est très sérieuse! _____ (une fille)
5. Pascal est amusant! _____ (un garçon)
6. Joël est distrait et paresseux. _____ (un garçon)
7. Michelle est très bonne en maths. _____ (une fille)
8. André est très grand pour son âge! _____ (un garçon)
9. Pascale est moins grande. _____ (une fille)
10. Joëlle est très bonne en dessin. _____ (une fille)
11. Michel est très timide et un peu paresseux. _____ (un garçon)
12. Renée aussi est un peu timide mais c'est une très bonne élève. _____ (une fille)

Now check your answers. *Read each item again, giving the correct answer.*

	1	2	3	4	5	6	7	8	9	10	11	12
une fille												
un garçon												

Discrimination between [e] and [ɛ]; corresponding spellings (39)

9. Listening and Speaking Exercise

Listen carefully to the way the word *élève* is pronounced: élève, élève. Watch for the difference between the two vowels: é-lève, é-lève. They are quite different. The first sounds [e], [e], [e]. The second sounds [ɛ], [ɛ], [ɛ], [ɛ]. Sometimes, to describe the difference between the two, one says the first vowel is "closed" and the second "open," because when you say [e], your mouth is more closed than when you say [ɛ]. To say [ɛ] you have to open more. Practice saying the word: élève, élève.

Now notice how those two sounds are represented. Look at number 1.

1. élève

The difference between the two sounds is indicated by the accent on the **e.** The accent on the first **e** is called, in French, *accent aigu.* It represents the "closed" sound [e], [e]. The accent on the second **e** is called *accent grave.* It represents the "open" sound [ɛ], [ɛ].

Look at the words in number 2. Say the words, imitating the model. Notice that the letter **e** with the *accent aigu* represents the "closed" sound, [e].

2. une conférence   une bonne réponse   préférence
c'est différent   un bon numéro   à côté

Now repeat the sentences that you see in number 3.

3. François va à l'école à vélo.
Il étudie la géographie.
Il est doué et sérieux.

Of course, this sound is represented in several other ways. Let's look for some of them. Look at the examples in number 4. Repeat after the model.

4. Allez au tableau!
Regardez!
Ne bavardez pas!

You see that the spelling **-ez** is one way of representing this "closed" [e]-sound.

Here is another. Look at the examples in number 5.

5. J'aime bricoler.   Il faut corriger les fautes.
Il faut écouter.   Tu as le cahier d'Olivier?

As you can see, **-er** at the end of a word usually represents the "closed" [e]-sound. This is true, in particular, of all infinitives ending in **-er.**

Now, repeat the words in number 6.

6. efface   Je suis paresseux.

You see that here the sound is represented by the letter **e** followed by a double consonant (plus vowel).

10. Dictation Exercise

Write down what you hear. Watch out for the different spellings of the [e]-sound.

1. Ouvrez vos cahiers!   3. Il faut écouter!
2. Ne bavardez pas!   4. Effacez le dessin.

To verify your spelling, see the answer key at the end of your *Activity Book.*

11. Speaking Exercise

Now let's consider the open [ɛ]-sound. We have seen that it can be represented in writing by the letter **e** with a grave accent: **è**. Repeat the examples in number 1.

1. Le Sève   une matière   l'après-midi
     le collège   en quatrième   la bibliothèque

Now watch for the same sound in the words listed in 2. Repeat each item. Make sure you pronounce an ''open'' [ɛ]-sound.

2. il aime   s'il vous plaît
     l'anglais   au vestiaire

You see that in these words the sound [ɛ] is represented by the letters **a-i**.

Now look at number 3.

3. elle   Mademoiselle
     à quelle heure   les travaux manuels

Here the [ɛ]-sound is represented by **e** followed by **l-l-e** or just **l**. (In the plural, **e** is followed by **l-s** or **l-l-e-s.**)

Here is another group now. Look at number 4.

4. cette
     cassette
     bicyclette

Here the ''open'' [ɛ]-sound is represented by **e** followed by **t-t-e.** In fact, the letter **e** followed by any double consonant, plus the letter **e,** (pronounced [ə]) always represents the ''open'' [ɛ]-sound.

Now repeat the words in number 5.

5. les échecs
     la technologie

Here the ''open'' [ɛ]-sound is represented by **e** followed by **c** or **ch.**

Here is another group. Read number 6.

6. un exercice
     extraordinaire

Here the ''open'' [ɛ]-sound is represented by **e** followed by **x.**

Here is still another group. Read number 7.

7. mercredi
     Bernard

Here the sound is represented by **e** followed by a pronounced consonant (**r** or any other).

That makes seven different ways of writing this ''open'' [ɛ]-sound. That's a lot, but there are a few more. Look at the words in number 8, and repeat.

8. Qu'est-ce que c'est?
     Vous êtes bon en maths?
     l'enseignement

Let's practice some more with this ''open'' [ɛ]-sound. Say the following sentences before you hear them. Look at number 9.

9. Le Sève est un élève de quatrième.
     Il est dans un Collège d'Enseignement Secondaire.
     Il fait de l'anglais.
     Il aime bien la technologie.
     Il n'est pas mauvais en français.
     Mais il est très distrait.
     Le mercredi après-midi il va à la bibliothèque.
     Il joue aux échecs avec Bernard et il perd!

12. Dictation Exercise

Write the following sentences. Pay special attention to the spelling of the [ɛ]-sound.

1. Michelle est en quatrième.
2. Dans un Collège d'Enseignement Secondaire.
3. Elle va à l'école à bicyclette.
4. Elle est un peu distraite mais ce n'est pas une mauvaise élève.

To verify your spelling, see the answer key at the end of your *Activity Book*.

CHAPITRE 5

To practice new vocabulary in unit (1)

1. Listening Comprehension Exercise

You will hear a number of questions. For each question you hear, find the most appropriate answer among those you see in front of you. Then write the number of the question next to the best answer. Each answer is to be used only once. Let's begin.

1. Avec qui est-ce que vous allez à Dieppe? _____ *(Avec mes amis. 1)*
2. Comment est-ce que vous allez à Dieppe? _____ *(En voiture. 2)*
3. Pourquoi est-ce que vous allez à Dieppe? _____ *(Parce que nous n'avons pas classe. 3)*
4. Où est-ce que vous allez? _____ *(Au cinéma. 4)*
5. A quelle heure est-ce que le film commence? _____ *(A deux heures. 5)*
6. Qu'est-ce que vous allez voir? _____ *(Un film de science-fiction. 6)*
7. Quand est-ce que vous partez? _____ *(Dans cinq minutes. 7)*
8. Vous allez aux Ambassadeurs? _____ *(Oui. 8)*

Oui. _____   Avec mes amis. _____
Au cinéma. _____   Dans cinq minutes! _____
A deux heures. _____   Un film de science-fiction. _____
En voiture. _____   Parce que nous n'avons pas classe. _____

The nasal vowel [ã] and its spelling (16)

2. Speaking Exercise

Listen carefully to the vowel sounds in the following words: *un, en, on, hein?* Are they different? How many different sounds do you hear? Listen again: *un, en, on, hein?* There are four different sounds: *un,* that's one; *en,* that's two; *on* is the third, and *hein* is the fourth. These four vowel sounds are different, but they do have something in common. When you pronounce them, part of the air goes through the back of your mouth and nose. That's why they are called "nasal" sounds: because they are pronounced partly through the nose.

Now take the word "sandwich." It is a French word as well as an English word. As a matter of fact, the French borrowed it from English; it comes from the name of the fourth Earl of Sandwich, an eighteenth-century Englishman who invented the sandwich so that he could eat without leaving the gaming table. Compare the way it sounds in English and in French: *(American)* "sandwich"; *(French) sandwich.* Listen carefully to the first syllable: *(American)* "sandwich"; *(French) sandwich.* It is quite different, isn't it? The principal difference is that there is no trace of any [n]-sound in the French word. Listen: *(American)* "sandwich"; *(French) sandwich—san, an, an.* You see, [ã] is a pure vowel sound. There is no trace of any consonant [n]-sound in it. If you wish to sound French when you speak French, it is very important that you avoid the [n]-sound in nasals, whether the nasal is [œ̃], [ã] [ɔ̃], or [ɛ̃]. Try to say "sandwich" the French way: *sandwich.*

Now try the word *envie.* In English you say "envy" with an [n]. Not in French. In French there is no trace of an [n]: *envie.* Say it once more: *envie.*

Let's practice with a few words. Repeat each phrase you hear.

en France	dans la voiture	Il est grand.
quatre ans	trois francs	Cet enfant est amusant!

Spellings of the nasal sound [ã] *(16)*

3. Reading and Speaking Exercise

Let's read the following phrases aloud. Look at number 1.

1. C'est François.   Il est dans la voiture.   un sandwich . . .
Il est amusant.   Il mange . . .   un grand!

You see that the nasal vowel [ã] is often represented in writing by **a-n.**

Now let's read the dialog in number 2.

2. —Qu'est-ce qu'on prend?
—Tu as de l'argent?
—Tu penses! Attends! . . . Trente centimes!
—Seulement?

You see that the nasal vowel [ã] is also often spelled with e-n.

Now read the items in number 3.

3. de l'argent   ils partent
seulement   ils sortent

You see that **e-n-t** at the end of a word often represents the nasal sound [ã], but sometimes it does not. Can you tell when it does not? What do *ils partent* and *ils sortent* have in common? They are verbs in the third person plural form. When **e-n-t** is the third person plural ending of a verb, this combination does not represent a nasal sound. As a matter of fact it represents no sound at all!

Now read the items in number 4.

4. un pamplemousse   l'emploi
du jambon   du temps
aux Ambassadeurs   du camembert

You see that this nasal vowel [ã] can also be spelled **a-m** or **e-m.** When? Can you figure it out?

Look at the words in number 5.

5. un pamplemousse   du jambon
l'emploi   aux Ambassadeurs
du temps   du camembert

You see that the nasal vowel [ã] is spelled **a-m** or **e-m** in front of **p** or **b.**

In conclusion, we say that the nasal sound [ã] is represented in writing by the combination of the letters **a** or **e** with the letter **n;** or with the letter **m** in front of **b** or **p.**

Of course, you realize that the combination of the letters **a** (or **e**) and **n** (or **m**) does not always represent the nasal sound [ã]. Take the word *panier,* for example. You have the combination **a-n,** but you don't hear any nasal sound. The **a** is pronounced as a non-nasal vowel [a], and **n** is pronounced as the consonant sound [n].

Look at the words in number 6.

6. panier   ami
Canada   venir
animé   pamplemousse

Can you tell why these combinations of **a** or **e** and **n** (or **m**) do not represent the nasal sound? Look carefully: what do they have in common? They are all followed by a vowel sound. So you see, the combination of **a** or **e** with **n** or **m** does not represent a nasal vowel sound when a vowel sound follows it.

Now read the items in number 7.

7. Anne-Marie   tennis
Cannes   femme
programme

In these words we have combinations of **a** or **e** with **n** or **m** which do not represent a nasal sound. Do you see why? What's special here? We have a double **n** or a double **m**. So we can say: the combination of **a** or **e** with a double **n** or **m** does not represent a nasal vowel sound.

Well, is that always true? Almost. . .but do you remember a word that has an **e** plus a double **n** combination representing a nasal sound? Yes, you have seen one: look at the word *ennuyeux,* number 8.

8. ennuyeux

In *ennuyeux,* as an exception, we have a nasal vowel sound followed by the consonant sound /n/.

4. Dictation Exercise

Let's see now if you can write some of the words that you have been practicing. Fill in the blanks in each sentence in front of you, as you listen to the dialog. Let's begin.

1. —Tu as de l'argent?
2. —Attends . . . Oui! Trente francs!
3. —Alors, qu'est-ce qu'on mange?
4. —Eh bien . . . on prend un grand sandwich. Du jambon . . . du camembert, un pamplemousse.
5. —Seulement? C'est tout?

To verify your spelling, see the answer key at the end of your *Activity Book.*

Comprehension of new vocabulary in unit. Use of avoir faim, soif (16)

5. Listening and Speaking Exercise

You will hear someone offering you various kinds of things to eat or drink. You are to refuse everything and give a reason why. For example, if offered something to eat, you may say: *Non merci, je n'ai pas faim.* If offered something to drink, you say: *Non merci, je n'ai pas soif.* After your answer you'll hear the correct response. Let's begin.

1. Tu veux du jambon? (   ) *Non merci, je n'ai pas faim.*
2. Tu prends un sandwich? (   ) *Non merci, je n'ai pas faim.*
3. Qu'est-ce que tu veux, un jus de fruit? (   ) *Non merci, je n'ai pas soif.*
4. Prends du camembert! (   ) *Non merci, je n'ai pas faim.*

5. Je vous apporte une limonade? (   ) *Non merci, je n'ai pas soif.*
6. Tu ne veux pas de gruyère? (   ) *Non merci, je n'ai pas faim.*
7. Allons, mange ce pâté, il est bon! (   ) *Non merci, je n'ai pas faim.*
8. Tu veux du lait? (   ) *Non merci, je n'ai pas soif.*

To practice new vocabulary in unit (16)

6. Listening and Speaking Exercise

In front of you are pictures of good things to eat or drink. For each picture you will hear a question. Answer the question with a complete sentence referring to what you see in the picture. After your answer you'll hear a suggested response. Let's begin.

1. Vous avez faim? Qu'est-ce que vous allez prendre? (   ) *Du jambon — un sandwich au jambon.*
2. Je vous donne des rillettes? (   ) *Non, donnez-moi du saucisson.*
3. Quel genre de sandwich est-ce que je vous donne? (   ) *Un sandwich au pâté!*
4. Vous aimez le fromage? Qu'est-ce que je vous donne? (   ) *Du camembert.*
5. Je vous donne du camembert? (   ) *Non, du gruyère.*
6. Vous avez soif? Qu'est-ce que vous voulez? (   ) *Un jus de fruit.*
7. Vous voulez du Coca Cola? (   ) *Non, donnez-moi une limonade.*
8. Je vous donne de l'eau? (   ) *Non, du lait, s'il vous plaît.*
9. Vous avez soif? (   ) *Non, je vais prendre une glace.*

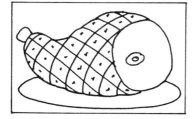 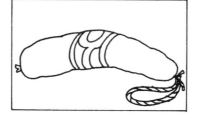 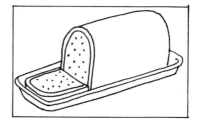

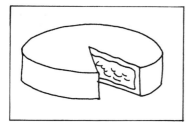 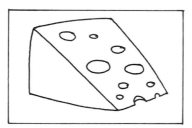 

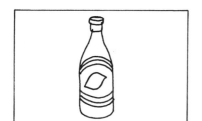  

Practice with the vocabulary of the unit and the verb choisir (38)

7. Listening and Speaking Exercise

You are about to go to the movies with a group of friends. You are looking at the newspaper page trying to make a decision. Each of you would like to see something else. Answer each of the following questions, using as a cue the picture that's numbered the same as the question. Use complete sentences. After your response you'll hear the correct answer. Let's begin.

1. Qu'est-ce que tu choisis? (   ) *Je choisis le western.*
2. Et Dominique? (   ) *Il choisit le film policier.*
3. Et Philippe? (   ) *Il choisit le film comique.*
4. Et Catherine? (   ) *Elle choisit l'histoire d'amour.*

Preparation for Conversation Exercise 46

8. Listening Exercise

The following dialog took place on a Wednesday morning at the Signorets. Madeleine Signoret was asking her younger brother Marc what he was going to do that day. Listen to what they said.

MADELEINE	Qu'est-ce que tu vas faire aujourd'hui?
MARC	Je vais travailler un peu ce matin: je vais faire mon devoir d'anglais et puis, cet après-midi, je vais sortir.
MADELEINE	Avec qui?
MARC	Avec des copains du lycée, Eric et Arnaud et puis Sylvie, sans doute.
MADELEINE	Qu'est-ce que vous allez faire?
MARC	On va sûrement aller au cinéma.
MADELEINE	Qu'est-ce que vous allez voir?
MARC	Il paraît qu'on joue un film policier à l'Apollo. On va sûrement aller voir ça. Il paraît que c'est bien.
MADELEINE	Toi et tes copains, vous allez toujours voir des films policiers! Vous n'avez pas beaucoup d'imagination . . .
MARC	Pourquoi? C'est très bien, les films policiers! Justement, il y a beaucoup d'imagination dans les films policiers!

MADELEINE	Je ne comprends pas comment vous pouvez aimer toutes ces histoires de crimes ...
MARC	Oh ben, c'est plus amusant que les histoires d'amour ...
MADELEINE	Bah! Tu es trop jeune pour comprendre.
MARC	Oui, grand-mère!
MADELEINE	Vous rentrez tout de suite après le cinéma?
MARC	Ouais ... enfin ... on va sans doute aller boire un Schweppes ou un jus de fruit avec les copains.
MADELEINE	Tu as de l'argent?
MARC	Ben non, justement ... pas trop. Tu ne peux pas me donner 20 francs?
MADELEINE	Oh la la! Tiens, voilà 20 francs! Tu es content?
MARC	Merci.

CHAPITRE 6

Practice with the nasal sounds [ɔ̃], [œ̃], [ɛ̃] *(1)*

1. Speaking Exercise

We saw that there were four nasal vowels in French—[ã], [ɔ̃], [œ̃], [ɛ̃] —and we studied the nasal [ã] in some detail. Today we will practice the other three: [ɔ̃], [œ̃], [ɛ̃]. As you repeat the following words, try to do two things. First, make sure you do not put any trace of the consonant **n** in your nasal sounds. Second, make each one of the four nasals sound different from the others. Imitate the model as closely as possible.

an   on   un   hein

Now, the last two may be pretty tricky to distinguish. As a matter of fact, many French people do not make any distinction between them. But others do. So try to make them different. Repeat the following words and phrases:

on	hein!	un
bon	cinq	lundi
bonjour	dessin	

Allons-y!	C'est bien!
Allons-y lundi!	C'est un bon dessin.
Allons-y lundi matin!	

Representation of the nasal sounds [ɔ̃], [ɛ̃], [œ̃] *(1)*

2. Reading and Speaking Exercise

Look at the words in number 1.

1. Bonjour!   Combien?
Dis donc!   Compose le numéro.
Ils font leurs devoirs.   Comptez!

You see that the nasal sound [ɔ̃] is represented by a combination of **o** and **n,** or **o** and **m** before a **b** or a **p.** Whenever you see these two combinations **o-n** and **o-m,** you may expect them to represent the nasal sound [ɔ̃], unless they are followed by a vowel, as in *limonade* (number 2):

2. li-mo-nade

. . . or unless you have a double **n,** as in ça *sonne,* or a double **m,** as in *comme* (number 3):

3. ça sonne   comme

Yet, there is one important exception. Look at the word in number 4.

4. Monsieur

Monsieur is spelled with an **o-n,** but it is not pronounced with a nasal sound! One says *monsieur* with an [ø].

Now let's look at the words in number 5:

5. le latin   impossible
intelligent   un timbre
maintenant   il a faim
bien!

You see that the nasal [ɛ] can be represented by several combinations of letters: **i-n** (or **i-m**), **a-i-n** (or **a-i-m**), or even sometimes **e-n** (mostly when **e-n** comes after **i**). This rule holds true unless these combinations are followed by a vowel, or unless you have a double **n** or double **m,** as we have seen with the rules for [ã] and [ɔ̃].

Now look at number 6:

6. un   lundi

The nasal sound [œ̃] is represented by **u-n.**

What we said about the representation of other nasal sounds is also true for this one:

a. In front of a **b** or a **p,** the **n** is replaced by an **m.**
b. In front of a vowel, or when there are two **n**'s or two **m**'s, the **u-n** or **u-m** combination does not represent a nasal sound.

3. Reading and Speaking Exercise

Read the following dialog aloud line by line. Try to say each line before you hear it. You will hear each line said once. Check with what you have said. Pay attention to the spelling, particularly for all words underlined.

Françoise téléphone à une amie, Christine.

1.	FRANÇOISE	<u>Dis donc!</u>
2.		Qu'est-ce que tu es en train de faire <u>maintenant?</u>
3.	CHRISTINE	<u>Moi?</u> . . . Je ne fais rien!
4.	FRANÇOISE	<u>Ça tombe bien!</u>
5.		Sortons!
6.		<u>Allons</u> au cinéma.
7.		Il paraît qu'il y a <u>un</u> dessin animé.
8.	CHRISTINE	Non! J'ai faim!
9.	FRANÇOISE	<u>Eh bien,</u> alors, viens à la maison.
10.		Il y a du <u>jambon</u> et du <u>saucisson.</u>
11.		<u>On va faire des sandwiches.</u>
12.	CHRISTINE	<u>Bon!</u>

4. Listening and Spelling Exercise

Listen to this exchange.

CHRISTINE   Dis donc, qu'est-ce qu'on fait maintenant?
FRANÇOISE   J'ai faim, moi!
CHRISTINE   Ça tombe bien, moi aussi!
FRANÇOISE   Eh bien, on va faire un sandwich.

CHRISTINE	Deux sandwichs! Un pour toi, un pour moi!
FRANÇOISE	D'accord. Jambon ou saucisson pour toi?
CHRISTINE	Jambon!
FRANÇOISE	Bon! Allons-y!

You have an incomplete text of this dialog in your *Activity Book*. Write in the missing words as you hear the exchange again.

1. CHRISTINE   Dis _____! Qu'est-ce qu'_____ fait _____?
2. FRANÇOISE   J'_____ _____, moi!
3. CHRISTINE   Ça _____ _____, moi aussi!
4. FRANÇOISE   Eh _____, _____ va faire _____ _____.
5. CHRISTINE   Deux _____! _____ pour toi, _____ pour moi.
6. FRANÇOISE   D'accord. _____ ou _____ _____ _____?
7. CHRISTINE   _____.
8. FRANÇOISE   _____! _____-y!

To verify your spelling, see the answer key at the end of your *Activity Book*.

5. Listening Exercise

The scene you are about to hear was recorded in a café in which Eric Leroy has stopped to make a telephone call. He is with a friend, Arnaud Périer. It's a good thing that Arnaud is with him, because Eric does not know what he is doing! By the way, this telephone works in a slightly different way from the one in the unit. The conversation begins with Eric and Arnaud talking to the cashier.

Part 1

E   Pardon madame, pour téléphoner s'il vous plaît?
C   C'est 60 centimes.
A   Oui mais où est l'appareil?
C   Vous avez une cabine au fond de la salle.
E   Bon, merci madame.
A   Où vas-tu?
E   Eh bien, je vais téléphoner!
A   A qui?
E   A Martine!
A   Ah bon! Tu as son numéro?
E   Ah non!
A   Eh bien, alors, regarde dans l'annuaire. Tu sais comment elle s'appelle?
E   Oui, bien sûr . . . Elle s'appelle Martine!
A   Martine, Martine! . . . évidemment qu'elle s'appelle Martine! Mais Martine comment?
E   Eh bien . . . Martine . . . attends . . . Ah bien oui! Dupuis; oui, c'est ça, Martine Dupuis.
A   Attends, passe-moi l'annuaire . . . Je vais chercher.
    (sound effect: shuffling of telephone-book pages)
A   Eh bien, tu n'as pas de chance.
E   Pourquoi?
A   Parce que des Dupuis, il y en a beaucoup. Regarde. Il y en a deux pages! C'est Dupuis avec *is* ou Dupuy avec un *y*?
E   Dupuis, *is* . . . ou peut-être Dupuy, *y* . . . . Non, non . . . c'est Dupuis, -*is*.
A   Tu es sûr?
E   Non.

A   Et son père, comment est-ce qu'il s'appelle?
E   Georges . . . Jean . . . ou Jacques peut-être.
A   Il y a un Jacques Dupuis 252-35-60.
E   Bon, je vais faire ça . . . 2-5
A   Eh bien décroche!
E   Ah oui . . .
    (sound effect: receiver taken off the hook)

Part 2

E   Voyons . . . . Qu'est-ce que tu as dit : 242 . . .
A   Non! Deux-cent-cin-quant-te-deux, tren-te-cinq, soi-xante!
E   Ah bon. Alors 2-5-2.
A   Mais . . . mets les pièces dans l'appareil!
E   Ah oui.
    (sound effect: 3 coins inserted in slot)

Part 3

E   2-5-2, 45-
    (sound effect: dialing)
A   Non! pas 45! Je te dis 252-35-60. C'est simple, non!
E   Bon, bon! . . . Alors, qu'est-ce que tu dis : 55 . . .?
A   Mais non. 35. Mais raccroche maintenant et refais le numéro!
    (sound effect: hanging up)

Part 4

    (sound effect: coins falling)
E   Qu'est-ce que c'est?
A   Eh bien, les pièces!
E   Qu'est-ce que je fais?
A   Remets-les dans l'appareil!
E   Ouais . . .
    (sound effect: 3 coins being introduced in slot and falling)

Part 5

A   Eh bien décroche! Maintenant!
    (sound effect: receiver being taken off the hook)

Part 6

E   Voilà! Bon! Alors, je fais le numéro . . . . Qu'est-ce que c'est déjà? Ah oui, 252-35-60!
    (dialing: two, five, two, three, five, six, zero)

Part 7

    (sound effect: busy signal, faint)
A   Ça ne répond pas?
E   Non.
A   Ça sonne?
E   Oui . . .

A   Voyons, donne . . .
E   Tiens, écoute . . .
    (sound effect: busy signal, stronger)
A   C'est occupé.

Part 8

E   Eh bien alors, raccroche! On va attendre un peu et puis on va recommencer.
    (sound effect: hanging up — 3 coins returned, falling.)
E   Qu'est-ce que c'est?

Part 9

A   Les pièces!!
E   Ah oui!
A   Bon, j'y vais? Je fais le numéro.
E   Oui, vas-y.
    (sound effect: 3 coins inserted in a slot; taking receiver off the hook; dialing; receiver taken off the hook at other end)
M.D   Allô!
A   Allô! Allô! Euh . . . Bonjour Monsieur . . . C'est bien Monsieur Dupuis, Monsieur Jacques Dupuis?
M.D   Oui, lui-même.
A   Ah bon, ne quittez pas, je vous passe Eric Leroy.
E   Allô. Ici Eric Leroy . . . Bonjour Monsieur. Excusez-moi de vous déranger . . . Est-ce que je pourrais parler à Martine, s'il vous plaît?
M.D   A qui?
E   A Martine.
M.D   Martine?? Quelle Martine? Il n'y a pas de Martine ici.
E   Mais vous êtes bien M. Dupuis?
M.D   Oui! Mais je ne connais pas de Martine.
E   Ah bon! Ça doit être une erreur, alors!
M.D   Oui, c'est sûrement une erreur! . . .
E   Excusez-moi, Monsieur.
    (sound effect: hanging up)
A   Oui, eh bien, le père de Martine ne s'appelle sûrement pas Jacques!
E   Il s'appelle peut-être Jacques . . . mais avec un *y.*
A   Jacques avec un *y*?!!!
E   Non! Jacques Dupuy avec un *y.* Cherche dans l'annuaire! Il y a un Jacques Dupuy avec un *y*?
    (sound effect: shuffling pages of telephone book)

Part 10

A   Il y a un Sigismond, Siméon, Théophile, mais il n'y a pas de Jacques!
E   Alors c'est Georges! Cherche. Il y a un Georges Dupuis?
A   Georges Dupuy avec *y*? Non!
E   . . . Alors cherche Dupuis avec *s.*
A   Voyons . . . Ferdinand, Gaston . . . Georges! Oui, oui, il y a un Georges Dupuis. C'est le 347-26-58.
E   Bon! Allons-y!
    (sound effect: 3 coins inserted in slot; receiver being picked up; dialing: three, four, seven, two, six, five, eight; sound effect: telephone ringing)

Part 11

> *(receiver picked up at the other end — woman's voice)*

Mme D Allô?...

  E Allô. C'est bien le 347-26-58?

Mme D Oui.

  E C'est bien Madame Dupuis?

Mme D Oui, elle-même!

  E Ah. Bonjour, Madame. Excusez-moi de vous déranger ... Est-ce que je pourrais parler à Martine, s'il vous plaît.

Mme D Ah non!... Martine n'est pas là.

  E Ah ... elle n'est pas là?

Mme D Non, elle n'est pas là!

  E Ah ... elle est sortie, peut-être?

Mme D Oui, elle est sortie!

  E Ah ... elle est allée au cinéma peut-être? Voir le dessin animé?

Mme D Eh bien, je ne sais pas au juste. Ou bien elle est au cinéma avec Philippe, ou bien elle fait ses devoirs de maths avec Eric Leroy et Arnaud Périer.

  E Ah! Ah bon! Merci beaucoup Madame. Excusez-moi de vous avoir dérangée. Au revoir, Madame.

6. Listening and Speaking Exercise

You will hear the same scene again. This time it will be interrupted by a few questions. Try to answer the questions.

(dialog, Part 1)
Vous entendez ce bruit? Qu'est-ce que c'est? Qu'est-ce qu'Eric fait? ( ) *Il décroche.*

(dialog, Part 2)
Qu'est-ce que c'est ce bruit? Qu'est-ce qu'Eric fait? ( ) *Il met les pièces dans l'appareil.*

(dialog, Part 3)
Et là, qu'est-ce qu'Eric fait? ( ) *Il raccroche.*

(dialog, Part 4)
Et maintenant, qu'est-ce qu'il fait? ( ) *Il remet les pièces dans l'appareil.*

(dialog, Part 5)
Et maintenant? ( ) *Il décroche.*

(dialog, Part 6)
Qu'est-ce qu'Eric fait maintenant? ( ) *Il fait le numéro.*

(dialog, Part 7)
Ça répond? ( ) *Non, c'est occupé.*

(dialog, Part 8)
Oui, qu'est-ce que c'est? ( ) *Les pièces.*

(dialog, Part 9)
Qu'est-ce qu'Arnaud est en train de faire? ( ) *Il cherche dans l'annuaire.*

(dialog, Part 10)
Est-ce que c'est occupé? ( ) *Non, ça sonne.*

(dialog, Part 11)

CHAPITRE 7

*Spelling **s** and **ss** (4)*

1. Reading and Speaking Exercise

Read aloud the following sentences. Look at number 1.

1. Assez!   Elle est rousse.   Elle ressemble à Papa.

Note that the **s-s** spelling represents the sound [s].

Now read the sentences in number 2.

2. Passez!   Elle aussi.
Prenez ma tasse.   Ils essayent de travailler.
Il est dessinateur.   Ils finissent à huit heures.
Elle est professeur.   C'est impossible.

This is a very reliable spelling: whenever you see a double **s,** you may assume it represents the sound [s].

Now read the items in number 3.

3. Mais si!   souvent
Bien sûr!   salle

You can see that the spelling "**s** plus vowel" at the beginning of a word represents the sound [s].

Read the sentence in number 4.

4. Sylvie et sa sœur Sophie sortent souvent le samedi soir.

This is a reliable spelling also. Whenever you see an **s** followed by a vowel at the beginning of a word, you may assume it represents a sound·[s].

Now let's see what happens when the letter **s** is followed by a consonant. Read number 5.

5. Restez!   Juste un moment.   Ecoutez mon disque.

You can see that **s** followed by a consonant represents the sound [s].

Now read number 6.

6. Elle est journaliste . . . ou dentiste . . . ou professeur d'histoire . . . ou de gymnastique.

This is also a fairly reliable spelling.

The letter **s** does not always represent the [s]-sound, however! Look at number 7.

7. Vous désirez?   Proposez quelque chose!

The letter **s** between two vowels represents the sound [z]. Read the sentences in number 8.

8. Mes cousins lisent sur la pelouse.   Ce n'est pas amusant.
Ils n'ont pas la télévision?   La musique est bien mauvaise!

Liaison provides one example of **s** pronounced [z] when between vowel sounds. Read the sentences in number 9.

9. Allons-y! Il est trois heures.   Ils ont les yeux bleus.
Vous avez vos occupations!   Vous allez aux Etats-Unis tous les ans?

Now read number 10.

10. Consultez un catalogue!

Note that the letter **s** represents the sound [s] when it follows a nasal vowel spelling within a word.

You can summarize what has been presented in the preceding exercises by going over the following chart.

Spelling	Sound
-ss-	[s]
s- at the beginning of a word	[s]
s- plus consonant	[s]
-s after nasal	[s]
-s- between vowels	[z]
-s in *liaison*	[z]

Distinction between [s] and [z] sounds (1)

2. Reading and Speaking Exercise

In this exercise you will apply what you have just learned. Try to read aloud the following words. Some you have seen; others you have not. But if you remember what you have just studied about the sounds represented by **s** and **s-s,** you should be able to figure out how these words sound in French. After each item, you'll hear the correct response. Let's begin.

Elle te ressemble.	la télévision
C'est le dessert.	une révision
une passion	usuel
une issue	isolation
une assurance	un vase

3. Reading and Speaking Exercise

Here is another exercise in which you will apply what you have just studied. Say the following sentences before you hear them. Pay special attention to the way you pronounce the underlined **s**'s.

Il_s ont une belle mai_son.	Il _s'appelle Dupont.
Il_s sont à la mai_son.	Il_s appellent Dupont.
Elle_s ont deux sœurs.	Li_sez le_s instructions!
Elle_s sont deux sœurs.	_Son cou_sin travaille dan_s une u_sine.

4. Dictation Exercise

Listen to the dialog and complete the sentences in front of you.

DENISE   Ce n'est pas Sylvie!
CHRISTINE   Mais si!
DENISE   C'est impossible!
CHRISTINE   Elle ne ressemble pas à sa sœur.
DENISE   Elle a les yeux bleus.
CHRISTINE   Comme ses cousins des Etats-Unis!
To verify your spelling, see the answer key at the end of your *Activity Book.*

Practice with the vocabulary of the unit and review of adjectives (4)

5. Listening Comprehension Exercise

In this exercise, you will hear statements about members of the Blanche and Lenoir families. Now these two families are quite exceptional!

Mrs. Blanche and Mrs. Lenoir are sisters, you see. When each one had children, she named them after her grandparents: Grandfather Frédéric, Grandmother Marcelle, Grandfather Paul, and Grandmother Renée, and also after their Aunt Andrée and their Uncle Christian.

Now it just so happened that Mrs. Blanche had only girls. Six girls! And Mrs. Lenoir had only boys. Six boys! So, out of the twelve cousins, six are girls and six are boys, but they have practically the same names. This is sometimes quite confusing. It's hard to tell whether one is talking about a girl of the Blanche family or a boy of the Lenoir family.

Let's see whether you can tell. You have in front of you a chart with the names of the twelve cousins. For each statement you hear, try to decide to which of the 12 cousins it refers. Write the number of each statement next to the name it refers to. Let's begin.

1. Frédéric est blond.   *(un garçon)*
2. Marcelle est brune.   *(une fille)*

3. Paul est roux. *(un garçon)*
4. Renée aussi est rousse. *(une fille)*
5. André est très brun. *(un garçon)*
6. Christiane au contraire est très blonde. *(une fille)*
7. Frédérique est dynamique, énergique et intelligente. *(une fille)*
8. Christian est très intelligent mais un peu distrait. *(un garçon)*
9. Paule est un peu paresseuse mais elle est assez bonne en maths. *(une fille)*

Now check your answers. *Read each statement again, and give the correct answer as indicated.*

Famille Blanche (6 filles!)		Famille Lenoir (6 garçons!)	
Frédérique	_____	Frédéric	_____
Marcelle	_____	Marcel	_____
Paule	_____	Paul	_____
Renée	_____	René	_____
Andrée	_____	André	_____
Christiane	_____	Christian	_____

Practice with the vocabulary of the unit (27)

6. Listening Comprehension Exercise

You will hear five short passages. Try to figure out what or whom is being talked about in each of these passages. Your choices are printed in front of you. Let's begin.

1. Non, non, elle n'est pas à l'hôpital, elle est à la maison. Elle ne travaille pas le lundi. *(Madame Lardan, D)*
2. Elle! Elle n'a rien à faire? Hah! Elle a 82 ans mais elle travaille tout le temps. Elle enseigne le piano. *(La grand-mère de Catherine, F)*
3. —Où est-ce qu'il est? Je ne le vois pas.
   —Il n'est pas dans la maison.
   —Ah, je le vois. Il est sur la pelouse.
   —Il court après le chat! le vilain! *(Toupie, le chien, G)*
4. C'est mercredi aujourd'hui, il ne va pas au lycée. En général le matin il va jouer au football et l'après-midi il va au cinéma. *(Philippe, le frère de Catherine, B)*
5. Allô! Oui, il est là... Oh non! il ne va pas à l'usine le dimanche!... Il est en train de tondre la pelouse.... Attendez une minute, ne quittez pas. Je l'appelle. *(Monsieur Lardan, C)*

Now check your answers. *Read each item once again, and give the correct answer.*

		1	2	3	4	5
A	Catherine Lardan					
B	Philippe, le frère de Catherine					
C	Monsieur Lardan					
D	Madame Lardan					
E	Le grand-père de Catherine					
F	La grand-mère de Catherine					
G	Toupie, le chien.					

7. Listening and Speaking Exercise

In this exercise you will hear a girl, Claire Poirier, talking with a friend, Arnaud. They are at Claire's house, and Arnaud has just noticed a photograph on the piano in the living room. Listen.

ARNAUD   Qui est-ce? C'est ta sœur? C'est Denise?

CLAIRE   Ça? Non, ce n'est pas Denise. C'est une sœur de ma mère. C'est ma Tante Henriette. Denise lui ressemble, c'est vrai, mais elle est plutôt rousse et Tante Henriette est très blonde. Et puis elle est un peu plus grande que Denise aussi.

ARNAUD   Quel âge a-t-elle?

CLAIRE   Maintenant elle a 26 ou 27 ans. Elle est plus jeune que Maman!

ARNAUD   Elle habite ici?

CLAIRE   Non, elle habite à Paris.

ARNAUD   Ah, c'est elle qui est médecin?

CLAIRE   Non, c'est Tante Jacqueline, la sœur de Papa qui est médecin. Tante Henriette est dentiste.

Now that you have heard the dialog between Claire Poirier and her friend Arnaud, let's see if you can answer the questions. After your response you will hear a suggested answer. Let's begin.

1. Qui est Denise? (   ) *C'est la sœur de Claire.*
2. Comment s'appelle la sœur de Mme Poirier? (   ) *Elle s'appelle Henriette.*
3. A qui Denise ressemble-t-elle? (   ) *A sa Tante Henriette.*
4. Est-ce que Denise est blonde, comme Tante Henriette? (   ) *Non, elle est rousse.*
5. A quelle heure est-ce que le film commence? _____ *(A deux heures. 5)*
6. Qu'est-ce que vous allez voir? _____ *(Un film de science-fiction. 6)*
7. Quand est-ce que vous partez? _____ *(Dans cinq minutes. 7)*
8. Et la sœur de Monsieur Poirier, qu'est-ce qu'elle fait? (   ) *Elle est médecin.*

CHAPITRE 8

The sound [r] *(17)*

1. Pronunciation Exercise

Listen carefully to the way the [r]-sound is pronounced in the following French words.
> une orange   de l'eau minérale   un fruit   des carottes

The French [r]-sound is quite different from the American [r]. To pronounce a French [r] you should keep the tip of your tongue pressed against your lower teeth. The back of the tongue should be arched upward. It should almost completely block the passage of air in the back of the throat, as you force the air through. Try it. The French [r] requires more energy than the American one. Don't overdo it, though!

Listen and repeat.

à la boulangerie	des radis	des frites
à l'épicerie	des rillettes	du fromage
à la boucherie	des carottes	des fruits
à la charcuterie	du raisin	des fraises
à la crèmerie	des pommes de terre	des haricots verts

2. Listening Comprehension and Speaking Exercise

In this exercise you will pretend to go to several stores. In each store the merchant will offer you a number of things to buy. He will give you all the prices as he goes. Pay attention to the prices, because your problem is to choose one thing to buy and, since you don't have too much money, you want to choose the least expensive of the things offered. So, as soon as the merchant is through speaking, ask for the cheapest item. For example, if you are at the first store and bananas are the cheapest fruit there, you say: *Donnez-moi des bananes.* Now, don't hesitate too long. Try to make up your mind, and speak up as soon as each merchant is through. After your answer you'll hear the correct response.

Of course, it will be easier to understand what the merchants say if you see what they are talking about. So look at the pictures of the items sold in each shop. As you listen, you may even want to jot down the price of each item next to its picture. Let's begin.

1. Vous êtes dans une boulangerie-pâtisserie.
    —Alors, qu'est-ce que je vous donne? Petit pain, croissant, brioche? Les petits pains sont à 0.40 F pièce, les croissants 1.10 F et les brioches 1.20 F. (   ) *Donnez-moi un petit pain.*

2. Chez le marchand de légumes.
    —Haricots verts! Voyez, les haricots verts! Voyez comme ils sont beaux! 10 F le kilo. Regardez les carottes! C'est pas cher. 2 F le kilo. Tomates! Regardez les belles tomates! 2.90 F les tomates! (   ) *Donnez-moi des carottes!*

3. Chez le marchand de fruits.
    —Voyez le raisin, s'il est beau! C'est du chasselas! 5.20 F le kilo, le raisin! Les poires, elles sont belles, elles sont mûres! C'est des duchesses ça, Madame! 8 F le kilo de poires. 7 F les pommes. C'est cher, oui, mais c'est pas encore la saison! Prenez des pêches, 4 F le kilo! Regardez les belles fraises, 5.80 F les fraises! (   ) *Donnez-moi des pêches.*

4. Chez le charcutier.
    —Qu'est-ce que je vous donne? du jambon, du saucisson, du pâté, des rillettes? Le jambon c'est 48 F le kilo. Le saucisson pur porc, bien sec—c'est 37 F le kilo. Le pâté c'est 29 F le kilo. Les rillettes sont extra, c'est des rillettes du Mans. C'est 35 F le kilo, les rillettes. (   ) *Donnez-moi du pâté.*

1. Dans une boulangerie-pâtisserie

2. Chez le marchand de légumes

3. Chez le marchand de fruits

4. Chez le charcutier

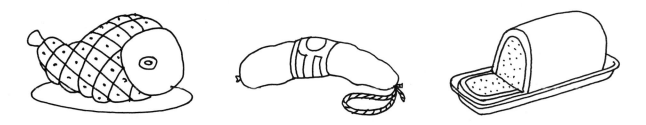

3. Reading Exercise

Look at the words in number 1 and listen.

1. (**c** plus **a**)   (**c** plus **o**)   (**c** plus **u**)
un camarade   à côté   la cuisine
un café   un cousin   une cuillère
une cabine   de la confiture

The letter **c** used before the letters **a, o,** or **u** represents the sound [k].

Now read the words in number 2.

2. des carottes   une côtelette   de la charcuterie
un camembert   des haricots   l'agriculture

Let's see what happens when the letter **c** appears in front of an **e,** an **i,** or a **y.** Read the words in number 3.

3. une place   voici   à bicyclette
dix centimes   cinq

The letter **c** followed by **e, i,** or **y** represents the sound [s].

Now read the words in number 4.

4. deux pièces   principal
à Nice   Il est médecin.
Effacez!   Ici!

You may have noticed that sometimes the letter **c** is written with a little sign that looks like a tiny question mark, or like a backwards **c** hanging down. That's called a *cedilla.* Whenever the letter **c** is written with a *cedilla,* it represents the sound [s]. Read the items in number 5.

5. Ça va?   Commençons!   François est français?

Of course, the cedilla is used only in front of **a, o,** or **u,** since in front of **e, i,** or **y** the letter **c** represents the sound [s] even without a cedilla.

4. Reading and Pronunciation Exercise

Read each of the following sentences before you hear them. Let's begin.

1. Ce n'est pas comme ça qu'on met le couvert!
2. On met la cuillère à côté du couteau!
3. Commençons avec des tomates provençales.
4. Garçon! Le service est compris?
5. L'épicerie est en face.
6. L'épicier est un bon commerçant.
7. Il a des cerises délicieuses,
8. des concombres,
9. des haricots,
10. du camembert,
11. du saucisson,
12. du café . . .

To practice new vocabulary in unit (32)

5. Listening Comprehension and Reading Exercise

You will hear several sentences. For each one, you have in front of you a number of suggested rejoinders. Decide which rejoinder goes best with the sentence, and put a check mark in the appropriate row. Let's begin.

Part 1

1. Qu'est-ce qu'on prend pour boire, du vin? _____ *(Non, de l'eau minérale, C)*
2. Tu as soif? _____ *(Oui, donne-moi un peu d'eau, A)*
3. Elle n'est pas bonne ma salade? _____ *(Si, mais il y a trop de vinaigre, B)*
4. Tu veux du fromage de chèvre? _____ *(Non, je préfère le gruyère, E)*
5. Je veux le café! _____ *(Non, on n'a pas encore fini le dessert, D)*

Now check your answers. *Read each item again and give the correct answer.*

		1	2	3	4	5
A	Oui, donne-moi un peu d'eau.					
B	Si, mais il y a trop de vinaigre.					
C	Non, de l'eau minérale.					
D	Non, on n'a pas encore fini le dessert.					
E	Non, je préfère le gruyère!					

Part 2

Now look at the second group of rejoinders. Listen to each sentence and make your choice.

1. Je vais chez le boucher. _____ *(Bon, alors, achète un bifteck, D)*
2. Qu'est-ce que je prends comme viande pour demain, des côtelettes? _____ *(Non, je n'aime pas l'agneau, B)*
3. J'achète des œufs? _____ *(Oui, on va faire une omelette, E)*
4. Je vais chez le boulanger? _____ *(Oui, prends une baguette et des croissants, C)*
5. J'achète des pêches? _____ *(Non, elles sont trop chères. Prends des pommes, A)*

Now check your answers. *Read each item again and give the correct answer.*

		1	2	3	4	5
A	Non, elles sont trop chères. Prends des pommes.					
B	Non, je n'aime pas l'agneau.					
C	Oui, prends une baguette et des croissants.					
D	Bon, alors, achète un bifteck.					
E	Oui, on va faire une omelette.					

To practice new vocabulary in unit (32)

6. Listening Comprehension Exercise

When you are in a foreign country, you have to recognize readily the names of different foods. If you don't, you may be in for a few surprises, like getting snails in garlic butter when you anticipated a dessert. Let's see what the chances are of such a thing happening to you. You will hear the names of 24 different foods or drinks, said fairly fast. Try to decide quickly what category each belongs to. Then put a check mark in the appropriate row. Let's begin.

1. un gigot d'agneau _____ *(plat de viande)*
2. une tranche de pâté _____ *(hors-d'œuvre)*

3. des fraises à la crème _____ *(dessert)*
4. des carottes à la crème _____ *(plat de légumes)*
5. une poire Belle Hélène _____ *(dessert)*
6. des tomates provençales _____ *(hors-d'œuvre)*
7. une pêche melba _____ *(dessert)*
8. des rillettes _____ *(hors-d'œuvre)*
9. des haricots verts _____ *(plat de légumes)*
10. une bouteille d'eau minérale _____ *(boisson)*
11. du raisin _____ *(dessert)*
12. des pommes de terre lyonnaises _____ *(plat de légumes)*
13. une tarte aux pommes _____ *(dessert)*
14. une côtelette de porc _____ *(plat de viande)*
15. du saucisson _____ *(hors-d'œuvre)*
16. du vin rouge _____ *(boisson)*
17. un rôti de porc _____ *(plat de viande)*
18. une salade de concombres _____ *(hors-d'œuvre)*
19. un poulet rôti _____ *(plat de viande)*
20. du lait _____ *(boisson)*
21. un ananas frais au Kirsch _____ *(dessert)*

Now check your answers. *Read each item again, and give the correct answer.*

	1	2	3	4	5	6	7	8	9	10	11	12	13	14	15	16	17	18	19	20	21
hors-d'œuvre																					
plat de viande																					
plat de légumes																					
dessert																					
boisson																					

Preparation for Conversation Exercise 43

7. Listening Exercise

Hélène, one of Claire's friends, is coming for lunch at Claire's tomorrow. Listen to Claire and her mother as they discuss what they will have.

MOTHER   Alors, qu'est-ce qu'on va faire demain pour le déjeuner? Qu'est-ce que tu veux?
CLAIRE   Eh bien, on va faire une grosse tarte aux pêches, une mousse au chocolat, et puis on va acheter un gros gâteau chez le pâtissier.
MOTHER   Allons, allons, ne dis pas de bêtises! Je parle sérieusement.
CLAIRE   Mais je suis sérieuse! Je suis tout à fait sérieuse!
MOTHER   On ne va pas avoir trois desserts!
CLAIRE   Pourquoi pas?
MOTHER   Parce que! Il faut manger autre chose! On ne peut pas manger que des desserts!
CLAIRE   Moi si, je peux! Et Hélène aussi, je suis sûre!
MOTHER   Et si je faisais une bonne soupe de légumes pour commencer!
CLAIRE   Une soupe! Ah non, alors! Hélène n'aime pas ça!
MOTHER   Alors une bonne salade de tomates.
CLAIRE   Heuh oui ... peut-être, je ne sais pas ...

MOTHER	Tu préfères une salade de concombres?
CLAIRE	Oh non, non!
MOTHER	Alors des carottes râpées.
CLAIRE	Non, Hélène n'aime pas les carottes crues . . . ni les carottes cuites d'ailleurs. Pourquoi pas du pâté, et du jambon, mais pas du jambon d'York, non, du jambon cru, du jambon de montagne.
MOTHER	Non, le charcutier est fermé demain.
CLAIRE	Alors, du saucisson. Il y en a à la maison?
MOTHER	Oui.
CLAIRE	Alors comme hors-d'œuvre du saucisson, avec du beurre et des olives.
MOTHER	Bon, et ensuite comme viande?
CLAIRE	Eh bien, du bifteck avec des frites.
MOTHER	Mais non, elle en mange tous les jours du steak et des frites! Ce n'est pas très original. Et si je faisais un poisson, au lieu de faire de la viande?
CLAIRE	Non, pas de poisson . . . Hélène n'aime pas ça. Et puis le poisson, c'est difficile à manger.
MOTHER	Alors, des côtelettes d'agneau?
CLAIRE	Non! Je sais! un gigot de mouton.
MOTHER	Mais non! Tu n'y penses pas. Un gigot de mouton c'est beaucoup trop gros pour nous trois!
CLAIRE	Oui mais c'est bon!
MOTHER	Ecoute! Je sais! Je vais acheter une tranche de gigot. Une tranche de gigot grillée et des petits haricots verts comme légumes.
CLAIRE	Oh non, une tranche de gigot, ce n'est pas amusant. Et puis Hélène n'aime pas les haricots verts.
MOTHER	Quoi alors? Un petit poulet rôti.
CLAIRE	Oui, c'est ça, un poulet! Un poulet avec des frites.
MOTHER	Une petite salade . . .
CLAIRE	Oh non, la salade, ce n'est pas indispensable. Hélène, elle n'aime pas la salade, je le sais.
MOTHER	Oui, mais il faut manger de la salade . . . C'est bon pour la santé. A cause des vitamines! Et puis du camembert, ou un fromage de chèvre?
CLAIRE	Non, non pas de fromage; un dessert.
MOTHER	Mais vous pouvez avoir du fromage et un dessert après.
CLAIRE	Et si on n'a pas de fromage, est-ce qu'on peut avoir deux desserts?
MOTHER	Non, im-pos-sible! Alors qu'est-ce que tu veux comme dessert? De la mousse au chocolat, de la glace, des fraises à la crème fraîche, une tarte aux pommes? Choisis!
CLAIRE	Un gâteau. Un gâteau de chez le pâtissier, avec beaucoup de crème!

CHAPITRE 9

The spelling **g** *plus vowel (1)*

1. Listening and Reading Exercise

Listen to the words in number 1 and repeat them. Watch for the sound represented by the letter **g.**

1. les gâteaux   les légumes   la gomme

The letter **g** represents the hard [g] sound when it is followed by the letters **a, u,** or **o.**

Now listen to the words in number 2.

2. rouge   Montargis   gymnase

The letter **g** represents the soft sound [ʒ] when followed by the letters **e, i,** or **y.**

Notice what's special in the words in number 3.

3. guitare   fatigué   bague

The letter **g** followed by a **u** represents the hard sound [g], as in *légume*. But here the letter **u** does not represent the sound [y]. It represents no sound; it's used only to indicate that the letter **g** represents the hard sound [g], even though it is followed by an **i** or an **e.**

This is similar to what happens with a **u** following a **q.** Read the words in number 4.

4. musique   qualité

Let's read the words in number 5.

le gigot	ranger	l'âge	de l'argent	des langues
Brigitte	changer	le coquillage	des gens	une bague
Montargis	mélanger	le village		une baguette
la Belgique	léger	du fromage		blaguer
la gymnastique	un ingénieur			guitare

The sound [a] *(1)*

2. Speaking Exercise

Listen to the way the word "Coca Cola" sounds in French. One says *un Coca,* or *un Coca Cola.* Listen carefully to the last sound: *Coca, Coca Cola.* You see that the French [a] at the end of these words is quite different from what you use in English. To sound French, you will have to practice pronouncing that French [a]. It requires a little attention, especially in words that resemble English words. Try not to be influenced by what you would say in English. Listen and repeat.

Il y a du Coca Cola.	à table	Les amis arrivent.	Ça marche.
de la grenadine	une carotte	Papa est là.	C'est rapide.
du café glacé	de la salade	Ça va mal.	C'est pratique.
une carafe	de la moutarde		

Now listen carefully and compare: *ta chanson — des tas de chansons.* If you pay very close attention, you will notice that the [a]-sound is not quite the same in the two phrases: *ta — des tas.* There are two different [a]-sounds in French. The second one occurs rather infrequently. Here are a few examples: *des pâtes, du pâté; des gâteaux, des tas de gâteaux.* Many French speakers, however, tend to neglect this distinction, so you do not have to worry too much about it.

Practice with tenses: present, future, past (6)

3. Listening Comprehension Exercise

You will hear a number of short sentences. For each one, indicate whether it refers to the present, to the past, or to the future. Let's begin.

1. Vous mangez déjà? _____ *(present)*
2. J'ai mangé. _____ *(past)*
3. Vous avez déjà mangé? _____ *(past)*
4. Vous avez dormi? _____ *(past)*
5. Je vais manger. _____ *(future)*
6. Il a dormi. _____ *(past)*
7. Vous dormez? _____ *(present)*
8. Vous avez choisi? _____ *(past)*
9. Qu'est-ce que vous allez choisir? _____ *(future)*
10. Elle choisit une robe. _____ *(present)*
11. Elle les a finis. _____ *(past)*
12. Elle va finir. _____ *(future)*
13. Elle les finit. _____ *(present)*
14. Ils ne vont pas trouver. _____ *(future)*
15. Ils n'ont pas trouvé. _____ *(past)*
16. Vous ne trouvez pas? _____ *(present)*

Now check your answers. *Repeat each sentence and give the correct answer.*

	1	2	3	4	5	6	7	8	9	10	11	12	13	14	15	16
Present																
Past																
Future																

Practice with the vocabulary of the unit (21)

4. Listening Comprehension Exercise

You will hear a number of people talk. Look at the list in front of you and try to figure out what or whom they are talking about.

1. Je ne peux pas mettre ça! C'est trop lent! _____ *(un disque)*
2. Je ne peux pas mettre ça! C'est trop grand! _____ *(un pantalon)*
3. Oui, oui, ça y est! C'est rangé et balayé. _____ *(le sous-sol)*
4. Non . . . je l'ai rangé! Je ne le mets pas. Il ne me va pas bien. _____ *(un pantalon)*
5. Il marche, mais il me semble que c'est un peu lent! _____ *(l'électrophone)*
6. Il est fatigué, il n'a pas bien dormi. _____ *(Philippe)*
7. Il met toujours de la musique quand il travaille. _____ *(Philippe)*
8. On l'a toute bue! _____ *(la limonade)*
9. Je ne peux pas les faire; il n'y a pas de pain! _____ *(des sandwiches)*

Now check your answers. *Read each sentence again and give the correct answer.*

	1	2	3	4	5	6	7	8	9
la limonade									
le sous-sol									
l'électrophone									
Philippe									
un disque									
des sandwiches									
un pantalon									

Preparation for Conversation Exercise 33

5. Listening Exercise

Denise gave a great party last Thursday. Everybody is still talking about it. It was the great social event of the month. Let's interview some of the kids who went:

QUESTION   Bonjour, Christine, tu es allée à la boum de Denise, la semaine dernière?
CHRISTINE Oui.
QUESTION   C'était bien? Tu t'es amusée?
CHRISTINE Oh oui!
QUESTION   Qu'est-ce que tu as mis pour y aller?

CHRISTINE	Eh bien, j'ai mis un jean et puis un pull noir et beaucoup de bracelets aux deux bras! Et puis j'ai mis des bottes.
QUESTION	Et toi, Sylvie?
SYLVIE	Moi, j'ai mis ma jupe rouge et un chemisier blanc, avec un collier et puis des sandales.
QUESTION	Tu n'as pas mis de bottes, toi?
SYLVIE	Non, pour danser, les bottes, ce n'est pas tellement bien, je préfère les sandales.
QUESTION	Et toi, Arnaud? tu es allé à la boum?
ARNAUD	Oui, j'y suis allé. C'était très bien.
QUESTION	Et qu'est-ce que tu as mis?
ARNAUD	Oh . . . j'ai mis un pantalon . . . un pantalon gris, quoi! et puis une chemise et un pull . . . un pull bleu.
QUESTION	Et toi, Monique?
MONIQUE	Moi, j'ai mis ma robe verte, et puis un bracelet. J'ai aussi une robe jaune qui est très bien. Mais je ne l'ai pas mise, parce que le jaune ne me va pas bien!
QUESTION	Et toi, Marc?
MARC	Moi, j'ai mis mon jean, une chemise bleue et mon blouson, et puis mes bottes . . . D'ailleurs, je n'avais pas le choix: je n'ai pas d'autres chaussures.
QUESTION	Et qu'est-ce que vous avez mangé et bu?
MONIQUE	Des petits sandwiches au saucisson, des sandwiches avec du fromage.
ARNAUD	Des petits gâteaux, de la glace . . .
CHRISTINE	Et puis aussi des œufs durs avec de la mayonnaise, du pâté, de toutes petites tomates, vous savez des tomates miniatures . . .
SYLVIE	Et puis on a bu de la limonade, des jus de fruits.
CHRISTINE	Du sirop de grenadine . . . avec de l'eau, évidemment, pas comme ça!
QUESTION	Et qu'est-ce que vous avez fait?
SYLVIE	On a passé des disques, on a parlé, on a joué à des jeux.
QUESTION	Vous avez dansé?
CHRISTINE	Oui, on a un peu dansé.
QUESTION	Enfin, c'était bien?
MONIQUE	Oh oui, c'était bien! C'était très bien, même!

CHAPITRE 10

The letter i and the [i]-sound

1. Reading and Speaking Exercises

Notice how the letter **i** sounds in the following English words. Look at number 1.

1. residence   reside
      visit   site

It sounds one way in ''residence'' and ''visit'' and quite differently in ''reside'' and ''site.''

Now listen to how the letter **i** is pronounced in the following French words. Look at number 2.

2. résidence   résider
      visite   site

Notice that it is pronounced the same way, [i], in all four words. The letter **i** usually represents the sound [i] in French, with a few exceptions.

Read the words in number 3. Be sure to produce an [i]-sound for each letter **i** you see. After you say each word, you'll hear it spoken.

3. guide   pilote   silence   disciple   pile
    rite   file   vice   vile   Simon

Now repeat the following words. Look at number 4.

4. Marie   mairie   prairie   sortie   vie
    industrie   géométrie   géographie   pharmacie   amie

Now look at the French words in number 5. How would you pronounce them? Guess!

5. pie   lie   mie   Julie
    loterie   métallurgie   poterie   barbarie

Listen to the pronunciation of the word in number 6.

6. Sylvie

You hear the sound [i] twice. The first time, it is represented by **y,** and the second time by the letter **i.** The letter **y** is the other way of representing the sound [i] in French. (Note that in English there are also several ways, such as **e-e,** as in ''see'' or **e-a,** as in ''sea.'')

Say the words in number 7.

7. Sylvie   vas-y   bicyclette   Roissy

In French the sound [i] is pretty much the same in all the words in which it occurs. The [i] in *Paris* is not any longer than the [i] in *Denis* or *ville,* for example. The [i] in *cousine* is no shorter than the one in *machine.*

Say the French words in number 8. Pronounce every *i* the same way.

8. l'église   la boucherie   visible   machine

Discrimination between le, la, and les (11)

2. Listening Comprehension Exercise

Each one of the sentences you will hear in this exercise is about one of the people or groups of people you see below. You are to guess which. You will notice that each sentence contains one of the pronouns *le, la,* or *les.* That's the clue. If you can tell which pronoun you heard, you should be able to tell which person or group of persons the sentence is about. Indicate your guess by putting a check mark in the appropriate column. Let's begin!

1. —Regarde-le! _____ *(Jérôme)*
2. —Ecoute-la! _____ *(Marie-Paule)*
3. —Invitons-le! _____ *(Jérôme)*
4. —Je les ai rencontrés. _____ *(Christine et Denis)*
5. —Tu la connais? _____ *(Marie-Paule)*
6. —Emmène-la! _____ *(Marie-Paule)*
7. —Comment est-ce que tu les trouves? _____ *(Christine et Denis)*
8. —Je les ai suivis. _____ *(Christine et Denis)*
9. —Nous ne le connaissons pas. _____ *(Jérôme)*
10. —Suis-les! _____ *(Christine et Denis)*
11. —Pierre me les a présentés. _____ *(Christine et Denis)*
12. —Je les vois souvent. _____ *(Christine et Denis)*
13. —Nous la voyons tous les jours. _____ *(Marie-Paule)*
14. —Philippe les connaît. _____ *(Christine et Denis)*
15. —Jacques le trouve très sympathique. _____ *(Jérôme)*

Now check your answers. *Repeat each item and give the correct answer.*

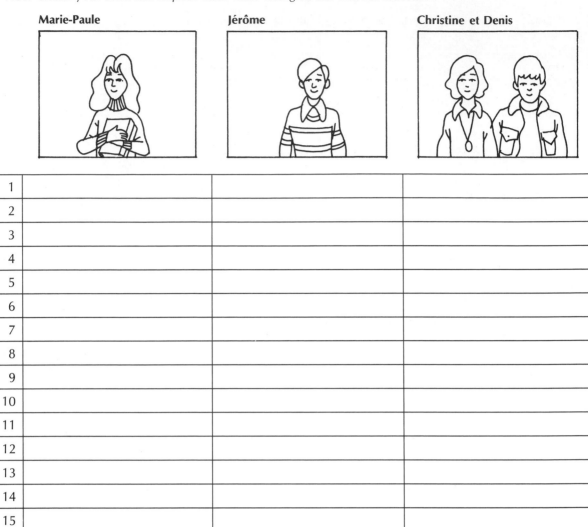

	Marie-Paule	Jérôme	Christine et Denis
1			
2			
3			
4			
5			
6			
7			
8			
9			
10			
11			
12			
13			
14			
15			

Practice with past participles (11)

3. Reading Exercise

Each of the sentences printed in your *Activity Book* refers to one of the four persons or groups of persons that you see. You must determine which it is. Although each sentence will be spoken, merely hearing the sentence will not give you enough of a clue. To know each answer for sure, you have to look carefully at the spelling of the past participle. Put the number of the sentence you hear next to the picture it refers to. Let's begin.

1. Vous les avez vus?
2. Vous l'avez rencontrée?
3. Je les ai vues à Saint-Moritz.
4. Je l'ai recontré à la Maison des Jeunes.
5. Je l'ai vue à la piscine hier.
6. Je les ai trouvées très sympathiques.
7. Nous les avons invités à venir jouer au tennis.
8. Je les ai rencontrées dans l'ascenseur ce matin.

9. Nous l'avons suivi jusquà Versailles.   10. Jacques l'a trouvé très sympathique.

Now check your answers. The numbers from left to right are *A: 4, 9, 10; B: 2, 5; C: 1, 7; D: 3, 6, 8.*

| Jérôme | Christine | Marie-Paule et Stéphane | Les trois soeurs Malassis |

A. _____ _____ _____   B. _____ _____ _____   C. _____ _____   D. _____ _____ _____

Practice with the vocabulary of the unit (31)

4. Listening Comprehension Exercise

You will hear ten fragments of conversation. Try to guess what each fragment is about; then indicate your answer by putting a check mark in the appropriate row. But watch it. It's not always easy to guess. In fact, sometimes it's pretty tricky. Sometimes the only way you can tell is by noticing the difference between a masculine and a feminine form. Let's begin.

1. Suivez-le. Il va vous montrer le chemin. _____ *(un guide)*
2. Il ne marche pas. Il faut monter à pied. _____ *(un ascenseur)*
3. C'est en face de la gare. Il y a 15 étages. _____ *(un immeuble)*
4. Prenez la première à gauche. _____ *(une rue)*
5. C'est assez grand. Il y a quatre pièces. _____ *(un appartement)*
6. Suivez-la jusqu'au croisement. _____ *(une rue)*
7. Elle est entre la salle de séjour et la chambre de mes parents. C'est la plus grande et la plus agréable. _____ *(une chambre)*
8. Elle est en face de l'église, entre la poste et la mairie. _____ *(une piscine)*
9. C'est au rez-de-chaussée. C'est tout petit. Il y a juste une chambre, une cuisine et une salle de bains minuscule. _____ *(un appartement)*
10. Elle est au fond du couloir à gauche. _____ *(une chambre)*

Now check your answers. *Read each item again and give the correct answer.*

	1	2	3	4	5	6	7	8	9	10
une chambre										
une rue										
un immeuble										
un ascenseur										
un appartement										
une piscine										
un guide										

5. Listening Comprehension Exercise

Jeu des pièces de la maison

Look at this house plan. This is your house, a nice house with a garden and a garage, on the *rue de la République*. As you may see, this house has a lot of doors—nineteen, to be exact. It has to—otherwise the game wouldn't be much fun.

Now here are the rules of the game. You are outside the house, in the garden, to the left. Night is falling, and it's getting chilly. You decide to go to bed. Do you see it? Do you see your bed in the bedroom? That's where you want to go. But before going to bed, you must close and lock all the doors—all of them, including the big garden gate and the garage door, both of which open onto the street. You may go through each door only once. (Once you have passed a door, you must lock it, and you are not supposed to unlock it again. That's the rule of the game!) However, you may go into a room more than once, provided you do not go twice through the same door. You may also go in and out of the house into the garden or the street as many times as you wish. Stop the recording while you try to figure out the problem. Start the recording again when you wish to check your solution. The recording will give you one solution. There may be others.

Solution

Voici une solution du problème. Vous sortez du jardin et vous allez dans la rue de la République. Vous fermez la grande porte du jardin. Voilà une porte fermée! Vous tournez à droite dans la rue de la République et vous allez jusqu'au garage. Vous entrez dans le garage. Vous fermez la porte du garage. Ça fait 2 portes! Vous sortez du garage et vous entrez dans le couloir. Evidemment vous fermez la porte entre le garage et le couloir: ça fait 3 portes. Vous passez dans la salle de bains et vous fermez la porte. Ça fait 4 portes de fermées. Vous entrez dans la cuisine et vous fermez la porte. Ça fait 5 portes.

Alors là, attention: vous sortez de la cuisine par la petite porte de la rue de la République. Ça fait 6 portes. Bon! Vous êtes donc dans la rue. Vous tournez à gauche et vous rentrez dans la maison par la grande porte d'entrée. Ça fait 7 portes. Vous êtes maintenant dans l'entrée. Vous allez dans la salle à manger et vous fermez la porte. Ça fait 8 portes. Vous tournez à gauche et vous passez dans la salle de séjour. Ça fait 9 portes. Vous tournez à droite et vous entrez dans le petit salon. Vous fermez donc la porte entre la salle à manger et le petit salon. Ça fait 10 portes. Maintenant vous revenez dans la salle à manger. Vous fermez la porte entre le petit salon et la salle à manger. Ça fait 11 portes. Vous tournez à gauche et vous sortez dans le jardin. Ça fait 12 portes. Vous tournez à gauche et vous rentrez dans le petit salon. Ça fait 13 portes. Vous ressortez dans le jardin par l'autre porte, à droite. Ça fait 14 portes.

Vous voilà dans le jardin derrière la maison. Vous rentrez dans la salle de séjour par la porte du jardin. Ça fait 15 portes. Vous passez dans l'entrée. Ça fait... 16 portes! Vous allez tout droit, vers la porte d'entrée sur la rue, mais vous tournez à droite pour entrer dans la cuisine. Ça fait 17 portes. Maintenant c'est simple! Vous sortez de la cuisine par la porte du couloir. Ça fait 18 portes. Vous entrez dans votre chambre. Vous fermez la porte. C'est la 19ᵉ porte que vous fermez! Maintenant vous pouvez aller au lit! Bonsoir. Dormez bien.

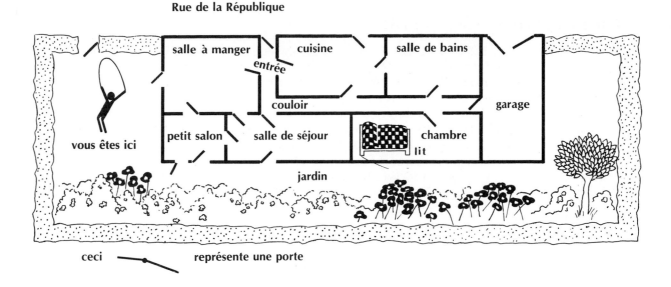

Rue de la République

vous êtes ici

ceci ————•———— représente une porte

6. Listening and Speaking Exercise

Look at the floor plan of the Pierres' apartment. Stéphane has just come in. It's his first visit, so he does not know the apartment at all. He asks questions. You answer him. For example, Stéphane asks: Où est la chambre de Denis? You answer: C'est la deuxième porte à droite. After your response you will hear a suggested answer. Let's begin.

1. Où est la salle à manger? (   ) *C'est la première porte à gauche.*
2. Où est la chambre des parents? (   ) *C'est la troisième porte à gauche.*
3. Où est la cuisine? (   ) *C'est la première porte à droite.*
4. Où est la chambre de Christine? (   ) *C'est la troisième porte à droite.*
5. Où est la salle de séjour? (   ) *C'est la deuxième porte à gauche.*

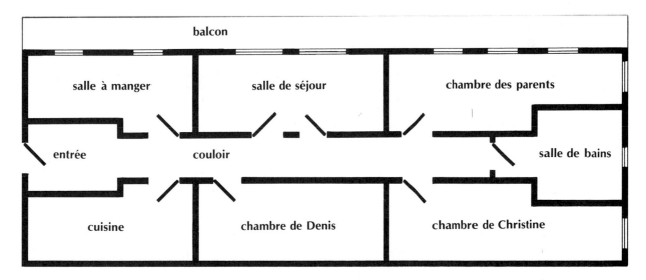

7. Dictation Exercise

You will hear four short exchanges (questions and answers) about people you know (Marie-Paule, the Sitbon brothers, Denis, Christine). Though you will hear the questions, they do not appear in your *Activity Book*. The answers are printed in your *Activity Book,* but they are incomplete. You must fill in the missing word. In each case the missing word is a past participle. You must write it down with the proper ending. Remember that this ending depends on the direct object; here the direct object is always the person or people we are talking about. If we are talking about one girl, the past participle should have a feminine singular ending—that is to say, an extra **e.** If we are talking about several boys, or boys and girls, it should have a masculine plural ending—that is to say, an extra **s.** If we are talking about several girls, it should have a feminine plural ending—that is to say, an extra **es.** Let's begin.

1. Tu as rencontré Marie-Paule? Oui, je l'ai trouvée très sympathique.
2. Vous savez où est Christine? Non, nous ne l'avons pas vue.
3. Tu crois que les frères Sitbon sont chez eux? Non, je les ai vus à la piscine tout à l'heure.
4. Denis et Christine sont là? Non, leur mère les a emmenés à Paris.
5. Comment! Tu connais Christine et Marie-Paule? Oui, je les ai rencontrées à la Maison des Jeunes.

Now check your answers. To verify your spelling, see the answer key at the end of your *Activity Book.*

1. Oui, je l'ai _____ très sympathique.
2. Non, nous ne l'avons pas _____ .
3. Non, je les ai _____ à la piscine tout à l'heure.
4. Non, leur mère les a _____ à Paris.
5. Oui, je les ai _____ à la Maison des Jeunes.

Preparation for Conversation Exercise 42

8. Listening Exercise

Christine calls her new friend, Sylvie, on the phone.

CHRISTINE   Allô, Sylvie, c'est toi? Ça va?
SYLVIE   Ça va, et toi?
CHRISTINE   Ça va. Dis donc, qu'est-ce que tu fais? Tu travailles? Tu es occupée?
SYLVIE   Non, pourquoi?
CHRISTINE   Mon frère a acheté des disques. Tu veux venir les écouter?
SYLVIE   Oui . . . quand? Maintenant? Tout de suite?
CHRISTINE   Oui, viens maintenant, si tu n'as rien à faire.
SYLVIE   Bon, j'arrive . . . Mais où est-ce que tu habites?
CHRISTINE   113 Avenue du Général de Gaulle. Tu sais où c'est?
SYLVIE   Non, pas du tout. C'est loin du lycée?
CHRISTINE   Non, pas très. Je vais t'expliquer. Voyons . . . Tu sais où est le lycée?
SYLVIE   Ben, ça, oui!
CHRISTINE   Bon, alors, quand tu sors du lycée tu prends la rue Gambetta, juste en face. Tu vas jusqu'à la place de la Mairie . . . Tu me suis?
SYLVIE   Oui, oui. Jusque là, ça va, continue.
CHRISTINE   Bon, quand tu es sur la place de la Mairie, tu tournes à gauche. Tu me suis, oui?
SYLVIE   Oui, oui, je tourne à gauche.

CHRISTINE	Mais attention, hein, c'est à gauche quand tu regardes la Mairie. Ne te trompe pas.
SYLVIE	Non, non, j'ai compris, continue.
CHRISTINE	Bon, alors tu tournes à gauche dans la rue Victor Hugo. Tu continues jusqu'à l'église, et à l'église tu tournes à droite. C'est l'avenue du Général de Gaulle.
SYLVIE	Ah oui, je vois, je connais . . . Il y a une pharmacie?
CHRISTINE	Oui, tu passes devant la pharmacie . . .
SYLVIE	Et puis il y a la poste, et puis une banque?
CHRISTINE	C'est ça, et après la banque, tu vois une très belle maison.
SYLVIE	Avec un grand jardin devant?
CHRISTINE	Oui, avec beaucoup de fleurs, un grand garage pour deux voitures, et il y a toujours une grosse Cadillac arrêtée devant. Tu vois ce que je veux dire?
SYLVIE	Oui, oui.
CHRISTINE	Eh bien, ce n'est pas là! C'est en face. Le grand immeuble en briques. J'habite au sixième. A tout à l'heure!

CHAPITRE 11

The spellings **i** *plus vowel and* **y** *plus vowel (2)*

1. Reading and Speaking Exercise

Listen carefully to the way the word *bien* is pronounced. (See number 1.)

1. bien

How many distinct sounds do you hear? Listen: *bien*. There are three sounds—the consonant sound /b/, then the sound /j/, and finally the vowel sound /$\tilde{\varepsilon}$/. Listen again: *bien*.

The sound /j/ resembles the sound /i/ but it is nòt /i/. Listen: /j/, /j/. It is not a real vowel like /i/. It is not a real consonant either. It is something in between. It is called a semi-vowel: half vowel, half consonant. (You have something quite similar in English. For example the first sound in the words "you," "yesterday.")

Now look at the words in number 2, and repeat after the voice.

2. C'est bien!   C'est mieux!   Etudiez!

You see that in these three words the letter **i** represents the sound /j/. You will notice also that in each one of these three words, the letter **i** is followed by a spelling representing a vowel sound:

- In *bien* the spelling **e-n** represents the vowel sound [$\tilde{\varepsilon}$].
- In *mieux* the spelling **e-u-x** represents the vowel sound [ø].
- In *étudiant* the spelling **a-n-t** represents the vowel sound [ã].

Now look at number 3.

3. il y a longtemps

You hear the same /j/ sound before the vowel sound /a/. But this time, the sound /j/ is represented by the letter **y.** It seems, then, that the letter **i** or the letter **y,** followed by a spelling representing a vowel sound, represents the sound /j/.

Read and pronounce the words in number 4:

4. C'est ancien!   C'est égyptien.   C'est du treizième siècle.
C'est bien!   C'est mieux!   C'est le lieu.
Dans une demi-heure!   Il y est.   Il y a des étudiants.

Now here is a little problem for you. It's fairly easy. Look at the words in number 5 and try to pronounce them.

5. une amie   la mairie   je vous en prie

Does the letter **i,** in these words, represent the sound /j/? No! Can you guess why? Because it is not followed by a vowel sound. In these words the **e** that follows the **i** does not represent a vowel sound. In fact, it does not represent any sound at all.

2. Listening and Speaking Exercise

You remember the day when you took that terrific walk through Paris? No? You don't? Come on! That was the last time you saw Paris! You took such a terribly long walk. You were exhausted! You walked for hours and went everywhere, almost! Tell us about it! Try to remember what you did! To help you remember, there is a map in your *Activity Book*. As a matter of fact, you had noted down the time at which you reached the different points of your walk. That should help a lot. Let's see what you can tell us, and if you don't remember exactly, you can always invent a little. Ready? Here we go.

Voyons, vous êtes arrivé à Paris à 10 heures, ce jour-là. Vous êtes arrivé, par le train, à 10 heures. A quelle gare est-ce que vous êtes arrivé à 10 heures? Vous ne savez pas? Mais si, c'est une gare au nord . . . oui sur la Rive Droite . . . au nord . . . non, pas la gare du nord. Non! C'est au nord et un peu à l'ouest. Ça y est? Vous l'avez trouvée, cette gare? Oui . . . au nord de l'Eglise de la Madeleine! Bon, vous y êtes! Alors à quelle gare vous êtes arrivé à 10 heures? (   ) *A la gare Saint-Lazare.*

Est-ce que vous y êtes resté? Non, vous n'y êtes pas resté . . . ! Vous êtes reparti tout de suite. Vous êtes parti, vers l'ouest. Vous avez marché une heure et où est-ce que vous êtes arrivé à 11 heures? (   ) *Je suis arrivé à l'Arc de Triomphe.*

C'est ça, vous êtes arrivé à l'Arc de Triomphe de l'Etoile. Et comment est-ce que vous êtes arrivé à l'Arc de Triomphe? Quand vous êtes sorti de la Gare Saint-Lazare, vous avez tourné à droite . . . oui, à droite, et vous êtes passé devant une église, l'Eglise Saint-Augustin, et vous avez continué vers l'Arc de Triomphe. Vous **avez** suivi l'Avenue de Friedland et vous êtes arrivé à l'Arc de Triomphe. Mais vous n'y êtes pas monté, vous avez continué. Vous avez continué à marcher. Vous avez suivi l'Avenue Kléber et à 11 heures et demie, vous êtes arrivé au Palais de Chaillot. Et après, où est-ce que vous êtes allé? Voyons, cherchez! Où est-ce que vous êtes arrivé à midi? (   ) *A la Tour Eiffel.*

Oui, vous êtes arrivé à la Tour Eiffel. Et qu'est-ce que vous avez fait pour arriver à la Tour Eiffel? (   ) *J'ai traversé la Seine.*

Oui, vous avez traversé la Seine, sur le pont d'Iéna. A midi et demie, vous êtes arrivé à l'Ecole Militaire . . . pas très intéressant . . . vous avez continué et où est-ce que vous êtes arrivé à 1 heure? (   ) *Au Pont Alexandre III au bord de la Seine.* Qu'est-ce que vous avez vu entre l'Ecole Militaire et le Pont Alexandre III? (   ) *Les Invalides.*

Oui, vous êtes passé devant les Invalides. Vous avez traversé la Seine et vous êtes arrivé au Grand Palais à 1 h 15. Et puis, qu'est-ce que vous avez fait? (   ) *Je suis allé à la Place de la Concorde.*

Oui, vous avez traversé la Place de la Concorde à 1 heure et demie et vous avez acheté un sandwich rue de Rivoli. Puis vous êtes allé manger votre sandwich dans le jardin des Tuileries. Vous avez traversé le jardin des Tuileries. Et où est-ce que vous êtes arrivé à 2 heures et quart? (   ) *Au Louvre.*

Vous n'êtes pas entré au Louvre et vous êtes allé à la Tour Saint-Jacques. Quelle rue est-ce que vous avez prise pour aller à la Tour Saint-Jacques? (   ) *La rue de Rivoli.*

Quand vous êtes arrivé à la Tour Saint-Jacques, vous avez continué vers le sud, et vous êtes passé devant la Sainte-Chapelle. Vous n'y êtes pas entré. Vous avez continué dans la même direction et à 3 h 30 vous êtes arrivé à la Sorbonne. Qu'est-ce que vous avez fait pour aller de la Sainte Chapelle à la Sorbonne? (   ) *J'ai traversé la Seine sur un pont et j'ai suivi le Boulevard Saint-Michel.*

Et à 3 h 45 où est-ce que vous êtes arrivé? (   ) *Au Panthéon.* Où est-ce que vous êtes arrivé à 4 heures? (   ) *Au croisement du Boulevard Saint-Michel et du Boulevard Saint-Germain.* Et après ça, où est-ce que vous êtes allé? (   ) *A Notre-Dame.*

C'est ça. Et puis vous avez pris le métro jusqu'à la Gare Saint-Lazare et vous êtes rentré . . . bien fatigué! Oh la la, que vous étiez fatigué!

3. Listening Comprehension Exercise

You have in front of you eight photographs. You will hear eight fragments of conversation, in which Antoine and Isabelle tell about what they did in Paris. As you hear them speak, look at the photographs and try to figure out what they are talking about. Write the number of each conversation below the photograph to which it refers. Listen.

1. On est arrivés à peine quelques minutes avant la fermeture. On a juste eu le temps d'aller voir ''La Joconde''. On n'a rien pu voir d'autre.
2. —Oui, j'y suis monté. Je suis monté tout en haut, au troisième étage.
   —A pied!
   —Ah non, pas à pied. Par l'ascenseur! Non, mais dis! Monter trois cents mètres à pied!
   —C'est possible! Il y a un escalier.
   —C'est possible, mais c'est fatigant!
3. J'ai acheté tout un tas de choses. J'ai acheté un pantalon, pour moi. Et puis des cadeaux: un disque pour mon frère un bracelet pour ma sœur, un foulard pour maman et un livre pour papa.
4. On s'est bien promenés. On a rencontré 6 bateaux et on est passés sous 20 ponts.
5. On est allés boire une limonade dans un café en face d'une vieille Eglise.
6. Et puis après on est allés à Montmartre. J'ai fait une photo du Sacré Cœur: l'église avec des pigeons; mais elle n'est pas très réussie.
7. On est passés au Quartier Latin. On a vu de vieilles rues avec de vieilles maisons et beaucoup de gens dans les rues.
8. Après ça on est allés se promener dans un grand jardin, avec des fleurs. —Oui, on est allés au Luxembourg.

Now check your answers. The numbers below the photographs should read, from left to right: *4, 5, 7, 1, 2, 6, 8, 3.*

4. Listening Comprehension Exercise

You will hear a number of sentences. Some are in the present, others in the past. You will have to tell which ones are present and which ones are past. To do this, you must know what the verb is in each sentence. So we will go about it in two steps. The first time around, you will try to figure out what the verbs are in the sentences. Then we will go through the sentences again, and you will determine whether they are in the present or the past.

Part 1

Here is the first round. For each sentence you hear, indicate the verb by placing a check mark in the appropriate row of the first chart. The verbs you must choose among are *être, avoir, aller, partir, voir, rester, acheter, faire, passer.* You'll hear the infinitive of the correct verb after you make your check mark for each sentence. Let's begin.

1. Elle est au musée. _____ *(être)—(présent)*
2. Elle est allée au musée. _____ *(aller)—(passé)*
3. Nous sommes à Paris. _____ *(être)—(présent)*
4. Nous sommes partis. _____ *(partir)—(passé)*
5. Qu'est-ce que tu vois? _____ *(voir)—(présent)*
6. Tu y vas? _____ *(aller)—(présent)*
7. Tu l'as vu? _____ *(voir)—(passé)*
8. Il est resté à Paris. _____ *(rester)—(passé)*
9. Il reste à Paris. _____ *(rester)—(présent)*
10. Qu'est-ce que tu fais? _____ *(faire)—(présent)*
11. Qu'est-ce que tu as fait? _____ *(faire—(passé)*
12. Ils sont tous allés dans le même quartier. _____ *(aller)—(passé)*
13. Ils n'ont pas assez de temps. _____ *(avoir)—(présent)*
14. Ils sont passés au Louvre. _____ *(passer)—(passé)*
15. Ils n'ont pas été contents. _____ *(être)—(passé)*

Part 2

Now listen to the sentences again, and indicate whether each verb is in the present or in the past by placing a check mark in the appropriate row of the second chart. After you make your check mark, you'll hear the correct answer. Let's begin.

(Read the exercise again, and indicate the answers.)

	1	2	3	4	5	6	7	8	9	10	11	12	13	14	15
être															
avoir															
aller															
partir															
voir															
rester															
acheter															
faire															
passer															

	1	2	3	4	5	6	7	8	9	10	11	12	13	14	15
présent															
passé															

CHAPITRE 12

Spellings **oi** *and* **oin** *(1)*

1. Reading and Speaking Exercise

Listen carefully to the following words: *moi, toi, fois, doit, voit.* How many distinct sounds can you hear in each one of these words? Listen again: *moi, toi, fois, doit, voit.* Let's take *moi,* for example. How many sounds are there? *moi;* /m/w/a/. How many do you find? Two? Three? I count three. First you have the consonant [m] — *moi.* Then you get the sound [w], something between a consonant and a vowel, a semi-consonant as they say. Then you have the sound [a] — *moi.* Now let's see how these words are spelled. Look at number 1.

       1. moi   toi   fois   doit   voit

You see that all these words have the spelling **o-i** in common. The spelling **o-i** represents the sound [wa] (the semiconsonant [w] followed by the vowel [a]). You have already seen many words with this spelling. Practice saying those in number 2.

       2. Voici l'étoile.   Choisissez, Mademoiselle.
          C'est la troisième fois, je crois.   Le poisson, c'est bon!

Now here are a few French words and phrases that you may have never seen. They all have the **o-i** spelling. Try to say them. Make sure to pronounce **o-i** as [wa]. Look at number 3 in your *Activity Book.*

       3. un bourgeois   une vichyssoise
          une soirée   la joie de vivre

Now look at the words in number 4 and hear how they sound.

       4. loin   moins

We do have an **o-i** spelling in these words, yet the sound is different, right? You do not hear [wa] but [wɛ̃]: *loin.* Why? It's simple! Actually we do not have the spelling **o-i** but **o-i-n,** which represents the sound [wɛ̃]. It is made up of the semiconsonant [w] (the same we observed in [wa]) followed by the nasal vowel [ɛ̃] (which, you remember, is usually represented by **i-n**). Say the following French words, which all have this **o-i-n** spelling. You may never have encountered some of them, but you should be able to figure out how they sound. Look at number 5 in your *Activity Book.*

       5. loin   moins
          un point   une pointure
          un joint   une jointure

Now, pronounce the word in number 6.

       6. Antoine

Antoine, right! Why? Don't we have the **o-i-n** spelling? Well, not really! What we have here is the spelling **o-i** as in *toi,* followed by the spelling **n-e** as in the negation *ne, ne . . . pas.* In other words, the **n** here does not go with the **o-i.** It goes with the **e** that follows. It would be the same if the **n** was followed by any other letter representing a vowel sound — an **o** for example. *Moinot,* for example, is a family name. It is spelled **M-o-i-n-o-t.** Look at number 7.

       7. Moinot

Now say the words under number 8.

8. Antoine   Antoinette
un moine   Monsieur Moinot

Practicing with dates (12)

2. Listening and Writing Exercise

Now look at the pictures in front of you. You will be told when each of these girls and boys was born. Write this information down, in French, in the space provided under each picture. Make sure you write clearly, because later you will be asked to give that information yourself. Let's begin.

1. Arnaud est né le 20 février 1969.
2. Sylvie est née le 16 juillet 1965.
3. Caroline est née le 6 janvier 1967.

4. Muriel est née le 1er mars 1972.
5. David est né le 27 novembre 1970.
6. Eric est né le 15 avril 1968.

Let's see if you got all the dates right. *(Repeat each sentence.)*

Arnaud
né le _____

Sylvie
née le _____

Caroline
née le _____

Muriel
née le _____

David
né le _____

Eric
né le _____

3. Listening and Speaking Exercise

Now you know when each one of these boys and girls was born. So you can tell when his or her birthday is. For example, Arnaud was born on February 20, 1969. When is his birthday? On February 20! Right. Could you answer such a question in French? Let's try. *Quel jour est l'anniversaire d'Arnaud?* (   ) *Le 20 février; l'anniversaire d'Arnaud est le 20 février.* Now you should be able to do the following exercise. Answer the questions. After each response you'll hear the correct answer. Let's begin.

1. Quel jour est l'anniversaire de David? (   ) *le 27 novembre*
2. En quelle année est-ce qu'il est né? (   ) *en 1970*
3. En quelle année Caroline est-elle née? (   ) *en 1967*
4. Quel jour? (   ) *le 6 janvier*
5. Quand est l'anniversaire de Sylvie? (   ) *le 16 juillet*
6. En quelle année est-ce qu'elle est née? (   ) *en 1965*
7. Quel jour est-ce que Muriel est née? (   ) *le 1er mars 1972*

8. Et Arnaud? ( ) *le 20 févier 1969*
9. Et Eric? ( ) *le 15 avril 1968*
10. Qui est-ce qui est né le 6 janvier? ( ) *Caroline*
11. Qui est-ce qui est né en 1970? ( ) *David*
12. Qui est-ce qui a son anniversaire en février? ( ) *Arnaud*
13. Qui est-ce qui a son anniversaire le 1er mars? ( ) *Muriel*

4. Listening and Speaking Exercise

One has to deal a lot with dates when studying history, of course; but there are many other situations in which one mentions dates. One of the most common occasions, perhaps, is in talking about birthdays. Listen to the following conversation about birthdays. It is a conversation between a boy, Jacques, and a girl, Marie-Christine.

JACQUES	Quand est-ce que tu es née?
MARIE-CHRISTINE	En juin; et toi?
JACQUES	Moi, je suis né au mois d'août.
MARIE-CHRISTINE	Au mois d'août! Sans blague! Quel jour?
JACQUES	Le 10.
MARIE-CHRISTINE	Le 10 août! Ça alors! Tu as le même anniversaire que mon frère!
JACQUES	Qui ça, Patrick?
MARIE-CHRISTINE	Non, le petit, Marc.
JACQUES	En quelle année est-ce qu'il est né?
MARIE-CHRISTINE	En 1971.
JACQUES	Oh! Moi, je suis né en 1966!

Did you get it? Let's see if you did. Listen to the questions, and try to answer them before the voice on the recording gives the correct answer.

1. Quand est-ce que Marie-Christine est née? ( ) *En juin. Elle est née en juin.*
2. Et Jacques? ( ) *En août. Il est né en août.*
3. Quel jour? ( ) *Le dix. Le dix août.*
4. En quelle année est-ce que Marc est né? ( ) *En 1971.*
5. Et Jacques? En quelle année est-ce qu'il est né? ( ) *En 1966. Jacques est né en 1966.*

Discrimination between present, future, and past (20)

5. Listening Exercise

You will hear a number of questions. Some will be in the present, others in the past, and still others in the immediate future. For each question you hear, indicate which tense it refers to. Let's begin.

1. Vous allez bien? _____ *(present)*
2. Vous allez partir? _____ *(future)*
3. Vous avez vu Christine? _____ *(past)*
4. Elle écrit souvent? _____ *(present)*
5. Elle vous a écrit? _____ *(past)*
6. Tu vas lui écrire? _____ *(future)*
7. Tu vas être fatigué? _____ *(future)*
8. Ils ont descendu la télé au sous-sol? _____ *(past)*
9. Ils vont retourner au musée? _____ *(future)*
10. Ils sont montés à la Tour Eiffel? _____ *(past)*

11. Vous allez y monter? _____ *(future)*
12. Tu vois quelque chose? _____ *(present)*
13. Vous faites quelque chose? _____ *(present)*
14. Les courses, vous les avez faites? _____ *(past)*

Now check your answers. *Read each sentence again and give the correct answer.*

	1	2	3	4	5	6	7	8	9	10	11	12	13	14
Past														
Present														
Future														

CHAPITRE 13

The spellings **ai, ei, ain, ein, ail** *(35)*

1. Reading and Speaking Exercise

We have already seen (in Unit 4) that the **a-i** combination represents the sound [ɛ]. Look at the sentence in number 1:

1. Je v<u>ai</u>s t'<u>ai</u>der à f<u>ai</u>re la v<u>ai</u>sselle.

In that sentence, there are four such **a-i** combinations. Some represent the sound [e] and others the sound [ɛ], but since French speakers vary a great deal in distinguishing between [e] and [ɛ], we will not worry too much about that distinction. We also know that the **e-i** combination represents the sound [ɛ], as in the words in number 2.

2. treize   seize   la Seine

Now, the combinations **a-i-n** and **e-i-n** represent the nasal sound [ɛ̃], right? Look at the words in number 3.

3. le pain   éteint
     maintenant   plein

This nasal sound [ɛ̃] is a vowel. The consonant sound [n] is not heard. Yet if the letter **n** is followed by the letter **e** (or any other letter or combination representing a vowel sound), then the **n** is heard as a consonant, and we have an [ɛ]-sound instead of the nasal [ɛ̃]. Look at the words in number 4.

4. la main   *but*   le Maine
     L'île de Sein *(off the coast of Britanny)*   *but*   la Seine

So much for **a-i** or **e-i** followed by **n**. Now let's see what happens when **a-i** and **e-i** are followed by **l** or **l-l**. How do the words in number 5 sound?

5. le réveil   elle se réveille

The last sound is a [j], not quite a consonant, not a vowel either, but something in between: a "semi-consonant" as they say. Now look at the words in number 6.

6. le travail   elle travaille

We still have that semiconsonant [j], but the vowel before is no longer [ɛ] but [a]: *travail.*

Let's see if you can remember all that. Say the words in 7. When you pronounce the [ɛ]-sound make sure you do not "glide" from one vowel sound to another. Say [ɛd] rather than [ɛid] as you would in English.

7. aide   air   chaise
     raison   prairie   laissez-faire
     seize   peignoir   seigneur

For the words in number 8, make sure to distinguish between *main* (nasal [ɛ̃] and no consonant [n]), and *Maine* (vowel [ɛ] and consonant [n]).

8. le pain   une plainte   le train
la main   le Maine   la plaine
plein   pleine   à peine

Now let's try the words in number 9.

9. réveil   pareil   pareille
nous travaillons   un détail   le rail

Practice with the vocabulary of the unit (35)

2. Listening Exercise

You have in front of you ten photographs representing ten different situations. You will hear various people talking. Each one of the ten short talks is identified by a letter and corresponds to one of the ten situations represented in the photographs. Try to find out which one it is, and then write the letter of each talk under the photograph to which it corresponds. You may not understand every single word that is said, but many of the words and phrases you will hear were used in Unit 13. You should recognize enough of them to figure out what it is all about. You may get your clue from the actions mentioned, or the places, or the character. Does it involve a boy or a girl? One person or several? Watch the subject pronouns and the verb forms; they will tell you a lot. Let's begin.

A. —Qui est-ce qui est à la cuisine? C'est toi, Eric?
   —Non, c'est moi.
   —Qu'est-ce que tu fais? Tu déjeunes?
   —Non, j'ai fini. Je lave mon assiette.

B. —Où est-ce que tu es?
   —A la cuisine.
   —Qu'est-ce que tu fais? Tu fais la vaisselle?
   —Non, j'ai fini. Je me lave les mains.

C. —Après le dîner nous faisons la vaisselle. Moi je la lave et, elle, elle l'essuie.

D. —Il fait presque toujours beau. Alors elle fait souvent la vaisselle et la cuisine en plein air.

E. —C'est le soir. Elle doit se lever tôt demain matin, alors elle remonte son réveil avant de se coucher.

F. —Quand il fait beau, elle s'installe dans un hamac, en plein air, dans le jardin, pour se détendre un peu. Elle lit, elle se repose.

G. —Quand elle rentre à la maison elle n'a pas envie d'aller se coucher tout de suite. Elle aime bien travailler dans le jardin. Elle s'occupe de ses fleurs. Elle s'assure qu'elles ont assez d'eau.

H. —C'est le matin. Il se réveille. Mais il ne se lève pas d'un bond. Il n'a pas tellement envie de se lever.

I. —Elle reste debout toute la journée. Alors quand elle rentre à la maison, elle est épuisée et elle s'écroule dans un fauteuil. Quelquefois, même, elle s'endort.

J. —Elle est habillée, mais elle n'est pas prête. Sa sœur est en train de la peigner.

Now check your answers. The letters under the photographs should read from left to right: E, C, F, H, J, I, G, D, A, B.

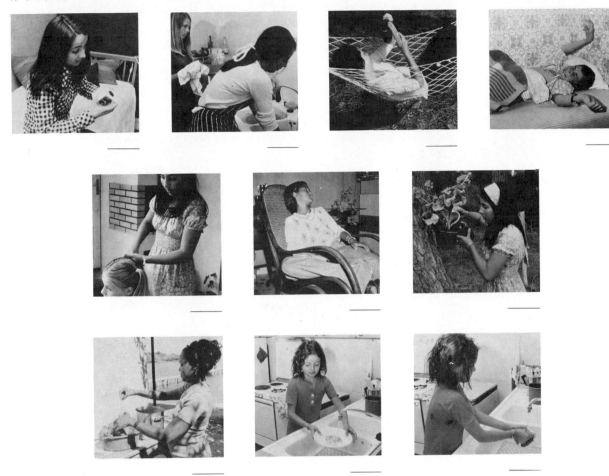

3. Listening and Speaking Exercise

In this exercise we will talk about the same pictures that you used for Exercise 2. So look at the pictures, listen, and give a response whenever you are asked a question.

1. Commençons par la photo nº 5! Regardez la photo nº 5. Voyons... Qui est-ce? Ce sont deux garçons? (   ) *Non, ce sont deux filles, Christine et Caroline.* Caroline est assise. Et Christine? (   ) *Elle est debout.* Qu'est-ce qu'elle fait? Elle se peigne? (   ) *Non, elle peigne Caroline.*

2. Voyons la photo nº 2 maintenant. Qui est-ce? (   ) *Caroline et Christine.* Où sont-elles? (   ) *Dans la cuisine.* Qu'est-ce qu'elles font? Elles se lavent? (   ) *Non! Elles font la vaisselle... elles lavent la vaisselle.*

3. Et sur la photo nº 3. C'est Caroline? (   ) *Non, c'est Christine.* Où est-elle? Elle est au lit, dans sa chambre? (   ) *Non, elle n'est pas dans sa chambre. Elle est dans le jardin... en plein air.* Elle n'est pas au lit... elle est dans un hamac. Qu'est-ce qu'elle fait? Elle travaille? (   ) *Non, elle ne travaille pas. Elle se repose. Elle lit pour se détendre.*

4. Maintenant, regardez la photo nº 6. C'est Doris. Où est-elle? Elle est au lit? (   ) *Non, elle est dans un fauteuil.* Qu'est-ce qu'elle fait, elle lit? (   ) *Non, elle se repose.*

5. Passons à la photo n° 1. Voyons, qui est-ce? (   ) *C'est Christine. Et où est-elle? Dans le jardin?* Dans la cuisine? (   ) *Non, elle est dans sa chambre. Où est-elle assise, dans un fauteuil? (   )* *Non, sur son lit. Qu'est-ce qu'elle fait, elle lit? (   ) Non, elle remonte son réveil. Vous croyez* que c'est le matin, ou le soir? (   ) *C'est le soir.*

6. Sur la photo n° 4, c'est Eric. Vous croyez que c'est le soir ou le matin? (   ) *C'est le matin.* Où est Eric? (   ) *Au lit. Il est dans un lit. Il est couché dans son lit. Qu'est-ce qu'il fait? (   ) Il dort.*

7. Qui est-ce sur la photo n° 7? Vous la reconnaissez? (   ) *C'est Christine. Où est-elle? Dans la* maison? (   ) *Non, elle est dans le jardin. De quoi s'occupe-t-elle? Elle s'occupe de son chien?* (   ) *Non, elle s'occupe de ses fleurs.*

8. Sur la photo n° 8 c'est Madame Dubois. Qu'est-ce qu'elle fait? Elle se repose ou elle travaille? (   ) *Elle travaille, oui. Elle fait la cuisine. Est-ce qu'elle fait la cuisine dans sa cuisine ou en plein air? (   )* *Elle fait la cuisine en plein air.*

9. Sur la photo n° 9 c'est Catherine. Où est-elle? (   ) *Dans la cuisine. Qu'est-ce qu'elle fait? (   )* *Elle fait la vaisselle. Elle lave une assiette.*

10. Et sur la photo n° 10, elle se lave la tête ou elle se lave les mains? (   ) *Elle se lave les mains.*

CHAPITRE 14

The spelling **tion** *(1)*

1. Speaking and Reading Exercise

Look at the words in number 1. How are these two French words pronounced?

1. composition   addition

You notice that in these two words the **t** is not pronounced like the first **t** in *petit,* for example, but like **s** as in *si.* Note that it is an [s]-sound—*composition*—and not [ʃ] as it would be in English. Now say the words in number 2.

2. une répétition   une collection   une occupation
       une exposition   une grande attention

They all end with **t-i-o-n,** which represents the sound [sjõ]. Now, all these words are nouns, right? And what is their gender? Are they masculine or feminine? They are all feminine. Well, whenever you find a French word that ends in **t-i-o-n,** you may be pretty sure of a few things: that this word is pronounced [sjõ] at the end, that it is a noun, and that it is feminine. Let's make use of this discovery. Look at number 3, and say each one of these words with the proper article.

3. *(une)* opération   *(une)* addition   *(une)* réduction
       (une) multiplication   *(une)* fraction   *(une)* administration
       (une) nation   *(une)* constitution   *(une)* invitation
       (une) installation   *(une)* opposition   *(une)* potion
       (une) option   *(une)* organisation

Now what about the word *question* in number 4? This word ends in **t-i-o-n,** yet the **t** represents the sound [t], not the sound [s]. Let's look at the words in number 4.

4. une question   une gestion
       une indigestion   une congestion

What's common to all these words? They all end in **s-t-i-o-n.** So, what we said about the ending **t-i-o-n** does not apply to the ending **s-t-i-o-n.** It is an exception.

2. Listening and Speaking Exercise

You see in front of you the names Sylvie, David, Caroline, Arnaud, Doris, and Eric. Each plays an instrument. The instruments they play are represented around them. First we will identify everybody's instrument. As soon as you have found out who plays what, make a note of it on the page. The simplest way might be to draw a line to connect each boy or girl with his or her instrument. Make sure you draw it clearly, because you will have to use that information later.

1. Commençons par Sylvie. Elle, elle joue du violon. Bon! Vous voyez le violon de Sylvie? Oui? C'est un petit violon *(sound)* pas un gros violoncelle *(sound)*. Non, un violon. Ça y est? Vous tracez une ligne entre la photo de Sylvie et son violon.
2. David, maintenant. David, lui, il joue de la guitare *(sound)*. Vous voyez la guitare de David? Alors tracez la ligne. Ça y est? — Bon.
3. Arnaud, lui, joue de la trompette *(sound)*. Pas de la flûte . . . *(sound)*. Non, non, de la trompette. Vous la voyez la trompette d'Arnaud? Tracez la ligne. Bien . . .
4. Et toi, Caroline, de quoi est-ce que tu joues? Moi, je joue de la flûte *(sound)*. Vous voyez la flûte de Caroline? Vous avez tracé la ligne?
5. Alors, passons à Doris. Tu sais de quoi elle joue, Doris? Elle joue du piano *(sound)*. Oh, mais . . . elle joue très bien! Bon, vous y êtes? Doris, c'est le piano.
6. Il ne reste plus qu'Eric. De quoi est-ce que tu joues, Eric? Moi, je joue du violoncelle *(sound)*. Du violoncelle? . . . Eh bien tu vois, on s'en doutait un peu. Alors, Eric, c'est le violoncelle.

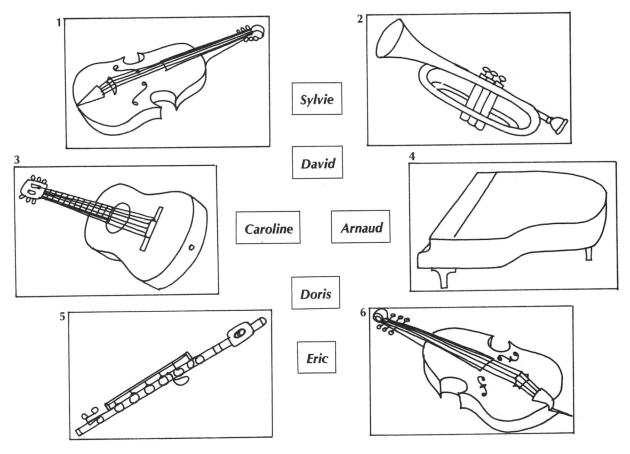

All right! Let's see whether you got it right or not. Answer the questions. Don't forget to pay attention to the gender. Remember that it's *du piano,* but *de la flûte!*

1. Commençons par Sylvie. De quel instrument est-ce qu'elle joue? (   ) *Elle joue du violon.*
2. Et David de quoi est-ce qu'il joue? (   ) *Il joue de la guitare.*
3. Et Arnaud! Il joue du piano, Arnaud? (   ) *Non, il joue de la trompette.*
4. Et Doris elle joue de la flûte? (   ) *Non, elle joue du piano.*
5. Et Eric, de quoi est-ce qu'il joue, du violon? (   ) *Non, il joue du violoncelle.*
6. Voyons . . . nous avons tout le monde? . . . Non! . . . Caroline! De quoi est-ce qu'elle joue, Caroline?
   (   ) *De la flûte, c'est ça! Elle joue de la flûte.*

Practice with the vocabulary of the unit (31)

3. Listening Comprehension Exercise

You will hear the first half for each of three short exchanges. The second half, the rejoinder to each of these exchanges, is printed in your *Activity Book.* However, these rejoinders are not printed in the right order. For each first half you hear, you will have to look for the best rejoinder and say it. Say it before you hear the answer on the tape. Now be careful. It may be a little tricky at times. You will have to pay attention to every little detail. Check whether what you hear is a question, an exclamation, or a simple statement. First, listen to the three rejoinders you will have to choose from.

Group 1
A Bien sûr, le haut parleur n'est pas branché!
B Bien sûr, tu as oublié d'appuyer sur le bouton d'enregistrement!
C Oui, baisse!

Now listen to the first halves of the exchanges, quickly select the best rejoinder, and say it.

1. On n'a rien enregistré! (   ) *Bien sûr, tu as oublié d'appuyer sur le bouton d'enregistrement! (B)*
2. C'est trop fort maintenant? (   ) *Oui, baisse! (C)*
3. On n'entend rien! (   ) *Bien sûr, le haut parleur n'est pas branché! (A)*

Here is the second group of three. Let's first read the rejoinders.

Group 2
A Non, c'est celle de Monique.
B Non, c'est une chanteuse.
C Non, de la clarinette.

Now listen to the first halves of the exchanges and say the most appropriate rejoinder.

1. Tu joues de la flûte? (   ) *Non, de la clarinette. (C)*
2. C'est ta guitare? (   ) *Non, c'est celle de Monique. (A)*
3. Qui c'est, cette Mireille Mathieu? Elle joue d'un instrument? (   ) *Non, c'est une chanteuse. (B)*

Here is the third group. Let's read the rejoinders.

Group 3
A Eh bien! Il faut le réparer!
B On va voir! On va faire un essai.
C Lequel?

Listen and say the most likely rejoinder.

1. Voilà, j'ai tout installé, mais je ne sais pas si ça va marcher. (   ) *On va voir! On va faire un essai. (B)*
2. Le magnétophone ne marche pas! (   ) *Eh bien, il faut le réparer! (A)*
3. Il y a un des haut-parleurs qui est débranché. (   ) *Lequel? (C)*

Practicing with celui, celle (38)

4. Listening and Speaking Exercise

Look again at the instruments that Sylvie, David, and the others play. Note that each picture of an instrument is identified by a number from 1 to 6. Listen and answer the questions.

Regardez le numéro 1. Qu'est-ce que c'est? C'est un violoncelle? (   ) *Non, c'est un violon.* C'est le violon d'Eric? (   ) *Non, c'est le violon de Sylvie. C'est celui de Sylvie.*

Maintenant regardez le numéro 2. Qu'est-ce que c'est? (   ) *Oui, c'est une trompette.* Vous savez, David a une guitare, oui, mais il a aussi une trompette! Oui, oui, oui! Maintenant cette trompette, là, au numéro 2, c'est la trompette de David? (   ) *Non, c'est celle d'Arnaud.*

Bien, Eric a un violoncelle, mais il a aussi une guitare. Regardez le numéro 3. Est-ce que c'est la guitare d'Eric? (   ) *Non, c'est celle de David.*

Caroline joue de la flûte, mais elle a aussi un piano. Regardez le numéro 4. Est-ce que c'est le piano de Caroline? (   ) *Non, c'est celui de Doris.*

CHAPITRE 15

*The spelling **ti** (1)*

1. Reading and Speaking Exercise

You remember that in Unit 14 we saw that the letter **t** represented the sound (s) in the **t-i-o-n** ending of nouns, as in *condition, nation, attention*. In Unit 10 you saw the word *résidentiel*. Look at number 1 in your *Activity Book*.

      1. C'est un quartier résidentiel de Montréal.

In this word, as well, the **t** represents an [s]-sound. This is true of all adjectives that end in **t-i-e-l** (or **t-i-e-l-l-e** in the feminine). It is likewise true of most adjectives that end in **t-i-a-l** (or **t-i-a-l-e** in the feminine). Knowing this, you should be able to pronounce all the words in number 2 even though you may have never heard them pronounced in French. Let's try. Say the words in number 2.

    2. résidentiel   essentiel
         présidentiel   confidentiel
         initial   partiel

Do you recognize these words? All these words are also found in English. The English version, though, is always spelled **t-i-a-l** at the end.

Of course, there are many words in which a **t** followed by an **i** does *not* represent the sound [s] but the sound [t]. You will find some of them, which we have already encountered, in number 3. Let's say them, pronouncing the letter **t** as a [t]-sound. The French [t]-sound is quite similar to the English sound, yet there is some difference. In English the [t]-sound is usually followed by a sort of little explosion. For example, in English you say "tic, taboo," but in French, you say *tic, taboo,* without any explosion or aspiration of the [t]-sound. So, when saying the words in group 3, try not to "explode" your **t**'s.

3. partie   sortie   rôti   fatigué
continuer   bâtiment   antiquité   tartine
dentifrice   gentillesse   charcutier   utiliser
petit

Practice with the vocabulary of the unit (11)

2. Listening Comprehension Exercise

You will hear eight spoken items. For each item you hear, try to find the best rejoinder among the eight sentences that you see printed in your *Activity Book.* Let's begin.

1. Pourquoi est-ce qu'elle n'écrit pas? *(D)*
2. Ton frère ne vient pas skier avec nous? *(C)*
3. Vous n'allez pas skier cet hiver? *(H)*
4. Elle va louer des skis? *(B)*
5. Vous ne prenez pas le télésiège? *(F)*
6. Tu t'es fait mal? *(A)*
7. Vous montez à pied? *(E)*
8. Oh, la la! Ce que j'ai froid aux pieds! *(G)*

Now check your answers. *Repeat each question once and give the correct answer.*

		1	2	3	4	5	6	7	8
A	Oui, je suis tombée!								
B	Oui, elle a cassé ses skis.								
C	Non, il s'est cassé la jambe.								
D	Elle s'est cassé le bras en faisant du ski.								
E	Oui, le télésiège ne marche pas.								
F	Non, il faut faire la queue au moins une heure!								
G	Viens te réchauffer près du feu!								
H	Non, il n'y a pas de neige.								

Practice with the vocabulary of the unit (14)

3. Listening Exercise

Imagine you are about to take up skiing. You have never done any before, so you don't have any equipment. You look in a sports catalog to find out how much it will cost you to get equipped. So let's establish a budget. Look at the catalog page in your *Activity Book,* and as we discuss what you will need, look up the price for each item. Then write it down in the space provided. Write carefully so that it will be easy to add up all prices at the end. (See p. 132.)

Bon, allons-y. D'abord il vous faut des skis, une bonne paire de skis. Ça fait combien une paire de skis? Vous avez trouvé? Bon, alors marquez le prix de la paire de skis. Ça y est?

Ensuite il vous faut des bâtons. Une paire de bâtons, ça fait combien? Ça c'est moins cher que les skis. Notez le prix de la paire de bâtons.

Des raquettes . . . non, des patins à glace non plus! mais des lunettes oui! Il vous faut des lunettes.

C'est indispensable avec la lumière sur la neige . . . et puis le vent dans les yeux pendant les descentes à toute vitesse! Voyons, combien ça coûte les lunettes? Vous avez trouvé? Alors ajoutez le prix des lunettes.

Maintenant il faut vous habiller. Voyons, qu'est-ce qu'il vous faut comme vêtements? Des chaussettes? Non, des chaussettes vous en avez. Ce n'est pas la peine d'en acheter. Mais il vous faut des gants ou des mouffles. Prenez des mouffles. C'est très bien pour le ski, et c'est un peu moins cher que les gants. Alors notez le prix d'une paire de mouffles.

Il vous faut aussi un bonnet de laine bien chaud. Parce qu'il fait froid sur les pentes. Vous allez avoir froid aux oreilles! Alors, un bonnet, ça fait combien? Ajoutez le prix du bonnet.

Voilà. C'est tout? Ah non! Il vous faut aussi un anorak. C'est cher ça! Mais c'est indispensable pour couper le vent. Ajoutez le prix de l'anorak.

Maintenant nous avons tout. Il ne reste plus qu'à faire l'addition. Allez-y, faites l'addition! Additionnez tous les prix. Ça fait combien? Quel est le total? Combien est-ce que vous trouvez? 810 F?

Voyons, vérifions:

une paire de skis	400 F
une paire de bâtons	75 F
des lunettes	30 F
une paire de mouffles	30 F
un bonnet	25 F (ça n'est pas cher!)
un anorak	250 F
	810 F

Additionnez: cinq et cinq = dix. 0 et je retiens un.

7 et 1 = 8, et 3 = 11, et 3 = 14, et 2 = 16, et 5 = 21. Je pose 1 et je retiens 2.

2 et 4 = 6, et 2 = 8.

Ça fait donc 810 F. C'est ça?

4. Speaking Exercise

To do this exercise, you will have to look once more at the sports catalog page reproduced in your *Activity Book*.

You will be asked which one item you can buy with a specific amount of money. Answer each question, naming the most expensive item you can buy. For example, you hear: *Vous avez 30 F. Qu'est-ce que vous pouvez acheter?* And your answer: *Une paire de mouffles ou des lunettes.* Or if you wish you may say: *Je peux acheter une paire de mouffles ou des lunettes.* OK? Here we go.

Si vous avez 20 F, qu'est-ce que vous pouvez acheter avec ces 20 F? ( ) *des chaussettes, je peux acheter une paire de chaussettes.* Si vous avez 25 F, qu'est-ce que vous pouvez acheter? ( ) *un bonnet, je peux acheter un bonnet.* Et si vous avez 35 F, qu'est-ce que vous pouvez acheter? ( ) *une paire de gants. Je peux acheter une paire de gants.* Et avec 75 F. Qu'est-ce que vous pouvez avoir? ( ) *des bâtons. Avec 75 F je peux avoir une paire de bâtons.* Et avec 200 F qu'est-ce qu'on peut avoir? ( ) *Avec deux cents francs on peut avoir des raquettes.* Et avec 250 F? ( ) *Avec 250 F on peut avoir un anorak.* Et avec 300 F? ( ) *Avec 300 F on peut avoir une paire de chaussures de ski.* Et avec 400 F? ( ) *Avec 400 F on peut avoir une paire de skis.*

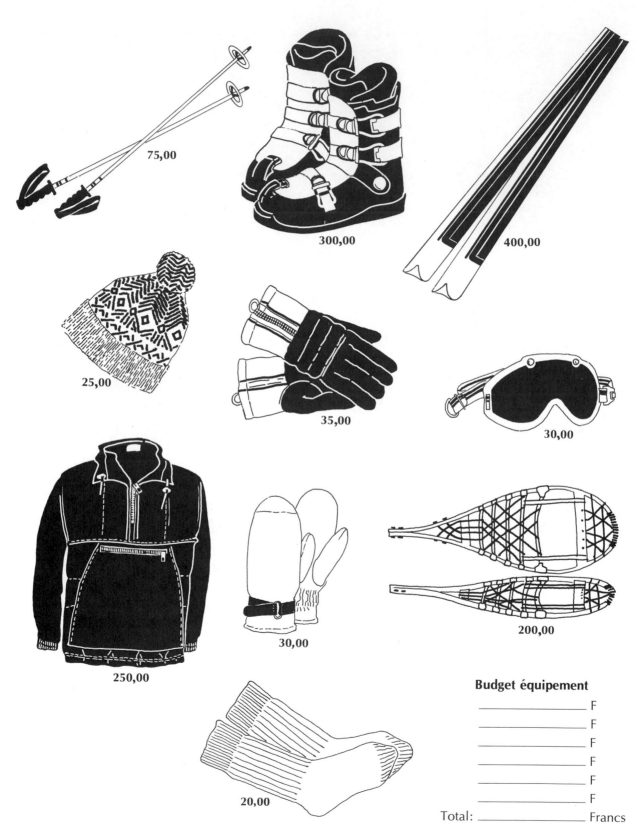

75,00

300,00

400,00

25,00

35,00

30,00

250,00

30,00

200,00

Budget équipement

_____ F
_____ F
_____ F
_____ F
_____ F
_____ F
Total: _____ Francs

20,00

5. Listening Exercise

Alain and Patrick are talking between two classes at the lycée, in Bagnères de Bigorre, in the Pyrénées, on a Thursday morning.

ALAIN Qu'est-ce que tu as fait hier? Tu as travaillé?

PATRICK Non, je suis allé faire du ski.

ALAIN Où est-ce que tu es allé?

PATRICK A la Mongie, bien sûr.

ALAIN Tu y es allé avec tes parents?

PATRICK Non, mon père travaille le mercredi! J'y suis allé avec mon frère. On a pris le bus.

ALAIN Il a fait beau?

PATRICK Oui, très beau. Froid! Mais beau.

ALAIN Tu as loué des skis, ou tu as des skis à toi?

PATRICK Oui, j'ai des skis à moi, mais je suis tombé et j'ai cassé un ski dimanche dernier, alors hier, j'ai pris les skis de ma mère.

ALAIN Et tu ne les as pas cassés?

PATRICK On non non! J'ai été prudent. Je suis resté sur la piste jaune. De toute façon, j'ai encore mal à la jambe depuis dimanche. Hier, j'ai fait quatre ou cinq descentes, puis à 3 heures, je suis allé boire un chocolat au chalet du Ski Club. J'y ai vu la sœur de Chabot.

ALAIN Jacqueline?

PATRICK Oui, on a parlé un peu. Elle est assez sympa! Elle n'avait pas trop envie d'aller se casser une jambe sur les pistes, elle non plus, alors on a pris un autre chocolat et on est restés là jusqu'à l'heure du bus.

CHAPITRE 16

Practice with the vocabulary of the unit (11)

1. Listening Comprehension Exercise

We are paying a visit to the Bouvier's farm. But nobody is home except old Grandfather Bouvier. Everybody else is out somewhere, working. If we want to see the rest of the family, we will have to find out from Grandfather Bouvier where everybody else is.

Grandfather Bouvier is very old. He is in his nineties. What he says is not always perfectly clear, but if we pay attention, we should be able to figure out from what he says where each member of the family is. It shouldn't be too hard because, though he does not speak too clearly, he tends to repeat himself quite a bit and that may be a help. Even so, it will help you to know *who* the members of the family are. So look at the picture you have in front of you. First, of course, there is old Grandfather Bouvier. No problem about him. He is at home. Then there is the grandmother, then Mr. and Mrs. Bouvier, Uncle Victor, and the five children: three boys (Charles, René, and Petit Louis) and two girls (Marie-Louise and Josiane). It will also help to have in mind the different places where they could be. The places are represented on your answer page by boxes, six of them. As you see, any member of the family can be *au champ, au pré, à la grange, à l'étable, au jardin, sous le hangar.*

So now listen, and try to figure out where everyone is. Indicate it on the page by drawing a line between each person and the place where he or she is.

LE VISITEUR Bonjour Grand-Père! Ça va?

LE GRAND-PÈRE Ça va! . . . Ça va . . . heu, pas trop non.

LE VISITEUR	Vous êtes tout seul? Où est tout le monde?
LE GRAND-PÈRE	Ouais . . . je suis tout seul. Tout le monde est parti, tout le monde travaille . . . Y a que moi qui travaille pas[1]! Je suis trop vieux. Qu'est-ce que vous voulez! Ce sont les jambes! . . . les rhumatismes . . . C'est l'âge . . . Je peux rien faire . . . suis plus bon à rien!
LE VISITEUR	Mais si, vous gardez la maison!
LE GRAND-PÈRE	Oh, garder la maison . . . garder la maison . . . C'est pas moi qui garde la maison, c'est Farou . . . Là, là! Couché, Farou! Oui, oui, tu es un bon chien.
LE VISITEUR	Et la grand-mère, elle est là? Elle va bien?
LE GRAND-PÈRE	Oh, elle! Elle va bien, oui. Elle est jeune, elle. Elle travaille.
LE VISITEUR	Où est-ce qu'elle est en ce moment?
LE GRAND-PÈRE	Aux moutons . . . Elle garde les moutons. Oui!
LE VISITEUR	Et Monsieur Bouvier, il est là?
LE GRAND-PÈRE	Non, il est pas là! Il fait les foins, avec le voisin. Oui! Y a le voisin qui l'aide à faire les foins . . . c'est qu'il y a du travail pour faire les foins! Et moi, je peux plus l'aider . . . je suis trop vieux! Autrefois je faisais les foins . . . maintenant je peux plus rien faire. C'est l'âge, qu'est-ce que vous voulez!
LE VISITEUR	Et l'oncle Victor, je peux le voir?
LE GRAND-PÈRE	Eh non! Il est pas là. Toujours à se promener! Il est jeune, lui! Il est allé voir si le blé est mûr, oui! L'est allé voir si le blé est assez mûr pour faire la moisson.
LE VISITEUR	Et Madame Bouvier, elle va bien?
LE GRAND-PÈRE	Oh oui. Elle est jeune, elle! Ça va!
LE VISITEUR	Elle n'est pas là non plus?
LE GRAND-PÈRE	Non, elle n'est pas là. Mais elle n'est pas loin. Elle est en train de planter des tomates. Ouais . . . vous la trouverez en train de planter ses tomates.
LE VISITEUR	Et les enfants ça va?
LE GRAND-PÈRE	Oh, oui, les enfants . . . ça va! Ils sont jeunes, eux! Ils sont jamais là!
LE VISITEUR	Où est Marie-Louise?
LE GRAND-PÈRE	Marie-Louise? Elle est en train de traire les vaches. Oui! C'est une brave petite, oui! Elle travaille toute la journée! C'est toujours elle qui trait les vaches . . . Moi, je ne peux plus, traire les vaches . . . ! Suis trop vieux, qu'est-ce que vous voulez! Je ne suis plus bon à rien!
LE VISITEUR	Et René, qu'est-ce qu'il fait?
LE GRAND-PÈRE	Oh, lui, ça va! Il est jeune, lui, il peut travailler! Il est en train de faire la litière des vaches. Seulement on n'a plus beaucoup de paille en cette saison.
LE VISITEUR	Et Petit Louis? Il va bien?
LE GRAND-PÈRE	Oh lui, oui! Qu'est-ce que vous voulez, il est jeune! Les jeunes ça va toujours bien! Ce n'est pas comme moi! Il est allé chercher du foin pour le cheval, Petit Louis. C'est lui qui s'occupe du cheval. Il va lui chercher du foin. C'est du foin de l'année dernière. Il nous en reste encore pas mal de l'année dernière. Voilà, où il est, Petit Louis: il est allé chercher du foin.
LE VISITEUR	Et Charles, il est toujours là?
LE GRAND-PÈRE	Il est à côté, là. Il est en train de réparer le vieux tracteur. Tenez, c'est lui là, vous l'entendez? Ça fait deux jours qu'il y travaille sur le vieux tracteur! Je ne sais pas ce qui ne marche pas! le carburateur, ou la transmission . . .
LE VISITEUR	Et Josiane?
LE GRAND-PÈRE	Oh Josiane! Elle, ça va! Elle est en train de cueillir des haricots verts. C'est elle qui s'occupe de la cuisine. Elle aide bien sa mère! Elle travaille . . . ! Qu'est-ce que vous voulez? Elle est jeune! Ce n'est pas comme moi!

[1] This transcription reflects the slurring that takes place in actual speech. (For instance, the word *ne* is omitted in most negative sentences.)

2. Speaking Exercise

Now let's see if you got it all right. Let's see if you can tell where everybody is. For example, if you are asked: *Où est le grand-père Bouvier?* you can answer: *A la maison, il est à la maison.* You could also try to say what everybody does if you wish . . . and if you can remember. For example, for the grandfather you can say, *Il est à la maison . . . Il ne travaille pas. Il ne fait rien!* Let's try.

1. Où est la grand-mère? (   ) *Elle est au pré. Elle garde les moutons.*
2. Où est M. Bouvier? (   ) *Il est au pré. Il fait les foins.*
3. Où est l'oncle Victor? (   ) *Il est au champ. Il regarde si le blé est mûr.*
4. Où est Marie-Louise? (   ) *Elle est à l'étable. Elle trait les vaches.*
5. Où est René? (   ) *Il est à l'étable. Il fait la litière des vaches.*
6. Où est Petit Louis? Qu'est-ce qu'il est allé chercher? (   ) *Il est à la grange. Il est allé chercher du foin pour le cheval.*
7. Où est Charles? (   ) *Il est sous le hangar. Il répare le vieux tracteur.*
8. Où est Josiane? (   ) *Elle est au jardin. Elle cueille des haricots verts.*
9. Où est Madame Bouvier? (   ) *Elle est au jardin. Elle plante des tomates.*

3. Reading Exercise

We saw in Units 14 and 15 that the letter **t** followed by the letter **i** was often pronounced [s].
We saw in Unit 14 that this was true for many nouns that end in **t-i-o-n.** You remember such nouns as these in number 1:

1. composition   sonorisation   attention
répétition   collection   exposition

Yet not all words with **t-i-o-n** at the end are pronounced that way. Take, for example, the words in number 2. How do you pronounce them?

2. nous partions   nous sortions

We do have a **t-i-o-n** spelling in these words, but the **t** is not pronounced [s]. It is pronounced [t]. How are these words different from the nouns in number 1? (   ) Well, they do have an **s** at the end. True, but that's not what makes them different. We could have the nouns in number 1 in the plural, and then they would have an **s** at the end too! Look at number 3.

3. des compositions   des collections
des répétitions   des expositions

The **t** is still pronounced [s]. So the final **s** makes no difference. What then is the big difference between the words in 1 and those in 2? The words in 1 are nouns. What about the words in 2? Are they nouns? (   ) No, they are verbs. *Nous partions* and *nous sortions* are forms of the imperfect tense of the verbs *partir* and *sortir*. That's what makes the difference. A letter **t** pronounced [t] at the end of a verb will still be pronounced [t] when followed by the ending of the imperfect, **i-o-n-s.** So, we have **t-i-o-n-s** endings that are pronounced [sjõ] and others that are pronounced [tjõ]. This leads to a rather curious oddity: You can find words that are spelled exactly alike, that *look* exactly the same, but that are pronounced differently. Look for example at number 4:

4. nous inventions   des inventions

Nous inventions is a verb—the imperfect of the verb *inventer*. Therefore, the **t** is pronounced [t]: *nous inventions*. But *des inventions* is a noun. So **t** is pronounced [s]: *des inventions*. The same thing is true for *nous portions, des portions*. We say *nous portions*, but *des portions*. Here *nous portions* is the imperfect of the verb *porter,* and *des portions* is a noun. Note that there is no connection between the meaning of this verb and noun as there was between *inventer* and *invention* or as there is in *nous inspections* and *des inspections* or *nous options* and *des options. Nous inspections* is the imperfect of the verb *inspecter,* and *nous options* is the imperfect of the verb *opter*. In the next lesson we will look more closely at these imperfect endings—at how they are spelled and how they sound.

4. Listening Comprehension Exercise

Grandfather Bouvier does not leave the house, but from his armchair near the window he sees everything. Nothing escapes him. So, if you want to know what's happening on this farm, just ask him. From what he tells you, you should be able to figure out where everybody went and what they did.

Let's try it with Petit Louis. Petit Louis has been busy feeding the animals. By using what his grandfather says, you should be able to guess which animals he fed and in which order he did it.

Do you see Petit Louis in the picture in your *Activity Book?* Do you see the five dots—one for Petit Louis, one for the horse, one for the rabbit, one for the cat, one for the chicken? Now listen to what his grandfather says, and draw a line from one dot to the other to show where Petit Louis went. Your starting point, of course, is the dot for Petit Louis.

Le Visiteur	Grand-Père, tu as vu Petit Louis?
Grand-Père	Oui, je l'ai vu. D'abord je l'ai vu passer avec des carottes et de l'herbe. Oui, il portait des carottes et de l'herbe. Ensuite je l'ai vu passer avec du foin et de l'avoine. Ouais, ouais il portait du foin et aussi de l'avoine. Après il est passé avec du maïs. Et puis après il est passé avec du lait.
Le Visiteur	Du lait?
Grand-Père	Oui, oui, du lait. Il portait du lait dans une tasse.

5. Speaking Exercise

Let's see how well you understood *Grand-Père*. Try to answer the questions.

A qui est-ce que Petit Louis a porté les carottes et l'herbe? Aux poules? Non! On ne donne pas d'herbe aux poules... ni de carottes d'ailleurs. Alors à qui est-ce qu'il a porté l'herbe et les carottes? *Au lapin! Oui.* A qui est-ce qu'il a porté le foin et l'avoine? Mais non, pas aux poules! L'avoine, peut-être. On peut donner de l'avoine aux poules, oui! mais on ne leur donne pas de foin. Qui est-ce qui peut manger de l'avoine et aussi du foin? *Le cheval! Oui! Il a porté l'avoine et le foin au cheval.* Et le lait alors? A qui est-ce qu'il a porté le lait? *Au chat, sûrement!*

Preparation for Conversation Exercise 34

6. Listening Exercise

Madeleine Signoret and Brigitte Flon are talking in a sidewalk café on the *Boulevard Saint-Michel*. They are both students at the *Sorbonne*. They are old friends because they used to be together at the *lycée*

Fénelon when they both were in "6ᵉ." They like to talk about those years. Let's listen in! It's not very polite, but I don't think they will mind... even if they find out! They are good friends of mine.

B.F.   Je passais mes vacances en Normandie, au bord de la mer. Mes parents avaient une petite maison, tout près de la plage.

M.S.   Moi, non! Je passais toutes mes vacances en Sologne. Chez mes grands-parents... ils avaient une ferme.

B.F.   C'était bien? Tu t'amusais?

M.S.   Oui j'aimais bien! Je travaillais dans les champs. J'aidais mes grands-parents. Je m'occupais des animaux. Ils avaient des lapins et des tas de poulets. J'allais leur porter du grain tous les matins. Ils me connaissaient. Ils venaient manger le grain dans ma main. Et puis j'aimais bien quand on faisait les foins. Je montais sur les charrettes pleines de foin pour revenir à la ferme, c'était bien! C'était très confortable. Et puis c'était très haut, on voyait loin. Et puis, quelquefois, mon grand-père me laissait conduire le tracteur. J'aimais bien. C'était bien! C'était un gros tracteur—énorme! tu sais? Mon grand-père était gentil! Il me laissait faire tout ce que je voulais. Quelquefois je prenais le tracteur pour aller cueillir des mûres. Il y avait des tas de mûres délicieuses! Ma grand-mère faisait une confiture de mûres! Hmmm...

B.F.   Moi, je n'aime pas tellement les mûres. Ce que j'aime, ce sont les figues!

M.S.   Il n'y avait pas de figues. Je crois qu'il ne fait pas assez chaud en Sologne.

B.F.   Et des noisettes?

M.S.   Oui des noisettes, il y en a! mais elles n'étaient jamais mûres quand j'y étais. Je partais toujours en septembre... les noisettes n'étaient pas encore vraiment mûres. Les pommes et les poires non plus n'étaient pas mûres. Je partais trop tôt.

B.F.   Eh oui! Moi aussi, je rentrais toujours à Paris en septembre. C'est dommage parce qu'il y avait toujours de grosses tempêtes en septembre, et j'adorais ça. C'était formidable!

M.S.   Ouais! Tu as toujours été une grande romantique! Moi, je suis plutôt du type bucolique... les champs, les fleurs, les petits oiseaux...

CHAPITRE 17

*The spelling **ai** and the endings of the imperfect (14)*

1. Reading and Speaking Exercise

We said in Units 13 and 14 that **a-i** represents either the open [ɛ]-sound or the closed [e]-sound. French people are not entirely consistent in their use of [ɛ] as opposed to [e], but there are some general rules about what is pronounced [ɛ] and what is pronounced [e]. Let's look at the words in number 1 and say them.

1. martiniquais martiniquaise mauvais mauvaise
      faire   primaire   corsaire baigne
      aime   plaine   saison   naissance

In all the words above, the combination **a-i** represents the open [ɛ]-sound. Note that in these words the spelling **a-i** never occurs in a verb ending. Well, let's see what happens in verb endings. Let's say the words in number 2.

2. Il faisait beau. C'était fantastique!
    Je poursuivais des poissons. Ils allaient vite!
Here again, the spelling **a-i** represents the open [ε]-sound. Yet, watch what happens in 3.

3. J'ai un poisson! J'ai attrapé un poisson!

Here the **a-i** combination is at the end of a verb form, as in number 2, but this time the verb ends in just **a-i**; there is nothing else after the **i**. You heard a closed [e]-sound. Most French people will pronounce an [e]-sound in this instance. In conclusion, you could say that **a-i** represents the [ε]-sound except in verb endings that are just **a-i,** with no other letter after the **i**. In the latter instance, the spelling represents the [e]-sound. Let's see whether you got it straight. Say aloud what you see in number 4.

4. J'ai fait du bateau dans la baie.
    Mais c'est vraiment la mauvaise saison pour se baigner!
    Il fait plutôt frais!
    J'ai eu froid pendant que je me baignais.
    Il y avait du vent.
    Les vagues étaient énormes.

Note that in the endings of the imperfect, **a-i** is always followed by something else. It is always pronounced [ε] (open [ε]). Look at number 5.

5. J'allais à la pêche. Il allait à la pêche.
    Tu allais à la pêche. Elles allaient à la pêche.

Let's now have a look at the other two endings of the imperfect, which are shown in 6.

6. *Imperfect* *Present*
    Nous allions à la pêche. Nous allons à la pêche.
    Vous alliez à la pêche. Vous allez à la pêche.

Compare these endings with the endings of the present:
    Nous allions Nous allons
    Vous alliez Vous allez

Do you hear the difference between the two? There is a [j]-sound in the imperfect that is not there in the present. That's the way you can tell whether the verb is in the present or in the imperfect.

Discrimination between present and past (20)

2. Listening Comprehension Exercise

It's always important to know whether someone is talking in the present or in the past. For example, it does make a difference whether one says "I am rich" or "I was rich." How can you tell present from past? One way is to watch for words that indicate time. For example, if you hear *en ce moment* or *maintenant,* chances are that the speaker is referring to the present. If you hear *autrefois, ce jour-là, hier,* or *hier soir,* chances are that the speaker is referring to the past.

But there are words referring to time that don't tell you for sure whether the sentence is in the present or the past. Take the sentences in number 1, for example. If you hear: *Il fait beau aujourd'hui,* the speaker is referring to the present. But if you hear: *Je me suis levé tôt aujourd'hui,* the speaker is referring to the past, though the same word, *aujourd'hui,* is used.

1. Il fait beau aujourd'hui.
    Je me suis levé tôt aujourd'hui.

Look at number 2.

2. *Past* *Present* *Variable*
    hier maintenant aujourd'hui
    autrefois en ce moment alors
    ce jour-là   déjà
    lundi dernier   cette semaine

If you hear *hier, autrefois, ce jour-là,* or *lundi dernier,* you may be pretty sure that the speaker is talking about the past. If you hear *maintenant* or *en ce moment,* chances are that it is about the present. But if you hear *aujourd'hui, alors, déjà,* or *cette semaine,* then you can't be sure. You had better look for some other clues. The best place to look for clues is the verb. The easiest verb tense to recognize is the *passé composé,* because the verb is made up of two parts. There is the past participle, which identifies the verb, and in front of it the auxiliary, a form of *avoir* or *être: J'ai dormi, je me suis réveillé, nous sommes partis.* However, if the verb is in the imperfect, it may be more difficult for you to identify. You will have to go by the endings. If you hear a [jõ] or [je] ending, such as *nous faisions du bateau* or *vous pêchiez?* chances are that the verb is in the imperfect. In most verbs you hear the difference quite clearly between the present *(nous faisons du bateau)* and the imperfect *(nous faisions du bateau).* But it becomes a bit trickier with verbs that already have the sound [i] or [j] just before the ending. Let's try a few. Look at number 3.

3. *Present*

Vous oubliez tout!
Nous vérifions tout.

Vous travaillez trop!
Nous nous réveillons tôt.

Nous essayons!
Vous croyez ça?
Qu'est-ce que vous voyez?

Imperfect

Vous oubliiez tout!
Nous vérifiions.

Vous travailliez trop!
Nous nous réveillions tôt.

Nous essayions!
Vous croyiez ça?
Qu'est-ce que vous voyiez?

There is a difference. But there isn't much!

Now, what if you hear an [ɛ]-sound at the end? Well, chances are that the verb is in the imperfect, though there are a few verbs that end with an [ɛ]-sound in the present, such as those in number 4.

4. **savoir**	**faire**	**essayer**	**aller**
je sais	je fais	j'essaie	je vais
tu sais	tu fais	tu essaies	
il sait	il fait	il essaie	
		ils essaient	

So, if it is not the verb *savoir,* or *aller (je vais),* or a verb with the infinitive in **a-i-r-e** or in **a-y-e-r,** then a verb form that ends with the [ɛ]-sound is probably in the imperfect.

Somewhat troublesome are forms ending with the sound [e], as in number 5.

5. vous savez   vous avez   vous pêchez

When you just hear those forms, how can you tell they are not in the imperfect? Compare the examples in number 6.

6. *Present*	*Imperfect*	*Present*	*Imperfect*
	je savais		je pêchais
vous savez	tu savais	vous pêchez	tu pêchais
	elle savait		il pêchait
	ils savaient		elles pêchaient

Now let's see how good you really are at deciding whether a verb in a sentence is in the present or the imperfect. Look out for the words that tell time, if there are any, and above all watch for the forms of the verb. Is the verb one word or in two parts? Is the verb ending pronounced [e] or [ɛ]? Is it a *vous*-form or not? Listen and check the proper box.

1. Ils se sont baignés.
2. Vous nous attendez?
3. Je ne me suis pas baigné aujourd'hui.

4. Vous nous attendiez?
5. Autrefois nous skiions beaucoup.
6. Qu'est-ce que vous vérifiez maintenant?

7. En ce moment nous nous réveillons très tôt.
8. Pourquoi est-ce que vous riiez comme ça hier, au cours de maths?
9. Vous ne pouviez pas vous arrêter.
10. Il ne savait pas nager.
11. Ils attrapaient beaucoup de poissons.
12. Qu'est-ce que vous avez attrapé?
13. Vous attrapiez des langoustes?
14. La semaine dernière, nous essayions de travailler.
15. Pourquoi est-ce que tu n'essaies pas?

	1	2	3	4	5	6	7	8	9	10	11	12	13	14	15
Present															
Past															

Practice with the vocabulary of the unit (26)

3. Listening Comprehension Exercise

In this exercise, you will hear Doris talking with her friend Claude, who has just arrived in Martinique from metropolitan France. Doris is showing her some pictures that she took on an excursion around the island.

The pictures are shown on the page in front of you. Unfortunately, they are not in order, so you may have a little trouble finding them. So, listen to what the two girls say, and try to identify the pictures they are talking about. Before you begin, you should have a quick look at each of the ten pictures.

Now listen to the two girls talking. Figure out which picture they are discussing, and write the number of each comment or brief dialog below the picture it matches. Let's begin.

1. D'abord, on est allés au marché pour acheter des provisions. Ça, c'est une femme qui vendait des légumes et des fruits. Elle avait un gros tas d'oranges devant elle par terre.

2. DORIS   Ça aussi, c'est au marché. C'est une femme qui vendait des anthuriums.
   CLAUDE   Des anthuriums? Qu'est-ce que c'est?
   DORIS   Ce sont de grandes fleurs, en forme de cône. C'est très joli. Il y a beaucoup de fleurs à la Martinique, tu sais, mais celle-là, c'est celle qu'on voit le plus souvent. Il y en a en toute saison.

3. Ça, c'est encore au marché. C'est un homme qui vendait du poisson. C'était sûrement un pêcheur. Il vendait le poisson qu'il avait attrapé. Il avait un gros poisson sur une petite table en bois.

4. DORIS   Ça, c'est une plage où on s'est arrêtés pour déjeuner.
   CLAUDE   C'est très joli. C'est votre bateau?
   DORIS   Non, c'est celui d'un pêcheur.
   CLAUDE   C'est celui de M. Daquin?
   DORIS   Oui, c'est ça.

5. DORIS   Ça, c'est mon petit frère. Quand on s'est arrêtés pour déjeuner sur cette plage, lui, tout de suite, il est allé à la pêche (il va tout le temps à la pêche, mon petit frère). Et il a attrapé un petit poisson. Il n'était pas bien gros, le poisson, mais il était tout content (mon petit frère, pas le poisson!)

CLAUDE Vous l'avez mangé?
DORIS Mon petit frère?
CLAUDE Non, le poisson!
DORIS Oui, bien sûr, on l'a mangé, le soir, quand on est rentrés à la maison.

6. CLAUDE Et ça, qui c'est? C'est ton père?
DORIS Non, c'est un pêcheur du village qui revenait de la pêche.
CLAUDE Qu'est-ce qu'il tient? Ce n'est pas un poisson?
DORIS Non, c'est une pieuvre, une grosse pieuvre.
CLAUDE Pouah!
DORIS Pourquoi « Pouah »? Ce n'est pas joli, mais c'est très bon.
CLAUDE Tu en as mangé?
DORIS Bien sûr, que j'en ai mangé. Quand c'est bien préparé, c'est délicieux.

7. DORIS Ça c'est à Saint-Pierre. C'est l'église.
CLAUDE L'église? Où est-ce que tu vois une église? Il n'y a pas d'église.
DORIS Non, mais c'est là qu'elle était. Tu sais bien que toute la ville de Saint-Pierre a été détruite en 1902 par une éruption de la Montagne Pelée! L'église a été complètement détruite avec le reste de la ville. Il ne reste que quelques marches d'escalier, des morceaux de colonnes et de gros blocs de pierre.

8. CLAUDE Ça c'est toi!
DORIS Oui, c'est moi.
CLAUDE Je ne savais pas que tu jouais de la flûte.
DORIS Mais je ne joue pas de la flûte, que tu es bête!
CLAUDE Tu ne joues pas de la flûte? Mais qu'est-ce que tu fais alors? Ce n'est pas une flûte que tu tiens?
DORIS Mais non, ce n'est pas une flûte, c'est un morceau de canne à sucre. Je suis en train de boire le jus de canne.
CLAUDE C'est bon?
DORIS Oui, ce n'est pas mauvais! C'est sucré, c'est frais. Quand on a soif, c'est bon.

Now check your answers. The numbers next to the pictures should read from left to right: *3, 6, 5, 8, 2, 1, 4, 7.*

Preparation for Conversation Exercise 25

4. Speaking Exercise

Now that you have identified and numbered these pictures, you will be asked a few questions about them. We will do them in order, starting with number 1. Can you find number 1? Do you have it? Here we go.

1. Où est-ce que c'est? Sur la plage? (   ) *Non, c'est au marché.* Qu'est-ce qu'elle vend, cette femme? (   ) *Des fruits et des légumes.*

2. Et celle-là, qu'est-ce qu'elle vend? des légumes? (   ) *Non, elle vend des fleurs.*
3. Ça c'est un pêcheur. Où est-ce qu'il est ce pêcheur? Sur son bateau? (   ) *Non, il est au marché.* Qu'est-ce qu'il vend? (   ) *Du poisson.*
4. Où est ce bateau? Sur la mer? (   ) *Non, il est sur la plage.*
5. Qu'est-ce que le petit frère de Doris a attrapé? (   ) *Un poisson. Il a attrapé un petit poisson.*
6. Et ça, c'est le petit frère de Doris? (   ) *Non, c'est un pêcheur.* Qu'est-ce qu'il a attrapé? (   ) *Une pieuvre.*
7. Qu'est-ce qui est arrivé à l'église de Saint-Pierre? (   ) *Elle a été détruite par une éruption volcanique.*
8. Qu'est-ce que Doris tient, sur cette photo? C'est une flûte? (   ) *Non, c'est un morceau de canne à sucre.*

CHAPITRE 18

The circumflex accent (1)

1. Reading Exercise

You have noticed that vowel letters are often written with accents over them. In Unit 4, for example, we discussed acute and grave accents, which are often found on the letter **e,** as in the word *élève* in number 1.

1. élève

Now look at the words in 2.

2. se dépêcher   s'arrêter
une pêche   rêver
pêcher   un pêcheur
la pêche

You notice an accent on these words, which is neither an acute nor a grave accent. It is called a circumflex accent. What does that accent mean to us? Well, it may tell us several things. Let's first observe the sound of the vowel marked with this accent in the following words in number 3.

3. Alors, quoi, tu te dépêches?   Tu rêves!

Compare, for example, the two vowel sounds represented by the letter **e** in *dépêches.* Are they the same? The first one is marked with an acute accent. It is a closed [e]. The second, which is marked with a circumflex accent, is more open and longer. A circumflex accent over an **e,** then, indicates that this **e** is pronounced as an open [ɛ], just as if it had a grave accent.

Let's practice with the words in number 4. Make sure to pronounce the **e**-circumflex as open [ɛ].

4. A quoi tu rêves?   Oui, je me dépêche!
Tu as mis tes vêtements de pêche?   Arrête-toi, quand même!

Now look at the words in number 5.

5. Nous avons dîné très tôt.   Il y avait un très bon gâteau.   Bien sûr, il faut connaître.

You can see that the circumflex can be found on vowels other than **e.** It can be found on **a, i, o,** or **u,** as well as **e.**

Let's first have a look at the letter **o** with a circumflex accent. Compare the two sentences in number 6.

6. C'est notre bateau.   C'est le nôtre.

The first *notre* is written without any accent. The second is written with a circumflex accent. Why?

Well, they are not exactly the same words. As a matter of fact, they don't sound the same. Listen: *C'est notre bateau. C'est le nôtre.* The **o** in the second sentence is longer, and also has a different sound: *notre, nôtre.* The circumflex accent helps us to distinguish between these two words, which have the same letters and yet are different words. One is an adjective—*notre bateau*—and the other is a pronoun —*le nôtre.*

Now look at the words in number 7.

> **7.** François est sur la plage?
> Oui, je suis sûr qu'il est sur la plage.

Here you have two words **s-u-r.** They are spelled alike (except for the circumflex accent), and they sound alike. Yet they are two different words. In the phrase *sur la plage, sur* is a preposition. In the phrase *je suis sûr, sûr* is an adjective. The distinction between the two is marked by placing a circumflex accent over the **u** of the adjective.

In number 8, we have still another example.

> **8.** Le raisin qui est contre le mur est mûr.

Here again we have two words that sound and look alike, except for the circumflex accent. Yet they are two totally different words. The distinction is marked, in writing, by placing a circumflex accent on the **u** of one of them.

In conclusion, you might say that the circumflex accent is sometimes used to distinguish between two words that would have been spelled exactly the same without that accent, but are in fact two different words. But the circumflex accent in certain words can tell us something else. Let's have a look at the words in number 9.

> **9.** une tempête   une forêt   un hôpital

Do these words look somewhat like English words you know? Let's compare the French word *tempête* and the English word "tempest," for example. What's the main difference? There is an **s** in the English word that is not in the French word. The French word has a circumflex accent instead. It is the same with *forêt* and "forest," *hôpital* and "hospital." Now let's look at the words in number 10.

> **10.** La côte   le rôti

What English word is close to the French *côte?* "Coast," spelled: **c-o-a-s-t.** And what is close to *rôti?* The word "roast," **r-o-a-s-t.** Here the resemblance between the English and the French words is not as close, but here, as in number 9, the circumflex accent in the French word corresponds to an **s** in the English word.

There are many words like that. Why? Because these English and French words have a common origin. In most instances, English borrowed the word from French at a time when the French word still had an **s.** Since that time, the French word has evolved, the **s** has disappeared, and its place is marked by a circumflex accent. In English, however, the **s** has remained in both the pronunciation and the spelling.

Now, this little piece of historical information may be quite useful to you. Suppose you are reading French and you find an unfamiliar word spelled with a circumflex accent. It may be one of those words in which the circumflex accent replaces an **s** that is still preserved in the English word. So you could try to put that **s** back (after the vowel with the circumflex accent). Then say the word to see whether it reminds you of some English word. If it does, chances are that the French word is related to the English word and that its meaning is also related. But remember that "related" does not mean "the same"! You will have to go by the context to figure out what the meaning really is. Look at the words in number 11, and try to find English words related to the French words.

> **11.** un mât   la hâte   une râpe   un hôte   une fête
> la pâte   une bête

2. Listening and Writing Exercise

You will hear fourteen sentences. For each sentence you hear, you have, in number 2, an incomplete sentence that corresponds to it. The sentence you see can be completed with one of the words contained in the sentence you heard. Decide which word it is, and fill in the blank. The words to be used in the blanks are listed below in alphabetical order. Let's have a quick look at them.

bête — bêtes — fête — fêter — hâte — hôtes — mât — pâte — pâtes — râpé

1. Il ne se dépêchait pas mais quand on lui a dit que Catherine l'attendait il est parti en hâte. Il est parti en _____.
2. Nous avons vu passer un gros bateau avec trois mâts. Il avait un grand _____ et deux _____ plus petits.
3. Je ne peux pas me brosser les dents; je n'ai pas de pâte dentifrice! Il faudra acheter de la _____ dentifrice!
4. Qu'est-ce que c'est que cette pâte? C'est pour faire un gâteau? Non, c'est pour faire du pain. C'est de la _____ à pain.
5. Tu aimes les pâtes? Oui, mais je n'aime pas trop les macaronis; je préfère les spaghettis. En Italie on mange des _____ presque tous les jours!
6. Passe-moi la râpe à fromage, je vais râper du fromage pour les spaghettis. J'aime le fromage _____ sur les pâtes.
7. Nous avons passé une semaine dans une famille en Angleterre. Nos hôtes s'appelaient Smith, et ils étaient anglais, évidemment. Nos _____ nous ont très bien reçus!
8. Nous sommes allés à la fête du village. Nous avons dansé une partie de la nuit. Il y a toujours un bal pour la _____ du village.
9. La fête nationale est le 14 juillet. C'est la _____ nationale.
10. Regarde j'ai fait un gâteau pour maman! C'est sa fête? C'est la _____ des mères.
11. Nous fêtons l'anniversaire de Claire. Elle a 14 ans aujourd'hui! Il faut _____ son anniversaire!
12. Quand on a une ferme, il y a beaucoup de travail. Il faut s'occuper des bêtes. Il faut s'occuper des _____ tous les jours.
13. Camper, coucher sous la tente, c'est très bien; mais il y a toujours des petites bêtes qui entrent dans la tente et qui courent partout. Il y a même des petites _____ qui rentrent dans votre sac de couchage! Moi, je n'aime pas ça du tout!
14. Catherine n'est pas plus bête que sa sœur! Elle est peut-être même plus intelligente qu'elle! Elle n'est pas _____ du tout!

Now check your answers. *Read each sentence again and give the correct answer.*

Practice with the vocabulary of the unit (9)

3. Listening and Speaking Exercise

The six pictures you see in your *Activity Book* relate to the experiences of François and his friends in the sailing camp where they spend their vacation. Listen to the questions and then answer each one, making use of the information suggested by the corresponding picture.

1. Qu'est-ce que les camarades de François ont fait pendant la nuit? (   ) *Ils ont dormi (à poings fermés) sous la tente.*
2. François, lui, n'a pas passé la nuit sous la tente. Il a passé la nuit tout en haut du sémaphore. Qu'est-ce qu'il a fait? (   ) *Il a regardé les étoiles . . .*
3. Mais le lendemain, François a dormi sous la tente. Est-ce qu'il a eu froid? (   ) *Non, il avait son sac de couchage.*
4. « Aïe, aïe! Au secours! » Pourquoi est-ce que François est sorti de la tente en criant « au secours »? (   ) *Il y avait une vipère!*
5. Qu'est-ce que François a fait le matin en se levant? (   ) *Il est allé se laver à la pompe.*
6. Et puis après, qu'est-ce qu'il est allé faire? (   ) *Il est allé faire de la voile.*

T146

Preparation for Conversation Exercise 18

4. Listening Exercise

MARIE-CHRISTINE	Tiens! c'est toi, Lefèvre! Tu ne me reconnais pas?
MARTINE	Attends . . . je ne vois pas.
MARIE-CHRISTINE	Mais si, voyons! . . . Cherche un peu. Tu vas te rappeler! Tu n'étais pas au lycée Fénelon, en 6ᵉ?
MARTINE	Si. Tu y étais aussi?
MARIE-CHRISTINE	Oui. Il y avait aussi Delphine Brunoy, et Blanchette Raynaud . . . Tu ne te rappelles pas? Blanchette Raynaud qui achetait toujours des disques de musique pop . . . Et Madeleine Signoret qui faisait du cheval . . . en vacances parce que son père avait une ferme en Sologne! Moi j'étais très amie avec Suzanne Simon. Nous jouions au tennis ensemble.
MARTINE	Oui, ça, je me rappelle Suzanne Simon. Elle était blonde, avec de longs cheveux . . . et elle avait une mère qui était dentiste.
MARIE-CHRISTINE	Tu ne te rappelles pas, un dimanche on est allées dans la Forêt de Fontainebleau ensemble, à vélo. On était parties à 5 ou 6 heures du matin pour être sûres d'être à Fontainebleau pour pique-niquer à midi. Il faisait beau! Il faisait chaud. C'était au mois de juin, je crois. Il y avait des fleurs partout.
MARTINE	Ben non, je ne me rappelle pas!
MARIE-CHRISTINE	Une autre fois, les parents de Brigitte Leroy nous ont invitées à aller passer le weekend dans leur maison au bord de la mer, en Normandie. Il faisait un froid! C'était à Pâques,

je crois, au mois de mars ou d'avril. On est allées faire une promenade en bateau. Il y avait du vent!... des vagues... comme des maisons! Terrible! La tempête, quoi! Tu étais malade!...

MARTINE   Moi, je n'ai jamais été malade en mer... d'ailleurs, je ne suis jamais allée sur un bateau de ma vie, je t'assure!

MARIE-CHRISTINE   Allons, voyons! Rappelle-toi! Pendant les vacances d'été, on est allées chez Madeleine Signoret, dans sa ferme, en Sologne. On mangeait du poulet et des carottes tous les jours. Ils avaient un jardin plein de carottes. Et on buvait du lait. Tu étais malade toutes les nuits, parce que tu buvais trop de lait.

MARTINE   C'est pas possible. Je n'aime pas le lait. Je n'en bois jamais.

MARIE-CHRISTINE   Mais si, voyons! On faisait du cheval. Mais ils n'avaient qu'un cheval... Un vieux cheval fatigué. Alors, il y en avait une qui faisait du cheval dans la cour de la ferme pendant que les autres attendaient leur tour. On tricotait pour s'occuper. Et même un jour, tu es tombée de cheval, tu t'es cassé la jambe. On t'a amenée à l'hôpital de Bourges. Et on ne t'a jamais revue.

MARTINE   Ah bon, maintenant, je comprends. Ce n'est pas moi, c'est ma cousine...

MARIE-CHRISTINE   Comment, tu n'es pas Claudia Lefèvre?

MARTINE   Non, Claudia, c'est ma cousine. Elle a été à Fénelon aussi, mais deux ans avant moi! Moi, je suis Martine Lefèvre!

MARIE-CHRISTINE   Ah, c'est pour ça! Je me disais aussi! C'est extraordinaire comme tu ressembles à Claudia!

MARTINE   Ce n'est pas étonnant, puisque c'est ma cousine!

CHAPITRE 19

The spelling **gn** *(1)*

1. Reading and Speaking Exercise

Look at the words in number 1, and listen to how they are pronounced:

       1. enseigner   compagnie

In these words, the letter **g** does not represent the sound [g], because it is followed by the letter **n.** The combination of **g** and **n** represents the sound [ɲ]. No [g]-sound is heard. This is generally true, except for a very few rather learned words which we won't need to bother with. Let's practice saying the words in number 2. Make sure you pronounce the **g-n** combination as [ɲ], without any [g] sound.

2. Vous avez gagné.	éteignez	en Allemagne
Nous nous baignons.	un agneau	en Espagne
un peigne	une compagnie aérienne	les Espagnols
des renseignements		

Now suppose you are in a restaurant. With your best French accent, you order the dishes listed in number 3:

       3. Un filet-mignon!   Des rognons d'agneau!   Des champignons!

Now let's try some other French words. Look at number 4.

       4. Un signal lumineux!   Qu'est-ce que ça signifie?

            Mais, c'est magnifique!   C'est un système magnétique.

C'est ignoble!   C'est une ignominie!
C'est un ignorant!   Quelle dignité!

Practice with the vocabulary of the unit (1)

2. Listening Comprehension Exercise

You will hear ten statements. Decide whether each one refers to our friend, to our boat, or to a plane. Then put a check mark in the appropriate row. Let's begin.

1. C'est celui que nous devions prendre pour aller à Bruxelles, mais nous l'avons raté! (   ) *C'est l'avion d'Air France que nous avons raté!*
2. Il nous attend à côté du tableau des arrivées. (   ) *C'est notre ami qui nous attend!*
3. Nous l'avons tiré sur la plage pour réparer la voile. (   ) *Ça, c'est notre bateau.*
4. Il dormait à poings fermés. (   ) *C'est notre ami qui dormait!*
5. Il vient juste de décoller! (   ) *C'est l'avion d'Air France qui vient de décoller.*
6. Il est tellement bronzé que d'abord je ne l'ai pas reconnu! (   ) *C'est notre ami qui est bronzé.*
7. Nous l'avons acheté à un vieux pêcheur (   ) *Notre bateau.*
8. Il n'a pas pu atterrir à cause du brouillard. (   ) *C'est l'avion d'Air France qui n'a pas pu atterrir.*
9. Je l'ai rencontré à l'aéroport. (   ) *C'est notre ami que j'ai rencontré.*
10. Nous avons plongé parce qu'il s'est cassé contre les rochers. (   ) *C'est notre bateau qui s'est cassé contre les rochers.*

	1	2	3	4	5	6	7	8	9	10
notre ami										
notre bateau										
l'avion d'Air France										

Practice with geographical names and adjectives of nationality (24)

3. Listening Comprehension and Writing Exercise

You will hear a few statements about the people whose names appear on your *Activity Book* page. Try to guess what nationality each person is, and write it down under the name.

Lili   Françoise   Claudia   Paul

_____   _____   _____   _____

Gloria   Idris   Lisa   Andrea

_____   _____   _____   _____

Lili: Elle a toujours habité à Hambourg en Allemagne, mais ses parents sont nés à Berlin. Elle joue du violon; elle aime beaucoup Mozart et Schubert.

Françoise: Elle est née à Mons pas très loin de Bruxelles, savez-vous! Elle parle français évidemment, elle aime beaucoup la bière, les frites, les moules, et les endives.

Claudia: Elle habite à Londres, mais elle est née à Liverpool. Elle n'a jamais quitté l'Angleterre, ses parents non plus.

Paul: Il est né à Québec, mais maintenant sa famille est à Montréal. Il parle français.

Gloria: Elle est née à Barcelone, mais maintenant elle habite à Madrid. Ses parents sont andalous : ils viennent de Grenade en Andalousie.

Idris: Lui, il habite à Casablanca, mais ses parents sont nés à Rabat. Son père est exportateur de phosphates. Il est musulman, il parle français.

Lisa: Sa mère est vénitienne et son père florentin. Maintenant ils habitent à Rome, mais elle est née à Bologne.

Andrea: Elle est née dans le Maine, mais elle habite à Detroit. Son père travaille pour une compagnie qui fabrique des automobiles. Elle parle anglais.

4. Speaking Exercise

Now let's see how many you got right. Answer the questions:

1. Quelle est la nationalité de Lili? (   ) *Elle est allemande.*
2. Et Françoise, qu'est-ce qu'elle est? (   ) *Elle est Belge.*
3. Et Claudia? (   ) *Elle est anglaise.*
4. Et Paul, quelle nationalité a-t-il? (   ) *Canadienne. Il est Canadien.*
5. Et Gloria? (   ) *Elle est espagnole.*
6. Et Idris? (   ) *Il est marocain.*
7. Quelle est la nationalité de Lisa? (   ) *Italienne.*
8. Et Andrea? (   ) *Elle est américaine.*

5. Listening and Speaking Exercise

Of course, you realize that you cannot invent French. Yet, within certain limits, and if you go about it with prudence, you may be able to discover some French on your own. This is possible because French, like any other language, follows patterns — at least, up to a point.

In this discovery exercise, you will have the chance to observe such patterns, and to guess a few words that you have not yet encountered. We will start with things you know. The point is for you to discover the pattern or system. Then you can push on a little further to make some educated guesses.

You will be told that someone was born in a certain country. You will then say what nationality this person is, at least by birth. For example, you are told: *Il est né en France,* and you say: *Il est français.* Now watch it — if you hear: *Elle est née en France,* you say, of course: *Elle est française.* Then you will hear: *Il est né en Ecosse* and, following the pattern *France — français,* you will think "*Ecosse — écossais*" and you will say: *Il est écossais.* Let's see how far we can go with the *France — français* pattern.

Il est né au Sénégal. (   ) *Il est sénégalais.*
Elle est née au Sénégal. (   ) *Elle est sénégalaise.*
Elle est née en Ecosse. (   ) *Elle est écossaise.*
Elle est née en Irlande. (   ) *Elle est irlandaise.*
Il est né en Hollande. (   ) *Il est hollandais.*
Elle est née en Finlande. (   ) *Elle est finlandaise.*
Il est né en Thaïlande (   ) *Il est thaïlandais.*
Elle est née au Groënland (   ) *Elle est groënlandaise.*
Elle est née au Japon. (   ) *Elle est japonaise.*
Il est né au Liban. (   ) *Il est libanais.*
Il est né au Soudan. (   ) *Il est soudanais.* (Notice that the nasal sound at the end of *Liban, Soudan,* is no longer nasal when one adds a vowel at the end: *Liban — libanais, Soudan — soudanais.*)

Il est né en Iran. (   ) *Il est iranien.* Yes! *Il est iranien!* You see that you have to be cautious. You can trust a pattern only to a certain point. A given pattern will go only so far; it stops when another starts. *Il est né au Soudan. Il est soudanais.* But: *Il est né en Iran. Il est iranien.*

Il est né en Israël. (   ) *Il est israélien.*
Sophia Loren est née en Italie. (   ) *Elle est italienne.*
Bourguiba est né en Tunisie. (   ) *Il est tunisien.*
Elle est née en Lybie. (   ) *Elle est lybienne.*
Il est né en Ethiopie. (   ) *Il est éthiopien.*
Elle est née en Australie. (   ) *Elle est australienne.*
Il est né en Colombie. (   ) *Il est colombien.*
Elle est née en Bolivie. (   ) *Elle est bolivienne.*
Il est né au Brésil. (   ) *Il est brésilien.*
Elle est née en Autriche. (   ) *Elle est autrichienne.*
Elle est née en Norvège. (   ) *Elle est norvégienne.*
Il est né au Cambodge. (   ) *Il est cambodgien.*
Elle est née au Vietnam. (   ) *Elle est vietnamienne.*

Let's go to a third pattern: *Amérique — américain.*

Elle est née en Amérique. (   ) *Elle est américaine.*
Il est né au Maroc. (   ) *Il est marocain.*
Il est né en Afrique. (   ) *Il est africain.*
Elle est née au Mexique. (   ) *Elle est mexicaine.*
Il est né à Porto Rico. (   ) *Il est portoricain.*
Il est né à Costa Rica. (   ) *Il est costaricain.*
Elle est née à Cuba. (   ) *Elle est cubaine.*

Let's try a fourth one: *Turquie — turc.*

Il est né en Turquie. (   ) *Il est turc.*
Elle est née en Tchécoslovaquie. (   ) *Elle est Tchécoslovaque.*
Il est né en Yougoslavie. (   ) *Il est yougoslave.*
Elle est née en Bulgarie. (   ) *Elle est bulgare.*
Elle est née en Normandie. (   ) *Elle est normande.*
Il est né en Normandie. (   ) *Il est normand.*

We could even go a little further. For example: *Chine — chinois.*

Confucius et Mao sont nés en Chine. (   ) *Il sont chinois.*
Nobel, qui a inventé la dynamite, et Ingmar Bergman, le cinéaste, sont nés en Suède. (   ) *Ils sont suédois.*
Quelqu'un qui est né à Nice, sur la Côte d'Azur, est (   ) *niçoise.*
Et la salade qu'on fait à Nice, c'est la salade (   ) *niçoise.*

Preparation for Conversation Exercise 32

6. Listening Exercise

Listen to this boy and girl, who are talking in front of the *lycée* in Montpellier, in the South of France.

ISABELLE	Tu t'appelles Carlo?
CARLO	Oui, Carlo Adjani!
ISABELLE	Tu es italien, alors?
CARLO	Non, je suis français.
ISABELLE	Tu es né en France?
CARLO	Oui, je suis né à Marseille.
ISABELLE	Tes parents aussi?
CARLO	Ma mère oui, elle est née à Marseille, mais mon père est né à côté de Tunis.
ISABELLE	Ah! alors, il est Tunisien?
CARLO	Ben, oui . . . mais mon grand-père était italien. Il est né à Naples. Et toi tu t'appelles Isabelle?
ISABELLE	Oui, Isabelle Sanchez.
CARLO	Tu es espagnole?
ISABELLE	Non, pas vraiment. Mon père est algérien.
CARLO	Il s'appelle Sanchez et il est algérien?
ISABELLE	Eh bien oui! Il est né en Algérie, à Oran, mais ses parents, ou ses grands-parents, je ne sais plus, étaient espagnols.
CARLO	Et tu parles arabe ou espagnol?
ISABELLE	Non, moi je suis née en France! Et ma mère est née dans un petit port près de Lisbonne.
CARLO	Au Portugal?
ISABELLE	Oui.
CARLO	Alors, elle est portugáise?
ISABELLE	Oui.
CARLO	Et tu parles portugais?
ISABELLE	Oh . . . un peu, quelques mots. Et toi, tu parles italien?
CARLO	Oh . . . quelques mots. Ciao!
ISABELLE	Ciao!
CARLO	Tu sais l'italien?
ISABELLE	Oui, assez bien.
CARLO	Où est-ce que tu l'as appris?
ISABELLE	Au lycée!
CARLO	Moi, je fais de l'anglais . . . Allez, je m'en vais! Ciao!
ISABELLE	Goodbye!

CHAPITRE 20

The spelling **ill** *(3)*

1. Reading and Speaking Exercise

In Unit 13 you saw that in words like *je travaille, je me réville,* the spelling **i-l-l** represents the sound [j]. This is true whenever **i-l-l** is preceded by a vowel, and is therefore true for all the underlined words in number 1. Say these sentences, making sure to pronounce **i-l-l** as [j].

1. C'est une vieille histoire!

J'ai veillé toute la nuit.

Il y avait du brouillard.

Nous avons cueilli des fruits.

Monsieur Lafeuille a été très accueillant.

Il nous a prêté un maillot.

D'ailleurs, il est tailleur.

So, if you find **i-l-l** preceded by a vowel, you can be pretty sure it is pronounced as [j].

Now, what if **i-l-l** is preceded by a consonant? Well, in most cases, it also represents the sound [j]. Say the sentences in number 2.

2. Aux Antilles nous avons trouvé de très beaux coquillages.
Des poissons brillants sautaient dans le sillage du bateau.
Nous avons fait griller des sardines.

Yet, there are a few words in which **i-l-l** does not represent [j], but rather [il]. It is true for *ville, village,* and for more or less learned, scientific words like *penicilline* or *oscillation*. Say the sentences in number 3.

3. Lille est une grande ville.
Un petit village tranquille, caché dans les bougainvilliers . . .
A la Martinique, on distille le jus de la canne à sucre pour faire du rhum.
Ça oscille entre mille et un million.
On lui a donné de la pénicilline.

The sound /yi/ (16)

2. Pronunciation Exercise

In Unit 20 you encountered the words that you see in number 1:

1. cuir   cuivre   cuisine

These words are interesting from the point of view of pronunciation. You notice that they are spelled with a **u** followed by an **i**. This combination represents the sound [yi], which sounds somewhat like [y] followed by [i]. Yet what you hear is not exactly the vowel [y] but rather a semi-vowel. Let's practice saying words that contain this sound. Of course, you must be sure to say [yi] and not [wi]. This is the difference between *lui* and *Louis,* which you see in number 2.

2. Lui   Louis

Now say the words in number 3.

3. le cuir   le cuivre
la cuisine   C'est cuit dans l'huile.
C'est la nuit.   N'appuie pas!

Interrogation (16)

3. Listening Comprehension Exercise

In Unit 20, you saw several interrogative phrases that sound quite similar: *Qu'est-ce qui, qui est-ce qui, qu'est-ce que, qui est-ce que*. They sound similar, yet there are little differences. And these differences are quite important because they correspond to different meanings. For example, if you hear, *Qu'est-ce que. . . ,* you know it refers to a thing, not a person. But, if you hear, *Qui est-ce que. . . ,* you know it refers to a person, not a thing. And, if you hear, *Qui est-ce qui. . . ,* you know that it is a question about who is doing something. In other words, it is a question about the subject of the verb. But if you hear *Qui est-ce que. . . ,* you know that it is a question about the object of a verb. As you see, those little differences are in the *qui's* and *que's* at the beginning and at the end of these interrogative phrases. That's what you have to watch if you want to get the question right.

Let's see whether you can understand questions correctly. You will hear a few questions with *qui est-ce qui, qu'est-ce que,* and so on. On your *Activity Book* page, you see four answers: *Mme Slim, le mouton, midi, le commerce*. For each question you hear, select the most likely answer among the four. Indicate your choice by checking the appropriate box.

1. Qu'est-ce qui cuit à la cuisine? _____ *(le mouton   B)*
2. Qui est-ce qui fait la cuisine? _____ *(Mme Slim   A)*
3. Qu'est-ce qui fait un bon couscous? _____ *(le mouton   B)*
4. Qui est-ce qui fait un bon couscous? _____ *(Mme Slim   A)*
5. Qu'est-ce qui est le plus cher? _____ *(le mouton B)*
6. Qui est-ce que tu cherches? _____ *(Mme Slim   A)*
7. Qu'est-ce qui rapporte? _____ *(le commerce   D)*
8. Qu'est-ce qui sonne? _____ *(midi   C)*

Now check your answers. *(Read each sentence again, and give the correct answer.)*

		1	2	3	4	5	6	7	8
A.	Mme Slim								
B.	le mouton								
C.	midi								
D.	le commerce								

4. Listening and Speaking Exercise

You will hear statements which all give some rather vague information, such as "I hear something." You are to ask for more precise information, such as "What do you hear?"

1. Il y a quelque chose qui cuit dans la marmite. (   ) *Qu'est-ce qui cuit dans la marmite?*
2. Je connais quelqu'un qui fait un très bon couscous. (   ) *Qui est-ce qui fait un très bon couscous?*
3. Mme Slim épluche quelque chose. (   ) *Qu'est-ce qu'elle épluche?*
4. Nadia cherche quelque chose. (   ) *Qu'est-ce qu'elle cherche?*
5. Quelqu'un a pris mon portefeuille! (   ) *Qui est-ce qui a pris mon portefeuille?*
6. Je cherche quelqu'un. (   ) *Qui est-ce que tu cherches?*

Practice with the vocabulary of the unit (16)

5. Listening Comprehension Exercise

You will hear a series of twelve sentences. Each sentence can be followed logically by one of the six sentences you see printed on your *Activity Book* page. Indicate your choice by putting a check mark in the appropriate row. Let's first read the printed sentences. *(Read sentences from answer grid.)* Now listen:

1. Achète un gigot. _____ *(Il n'y a rien à manger dans la maison.   A)*
2. Il va falloir acheter un couteau! _____ *(Il n'y a rien pour éplucher les légumes!   B)*
3. N'oublie pas d'acheter le mouton! _____ *(Il n'y a rien à manger dans la maison!   A)*
4. Passe chez le cordonnier! _____ *(Il faut faire réparer tes chaussures!   F)*
5. Je vais acheter de la semoule. _____ *(Il n'y a rien à manger dans la maison!   A)*
6. Je vais passer chez le tailleur. _____ *(Je n'ai rien à mettre pour sortir!   D)*
7. Achète du couscous. _____ *(Il n'y a rien à manger dans la maison!   A)*
8. Passe chez le charcutier! _____ *(Il n'y a rien à manger dans la maison!   A)*
9. Je vais acheter une robe. _____ *(Je n'ai rien à mettre pour sortir!   D)*
10. Il faut acheter une marmite. _____ *(Il n'y a rien pour faire cuire les légumes!   C)*
11. Je vais acheter un portefeuille. _____ *(Je n'ai rien pour mettre mon argent!   E)*
12. Je vais acheter un chemisier. _____ *(Je n'ai rien à mettre pour sortir!   D)*

Now check your answers. *(Read each sentence again, and give the correct response.)*

		1	2	3	4	5	5	7	8	9	10	11	12
A	Il n'y a rien à manger dans la maison!												
B	Il n'y a rien pour éplucher les légumes!												
C	Il n'y a rien pour faire cuire les légumes!												
D	Je n'ai rien à mettre pour sortir!												
E	Je n'ai rien pour mettre mon argent!												
F	Il faut faire réparer tes chaussures!												

6. Listening Comprehension and Speaking Exercise

Now you will hear sentences like those you saw printed in the preceding exercise. What could you say as a logical sequence? For example, you hear: *Je n'ai rien à mettre pour sortir!* What could you say? You could say: *Je vais acheter un chemisier, une robe, un pantalon, un pull,* etc.

1. Il n'y a rien à manger dans la maison! (   ) *Je vais acheter du mouton, du couscous, des légumes, des côtelettes, du jambon, des fruits, etc.*
2. Il n'y a rien pour éplucher les légumes! (   ) *Je vais acheter un couteau.*
3. Il n'y a rien pour faire cuire les légumes. (   ) *Je vais acheter une marmite.*
4. Je n'ai rien pour mettre mon argent! (   ) *Je vais acheter un portefeuille.*
5. Il faut acheter des côtelettes de porc, et du pâté. (   ) *Je vais passer chez le charcutier.*
6. Il faut acheter du bifteck. (   ) *Je vais passer chez le boucher.*
7. Il faut acheter de la semoule et du sucre. (   ) *Je vais passer chez l'épicier.*
8. Il faut faire réparer nos chaussures. (   ) *Je vais passer chez le cordonnier.*
9. Il faut acheter des poissons, des oranges, des pommes de terre, et des fleurs. (   ) *Je vais passer au marché.*

Preparation for Conversation Exercise 26

7. Listening Exercise

Isabelle Sanchez, who lives in the South of France, not very far from Marseille, has come to Marseille to visit for the day. She has been walking through the picturesque streets around the *Vieux Port,* the *Cannebière,* and the *Cours Belsunce,* where there are many Oriental and North African people and shops. She has stopped at one of the shops, which displays hundreds of intriguing objects on the sidewalk, as well as inside. This is what we were able to record. Listen:

LE MARCHAND   Alors, qu'est-ce que tu veux, Mademoiselle? Tu veux un beau tapis? Regarde celui-là, s'il est beau!

ISABELLE   Oh non! C'est sûrement trop cher pour moi.

LE MARCHAND   Oh non, celui-là, je te le donne avec le plateau, là. Tu achètes le plateau et je te donne le tapis.

ISABELLE   Il est en or, le plateau?

LE MARCHAND   Non, c'est du cuivre, mais c'est du travail d'artiste, ça! C'est fait en Tunisie, ce n'est pas cher: 1000 francs et je te donne le tapis avec!

ISABELLE   Oh la la! c'est beaucoup trop cher!

LE MARCHAND	Alors, qu'est-ce que tu veux?
ISABELLE	C'est combien la robe bleue, là, avec les broderies en or?
LE MARCHAND	Ce n'est pas une robe, c'est un caftan marocain. Au Maroc, on vend ça 600 francs, mais pour toi, c'est 300 francs!
ISABELLE	C'est joli, mais c'est trop cher pour moi.
LE MARCHAND	Allez! Tiens! Je te le donne pour 200 francs!
ISABELLE	Non, c'est encore trop cher!
LE MARCHAND	200 francs. Tu prends le caftan pour 200 francs et je te donne cette ceinture en cuir avec. Regarde, c'est une belle ceinture.
ISABELLE	Oui, elle est jolie . . . C'est combien, la ceinture sans le caftan?
LE MARCHAND	150 francs.
ISABELLE	150 francs!
LE MARCHAND	Oui, c'est un prix d'ami. Tu ne la veux pas?
ISABELLE	Non.
LE MARCHAND	Alors, qu'est-ce que tu veux? Des sandales de cuir avec des broderies d'argent? 300 francs.
ISABELLE	Vous me prenez pour une millionaire!
LE MARCHAND	200 francs.
ISABELLE	Non, c'est beaucoup trop cher.
LE MARCHAND	Combien pour toi?
ISABELLE	50 francs.
LE MARCHAND	Ah non. 50 francs, je ne peux pas.
ISABELLE	60. Pas un franc de plus.
LE MARCHAND	55, parce que c'est pour toi.
ISABELLE	Bon, je les prends!

CHAPITRE 21

The spelling **ch** *(2)*

1. Reading and Speaking Exercise

How do you say the words that you see listed in number 1?

1. à cache-cache   une machine   à gauche
cochon   vache   cheval
un sac de couchage   très chaud   défense d'afficher

In all these words, the spelling **c-h** corresponds to the sound [ʃ]. Notice that this sound [ʃ] is very different from the [tʃ]-sound which is so common in English.

Look at the word in number 2.

2. charter

This is an English word. And it is also a French word. French people use the word in speaking of planes, just as we do in English. But the French pronounce it in the French way. Can you guess how it sounds in French? Try to say it the way French people do: *charter*. You hear the difference! "Charter" (English) and *charter* (French).

Say the words in number 3. Remember that the **c-h** spelling, in French, does not represent the sound /tʃ/.

3. Charles a de la chance. Il est riche.

Elle est charmante. Et pour éplucher les légumes, c'est une championne!

Je ne sais pas marchander, mais ça ne m'a pas empêché d'acheter de belles pêches.

Now in number 4, let's compare the pronunciation of the words in column A with those in column B.

	A	B
4.	un chantier	c'est très technique
	des choses	du chlore
	chéri	Christine

You see that in the words in column A, **c-h** corresponds to [ʃ]. But in the words in column B, the same **c-h** corresponds to the sound [k]. Why is that? What difference is there between the words in the two columns? In column A, **c-h** is followed by a vowel, whereas in column B, **c-h** is followed by a consonant. So that seems to be the way it works: **c-h** plus vowel is pronounced [ʃ], but **c-h** plus consonant is pronounced [k].

Well, let's look at the words in number 5. Do you know how they are pronounced?

5.	un orchestre	c'est archaïque
	quel chaos!	c'est une chiromancienne

Yes! In these words, **c-h** is followed by a vowel, and yet the **c-h** is pronounced [k]! But there are not too many words like that; and they are not used too often, either. Anyhow, you may be able to spot them. First, they are rare, learned words—Greek words. And then, most of them are used in English, and the **c-h** is also pronounced [k] in English. So you may be able to identify them that way.

Now let's see whether you can pronounce the **c-h** spelling correctly in the following words. Remember! In front of a vowel, **c-h** is pronounced [ʃ], unless it is one of those few, Greek terms which are also pronounced with a [k] in English. In front of a consonant, **c-h** is pronounced [k].

6.	une chaîne	un chapelain	du chocolat
	une charade	une chapelle	un charlatan
	un chariot	du chloroforme	un chimpanzé
	l'archéologie	un challenge	chic!
	une charge de cavalerie	de la chicorée	le Chili

Practice with the future tense (9)

2. Speaking Exercise

You have become quite clairvoyant. By looking into a crystal ball, you can see the future. You are going to tell a young lady her fortune. Look into your crystal ball, and tell her what she will do. What you see in the crystal ball is represented in the six pictures in front of you. Look at them one by one, and tell your customer what will happen to her.

1. (   ) *Vous deviendrez championne de ski.*
2. (   ) *Vous gagnerez beaucoup d'argent à la loterie.*
3. (   ) *Vous ferez un long voyage.*
4. (   ) *Vous irez à Paris.*
5. (   ) *Vous vous marierez.*
6. (   ) *Vous aurez trois enfants.*

Practice with the vocabulary of the unit (15)

3. Listening Comprehension and Speaking Exercise

You will hear young people talking about their experiences at the traveling fair. Unfortunately, what they say is incomplete. The last word they said has been cut off! Can you guess what it probably was? Actually, we have picked up the lost words for you. You will find them in front of you. They are:

bleus — cache — carton — chance — froussard — plaire — tamponneuses — vertige

Listen and try to complete each sentence by saying the word that is missing. Don't wait — say it right away. Say it before it is given to you!

1. Où est Muriel? Elle était là tout à l'heure. Je ne la vois plus. Qu'est-ce qu'elle fait? Ça fait deux fois qu'on la perd! Pas possible, elle joue à cache (   ) *cache!*
2. Regarde Jacques sur le grand huit! Il est vert! Je crois qu'il n'aime pas ça . . . Non, ça n'a pas l'air de lui (   ) *plaire.*
3. Nous sommes allés au stand de tir, faire un (   ) *carton.*
4. Puis après nous sommes allés au stand de la loterie pour tenter notre (   ) *chance.*
5. Oh la la, non! Je ne veux pas monter dans la grande roue. C'est trop dangereux. J'ai peur, moi! J'ai toujours été un (   ) *froussard.*
6. Je n'ai pas aimé ça du tout, la grande roue! Dès que je suis monté, j'ai commencé à avoir le mal de mer. Et quand je me suis vu, tout en haut, alors là, j'ai eu le (   ) *vertige.*
7. Les manèges, c'est pour les bébés. Ce n'est pas drôle. Ça tourne, c'est tout—ce n'est pas très amusant. Moi, j'ai envie d'un peu d'action! Allons faire un tour sur les autos (   ) *tamponneuses.*
8. Les autos tamponneuses, c'est très bien! Il y a de l'action! Ça oui! Il y en a même un peu trop! La dernière fois que j'y suis monté il y avait deux garçons qui s'amusaient à nous rentrer dedans . . . des brutes! Dès qu'ils pouvaient, ils fonçaient sur nous! Quand je suis descendu, j'étais couvert de (   ) *bleus.*

Preparation for Conversation Exercise 22

4. Listening Exercise

Monday morning, Eric and Muriel meet in front of the *lycée.*

ERIC   Qu'est-ce que tu as fait hier? Tu es allée au cinéma?

MURIEL   Non, je suis allée à la Fête des Loges avec mon frère.

ERIC   Ah oui? C'était bien? Tu t'es bien amusée?

MURIEL   Oui, c'était bien.

ERIC   Qu'est-ce que tu as fait?

MURIEL   Je suis allée partout! sur les manèges, sur les autos tamponneuses, sur le grand huit, sur la grande roue!

ERIC   Tu aimes ça, toi!

MURIEL   Oui, pas toi?

ERIC   Ah non, alors!

MURIEL   Pourquoi? Tu as peur? Je ne savais pas que tu étais froussard comme ça!

ERIC   Je n'ai pas peur, mais ça me donne le vertige. Je ne trouve pas ça amusant du tout.

MURIEL   Et les autos tamponneuses, alors? Pourquoi est-ce que tu n'aimes pas ça? Ça ne te donne pas le vertige quand même!

ERIC   Je trouve ça brutal! Je n'aime pas les jeux violents, moi! Rentrer dans les gens . . . Je ne trouve pas ça particulièrement amusant!

MURIEL   Et le tir? le tir à la carabine, tu aimes ça?

ERIC   Non!

MURIEL   Moi si! Je suis allée faire un carton. Je suis très bonne au tir! J'ai mis 7 balles sur 10 dans le disque rouge au centre! C'est pas mal! Mon frère, lui, il n'en a pas mis une seule! Et puis, j'ai vu un magicien . . .

ERIC   Ah oui? Qu'est-ce qu'il faisait?

MURIEL   Oh, les trucs classiques! Il a sorti un lapin du gant d'une dame et une pièce de cinq francs des cheveux d'un petit garçon!

ERIC   C'est amusant!

MURIEL   Tu trouves? Tu sais ce que j'ai préféré?

ERIC   Non.

MURIEL   Les frites! Il y avait des frites formidables! Je n'ai jamais mangé de frites aussi bonnes! . . .

5. Listening Comprehension Exercise

You will hear Marc, Muriel's brother, talking about what he did and saw at the traveling fair. Try to figure out what he is referring to. You will find a list on your *Activity Book* page, with a grid. Listen, and check the appropriate box. Let's begin.

1. Il m'a prédit que j'allais faire un grand voyage et un très beau mariage. _____ *(le fakir)*
2. Je n'ai pas eu de chance! Je suis allé faire un tour, mais j'ai eu le vertige! J'ai eu le mal de mer. J'étais vraiment malade, hein! _____ *(la grande roue)*
3. J'ai eu de la chance. J'ai joué une fois, et j'ai gagné une bouteille de champagne! Hein! Une bouteille de champagne pour 1 franc, ce n'est pas mal! _____ *(la loterie)*
4. J'ai fait un carton et j'ai mis deux balles en plein dans le mille. Et pourtant je ne suis pas très fort. J'ai eu de la chance, c'est tout! _____ *(le tir)*
5. Oh non, moi je n'aime pas ça! J'ai peur. Il y a toujours des imbéciles qui s'amusent à vous rentrer dedans. Quand on sort de là, on est plein de bleus partout. _____ *(les autos tamponneuses)*
6. Il est peut-être très fort... oui... pour profiter de la crédulité du public. Mais toutes ses histoires de signes, de Poissons, de Verseau, d'étoiles, et de boules de cristal, moi, je n'y crois pas. Ce sont des idioties! _____ *(le fakir)*

Now check your answers. *Read each item again and give the correct answer.*

	1	2	3	4	5	6
la grande roue						
les autos tamponneuses						
le tir						
le fakir						
la loterie						

CHAPITRE 22

Practice with the vocabulary of the unit (2)

1. Listening Comprehension Exercise

Now we will describe eight calisthenic exercises. We will not ask you to perform them, because we are not sure you could . . . and we are not sure what good it would do you, either! So we'll let the character in the drawings follow the instructions for you. Listen to each set of instructions and try to find the drawing that shows how the exercise looks. Each exercise is identified by a letter of the alphabet—but these letters are not in ABC order. Just be sure you get the correct letter each time, and write it in the box below the appropriate drawing. Ready? Let's begin.

1. Le mouvement A : Couchez-vous sur le dos, les bras tendus derrière la tête. Appuyez-vous au sol avec le dos, les épaules, les bras, et levez les deux jambes et la tête. La tête ne doit pas rester appuyée sur le sol. Vous y êtes? C'était le mouvement A.
2. Le mouvement C : Appuyez-vous sur les coudes et les genoux. Alors, là, attention! Les genoux sont sur le sol, mais pas les pieds! Levez les pieds, ne vous appuyez pas sur les pieds. Ne vous appuyez

pas sur les mains non plus. Les mains ne doivent pas toucher le sol. Bon. Maintenant avancez sur les coudes et les genoux. C'était le mouvement C.

3. Le mouvement H : Les pieds au sol. Mettez vos mains sur les cuisses, écartez les genoux, et baissez-vous lentement, la tête droite. C'était le mouvement H.

4. Le mouvement I : Couchez-vous sur le ventre. Vous vous appuyez au sol sur la poitrine et le ventre; maintenant levez les deux jambes, les deux bras, et la tête—levez-les aussi haut que possible, et restez dans cette position aussi longtemps que póssible. C'était le mouvement I.

5. Le mouvement M : Commencez par vous coucher sur le dos. Appuyez-vous sur la main droite et le pied droit. Levez-vous. Levez la jambe gauche et le bras gauche. Voilà! Seuls la main droite et le pied droit sont au sol. La main gauche et le pied gauche ne touchent pas le sol. C'était le mouvement M.

6. Le mouvement N : Mettez-vous à 50 centimètres du mur. Appuyez votre épaule droite contre le mur. Levez la jambe droite et le bras gauche. Essayez de toucher le mur au-dessus de votre tête avec votre main gauche. C'était le mouvement N.

7. Le mouvement O : Mettez-vous à 50 centimètres du mur, le dos au mur. Appuyez votre dos contre le mur. Les deux épaules doivent toucher le mur. Maintenant levez la jambe gauche et le bras gauche. Essayez de toucher le mur au-dessus de votre tête avec votre main gauche . . . mais vous n'y arriverez sûrement pas! C'était le mouvement O.

8. Le mouvement P : Appuyez-vous sur la tête et les deux mains. Levez les jambes. Tenez-vous droit! Restez en équilibre sur la tête et les mains. Ça c'est un des mouvements les plus difficiles. C'était le mouvement P.

Now let's see how well you did. If you did everything right, the letters you wrote under the drawings should spell the word "CHAMPION." *Vous êtes un Champion!*

2. Listening and Speaking Exercise

Look again at the drawings for Exercise 1, and answer the following questions. We'll go in order, left to right.

1. Regardez le dessin qui représente le mouvement C. Qu'est-ce qui appuie sur le sol dans ce mouvement? ( ) *Le coudes et les genoux.*
2. Où sont les mains dans le mouvement H? ( ) *Sur les cuisses. Elles sont appuyées sur les cuisses.*
3. Dans le mouvement A, qu'est-ce qui appuie sur le sol? ( ) *Le dos et les bras.* Qu'est-ce qu'il faut faire avec les jambes? ( ) *Il faut les lever.*
4. Dans le mouvement M, sur quoi faut-il se tenir en équilibre? Qu'est-ce qui reste appuyé sur le sol? ( ) *La main droite et le pied droit.* Qu'est-ce qu'on lève? ( ) *Le bras gauche et la jambe gauche.*
5. Et dans le mouvement P, sur quoi se tient-on en équilibre? Sur quoi s'appuie-t-on? ( ) *Sur la tête et les mains.*
6. Qu'est-ce qui appuie sur le sol dans le mouvement I? ( ) *Le ventre et la poitrine.* Qu'est-ce qu'on fait avec les bras et les jambes? ( ) *On les lève.*
7. Dans le mouvement O, qu'est-ce qui appuie contre le mur? ( ) *Les épaules et le dos.* Qu'est-ce qui appuie sur le sol? ( ) *Le pied droit.* Avec quoi est-ce qu'on essaie de toucher le mur au-dessus de sa tête? ( ) *Avec la main gauche.*
8. Dans le mouvement N, qu'est-ce qui appuie contre le mur? ( ) *L'épaule droite.* Qu'est-ce qu'on essaie de faire avec la main droite? ( ) *On essaie de toucher le mur au-dessus de sa tête.*

The spellings o, ô, au, and eau (12)

3. Reading and Speaking Exercise

Look at the words in number 1. Listen to the way they sound, and repeat each one.

1. Elle dort.   Hop!   le sol   Un bel effort!
à l'école   d'abord   la voltige   Elle est bien bonne!

All these words are spelled with an **o.** And in all these words, the letter **o** represents the same sound [ɔ]. So we are tempted to say that the letter **o** represents the sound [ɔ].

However, look at the words in number 2, and listen to the way they sound:

	A	B
2.	une dose	le dos
	une chose	un javelot
	une rose	à vos marques!

All these words are spelled with an **o.** Does the letter **o** represent the same sound as in the words of number 1? Compare: *elle dort* and *une dose : dort, dose.* Is it the same vowel sound? No. In *dort* we have the sound [ɔ], which is called an open **o,** while in *dose,* we have the sound [o], which is called a closed **o.** It's the same sound that you find in *dos* and in all the other words in number 2.

So the letter **o** does represent the sound [ɔ] in many cases (for example, in all the words in number 1), but it also represents the sound [o] in other cases (for example, in all the words in number 2).

Can we figure out when it is the open [ɔ] and when it is the closed [o]? Look for example at the words in number 2, column A: *dose, chose, rose.* Do you notice something special about these words? What do they have in common? They all end in the sound [z]. The letter **o** is part of a syllable that ends in the consonant sound [z]. So we can say that the letter **o** represents the sound [ɔ] as in *elle dort,* except if it is part of a syllable ending in [z], as in *une dose.*

Now, what about the words in number 2, column B: *le dos, le javelot, à vos marques.* They have the same closed [o], yet the syllable does not end in [z]. So what is the story here? What do these words have in common? And how do they differ from the words in number 1? What is the difference between *elle dort* and *le dos?* Can you see? Well, in *dos,* the syllable ends with what? With [o], with the vowel sound [o]. What about *dort?* What does the syllable end with? With [r] — it ends with the consonant sound [r]. That's the difference. If the syllable ends with the vowel sound [o], the letter **o** represents the closed [o]. But if the syllable ends with any other consonant, like [r] in *elle dort,* [p] in *hop!* [l] in *voltige,* and so on, then the letter **o** represents the open [ɔ]-sound.

In conclusion, the letter **o** represents the sound [ɔ] unless it is in a syllable that ends with a vowel or in a syllable that ends with the consonant [z]. As you can see, this is one reason why it is important to know how to divide words into syllables.

You may have heard of a famous and fashionable resort on the French Riviera called *Saint-Tropez* (number 3).

3. Saint-Tropez

Here, the **o** is pronounced [o] because it is in a syllable which ends with a vowel: the name is divided into three syllables, like this: *Saint-Tro-pez*.

Now the people who want to sound very "in" shorten the name of the place to *Saint-Trop'* (number 4).

4. Saint-Trop'

And then the o sounds like [ɔ] because it is no longer in a syllable that ends with a vowel. It is in a syllable that ends with the consonant [p].

Look now at the words in number 5, and listen to the way they sound.

5. à côté   aussi   c'est beau

They all have the sound [o], the closed [o], though this [o]-sound is represented by three different spellings: **o** with a circumflex accent, **a-u,** and **e-a-u.**

These spellings always represent the closed [o]-sound. Always . . . well, there is one little exception: when **a-u** is in a syllable that ends in [r], as in the girl's name *Laure* (number 6), then it represents the open [ɔ]. But you shouldn't worry about it, because it is a rare exception. There are not too many words like this. You will find two in number 6: *Laure,* the girl's name, and *Faure,* which is a common family name. (Edgar Faure is a French politician who was Prime Minister in the 1950's, and Minister of National Education.)

6. Laure   Edgar Faure

Let's see if you can apply what we have just said. Read aloud the words in number 7.

7. une corde   un record   d'abord
   et alors?   hop!   top!
   à vos marques   sur le dos   le javelot
   le chronomètre   l'oreille   polyvalent
   il le faut   les épaules   aussi
   les anneaux
   un pot   la peau
   au saut en hauteur   au sol   l'école est à côté
   c'est un beau trophée   c'est une autre catégorie

CHAPITRE 23

Open /œ/ and closed /ø/ (13)

1. Reading and Speaking Exercise

Compare the sound of the two words in number 1:

1. un neuf   un œuf

The vowels in *neuf* and in *œuf* sound the same, yet the way they are spelled is not quite the same. The spelling **e-u** is the most common one for this vowel [œ], but in a few words it is spelled **o-e-u.**

Actually, there is a third way of spelling this [œ] vowel. Look at the words in number 2:

2. une feuille   elle cueille

We have the same vowel sound [œ] in *feuille* and in *cueille.* Yet they are not spelled quite the same. The **e-u** spelling is inverted in *cueille,* right? Can you guess why? Well, maybe you remember that if **c** or **g** are to be pronounced [k] and [g] when followed by an **e,** there must be a **u** after the **c** or **g,** otherwise they would be pronounced [s] and [ʒ]. By inverting the **e-u** spelling, you get that **u** in the right place to make the **c** sound [k] Clever, isn't it?

Now compare the vowel sounds in *un œuf — des œufs.* Is it the same vowel sound? It is not quite the same, is it? Listen: *un œuf — des œufs.* The first sound is [œ]; the second is [ø].

So, there are two variants of that vowel, [œ] and [ø]. To distinguish them, we say that [œ] is "open" and [ø] is "closed," because you have to open your mouth more to say [œ] than to say [ø]. Listen to the way the words in number 3 are pronounced. Repeat each pair.

3. *"open" sound*   *"closed" sound*

"open" sound	"closed" sound
un œuf	des œufs
un bœuf	des bœufs
elles peuvent	elle peut
sœur	ceux
peur	peu

You see that the "closed" sound occurs in syllables that end with a vowel sound: *œufs, bœufs, peut, ceux.*

As a rule, you find the "closed" sound [ø] in an "open" syllable—that is to say, a syllable that ends in a vowel sound.

Now compare the way the words in number 4 are pronounced. Repeat each pair.

4. *"open" sound*   *"closed" sound*

"open" sound	"closed" sound
chanteur	chanteuse
menteur	menteuse
une épreuve	périlleuse
une côte de bœuf	délicieuse
fauteuil	gracieuse

The words in the left-hand column have an open [œ]-sound. This open [œ]-sound occurs in a "closed" syllable. The syllables in these words are closed by a [r]-sound *(chanteur),* a [v]-sound *(épreuve),* a [f]-sound *(bœuf)* and a [j]-sound *(fauteuil).*

Now, in the right-hand column we have closed [ø]-sounds which occur also in closed syllables. But this time the syllables are closed by a [z]-sound; that's different! Let's sum it up. Look at the chart numbered 5.

5.

> *Open syllable = closed vowel:*
>
> d<u>eu</u>x, p<u>eu</u>, banli<u>eu</u>e, h<u>eu</u>r<u>eu</u>x
>
> ---
>
> *Syllable closed by [z] = closed vowel:*
>
> courag<u>eu</u>se, graci<u>eu</u>se, ment<u>eu</u>se, chant<u>eu</u>se
>
> ---
>
> *Syllable closed by [r], [f], [v], [j] = open vowel:*
>
> l<u>eu</u>r, s<u>œu</u>r, b<u>œu</u>f, épr<u>eu</u>ve, faut<u>eu</u>il

Now let's see if you can correctly pronounce the vowels in the following words. Look at number 6.

6. Il pleut!   C'est bleu.   C'est un peu mieux!

Il pleut!	C'est bleu.	C'est un peu mieux!
Heureusement!	Quel bonheur!	Quelles belles fleurs!
A tout à l'heure!	C'est un vieux pêcheur.	Quel menteur!
C'est une chanteuse connue.	Quelle menteuse!	C'est sa sœur!

C'est un grand amateur d'autos tamponneuses.
C'est la meilleure skieuse. Elle a gagné l'épreuve comme dans un fauteuil!

2. Listening Exercise

In this exercise you will hear two young people talking. They are in a big department store with all kinds of nice things that would make wonderful gifts for all their friends. So they are pretending they have lots of money, and are selecting a gift for each one of their friends. Try to figure out what they choose for everyone. You will have to listen carefully, because they don't name the objects they are talking about. (They don't have to, because the objects are right there, in front of them.) You see the names of the nine friends mentioned, and the names of each of the gifts. Indicate who is getting what, by drawing a line between the name of each friend and the gift selected for each.

1. Voilà ce qu'on va acheter à Bernard pour son anniversaire! Il ne sait jamais l'heure qu'il est, et il est toujours en retard! _____ *(une montre)*
2. Et à Cécile on va lui acheter ça parce qu'elle aime écrire. Elle écrit à toutes ses amies au moins une fois par semaine. _____ *(du papier à lettres)*
3. Et voilà pour Marc! Il aime le cuir, tout ce qui est en cuir . . . il pourra le prendre pour aller au lycée. Il perd toujours tous ses livres! _____ *(un porte-documents)*
4. Et ça, ça sera un cadeau formidable pour Vincent, parce que lui aussi, il aime le cuir . . . mais lui, c'est son pantalon qu'il perd! _____ *(une ceinture)*
5. Et pour Christine, voyons . . . elle aime la soie . . . et elle a toujours froid au cou. _____ *(une écharpe)*
6. Voilà ce qu'il faut à François pour mettre avec sa nouvelle chemise. _____ *(des boutons de manchettes)*
7. Pour Françoise, il nous faut quelque chose en or. Voyons, oui, ça! Elles iront très bien avec son collier. _____ *(des boucles d'oreille)*
8. Et ça, pour Xavier; il perd toujours son argent! _____ *(un porte-monnaie)*

Now check your answers. *Read each item again and give the correct answer.*

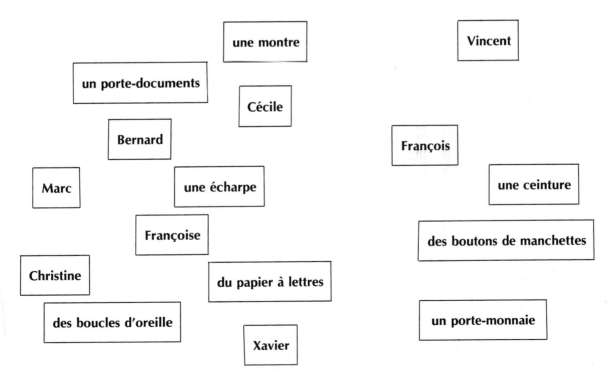

3. Listening and Speaking Exercise

Look at the chart showing our nine friends and the gifts that would be nice for each one of them. Let's see if you remember why these gifts are appropriate for the people who will get them. Try to answer each question before you hear the answer.

1. Qu'est-ce qu'on pourrait donner à Bernard? (   ) *Une montre.* Pourquoi est-ce qu'une montre serait bien pour lui? (   ) *Parce qu'il est toujours en retard; il ne sait jamais l'heure qu'il est.*
2. Et pour Cécile, qu'est-ce qu'on va acheter? (   ) *Du papier à lettres.* Pourquoi? (   ) *Parce qu'elle aime écrire; elle écrit beaucoup; elle écrit à ses amies au moins une fois par semaine.*
3. Qu'est-ce qu'on va acheter pour Marc? (   ) *Un porte-documents.* En quoi est-il, ce porte-documents? (   ) *En cuir.*
4. Et pour Christine, qu'est-ce qu'on achète? (   ) *Une écharpe.* Où Christine a-t-elle toujours froid? (   ) *Au cou.* En quoi est l'écharpe qu'on va lui acheter? (   ) *En soie.*
5. Qu'est-ce qui serait bien pour François? (   ) *Des boutons de manchettes.* Avec quoi pourrait-il les mettre? (   ) *Avec sa nouvelle chemise.*
6. Qu'est-ce que Françoise aimerait? (   ) *Des boucles d'oreille.* Des boucles d'oreille en quoi? (   ) *En or!*
7. Qu'est-ce qu'on pourrait acheter pour Xavier? (   ) *Un porte-monnaie.* Pourquoi? (   ) *Parce qu'il perd toujours son argent.* En quoi est-il, ce porte-monnaie? (   ) *En cuir.*
8. Et pour Vincent, qu'est-ce qu'il faudrait? (   ) *Une ceinture.* Pourquoi? (   ) *Il perd toujours son pantalon!* En quoi est-elle, cette ceinture? (   ) *En cuir.*

Preparation for Conversation Exercise 36

4. Listening Exercise

We overheard this apparently not very serious conversation, and luckily we were able to record it for you.

—Qu'est-ce que tu ferais si tu avais beaucoup d'argent?
—D'abord j'achèterais un grand sac à main pour mettre mon argent.
—Et puis après?
—Et puis après, j'achèterais une bijouterie, comme ça quand j'aurais envie d'un bracelet, je pourrais en choisir un. Je pourrais avoir un collier ou des boucles d'oreille différents tous les jours.
—Et puis après?
—Et puis après j'achèterais un grand rasoir électrique pour papa, parce que le sien ne marche pas, et une maison avec un grand jardin.
—Pour toi?
—Non, pour maman, parce qu'elle aime les fleurs. Pour moi, je m'achèterais un grand bateau à voiles; je ferais le tour du monde, et tous les soirs, j'irais au restaurant et au cinéma.
—Tu aurais un cinéma sur ton bateau?
—Non, mais tous les soirs, je m'arrêterais dans un port. Le matin j'irais dans les magasins et j'achèterais des cartes postales et des cadeaux que j'enverrais à mes amis. Et toi, qu'est-ce que tu ferais si tu avais beaucoup d'argent?
—Moi, j'achèterais un très gros gâteau au chocolat.
—Un bateau en chocolat?
—Non, un *gâteau* au chocolat.
—Et puis tu le mangerais, et c'est tout?
—Non, avant de le manger, j'y mettrais des bougies, je ferais le vœu d'avoir un autre très gros gâteau au chocolat, je soufflerais très fort, j'éteindrais toutes les bougies d'un coup, et comme ça j'aurais toujours des gâteaux au chocolat.

—Oui, mais ton vœu ne se réaliserait que si c'était le jour de ton anniversaire!
—Ça ne ferait rien; parce que si j'avais beaucoup d'argent, je pourrais acheter un gâteau au chocolat tous les jours, même quand ce ne serait pas mon anniversaire. Je pourrais même acheter une moto.
—Une moto en chocolat?
—Mais non, une vraie, pour aller me promener.

CHAPITRE 24

*Aspiration and spelling **h** (1)*

1. Reading and Speaking Exercise

Listen carefully to the words in number 1. Compare the way they are pronounced in English with the way they are pronounced in French.

1. *English*   *French*
the hostess   l'hôtesse
hockey   le hockey
the hall   le hall
the hospital   l'hôpital

There are many differences, of course. Note particularly the beginning of the words: "hostess," *hôtesse.* There is obviously an aspiration at the beginning of the English word but none at the beginning of the French one. This is a very general difference between French and English. In English many sounds are accompanied by some "air noise": you hear air being aspirated or blown out. Such "air noises" are much less noticeable in French, if they are there at all.

Here is another example. Compare the pronunciation of the English and the French words in number 2:

2. *English*   *French*
Impossible!   Impossible!
Immediately!   Immédiatement!

You may have noticed that there is a little "air noise" at the beginning of the English words, while the attack of the French words is much quieter. Now compare the pronunciation of the English and the French words in number 3:

3. *English*   *French*
park   parc
terrible   terrible
capital   capitale

If you listen very carefully, you will notice that one of the differences between the English and the French is that in English there is a slight "air noise." Here it is more like an explosion, air being released or blown out, after the /p/-, the /t/-, and the /k/- sounds, while there is no such "air noise" in the French words. Listen again:

park   parc
terrible   terrible
capital   capitale

Let's practice with a few words. Say the words in 4A and 4B, being careful not to make any "aspiration" or "air noise" at the beginning of the words. By the way, remember not to put any stress at the beginning of the word. This will help you to avoid the "aspiration."

4. A. accident   impossible   hôtesse
arabe   idiot   hockey

adresse	intéressant	hôpital
artiste	immédiatement	
animal	intelligent	
auto	immoral	

B.
parc	tour	capitale
population	terrible	conversation
permission	tableau	culturel
poste	terrasse	café
paysan	télévision	camarade
peintre	tennis	camp
pays		
publicité		

When you consider French words like those in number 5 and the way they are pronounced—

5. hôtesse   hockey   hôpital

you realize that there is no "aspiration" at the beginning, even though there is an **h** in the spelling. You might say that an **h** at the beginning of a French word does not mean much . . . at least as far as pronunciation is concerned!

As you know, all words beginning with an **h** do not behave in the same way. Look at the words in number 6 as you listen to them.

6. le haricot   l'harmonica
    un haricot   un harmonica

There is *élision* or *liaison* with *harmonica (l'harmonica, un harmonica),* but not with *haricot (le haricot, un haricot).* So it would seem that in *harmonica,* the **h** does not count at all. It is just as if it were not there. The word *harmonica* begins with the vowel sound /a/, while the word *haricot* seems to be different. There is no *élision* since you say le haricot, and no *liaison* since you say *un haricot,* so it would seem that the word *haricot* does not begin with the vowel sound /a/ but with some kind of consonant sound that is represented by the letter **h.** It seems there should be some consonant sound before the /a/-sound. Actually there is none, for there is no real aspiration: *haricot, harmonica.* Both start with the same /a/-sound. The **h** does not represent any real sound in either word. All we can say is that there is no *élision* or *liaison* with *haricot.* We might perhaps say that in *haricot* the **h** represents a little pause that prevents any *élision* or *liaison.*

In number 7 you will see two columns of words. The words in column A do not have *liaison* or *élision.* The words in column B do. Say each pair as you see it, and then say the plural. For example, you see: *un haricot—un harmonica,* and you say *un haricot, un harmonica.* Then you say the plurals: *des haricots, des harmonicas.*

A	**B**
7. un haricot	un harmonica
un haut-parleur	un habitant
une haie	une histoire
un hangar	un hôpital
un hall	un hôtel
une hauteur	une heure
un hors-d'oeuvre	une herbe

One last thing about the letter **h.** Look at the words in number 8, and listen to the way they are pronounced:

8. une panthère   un thermomètre
    ethnique

You see that these words are spelled with a **t-h,** which is pronounced /t/. The **h** does not represent any sound in these words. Let's say the words in number 9.

9. une panthère
un groupe ethnique
l'éther
la théologie
pathétique

un thermomètre
les mathématiques
l'athéisme
la thérapie
la sympathie

Distinction between future and conditional (8)

2. Listening Comprehension Exercise

You will hear 12 sentences, which are either in the future or in the conditional. In your *Activity Book* you see two phrases: *si c'est possible* and *si c'était possible*. Match each sentence you hear with one of the two phrases and check the appropriate row. Let's begin.

1. Nous irions au Sénégal. _____ *(conditionnel)*
2. Vous voudrez voyager? _____ *(futur)*
3. Il aurait un bateau à voile. _____ *(conditionnel)*
4. Il ira à Paris. _____ *(futur)*
5. Vous voudriez partir? _____ *(conditionnel)*
6. Il serait peintre. _____ *(conditionnel)*
7. C'est ce qu'il fera. _____ *(futur)*
8. Nous le saurions! _____ *(conditionnel)*
9. Ils viendraient. _____ *(conditionnel)*
10. Vous le saurez. _____ *(futur)*
11. Elles viendront. _____ *(futur)*
12. Tu aurais la télévision? _____ *(conditionnel)*

Now check your answers. *Read each sentence again and give the correct answer.*

	1	2	3	4	5	6	7	8	9	10	11	12
futur: si c'est possible												
conditionnel: si c'était possible												

Practice with the vocabulary of the unit (13)

3. Listening Comprehension Exercise

You will hear six short comments. Each one relates to one of the pictures you see in front of you. Match up each comment with a picture, by writing the number of the comment under the picture it refers to.

1. Moi, j'adore les singes! Ils sont tellement amusants!
2. Moi, j'adore l'eau minérale. C'est frais, c'est pétillant, c'est tellement agréable quand on a soif!
3. Mais éteins-le ou règle-le! C'est agaçant, à la fin! C'est trop sombre, on n'y voit rien, c'est flou, et l'image saute tout le temps!
4. Je ne peux pas me peigner, mon peigne est cassé! Je ne peux pas me peigner avec mes doigts, non?
5. Il est peintre. Il fait de très jolis paysages.
6. Si vous voulez bien bronzer, il ne faut pas trop bouger.

Now check your answers. The numbers under the pictures should read: *5, 2, 3, 1, 6, 4.*

4. Speaking Exercise

Now that you have numbered each one of the 6 pictures in your Activity Book, you will be asked a few questions about each one.

Let's start the picture under which you put a 5, since it is the top one to the left.

A. Qui est ce Monsieur? C'est un ingénieur, un médecin? (　　) *C'est un peintre.*
   Qu'est-ce qu'il est en train de peindre? Un portrait? (　　) *Non, un paysage.*
B. Qu'est-ce qu'il y a dans cette bouteille et ce verre? Vous croyez que c'est du lait? (　　) *Non, c'est de l'eau minérale.*
   Pourquoi est-ce qu'elle ressemble à du champagne, de la limonade ou du soda? (　　) *Elle est pétillante.*
C. Est-ce que ce poste de télévision marche bien? Qu'est-ce qui ne va pas? (　　) *C'est flou, l'image saute, c'est trop sombre.*
   Alors, qu'est-ce qu'il faut faire? (　　) *Il faut le régler (ou l'éteindre).*
D. Qu'est-ce que c'est, cet animal? C'est un rhinocéros? Un crocodile? (　　) *Non, c'est un singe.*
E. Pourquoi est-ce que cette fille reste au soleil sans bouger? Qu'est-ce qu'elle veut faire? (　　) *Elle veut bronzer.*
F. Pourquoi est-ce que cette fille n'est pas contente? Qu'est-ce qu'elle ne peut pas faire? (　　) *Elle ne peut pas se peigner.*

Preparation for conversation exercise (19)

5. Listening Exercise

Look at the TV program on p. 255 of your book, and listen to Christine and Marc talking.

C Si tu pouvais regarder tout ce que tu veux, qu'est-ce que tu regarderais, aujourd'hui?

M Je ne sais pas, quelque chose d'amusant...

C Quoi? L'Ile aux Enfants?

M Où est-ce que tu vois ça?

C Sur la troisième chaîne à 18:40.

M Bah! C'est sûrement pour les bébés! avec des chansons, des marionnettes! Je préférerais du théâtre, du vrai, avec de vrais acteurs.

C Ben là, alors, tu n'as pas de chance. Il n'y a pas de théâtre aujourd'hui. Si tu veux des acteurs, tu peux regarder la Nuit des Césars, à 20:30 sur la deuxième chaîne.

M Bah! Ce n'est sûrement pas amusant! Pour voir des acteurs qui viennent chercher leur prix!

C Eh bien alors, tu as un film à 20:30 aussi, mais sur la troisième chaîne.

M Bof! C'est un vieux film! 1969! Et puis pour voir quelqu'un qui revient en France... Ce n'est pas intéressant. J'aimerais mieux le voir aux Etats-Unis, ce Bruno! Ça oui, ce serait intéressant! On verrait les Etats-Unis, New York, Chicago, les gratte-ciel, les grosses voitures, les cow-boys et les Indiens!

M Tu crois qu'il y en a encore des gangsters?

C Des gangsters et des policiers, oh oui, sûrement.

M Bon, alors je voudrais voir un film avec des gangsters et des policiers.

C Alors, peut-être *Chapeau Melon et Bottes de Cuir,* à 21:45 sur la première chaîne.

M Tu crois que c'est américain?

C Oui, sûrement, avec Steed et Emma Peel... Ce sont des noms américains, non?

M Hum! Ça pourrait être des noms anglais?

C Peut-être... mais regarde: ''le plus grand hold-up du siècle''. Quand tu vois ''le plus grand quelque chose du monde''... c'est toujours américain!

M Tu aimes ça, toi, les histoires policières, avec des criminels, des détectives?...

C Ouais!

M Eh bien alors, tu en as une autre, là, sur la deuxième chaîne, 22:30. L'Affaire de l'Emeraude, que ça s'appelle!

Moi, je préférerais quelque chose de vraiment amusant... Des clowns!

C Alors regarde sur la troisième chaîne, à 19:20, tu as une émission qui s'appelle ''Eh bien, raconte!'' Ce sont des histoires drôles! Ça doit être amusant.

M Ça dépend si c'est bien raconté.

C Moi, tu vois, ce que j'aimerais, c'est des histoires d'animaux. Des histoires de chats ou de tigres.

M Pour les chats, tu n'as pas de chance. Je ne vois pas de chats au programme. Mais tu as des chiens. A 18:05, sur la première chaîne, tu as ''Les chiens de traîneaux''. Ça doit se passer chez les Esquimaux... en Alaska ou au Pôle Nord... Ça doit être bien! Ou alors tu as une autre histoire de chien sur la deuxième chaîne à 17:30.

C Oh, un chien qui va voir tous les jours la tombe de son maître au cimetière... oh non! Ça doit être trop triste...

M Et le championnat de France de danse, tu crois que tu aimerais ça? Ça, ça ne doit pas être triste!

C Où est-ce que tu vois ça?

M Sur la première chaîne, à 15:05.

C Non, je crois que je préférerais ce qu'il y a juste au-dessus, à 14:05. Ce doit être une émission scientifique.

M Cosmos 1999... ''violente tempête sur la lune...'' Hum! C'est peut-être de la science-fiction. Mais si tu veux une émission scientifique, tu en as une sur la troisième chaîne à 13:40 ''Les planètes''. Ça, c'est sûrement une émission scientifique sérieuse!

C C'est ce que tu regarderais, toi?

M Oh non! Moi, j'attendrais 16:45 et je regarderais les dessins animés. C'est sûrement ce qu'il y a de mieux!

C Tu n'es pas sérieux!...

Scope and Sequence Chart

NOS AMIS

Learning Objectives	Basic Material	Grammar	Activities, Realia, and Supplementary Readings	Areas for Cultural Awareness[1]
(opener)				
1. To ask someone's name and to tell yours —using the verb s'appeler (singular) —practicing boys' and girls' names	Comment t'appelles-tu? 2	What is your name? 2	map showing where some of our friends live Noms de garçons, Noms de filles 2	places where French is spoken boys' and girls' names currently popular in France
2. To ask someone's age and to tell yours —using numbers from 1 to 20 —using the verb avoir (singular) —practicing numbers by playing a game	Quel âge as-tu? 3 Les nombres de 1 à 20. 3	How old are you? 3	Le jeu de loto. 3	
3. To talk about where one lives —using the verb habiter (singular) —learning the gender of nouns —practicing the gender of nouns by talking about the geography of France	Où habites-tu? 4 For Reference 9 Word List 10	Where do you live? 6 Gender and Gender Markers 6	En France 8 (map of France)	variety of houses and landscapes in France and French-speaking countries names of main provinces; major cities; major rivers; mountains; seas

[1] This column, "Areas for Cultural Awareness," by no means exhausts the possibilities for cultural awareness in the program. The themes and cultural content of the individual units are discussed in the section titled "Teaching Suggestions for Each Unit," which begins on page T11.

Unit 2

LES SPORTS

Learning Objectives	Basic Material	Grammar	Activities, Realia, and Supplementary Readings	Areas for Cultural Awareness
1. To talk about sports —learning names of sports —using the verb faire and all subject pronouns	Ils font du vélo. 12 Qu'est-ce qu'ils font comme sports? 12	Pronouns and the Verb faire 13		young people's favorite sports in France and Canada
2. To talk about other sports —learning about a soccer field and the positions of the players —talking about a variety of other sports and sports equipment —using the verb jouer	A quoi est-ce qu'il joue? 14 On joue au football? 14 A quoi est-ce que vous jouez? Avec quoi? 15	Verbs Ending in -er 15	(soccer field with names of positions in French) 14	importance of soccer in France
3. To discuss preferences in sports —talking about sports —learning liaison and élision —learning names of colors —talking about colors of sports teams	Qu'est-ce qu'elles aiment comme sports? 17 Les couleurs. 19 For Reference 19 Word List 20	How to Talk About Sports 17 Liaison and Elision 17	Quelles sont les couleurs de ces équipes? 19	colors for some French soccer teams

T173

LES PASSE-TEMPS

Learning Objectives	Basic Material	Grammar	Activities, Realia, and Supplementary Readings	Areas for Cultural Awareness
1. To talk about leisure activities —using plural markers	Qu'est-ce que ces jeunes aiment faire? 22	Plural Markers: Articles with Nouns 23		favorite leisure activities of young people
2. More about other spare-time activities —using the verb être —learning the names of objects to collect —using negative constructions —using numbers from 20 to 1,000	Qu'est-ce qu'ils ont comme passe-temps? 25 Vous êtes collectionneurs (collectionneuses)? Qu'est-ce que vous collectionnez? 26 Les nombres de 20 à 1.000. 28	The Verb être 25 Negation—ne . . . pas (de) 26		
3. To talk about winning and losing —learning the names of games to play —using the verb avoir —using oui or si in response to a negative question —reviewing numbers by playing a card game	C'est à qui de jouer? 29 A quel jeu est-ce que tu veux jouer? 29 For Reference 31 Word List 32	The verb avoir 30 Answering a Negative Question 30	Le Barbu 31	card game popular among French young people

Unit 4

L'ECOLE

Learning Objectives	Basic Material	Grammar	Activities, Realia, and Supplementary Readings	Areas for Cultural Awareness
1. To talk about school —learning names of school subjects —using the verb aller —telling time	(François va à l'école.) 33 (L'emploi du temps de François.) 33	The Verb aller 34 Quelle heure est-il? 34	(François' schedule) 33	schedule of classes; days of the week; school subjects expressions for telling time
2. To talk about the school building —learning names of various school rooms —using contractions	Voilà l'école de François. 35 François rencontre un nouveau, Olivier, dans la cour du CES. 35	Contractions with à and de 36	(layout of a French school) 35	
3. To talk about what goes on in class —using tu and vous —understanding and giving directions	La classe de François. 37	The Formal vous 38 Giving Commands 38		teacher/student exchanges formal and informal address
4. To learn names of school supplies —practicing vocabulary by playing a game			Dans le cartable de François. 39 Dans la trousse de François. 40 Chaîne de mots. 40 (words in a chain)	French school supplies
5. To talk about report cards —using adjectives	Le bulletin trimestriel de François. 40 For Reference 43 Word List 43	Adjectives: Gender Agreement 41	(French report card) 40	the French grading system

Unit 5

UNE SORTIE

Learning Objectives	Basic Material	Grammar	Activities, Realia, and Supplementary Readings	Areas for Cultural Awareness
1. To discuss going out with friends —using the verbs sortir and partir —learning names of different places to go —asking questions	Qu'est-ce qu'on fait cet après-midi? 46 Où est-ce qu'on va? 47	Verbs Ending in -ir 46 How to Ask Questions 48		how young people spend their leisure time in France; minimum age for driving
2. To order lunch in a café —using quantities —using de in negative constructions	Qu'est-ce qu'on prend? 49	How to Indicate Quantity 50 Use of de in Negative Constructions 51	*(menu from a café)* 49	cafés as meeting places for young people; foods available at cafés; expressions for ordering
3. To decide on a film to see —learning names of kinds of films —using the verbs choisir and finir —expressing future time	On va voir un film? 52 Qu'est-ce que vous aimez comme films? 52 For Reference 55 Word List 56	More Verbs Ending in -ir 53 Expressing Future Time 54	*(newspaper listings for films)* 52 L'argent français: les billets et les pièces 53	kinds of films French teenagers like French money: bills and coins

AU TELEPHONE

Chapitre de Révision *(Review Unit)*

Learning Objectives	Basic Material	Grammar	Activities, Realia, and Supplementary Readings	Areas for Cultural Awareness
1. To make telephone calls: expressions used for telephone conversations —reviewing articles	Martine Dupuis téléphone à Evelyne Bouquet 58	Articles 59		use of the phone in France; how to use a public phone; greetings
2. To learn more expressions used for telephone conversations —reviewing adjectives	Didier Jolibois téléphone à Evelyne Bouquet 60	Adjectives: Agreement 61		French phone numbers
3. To read a page from a telephone book, reviewing numbers	For Reference 63 Word List 64		Téléphonez aux Renseignements. 63 *(excerpt from a French phone book)*	calling information

Unit 7 LA FAMILLE DE CATHERINE LARDAN

Learning Objectives	Basic Material	Grammar	Activities, Realia, and Supplementary Readings	Areas for Cultural Awareness
1. To talk about family members and relationships —describing physical characteristics of people —using adjectives —practicing new vocabulary by playing a game —using possessive articles	(Catherine montre son album à son amie Sylvie.) 65 Le jeu des ressemblances. 66	Adjectives: Position 66 Possessive Articles 67	Devinez qui c'est. 67	the French family
2. To talk about professional occupations —learning the names of more occupations —learning gender counterparts for names of occupations —using negatives	Qu'est-ce qu'ils font dans la famille de Catherine? 68 Autres professions. 69 Qu'est-ce qu'ils font, ton père et ta mère? 69	Negation: Other Negative Words 70		variety of occupations for men and women
3. To read about the life of a French family —using -re verbs —using independent pronouns —reading a cartoon	Comment vivent les Lardan. 71 Word List 74	Verbs Ending in -re 72 Using Independent Pronouns 73	Un fils fier de son père. 73	how a typical French family lives; weekly Sunday gathering; close family ties; how young people make money

Learning Objectives	Basic Material	Grammar	Activities, Realia, and Supplementary Readings	Areas for Cultural Awareness
1. To learn expressions used when one shops for food; names of fruits —using pronouns to refer to things	(Jean-Marcel va faire les courses.) 75	Pronouns Referring to Things: il/elle, ils/elles 76		Provence and the Côte d'Azur; products of the area; shopping in an open market; typical vegetables and fruits
2. To learn to use metric weights and to learn names of vegetables —using the verb acheter	Combien est-ce que les Giuliani dépensent pour les légumes? 77	The Verb acheter 78		metric weights; grams and kilograms
3. To learn the names of specialty food stores and the foods they sell —reviewing names of food items by playing a game —learning expressions of quantity —using the verb prendre	Chez les commerçants. 79	How to Express Quantity 80 The Verb prendre 81	Le jeu de l'odorat. 80	system of individual stores in France; names of food stores; groceries more metric capacities; packages that foods are sold in
4. To read about the eating habits of the French —reading about meals in France; foods; table setting —playing a game —using indirect objects —making a Provençal specialty	Les Giuliani déjeunent. 82 Les repas. 83 Word List 86	Indirect-Object Pronouns: lui and leur 83	Charade. 83 Une spécialité provençale: le pain-bagnat. 85	French table setting; typical French lunch the meals of the day and what they usually consist of special kinds of cooking in the South; recipe to make a Provençal sandwich

LA SURPRISE-PARTIE

Learning Objectives	Basic Material	Grammar	Activities, Realia, and Supplementary Readings	Areas for Cultural Awareness
1. To speak about preparing for a party —using past time	Tout est prêt! 88	Expressing Past Time: The Passé Composé with avoir 89	(*last-minute checklist*) 88	how some French young people give a party; useful information on how to give a party
2. To talk about what to wear to a party —using the verb mettre —learning the names of more articles of clothing —learning past participles of irregular verbs	Quels vêtements est-ce qu'ils mettent? 90? Et vous, qu'est-ce que vous mettez quand vous sortez? 91	The Verb mettre 90 More on Past Participles 91		casual clothes French teenagers wear to parties and elsewhere
3. To talk about a party —using the verb boire —using the pronoun en	La surprise-partie bat son plein. 92	The Verb boire 93 The Pronoun en 93		a typical French teenagers' get-together; bringing things to the party; party talk—asking someone to dance, offering food and drink
4. To read about planning a party	Word List 96		Les Secrets d'une Bonne Surprise-Partie 95	suggestions for planning a party; invitations; music; drinks; food; games

A VILLE D'AVRAY

Learning Objectives	Basic Material	Grammar	Activities, Realia, and Supplementary Readings	Areas for Cultural Awareness
1. To talk about life in a suburban town —describing neighbors	La banlieue de Paris. 98 A la Résidence Musset. 98			a residential suburb of Paris a French apartment house; floor numbering
—using ordinal numbers		From Cardinal Numbers to Ordinal Numbers 99		
—practicing ordinal numbers by playing a game —using the verb connaître		The Verb connaître 100	Chaîne de mots. 99	
—using direct-object pronouns		The Direct-Object Pronouns le, la, les 100		
2. To talk about one's town —learning the names for the various buildings of a town; expressions to give directions	Allons en ville! 101 Suivons sur le plan! 102		(street map of Ville d'Avray) 102	naming of streets in a French town
—using the verb suivre —using more object pronouns		The Verb suivre 103 The Object Pronouns me, te, nous, vous 103		French apartments
3. To talk about one's house	L'appartement de la famille Pierre. 105		(floor plan of a French apartment) 105	French apartments; a French teenager's room
—learning names of rooms —using object pronouns with the passé composé		Object Pronouns with the Passé Composé: Agreement of Past Participle 106		
	Word List 108			

Unit 11

PARIS

Learning Objectives	Basic Material	Grammar	Activities, Realia, and Supplementary Readings	Areas for Cultural Awareness
1. To talk about visiting a city —using past time	Premier jour à Paris. 110	The Passé Composé with être 112	(map showing route followed by bateaux-mouches) 111	Paris: its buildings and monuments, history and treasures
2. To talk about landmarks one has seen —playing a game —using the verb voir —using the pronoun y —getting better acquainted with Paris by playing a game	En haut de la Tour Eiffel. 114	The Verb voir 115 The Pronoun y 116	Devinettes. 115 (riddles about Paris monuments) Suivez la piste! 117 (map of Paris)	
3. To read impressions of a visit to Paris	For Reference 120 Word List 120		Dernier coup d'œil sur Paris. 118	

LA LETTRE

Chapitre de Révision (Review Unit)

Learning Objectives	Basic Material	Grammar	Activities, Realia, and Supplementary Readings	Areas for Cultural Awareness
1. To write a letter to a friend	La Lettre 121		(postage stamps) 121	Monaco, the French-speaking principality on the Côte d'Azur—its beauty; its contribution to oceanography
2. To use the appropriate forms in letter-writing	Comment écrire une lettre. 122			style of an informal letter; care in French letter-writing style
—using the verb écrire		The Verb écrire 123		
—learning the months	Quels sont les mois de l'année? 123			names of the months; reading dates
—learning the date	Quelle est la date aujourd'hui 123			
—becoming acquainted with the Oceanographic Museum			Au Musée Océanographique. 123	
—reviewing pronouns		Pronouns—Summary 124		
—reviewing how to express time		Expressing Time: Present, Future, and Past 125		
3. To learn steps to follow when one visits a museum	Comment visiter le Musée Océanographique. 126			a guide to museum-visiting
4. To learn how to address an envelope	Comment adresser une enveloppe. 127			addressing an envelope
—becoming familiar with a French post office			Il va mettre sa lettre à la poste. 127	
—asking questions at the post office			A la poste. 128	expressions to use at the post office
	Word List 128			

LA JOURNEE DE VIVIANE

Learning Objectives	Basic Material	Grammar	Activities, Realia, and Supplementary Readings	Areas for Cultural Awareness
1. To talk about getting ready in the morning —using reflexive constructions —learning the names of toilet articles —practicing new vocabulary by playing a game	Tôt le matin. 130 Qu'est-ce que Viviane utilise comme objets de toilette? 132	Reflexive Constructions 131	Devinettes. 132	an industrial suburb of Paris a day in the life of a 16-year-old girl working in Paris morning preparations; French toilet articles
2. To talk about getting to work or school —using reflexives —playing a game by following a subway map —using negatives	La matinée. 133	More on Reflexive Verbs 134 rien and personne 136	Dans le métro. 134 (map of Paris subway)	morning: getting to work; at work in a boutique how to get around by subway in Paris
3. To talk about what one can do on lunch hour —using more reflexives	L'heure de déjeuner. 137	More Reflexive Verbs 138		lunch time in the fashionable center of Paris
4. To read about the end of the day: returning home, dinner with the family, bedtime	L'après-midi et le soir. 139 Word List 140			afternoon and evening

Learning Objectives	Basic Material	Grammar	Activities, Realia, and Supplementary Readings	Areas for Cultural Awareness
1. To meet the members of a jazz group and learn what instruments they play —learning the names of more instruments —using the verb venir —using venir de + infinitive	Les Canards à l'Orange. 142 Et vous, de quels instruments est-ce que vous jouez? 143	The Verb venir 144 Expressing Past Time: venir de + infinitive 144		music popular with French teenagers
2. To talk about kinds of music —using interrogative adjectives —using the verb préférer —learning more about the past participle	La répétition. 145	Interrogative Adjectives: quel, quelle, quels, quelles 146 The Verb préférer 146 More on Agreement of the Past Participle 146		
3. To talk about sound equipment —learning expressions for how to use a tape recorder —using interrogative pronouns —using demonstrative pronouns —practicing names of instruments by singing a song	«Et voici les Canards à l'Orange!» 147 Comment se servir d'un magnétophone. 148 Word List 150	The Interrogative Pronouns: lequel, laquelle, lesquels, lesquelles 148 The Demonstrative Pronouns: celui, celle, ceux, celles 149	Chanson: L'Orchestre. 150	"kermesse"—community festival French onomatopoeia for sounds made by various musical instruments

Unit 15

SKI AU QUEBEC

Learning Objectives	Basic Material	Grammar	Activities, Realia, and Supplementary Readings	Areas for Cultural Awareness
(opener)			(map of Laurentian area) 151	
1. To talk about the weather —learning expressions to describe the weather and names of seasons —using degrees centigrade; converting F° to C°	Le ski avant tout! 152 Quelle saison est-ce? Quel temps fait-il? 153 Ça fait combien en Fahrenheit? Ça fait combien en Celsius? 153			where to go skiing north of Montreal temperature in degrees centigrade (Celsius)
2. To talk about skiing —learning names for ski equipment —practicing vocabulary —expressing past time	Sur les pistes. 154 L'équipement d'une bonne skieuse. 155	Expressing Past Time: Reflexive Constructions 156	Chaîne de mots. 155	
3. To talk about a minor ski accident —reviewing interrogative pronouns by playing a game —using interrogative pronouns	Au chalet. 157	More on Interrogative Pronouns: Contractions with à and de 158	Le jeu des stations. 158	first-aid services on the slopes
4. To read some do's and don'ts for good, safe skiing	Word List 160		Skier. 159	

Learning Objectives	Basic Material	Grammar	Activities, Realia, and Supplementary Readings	Areas for Cultural Awareness
1. To describe a farm and its surroundings —using beau, nouveau, and vieux	Ore. 162	The Adjectives beau, nouveau, vieux 164		rural, mountainous area of southwestern France
2. To talk about farm activities	A la ferme. 165	The Verb savoir 166 connaître or savoir 167		work on a French farm; how it is shared by the whole family
—using the verb savoir —contrasting the verbs connaître and savoir —learning names of animals and the foods they eat	Savez-vous ce que ces animaux mangent? 167			animals and their feed
—practicing names of animals by playing a game —learning the French words for sounds farm animals make			Devinettes. 168 Les cris des animaux . . . en français! 168	French onomatopoeia for animal sounds
3. To talk about old times	C'était le bon temps! 168	Expressing Past Time: The Imparfait 169		
—using the imparfait				
—reviewing the vocabulary on the farm by playing a game			Le jeu de la ferme. 171	
—reading farm sayings about the weather			La météo du fermier. 172	
	Word List 172			

Unit 17

LA MARTINIQUE

Learning Objectives	Basic Material	Grammar	Activities, Realia, and Supplementary Readings	Areas for Cultural Awareness
1. To talk about the French-speaking island of Martinique —comparing kilometers with miles —using the verbs pouvoir and vouloir —learning songs about water and beaches	La Martinique 173 (Voici deux circuits) 176	The Verbs pouvoir and vouloir 178	(*map of the Caribbean*) 174 (*map of Martinique*) 176 Chansons. 178	Martinique comparing kilometers with miles
2. To talk about life on the island —meeting the Dubois family	Une famille martiniquaise. 179			family life in Martinique: occupations, leisure time
3. To talk about a fishing expedition —learning the names of various fish by playing a game —learning the names of scuba-diving equipment —comparing the imparfait and passé composé	Une sortie en mer. 179 Danou va plonger. 181	Imparfait or Passé Composé 181	Dans la mer des Caraïbes. 180	
4. To read about the fate of the town of St-Pierre	Word List 184		Une excursion à St-Pierre. 183	historical volcanic eruption that destroyed St-Pierre in 1902

FRANÇOIS A L'ECOLE DE VOILE
Chapitre de Révision (*Review Unit*)

Learning Objectives	Basic Material	Grammar	Activities, Realia, and Supplementary Readings	Areas for Cultural Awareness
1. To talk about summer camp—getting there, settling in, getting adjusted —reviewing reflexives	Mon journal de bord: 1er jour 186	Reflexive Constructions 187		summer sailing camp
—learning the French alphabet by playing a game			Le jeu des messages. 188	Morse code and nautical flags
2. To talk about life at camp —daily routines, special duties —reviewing the passé composé and imparfait —using the passé composé and the imparfait by playing a game —learning four nautical knots	Mon journal de bord: 3e jour 189	Passé Composé or Imparfait 190	Histoire en chaîne. 190 Quatre nœuds. 192	how camp is organized; group activities, individual and group responsibilities learning how to make nautical knots
	Word List 192			

Learning Objectives	Basic Material	Grammar	Activities, Realia, and Supplementary Readings	Areas for Cultural Awareness
1. To talk about traveling by plane —using reflexive constructions	A l'aéroport Charles-de-Gaulle. 194	More on Reflexive Constructions 195		modern Paris airport
2. To learn names of countries —practicing the names of countries and their capitals by finding them on a map —learning prepositions to use with names of countries —playing a game	Devant le tableau des arrivées. 195 Et vous, êtes-vous bon (bonne) en géographie? 196	Names of Countries 196	Bon Voyage! 197 (map of Europe, North Africa, and Middle East)	flight schedules locating European, North African, and Middle Eastern countries on map
3. To talk about nationalities and languages —using the verb dire —learning adjectives and nouns of nationality; names of languages —relating the names of countries to nationalities and languages —to read a cartoon on some do's and dont's of traveling abroad	A l'arrivée. Epilogue. 198 Pays, nationalités et langues. 199 Word List 202	The Verb dire 199 Nationalities and Languages 199	Si vous allez dans un pays étranger. 201	what to do and not to do when traveling abroad by plane

Unit 20

EN TUNISIE

Learning Objectives	Basic Material	Grammar	Activities, Realia, and Supplementary Readings	Areas for Cultural Awareness
1. To read about Tunisia			A Sousse, en Tunisie. 204	French spoken in Arab North Africa; what cities look like; how people live
2. To talk about everyday life in a Tunisian city —using interrogative pronouns	Dans la médina. 205	Interrogative Pronouns 206		the markets; craftspeople; bargaining
3. To meet and talk about a Tunisian family —talking about preparing a Tunisian meal —using verbs followed by infinitives	Chez les Slim. 209 La cuisine tunisienne. 210	Verb + Infinitive 211		close family relationships in Tunisia typical Tunisian dishes
4. To read about Tunisian customs and Tunisian hospitality			Thé à la tunisienne. 213	customs for serving tea to guests
5. To practice new vocabulary by playing a game	Word List 214		Le jeu des photos. 214	

Learning Objectives	Basic Material	Grammar	Activities, Realia, and Supplementary Readings	Areas for Cultural Awareness
1. To talk about an amusement park; expressions of excitement and fear	Anna et Sylvie à la fête. 216			amusement park; rides and activities
2. To talk about the future —using the future tense	Anna, Sylvie et le fakir. 218	The Future Tense 218		
3. To talk about riding bumper cars —using prepositions followed by infinitives —practicing après + past infinitive by playing a game —reading one's own future in a horoscope —reviewing the future tense by playing a game	Anna et Sylvie dans les autos tamponneuses. 220	Preposition + Infinitive 221	Chaîne de mots. 222 Que dit votre horoscope? 222 Le jeu de l'horoscope. 222	
4. To read a horoscope	Word List 224		Votre horoscope 223	what French teenagers might like to do during their summer vacation

GYMNASTIQUE ET ATHLETISME

Learning Objectives	Basic Material	Grammar	Activities, Realia, and Supplementary Readings	Areas for Cultural Awareness
1. To talk about gym class	La mise en train. 226			gym class in Canada
—learning names for parts of the body				
—learning different kinds of gymnastic exercises	Qu'est-ce qu'on peut faire encore comme exercices? 227			
—using articles with nouns referring to the body		The Articles le, la, and les with nouns referring to the body 228		
—practicing names for parts of the body by playing a game			Le jeu de «Jacques a dit». 228 (*"Simon says . . ."*)	
—using adverbs		From Adjective to Adverb 228		
—practicing using adverbs by playing a game			Le jeu des adverbes. 228	
2. To talk about athletics	L'entraînement. 229			meters and centimeters
—using the verb courir		The Verb courir 230		
—measuring distances in meters and centimeters		Mesurons en mètres et centimètres 230		
—measuring one's height using the metric system			Combien est-ce que vous mesurez? 230	
—using the comparative forms of adjectives and adverbs		Making Comparisons 231		
—comparing performances	Comparons les performances de Jean-François et de Louis. 232		(*personal progress sheets*) 232	personal record sheets of times and distances
3. To read an account of a championship	Trophées Scolaires 233	Making Comparisons: Superlatives 234		
—using superlative forms of adjectives and adverbs	Word List 236			

POUR MAMAN

Unit 23

Learning Objectives	Basic Material	Grammar	Activities, Realia, and Supplementary Readings	Areas for Cultural Awareness
1. To talk about choosing a birthday present —learning the names of some presents for one's mother —using the conditional	L'embarras du choix. 238 Et vous, qu'est-ce que vous aimeriez acheter à votre mère? 238	The Conditional 239		French-speaking Liège, in Belgium; kinds of gifts chosen for parents
2. To talk about getting presents and about shops where they are sold —learning the names of some presents for one's father —using conditions —practicing conditions by playing a game	A la galerie marchande. 240 Si c'était l'anniversaire de votre père, qu'est-ce que vous lui achèteriez? 242	Expressing Conditions 243	Le jeu des portraits chinois. 244	shops where one buys presents and cards
3. To talk about how to write a birthday card —using possessive pronouns	Derniers préparatifs. 244	Possessive Pronouns 245		things to say on a card
4. To read about the birthday celebration —reading a recipe for a birthday cake	Word List 248		Bon Anniversaire, Maman! 246 Gâteau d'anniversaire 247	expressions to thank people birthday customs in Belgium and France

Unit 24

LA TELEVISION

Chapitre de Révision (*Review Unit*)

Learning Objectives	Basic Material	Grammar	Activities, Realia, and Supplementary Readings	Areas for Cultural Awareness
1. To talk about the kinds of TV programs young people like to watch —how to use a TV set	Le genre d'émissions que nos amis aiment. 249 Quand Suzanne veut regarder la télévision. 250			some of the TV shows French-speaking teenagers like; young people's attitudes toward TV; French TV system
2. To discuss a particular show —reviewing the future and the conditional	Documentaire sur le Sénégal. 250	The Future and the Conditional 252		Sénégal: its people, places, culture, way of life
3. To talk about commercials on TV —reviewing comparatives and superlatives	Quelques publicités. 253	Comparatives and Superlatives of Adjectives 254		
4. To read a French TV guide	Word List 256		Samedi 19 Février 255 (*excerpt from French TV guide*)	

WRITING AND CONSULTING STAFF
CENTER FOR CURRICULUM DEVELOPMENT

RESEARCH AND WRITING

Writers   KATIA BRILLIÉ LUTZ, FRANÇOISE PÉRIN LEFFLER

Consulting Editor   MARINA LIAPUNOV

Consulting Linguist   ANN TUKEY HARRISON, Michigan State University, East Lansing, Mich.

Editor   ARTHUR WOLSONCROFT

CONSULTANTS

General Consultant   NELSON BROOKS, New Haven, Conn.

Culture Consultant   JEAN-PAUL CONSTANTIN, Université de Paris X, France

TEACHER CONSULTANTS   RHEBA BURGESS, Norview High School
Norfolk, Va.
ROBERT DIDSBURY, Weston High School
Weston, Conn.
JOHN V. GORMLEY, Mount Miguel High School
Spring Valley, Calif.
JOSEPH F. HERNEY, Briarcliff High School
Briarcliff Manor, N.Y.
MAX PARIENTI, Springfield High School
Springfield, Ill.
ROSALIE G. ROGERS, Briarcliff Middle School
Briarcliff Manor, N.Y.

nos Amis

french 1

HARCOURT BRACE JOVANOVICH, PUBLISHERS

Orlando   New York   Chicago   San Diego   Atlanta   Dallas

PICTURE CREDITS

Positions are shown in abbreviated form, as follows: *t*, top; *c*, center; *b*, bottom; *l*, left; *r*, right.

PLATES All HBJ photos as noted, except Pl 32 #1 Mark Antman. Pl 1: #1 Oscar Buitrago; #2, #8 Patrick Courtault; #3 O. Buitrago; #4, #5 M. Antman; #6 Marc Riboud, Magnum; #7 Eugene Gordon; #8 P. Courtault. Pl 2/3: HBJ Art. Pl 4: #1, #2 Stephen Colwell; #3 Philippe Bérard. Pl 5: #4, #5, #8 S. Colwell; #6 Dominique Lacarrière; #7 Pierre Capretz. Pl 6: #1 O. Buitrago; #2 Gerhard Gscheidle; #3 C. Bear, Shostal; #4 R. Fawcett, Shostal. Pl 7: #5, #6 P. Courtault; #7, #8 M. Antman. Pl 8: #1 M. Antman; #2, #3, #4 E. Gordon. Pl 9: M. Antman. Pl 10: #1 O. Buitrago; #2, #3 S. Colwell; #4 P. Courtault. Pl 11: #5, #9 S. Colwell; #6 P. Courtault; #7, #8 M. Antman. Pl 12: #1 P. Courtault; #2, #3 P. Capretz; #4 M. Antman. Pl 13: #5, #9 O. Buitrago; #6 S. Colwell; #7 M. Antman; #8, #10 P. Capretz. Pl 14: #1, #3 P. Courtault; #2 P. Capretz; #4 M. Antman. Pl 15: #5, #6, #7 M. Antman; #8 P. Capretz; #9 P. Courtault. Pl 16: M. Antman. Pl 17: S. Colwell. Pl 18: #1 G. Gscheidle; #2 P. Courtault; #3, #4 S. Colwell; #5 M. Antman. Pl 19: #6 P. Courtault; #7 S. Colwell; #8 G. Gscheidle; #9 Robin Forbes. Pl 20: P. Courtault. Pl 21: #2, #4, #5 S. Colwell; #3 M. Antman. Pl 22: #1 P. Courtault; #2, #3, #5 S. Colwell; #4 O. Buitrago. Pl 23: #1, #3 S. Colwell; #2 D. Lacarrière; #4 P. Courtault. Pl 24: #1, #2, #4, #5 M. Antman; #3 S. Colwell. Pl 25: S. Colwell. Pl 26: #1, #3 M. Antman; #2, #4, #5 P. Courtault. Pl 27: M. Antman. Pl 28: M. Antman. Pl 29: M. Antman. Pl 30: P. Capretz. Pl 31: #1, #2, #4 S. Colwell; #3 P. Courtault. Pl 32: #2, #3, #4, #5 O. Buitrago.

TEXT PHOTOS F1: Ciganovic, FPG. F2: #1, #5 P. Capretz; #2 Air France; #3, #4 P. Courtault. F3: #6, M. Antman; #7, #8, #9 S. Colwell; #10, #11 O. Buitrago. F4: #1, #3, #4 O. Buitrago; #2, #5 S. Colwell. F5: #6 P. Courtault; #7 S. Colwell; #8, #9, #10 P. Capretz; #11 O. Buitrago. F6: #1 (Musée du Louvre) P. Capretz; #2, #3 P. Courtault; #4 (Collection du Louvre) S. Colwell. F7: #5 M. Antman; #6 P. Capretz; #7 O. Buitrago; #8 Berreetly, Photo Researchers; #9 H. Namuth, Photo Researchers. F8: O. Buitrago. F9: #3, #5 O. Buitrago; #4 TWA. F10: O. Buitrago; #3 Courtesy of William H. Van Vleck, Inc. Brooklyn, N.Y. F11: #1, #2 O. Buitrago; #3 "W"/ Fairchild Publications. F12: #1 I. Berry, Magnum; #2 UN; #3, #4 M. Antman. F13: #1 G. Gahan, Photo Researchers; #2, #3 O. Buitrago; F14: O. Buitrago. F15: #1, #2, #3 O. Buitrago; #4 Museum of Modern Art. F16: #1 L'Oréal; #2 Allibert; #3 Péchiney Ugine Kuhlmann; #4 Guerlain. Page 1: #1, #3, #4 P. Courtault; #2, #5 P. Capretz; #6 O. Buitrago. 2: P. Courtault. 3: #3 P. Capretz; #4 P. Courtault. 4: #1, #2 P. Capretz; #3, #4 O. Buitrago. 5: #3, #5, #6 P. Courtault; #4, #7, #8 P. Capretz. 11: D. Vine, Shostal. 12: #1*tr*, #1*tl*, #3, #4 P. Capretz; #2 O. Buitrago. 17: P. Capretz. 21: O. Buitrago. 22: P. Courtault. 25: P. Capretz. 29: P. Courtault. 31: O. Buitrago. 33, 37: P. Capretz. 45, 46, 49: P. Courtault. 53: O. Buitrago. 58, 60, 65, 68, 71: P. Courtault. 75, 78, 81, 82, 83, 85: S. Colwell. 87, 88, 90, 92, 97, 98, 99, 105, 106: P. Courtault. 109: Lauros-Giraudon, Paris. 110: #1, P. Capretz, #2, #3 M. Antman. 111: #4 S. Colwell; #5 (Musée du Louvre) Jim Theologos. 113: P. Capretz. 114: #1 P. Capretz; #2, #3, #4, #5 M. Antman. 118, 119: M. Antman. 121: O. Buitrago. 123, 126 (Musée Océanographique de Monaco), 127: S. Colwell. 129, 130, 133, 137, 139: P. Capretz. 141, 142, 145: P. Courtault. 147: Philippe Beadle. 152, 154, 157, 160: O. Buitrago. 161: P. Capretz. 162: *tl* P. Capretz; *tr*, *bl*, *br* P. Courtault. 165: #1, #3, #4, #5, #6 P. Capretz; #2 P. Courtault. 166: #7 P. Courtault; #8 P. Capretz. 168, 173, 174, 175, 176, 179, 183 (Musée Vulcanologique de Saint-Pierre), 185, 186, 189: P. Capretz. 193: Halary, Photo Researchers. 194: #1 (Aéroport de Paris) P. Courtault; #2 (Aéroport de Paris) P. Capretz. 198: P. Capretz. 203: decorative background, Office National du Tourisme Tunisien. 203, 204, 205: P. Courtault. 206: *l*, K. D. Franke, Peter Arnold; *r*, W. Hamilton, Shostal. 207: *l*, H. Lanks, Monkmeyer; *r*, G. Torton, Photo Researchers. 209, 210, 213: P. Courtault. 215, 216, 217, 218, 220: S. Colwell. 226, 229: O. Buitrago. 233: #1, #2, #3 M. Antman; #4, #5 O. Buitrago. 237: O. Buitrago. 238: P. Courtault. 240: #1 O. Buitrago; #2 P. Courtault. 241: #3, #4, #5, #6 P. Courtault; #7 M. Antman; #8 P. Capretz. 244, 246, 247: P. Courtault. 249: *tr*, M. Antman; *tl*, E. Gordon; *bl*, Columbia Pictures Television Industries, Inc; *br*, © Paramount Pictures Corporation. 251: #1 P. J. Meyer; #5 G. Holton; #6 B. Wolff, All Photo Researchers; #2, #3, #4 E. Gordon; #7 M. Riboud, Magnum; #8 Animals, Animals.

ART HBJ: Page 1, 34, 153 Middle, 174, 176, 197. DON CREWS: 8, 14, 35, 57, 102, 105, 111, 117, 128, 151, 153*t*, 155, 159, 181, 188, 223, 225. MANNY HALLER: 13, 66, 69, 73, 142, 167, 171, 180, 192, 201, 227, 247. ZORAN ORLIC: 15, 19, 26, 29, 39, 40, 47, 52, 76, 77, 79, 82, 85, 91, 95, 132, 143, 238, 242, 253.

SONGS "La plage calme" paroles de René Livron, "Ho et Hisse et Ho" paroles de Christian Loire, extraits de ''1000 chants 2'' de Jean-Edel Berthier, Les Presses d'Ile de France.

Acknowledgments

We wish to express our gratitude to the young people pictured in this book, to their parents for their cooperation, and to the many people who assisted us in making this project possible.

Our Friends: Some of our friends have been renamed in the units to avoid any confusion between names. In the list that follows, the fictional names appear in parentheses next to the real names. Arnaud and Richard Aché, Units 1, 2, 19; Anna Angeli, Unit 21; Catherine and Philippe Beadle (Lardan) with family and friends, Cover, Units 1, 3, 5, 7, 9, 14; Pierre Bize, Unit 16; Evelyne Bouquet, Unit 6; Suzanne Côté, Units 22, 24; Stéphane Debras, Unit 10; François Denis-le-Sève and classmates, Units 1, 2, 4, 6, 18; Danou and Doris Dubois with family, Cover, Units 1, 3, 17, 24; Paul Dufresne, Unit 15; Françoise and Vincent Dupont with family, Units 7, 23; Dominique and Philippe (Bernard) Ecrepont with friends, Units 5, 14; Denis Félix (Pierre), Unit 10; Jean-François and Monique Fort with family, Units 1, 16; Ghislaine Gignère, Unit 22; Jean-Marcel Giuliani with family, Units 8, 12; Denise and Louise Goulet with family and friends, Cover, Units 1, 2, 15; Didier Jolibois, Units 2, 4, 6; Louis Laferrière, Unit 22; Hélène Lapierre, Unit 22; Yves Lefort, Unit 22; Antoine Masson, Unit 11; Christine Pierre, Unit 10; Jean-François Plante, Unit 22; Jean-Raymond Poliquin, Unit 22; Christine (Isabelle) Sautelet, Unit 11; Viviane Simorre and friend, Unit 13; Aziz and Nadia Slim with family, Cover, Units 20, 24; Martine Thierry (Dupuis), Unit 6; Catherine (Sylvie) Vanheeghe, Units 3, 9; Sylvie Vincent, Units 21, 24.

Our special thanks to the following people who introduced us to some of our friends: Claude Beadle, Raymond Côté, Françoise Denis-le-Sève, Solange Dupont Dispas.

Contents

● *basic material*
▲ *grammar*
■ *materials for fun and cultural awareness*
▼ *reference*

PHOTO ESSAY   **City Life**   Plates 9–16

PHOTO ESSAY **Festivals** Plates 25–32

Foreign Language and You

When you arrive in a French-speaking country, you'll find it a big help to know the language. As soon as you step off the plane, you'll have to communicate with the customs officer, who almost certainly will not speak English. Also, if you speak French, you'll have no trouble taking a taxi or the airport bus to your next destination.

1

2

3

4

5

6

7

Knowing the language will help, no matter what means of transportation you use. If you travel by car, you have to understand road signs. If you travel by train, you have to be able to figure out schedules and ticket prices. You might be eligible for a discount fare! Besides, you would not want to miss the fun of meeting and talking to your traveling companions.

🚃 30
🚗 50

8

RESPECTEZ LA DISTANCE DE 50m ENTRE VÉHICULES

9

Si vous avez moins de 23 ans

INTER RAIL

un mois de voyages à l'étranger par le train pour 700 francs.

10

25¢ AUTOMOBILES AVEC MONNAIE EXACTE SEULEMENT AUTOMOBILES

11

Once you arrive at your destination, you have to find a hotel room. You also have to eat, and ordering a meal when you don't know the language can be quite an adventure! Then you may want to go into the local stores and buy presents for family and friends, or for yourself.

When you don't know the language, everyday life can be full of pitfalls. You have to know how much money to leave in the parking meter. The subway may not run all night, and you may end up stranded somewhere. You have to be able to discuss things with the bank teller, the cleaner, the pharmacist.

6 7

8 9

10

11

When you know the language of a country, you understand its culture better. Its history will come alive when you actually walk on the ground where famous historical figures walked centuries ago. Museums contain treasures well worth investigating. Here, the best source of information is usually the guard, who will tell you not only historical facts but also interesting, unpublished anecdotes.

1

2

3

4

5

6

7

8

9

Art plays an important role in the culture of any country. It manifests itself in different forms: in architecture—whether a Gothic cathedral or an ultra-modern structure—in the plastic arts, in the theater, and also in forms that are specific to an area, like the fine porcelain of Limoges.

1

Foreign language skills are important not only when you travel, but also when you look for a job. The next several pages suggest some of the ways you can use foreign language in a career. For example, travel agents and tour guides, who deal with travelers from many countries, often need to know several languages.

2

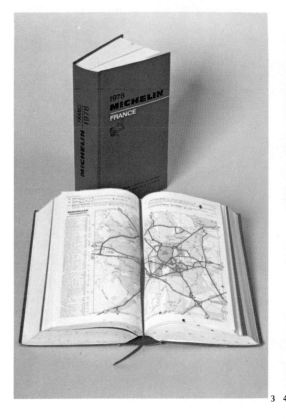

3 4

Printed travel guides, airlines, and tourist offices can suggest standard tours to popular places. But when a travel agent has to plan a trip to some place off the beaten path, brochures from the country itself—printed in the foreign language—are the only source of information. For jobs like these, knowing a foreign language can be a definite asset. For certain other jobs, the knowledge of a foreign language is essential. Stewards and stewardesses on flights to non-English-speaking countries are required to speak at least one language besides English. And in hotels of international stature, which attend to the needs of tourist and business people from all over the world, the hotel manager must often speak three or more foreign languages.

5

People who work in the food industry often have to travel to foreign countries, where they sample and buy local products and are in close contact with local merchants. Very often, the only way food importers can keep up with product changes is to go to the foreign country themselves. This is especially true in the wine industry, where a good rapport between wine brokers and growers or distributors is essential.

1

Fromages de France

2

3

In recent years, the French fashion industry has greatly expanded. Many designers have opened stores in cities all over the world, and in these stores most of the employees are required to speak French. Even American stores often have French-speaking employees, especially stores specializing in fine textiles, such as bath towels, men's shirts, and sheets. Such items are especially prized by French tourists, because they are much cheaper in the United States than in France.

Jobs in communications are often very exciting, and many of them require the use of foreign languages. Reporters and camera teams need to know foreign languages when they cover international events. International organizations in the United States and abroad depend on interpreters. So do the many international conventions set up annually all over the world. In the work of international diplomacy, the language most frequently used, after English, is French.

In many fields, people with highly developed professional skills find foreign languages an asset. For example, economists sometimes deal with foreign countries. Financial experts may work in the international commodity and money markets. And lawyers often represent clients from foreign countries. For United States lawyers who handle cases in French-speaking Canada, or who handle negotiations with companies in French-speaking countries, French language skills are essential.

Foreign languages are the cornerstone of many academic careers. Some people make a career of foreign language teaching. Librarians find it very useful to know more than one language. And in the field of publishing, writers and editors use foreign language skills to produce teaching materials and textbooks like this one.

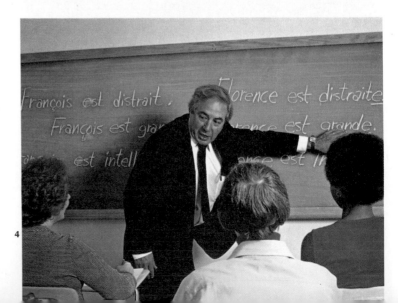

F14

1

Many careers involving art or literature benefit from the knowledge of foreign languages. Antique dealers and museum curators often go abroad to buy items for their trade. In another domain, translators need a perfect command of the foreign language, as well as an understanding of the foreign culture.

2

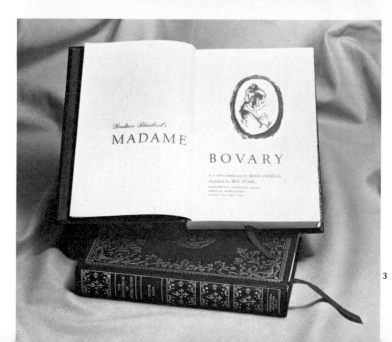

Gustave Flaubert's

MADAME

BOVARY

in a new translation by JOAN CHARLES
illustrated by BEN STAHL

3

4

In industry, the knowledge of foreign languages is becoming more and more important as companies become multinational. Many French companies now have branches in the United States, where the managers are required to speak French. Meanwhile, American companies have to deal with companies from French-speaking countries all over the world.

By enhancing your professional skills and enlarging your view of the world, foreign languages can help you in almost any field.

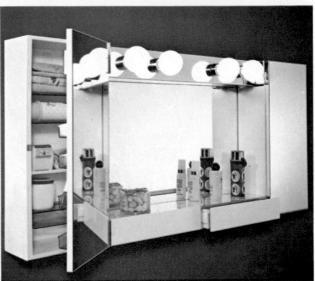

Catherine Lardan
15 ans
Luneray, France

Richard Aché
15 ans
Paris, France

Denise Goulet
12 ans
Montréal, Canada

François Le Sève
14 ans
Montargis, France

Doris Dubois
13 ans
Fort-de-France,
Martinique

Jean-François Fort
12 ans
Ore, France

The correct pronunciation of these names will
be practiced in Oral Exercise No. 4. These young
people appear at least once more in the
book: Catherine, Units 3, 5, 7, 9, 14;
Richard, Units 2, 19; François, Units 2, 4,
6, 18; Jean-François, Unit 16; Doris,
Units 3, 17; Denise, Unit 15.

1

NOS AMIS

These young people live in different parts of France and the world. Richard lives in Paris, the capital of France; François, in the town of Montargis, about seventy miles south of Paris. Jean-François lives in southwestern France, in a village in the Pyrenees, the mountains separating France and Spain; and Catherine lives in the small town of Luneray, to the west of Paris, in Normandy. Doris and Denise live on the other side of the Atlantic Ocean from France. Doris' home is the island of Martinique in the Caribbean. Denise lives in Montreal, the largest city in Canada. Nevertheless, all of these young people have one thing in common: they are all French-speaking. Naturally, they do not all sound the same when they talk. They have regional accents and use regional expressions, just as we do, but their language is the standard French that can be heard on radio and television.

All French-speaking countries in the world are shown on the map, Plates 2-3.

For presentation of Basic Material, see section called Recording Materials: Format and Samples, p. T56.

2 Comment t'appelles-tu? ⊗

Catherine parle à Jean-François.
- C. Comment t'appelles-tu?
- J.-F. Qui? Moi?[1] Je m'appelle Jean-François. Et toi?
- C. Moi, je m'appelle Catherine.
- J.-F. Catherine comment?
- C. Catherine Lardan.
- J.-F. Et ce garçon, il s'appelle François?
- C. Non, lui, il s'appelle Richard.
- J.-F. Et cette fille, elle s'appelle Doris ou Denise?
- C. Elle, elle s'appelle Denise.
- J.-F. Ah oui, Denise Goulet!

1

2

3 Look at the photographs on page 1 and answer the questions. ⊗

(photo 1) Comment s'appelle cette fille?	Elle s'appelle Catherine.
Catherine comment?	Catherine Lardan.
(photo 4) Comment s'appelle ce garçon?	Il s'appelle Jean-François.
Jean-François comment?	Jean-François Fort.
(photo 6) Comment s'appelle cette fille?	Elle s'appelle Denise.
Denise comment?	Denise Goulet.

Ask these questions for the other young people in the photos, too, as well as for the students in your class.

4 ORAL EXERCISE

5 Ask a classmate:
Answers here should use only students' own English names.

Comment t'appelles-tu?	Moi, je m'appelle…
Et comment s'appelle cette fille?	Elle s'appelle…
Et ce garçon?	Il s'appelle…
Et lui? Et elle?	Il s'appelle… Elle s'appelle…

6 What is your name?

Only singular subject pronouns and verb forms are introduced in Unit 1. Plurals are introduced in Unit 2.

Je m'appelle Catherine.	*My name is Catherine.*
Tu t'appelles François?	*Your name is François?*
Il s'appelle Jean-François.	*His name is Jean-François.*
Elle s'appelle Denise.	*Her name is Denise.*

7 Noms de garçons ⊗

Alain	François	Olivier
Arnaud	Jean-Pierre	Patrick
Bernard	Jean-Marc	Philippe
Christian	Marc	Richard
Daniel	Mathieu	Serge

Noms de filles ⊗

Brigitte	Danielle	Michelle
Catherine	Florence	Nathalie
Cécile	Françoise	Sophie
Christine	Isabelle	Sylvie
Claire	Marie-Claire	Véronique

You may want to tell students what the equivalents (if any) of their names are. Then redo Ex. 5 with French names.

[1] **Moi, toi, lui, elle** mean *me, you, him, her.* They are used independently as one-word questions or answers. They can also be used to emphasize **je, tu, il, elle,** as these examples show.
Independent pronouns are introduced in Unit 7.

8 Quel âge as-tu? ⊗

Doris parle à François.
D. Quel âge as-tu?
F. J'ai presque quinze ans. Et toi?
D. Moi, j'ai treize ans, comme Denise.
F. Ah non, elle, elle a douze ans.
D. Et Jean-François?
F Il a douze ans aussi.

9 Les nombres de 1 à 20. ⊗

1	2	3	4	5	6	7	8	9	10
un	deux	trois	quatre	cinq	six	sept	huit	neuf	dix

11	12	13	14	15	16	17	18	19	20
onze	douze	treize	quatorze	quinze	seize	dix-sept	dix-huit	dix-neuf	vingt

Point out the different pronunciations of 1, 2, 3, 6, 9, 10, 19, and 20 when used alone and when followed by "an(s)"

10 Look at the photographs on page 1 and answer the questions. ⊗

Quel âge a Catherine? Elle a quinze ans.
Quel âge a Richard? Il a quinze ans.
Et Denise? Et François? Elle a douze ans. Il a quatorze ans.
Et Doris? Et Jean-François? Elle a treize ans. Il a douze ans.

11 ORAL EXERCISE ⊗

12 How old are you?

J'ai quinze ans.	*I am fifteen years old.*
Tu as quinze ans?	*You are fifteen years old?*
Il a quinze ans.	*He is fifteen years old.*
Elle a quinze ans.	*She is fifteen years old.*

The verb avoir with the meaning "to have" is introduced in Unit 3.

13 Ask some of your classmates about themselves and others :

Quel âge as-tu? J'ai presque…
Et toi? Moi, j'ai…
Et lui? Et elle? Lui, il a… Elle, elle a…

14 Le jeu de loto.

Draw a rectangle and divide it into twenty squares as shown. Number the squares from 1 to 20 in any order you choose. Use each number only once. Someone will call numbers from 1 to 20 in random order. The winner is the first one to fill in a horizontal line.

8	2	5	13	14
7	1	6	4	15
9	10	3	19	17
18	11	16	12	20

15 Où habites-tu? ⊗

DENISE   Où habites-tu? En France?
RICHARD   Oui, à Paris. Toi, tu habites aux Etats-Unis, n'est-ce pas?
DENISE   Non, j'habite au Canada, à Montréal.

Refer to map of France, p. 8, for location of Paris.

The population of Paris is about two and a half million, and with the suburbs it reaches about ten million.

Paris is the topic of Unit 11, p. 109. More photographs of Paris can be found there.

1

Richard habite à Paris. Paris est une très grande ville. C'est la capitale de la France. Richard habite dans un appartement.

Point out location of Canada and Montreal on a map of North America.

The population of Montreal is about three million, of whom about two-thirds speak French.

2

Denise habite à Montréal, au Canada. Montréal est une très grande ville aussi. Denise habite dans une petite maison.

The map on p. 8 will show distances between Luchon and Montargis and Paris. More photographs of Ore can be found in Unit 16, p. 161.

3

Jean-François habite à Ore. C'est un petit village près de Luchon. (C'est très loin de Paris.)

4

François habite à Montargis. C'est une petite ville près de Paris.

Dieppe is a fishing and commercial port, pop. about 30,000. It also serves as one of several Channel ferry ports. See map p. 8. More photographs of Dieppe can be found in Unit 5, p. 45.

5

Catherine habite à Luneray. C'est un village près de Dieppe.

6

Dieppe est un grand port.

7

Doris habite à Fort-de-France. C'est à la Martinique.

8

La Martinique est une petite île dans la mer des Caraïbes.

Refer to map of the world (Photo Essay "French Throughout the World," Plates 2-3) for location of Martinique, also to map of Caribbean, p. 174, and to map of Martinique, on p. 176. Martinique is the topic of Unit 17, p. 173, where more photographs can be found.

16 **Look at the photographs on pages 4 and 5 and answer these questions.** ⊗

Où habite Catherine?	Elle habite à Luneray.
C'est une grande ville?	Non, c'est un village.
C'est près de Dieppe?	Oui, c'est près de Dieppe.
C'est au Canada, Dieppe?	Non, c'est en France.
Où habite François?	Il habite à Montargis.
C'est près de Dieppe?	Non, c'est près de Paris.
Où habite Doris?	A Fort-de-France, à la Martinique.
La Martinique, c'est une ville?	Non, c'est une île dans la mer des Caraïbes.

17 **ORAL EXERCISE** ⊗

18 **Where do you live?**

J'habite à Paris.	*I live in Paris.*
Tu habites à Paris?	*You live in Paris?*
François / **Il** **habite à Montargis.**	*François* / *He lives in Montargis.*
Catherine / **Elle** **habite à Luneray.**	*Catherine* / *She lives in Luneray.*

19 **Ask one of your classmates :** Elicit personal responses

Où habites-tu?	J'habite à...
C'est une grande ville?	Oui, c'est une très grande ville.
	Non, c'est un village.
C'est près d'une grande ville?	Oui, c'est près de...
Tu habites dans un appartement?	Non, j'habite dans une petite maison.

20 **CONVERSATION EXERCISE**

Now when you meet someone, you can find out about each other by asking these questions :
1. Comment t'appelles-tu?   2. Quel âge as-tu?   3. Où habites-tu?

You might set up a situation of students meeting each other in a new class. Use "Bonjour" or "Salut" and a handshake, and ask questions. "Et toi?" will continue the conversations.

21 **GENDER AND GENDER MARKERS**

A sample of the recording of grammar presentations is given on p. T56.
Answer the questions which follow the examples. ⊗

C'est **un garçon.**   C'est **une fille.**
Is **un** or **une** used with **garçon?** Is **un** or **une** used with **fille?**
C'est **un village.**   C'est **une ville.**
Which of these words, **un** or **une,** is used with **village?** Is it the same as the word used with **garçon?** Which of these words, **un** or **une,** is used with **ville?** Is it the same as the word used with **fille?**

22 Read the following generalization.

1. All French nouns are classed as either masculine or feminine. These classes are called gender. The gender classes masculine and feminine do not always refer to males and females but refer also to objects and ideas that have nothing to do with males and females at all. For instance, **un village** is masculine as is **un garçon,** and **une ville** is feminine as is **une fille.** The gender of many words, such as **village** and **ville,** cannot be determined from the meaning. You will have to look and listen for other words which mark their gender, such as **un/une** or **le/la.**

2. The following chart includes all the gender markers you have seen so far.

Markers	Masculine			Feminine		
Articles	C'est · Où est Où est	**un** **le** **ce**	village. village? village?	C'est Où est Où est	**une** **la** **cette**	ville. ville? ville?
Adjectives	C'est un C'est un	**petit** **grand**	village. village.	C'est une C'est une	**petite** **grande**	ville. ville.

3. Here is a list of the nouns you have seen so far with the articles that mark their gender:

Masculine: **un appartement, un garçon, un port, un village.**
Feminine: **une capitale, une fille, une île, une maison, une mer, une ville.**

23 Ask your classmates these questions: ⊗
(*Vary the questions by using* **ce** *or* **cette**, *then* **petit** *or* **petite**.)

Qui est le garçon?

Qui est ce garçon?
Qui est ce petit garçon?

Il habite dans une maison? Il habite dans cette (petite) maison?
C'est dans une ville? C'est dans cette (petite) ville?
Comment s'appelle la fille? Comment s'appelle cette (petite) fille?
Elle habite dans un village? Elle habite dans ce (petit) village?

24 LISTENING EXERCISE ⊗

	0	1	2	3	4	5	6	7	8	9	10
Masculine	✓										
Feminine											

Scripts for Listening Exercises are given in Teaching Suggestions for a given Unit. Unit 1 script, p. T14.

25 WRITING EXERCISE

a. Write the responses for Exercise 23.
b. Rewrite each sentence below, using the proper gender marker.
1. (ce/cette)   Où habite __cette__ fille?
2. (un/une)   Elle habite à Luneray. C'est _____un_____ village.
3. (un/une)   C'est près d' __une__ ville?
4. (un/une)   Oui, de Dieppe. Dieppe est aussi _____un_____ port.
5. (grand/grande)   Un __grand__ port!

26   EN FRANCE ⊗

Long before France was united into the nation we know now, it was many separate provinces. These provinces, in time, developed their own particular characters and their own regional specialties, which they have kept. It is because of the traits, the products, and the natural

The map shows some of the main products of the provinces and regions listed on the next page — e.g., Normandy is well known for its cows and dairy products, and for its apple orchards and cider.

differences in geography of these old provinces that France as a nation is known for its tremendous variety and richness. Burgundy, for instance, is always associated with its wines, Normandy with its butter and cheeses, Provence with its sun. Here are the names of six of these provinces along with the names of seas, rivers, mountains, and cities of France.

PROVINCES: l'Alsace, l'Aquitaine, la Bourgogne, la Bretagne, la Normandie, la Provence.
VILLES: Bordeaux, Brest, Lille, Lyon, Marseille, Nantes, Nice, Strasbourg, Rouen.
MERS: la mer du Nord, la Manche, l'océan Atlantique, la mer Méditerranée.
FLEUVES: la Garonne, la Loire, la Seine, le Rhin, le Rhône.
MONTAGNES: les Vosges, le Jura, les Alpes, les Pyrénées, le Massif central.

VOCABULARY: **provinces** *provinces;* **mers** *seas;* **fleuves** *rivers;* **montagnes** *mountains.*

27 CONVERSATION EXERCISE

You may want to add to the list of cities and provinces, but limiting your choices to feminine names of provinces, like Auvergne and Champagne, would avoid confusion between "en" and "dans le" (used with masculine names like Languedoc).

1. Say to a friend:
   Montre-moi Rouen.
   C'est une grande ville?
   C'est en Bretagne?
   C'est sur la Loire?
   C'est un petit port?

   Your friend answers:
   Voilà Rouen.
   Oui, c'est une grande ville.
   Non, c'est en Normandie.
   Non, c'est sur la Seine.
   Non, c'est un grand port.

2. Ask the same questions about Bordeaux, Strasbourg, Marseille, Nantes.

VOCABULARY: **montre-moi** *show me;* **voilà** *here is;* **en** *in;* **sur** *on.*

Variation: Do the same with other cities, big and small. Questions will, of course, vary according to the place chosen. They could be: C'est une petite ville? C'est dans le Massif central? C'est sur l'océan Atlantique?

28 FOR REFERENCE

	Nos Amis	Our Friends
2	Comment t'appelles-tu?	What's your name?
	Catherine parle à Jean-François.	Catherine is talking to Jean-François.
	C. Comment t'appelles-tu?	What's your name?
	J.-F. Qui? Moi? Je m'appelle Jean-François. Et toi?	Who? Me? My name is Jean-François. And yours?
	C. Moi, je m'appelle Catherine.	My name is Catherine.
	J.-F. Catherine comment?	Catherine what?
	C. Catherine Lardan.	Catherine Lardan.
	J.-F. Et ce garçon, il s'appelle François?	And that boy, his name is François?
	C. Non, lui, il s'appelle Richard.	No, his name is Richard.
	J.-F. Et cette fille, elle s'appelle Doris ou Denise?	And that girl, is her name Doris or Denise?
	C. Elle, elle s'appelle Denise.	Her name is Denise.
	J.-F. Ah oui, Denise Goulet!	Oh yes, Denise Goulet!
7	Noms de garçons.	Boys' names.
	Noms de filles.	Girls' names.
8	Quel âge as-tu?	How old are you?
	Doris parle à François.	Doris is talking to François.
	D. Quel âge as-tu?	How old are you?
	F. J'ai presque quinze ans. Et toi?	I'm almost fifteen. And you?
	D. Moi, j'ai treize ans, comme Denise.	I'm thirteen, like Denise.
	F. Ah non, elle, elle a douze ans.	Oh no, she's twelve.
	D. Et Jean-François?	And Jean-François?
	F. Il a douze ans aussi.	He's twelve too.
9	Les nombres de 1 à 20.	Numbers from 1 to 20.

15	Où habites-tu?	Where do you live?
	DENISE Où habites-tu? En France?	Where do you live? In France?
	RICHARD Oui, à Paris. Toi, tu habites	Yes, in Paris. And you, you live in the
	aux Etats-Unis, n'est-ce pas?	United States, don't you?
	DENISE Non, j'habite au Canada, à Montréal.	No, I live in Canada, in Montreal.
15.1	Richard habite à Paris.	Richard lives in Paris.
	Paris est une très grande ville.	Paris is a very large city.
	C'est la capitale de la France.	It is the capital of France.
	Richard habite dans un appartement.	Richard lives in an apartment.
15.2	Denise habite à Montréal,	Denise lives in Montreal,
	au Canada. Montréal est une très	in Canada. Montreal is a very
	grande ville aussi.	large city too.
	Denise habite dans une petite maison.	Denise lives in a little house.
15.3	Jean-François habite à Ore. C'est	Jean-François lives in Ore. It's
	un petit village près de Luchon.	a little village near Luchon.
	(C'est très loin de Paris.)	(It is very far from Paris.)
15.4	François habite à Montargis. C'est	François lives in Montargis. It's
	une petite ville près de Paris.	a small town near Paris.
15.5	Catherine habite à Luneray. C'est	Catherine lives in Luneray. It's
	un village près de Dieppe.	a village near Dieppe.
15.6	Dieppe est un grand port.	Dieppe is a large port.
15.7	Doris habite à Fort-de-France.	Doris lives in Fort-de-France.
	C'est à la Martinique.	It's in Martinique.
15.8	La Martinique est une petite île	Martinique is a little island
	dans la mer des Caraïbes.	in the Caribbean Sea.

29   WORD LIST

1–7

an(s) year(s)	**ce/cette** that, this	**Comment t'appelles-tu?** What is your name?
fille girl		
garçon boy	**de** of	**(Moi) Je m'appelle…** My name is . . .
noms names	**et** and	
nos amis our friends	**ou** or	**(Toi) Tu t'appelles…** Your name is . . .
chapitre unit	**qui** who	**(Lui) Il s'appelle…** His name is . . .
	comment what, how	
moi me	**oui** yes	**(Elle) Elle s'appelle…** Her name is . . .
toi you	**non** no	
lui him		
elle her		**parle à** is talking to

8–14

les nombres de 1 à 20 numbers from 1 to 20	le jeu de loto the game of lotto
à to	**Quel âge as-tu?** How old are you?
comme like, as	**J'ai quinze ans.** I am 15 years old.
de from	**Tu as quinze ans?** You are 15 years old?
	Il a quinze ans. He is 15 years old.
aussi too, also	**Elle a quinze ans.** She is 15 years old.
presque almost	

15–27

un appartement apartment	**Où habites-tu?** Where do you live?
une capitale capital	**J'habite…** I live . . .
une île island	**Tu habites…** You live . . .
une maison house	**Il habite…** He lives . . .
un port port	**Elle habite…** She lives . . .
un village village	
une ville city, town	**grand/grande** big, large
	petit/petite little, small
la France France	
la mer des Caraïbes Caribbean Sea	**c'est** it is
au Canada in Canada	**n'est-ce pas?** isn't it?
aux Etats-Unis in the United States	**à** in
en France in France	**dans** in
à la Martinique in Martinique	**loin de** far from
	où where
le/la the	
un/une a, an	**près de** near
	très very

2

LES SPORTS

Young people in France are very involved in active sports. Soccer is very popular; so is rugby, particularly among Southerners. Skiing attracts a large number of participants, and many clubs and groups have formed to help make skiing cheaper and therefore more available to more young people. Swimming and tennis along with horseback riding continue to grow in popularity.

Active sports usually take place outside school, especially on days off when there is more time for play. Teams and individuals from different schools and towns compete against each other in a spirit of fun as much as in a desire to win.

2 Ils font du vélo. ⊗

1

RICHARD ET ARNAUD : Ils font du vélo.

JOËLLE   Qu'est-ce que vous faites? Vous sortez?

RICHARD   Oui, nous allons faire du vélo.

JOËLLE   Vous n'allez pas regarder le match à la télé?

ARNAUD   Mais si, nous faisons un tour et nous rentrons regarder le match.

3 Qu'est-ce qu'ils font comme sports? ⊗

1

CLAIRE : Elle fait du cheval.

2

DENISE ET LOUISE : Elles font du ski.

3

FRANÇOIS ET DIDIER : Ils font de la natation.

4

JOËLLE ET PATRICK : Ils font du judo.

4 Answer the questions. Make sure students give answers in complete sentence with subject pronoun and verb.

1. Qu'est-ce qu'ils font, Richard et Arnaud?
2. Et Claire? Qu'est-ce qu'elle fait?
3. Et Denise et Louise? Qu'est-ce qu'elles font?
4. Qu'est-ce qu'ils font, François et Didier?
5. Et Joëlle et Patrick? Qu'est-ce qu'ils font?

5 ORAL EXERCISE ⊗

6 PRONOUNS AND THE VERB faire

Answer the questions which follow the examples. ⊗

Richard! Arnaud! Qu'est-ce que **vous** faites?　　**Nous** faisons du vélo.
If you were talking to Richard and Arnaud together, which word for "you" would you use?
Richard! Qu'est-ce que **tu** fais?　　**Je** fais du vélo.
If you were talking to Richard alone, which word for "you" would you use?

Richard fait du vélo?	Oui, **il** fait du vélo.
Claire fait du cheval?	Oui, **elle** fait du cheval.
François et Didier font de la natation?	Oui, **ils** font de la natation.
Denise et Louise font du ski?	Oui, **elles** font du ski.
Joëlle et Patrick font du judo?	Oui, **ils** font du judo.

In the sentences on the right, what word refers to **Richard?** What word refers to **Claire?** What word refers to **François et Didier?** What word refers to **Denise et Louise?** What word refers to **Joëlle et Patrick,** that is, to a girl and a boy?

7 Read the following generalization.

1. **Je, tu, il, elle, nous, vous, ils, elles** are called pronouns. The following chart shows how these pronouns are used with the verb **faire,** *to do.* The pronouns and verb forms on the left are singular; they refer to one person. Those on the right are plural; they refer to more than one person.

Point out that the singular forms of the verb faire all sound the same.

Singular			*Plural*		
Je	**fais**	un tour.	**Nous**	**faisons**	un tour.
Tu	**fais**	un tour?	**Vous**	**faites**	un tour?
Il	**fait**	un tour.	**Ils**	**font**	un tour.
Elle	**fait**	un tour	**Elles**	**font**	un tour.

Extensive work on tu/vous will be done in Unit 4, but a brief discussion might be in order here.

2. There are two pronouns equivalent to "you": **tu** and **vous.**
   • **Tu** is used when you talk to someone you know well.
   • **Vous** is used when you talk to more than one person.
   • **Vous** is also used when you talk to one adult who is not a member of your family.
   This use of **vous** will be discussed further in Unit 4.
   There are two pronouns equivalent to "they": **ils** and **elles.**

Il/elle, ils/elles, referring to things, will be treated in Unit 8.

   • **Ils** refers to a group that includes only boys or both boys and girls.
   • **Elles** refers to a group that includes only girls.
   In French, the verb forms change with the pronouns.

8 Qu'est-ce qu'ils font? Qu'est-ce qu'elles font? ⊗

For answers see p. T15.

1　　2　　3

9 Richard et Arnaud font du vélo. ⊗

Et toi, qu'est-ce que tu fais comme sport? Du vélo?

Oui, je fais du vélo.

Et vous deux, qu'est-ce que vous faites? Du cheval?

Oui, nous faisons du cheval.

Et Joëlle et Patrick, qu'est-ce qu'ils font? Du judo?

Oui, ils font du judo.

Et Denise et Louise, qu'est-ce qu'elles font? Du ski?

Oui, elles font du ski.

10 Now ask your classmates: See Teaching Suggestions, p. T15, for additional vocabulary your students may want to use to answer these questions.

Qu'est-ce que tu fais comme sports?

Je fais…

Qu'est-ce que vous faites comme sports?

Nous faisons…

11 WRITING EXERCISE

Rewrite the following sentences, using the proper form of the verb **faire.**
1. Joëlle et Patrick __font__ du judo.
2. Vous __faites__ du judo?
3. Moi, je __fais__ du cheval.
4. Claire aussi __fait__ du cheval.
5. Claire et moi, nous __faisons__ de la natation.
6. Et toi? Qu'est-ce que tu __fais__?

12 A quoi est-ce qu'il joue? ⊗

FRANÇOIS   Dans quelle équipe de football est-ce que tu joues?
DIDIER   Dans l'équipe de Montargis. Je joue « avant ».
FRANÇOIS   Lambert aussi est dans cette équipe?
DIDIER   Oui, c'est le capitaine.

13 On joue au football? ⊗

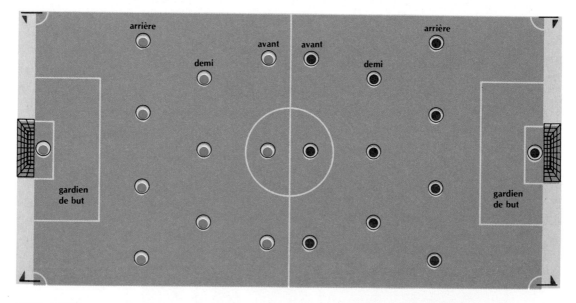

More specific terms for player positions on a soccer field are given in Teaching Suggestions, p. T15.

14 **Answer the questions.**

    1. Dans quelle équipe joue Didier?   3. Qui est aussi dans cette équipe?

    2. Qu'est-ce qu'il est dans cette équipe?   4. Qu'est-ce qu'il est dans cette équipe?

15 Point out that the verb jouer à is used only with sports like the ones mentioned here, involving rules,

A quoi est-ce que vous jouez? Avec quoi? ⊗ scoring, and two opposing sides.

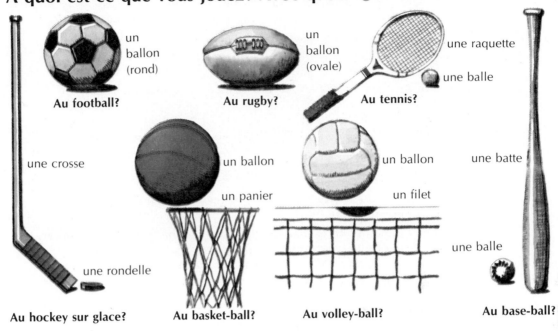

un ballon (rond)

Au football?

un ballon (ovale)

Au rugby?

une raquette

une balle

Au tennis?

une crosse

un ballon

un panier

Au basket-ball?

un ballon

un filet

une balle

Au volley-ball?

une batte

une balle

Au base-ball?

une rondelle

Au hockey sur glace?

Nous jouons au tennis. Avec une raquette.

16 In France, the word for puck is "un palet." In Canada it is called "une rondelle." We have chosen the
Ask a friend: Canadian usage, since hockey is more popular in Canada than in France.

    1. Qu'est-ce que tu fais comme sports?   4. Qui est le capitaine de l'équipe?

    2. Dans quelle équipe est-ce que tu joues?   5. Tu joues « avant »?

    3. Comment s'appelle cette équipe?

17 ORAL EXERCISE ⊗

18   VERBS ENDING IN -er

Answer the questions which follow the examples. ⊗

      Vous jouez au football?   Oui, **nous jouons** au football.

Which are the verbs in these sentences? What is the last sound in the verb when you use
vous? How is it spelled? What is the last sound in the verb when you use **nous?** How is it
spelled?

     Je joue au basket-ball.   **Il joue** au basket-ball.

     Tu joues au basket-ball.   **Ils jouent** au basket-ball.

Do these four verb forms sound alike? Are they spelled alike? Which part of the verb is the
same in these four verb forms as well as in the two verb forms in the first paragraph?

19 Read the following generalization.

1. The basic form of the verb is called the infinitive. It is the infinitive form that you find in dictionaries and word lists. The infinitive of the verb below is **jouer,** *to play.* It is made up of a stem, **jou-,** and an ending, **-er.** The stem is the part of the verb that does not change. The infinitives of a great many French verbs end in **-er.**
2. The following chart shows the forms of the verb **jouer.** Although there are spelling differences in the **je, tu, il,** and **ils** forms, they are pronounced alike.

Infinitive	Pronoun	Stem	Ending	
jouer	je		-e	Je **joue** au football.
	tu		-es	Tu **joues** au football.
	il / elle / on	jou	-e	Il / Elle / On **joue** au football.
	nous		-ons	Nous **jouons** au football.
	vous		-ez	Vous **jouez** au football.
	ils / elles		-ent	Ils / Elles **jouent** au football.

Notice that **on,** *one, people, they, we,* can have a plural meaning, but it is always used with the **il** form of the verb—a singular form.

3. Besides **jouer,** other **-er** verbs that you have seen are **habiter,** *to live,* **rentrer,** *to come (go) home,* and **regarder,** *to watch, to look (at).* Practice these verbs (after Ex. 21) with item substitution drills: Tu habites à Paris? Florence / Vous / Robert et Alain / Christine et Sylvie

20 Ils jouent au basket-ball. ⊗

A quoi est-ce que vous jouez? Nous jouons au basket-ball.
Et toi? Je joue au basket-ball.
Et Richard? Il joue au basket-ball.
Et François et Didier? · Ils jouent au basket-ball.
Et Catherine? Elle joue au basket-ball.
Et Denise et Louise? Elles jouent au basket-ball.

21 Ils regardent un match à la télé. ⊗

Qu'est-ce que vous faites? Nous regardons un match à la télé.
Et Richard? Il regarde un match à la télé.
Et toi? Je regarde un match à la télé.
Et Claire? Elle regarde un match à la télé.
Et Denise et Louise? Elles regardent un match à la télé.

22 WRITING EXERCISE

Rewrite the following sentences using the proper form of the verb in parentheses.

1. (jouer) A quoi est-ce que vous _jouez_ ?
2. (jouer) Nous _jouons_ au football.
3. (jouer) Didier et François _jouent_ au football aussi?
4. (regarder) Non, ils _____ le match à la télé. regardent
5. (rentrer) Qu'est-ce que tu fais? Tu _rentres_ ?
6. (rentrer) Oui, je _rentre_ .

23   Qu'est-ce qu'elles aiment comme sports? ⊗

Sabine parle à une amie.

SABINE   Tu aimes le tennis?

ANNE   Non, pas beaucoup. J'aime mieux le ping-pong.

SABINE   C'est amusant, le tennis!

ANNE   Moi, je trouve ça ennuyeux. Ce que j'aime vraiment, c'est le cheval.

SABINE   Pas moi!

ANNE   Pourquoi?

SABINE   Parce que c'est trop dangereux.

24   Answer the questions.

1. A qui est-ce que Sabine parle?
2. Sabine aime le tennis?

3. Qu'est-ce qu'Anne aime mieux?
4. Qu'est-ce qu'elle aime comme sports?

25

HOW TO TALK ABOUT SPORTS

Teach these forms as lexical items. Contractions will be taught in Unit 4.

Sports: Activities **FAIRE**	Je **fais**	**du** **de la**	cheval. natation.
Sports: Games **JOUER**	Je **joue**	**au**	tennis.
Sports: What you like **AIMER**	J'**aime**	**le** **la**	cheval. natation.

26   Ask one of your classmates: They may also ask about sports they might have talked about in No. 10.

1. Qu'est-ce que tu aimes comme sports?
2. Pourquoi?

3. Est-ce que tu trouves ça dangereux, le cheval? Et le ski? Et le football?

27   ORAL EXERCISE ⊗

28   LIAISON AND ELISION

Answer the questions which follow the examples. ⊗

Nous jouons au tennis.   **Nous aimons** le tennis.
Vous jouez au tennis?   **Vous aimez** le tennis?
Ils jouent au tennis.   **Ils aiment** le tennis.
Elles jouent au tennis.   **Elles aiment** le tennis.

In the sentences on the left, do the verbs begin with a consonant or a vowel sound? Do the verbs begin with a consonant or a vowel sound in the sentences on the right? What sound is added between the pronouns **nous, vous, ils, elles** and the verbs?

Je joue au tennis.   **J'aime** le tennis.

In the second sentence, what sound is missing from **je?** Does the spelling show that a sound is missing? How?

Point out in section 2 below that liaisons with numbers are obligatory: un‿an, deux‿ans, trois‿ans, six‿ans, neuf‿ans, dix‿ans, dix-neuf‿ans, vingt‿ans.

29 Read the following generalization.

1. A link is often made between two words if the second word begins with a vowel sound.
Liaison: the link is made by adding a consonant sound between the two words:

$$\text{vous}\stackrel{z}{\frown}\text{aimez} \qquad \text{un}\stackrel{n}{\frown}\text{ami} \qquad \text{cet}\stackrel{t}{\frown}\text{ami.}$$

Elision: the link is made by dropping a vowel sound from between the two words: **j'aime** (represented in writing by an apostrophe).

	Before Consonant Sound	Before Vowel Sound	
		Liaison	Elision
Pronouns	je joue nous jouons vous jouez ils jouent elles jouent	nous‿aimons vous‿aimez ils‿aiment elles‿aiment	j'aime
Articles	un garçon le garçon la fille ce garçon	un‿ami cet‿ami	l'ami l'amie

Notice the special liaison form **cet** before a masculine noun beginning with a vowel sound.

2. a. Some liaisons are obligatory; the speaker has no choice. Liaison must be made with certain words, such as the plural pronouns **nous, vous, ils,** and **elles.**

$$\text{nous}\stackrel{z}{\frown}\text{aimons} \qquad \text{vous}\stackrel{z}{\frown}\text{aimez} \qquad \text{ils}\stackrel{z}{\frown}\text{aiment} \qquad \text{elles}\stackrel{z}{\frown}\text{aiment}$$

In this book, we will indicate all obligatory liaisons.

b. Some liaisons are optional; you can either link or not link the two words. For example, you may say: **Nous jouon̸s au rugby,** or **Nous jouons‿au rugby.** These optional liaisons are often made in formal situations but not so often in everyday conversation.

c. Elision is never optional: **je joue,** but **j'aime.**

30 Ils aiment le ping-pong. ⊗ Have students answer in complete sentences, as shown in the model.

Tu joues au ping-pong?   Oui, et j'aime beaucoup ça.
Et François? / Et François et Didier? / Et vous deux?

il aime / ils aiment / nous aimons

31 LISTENING EXERCISE ⊗ For script, see Teaching Suggestions, p. T15.

	0	1	2	3	4	5	6	7	8
One person									
More than one	✓								
Cannot tell									

*Throughout this program, Et vous deux? requires a "nous" answer.

32 CONVERSATION EXERCISE

a. Ask one of your classmates:
1. Tu joues au football?
2. Tu aimes le basket-ball?
3. Qu'est-ce que tu aimes mieux, le football ou le basket-ball?
4. Qu'est-ce que tu aimes comme sports? Pourquoi?

b. Talk about the sports you like and those you don't like. Tell why.

33 Les couleurs. ⊗

Drill colors with available articles of clothing, pieces of cardboard, colors in the classroom, etc.

le blanc	le marron	l'orange	le bleu
le noir	le rouge	le jaune	le vert

34 Quelles sont les couleurs de ces équipes? ⊗

Paris	Lille	Tours	Lorient
Nantes	Nice	Marseille	Saint-Etienne

Les couleurs de l'équipe de Paris sont le bleu et le rouge. Quelles sont les couleurs de l'équipe de Marseille? Quelles sont les couleurs de votre équipe de football? De votre équipe de baseball préférée? Des Red Sox?

VOCABULARY: **Quelles sont** *What are;* **ces équipes** *these teams;* **votre équipe préférée** *your favorite team.*

In recent years, the teams from St-Etienne and Nantes have dominated soccer in France. The St-Etienne team, called "Les Verts," won the French championship three years in a row, and the Nantes team won it twice.

35 FOR REFERENCE

2		Ils font du vélo.	They go bike-riding.
	JOËLLE	Qu'est-ce que vous faites?	What are you doing?
		Vous sortez?	Are you going out?
	RICHARD	Oui, nous allons faire du vélo.	Yes, we're going to go bike-riding.
	JOËLLE	Vous n'allez pas regarder le match à la télé?	You're not going to watch the game on TV?
	ARNAUD	Mais si, nous faisons un tour et nous rentrons regarder le match.	Of course we are. We're taking a ride, and we're coming home to watch the game.
2.1		Ils font du vélo.	They are bike-riding.
3		Qu'est-ce qu'ils font comme sports?	What kinds of sports do they engage in?
3.1		Elle fait du cheval.	She goes horseback-riding.
3.2		Elles font du ski.	They ski.
3.3		Ils font de la natation.	They swim.
3.4		Ils font du judo.	They practice judo.

12	A quoi est-ce qu'il joue?	What does he play?
	FRANÇOIS Dans quelle équipe de football est-ce que tu joues?	What football team do you play for?
	DIDIER Dans l'équipe de Montargis. Je joue « avant ».	For the Montargis team. I play forward.
	FRANÇOIS Lambert aussi est dans cette équipe?	Lambert is on that team too, isn't he?
	DIDIER Oui, c'est le capitaine.	Yes, he's the captain.
13	On joue au football?	Shall we play football?
15	A quoi est-ce que vous jouez? Avec quoi?	What do you play? With what?
	Nous jouons au tennis. Avec une raquette.	We play tennis. With a racket.
23	Qu'est-ce qu'elles aiment comme sports?	What sports do they like?
	Sabine parle à une amie.	Sabine is talking to a friend.
	SABINE Tu aimes le tennis?	Do you like tennis?
	ANNE Non, pas beaucoup. J'aime mieux le ping-pong.	No, not very much. I like Ping-Pong better.
	SABINE C'est amusant, le tennis!	Tennis is fun.
	ANNE Moi, je trouve ça ennuyeux.	I think it's boring.
	Ce que j'aime vraiment, c'est le cheval.	What I really like is horseback-riding.
	SABINE Pas moi!	Not me!
	ANNE Pourquoi?	Why not?
	SABINE Parce que c'est trop dangereux.	Because it's too dangerous.

36 WORD LIST

2–11

les sports sports
un match game
le cheval horseback-riding
le judo judo
la natation swimming
le ski skiing
le vélo bike-riding

la télé TV
un tour a ride

faire to do
faire un tour to take a ride

Vous sortez? You're going out?
vous n'allez pas regarder...? you're not going to watch . . .?
nous allons faire... we're going to . . .
nous rentrons we're coming home

qu'est-ce que...? what . . .?

je I
tu you
il he
elle she
nous we
vous you
ils, elles they
comme for
mais si of course we are

12–22

le football soccer
le football américain football
le base-ball baseball
le basket-ball basketball
le hockey sur glace ice hockey
le rugby rugby
le tennis tennis
le volley-ball volleyball

une balle ball (baseball, tennis)
un ballon ball (football, soccer . . .)
une batte baseball bat
une crosse hockey stick
un filet net
un panier basket
une raquette racket
une rondelle hockey puck

une équipe team
un capitaine captain
un but goal
gardien de but goalkeeper
arrière fullback
demi halfback
avant forward

habiter to live
jouer to play
regarder to watch, to look (at)
rentrer to come (go) home

est is
est-ce que...? do (you, they) . . .?

quelle, quelles what, which
on one, people, they, we

quoi what

avec with

ovale oval
rond round

23–34

un(e) ami(e) friend
le ping-pong Ping-Pong
une couleur color
le blanc white
le bleu blue
le jaune yellow
le marron brown
le noir black
l'orange (m.) orange
le rouge red
le vert green

aimer to like
aimer mieux to prefer
parler to talk
trouver to find, to think

amusant fun
dangereux dangerous
ennuyeux boring

ça that
cet this, that
ce que what
parce que because
pourquoi why
pas not

beaucoup much, many, a lot
mieux better
trop too, too much
vraiment really

Chess is just one of the many pastimes
mentioned in this unit about what
young people in the French-speaking world
do with their leisure time. Chess players will
notice from the positions of the pieces on
the board that an actual game is in progress.
Here are some important words for
the chess players: chessboard—l'échiquier;
pawns—les pions; king—le roi; queen—la
reine; rook—la tour; bishop—le fou;
knight—le cavalier; check—échec;
checkmate—échec et mat.

3
LES
PASSE-TEMPS

1 Qu'est-ce que ces jeunes aiment faire? ⊗

PHILIPPE

CATHERINE

1 Il aime écouter des disques.
Il a aussi des cassettes.

4 Elle aime discuter avec son amie Sylvie.

2 Il aime bricoler : par exemple, il peut réparer les vélos, les vélomoteurs et les motos.

5 Les deux amies aiment regarder la
télévision.

3 Il aime lire des revues d'électronique.
Il lit aussi des livres de science-fiction.

6 Elles aiment écouter la radio et
tricoter.

2 Answer the questions.

1. Est-ce que Philippe aime bricoler?
2. Qu'est-ce qu'il peut réparer, par exemple?
3. Qu'est-ce qu'il aime écouter?
4. Qu'est-ce qu'il aime lire?
5. Et Catherine? Avec qui est-ce qu'elle aime discuter?
6. Qu'est-ce que les deux amies aiment faire?

3 Ask a friend:

1. Tu aimes discuter? Avec qui?
2. Tu aimes regarder la télévision?
3. Qu'est-ce que tu aimes mieux lire, des revues ou des livres de science-fiction?
4. Tu aimes bricoler? Qu'est-ce que tu répares?

4 ORAL EXERCISE ⊗

5 PLURAL MARKERS: ARTICLES WITH NOUNS

Answer the questions which follow the examples. ⊗

Il répare **un vélo** et **une moto.**	Il répare **des vélos** et **des motos.**
Il répare **le vélo** et **la moto.**	Il répare **les vélos** et **les motos.**
Il répare **ce vélo** et **cette moto.**	Il répare **ces vélos** et **ces motos.**

What articles indicate that the nouns on the left are singular? What articles indicate that the nouns on the right are plural? Which article do you use to make **un vélo** plural? Or **une moto?** Which article do you use to make **le vélo** plural? Or **la moto?** Which article do you use to make **ce vélo** plural? Or **cette moto?**

6 Read the following generalization.

1. The articles you have seen so far (**un/une, le/la, ce/cette**) are singular markers. The plural forms of these articles are shown in the following chart.

	Singular			*Plural*	
Il écoute	**un** **une**	disque. cassette.	Il écoute	**des** **des**	disques. cassettes.
Il écoute	**le** **la**	disque. cassette.	Il écoute	**les** **les**	disques. cassettes.
Il écoute	**ce** **cette**	disque. cassette.	Il écoute	**ces** **ces**	disques. cassettes.

Unlike singular articles, plural articles do not indicate gender: the same markers are used with both masculine and feminine nouns.

2. Liaison is obligatory with plural articles.

des‿amis   les‿amis   ces‿amis

3. As you know, an article gives information about the noun following it. A plural article indicates that the noun following it is a plural noun. The plural form of a noun usually sounds like its singular form. Therefore, you have to listen carefully to the article to determine whether the noun is singular or plural. In writing, however, the plural form of a noun is different from its singular form: it usually ends in **-s.**

Use vocabulary cards to practice gender and plural forms for all nouns learned so far.

un disque   **des disques**
une cassette   **des cassettes**

The plural forms of some words do not sound the same as the singular. They are also not written by adding **-s.** Words ending in **-al,** for example, form the plural by adding **-aux :** **un cheval,** *horse,* **des chevaux,** *horses.* Other examples will be indicated in the Word Lists.

7 Qu'est-ce qu'elle fait? ⊗

Elle écoute un disque.   Elle a des disques?
Elle écoute une cassette.   Elle a des cassettes?
Elle lit un livre d'électronique.   Elle a des livres d'électronique?
Elle lit une revue de science-fiction.   Elle a des revues de science-fiction?

8 Il aime bricoler. ⊗

Il peut réparer la moto?   Oui, il répare les motos.
le vélomoteur / la télévision / le vélo
les vélomoteurs / les télévisions / les vélos

9 Ces jeunes aiment discuter. ⊗

Elle discute avec cette fille.   Ces filles aiment discuter.
Il discute avec ce garçon.   Ces garçons aiment discuter.
Elle discute avec cette amie.   Ces amies aiment discuter.
Il discute avec cet ami.   Ces amis aiment discuter.

10 LISTENING EXERCISE ⊗ For script, see p. T16.

	0	1	2	3	4	5	6	7	8	9	10
Singular											
Plural	✓										

11 WRITING EXERCISE

Write the responses to Exercises 7, 8, and 9.

12 CONVERSATION EXERCISE

Ask your classmates what they like to do.   Start: Qu'est-ce que tu aimes faire?

Doris Dubois (from Unit 1) and her brother Danou live in Fort-de-France, Martinique. They and their family are the subject of Unit 17. Like most fishing boats in Martinique, the one behind Danou has a poetic name, "Cœur d' Acier," "Heart of Steel." The conch Danou is looking at is called "un lambi."

13 Qu'est-ce qu'ils ont comme passe-temps? ⊗

Doris est photographe amateur. Elle passe son temps à faire de la photo. Elle a un appareil-photo très simple, mais ses photos sont souvent extraordinaires.

Danou est collectionneur. Il collectionne les coquillages. Il n'a pas de difficultés à en trouver. Il habite à deux pas de la plage.

14 Answer the questions.

1. A quoi est-ce que Doris passe son temps?
2. Qu'est-ce qu'elle a comme appareil-photo?
3. Comment sont ses photos?
4. Qu'est-ce que Danou collectionne?
5. Est-ce qu'il a des difficultés à en trouver?
6. Pourquoi?

15

THE VERB être

Etre, *to be*, does not follow a pattern. Etre is an irregular verb. ⊗

	Singular			Plural	
Je	**suis**	photographe.	Nous	**sommes**	photographes.
Tu	**es**	photographe?	Vous	**êtes**	photographes?
Il / Elle / On	**est**	photographe.	Ils / Elles	**sont**	photographes.

16 Ils sont photographes amateurs. ⊗

Doris fait de la photo?   Oui, elle est photographe amateur.
Et Danou? / Et Catherine et Sylvie? / Et vous deux? / Et toi?

il est / elles sont / nous sommes / je suis

The motto seen on the coin — "Liberty, Equality, Fraternity" — is the motto of the French Republic. It can also be found on public buildings like town halls (see insert on Country Life, Plate 21, photograph #2).

The head on the coin is that of "Marianne," symbol of the French Republic. She is wearing the Phrygian cap, an ancient symbol of liberty, adopted by the French after the 1789 Revolution.

17 Vous êtes collectionneurs (collectionneuses)? Qu'est-ce que vous collectionnez? ⊗

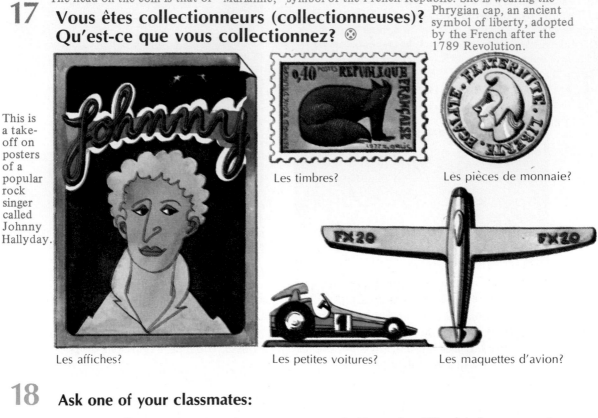

This is a take-off on posters of a popular rock singer called Johnny Hallyday.

Les timbres?

Les pièces de monnaie?

Les affiches?

Les petites voitures?

Les maquettes d'avion?

18 Ask one of your classmates:

1. Tu es collectionneur (-euse)?
2. Qu'est-ce que tu collectionnes?
3. Tu as des difficultés à en trouver?
4. Est-ce que tu fais de la photo?

You will probably want to supply the words your students need to identify their collections.

19 ORAL EXERCISE ⊗

20 WRITING EXERCISE   For answers, see p. T17.

Write the responses to Exercise 18.

21   NEGATION — ne... pas (de)

Answer the questions which follow the examples. ⊗

Il collectionne les timbres.   Il **ne** collectionne **pas** les timbres.
Il aime collectionner les timbres.   Il **n'**aime **pas** collectionner les timbres.

Which words make the sentences on the right negative? Where does the first negative word appear in relation to the main verb? Where does the second negative word appear?

Il a **un** vélomoteur?   Non, il **n'**a **pas de** vélomoteur.
Il a **une** radio?   Non, il **n'**a **pas de** radio.
Il a **des** timbres?   Non, il **n'**a **pas de** timbres.

Are **un, une,** and **des** used in negative constructions? What is used instead?

22 **Read the following generalization.** Use vocabulary cards to practice negation with all the verbs and verb forms seen so far.

1. In a negative construction with a verb, **ne** precedes the verb and **pas** follows it.

On	**ne**	discute	**pas.**
Je	**ne**	discute	**pas.**

Notice that élision occurs with **ne.** For example: **Il n'écoute pas.**

2. In a negative construction where a verb is followed by an infinitive, **ne** precedes the verb and **pas** follows it.

On	**ne**	peut	**pas**	discuter.
Je	**n'**	aime	**pas**	bricoler.

3. In a negative construction without a verb, **ne** is omitted and only **pas** is used.

Tu aimes collectionner les timbres?   Non, **pas** beaucoup.
J'aime faire de la photo.   **Pas** moi!

4. In negative constructions, **de** is used instead of **un, une,** and **des.**

Affirmative			Negative				
Elle a	**un**	vélo.	Elle	**n'**	a	**pas de**	vélo.
Elle a	**une**	radio.	Elle	**n'**	a	**pas de**	radio.
Elle a	**des**	disques.	Elle	**n'**	a	**pas de**	disques.

Notice that élision occurs with **de.** For example: **Il n'a pas d'amis.**

23 **Ils ne font pas ça!** ⊗

Doris répare les vélomoteurs.   Mais non! Elle ne répare pas les vélomoteurs.
Philippe collectionne les coquillages.   Mais non! Il ne collectionne pas les coquillages.
Danou regarde la télévision.   Mais non! Il ne regarde pas la télévision.
Catherine collectionne les timbres.   Mais non! Elle ne collectionne pas les timbres.
Sylvie collectionne les affiches.   Mais non! Elle ne collectionne pas les affiches.

24 **Qu'est-ce que tu fais?** ⊗

Tu tricotes?   Non, je n'aime pas tricoter.
Tu bricoles? / Tu collectionnes les timbres? / Tu discutes?
je n'aime pas bricoler / je n'aime pas collectionner les timbres / je n'aime pas discuter

25 **Qu'est-ce qu'il a, Danou?** ⊗

Des cassettes?   Non, il n'a pas de cassettes.
Une collection de timbres? / Des disques? / Un vélomoteur?
de collection de timbres / de disques / de vélomoteur

26 LISTENING EXERCISE ⊗ For script, see p. T17.

	0	1	2	3	4	5	6	7	8	9	10
Oui											
Non	√										

27 WRITING EXERCISE

Rewrite the following sentences in the negative.

1. François collectionne les photos.   François ne collectionne pas les photos.
2. Il trouve ça amusant.   Il ne trouve pas ça amusant.
3. Il fait de la photo?   Il ne fait pas de photo?
4. Oui, il a un appareil-photo.   Non, il n'a pas d'appareil-photo.
5. Il peut réparer cet appareil-photo?   Il ne peut pas réparer cet appareil-photo?
6. Oui, il répare les appareils-photo.   Non, il ne répare pas les appareils-photo.

28 CONVERSATION EXERCISE

Ask your classmates if they are collectors and, if so, what they collect.

29 Les nombres de 20 à 1.000. ⊗ Liaison is obligatory with numbers.

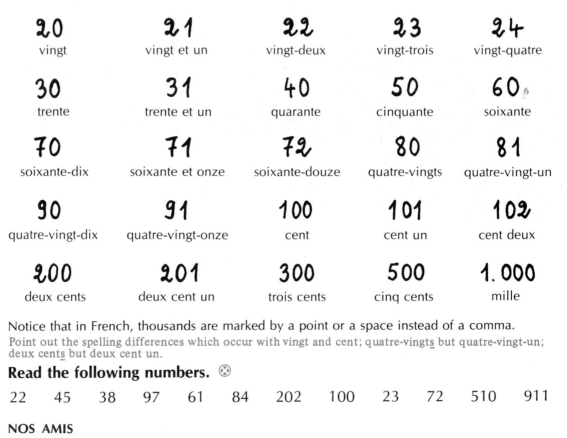

20 vingt	21 vingt et un	22 vingt-deux	23 vingt-trois	24 vingt-quatre
30 trente	31 trente et un	40 quarante	50 cinquante	60 soixante
70 soixante-dix	71 soixante et onze	72 soixante-douze	80 quatre-vingts	81 quatre-vingt-un
90 quatre-vingt-dix	91 quatre-vingt-onze	100 cent	101 cent un	102 cent deux
200 deux cents	201 deux cent un	300 trois cents	500 cinq cents	1.000 mille

Notice that in French, thousands are marked by a point or a space instead of a comma.

Point out the spelling differences which occur with vingt and cent; quatre-vingt<u>s</u> but quatre-vingt-un; deux cent<u>s</u> but deux cent un.

30 Read the following numbers. ⊗

22   45   38   97   61   84   202   100   23   72   510   911

31 C'est à qui de jouer? ⊗

Sylvie, Philippe, Catherine et Arnaud jouent
aux cartes (au Barbu). Catherine marque les
points.

PHILIPPE   C'est à toi de jouer, Catherine.
SYLVIE   C'est pour qui tous ces cœurs?
PHILIPPE   Pour toi!
SYLVIE   Ce n'est pas vrai!?
PHILIPPE   Mais si! Tu es en train de perdre, ma vieille!
SYLVIE   Qui est-ce qui gagne, alors?
CATHERINE   Philippe. Il a 25 points.
SYLVIE   Combien? 25 seulement? Tu es sûre?
CATHERINE   Mais certainement, je joue peut-être mal, mais je compte bien!

32 Answer the questions.

1. A quoi jouent Catherine, Sylvie, Arnaud et Philippe?
2. Qui est-ce qui marque les points?
3. Pour qui sont tous les cœurs?
4. Qui est-ce qui gagne?
5. Combien de points a Philippe?
6. Qu'est-ce que Catherine fait bien?

33 A quel jeu est-ce que tu veux jouer? ⊗

Aux dominos?   Aux dames?

Au monopoly?   Aux échecs?

34 Ask one of your classmates:

1. A quel jeu est-ce que tu aimes jouer?
2. Avec qui est-ce que tu joues souvent?
3. C'est toi qui marques les points?
4. Est-ce que tu comptes bien?
5. Tu gagnes souvent? Pourquoi?

35 ORAL EXERCISE ⊗

31 C'est à qui de jouer?
Sylvie, Philippe, Catherine et Arnaud
jouent aux cartes (au Barbu). Catherine
marque les points.

PHILIPPE C'est à toi de jouer, Catherine.
SYLVIE C'est pour qui tous ces cœurs?
PHILIPPE Pour toi!
SYLVIE Ce n'est pas vrai!?
PHILIPPE Mais si! Tu es en train de perdre,
ma vieille!
SYLVIE Qui est-ce qui gagne alors?
CATHERINE Philippe. Il a 25 points.
SYLVIE Combien? 25 seulement? Tu es sûre?
CATHERINE Mais certainement, je joue peut-être
mal, mais je compte bien!

Whose turn is it to play?
Sylvie, Philippe, Catherine, and Arnaud
are playing cards (lit.: "The Bearded Man"; like
Hearts). Catherine is keeping score.

It's your turn, Catherine.
Who are all those hearts for?
For you!
That's not true!?
Oh yes it is! You are losing,
old friend!
Well, who's winning then?
Philippe. He has 25 points.
How many? Only 25? Are you sure?
Of course. Maybe I play badly, but I
count well.

44 WORD LIST

1–12
une cassette *cassette*
un disque *record*
l'électronique (f.) *electronics*
les jeunes *young people*
un livre (de science-fiction)
  (science-fiction) book
une moto *motorcycle*
un passe-temps *pastime*
une radio *radio*
  écouter la radio *to listen to the radio*
une revue (d'électronique)
  (electronics) magazine
la science-fiction *science fiction*
une télévision *television*
  regarder la télévision *to watch television*
un vélo *bicycle*
un vélomoteur *moped*

bricoler *to tinker*
discuter *to talk over*
écouter *to listen to*
réparer *to fix*
tricoter *to knit*

il a *he has*
il lit *he reads*
il peut *he can*
il aime lire *he likes to read*

par exemple *for instance*

son *her*

ces *these*
des *some, any*
les *the*

13–30
une affiche *poster*
un appareil(-photo) *camera*
  des appareils(-photo) *cameras*
un collectionneur *collector*
une collectionneuse *collector*
un coquillage *shell*
une difficulté *trouble, difficulty*
une maquette d'avion
  model airplane
une photo *photograph*
un(e) photographe *photographer*
une pièce (de monnaie) *coin*
une plage *beach*
le temps *time*
un timbre *stamp*
une petite voiture *toy car*

collectionner *to collect*
être *to be*
faire de la photo *to take pictures*
passer *to spend (time)*
ils ont *they have*

amateur *amateur*
extraordinaire *exceptional*
simple *simple*

mais *but*
ne... pas *not*
souvent *often*
combien *how much, how many*

leur *their*
ses *her*
en *any*
à deux pas *a few feet from*

31–42
une carte *playing card*
un coeur *heart*
les dames (f.) *checkers*
les dominos (m.) *dominoes*
les échecs (m.) *chess*
un jeu *game*
un point *a point*
mon vieux! ma vieille! *old friend!*

avoir *to have*
compter *to count*
gagner *to win*
marquer *to mark down*
  marquer les points *to keep score*
tu veux *you want*
c'est à toi (de) *it's your turn (to)*
en train de... *in the process of . . .*
  en train de perdre *losing*
pour *for*
qui *whom*
qui est-ce qui... *who . . .*

quel *which*
sûre *sure*
tous *all*
vrai *true*

alors *then*
bien *well*
certainement *certainly, of course*
mal *badly*
peut-être *maybe*
seulement *only*
si *yes*

4

L'Ecole

EMPLOI DU TEMPS

	8 h	9 h	10 h	11h	2 h	3 h	4 h
LUNDI	Maths	Gym	Latin	Français	Histoire	Allemand	
MARDI	Latin	Maths	Technologie	Dessin	Français	Anglais	
MERCREDI							
JEUDI	Français	Latin	Allemand	Travaux Manuels	Anglais	Musique	
VENDREDI	Allemand	Français	Latin	Maths	Géographie	Sciences	
SAMEDI	Gym	Anglais	Maths	Histoire			

François Le Sève va à l'école au CES (Collège d'Enseignement Secondaire) de Montargis. Il est en quatrième. Il étudie 13 matières différentes. Les matières que François aime le mieux sont les maths et la musique. Il aime bien les langues vivantes (il étudie l'anglais et l'allemand), mais il n'aime pas tellement le latin. Comme tous les élèves de CES, il a des cours tous les jours, sauf le mercredi, le samedi après-midi et le dimanche, bien sûr! Les jours où il va en classe, il commence à huit heures et il finit à quatre heures (le lundi, le jeudi, le vendredi) ou à cinq heures (le mardi). Il a deux heures pour déjeuner.

François goes to a Collège d'Enseignement Secondaire ("collège" in French usually applies to a secondary school). This is his third year at this school, and he is now in "quatrième" (about ninth grade). His school day is long and full, as you can see. For each of the many subjects he takes, including three foreign languages, he has to prepare assignments, recitations, and, of course, many tests. But then come Wednesday and half of Saturday, which are his to do with as he wishes—if he doesn't have too much catching up to do!

4 Répondez aux questions. *Answer the questions.*

1. Où est-ce que François va à l'école?
2. En quelle classe est-ce qu'il est?
3. Combien de matières est-ce qu'il étudie?
4. Qu'est-ce qu'il aime le mieux?

5. Qu'est-ce qu'il étudie comme langues?
6. Est-ce qu'il va en classe le mercredi?
7. Combien de cours est-ce qu'il a le samedi?
8. Est-ce qu'il aime le latin?

5 Demandez à un(e) camarade. *Ask a classmate.*

Qu'est-ce que tu aimes le mieux?
1. Les maths ou les sciences? 2. Les travaux manuels ou la musique? 3. Le français ou l'anglais? 4. La géographie ou l'histoire? 5. La gymnastique ou la musique? 6. La technologie ou le dessin? 7. L'anglais ou l'allemand? 8. Le français ou le latin?

6 EXERCICE ORAL *Oral exercise* ⊗

7 THE VERB aller

The following are the forms of the verb **aller,** *to go.* ⊗

Je	**vais**	à l'école.	Nous	**allons**	à l'école.
Tu	**vas**	à l'école.	Vous	**allez**	à l'école.
Il / Elle / On	**va**	à l'école.	Ils / Elles	**vont**	à l'école.

8 François ne va pas en classe le mercredi. ⊗

Vous n'allez pas en classe le mercredi?
Et toi? / Et elle? / Et les garçons?
je vais / elle va / ils vont

Si, nous allons en classe le mercredi.

9 Quelle heure est-il? ⊗

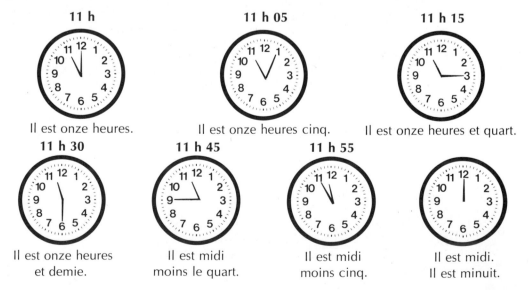

11 h
Il est onze heures.

11 h 05
Il est onze heures cinq.

11 h 15
Il est onze heures et quart.

11 h 30
Il est onze heures et demie.

11 h 45
Il est midi moins le quart.

11 h 55
Il est midi moins cinq.

Il est midi.
Il est minuit.

The 24-hour clock for official schedules is mentioned in Unit 5. Not dealing with it here will facilitate practice in telling time.

You may say **du matin,** *in the morning,* **de l'après-midi,** *in the afternoon,* and **du soir,** *in the evening,* to make it clear which part of the day you are talking about. **Midi** and **minuit** are the only ways to say *12-noon* and *12-midnight* in French.

10 **EXERCICE ORAL** ⊗

11 **Quelle heure est-il? Où est François?** ⊗

Regardez son emploi du temps, p. 33, et répondez.
lundi 8 h 15 • Il est huit heures et quart. François est au cours de maths.

mardi 10 h 30 • mardi 3 h 45 • jeudi 9 h 10 • vendredi 2 h 55 • samedi 11 h 40
technologie   français   latin   géographie   histoire

12 **Demandez à un(e) ami(e):**

1. A quelle école est-ce que tu vas?
2. A quelle heure est-ce que tu commences?
3. A quelle heure est-ce que tu déjeunes?
4. A quelle heure est-ce que tu rentres?

5. Tu étudies combien de matières?
6. Qu'est-ce que tu aimes le mieux?
7. Est-ce que tu vas en classe le mercredi?
8. Est-ce que tu vas en classe le samedi?

13 **Voilà l'école de François.** ⊗ Make sure students check the Word List for the gender of these nouns.

Many city schools have concrete courtyards. Trees are planted in openings in the concrete, protected by grillwork.

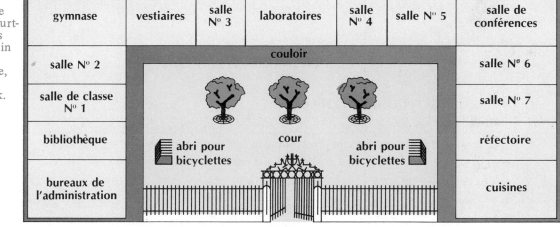

14 **François rencontre un nouveau, Olivier, dans la cour du CES.** ⊗

OLIVIER   Où sont les vestiaires, s'il te plaît?
FRANÇOIS   Là-bas, au fond de la cour.
OLIVIER   Il y a une bibliothèque?
FRANÇOIS   Oui, en face de toi.
OLIVIER   Où ça?
FRANÇOIS   Juste ici, à côté des bureaux. Viens avec moi...
OLIVIER   Merci, mais je ne vais pas à la bibliothèque tout de suite. Je vais d'abord au gymnase.

15 Répondez aux questions.

1. Il y a combien de salles de classe dans le CES de François?
2. Où sont les vestiaires? Et la bibliothèque?
3. Olivier va d'abord à la bibliothèque ou au gymnase?
4. Pour quel cours est-ce qu'on va au gymnase? Et au laboratoire?

16 EXERCICE ORAL ⊗

17 CONTRACTIONS WITH à AND de

1. **A** and **de** do not appear in combination with the articles **le** and **les**. Instead, the contractions **au** and **du, aux** and **des** occur.
2. Similar contractions do not occur with **à** and **de** and the articles **la** and **l'**.

Contraction					
à + le ⟶ **au**	Je vais **au** gymnase.		de + le ⟶ **du**	Je viens **du** gymnase.	
à + les ⟶ **aux**	Je vais **aux** bureaux.		de + les ⟶ **des**	Je viens **des** bureaux.	
No Contraction					
à + la ⟶ **à la**	Je vais **à la** cuisine.		de + la ⟶ **de la**	Je viens **de la** cuisine.	
à + l' ⟶ **à l'**	Je vais **à l'**école.		de + l' ⟶ **de l'**	Je viens **de l'**école.	

3. Liaison is obligatory with **aux** and **des**.

aux͜ Etats-Unis   des͜ Etats-Unis

18 Le nouveau rencontre François. ⊗

C'est là-bas, la bibliothèque?   Oui. Tu vas à la bibliothèque?
le gymnase / les vestiaires / le réfectoire / la salle de conférences / les bureaux
au gymnase / aux vestiaires / au réfectoire / à la salle de conférences / aux bureaux

19 Vrai ou faux. *True or false.* ⊗

Regardez le plan *(layout)* de l'école de François.
1. Les vestiaires sont au fond de la cour.   C'est vrai.
2. La bibliothèque est en face du gymnase.   C'est faux. La bibliothèque est en face du...

C'est faux. 3. Les cuisines sont à côté des bureaux. Les cuisines sont en face des bureaux.
C'est faux. 4. Les laboratoires sont à côté de l'abri. Les laboratoires sont à côté de la salle No. 3.
C'est faux. 5. Le réfectoire est près du gymnase. Le réfectoire est près des cuisines.
C'est faux. 6. Les bureaux sont à côté des vestiaires. Les bureaux sont à côté de la bibliothèque.

20 EXERCICE ECRIT *Writing exercise*

Faites le plan de votre école et dites où sont les laboratoires, la bibliothèque, le réfectoire et la salle de conférences. *Make a layout of your school and tell where the laboratories, the library, the lunchroom, and the auditorium are.*

21 La classe de François. ⊗

1 Le professeur d'anglais, Mme[1] Dubois, dit aux élèves : « Maintenant corrigeons les devoirs. François, allez au tableau et effacez. Les autres, ouvrez vos livres à la page 32, et ne bavardez pas, s'il vous plaît! »

2 Le professeur de maths, M. Perret, demande : « Tout le monde a compris? » Une élève, Florence, lève la main et répond : « Monsieur[2], s'il vous plaît, je ne comprends pas la réponse à la question numéro deux. »

3 Le professeur de dessin, Mlle Blondel, dit à la classe : « Maintenant, les enfants, regardons ces dessins. Commençons par le dessin de Florence. » See No. 25 for the uses of tu and vous.

4 Le professeur de technologie, M. Pujol, dit à un élève : « S'il te plaît, Bernard, fais attention! Il faut soigner la présentation des devoirs! » French students are required to write in ink and to hand in very neat papers.

22 Répondez aux questions.

1. Qu'est-ce que Mme Dubois dit d'abord?
2. A qui est-ce qu'elle parle?
3. Qu'est-ce qu'elle dit à François?
4. Qu'est-ce qu'elle dit aux autres?
5. Qu'est-ce que M. Perret demande?
6. Qu'est-ce que Florence répond?
7. A qui est-ce que Mlle Blondel parle?
8. Qu'est-ce qu'elle dit?
9. A qui est-ce que M. Pujol parle?
10. Qu'est-ce qu'il dit?

23 EXERCICE ORAL ⊗

---

[1] **Mme** and **Mlle** are abbreviations of **Madame** and **Mademoiselle. Monsieur** is abbreviated **M.**

[2] It is customary not to use last names when you are talking to adults but to say simply **Madame, Mademoiselle,** or **Monsieur.**

For script, see p. T18.

40 EXERCICE DE COMPREHENSION *Listening exercise* ⊗

	0	1	2	3	4	5	6	7	8	9	10
Un garçon	√										
Une fille											

41 Demandez à des camarades : ⊗ For answers, see p. T19.

Vous parlez de *(about)* François.　　　　Vous parlez de Florence.
Il est bon en français?　　　　　　　　　Elle est bonne en français?
Il est doué en latin?　　　　　　　　　　Elle est douée en latin?
Il est intelligent?　　　　　　　　　　　Elle est intelligente?
Il est paresseux?　　　　　　　　　　　Elle est paresseuse?
Il est doué pour les langues?　　　　　　Elle est douée pour les langues?
Il est distrait?　　　　　　　　　　　　Elle est distraite?

Variation: Vous parlez 1) à François, 2) à Florence: Tu es trop paresseux! (sérieux, distrait,
42 Parlons de Florence et de François. ⊗ timide) Resp.: Mais non, je ne suis pas paresseux!

Florence est bonne en français.　　　　　François aussi est bon en français.
Florence est un peu paresseuse.　　　　　François aussi est un peu paresseux.
Florence est douée en latin.　　　　　　François aussi est doué en latin.
Florence est un peu distraite.　　　　　François aussi est un peu distrait.
Florence est amusante.　　　　　　　　François aussi est amusant.

Variation: Florence est grande (intelligente, vivante, différente, ennuyeuse, paresseuse, douée,
43 Parlons de votre école. ⊗ timide). Et François?

Comment est la cour?　　　　　　　　　La cour est très grande.
Comment est le gymnase?　　　　　　　Le gymnase est très grand.
Comment est le réfectoire?　　　　　　　Le réfectoire est très grand.
Comment est la salle de conférences?　　La salle de conférences est très grande.
Comment est la bibliothèque?　　　　　La bibliothèque est très grande.
Comment est le vestiaire?　　　　　　　Le vestiaire est très grand.
Variation: response: La cour est petite.

44 Et vous?

1. Qu'est-ce que vous aimez le mieux comme matières?
2. Qu'est-ce que le professeur de français dit de votre travail?
3. Est-ce que vous êtes bon(ne) à l'oral en français?
4. Pour quelles matières est-ce que vous êtes doué(e)?

45 EXERCICE ECRIT

a. Ecrivez *(write)* les réponses des exercices No 42 et 43.
b. Ecrivez ce que vos professeurs écriraient *(would write)* sur votre bulletin trimestriel.

46 EXERCICE DE CONVERSATION

Décrivez une de vos journées à l'école. *Describe one of your days at school.*
Commencez : Le matin je commence à 8 h. Je vais d'abord au cours de maths. A 10 h…

21 La classe de François. ⊗

Le professeur d'anglais, Mme[1] Dubois, dit aux élèves : « Maintenant corrigeons les devoirs. François, allez au tableau et effacez. Les autres, ouvrez vos livres à la page 32, et ne bavardez pas, s'il vous plaît! »

Le professeur de maths, M. Perret, demande : « Tout le monde a compris? » Une élève, Florence, lève la main et répond : « Monsieur[2], s'il vous plaît, je ne comprends pas la réponse à la question numéro deux. »

Le professeur de dessin, Mlle Blondel, dit à la classe : « Maintenant, les enfants, regardons ces dessins. Commençons par le dessin de Florence. » See No. 25 for the uses of tu and vous.

Le professeur de technologie, M. Pujol, dit à un élève : « S'il te plaît, Bernard, fais attention! Il faut soigner la présentation des devoirs! » French students are required to write in ink and to hand in very neat papers.

22 Répondez aux questions.

1. Qu'est-ce que Mme Dubois dit d'abord?
2. A qui est-ce qu'elle parle?
3. Qu'est-ce qu'elle dit à François?
4. Qu'est-ce qu'elle dit aux autres?
5. Qu'est-ce que M. Perret demande?
6. Qu'est-ce que Florence répond?
7. A qui est-ce que Mlle Blondel parle?
8. Qu'est-ce qu'elle dit?
9. A qui est-ce que M. Pujol parle?
10. Qu'est-ce qu'il dit?

23 EXERCICE ORAL ⊗

[1] **Mme** and **Mlle** are abbreviations of **Madame** and **Mademoiselle. Monsieur** is abbreviated **M.**

[2] It is customary not to use last names when you are talking to adults but to say simply **Madame, Mademoiselle,** or **Monsieur.**

24 THE FORMAL vous

Répondez aux questions qui suivent les exemples. *Answer the questions which follow the examples.* ⊗

Didier! Tu rentres?   **Monsieur! Vous rentrez?**

When François talks to Didier, a boy about his own age, which word does he use for "you"? When he talks to his teacher, which word does he use for "you"? Why does he use a different pronoun in each case?

25 **Lisez la généralisation suivante.** *Read the following generalization.*

A rule of thumb might help: When in doubt say "vous"! To use "tu" in the wrong place can be embarrassing.

1. Both **tu** and **vous** are used to address one person. **Vous** is used in formal address, **tu** in informal or familiar address. The following will help you now in making your decision as to which pronoun to use:
   a. address people your own age or younger and members of your family as **tu;**
   b. address your teacher and all other older people as **vous,** even if they call you **tu.**

2. In general, such social factors as age, profession, and environment determine which pronoun to use. Sometimes personal preference enters into the decision, too. For instance, François and his classmates have now passed the age at which they would automatically be addressed as **tu.** Notice how their English teacher chooses to call them **vous,** but their technology teacher prefers **tu.** In this book we have chosen to address you as **vous.**

3. When you make a choice between **tu** and **vous,** various other elements are affected:
   a. the verb form changes: you would ask a friend, **"Où est-ce que tu vas?"** but you would ask an older person, **"Où est-ce que vous allez?";**
   b. and you would ask a friend, **"Quelle heure est-il, s'il te plaît?"** but you would ask an older person, **"Quelle heure est-il, s'il vous plaît?"**

4. **Vous** is the only form used to address more than one person.

26 **Vous demandez à un(e) camarade :**   **Vous demandez au professeur :** ⊗

Tu habites près de l'école?   Vous habitez près de l'école?
Tu regardes la télévision le soir?   Vous regardez la télévision le soir?
Tu commences à quelle heure le matin?   Vous commencez à quelle heure le matin?
Tu aimes bricoler?   Vous aimez bricoler?
Qu'est-ce que tu parles comme langues?   Qu'est-ce que vous parlez comme langues?

27 GIVING COMMANDS

Répondez aux questions qui suivent les exemples. ⊗

Vous ouvrez les livres.   **Ouvrez** les livres!
Tu fais attention.   **Fais** attention!
Nous regardons les dessins. **Regardons** les dessins!

Which sentences make statements and which give commands? What are the verb forms in the commands? Are they the same as the ones used in the statements? Which words are missing from the commands?

28 Lisez la généralisation suivante.

1. Commands are used to tell someone to do or not to do something. They are also used to make suggestions. In most cases the verb forms of the commands are exactly the same in sound and spelling as the **tu, vous,** and **nous** forms of verbs except that for commands the pronouns **"tu," "vous,"** and **"nous"** are not used.

	Statements	Commands
One person, familiar	**Tu fais** attention.	**Fais** attention!
One person, formal More than one person	**Vous faites** attention.	**Faites** attention!
A group including you	**Nous faisons** attention.	**Faisons** attention!

2. In the case of **-er** verbs and of the verb **aller,** the singular informal command is written without a final **-s.** For example: **Joue!   Va à l'école!**

3. In a negative command, **ne**… **pas** is added to the command: **Ne parlez pas!**

29 M. Pujol dit à Bernard… ⊗

de faire attention.   Fais attention, Bernard!
d'écouter / d'effacer le tableau / de corriger cette réponse
écoute / efface le tableau / corrige cette réponse

30 Mme Dubois dit à François… ⊗

de ne pas bavarder.   Ne bavardez pas, François!
de ne pas jouer en classe / de ne pas effacer / de ne pas parler
ne jouez pas en classe / n'effacez pas / ne parlez pas

31 François parle à Florence : ⊗

Tu vas au réfectoire avec moi?   Oui, allons au réfectoire.
Tu corriges ces devoirs avec moi? / Tu regardes ces dessins avec moi? / Tu étudies avec moi?
corrigeons ces devoirs / regardons ces dessins / étudions

32 Dans le cartable de François. ⊗

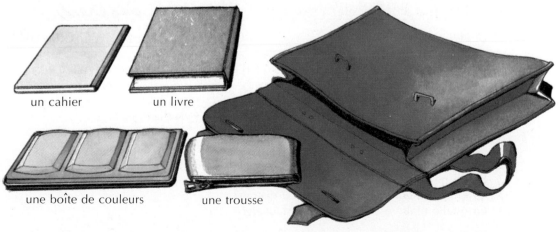

un cahier   un livre

une boîte de couleurs   une trousse

Add other items your students usually carry in their school bags.

Point out to students that the "de" construction indicates possession: l'école de François, la classe de François, le cartable de François, la trousse de François, le bulletin de François. Have students replace François by Florence, ce garçon, cette fille.

33 Dans la trousse de François. ⊗

The eraser shown here has two sides: one for ink, and one for pencil.

un crayon   un feutre   un stylo à bille   une gomme   une règle   un compas

34 Chaîne de mots. *Word chain.*

The type of ruler shown here is common in France. The flat type, similar to American school rulers, is also used in France, where it is called "un (double) décimètre."

ÉLÈVE 1 : Dans le cartable de François, il y a un livre de maths.
ÉLÈVE 2 : Dans le cartable de François, il y a un livre de maths et deux cahiers.
ÉLÈVE 3 : Dans le cartable de François, il y a un livre de maths, deux cahiers et un feutre.
ÉLÈVE 4 : Dans le cartable de François…

35 Le bulletin trimestriel de François. ⊗

NOM *Le Sève François*   ANNÉE SCOLAIRE 19 *79* –19 *80* CLASSE DE *4ᵉ*

This is only part of the bulletin trimestriel. Subjects, like "dessin," are not included. The principal's note, usually included, is not here either.

NOTES	MATIÈRES	APPRÉCIATIONS DES PROFESSEURS
14	COMPOSITION FRANÇAISE	*Bon élève, mais fait trop de fautes d'orthographe —*
7	ORTHOGRAPHE GRAMMAIRE	
13	RÉCITATION	
12	VERSION LATINE	*Élève doué, mais assez timide —*
11	THÈME LATIN	
9	HISTOIRE	*} Intelligent mais un peu*
10	GÉOGRAPHIE	*paresseux*
12	LANGUE VIVANTE I *anglais*	*Bon à l'oral, élève sérieux*
14	LANGUE VIVANTE II *allemand*	*Doué pour les langues —*
10	MATHÉMATIQUES	*Un peu distrait !*
8	TECHNOLOGIE	*Assez mauvais travail !*

Grades in French secondary schools are often indicated by numbers from 0 to 20. Teachers on the whole are not known for their generosity with grades, and students consider 10/20 satisfactory and 14/20 very good.

See notes in Teaching Suggestions, p. T17, for more on the grading system.

36 Répondez aux questions.

1. Pour quelles matières est-ce que François est doué?
2. Est-ce qu'il est bon en orthographe?
3. Quel professeur dit qu'il est un peu distrait?
4. En quelle matière est-ce qu'il est mauvais?

37 **EXERCICE ORAL** ⊗

38

ADJECTIVES: GENDER AGREEMENT

Répondez aux questions qui suivent les exemples. ⊗

François est **distrait.**	**Florence** est **distraite.**
François est **grand.**	**Florence** est **grande.**
François est **intelligent.**	**Florence** est **intelligente.**

Compare the first sentences in each of the two columns above. Is the same form of the adjective used to refer to a masculine noun and to a feminine noun? Is there a difference in sound in these two forms? Is there a difference in spelling? Answer the same questions for the second and third pairs of sentences.

François est **doué.** **Florence** est **douée.**

Do these two adjectives sound alike? Are they spelled alike?

François est **timide.** **Florence** est **timide.**

Do these adjectives sound alike? Are they spelled alike?

39 **Lisez la généralisation suivante.**

1. You already know that adjectives can be gender cues. Many adjectives have a masculine form and a feminine form which are different in both sound and spelling: **Il est distrait – Elle est distraite.**

2. Other adjectives have a masculine form and a feminine form which sound alike but are spelled differently: **Il est doué – Elle est douée.**

3. Still other adjectives have a masculine form and a feminine form which are alike in both sound and spelling: **Il est timide – Elle est timide.**

4. The chart below summarizes adjective agreements.

	Masculine		Feminine	
Different sound } *Different spelling*	**Il** est	**distrait.**	**Elle** est	**distraite.**
	Il est	**sérieux.**	**Elle** est	**sérieuse.**
Same sound } *Different spelling*	**Il** est	**doué**	**Elle** est	**douée.**
Same sound } *Same spelling*	**Il** est	**timide.**	**Elle** est	**timide.**

5. The following is a list of the adjectives you already know:

like **distrait, -e**		like **sérieux, -euse**	like **doué, -e**	like **timide**
amusant	**mauvais**	**dangereux**	**sûr**	**extraordinaire**
différent	**petit**	**ennuyeux**	**vrai**	**simple**
grand	**vivant**	**paresseux**		
intelligent				

Bon, bonne has a change in the vowel sound between the masculine and feminine.

For script, see p. T18.

40 EXERCICE DE COMPREHENSION *Listening exercise*

	0	1	2	3	4	5	6	7	8	9	10
Un garçon	√										
Une fille											

41 Demandez à des camarades : ⊗ For answers, see p. T19.

Vous parlez de *(about)* François.
Il est bon en français?
Il est doué en latin?
Il est intelligent?
Il est paresseux?
Il est doué pour les langues?
Il est distrait?

Vous parlez de Florence.
Elle est bonne en français?
Elle est douée en latin?
Elle est intelligente?
Elle est paresseuse?
Elle est douée pour les langues?
Elle est distraite?

Variation: Vous parlez 1) à François, 2) à Florence: Tu es trop paresseux! (sérieux, distrait,
timide) Resp.: Mais non, je ne suis pas paresseux!

42 Parlons de Florence et de François. ⊗

Florence est bonne en français.
Florence est un peu paresseuse.
Florence est douée en latin.
Florence est un peu distraite.
Florence est amusante.

François aussi est bon en français.
François aussi est un peu paresseux.
François aussi est doué en latin.
François aussi est un peu distrait.
François aussi est amusant.

Variation: Florence est grande (intelligente, vivante, différente, ennuyeuse, paresseuse, douée,
timide). Et François?

43 Parlons de votre école. ⊗

Comment est la cour?
Comment est le gymnase?
Comment est le réfectoire?
Comment est la salle de conférences?
Comment est la bibliothèque?
Comment est le vestiaire?

La cour est très grande.
Le gymnase est très grand.
Le réfectoire est très grand.
La salle de conférences est très grande.
La bibliothèque est très grande.
Le vestiaire est très grand.

Variation: response: La cour est petite.

44 Et vous?

1. Qu'est-ce que vous aimez le mieux comme matières?
2. Qu'est-ce que le professeur de français dit de votre travail?
3. Est-ce que vous êtes bon(ne) à l'oral en français?
4. Pour quelles matières est-ce que vous êtes doué(e)?

45 EXERCICE ECRIT

a. Ecrivez *(write)* les réponses des exercices No 42 et 43.
b. Ecrivez ce que vos professeurs écriraient *(would write)* sur votre bulletin trimestriel.

46 EXERCICE DE CONVERSATION

Décrivez une de vos journées à l'école. *Describe one of your days at school.*
Commencez : Le matin je commence à 8 h. Je vais d'abord au cours de maths. A 10 h...

2   François Le Sève va à l'école au CES (Collège d'Enseignement Secondaire) de Montargis. Il est en quatrième. Il étudie 13 matières différentes. Les matières que François aime le mieux sont les maths et la musique. Il aime bien les langues vivantes (il étudie l'anglais et l'allemand), mais il n'aime pas tellement le latin. Comme tous les élèves de CES, il a des cours tous les jours, sauf le mercredi, le samedi après-midi et le dimanche, bien sûr! Les jours où il va en classe, il commence à huit heures et il finit à quatre heures (le lundi, le jeudi, le vendredi) ou à cinq heures (le mardi). Il a deux heures pour déjeuner.

François Le Sève goes to school at the CES (School for Secondary Education) in Montargis. He is in 9th grade. He studies 13 different subjects. The subjects François likes best are math and music. He likes modern languages very much (he is taking English and German), but he is not terribly fond of Latin. Like all the students at the CES, he has classes every day, except Wednesday, Saturday afternoon, and Sunday, of course! On the days he goes to school, he starts at eight o'clock and he finishes at four o'clock (Mondays, Thursdays, Fridays) or five o'clock (Tuesdays). He has two hours for lunch.

9   Quelle heure est-il?

What time is it?

13   Voilà l'école de François.

Here is François' school.

14   François rencontre un nouveau, Olivier, dans la cour du CES.

François meets a new boy, Olivier, in the schoolyard of the CES.

OLIVIER   Où sont les vestiaires, s'il te plaît?
Can you tell me where the locker room is, please?

FRANÇOIS   Là-bas, au fond de la cour.
Over there, on the other side of the schoolyard.

OLIVIER   Il y a une bibliothèque?
Is there a library?

FRANÇOIS   Oui, en face de toi.
Yes, in front of you.

OLIVIER   Où ça?
Where?

FRANÇOIS   Juste ici, à côté des bureaux. Viens avec moi…
Right there, next to the offices. Come with me . . .

OLIVIER   Merci, mais je ne vais pas à la bibliothèque tout de suite. Je vais d'abord au gymnase.
Thanks, but I'm not going to the library right away. I'm going to the gym first.

21   La classe de François.
François' class.

21.1   Le professeur d'anglais, Mme Dubois, dit aux élèves : « Maintenant corrigeons les devoirs. François, allez au tableau et effacez. Les autres, ouvrez vos livres à la page 32, et ne bavardez pas, s'il vous plaît! »
The English teacher, Mrs. Dubois, says to her students: "Now let's correct the homework. François, go to the board and erase it. Everybody else, open your books to page 32, and don't talk, please."

21.2   Le professeur de maths, M. Perret, demande : « Tout le monde a compris? » Une élève, Florence, lève la main et répond : «Monsieur, s'il vous plaît, je ne comprends pas la réponse à la question numéro deux. »
The math teacher, Mr. Perret, asks: "Did everybody understand?" One student, Florence, raises her hand and answers: "Excuse me, sir, but I don't understand the answer to question two."

21.3   Le professeur de dessin, Mlle Blondel, dit à la classe : « Maintenant, les enfants, regardons ces dessins. Commençons par le dessin de Florence. »
The art teacher, Miss Blondel, says to the class: "Now, everybody, let's look at these drawings. Let's start with Florence's drawing."

21.4   Le professeur de technologie, M. Pujol, dit à un élève : « S'il te plaît, Bernard, fais attention! Il faut soigner la présentation des devoirs! »
The technology teacher, Mr. Pujol, says to a student: "Please be careful, Bernard! You have to make sure your homework is neat!"

35   Le bulletin trimestriel de François.
François' report card.
Bon élève mais fait trop de fautes d'orthographe.
Good student but makes too many spelling mistakes.
Elève doué mais assez timide.
Gifted student but rather shy.
Intelligent mais un peu paresseux.
Bright but a little lazy.
Bon à l'oral, élève sérieux.
Good oral work, serious student.
Doué pour les langues.
Talented in languages.
Un peu distrait!
Somewhat inattentive.
Assez mauvais travail.
Rather poor work.

WORD LIST

48

1–12 un CES *secondary school*	**aller** *to go*	**différentes** *different*
une classe *class*	**commencer** *to start*	**13 matières différentes** *13 different subjects*
en classe *in class*	**nous commençons** *we start*	
un cours *course, class*	**déjeuner** *to have lunch*	**le mieux** *best*
une école *school*	**étudier** *to study*	**aimer le mieux** *to like best*
un(e) élève *pupil, student*	**il finit** *he finishes*	

la quatrième   *9th grade*
un emploi du temps   *schedule*
une matière   *subject*
  l'allemand (m.)   *German*
  l'anglais (m.)   *English*
  le dessin   *drawing, art*
  le français   *French*
  la géographie   *geography*
  la gymnastique   *gym*
  l'histoire (f.)   *history*
  une langue vivante   *modern*
    language
  le latin   *Latin*
  les maths (m.)   *math*
  la musique   *music*
  les sciences (f.)   *science*
  la technologie   *technology*
  les travaux manuels (m.)   *shop*

un jour   *day*
  tous les jours   *every day*
  lundi (m.)   *Monday*
  le lundi   *on Mondays*
  mardi (m.)   *Tuesday*
  mercredi (m)   *Wednesday*
  jeudi (m.)   *Thursday*
  vendredi (m.)   *Friday*
  samedi (m)   *Saturday*
  dimanche (m.)   *Sunday*

à   *at*
en   *in*
sauf   *except*
bien sûr   *of course*
tellement   *terribly*

que   *which, that*

Quelle heure est-il?   *What time is it?*
Il est une heure.   *It's one o'clock.*
une heure (h)   *hour*
  …et quart   *quarter past*
  …et demie   *half past*
  …moins le quart   *quarter of / to*
l'après-midi (m.)   *afternoon*
  4 h de l'après-midi   *4 in the after-noon*
le samedi après-midi   *Saturday after-noon*
le matin   *morning*
  8 h du matin   *8 in the morning*
le soir   *evening*
  8 h du soir   *8 in the evening*
midi   *noon*
minuit   *midnight*

---

un abri (pour bicyclettes)   *(bicycle) shed*
une bibliothèque   *library*
un bureau (de l'administration)   *(administration) office*
  des bureaux   *offices*
un couloir   *hallway*
une cour   *courtyard, schoolyard*
une cuisine   *kitchen*
un gymnase   *gymnasium*
un laboratoire   *laboratory*
un réfectoire   *lunchroom*
une salle de classe   *classroom*
une salle de conférences   *auditorium*
un vestiaire   *locker room*

un nouveau   *a new boy*
une nouvelle   *a new girl*

rencontrer   *to meet*

viens   *come on*

il y a   *there is (are)*
voilà   *here is (are), there is (are)*
  Voilà l'école.   *Here is the school.*

à côté (de)   *next to*
au fond (de)   *at the far end (of)*
en face (de)   *in front of, facing*

d'abord   *first of all*
ici   *here*
juste ici   *right here*
là-bas   *over there*
tout de suite   *right away*

merci   *thanks*
s'il te plaît   *please*

---

un(e) autre   *another (person)*
un(e) camarade   *classmate*
un devoir   *homework*
un enfant   *child*
madame (Mme)   *Mrs.*
mademoiselle (Mlle)   *Miss*
monsieur (M.)   *Mr.*
un numéro   *number*
une page   *page*
  à la page 32   *on page 32*
la présentation   *appearance*

un professeur   *teacher*
une question   *question*
une réponse   *answer*
un tableau   *blackboard*

bavarder   *to talk*
commencer (par)   *to start (with)*
  commençons   *let's start*
corriger   *to correct*
  corrigeons   *let's correct*
demander   *to ask*
effacer   *to erase*
  nous effaçons   *we erase*
soigner   *to take pains with*

je comprends   *I understand*
Tout le monde a compris?   *Did everybody understand?*
elle (il) dit   *she (he) says*
faire attention   *to be careful*
il faut   *must, have to*
elle lève la main   *she raises her hand*
ouvrez   *open*
elle répond   *she answers*

maintenant   *now*
s'il vous plaît   *please*
tout le monde   *everybody*
vos   *your*

---

une année scolaire   *school year*
une appréciation   *comment*
un bulletin trimestriel   *report card*
une composition française   *com-position*
la grammaire   *grammar*
un nom   *name*
une note   *grade*
l'orthographe (f.)   *spelling*
  une faute d'orthographe   *spelling mistake*
la récitation   *recitation*
le thème latin   *translation into Latin*
le travail   *work*
la version latine   *translation from Latin*

une boîte de couleurs   *paintbox*
un cahier   *notebook*
un cartable   *schoolbag*
un compas   *compass*
un crayon   *pencil*
un feutre   *felt-tip pen*
une gomme   *eraser*
une règle   *ruler*
un stylo à bille   *ballpoint pen*
une trousse   *pencil case*

faire   *to make*

bon, bonne   *good*
différent, –e   *different*
distrait, –e   *inattentive*
doué, –e   *gifted, talented*
intelligent, –e   *intelligent*
mauvais, –e   *poor, bad*
paresseux, –euse   *lazy*
sérieux, –euse   *serious*
timide   *shy*

assez   *rather*

un peu   *a little*

de   *about*

Throughout this program, verb forms other than the infinitive are listed to show spelling changes.

Photo 1: Catherine, Philippe, Dominique, and Bernard in Bernard's car, "une 2 CV" (une deux chevaux Citroën). See notes, p. T19.
Photo 2: In front of movie theatre
Photo 3: On a beach between Luneray and Dieppe. Notice pebbles, typical of Dieppe. See notes, p. T19.
Photo 4: The fishing harbor of Dieppe.
Photo 4: At the café Les Ambassadeurs

5

UNE SORTIE

For recording sample, see p. T56.

1

Philippe Lardan (shown talking on the phone) and his sister Catherine were last seen in Unit 3.

Qu'est-ce qu'on fait cet après-midi? ⊗

C'est mercredi, aujourd'hui. Philippe et Catherine Lardan n'ont pas classe. Ils sont chez eux, mais ils ne veulent pas rester à la maison toute la journée. Ils ont envie de sortir avec des amis. Philippe téléphone à son ami Dominique pour lui demander s'il est libre.

PHILIPPE   Qu'est-ce que tu fais cet après-midi?

DOMINIQUE   Je sors avec Bernard. On va à Dieppe.

PHILIPPE   Vous allez aux Ambassadeurs[1]?

DOMINIQUE   Oui... Et après on pense aller au cinéma.

PHILIPPE   Est-ce qu'on peut venir avec vous? Il y a assez de place dans la voiture?

DOMINIQUE   Bien sûr! Quand est-ce qu'on passe vous prendre?

PHILIPPE   Quand vous voulez... Nous sommes prêts à partir!

DOMINIQUE   Ça tombe bien! Nous aussi. On est chez vous dans cinq minutes.

2

Refer students to opener, p. 45, and discuss details of pictures.
Catherine and her brother Philippe live in a very small village, Luneray. So for entertainment they have to go to the nearest big town, which is Dieppe. They are not old enough to drive, however (in France you have to be 18 to get a driver's license), and they depend on older friends and relatives to drive them. In this case Bernard, the brother of their friend Dominique, will do the driving.

3

Répondez aux questions.

1. Quel jour est-ce?
2. Est-ce que Philippe et Catherine vont à l'école le mercredi?
3. Qu'est-ce qu'ils ont envie de faire ce mercredi?
4. A qui est-ce que Philippe téléphone?
5. Qu'est-ce que Dominique fait cet après-midi?
6. Où est-ce qu'ils vont, Dominique et Bernard?
7. Est-ce que Catherine et Philippe vont à Dieppe avec Dominique et Bernard?

4

EXERCICE ORAL ⊗

5

For recording sample, see p. T58.

VERBS ENDING IN -ir

Répondez aux questions qui suivent les exemples. ⊗

Je sors avec Bernard.   **Nous sortons** avec Bernard.
Tu sors avec Bernard?   **Vous sortez** avec Bernard?
Elle sort avec Bernard.   **Ils sortent** avec Bernard.

Do the singular forms sound alike or different? Are they spelled alike? What consonant sound is present in the plural forms but not in the singular?

[1] A sidewalk café in Dieppe where Philippe and his friends like to go.

6 Lisez la généralisation suivante.

1. The following chart shows the forms of the verb **sortir,** *to go out.*

	Pronoun	Stem	Ending	
Singular	je tu il / elle / on	**sor**	-s -s -t	Je **sors** souvent. Tu **sors** souvent? Elle **sort** souvent.
Plural	nous vous ils / elles	**sort**	-ons -ez -ent	Nous **sortons** souvent. Vous **sortez** souvent? Ils **sortent** souvent.

2. There are other **-ir** verbs like **sortir : partir,** *to leave,* is one of them.

Use item substitution drills to practice partir.

7 Les trois amis sortent avec Bernard. ⊗

Qu'est-ce que tu fais cet après-midi?   Je sors avec Bernard.
Et vous deux? / Et Dominique? / Et Catherine et Philippe?

nous sortons / il sort / ils sortent

8 Les garçons partent dans cinq minutes. ⊗

Tu restes avec nous?   Non, je pars dans cinq minutes.
Et vous deux? / Et Philippe? / Et Dominique et Bernard?

nous partons / il part / ils partent

9 Où est-ce qu'on va? ⊗

Au café?

A la piscine?

A la patinoire?

Au bowling?

10 Et vous?

1. Qu'est-ce que vous faites quand vous n'avez pas classe?
2. Avec qui est-ce que vous sortez?
3. Où est-ce que vous aimez aller?

Use vocabulary cards
to review places men-
tioned in earlier units:
l'école, le bureau, la
bibliothèque, la plage, etc.

11 EXERCICE ECRIT

a. Ecrivez les réponses des exercices No 7 et 8.
b. Dites (*say*) ce que vous aimez faire le samedi après-midi.

12 HOW TO ASK QUESTIONS

Répondez aux questions qui suivent les exemples. ☺

Les jeunes partent.   Les jeunes partent?

Which of the two sentences is a statement? Which is a question? Can you hear a difference between the two sentences?

Les jeunes partent?   Est-ce que les jeunes partent?

What is the difference between these two questions?

Ils partent?   Quand est-ce qu'ils partent?
Est-ce qu'ils partent?   Pourquoi est-ce qu'ils partent?

Which of these questions ask for a yes / no answer? Which ask for specific information?

13 Lisez la généralisation suivante.

1. Questions answered by **oui** or **non.**
   a. A question to be answered **oui** or **non** can have the same form as a statement. The only change is in the rising intonation of the question: **Ils partent?**
   b. Another way of asking these **oui / non** questions is to add **est-ce que** at the beginning of the question. Notice that élision occurs with **est-ce que: Est-ce qu'**ils partent?

2. Information questions with **est-ce que.**
   A question that asks for some specific information is very often formed as follows:
   question word or phrase + **est-ce que** + (pro)noun + verb.
   It has a falling intonation: the voice starts at a high pitch on the question word and falls as it goes on.
   Question words you already know are:

Comment / A quelle heure / Pourquoi / Quand	est-ce que	tu pars?
A quoi / Avec qui / Où	est-ce que	tu joues?
Qu'	est-ce que	tu fais?

   When **qui** is the subject of the sentence, **est-ce que** is not used: **Qui joue au tennis?**

3. Questions are also formed in a third way, called inversion. You have seen examples of this construction:
   ### Comment t'appelles-tu? Quel âge as-tu? Quelle heure est-il?
   Except in these and a few other very common expressions, inversion is usually more formal in usage than the other forms you have learned.

14 Demandez à un camarade... ☺

s'il sort.   Est-ce que tu sors?
s'il part maintenant / s'il va au cinéma / s'il rentre tout de suite
Est-ce que tu pars maintenant? / Est-ce que tu vas au cinéma? / Est-ce que tu rentres tout de suite?

15 Demandez à une camarade... ☺

quand elle sort.   Quand est-ce que tu sors?
pourquoi elle sort / avec qui elle sort / à quelle heure elle sort
Pourquoi est-ce que tu sors? / Avec qui est-ce que tu sors? / A quelle heure est-ce que tu sors?

In addition to the beverages listed on this menu, coffee too is a popular drink. It can be ordered as "un express" (strong black coffee served in a small cup), as "un café-crème" or simply "un crème" ("un express" with cream). "Café au lait" refers only to coffee served at breakfast in a large cup or bowl with hot milk.

16 Qu'est-ce qu'on prend? ⊗

Il est une heure de l'après-midi quand les quatre amis arrivent aux Ambassadeurs. Et comme ils ont faim et soif, ils commandent tout de suite.

LE GARÇON	Vous désirez?
CATHERINE	Un Schweppes et un sandwich au pâté, s'il vous plaît.
LE GARÇON	Il n'y a plus de pâté. Du jambon, du saucisson et du camembert, seulement.
CATHERINE	Bon, alors donnez-moi un sandwich au saucisson.
DOMINIQUE	Moi, je vais prendre un jus de pamplemousse, s'il vous plaît.
CATHERINE	Tu n'as pas faim?
DOMINIQUE	Si, mais je n'aime ni le jambon ni le saucisson!
CATHERINE	Alors, prends un sandwich au camembert.

SANDWICHES

Jambon, Pâté	2,50*
Saucisson, Rillettes	2,50
Gruyère-Jambon	5,00
Gruyère, Camembert	2,50

BOISSONS

Limonade,* le quart	2,50
avec sirop	3,00
Eau Minérale, le quart	2,50
avec sirop	3,00
Jus de fruit	3,00
Schweppes Tonic	3,00
Coca-Cola	3,00
Lait froid	1,50

GLACES

Vanille, Café	3,50
Chocolat, Fraise	3,50
Pistache, Noisette	3,50

Le garçon apporte les sandwiches et les boissons. Tout le monde mange. Une fois terminé, il faut payer. Philippe appelle le garçon : « L'addition, s'il vous plaît! » Ils sortent tous leur argent. « Ça fait combien pour moi? » demande Catherine. « Six francs, trente-trois, service compris, » répond Philippe.

17

Catherine, Philippe, Dominique, and Bernard, like most French teenagers, spend a great deal of their free time at sidewalk cafés. They often have one, like Les Ambassadeurs, that is a favorite hangout and gathering place for them and their friends. They can meet and talk there, play pinball machines, and watch the world go by. They can also eat something, most likely sandwiches, and have a soft drink to go with it. The sandwiches they order are made from the long French breads called "baguettes," cut open and filled with meats or cheeses. Among the favorites are those mentioned here: ham (sometimes combined with cheese); a variety of cheeses, including Camembert and Gruyère; saucisson, a sliced hard sausage similar to the Italian salami; and pâté, a spreadable liver mixture. The bread is usually buttered, but the sandwich is not garnished.

* **2,50 = deux francs, cinquante (centimes).** In ordinary speech about money, the word **"francs"** is almost always added to the number, and when a price is written, a comma instead of a point indicates decimals. Remember, too, that in French a point or a space indicates thousands: **2.346,75. F** is the legal abbreviation for **franc: 2,50 F.**

*"Limonade" is a clear, carbonated, lemon-flavored drink. Lemonade is called "de la citronnade" in French.

18   **Répondez aux questions.**

1. Quelle heure est-il quand les quatre amis arrivent aux Ambassadeurs?
2. Qu'est-ce qu'ils font? Pourquoi?
3. Qu'est-ce que Catherine commande?
4. Qu'est-ce que Dominique commande?
5. Qu'est-ce qu'il aime le mieux, le jambon ou le saucisson?
6. Qu'est-ce qu'il faut faire une fois terminé?
7. Ça fait combien pour Catherine?

19   **Demandez à un(e) camarade :**

This Ex. drills items on menu, p. 49.

1. Qu'est-ce que tu aimes le mieux, la limonade ou l'eau minérale?
2. le jus de pamplemousse ou le lait froid?
3. le Schweppes ou le Coca-Cola?
4. le gruyère ou le camembert?
5. le saucisson ou les rillettes?
6. la glace au chocolat ou au café?
7. la glace à la pistache ou à la noisette?
8. la glace à la vanille ou à la fraise?

20   **EXERCICE ORAL** ⊗

21

HOW TO INDICATE QUANTITY

Répondez aux questions qui suivent les exemples. ⊗

J'aime **le Coca-Cola.** Vous avez **du Coca-Cola?** Alors, donnez-moi **un Coca-Cola.**
Which sentence refers to Coca-Cola in general? Which sentence refers to *some* Coca-Cola? Which sentence refers to a serving of Coca-Cola?

J'aime **la glace.** Vous avez **de la glace?** Alors, donnez-moi **une glace.**
Which sentence refers to ice cream in general? Which sentence refers to *some* ice cream? Which sentence refers to a serving of ice cream?

22   **Lisez la généralisation suivante.**

The following distinction is made in French:
1. **le Coca-Cola** means Coca-Cola in general.
2. **du Coca-Cola** means an unspecified quantity of Coca-Cola.
3. **un Coca-Cola** means a unit of Coca-Cola (a glass, a bottle, etc.).

in general		some		a unit	
le	Coca-Cola	**du**	Coca-Cola	**un**	Coca-Cola *(a glass, a bottle, a cup, etc.)*
le	jambon	**du**	jambon	**un**	jambon *(a whole ham)*
la	glace	**de la**	glace	**une**	glace *(a cone, a dish, etc.)*

Elision occurs: **de l'** is used instead of **du** or **de la** before a noun beginning with a vowel sound. For example: **Vous avez de l'eau minérale?**

Exercises 23, 24, 25, and 28 can be expanded by adding items.

23   **Ça tombe bien!** ⊗

J'aime beaucoup le jambon.
la limonade / le saucisson / l'eau minérale
de la limonade / du saucisson / de l'eau minérale

Ça tombe bien! Nous avons du jambon!

24 **Qu'est-ce que vous voulez comme boisson?** ⊗

Du Coca-Cola?   Oui, donnez-moi un Coca-Cola.
De la limonade? / Du lait froid? / De l'eau minérale?

  une limonade / un lait froid / une eau minérale

25 **Qu'est-ce que tu prends?** ⊗

De la glace?   Non, je n'aime pas la glace.
De l'eau minérale? / De la limonade? / Du lait froid?

  l'eau minérale / la limonade / le lait froid

26 # USE OF de IN NEGATIVE CONSTRUCTIONS

Répondez aux questions qui suivent les exemples. ⊗

  Nous avons **du** Coca-Cola.   Nous **n'**avons **pas de** Coca-Cola.
  Nous avons **de la** limonade.   Nous **n'**avons **pas de** limonade.
  Nous avons **de l'**eau minérale.   Nous **n'**avons **pas d'**eau minérale.

Are **du, de la,** and **de l'** used in negative constructions? What is used instead?

27 **Lisez la généralisation suivante.**

As you know, in negative constructions **de** is used instead of **un, une,** and **des; de** is also used instead of **du** or **de la.** Other articles do not change: **Je n'aime pas le Coca-Cola.**

	Affirmative			Negative	
Ils veulent	**un**	Coca-Cola.	Ils ne veulent pas	**de**	Coca-Cola.
	une	limonade.		**de**	limonade.
	des	sandwiches.		**de**	sandwiches.
	du	lait.		**de**	lait.
	de la	glace.		**de**	glace.
	de l'	eau.		**d'**	eau.

28 **Qu'est-ce que vous voulez?** ⊗

Du lait?   Non merci, pas de lait.
De la glace? / De l'eau? / Du Coca-Cola?

  Non merci, pas de glace. / Non merci, pas d'eau. / Non merci, pas de Coca-Cola.

29 **EXERCICE ECRIT**   For answers, see p. T20.

Mettez les phrases suivantes à la forme négative. *Make the following sentences negative.*
1. Ils veulent du Coca-Cola.   4. Dominique mange un sandwich.
2. J'ai de l'eau minérale.   5. Vous avez de la limonade?
3. Catherine aime le Schweppes.   6. Ils commandent des glaces.

30 **EXERCICE DE CONVERSATION**

Vous allez dans un café avec un(e) ami(e). Regardez la carte *(menu)* p. 49.
1. Le garçon arrive. Vous commandez. LE GARÇON : Vous désirez? VOUS : Je vais prendre…
2. Vous demandez à votre ami(e) : Qu'est-ce que tu prends?…

This movie listing is taken from the Dieppe newspaper <u>Les Informations Dieppoises</u>. Le Royal, le Casino, and le Rex are the names of Dieppe's movie theatres (a movie theatre is "un cinéma"). These movie titles in English are <u>Rio Bravo</u>, <u>Love in the Afternoon</u>, <u>The Aristocats</u>, and <u>Doctor Strangelove</u>.

31 On va voir un film? ⊗

DOMINIQUE Qu'est-ce qu'on fait maintenant? On va au cinéma?
PHILIPPE D'accord, mais qu'est-ce qu'on va voir comme film?
CATHERINE Attendez! Je vais regarder le programme dans le journal. Oh! Il y a *Les Aristochats* au Casino!
DOMINIQUE Qu'est-ce que c'est?
CATHERINE C'est un dessin animé de Walt Disney. Il paraît que c'est très bien.
DOMINIQUE On choisit ça?
BERNARD Oui, mais à quelle heure est-ce que ça va finir? Parce que moi, je dois rentrer avant six heures.
CATHERINE Oh, ça finit toujours vers cinq heures.
BERNARD Alors, allons-y!

32 Répondez aux questions.

1. Où est-ce qu'ils veulent aller?
2. Dans quoi est-ce que Catherine regarde le programme des cinémas?
3. Qu'est-ce que c'est *Les Aristochats?*
4. A quelle heure est-ce que le film commence?
5. A quelle heure est-ce qu'il va finir?

CINÉMA

ROYAL   84-21-82
Mardi 21 h
Un film de
HOWARD HAWKS
RIO BRAVO
avec John Wayne
et Dean Martin

**Mercredi 15 h   21 h
Jeudi 21 h**
Un film d'
ERIC ROHMER
**L'AMOUR
L'APRES-MIDI**

CASINO   84-16-58
**Mercredi 15 h   21 h
Jeudi 21 h**
Le grand dessin animé de
WALT DISNEY
LES ARISTOCHATS

REX   84-22-74
**Mardi 21 h
Mercredi 15 h   21 h**
Un film de
STANLEY KRAMER
DOCTEUR FOLAMOUR

33 Qu'est-ce que vous aimez comme films? ⊗

Les films comiques?

Les films policiers?

Les westerns?

Les histoires d'amour?

34 Et vous? Add other types of films, like "les films d'aventure," "les films de science-fiction," "les comédies musicales," or "les films d'épouvante" (horror movies).

1. Est-ce que vous allez souvent au cinéma?
2. Quand est-ce que vous allez au cinéma?
3. Avec qui?
4. Qu'est-ce que vous aimez comme films?
5. Vous aimez les histoires d'amour? Pourquoi?
6. Et les dessins animés? Vous trouvez ça amusant?

35 EXERCICE ORAL ⊗

¹ Official schedules use the 24-hour clock to avoid confusion among morning, afternoon, and evening. **15 h** *(12-noon plus 3)* means *3 o'clock in the afternoon,* and **21 h** *(12-noon plus 9)* means *9 o'clock in the evening.*

The coin "un demi-franc" is also referred to as "cinquante centimes." Point out that "dix francs" exists both as a coin and a bill. Pictures on French bills are of famous Frenchmen: <u>10 Francs</u>, old bill, Voltaire—not shown—18th c. philosopher; new bill, Berlioz, 19th c. composer. <u>50 Francs</u>: old, Racine—not shown—17th c. playright; new, Quentin de la Tour, 18th c. painter. <u>100 Francs</u>: Corneille, 17th c. playwright.

36

L'argent français : les billets et les pièces. ⊗

Regardez la carte p. 49. Choisissez ce que vous voulez. Calculez combien vous devez. Si le service n'est pas compris, laissez un pourboire (15 %) au garçon.

un centime   cinq centimes   dix centimes   vingt centimes

un demi-franc   un franc   cinq francs   dix francs

37

MORE VERBS ENDING IN -ir

Répondez aux questions qui suivent les exemples. ⊗

Je choisis le western.	**Nous choisissons** le western.
Tu choisis le western?	**Vous choisissez** le western?
Il choisit le western.	**Ils choisissent** le western.

Do the singular forms of the verb sound alike or different? Are they spelled alike? What consonant sound is present in the plural forms and not in the singular?

38 ### Lisez la généralisation suivante.

1. There are two kinds of **-ir** verbs: those of the type **sortir,** which you have already seen, and those of the type **choisir,** *to choose,* the forms of which are presented in the chart below.

	Pronoun	Stem	Ending	
Singular	je tu il / elle / on	chois	-is -is -it	Je **choisis** bien. Tu **choisis** bien. Il **choisit** bien.
Plural	nous vous ils / elles	choisiss	-ons -ez -ent	Nous **choisissons** bien. Vous **choisissez** bien. Ils **choisissent** bien.

2. There are other **-ir** verbs like **choisir : finir,** *to finish, to end,* is one of them.

Use item substitution drills to practice finir.

39 ### Regardons le programme dans le journal. ⊗

Qu'est-ce que tu choisis?   Je choisis le dessin animé.
Et vous deux? / Et Catherine? / Et les garçons?

nous choisissons / elle choisit / ils choisissent

40 **Il faut finir ces devoirs avant de sortir, les enfants!** ⊗

Tu es prêt?   Je finis ces devoirs et j'arrive!
Et vous deux? / Et Philippe? / Et les filles?
nous finissons . . . et nous arrivons / il finit . . . et il arrive / elles finissent . . . et elles arrivent

41 **EXERCICE DE COMPREHENSION** ⊗ For script, see p. T20.

	0	1	3	4	5	6	7	8
Singular								
Plural	√							

42   **EXPRESSING FUTURE TIME**

Répondez aux questions qui suivent les exemples. ⊗

Qu'est-ce que **tu fais?**   Qu'est-ce que **tu fais dans une heure?**
What time is expressed in the sentence on the left, present or future? And in the sentence on the right? How do you know? Is there any difference between the verb forms?

Je sors dans une heure.   **Je vais sortir** dans une heure.
What time is expressed in the sentence on the left, present or future? And in the sentence on the right? How do you know? What verb form expresses future time in the sentence on the left? What verb forms express future time in the sentence on the right?

Je **vais sortir** avec Bernard.   Nous **allons voir** un film.   Le film **va commencer** à 21 h.
Vais, allons, va are forms of what verb? What are the verb forms that follow called?

43 **Lisez la généralisation suivante.**

1. Most of the sentences you have been using so far have referred to present time. The verb forms used to express present time are said to be in the present tense.
Nous **sommes** prêts.   Je **regarde** la télévision.

2. Future time may be expressed by
   a. present-tense verb forms + a time expression: **Nous partons dans cinq minutes.**
   b. a present-tense form of **aller** followed by an infinitive, as this chart shows:

Je	vais	sortir	avec Bernard.
Tu	vas	regarder	le programme.
Il	va	aller	au cinéma.
Nous	allons	voir	un dessin animé.
Vous	allez	partir	tout de suite.
Ils	vont	rentrer	à six heures.

3. In the negative, **ne** comes right before the form of **aller** and **pas** comes immediately after it.
For example: **Je ne vais pas sortir avec Bernard.**

44 **Qu'est-ce que Catherine et Philippe vont faire cet après-midi?** ⊗

Téléphoner à Dominique?   Oui, ils vont téléphoner à Dominique.
Sortir avec Dominique et Bernard? / Aller aux Ambassadeurs? / Voir *Les Aristochats?*
ils vont sortir / ils vont aller / ils vont voir

45 Qu'est-ce qu'on va faire? ⊗

Tu téléphones à Dominique?
Vous jouez aux cartes, vous deux?
Tu sors avec Bernard?
Catherine va au cinéma?
Vous partez maintenant, vous deux?
Catherine et Philippe déjeunent aux
Ambassadeurs?

Oui, je vais téléphoner à Dominique.
Oui, nous allons jouer aux cartes.
Oui, je vais sortir avec Bernard.
Oui, elle va aller au cinéma.
Oui, nous allons partir maintenant.
Oui, ils vont déjeuner aux Ambassadeurs.

Variation: Ask for negative responses.

46 EXERCICE DE CONVERSATION

Cet après-midi, vous allez sortir avec des amis. Qu'est-ce que vous allez faire?

Commencez : Cet après-midi, je vais sortir avec...

Do this as a writing exercise after the conversation has been worked on.

47 FOR REFERENCE

1 Qu'est-ce qu'on fait cet après-midi?
C'est mercredi, aujourd'hui. Philippe et Catherine Lardan n'ont pas classe. Ils sont chez eux, mais ils ne veulent pas rester à la maison toute la journée. Ils ont envie de sortir avec des amis. Philippe téléphone à son ami Dominique pour lui demander s'il est libre.

PHILIPPE Qu'est-ce que tu fais cet après-midi?
DOMINIQUE Je sors avec Bernard. On va à Dieppe.
PHILIPPE Vous allez aux Ambassadeurs?
DOMINIQUE Oui... Et après on pense aller au cinéma.

PHILIPPE Est-ce qu'on peut venir avec vous? Il y a assez de place dans la voiture.
DOMINIQUE Bien sûr! Quand est-ce qu'on passe vous prendre?
PHILIPPE Quand vous voulez... Nous sommes prêts à partir!
DOMINIQUE Ça tombe bien! Nous aussi. On est chez vous dans cinq minutes.

What shall we do this afternoon?
Today is Wednesday. Philippe and Catherine Lardan don't have school. They are at home, but they don't want to stay home all day. They want to go out with some friends. Philippe calls his friend Dominique to ask him if he's free.
What are you doing this afternoon?
I'm going out with Bernard. We're going to Dieppe.
Are you going to the Ambassadors?
Yes, and afterwards we're thinking about going to the movies.
Can we come with you? Is there enough room in the car?
Oh, sure! When should we come by to pick you up?
Whenever you want to. . . . We're ready to leave now.
Terrific! We are too. We'll be at your place in five minutes.

9 Où est-ce qu'on va?
Au café? A la piscine?
A la patinoire? Au bowling?

Where shall we go?
To the café? To the pool?
To the skating rink? To the bowling alley?

16 Qu'est-ce qu'on prend?
Il est une heure de l'après-midi quand les quatre amis arrivent aux Ambassadeurs. Et comme ils ont faim et soif, ils commandent tout de suite.

LE GARÇON Vous désirez?
CATHERINE Un Schweppes et un sandwich au pâté, s'il vous plaît.
LE GARÇON Il n'y a plus de pâté. Du jambon, du saucisson, et du camembert, seulement.
CATHERINE Bon, alors donnez-moi un sandwich au saucisson.
DOMINIQUE Moi, je vais prendre un jus de pample-mousse, s'il vous plaît.
CATHERINE Tu n'as pas faim?
DOMINIQUE Si, mais je n'aime ni le jambon ni le saucisson!
CATHERINE Alors, prends un sandwich au camembert.
Le garçon apporte les sandwiches et les boissons. Tout le monde mange. Une fois terminé, il faut payer. Philippe appelle le garçon. « L'addition, s'il vous plaît. » Ils sortent tous leur argent. « Ça fait combien pour moi? » demande Catherine. « Six francs, trente-trois, service compris, » répond Philippe.

What shall we have?
It's one o'clock in the afternoon when the four friends get to the Ambassadors. And since they are hungry and thirsty, they order right away.
What would you like?
A Schweppes and a pâté sandwich, please.
There isn't any more pâté. Only ham, salami, and Camembert.
Okay, then give me a salami sandwich.
And I'll have a grapefruit juice, please.
Aren't you hungry?
Yes, but I don't like either ham or salami.
Then have the Camembert.
The waiter brings the sandwiches and the drinks. Everybody eats. Once they have finished, they have to pay. Philippe calls the waiter. "Check, please!" They all take out their money. "That's how much for me?" Catherine asks. "Six francs, thirty-three, service included," Philippe answers.

31 On va voir un film?		Shall we go to the movies?

31 On va voir un film? — Shall we go to the movies?

DOMINIQUE Qu'est-ce qu'on fait maintenant? On va au cinéma?
What shall we do now? Shall we go to the movies?

PHILIPPE D'accord, mais qu'est-ce qu'on va voir comme film?
Okay, but what kind of film shall we go see?

CATHERINE Attendez! Je vais regarder le programme dans le journal. Oh! Il y a *Les Aristochats* au Casino!
Wait a minute! I'll look at the movie listings in the paper. There's The Aristocats at the Casino!

DOMINIQUE Qu'est-ce que c'est?
What's that?

CATHERINE C'est un dessin animé de Walt Disney. Il paraît que c'est très bien.
It's an animated cartoon by Walt Disney. It's supposed to be very good.

DOMINIQUE On choisit ça?
Is that what we want?

BERNARD Oui, mais à quelle heure est-ce que ça va finir? Parce que moi, je dois rentrer avant six heures.
Yes, but what time will it be over? Because I have to be home before six o'clock.

CATHERINE Oh, ça finit toujours vers cinq heures.
Oh, it's always over about five o'clock.

BERNARD Alors, allons-y!
Okay, so let's go!

33 Qu'est-ce que vous aimez comme films? Les films comiques? Les films policiers? Les westerns? Les histoires d'amour?
What kinds of movies do you like? Comedies? Detective films? Westerns? Love stories?

48 WORD LIST

1–15

le cinéma *movies*	**partir** *to leave*	**libre** *free*
une journée *day*	**rester** *to stay*	**prêt, –e** *ready*
toute la journée *all day long*	**sortir** *to go out*	**après** *after*
une minute *minute*	**téléphoner (à)** *to call*	**aujourd'hui** *today*
une sortie *outing*	**avoir envie de** *to want to*	**quand** *when*
une voiture *car*	on peut venir *can we come*	**si** *if*
	pour lui demander *to ask him*	**assez de** *enough*
un bowling *bowling alley*	ils ne veulent pas *they don't want*	**assez de place** *enough room*
un café *café*	**vous voulez** *you want*	**chez** *at (to) someone's house*
une patinoire *skating rink*	on pense aller *we're thinking about going*	**chez eux** *at their house*
une piscine *swimming pool*	on passe vous prendre *we'll come by to pick you up*	**à la maison** *at home*
		Ça tombe bien! *Terrific!*

16–30

une boisson *drink*	**une glace** *ice cream*	**manger** *to eat*
l'eau minérale (f.) *mineral water*	une glace au café *coffee ice cream*	**nous mangeons** *we eat*
un jus de fruit *fruit juice*	le café *coffee*	**payer** *to pay*
un jus de pamplemousse *grapefruit juice*	le chocolat *chocolate*	**sortir** *to take out*
le lait *milk*	la fraise *strawberry*	**avoir faim** *to be hungry*
la limonade *lemon soda*	la noisette *hazelnut*	**avoir soif** *to be thirsty*
le sirop *flavoring syrup*	la pistache *pistachio*	**il appelle** *he calls*
un quart *¼ litre*	la vanille *vanilla*	**je vais prendre** *I'll have*
		on prend *we take*
une baguette *long French bread*	**une addition** *check*	**prends** *take*
un sandwich *sandwich*	**l'argent** (m.) *money*	
un sandwich au camembert *Camembert sandwich*	**un franc** *franc*	**froid, –e** *cold*
le camembert *Camembert cheese*	**un garçon** *waiter*	
le gruyère *Swiss cheese*		**ne... plus** *no more, not any more*
le jambon *ham*	**apporter** *to bring*	**ne... ni... ni...** *neither . . . nor*
le pâté *pâté*	**arriver** *to arrive*	**tous** *all of them*
les rillettes *potted pork*	**commander** *to order*	**Ça fait combien?** *How much?*
le saucisson *salami*	**désirer** *to want*	**une fois terminé** *once finished*
	donner *to give*	service compris *tip included*
	donnez-moi *give me*	

31–46

un journal *newspaper*	**calculer** *to figure out*	**avant (de)** *before*
un programme *listing of films*	**choisir** *to choose*	**vers** *about*
un film *a movie, film*	**finir** *to end, to finish*	
un dessin animé *animated cartoon*	**laisser** *to leave*	**toujours** *always*
un film comique *comedy*	**Allons-y!** *Let's go!*	
un film policier *detective film*	**Attendez!** *Wait a minute!*	**d'accord** *okay*
une histoire d'amour *love story*	je dois *I have to*	
un western *western*	combien vous devez *how much you owe*	
un billet *bill (money)*	**Qu'est-ce qu'on va voir?** *What shall we see?*	
une pièce *coin*	**il paraît que** *they say*	
un centime *a centime*		
un pourboire *tip*		

6
AU TELEPHONE
chapitre de révision

The most common type of French pay phone is the one shown here. In this kind of pay phone, the caller deposits money after the party being called has picked up the receiver.

1 Martine Dupuis téléphone à Evelyne Bouquet. ⊗

Martine veut donner un coup de téléphone à Evelyne. Mais, comme elle n'a pas le téléphone, elle appelle Evelyne d'une cabine téléphonique.

1

2

- Elle cherche le numéro d'Evelyne dans l'annuaire.
- Elle consulte les instructions.
- Elle prépare 40 centimes — c'est le prix de la communication.
- Elle décroche le combiné.
- Elle compose le numéro d'Evelyne (85–52–33).
- Elle attend qu'on décroche à l'autre bout du fil.
- Puis, elle met deux pièces de 20 centimes dans l'appareil.
- Et elle parle.

3

MARTINE	Allô. Bonjour, Madame. C'est Martine Dupuis à l'appareil. Est-ce que je pourrais parler à Evelyne, s'il vous plaît?

Expressions of greeting:
Allô! (phone conversation only)

MME BOUQUET	Mais oui. Ne quittez pas. (…) Evelyne! C'est pour toi.

Bonjour! (basic)
Salut! (young people or "buddies")

* * * * *

MARTINE	Salut, Evelyne! C'est Martine. Ça va?

Expressions for goodbye:
Au revoir! (basic)

EVELYNE	Ça va.

Salut! (informal)

MARTINE	Dis donc, est-ce que tu peux… *(grésillements)*

Bonjour! (French Canada)

EVELYNE	Qu'est-ce que tu dis? Je n'entends rien. La ligne est mauvaise.
MARTINE	Bon, alors raccroche; je te rappelle.
EVELYNE	D'accord, mais je suis un peu pressée maintenant.
MARTINE	Eh bien, je te rappelle ce soir.
EVELYNE	C'est ça. Au revoir.

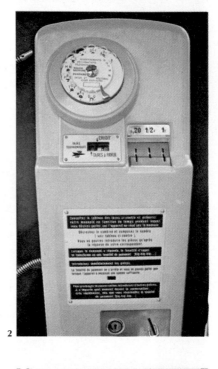

2

4

Being without a private phone is not uncommon in France. It costs a great deal to have a phone installed, but, more important, the P.T.T. (Postes et Télécommunications), the French Post Office and telephone company, cannot keep up with the demand for phones. People often have to wait as long as 3 years for a phone. Those who do not have phones go to a neighbor's house, or use public phones which can be found on the street, in post offices, and in cafés.

3

5 Répondez aux questions.

1. Qu'est-ce que Martine veut faire?
2. Pourquoi est-ce qu'elle appelle Evelyne d'une cabine téléphonique?
3. Dans quoi est-ce qu'elle cherche le numéro de téléphone d'Evelyne?
4. Quel est le prix de la communication?
5. Qui répond au téléphone?
6. Pourquoi est-ce que Martine dit à Evelyne de raccrocher?
7. Est-ce qu'Evelyne a le temps de parler au téléphone?
8. Quand est-ce que Martine va parler à Evelyne?

6 EXERCICE ORAL ⊗

7 Vous téléphonez à un(e) ami(e).

1. Vous voulez téléphoner, mais vous n'êtes pas à la maison. Qu'est-ce que vous faites?
   Vous répondez : « Je vais dans un café » ou « Je cherche une cabine téléphonique. »
2. Vous n'avez pas son numéro de téléphone. Qu'est-ce que vous faites? Je cherche le numéro dans l'annuaire.
3. Ce n'est pas votre ami(e) qui répond. Qu'est-ce que vous dites? Est-ce que je pourrais parler à . . .
4. C'est votre ami(e) qui répond. Qu'est-ce que vous dites? Salut . . . ! Ça va?   . . . s'il vous plaît?
5. La ligne est mauvaise. Qu'est-ce que vous faites? Je demande à mon ami(e) de raccrocher et je rappelle.

8   ARTICLES

Here is a review of the main points about articles that you have been studying.

1. An article gives information about the noun which follows it:
   a. it indicates the number (singular or plural) of the noun;
   b. if the noun is singular, it usually indicates its gender (masculine or feminine).

Singular		Plural	
un garçon **un** $\overset{\frown n\frown}{}$ élève **une** fille		**des** garçons **des** filles $\Big\}$	**des** $\overset{\frown z\frown}{}$ élèves
le garçon $\Big\}$ **l'** élève **la** fille		**les** garçons **les** filles $\Big\}$	**les** $\overset{\frown z\frown}{}$ élèves
ce garçon **cet** $\overset{\frown t\frown}{}$ élève **cette** fille		**ces** garçons **ces** filles $\Big\}$	**ces** $\overset{\frown z\frown}{}$ élèves

2. The articles **un/une, des,** and **du/de la** do not occur in negative constructions. Instead, **de** is used.

Singular			Plural		
un garçon **une** fille	pas **de** garçon $\Big\}$ pas **de** fille	pas **d'**élève	**des** garçons **des** filles	pas **de** garçons $\Big\}$ pas **de** filles	pas **d'**élèves

3. The articles **le** and **les** do not occur in combination with **à** and **de.** Instead, the contractions **au, aux** and **du, des** occur.

	Singular			Plural	
au **à la**	garçon fille }	**à l'**élève	**aux** **aux**	garçons filles }	**aux**‿élèves
du **de la**	garçon fille }	**de l'**élève	**des** **des**	garçons filles }	**des**‿élèves

9 Evelyne veut téléphoner d'un café. ⊗

Il y a un téléphone ici?

— Non, il n'y a pas de téléphone.
— Mais si, le téléphone est là-bas.

Il y a une cabine ici? / Il y a des annuaires ici?

. . . pas de cabine, . . . si, la cabine / . . . pas d'annuaires, . . . si, les annuaires sont

10 Martine est au téléphone. ⊗

Qui est-ce qu'elle appelle?
A qui est-ce qu'elle téléphone?
Qui est à l'appareil? / Qui répond? / A qui est-ce qu'elle parle?

Le professeur de maths.
Au professeur de maths.

Le professeur de maths. / Le professeur de maths. / Au professeur de maths.

11 EXERCICE ECRIT For answers, see p. T21.

Récrivez les phrases suivantes en mettant les mots soulignés au pluriel. *Rewrite the following sentences making the underlined words plural.*
1. Il y a un téléphone ici?
2. Où est le téléphone, s'il vous plaît?
3. La cabine est au fond du couloir.
4. Compose ce numéro.

12 Didier Jolibois téléphone à Evelyne Bouquet. ⊗

Pendant ce temps, Didier et son ami François Le Sève font leurs devoirs. Ils n'arrivent pas à faire leurs maths.

DIDIER Ces problèmes sont vraiment impossibles!
FRANÇOIS Téléphonons à Evelyne.
DIDIER Ou à Martine. Elles sont bonnes en maths toutes les deux.
FRANÇOIS Oui, mais Martine n'a pas le téléphone.

(*Didier fait le numéro d'Evelyne.*)

DIDIER Allô. Bonjour, Monsieur. Est-ce qu'Evelyne est là, s'il vous plaît?
L'HOMME Evelyne? Quel numéro demandez-vous?
DIDIER Le 85–52–33.
L'HOMME Ah, c'est une erreur. Ici, c'est le 85–53–33.
DIDIER Excusez-moi, Monsieur. (*Didier refait le numéro d'Evelyne.*)... Ah, pas de chance! Ça sonne occupé.

This picture of Didier on the phone shows the "écouteur" that most French phones have, enabling a third party to listen in on the conversation.

There are area codes for long-distance calls. The area code for Paris is 1, and for Montargis, 38. For "to call collect" in France, one says, "téléphoner en PCV" (from PERCEVOIR), and in Canada, "téléphoner en renversant les charges."

13 *Phone numbers in France have either six digits divided into three groups, as in Montargis: 85–53–33 (quatre-vingt-cinq, cinquante-trois, trente-trois); or seven digits also divided into three groups, as in Paris: 225–35–61 (deux-cent-vingt-cinq, trente-cinq, soixante-et-un).*

14 **Répondez aux questions.**

1. Qu'est-ce que François et Didier sont en train de faire?
2. Qui est bon en maths dans leur classe?
3. A qui est-ce que François va téléphoner?
4. Qui est-ce qui répond?
5. Qu'est-ce qu'il demande?
6. Pourquoi est-ce que François ne parle pas à Evelyne quand il refait son numéro?

15 **Et vous?**

1. Qui est bon en maths dans votre classe?
2. A qui est-ce que vous téléphonez quand vous n'arrivez pas à faire vos devoirs?
3. Quels sont leurs numéros de téléphone?
4. Quel est votre numéro de téléphone?

16 **EXERCICE ORAL** ⊚

17

ADJECTIVES: AGREEMENT

Here is a review of the main points about the agreement of adjectives that you have been studying.

1. Adjectives agree in gender and number with the noun or pronoun to which they refer.

Masculine		Feminine	
Singular	Plural	Singular	Plural
Il est **distrait.** **Il** est **sérieux.**	**Ils** sont **distraits.** **Ils** sont **sérieux.**	**Elle** est **distraite.** **Elle** est **sérieuse.**	**Elles** sont **distraites.** **Elles** sont **sérieuses.**
Il est **doué.**	**Ils** sont **doués.**	**Elle** est **douée.**	**Elles** sont **douées.**
Il est **timide.**	**Ils** sont **timides.**	**Elle** est **timide.**	**Elles** sont **timides.**

2. The plural form of an adjective sounds exactly like its singular form. In writing, however, it is different: it usually ends in **-s.**

Il est **distrait.**   Ils sont **distraits.**

Elle est **distraite.**   Elles sont **distraites.**

There are some exceptions to this rule. For example, no **-s** is added to adjectives ending in **-x,** like **sérieux.**

Il est **sérieux.**   Ils sont **sérieux.**

3. If an adjective refers to several nouns one of which is masculine, the masculine plural form of the adjective is used: Ce **garçon** et cette **fille** sont **distraits.**

18 Ces maths sont impossibles. ⊗

Téléphonons à François.
Téléphonons à Evelyne et Florence.
Téléphonons à Didier et Olivier.
Téléphonons à Martine.

Il est bon en maths?
Elles sont bonnes en maths?
Ils sont bons en maths?
Elle est bonne en maths?

19 A qui voulez-vous parler? ⊗

A François, s'il vous plaît.
A Evelyne et Martine, s'il vous plaît.
A Didier et François, s'il vous plaît.
A Olivier, s'il vous plaît.
A Florence, s'il vous plaît.

Ah, il est occupé.
Ah, elles sont occupées.
Ah, ils sont occupés.
Ah, il est occupé.
Ah, elle est occupée.

20 EXERCICE ECRIT

Récrivez les phrases suivantes en utilisant (*using*) la forme correcte des adjectifs.
1. (différent) Evelyne et Martine sont deux filles très _____ . différentes
2. (grand / timide) Evelyne est _____ et _____ . grande et timide
3. (petit / amusant) Martine est _____ et _____ . petite et amusante
4. (libre) Les deux amies sont _____ cet après-midi. libres
5. (prêt) Elles sont _____ à sortir avec François, Didier et Olivier. prêtes
6. (sérieux) Mais elles trouvent les trois garçons un peu trop _____ . sérieux

21 EXERCICE DE COMPREHENSION ⊗   For script, see p. T21.

	0	1	2	3	4	5	6
Un garçon	✓						
Une fille							

22 EXERCICE DE CONVERSATION

Vous téléphonez à des camarades.
1. Vous parlez de sports.
   Vous demandez à votre camarade…
   • à quoi il aime jouer.
   • pourquoi il aime jouer à ça.
   • avec qui il joue.
   • qui gagne.
2. Vous parlez de l'école.
   Vous demandez à votre camarade…
   • si elle est en train de faire les devoirs de maths.
   • si elle arrive à faire les deux problèmes.
   • si elle aime les maths.
   • ce qu'elle aime le mieux comme matières.
3. Vous parlez d'un nouveau à l'école.
   Vous dites à votre camarade…
   • comment il s'appelle.
   • où il habite.
   • à quels sports il joue bien.
   • en quelles matières il est bon.
4. Vous parlez de ce que vous allez faire.
   Vous demandez à votre camarade…
   • si elle veut sortir.
   • où elle veut aller.
   • si elle veut jouer aux cartes.
   • si elle veut aller au cinéma.
   • quel film elle veut voir.

To play this game, direct your students to the excerpt from the Montargis phone book below the dialog. The number (38) which precedes each telephone number is the area code and does not have to be given. They may notice that the telephone number of François' CES is on this page.

23 Téléphonez aux Renseignements°. ⊗

Vous voulez téléphoner à un(e) ami(e). Vous n'avez pas son numéro. Vous téléphonez aux Renseignements.

Vous	Allô, les Renseignements?
Téléphoniste°	Oui, j'écoute…
Vous	Est-ce que vous pouvez° me donner° le numéro de (Mme Chauvel), s'il vous plaît.
Téléphoniste	Où habite-t-(elle)?
Vous	(Elle) habite (36, rue° Paul Doumer).
Téléphoniste	Ne quittez pas… C'est le (85–48–46).
Vous	Le (85–48–46)… Merci!
Téléphoniste	Je vous en prie°.

VOCABULAIRE: **les Renseignements** *Information;* **le/la téléphoniste** *telephone operator;* **vous pouvez** *you can;* **me donner** *give me;* **rue** *street;* **je vous en prie** *you're welcome.*

24 FOR REFERENCE

1
Au téléphone. Chapitre de Révision.
Martine Dupuis téléphone à Evelyne Bouquet.
Martine veut donner un coup de téléphone à Evelyne.
Mais, comme elle n'a pas le téléphone, elle appelle Evelyne d'une cabine téléphonique.

On the telephone. Review Unit.
Martine Dupuis calls Evelyne Bouquet.
Martine wants to call Evelyne. But since she doesn't have a phone, she calls Evelyne from a phone booth.

2
• Elle cherche le numéro d'Evelyne dans l'annuaire.
• Elle consulte les instructions.
• Elle prépare 40 centimes—c'est le prix de la communication.

She looks up Evelyne's number in the phone book.
She looks at the instructions.
She gets out 40 centimes—the cost of a phone call.

• Elle décroche le combiné.
• Elle compose le numéro d'Evelyne (85–52–33).
• Elle attend qu'on décroche à l'autre bout du fil.

She picks up the receiver.
She dials Evelyne's number (85–52–33).
She waits for someone to pick up at the other end of the line.

• Puis, elle met deux pièces de 20 centimes dans l'appareil.

Then she puts two 20-centime coins in the phone.

• Et elle parle.

And she talks.

3	MARTINE	Allô. Bonjour, Madame. C'est Martine Dupuis à l'appareil. Est-ce que je pourrais parler à Evelyne, s'il vous plaît?	Hello? Hello, Mrs. Bouquet. This is Martine Dupuis. May I speak to Evelyne, please?
	MME BOUQUET	Mais oui. Ne quittez pas. (…) Evelyne! C'est pour toi.	Certainly. Hold on. . . . Evelyne! It's for you.
	MARTINE	Salut, Evelyne! C'est Martine. Ça va?	Hi, Evelyne! This is Martine. How are you?
	EVELYNE	Ça va.	Fine.
	MARTINE	Dis donc, est-ce que tu peux… (grésillements).	So listen, could you . . . (static).
	EVELYNE	Qu'est-ce que tu dis? Je n'entends rien. La ligne est mauvaise.	What are you saying? I can't hear anything. The connection is bad.
	MARTINE	Bon, alors, raccroche; je te rappelle.	Okay, then, hang up; I'll call you back.
	EVELYNE	D'accord, mais je suis un peu pressée maintenant.	Okay, but I'm kind of in a hurry right now.
	MARTINE	Eh bien, je te rappelle ce soir.	So I'll call you tonight.
	EVELYNE	C'est ça. Au revoir.	Good. Goodbye.

12		Didier Jolibois téléphone à Evelyne Bouquet. Pendant ce temps, Didier et son ami François Le Sève font leurs devoirs. Ils n'arrivent pas à faire leurs maths.	Didier Jolibois calls Evelyne Bouquet. During this time, Didier and his friend François Le Sève are doing their homework. They are not getting anywhere with their math.
	DIDIER	Ces problèmes sont vraiment impossibles!	These problems are really impossible!
	FRANÇOIS	Téléphonons à Evelyne.	Let's call Evelyne.
	DIDIER	Ou à Martine. Elles sont bonnes en maths toutes les deux.	Or Martine. They're both good in math.
	FRANÇOIS	Oui, mais Martine n'a pas le téléphone.	Yes, but Martine doesn't have a phone.

(Didier fait le numéro d'Evelyne.)

(Didier dials Evelyne's number.)

	DIDIER	Allô. Bonjour, Monsieur. Est-ce qu'Evelyne est là, s'il vous plaît?	Hello? Hello, Sir. Is Evelyne there, please?
	L'HOMME	Evelyne? Quel numéro demandez-vous?	Evelyne? What number do you want?
	DIDIER	Le 85–52–33.	85–52–33.
	L'HOMME	Ah, c'est une erreur. Ici, c'est le 85–53–33.	You have the wrong number. This is 85–53–33.
	DIDIER	Excusez-moi, Monsieur. *(Didier refait le numéro d'Evelyne.)*… Ah, pas de chance! Ça sonne occupé!	Excuse me, Sir. (Didier dials Evelyne's number again.) . . . Oh, no luck! It's busy!

25   WORD LIST

1–11

un annuaire *phone book*
un appareil *telephone*
une cabine téléphonique *phone booth*
un combiné *receiver*
une communication *call*
un coup de téléphone *phone call*
des **grésillements** (m.) *static*
des **instructions** (f.) *directions*
une ligne *line (phone connection)*
le prix *the cost*
le téléphone *phone*
  au téléphone *on the phone*

chercher *to look up*
composer *to dial*
consulter *to read*
décrocher *to pick up the receiver*
préparer *to get ready*
quitter *to leave*
  Ne quittez pas! *Hold on!*
raccrocher *to hang up (the phone)*
donner un coup de téléphone *to make a phone call*
elle **attend** *she waits for*
tu dis *you say*
Je n'entends rien. *I can't hear anything.*
elle **met** *she puts*
tu peux *you can*
je pourrais? *may I?*
je te rappelle *I'll call you back*
elle **veut** *she wants*

Allô. *Hello.*
Au revoir. *Goodbye.*
Ça va? *How's everything?*
Ça va. *Okay.*
Salut. *Hi.*

puis *then*

pressé, –e *busy, in a hurry*

dis donc *so listen!*
à l'autre bout du fil *at the other end of the line*

12–23

une erreur *mistake (wrong number)*
un homme *a man*
un problème *problem*

arriver à faire *to succeed in doing*
faire le numéro *to dial the number*
refaire le numéro *to dial the number again*
sonner *to ring*

excusez-moi *excuse me*

leurs *their*

impossible *impossible*
occupé, –e *occupied, busy*
tous les deux, toutes les deux *both of them*

pendant *during*

pas de chance *no luck*
Quel numéro demandez-vous? *What number do you want?*

French Throughout the World

Plate 1

CANADA

BELGIUM
LUXEMBOURG
SWITZERLAND

FRANCE
MONACO
TUNISIA

MOROCCO
ALGERIA
CHAD
NIGER
MAURITANIA
MALI
SENEGAL
UPPER VOLTA
GUINEA
IVORY COAST
FRENCH GUIANA

HAITI
GUADELOUPE

MARTINIQUE

TOGO
BENIN
CAMEROON
GABON
CENTRAL AFRICAN EMPIRE
CONGO REPUBLIC

PACIFIC OCEAN

POLYNESIAN ISLANDS

TAHITI

ATLANTIC OCEAN

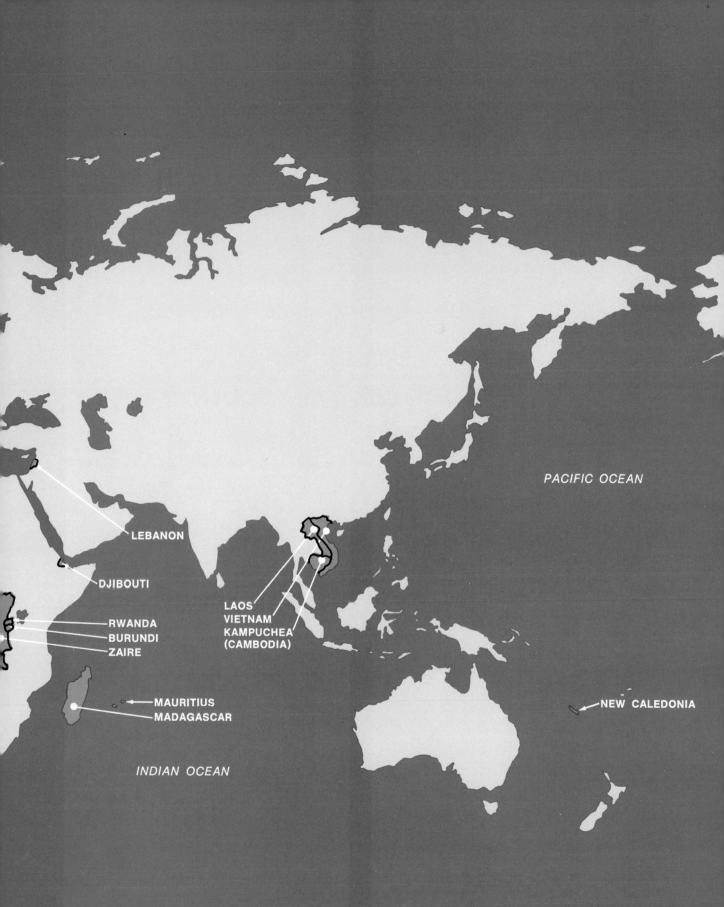

PACIFIC OCEAN

LEBANON

DJIBOUTI

LAOS
VIETNAM
KAMPUCHEA
(CAMBODIA)

RWANDA
BURUNDI
ZAIRE

MAURITIUS
MADAGASCAR

NEW CALEDONIA

INDIAN OCEAN

Of the 92 million people in the world who speak French, 52 million live in France. Although France is a small country — smaller than the state of Texas — her landscapes vary greatly, from high mountains to flat plains, from rocky coastline to sandy beaches. These photographs reflect this variety.

(1) The sunny, warm Côte d'Azur on the Mediterranean attracts tourists from everywhere.
(2) In Brittany, corn is likely to grow around prehistoric dolmens and menhirs.
(3) Many French kings chose green, hospitable Touraine, along the Loire River, to have their castles built.
(4) Peaceful canals are a very common sight in northern and eastern France.
(5) Vineyards can be found in many regions, like Champagne, Burgundy, and Provence.
(6) The marshes of Camargue, located in the Rhône delta, are used for the raising of bulls and horses.

Plate 4

(7) The ranges of the Alps have towering peaks: the highest one, the Mont-Blanc, rises 4807 meters (15,781 feet) above sea level.
(8) Black and white cows graze on the many pastures of Normandy, which produces most of the dairy products consumed in France.

The 40 million French-speaking people who live outside of France are scattered over all four continents. Although these people live in places that differ widely in their landscapes, climates, and cultures, they all do share in common the French language. On the American continent, French is spoken in the snows of Canada as well as in the tropics of Haiti, Guadeloupe, Martinique, and French Guiana, and the bayous of Louisiana. In Canada, most French-speaking people (5 out of 6 million) live in the eastern province of Quebec.

(1) The Château Frontenac in Quebec City, Quebec, Canada.
(2) The Jacques Cartier River in Quebec, "The Beautiful Province."
(3) Kyona Beach in Haiti.

In Asia, French is spoken in Vietnam, Laos, and Kampuchea (Cambodia).

(4) Vietnamese peasants working in rice paddies along the Ba River.

Plate 6

Outside of France in Europe, French is spoken in the lowlands of Belgium, the mountains of Switzerland, and the small territories like Luxembourg and Monaco. In Belgium, most French-speaking people live in the southern part of the country that borders on France. In the northern part, people speak Dutch. Brussels, the capital, and the region around it are bilingual.

(5) A street in Liège, which is, after Brussels, the largest city in French-speaking Belgium.

(6) Located on the Meuse River, Liège is an important port and a big industrial center.

In Switzerland, most French-speaking people live in the western cantons, which share a border with France. The rest of the Swiss speak German, Italian, or Romansh, a dialect derived from Latin.

(7) A village perched on the shore of Lake Geneva in Switzerland.

(8) A village in the Swiss part of the Jura mountains.

French is widely spoken on the African continent, from the mountains and (2) deserts of North Africa to (4) the savannahs and the lush jungles of sub-Saharan Africa.

In North African countries (Algeria, Morocco, and Tunisia), French is spoken along with Arabic. But in French-speaking sub-Saharan countries, French is often the only common language among Africans who speak completely different languages and dialects.

(1) Street scene in Abidjan, capital of the Ivory Coast, where French is the only official language.

(3) Street scene in a Moroccan city (notice the sign which is in both Arabic and French).

Plate 8

Only part of Catherine's family is shown here; more cousins, aunts, and uncles appear later, in Nos. 4 and 16.

Point out that grandmother's car is a collector's item, a 1930 Citroën. Her dogs are dachshunds (teckels).

Vincent, Françoise, Xavier, Oncle Claude, Tante Monique et Frédérique.

Papa

Grand-père

Grand-mère et ses chiens, Hector et Toupie.

Maman

Philippe

Catherine montre son album à son amie Sylvie. ✪

SYLVIE Tiens, qui sont ces gens?

CATHERINE Ce sont mes cousins de Belgique et leurs parents, mon oncle Claude et ma tante Monique.

SYLVIE Ce sont des cousins du côté de ton père?

CATHERINE Non, du côté de ma mère : Tante Monique est la sœur de Maman. Mon père, lui, n'a ni frère ni sœur.

SYLVIE Tes cousins ne viennent jamais à Luneray?

CATHERINE Si, ils viennent tous les ans passer le mois de juillet chez nos grands-parents.

SYLVIE Et vous, vous allez quelquefois chez eux, en Belgique?

CATHERINE Oui, mais pas assez souvent…

2 Répondez aux questions.

1. A qui est-ce que Catherine montre son album de photos?
2. Qui est Tante Monique?
3. Est-ce que le père de Catherine a des frères et des sœurs?
4. Où habitent Oncle Claude, Tante Monique et leurs enfants?
5. Quand est-ce qu'ils viennent à Luneray?
6. Est-ce que Catherine va quelquefois en Belgique chez son oncle et sa tante?

3 Et vous?

1. Est-ce que vous avez des frères et des sœurs? Combien?
2. Est-ce que vos grands-parents habitent près de chez vous?
3. Est-ce que vous avez des cousins et des cousines? Combien?
4. Est-ce qu'ils viennent souvent chez vous?

4 Le jeu des ressemblances.

Voici quelques cousins et cousines de Catherine. Qui lui ressemble le plus?   Answer: "Son cousin Marc."
Catherine est grande; elle est brune et elle a les yeux bleus.

Cousins Marc and Valérie are being introduced here. Vincent and Françoise were mentioned on the opening page.

Son cousin Marc?
Il est grand; il est brun
et il a les yeux bleus.

Sa cousine Valérie?
Elle est petite; elle
est rousse et elle a
les yeux verts. Elle
porte des lunettes.

Son cousin Vincent?
Il est de taille moyenne;
il est blond et il a les
yeux marron.

Sa cousine Françoise?
Elle est grande; elle
est blonde et elle a les
yeux gris.

5 EXERCICE ORAL

6 ADJECTIVES: POSITION

Adjectives in French usually follow the noun they refer to: **C'est un garçon sérieux.**
A few common adjectives precede the noun they refer to. You already know five of them:

bon, mauvais, grand, petit, and **autre.** Liaison is obligatory: **un grand album.**
Point out that the liaison sound for the letter d is [t].

7 Décrivez un(e) de vos camarades.

Dites comment il (elle) s'appelle; quel âge il (elle) a; de quelle couleur sont ses cheveux (*hair*); de quelle couleur sont ses yeux; s'il (elle) porte des lunettes; s'il (elle) est grand(e) ou petit(e); ce qu'il (elle) aime faire…

8 Devinez qui c'est. *Guess who it is.*

Un(e) élève sort de la classe. Les autres élèves choisissent le (la) camarade à identifier (*to be identified*). Quand l'élève rentre, il (elle) pose des questions (*ask questions*), comme : « C'est un garçon? Il est brun? Il est bon élève? etc. » Les autres élèves répondent oui ou non jusqu'à ce qu'il (elle) devine (*until he / she guesses*).

9 POSSESSIVE ARTICLES

1. Possessive articles indicate relationship or ownership. Like all other articles, they mark the gender and number of the nouns which follow them. ⊗

	Before singular noun				Before plural noun	
	Masculine		Feminine			
Je ressemble à	mon		ma		mes	
Tu ressembles à	ton	frère.	ta	sœur.	tes	
Il / Elle ressemble à	son		sa		ses	frères.
Nous ressemblons à	notre	frère.			nos	sœurs.
Vous ressemblez à	votre	sœur.			vos	
Ils / Elles ressemblent à	leur				leurs	

Notice that when you address a person as **tu**, you would use **ton, ta, tes.** When you address a person as **vous,** you would use **votre, vos.**

2. **Son, sa,** and **ses** may mean either *his* or *her*, depending on the context

Catherine ou Philippe		Catherine		Philippe	
Son	père est grand.	*Her*	*father is tall.*	*His*	*father is tall.*
Sa	mère est grande.	*Her*	*mother is tall.*	*His*	*mother is tall.*
Ses	parents sont grands.	*Her*	*parents are tall.*	*His*	*parents are tall.*

3. **Mon, ton,** and **son** are used before any singular word beginning with a vowel sound:

Ça, c'est **mon ami** Arnaud.   Ça c'est **mon amie** Sylvie.

4. Liaison is obligatory with **mon, ton, son** and all plural markers:

ton⁀amie   vos⁀amis

10 Sylvie regarde l'album de Catherine. ⊗

C'est ta tante?   Oui, c'est ma tante.
C'est ton oncle? / Ce sont tes cousines? / Ce sont tes cousins?
Oui, c'est mon oncle. / Oui, ce sont mes cousines. / Oui, ce sont mes cousins.

11 Sylvie regarde l'album de Catherine et de Philippe. ⊗

C'est votre tante?   Oui, c'est notre tante.

C'est votre oncle? / Ce sont vos cousines? / Ce sont vos cousins?

Oui, c'est notre oncle. / Oui, ce sont nos cousines. / Oui, ce sont nos cousins.

12 Ils sont tous bruns. ⊗

La mère de Catherine et Philippe est rousse.   Mais non! Leur mère est brune!

Les cousines de Catherine et Philippe sont rousses.   Mais non! Leurs cousines sont brunes!

Le père de Catherine et Philippe est roux.   Mais non! Leur père est brun!

Les grands-parents de Catherine et Philippe sont roux.   Mais non! Leurs grands-parents sont bruns!

13 L'album de Sylvie. ⊗

Voilà les parents de Sylvie.   Elle ressemble à ses parents!

le grand-père de Sylvie / les sœurs de Sylvie / la grand-mère de Sylvie

son grand-père / ses sœurs / sa grand-mère

14 Vous demandez…   … à un(e) camarade : … à votre professeur : ⊗

si ce sont ses livres.   Ce sont tes livres?   Ce sont vos livres?

si ce sont ses disques / si c'est sa radio / si c'est son électrophone

tes disques; vos disques / ta radio; votre radio / ton électrophone; votre électrophone

15 EXERCICE ECRIT

Ecrivez les réponses des exercices No 10, 11, 12 et 13.

16 Qu'est-ce qu'ils font dans la famille de Catherine? ⊗

Three members of Catherine's family not seen before appear in this photograph: Aunt Claire, little cousin Nicolas, and Uncle Roger.

1. Sa tante Claire élève le petit Nicolas.
2. Son grand-père est à la retraite: il ne travaille plus.
3. Sa grand-mère, elle, travaille encore: elle enseigne le piano.
4. Son père est ingénieur.
5. Son oncle Roger est journaliste.
6. Sa mère est infirmière.

17 Répondez aux questions.

1. Est-ce que le grand-père de Catherine travaille encore?
2. Qu'est-ce qu'il fait?
3. Et la grand-mère de Catherine, est-ce qu'elle travaille encore?
4. Qu'est-ce qu'elle fait?
5. Qu'est-ce qu'il fait, le père de Catherine?
6. Et sa mère, qu'est-ce qu'elle fait?
7. Et son oncle Roger?
8. Et sa tante Claire?

Notice the robe French lawyers wear when they plead in court. French farmers, especially the older ones, wear wooden clogs (des sabots), and the men often wear "un béret."

18 Autres professions. ⊗

| fermier | médecin | ouvrier | employée de bureau | avocat | commerçante |

19 Qu'est-ce qu'ils font, ton père et ta mère? ⊗

Mon père est...	Ma mère est...	Mon père est...	Ma mère est...
ingénieur.	ingénieur.	employé de bureau.	employée de bureau.
professeur.	professeur.	avocat.	avocate.
fermier.	fermière.	commerçant.	commerçante.
médecin.	médecin.	ouvrier.	ouvrière.
journaliste.	journaliste.	infirmier.	infirmière.
dentiste.	dentiste.	dessinateur.	dessinatrice.

20 Et dans votre famille, qu'est-ce qu'on fait?

1. Quelle est la profession de votre père? Et de votre mère?
2. Est-ce que vos grands-parents travaillent encore? Qu'est-ce qu'ils font?
3. Est-ce que vous avez des oncles et des tantes? Qu'est-ce qu'ils font?

21 EXERCICE ORAL ⊗

For an extended list of professions, which will be useful for Ex. 20, see Teaching Suggestions, p. T24.

22 NEGATION: OTHER NEGATIVE WORDS

1. You have already learned to use **ne… pas** to make a sentence negative. Several other negative expressions are used in the same way as **ne… pas** : **ne** precedes the verb and the other negative word follows it. Other negatives are **ne… plus, ne… jamais, ne… rien, ne… ni… ni…**

Ils **ne** travaillent **pas.**	They do <u>not</u> work.
Ils **ne** travaillent **plus.**	They <u>no longer</u> work.
Ils **ne** travaillent **jamais.**	They <u>never</u> work.
Ils **ne** font **rien.**	They do <u>nothing</u>.
Ils **ne** travaillent **ni** à la maison **ni** à l'école.	They work <u>neither</u> at home <u>nor</u> at school.

2. Remember that in a negative construction without a verb, **ne** is not used:

   Tu vas souvent à Dieppe? **Non, jamais.**

3. As you have seen in Unit 5, **un/une, des,** and **du/de la** are not used in negative constructions. **De** is used instead: **Il n'a plus d'argent. Il n'a jamais d'argent!** However, **de** is not used immediately following **ne… ni… ni… : Il n'a ni frères ni sœurs.**

23 Un camarade demande à Catherine : ⊗

Ton grand-père travaille encore? Non, il ne travaille plus.

Ta tante enseigne encore? / Ton frère joue encore au hockey? / Tes sœurs sont encore ici?

Non, elle n'enseigne plus. / Non, il ne joue plus au hockey. / Non, elles ne sont plus ici.

24 Une camarade demande à Catherine et Philippe : ⊗

Vos parents vont souvent en Belgique?	Non, ils ne vont jamais en Belgique.
Votre tante va quelquefois au Canada?	Non, elle ne va jamais au Canada.
Vos cousins viennent souvent ici?	Non, ils ne viennent jamais, ici.
Votre mère est libre l'après-midi?	Non, elle n'est jamais libre l'après-midi.
Votre père travaille le samedi?	Non, il ne travaille jamais le samedi.

25 Ni l'un ni l'autre. ⊗

Tu joues au football ou au rugby? Je ne joue ni au football ni au rugby.

Tu aimes le cheval ou le ski? / Tu vas au cinéma ou au café? / Tu as un cousin ou une cousine?

Je n'aime ni le cheval ni le ski. / Je ne vais ni au cinéma ni au café. / Je n'ai ni cousin ni cousine.

26 EXERCICE ECRIT

a. Ecrivez les réponses des exercices No 23, 24 et 25.

b. Répondez aux questions suivantes en utilisant les négations indiquées (*using the negatives indicated*).

1. Tu as un frère ou une sœur? (ne… ni… ni…) Je n'ai ni frère ni sœur.
2. Tu habites toujours là-bas? (ne… plus) Je n'habite plus là-bas.
3. Tu vas souvent au cinéma? (ne… jamais) Je ne vais jamais au cinéma.
4. Qu'est-ce que tu fais ce soir? (ne… rien) Je ne fais rien.
5. Où est-ce que tu vas? A la piscine ou à la patinoire? (ne… ni… ni…) Je ne vais ni à la piscine ni à la patinoire.

27 Comment vivent° les Lardan[1]. ⊗

This is common practice in France.

Pendant la semaine°, les Lardan ont chacun° leurs occupations : Catherine et Philippe vont au lycée° de Dieppe, Mme Lardan travaille à l'hôpital de Dieppe, et M. Lardan est à son usine° de Luneray. Parents et enfants rentrent chez eux pour le repas de midi°. Ils déjeunent entre midi et deux heures, et ils dînent° vers huit heures du soir.

Après le dîner, s'ils n'ont rien d'autre à faire, ils regardent la télévision, ils lisent° ou ils écoutent des disques. Quelquefois, ils font une partie de cartes° ensemble°.

Le mercredi est le jour que Catherine et Philippe attendent° avec impatience. Ce jour-là°, ils sont libres et leurs parents travaillent! Ils ont toute la maison à eux, et ils

peuvent° inviter leurs amis ou descendre° en ville avec eux.

Le samedi après-midi, Catherine et son frère essaient° de gagner un peu d'argent : elle, elle garde des enfants°, et lui, il tond des pelouses°.

Le dimanche est le jour des grands-parents et de leurs chiens, Hector et Toupie. Passer le dimanche ensemble est amusant pour tout le monde excepté Minou, le chat° de Catherine, car° Hector et Toupie courent° après lui toute la journée! Après le déjeuner, qui dure° en général trois bonnes heures, Grand-père propose° une promenade° dans les bois° : son passe-temps préféré est d'enregistrer° le chant des oiseaux°. Ils finissent leur dimanche tous ensemble, avec une tasse de thé° et un gâteau° fait par Grand-mère.

VOCABULAIRE : **vivent** *live;* **la semaine** *week;* **chacun** *each;* **lycée** *high school;* **usine** *factory;* **le repas de midi** *noon meal;* **dînent** *have dinner;* **lisent** *read;* **partie de cartes** *card game;* **ensemble** *together;* **attendent** *wait for;* **ce jour-là** *that day;* **peuvent** *can;* **descendre** *to go down;* **essaient** *try;* **garde des enfants** *baby-sits;* **tond des pelouses** *mows lawns;* **le chat** *cat;* **car** *for;* **courent** *run;* **dure** *lasts;* **propose** *suggests;* **une promenade** *a walk;* **les bois** *woods;* **enregistrer** *to record;* **le chant des oiseaux** *birdcalls;* **une tasse de thé** *a cup of tea;* **un gâteau** *cake.*

Point out that in this expression "là" gives the meaning "that."

28 Répondez aux questions.

1. Qu'est-ce que Catherine et Philippe font pendant la semaine?
2. Où est-ce que leurs parents travaillent?
3. Où est-ce que les Lardan déjeunent? A quelle heure?
4. A quelle heure est-ce qu'ils dînent le soir? Qu'est-ce qu'ils font après le dîner?
5. Pourquoi est-ce que Catherine et Philippe attendent le mercredi avec impatience?
6. Qu'est-ce qu'ils font ce jour-là? Et le samedi après-midi?
7. Est-ce que Minou aime le dimanche? Pourquoi?
8. Qu'est-ce que Grand-père propose après le déjeuner du dimanche? Pourquoi?
9. Comment est-ce qu'ils finissent leur dimanche?

[1] Family names in the plural do not have a final **-s.**

29 **EXERCICE ORAL** ⊗

30

VERBS ENDING IN -re

Répondez aux questions qui suivent les exemples. ⊗

J'**attends** la famille.	Nous **attendons** la famille.
Tu **attends** la famille?	Vous **attendez** la famille?
Il **attend** la famille.	Ils **attendent** la famille.

Do the three singular forms of the verb sound alike or different? Are they spelled alike? What consonant sound is present in the plural forms but not in the singular forms?

31 **Lisez la généralisation suivante.**

1. The following chart shows the forms of **attendre,** to wait (for).

	Stem	Ending		Stem	Ending
j'attends	**attend** {	-s	nous attendons	**attend** {	-ons
tu attends		-s	vous attendez		-ez
il / elle attend		–	ils / elles attendent		-ent

2. You have seen other **-re** verbs like **attendre : descendre,** to go down, **entendre,** to hear, **répondre,** to answer, and **tondre,** to mow.
Use item substitution drills to practice descendre, entendre, répondre, and tondre.

32 **Bernard va passer prendre ses amis.** ⊗

Qu'est-ce que tu fais, Sylvie? J'attends Bernard.
Et vous deux? / Et Dominique? / Et Catherine et Philippe?
nous attendons / il attend / ils attendent

33 **Tout le monde sort cet après-midi.** ⊗

Tu sors, Sylvie? Oui, je descends en ville.
Et Philippe? / Et vous deux? / Et les filles?
il descend / nous descendons / elles descendent

34 **EXERCICE DE COMPREHENSION** ⊗ For script, see p. T24.

	0	1	2	3	4	5	6	7	8
Philippe									
Catherine et Philippe	√								

35 **Et vous?**

1. Est-ce que vous déjeunez tous les jours avec vos parents?
2. Qu'est-ce que vous faites le samedi? Et le dimanche?
3. Quand est-ce que vous allez voir vos grands-parents?
4. Qu'est-ce que vous faites quand vous êtes en famille?
5. Qu'est-ce que vous faites pour gagner un peu d'argent?

36 USING INDEPENDENT PRONOUNS

1. You have been using the pronouns **moi, toi, lui,** and **elle.** They are called independent pronouns. The following chart includes both singular and plural independent pronouns and the corresponding subject pronouns.

Independent Pronouns	moi	toi	lui	elle	nous	vous	eux	elles
Subject Pronouns	je	tu	il	elle	nous	vous	ils	elles

2. Independent pronouns are used
   a. when there is no verb in the response: Qui? **Moi?**   **Lui** aussi?
   b. to emphasize a noun or a pronoun: **Moi,** j'ai un frère; Sylvie, **elle,** a une sœur.
   c. after **c'est** or **ce sont :** C'est **lui.** C'est **nous.** Ce sont **eux.**
   d. after prepositions (**avec, pour, loin de,** etc.): On déjeune souvent chez **lui.**

Make sure students use ce sont with eux and elles and c'est with other independent pronouns.

37 Que font-ils? ⊗

Son père est ingénieur. Et sa mère?   Elle aussi, elle est ingénieur.
Sa mère est médecin. Et son frère?   Lui aussi, il est médecin.
Son père est ouvrier. Et ses frères?   Eux aussi, ils sont ouvriers.
Sa mère est infirmière. Et ses sœurs?   Elles aussi, elles sont infirmières.
Son père est dentiste. Et son oncle?   Lui aussi, il est dentiste.

38 Qui est-ce, sur cette photo? ⊗

C'est ton frère?   Oui, c'est lui.
C'est ta grand-mère? / C'est toi et ton père? / Ce sont tes cousins? / Ce sont tes sœurs?
c'est elle / c'est nous / ce sont eux / ce sont elles

39 EXERCICE DE CONVERSATION

1. Vous êtes chez un(e) ami(e) et vous regardez son album de photos. Vous demandez qui est sur cette photo, etc.
2. Vous parlez de votre famille à un(e) camarade. Vous dites combien de frères et de sœurs vous avez; quel âge ils ont; ce que font vos parents; à qui vous ressemblez…

40 EXERCICE ECRIT

a. Fabriquez *(construct)* votre propre album *(your own album)* de photos. Identifiez chaque *(each)* photo en français.
b. Vous écrivez à votre correspondant français *(French pen pal)*. Décrivez votre famille.

41 Un fils fier de son père.   *A son proud of his father.*

Double subjects like "mon père, il" are often used for emphasis in colloquial French. "Un crétin" has the force of the English expression "a dummy." "Un crétin de fils" is equivalent to "un fils qui est un crétin."

1–15

une famille *family*
les parents (m.) *parents (mother, father)*
un père *father*
papa *dad, daddy*
une mère *mother*
maman *mom, mommy*
un enfant *child*
un frère *brother*
une sœur *sister*
des grands-parents (m.) *grandparents*
un grand-père *grandfather*
une grand-mère *grandmother*
un oncle *uncle*
une tante *aunt*
un(e) cousin(e) *cousin*

un album *album*
la Belgique *Belgium*
en Belgique *in Belgium*
un chien *dog*
les gens *people*
juillet *July*
des lunettes (f.) *eyeglasses*
un mois *month*
une ressemblance *resemblance*
les yeux (m.) *eyes*

montrer *to show*
passer *to spend*
porter *to wear*
ressembler (à) *to look like*
ils viennent *they come*

grand, –e *tall*
petit, –e *short*
de taille moyenne *of medium height*

blond, –e *blond*
brun, –e *dark (haired)*
roux, rousse *red (headed)*
bleu, –e *blue*
gris, –e *gray*
marron *brown*
des yeux marron *brown eyes*
vert, –e *green*

mon, ma, mes *my*
ton, ta, tes *your*
son, sa, ses *his / her*
notre, nos *our*
votre, vos *your*
leur, leurs *their*

du côté de ma mère *on my mother's side*
tous les ans *every year*
tiens *say!*
ne... jamais *never*
quelquefois *sometimes*
le plus *the most*
voici *here is, here are*

16–26

le piano *piano*

une profession *profession*
avocat, –e *lawyer*
commerçant, –e *merchant*
dentiste *dentist*
dessinateur, -trice *illustrator*
employé, –e de bureau *office worker*
fermier, –ière *farmer*
infirmier, –ière *nurse*
ingénieur *engineer*
journaliste *journalist*
médecin *doctor*
ouvrier, –ière *factory worker*

enseigner *to teach*
travailler *to work*
être à la retraite *to be retired*
Elle élève ses enfants. *She rears her children.*

encore *still*

ne... pas *not*
ne... plus *no longer*
ne... jamais *never*
ne... rien *nothing*
ne... ni... ni... *neither . . . nor . . .*

27–41

un bois *woods*
un chant *a song*
le chant des oiseaux *birdcalls*
un chat *cat*
un chien *dog*
un oiseau *bird*
des oiseaux *birds*
un déjeuner *lunch*
un dîner *dinner*
un gâteau *cake*
des gâteaux *cakes*
un hôpital *hospital*
des hôpitaux *hospitals*
un lycée *high school*
une occupation *occupation*
une partie (de cartes) *card game*
une pelouse *lawn*
une promenade *walk*
un repas *meal*
une semaine *week*
une tasse de thé *cup of tea*
le thé *tea*
une usine *factory*

dîner *to have dinner*
durer *to last*
enregistrer *to record*
essayer (de) *to try*
j'essaie, tu essaie, il essaie, ils essaient
gagner *to make (money)*
garder des enfants *to baby-sit*

inviter *to invite*
proposer *to suggest*

attendre *to wait for*
descendre *to go down*
entendre *to hear*
répondre *to answer*
tondre *to mow*

ils courent *they run*
ils lisent *they read*
ils peuvent *they can*
ils vivent *they live*

tout, toute, tous, toutes *all, the whole*
chacun, –e *each one*
fait, –e *made*

car *for*
entre *between*
excepté *except*
ce jour-là *that day*
en général *usually*
ensemble *together*
avec impatience *impatiently*
par *by*

Refer to culture note on the next page for background information about the area. Nice can be found on the map of France on p. 8.

Point out that many people living in the area so close to Italy have, like the Giulianis, Italian names.

8

BON APPÉTIT!

Jean-Marcel va faire les courses avec ses parents, M. et Mme Giuliani. Ils vont d'abord au Marché aux Fleurs. Là, on vend des fleurs, bien sûr, mais aussi beaucoup de fruits et de légumes différents.

JEAN-MARCEL	Maman! On peut acheter ce melon?
MME GIULIANI	D'accord; il a l'air bon.
JEAN-MARCEL	On achète aussi des pêches?
MME GIULIANI	Si elles ne sont pas trop chères. (*A la marchande*) Elles coûtent combien vos pêches?
LA MARCHANDE	3, 10 F le kilo, et elles sont délicieuses. Elles sont bien mûres, juteuses… Vous en prenez combien de kilos?
MME GIULIANI	Euh… Deux kilos, s'il vous plaît.

2 *The Giulianis live in Nice, the largest city on the Côte d'Azur. The Côte d'Azur is the part of the southern coast of France closest to the Italian border. It lies along the Mediterranean between the mountains and the sea and is one of the best-known resort areas in the world. Nice is not only an important resort city but is also a center for the perfume and flower industries of the South. The Marché aux Fleurs, in Nice, is a large and varied market where you can buy some of these flowers, like the famous mimosa and lavender. You can also buy beautifully ripened and fragrant fruits, vegetables, and herbs, like melons and peaches, fennel, and thyme.*

3 Répondez aux questions.

1. Où va Jean-Marcel? Avec qui?
2. Comment s'appelle le marché où ils vont?
3. Qu'est-ce qu'on vend dans ce marché?
4. Qu'est-ce que Mme Giuliani achète?
5. Combien de kilos de pêches est-ce qu'elle achète?
6. Combien est-ce que les pêches coûtent?

un ananas

du raisin

une pomme

des cerises

une poire   une banane   une orange

EXERCICE ORAL ⊗

5

PRONOUNS REFERRING TO THINGS
il / elle   ils / elles

Répondez aux questions qui suivent les exemples. ⊗

With "avoir l'air" the adjective can agree with either the subject of "avoir" or with "l'air". Agreement with the subject has been chosen here, since it is more common.

Je vais manger **ce pamplemousse.**   **Il** a l'air bon.
Je vais manger **cette pomme.**   **Elle** a l'air bonne.
Je vais manger **ces pamplemousses.**   **Ils** ont l'air bons.
Je vais manger **ces pommes.**   **Elles** ont l'air bonnes.

In the sentences on the right, do **il, elle, ils,** and **elles** refer to people or to things? Are the pronouns that refer to things the same as those that refer to people?

6 Lisez la généralisation suivante.

1. The pronouns **il/elle** and **ils/elles** refer to things as well as to people.

Ce melon	est bon.	**Il**	est bon.
Cette pomme	est bonne.	**Elle**	est bonne.
Ces melons	sont bons.	**Ils**	sont bons.
Ces pommes	sont bonnes.	**Elles**	sont bonnes.

2. Just as for people, **elles** refers to a group composed entirely of feminine nouns. **Ils** is used in all other cases.

Prends **cette pomme et cette pêche.**   **Elles** ont l'air mûres.
Prends **cette pêche et ce melon.**   **Ils** ont l'air mûrs.

The vegetables in No. 9 are shown as they are displayed in a French market. Notice the typical basket in which mushrooms are sold, and the typical wooden box (un cageot) where the green beans are displayed. Point out the shape of French cucumbers: long, skinny and pointed.

7 Jean-Marcel aime bien les fruits. ⊗

Elle est mûre, cette pomme?   Oui, elle est délicieuse.
Et cette poire? / Et ce melon? / Et ce raisin? / Et ce pamplemousse?
elle est délicieuse / il est délicieux / il est délicieux / il est délicieux

8 Mme Giuliani dit à la marchande: ⊗

Ces pêches ont l'air bonnes.   Oui, et elles ne sont pas chères.
Ces pamplemousses ont l'air bons.   Oui, et ils ne sont pas chers.
Ces pommes ont l'air bonnes.   Oui, et elles ne sont pas chères.
Ces cerises ont l'air bonnes.   Oui, et elles ne sont pas chères.
Ces poires ont l'air bonnes.   Oui, et elles ne sont pas chères.

9 Combien est-ce que les Giuliani dépensent pour les légumes? ⊗

Ils achètent un kilo et demi de pommes de terre,   deux concombres,   une livre de champignons,

un kilo de haricots[1] verts,   une livre de tomates,   et un kilo de carottes.

> Dans 1 kg (un kilogramme), il y a 1.000 g (grammes).
> Dans une livre, il y a 500 g.

10 Répondez aux questions.

1. Combien coûtent les pommes de terre? Et les carottes? Et les concombres? Et les tomates? Et les haricots verts? Et les champignons?

2. Combien est-ce que les Giuliani dépensent pour les pommes de terre? Et pour les carottes? Et pour les concombres? Et pour les tomates? Et pour les haricots verts? Et pour les champignons? Et pour tous ces légumes?

11 EXERCICE ORAL ⊗

[1] Even though the initial **h** is not sounded in **haricot** and some other words beginning with **h**, it still behaves like a consonant: that is, liaison and élision do not occur.

12 Cher ou pas cher? ⊗

Here are the vegetables from another market. You may assume that the prices from the first market (No. 9) are reasonable or average. Are these high or low by comparison?

60 centimes le kilo de pommes de terre!	Ce n'est pas cher!
15 francs le kilo de haricots verts!	C'est cher!
2 francs le kilo de tomates!	Ce n'est pas cher!
1 franc les 250 g de champignons!	Ce n'est pas cher!
4 francs le kilo de carottes!	C'est cher!

13 Calculons! ⊗

(Use the price list from No. 9.)
Combien est-ce que vous allez dépenser si vous achetez :

2 kg de carottes, 3 concombres et 750 g de champignons.	18,75 F
2 kg de haricots verts, 1 kg de tomates et une livre de pommes de terre.	32,95 F
une livre de champignons, 3 kg de carottes et un concombre.	16,50 F
1 kg de tomates, une livre de haricots verts et 2 kg de pommes de terre.	21,40 F

14 THE VERB acheter

The verb **acheter,** *to buy,* follows the same pattern as other verbs ending in **-er,** but it shows a change in the vowel sound of the **je, tu, il,** and **ils** forms. ⊗

J'	**achète**	des pêches.	Nous	**achetons**	des pêches.
Tu	**achètes**	des pêches.	Vous	**achetez**	des pêches.
Elle / Il	**achète**	des pêches.	Elles / Ils	**achètent**	des pêches.

Lever, *to raise,* and **élever,** *to rear,* follow the same pattern as **acheter.**

Use item substitution drills to practice lever and élever.

15 Les Giuliani sont au marché. ⊗

Jean-Marcel aime bien les tomates.	Il achète un kilo de tomates.
Mme Giuliani aime bien les carottes.	Elle achète un kilo de carottes.
M. Giuliani aime bien les pommes de terre.	Il achète un kilo de pommes de terre.
Les Giuliani aiment bien les haricots verts.	Ils achètent un kilo de haricots verts.

16 Et vous?

Qu'est-ce que vous achetez comme légumes?	J'achète…
Qu'est-ce que vous achetez comme fruits?	J'achète…
Et votre mère? Qu'est-ce qu'elle achète?	Elle achète…
Et vous deux? Qu'est-ce que vous achetez?	Nous achetons…

17 Chez les commerçants. ⊗

Après le Marché aux Fleurs, les Giuliani vont chez différents commerçants. Pour économiser un peu de temps, chacun va de son côté.

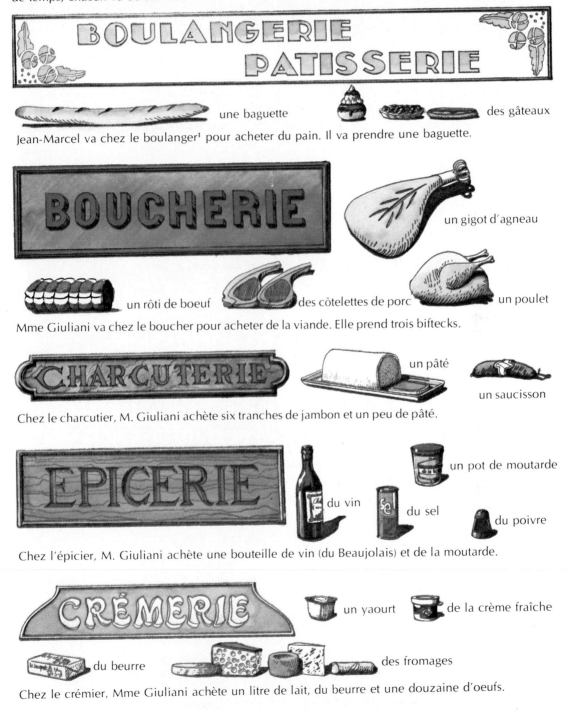

BOULANGERIE PATISSERIE

une baguette   des gâteaux

Jean-Marcel va chez le boulanger[1] pour acheter du pain. Il va prendre une baguette.

BOUCHERIE

un gigot d'agneau

un rôti de boeuf   des côtelettes de porc   un poulet

Mme Giuliani va chez le boucher pour acheter de la viande. Elle prend trois biftecks.

CHARCUTERIE

un pâté

un saucisson

Chez le charcutier, M. Giuliani achète six tranches de jambon et un peu de pâté.

EPICERIE

un pot de moutarde

du vin   du sel   du poivre

Chez l'épicier, M. Giuliani achète une bouteille de vin (du Beaujolais) et de la moutarde.

CRÉMERIE

un yaourt   de la crème fraîche

du beurre   des fromages

Chez le crémier, Mme Giuliani achète un litre de lait, du beurre et une douzaine d'oeufs.

[1] With the verb **aller,** French people very often prefer to use the name of the shopkeeper rather than the name of the shop. For example, they will say **Je vais chez le boucher** rather than **Je vais à la boucherie.**

18 **Répondez aux questions.**

1. Où vont les Giuliani après le Marché aux Fleurs?
2. Où va Jean-Marcel? Qu'est-ce qu'il achète?
3. Où va Mme Giuliani? Qu'est-ce qu'elle achète?
4. Où va M. Giuliani? Qu'est-ce qu'il achète?

19 **EXERCICE ORAL** ⊗

20 **Il n'y a plus rien!** ⊗

Il n'y a plus de pain!   Ça tombe bien! Je vais chez le boulanger.
Il n'y a plus de saucisson!
Il n'y a plus de beurre!   le charcutier
Il n'y a plus de viande!   le crémier
Il n'y a plus de lait!   le boucher
Il n'y a plus de vin!   le crémier
Il n'y a plus de jambon!   l'épicier
                                                           le charcutier

21 **Le jeu de l'odorat.** ⊗   See variation of this game, p. T25.

Bandez les yeux de vos camarades. Faites-leur sentir du fromage, des fruits, des légumes, du jambon, etc. Il faut qu'ils identifient ce que c'est, *sans toucher:* « C'est du fromage… C'est une orange… » Le gagnant est celui qui identifie le plus grand nombre d'objets.

VOCABULAIRE : **odorat**   *sense of smell;* **bandez les yeux**   *blindfold;* **faites-leur sentir**   *have them smell;* **le gagnant** *the winner;* **celui**   *the one;* **le plus grand**   *the greatest.*

22
HOW TO EXPRESS QUANTITY

Répondez aux questions qui suivent les exemples. ⊗

un pot de moutarde   **un peu de** pâté
une livre de beurre   **beaucoup de** pain

In each phrase, what are the words which express quantity? What word occurs in each of these expressions of quantity?

23 **Lisez la généralisation suivante.**

The following chart shows the expressions of quantity you know. Notice that each of these expressions includes **de.**

une douzaine	d'	œufs	beaucoup	de	beurre
une kilo	de	pêches	combien	de	kilos
une livre	de	beurre	un peu	de	lait
un pot	de	moutarde	trop	de	pain
une tranche	de	jambon	250 g	de	beurre
une bouteille	de	vin			
un litre	de	lait			

24   Vous désirez? ⊗

Des tomates, s'il vous plaît. Une livre.
Du lait, s'il vous plaît. Deux litres.
Du pâté, s'il vous plaît. 250 g.
Des œufs, s'il vous plaît. Une douzaine.
De l'eau minérale, s'il vous plaît. Trois
bouteilles.

Voilà une livre de tomates.
Voilà deux litres de lait.
Voilà 250 g de pâté.
Voilà une douzaine d'œufs.
Voilà trois bouteilles d'eau minérale.

25   Vous faites des sandwiches. ⊗

Tu veux du beurre?
Tu veux du saucisson?
Tu veux de la moutarde?
Tu veux du pâté?
Tu veux des rillettes?

Pas trop de beurre, s'il te plaît.
Pas trop de saucisson, s'il te plaît.
Pas trop de moutarde, s'il te plaît.
Pas trop de pâté, s'il te plaît.
Pas trop de rillettes, s'il te plaît.

26   THE VERB prendre

The following are the forms of the verb **prendre,** *to take.* ⊗

Je	**prends**	une baguette.	Nous	**prenons**	une baguette.
Tu	**prends**	une baguette.	Vous	**prenez**	une baguette.
Elle / Il	**prend**	une baguette.	Elles / Ils	**prennent**	une baguette.

27   Au marché. ⊗

Tu n'achètes pas de fruits?
Mme Giuliani / toi et ta sœur / tes cousins
elle prend / nous prenons / ils prennent

Si, je prends des pommes.

28   EXERCICE DE CONVERSATION

Vous faites les courses. Vous achetez : un
saucisson (6 F), 3 côtelettes d'agneau (15 F),
250 g de beurre (4,50 F), 1 litre de lait
(2,50 F), 1 douzaine d'œufs (4 F), une
baguette (1,50 F) et 4 gâteaux (8 F). Vous
allez d'abord chez le charcutier :
CHARC.   Vous désirez?
  VOUS   Un saucisson, s'il vous plaît.
CHARC.   Et avec ça?
  VOUS   C'est tout, merci.
CHARC.   Ça fait 6 francs.
Maintenant, chez les autres commerçants! 1

29   EXERCICE ECRIT

a. Ecrivez les réponses des exercices No 25 et 27.
b. Rédaction (*composition*) : Quelquefois, c'est moi qui fais les courses. D'abord, je vais…

30 Les Giuliani déjeunent. ⊗

Les Giuliani rentrent chez eux avec leurs provisions. Mme Giuliani commence à préparer le repas. M. Giuliani l'aide. Jean-Marcel, lui, met la table. « N'oublie pas le sel, le poivre et le pain! » lui dit sa mère. « Et mets bien les fourchettes à gauche et les couteaux à droite! Tu peux prendre des serviettes propres aujourd'hui! »

Most adult French people drink wine and mineral water with their meals. Bottled mineral water is widely used. Brands, like Perrier, Vichy, or Evian, have different properties. In some regions, like the East or the North, adults like beer (de la bière) with their meals.

Le Couvert

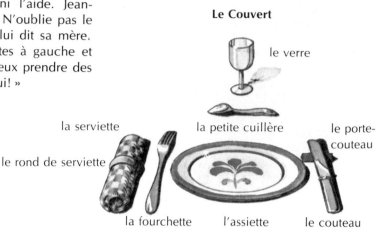

le verre

la serviette

la petite cuillère

le porte-couteau

le rond de serviette

la fourchette   l'assiette   le couteau

Tout est prêt. « A table! » dit Mme Giuliani. Aujourd'hui les Giuliani ont du melon et du jambon comme hors-d'œuvre. M. Giuliani sert Jean-Marcel. Il lui donne une grande tranche de jambon. Mme Giuliani a soif. M. Giuliani lui verse du vin. Jean-Marcel, lui, boit de l'eau minérale.

Après les hors-d'œuvre vient le plat principal : des biftecks avec des frites et des tomates provençales. Ensuite, ils mangent de la salade. Jean-Marcel apporte les fromages à ses parents. Puis il leur passe les fruits. C'est le dessert. A la fin du repas, M. et Mme Giuliani prennent du café.

"Tomates provençales" are tomatoes topped with bread crumbs, chopped parsley and garlic, and fried in olive oil.

31 Répondez aux questions.

1. Qui prépare le repas chez les Giuliani?
2. Qui met la table?
3. Qu'est-ce qu'il y a comme hors-d'œuvre?
4. Qu'est-ce que Mme Giuliani boit? Et Jean-Marcel?
5. Quel est le plat principal?
6. Qu'est-ce qu'il y a ensuite?
7. Qu'est-ce qu'ils ont comme dessert?
8. Qu'est-ce que les parents de Jean-Marcel prennent à la fin du repas?

Point out the "Mediterranean" atmosphere of Photo 2: because the weather is good most of the year, eating outdoors is almost always possible.

32 Les repas. ⊗

En France, le déjeuner est le repas principal de la journée. On commence par des hors-d'œuvre : une salade de tomates ou de concombres, des carottes râpées ou de la charcuterie. Après les hors-d'œuvre, il y a de la viande ou du poisson et des légumes. Ensuite vient la salade : l'assaisonnement est une vinaigrette. Après la salade, on sert des fromages variés : du camembert, du gruyère ou du fromage de chèvre. Comme dessert, il y a des fruits, une tarte ou une mousse au chocolat, par exemple. On finit le déjeuner avec une tasse de café noir.

Les deux autres repas de la journée sont plus légers. Au petit déjeuner, on boit du café au lait et on mange du pain, du beurre

See note on coffee p. 49.

et de la confiture. Le dimanche, on achète quelquefois des croissants et des brioches. Au dîner, on commence souvent par de la soupe. Après la soupe, on mange des œufs, une omelette, par exemple, ou des pâtes. Ensuite il y a de la salade, du fromage et un dessert.

33 EXERCICE ORAL ⊗

34 Et vous?

1. Qui prépare les repas chez vous?
2. Qui met la table?
3. Qu'est-ce qu'on boit à table chez vous?
4. Qu'est-ce que vous aimez comme viande?
5. Et comme légumes? Et comme fruits?
6. Quel est votre plat préféré?
7. Quel est votre dessert préféré?
8. Quelle est votre boisson préférée?

35 Charade.

Mon premier (*first*) est une boisson.
Mon deuxième (*second*) est une boisson.

Mon troisième (*third*) est une boisson.
Mon tout (*whole*) est une boisson.

SOLUTION : café au (eau) lait.

36   INDIRECT-OBJECT PRONOUNS
                             lui and leur

Répondez aux questions qui suivent les exemples. ⊗

Jean-Marcel passe le jambon **à son père**.   Jean-Marcel **lui** passe le jambon.
Jean-Marcel passe le jambon **à sa mère**.   Jean-Marcel **lui** passe le jambon.
In each sentence on the right, what does **lui** replace? Does **lui** refer to one or more than one person? Does it indicate gender?

Jean-Marcel apporte le plat **à ses parents**.   Jean-Marcel **leur** apporte le plat.
What does **leur** replace? Does it refer to one or more than one person?

37 Lisez la généralisation suivante.

1. In the following chart, each sentence is divided into four parts: the subject, the verb, the direct object of the verb, and the indirect object of the verb.

Subject	Verb	Direct Object	Indirect Object
M. Giuliani	donne	du jambon	à Jean-Marcel.
M. Giuliani	verse	du vin	à Mme Giuliani.
Jean-Marcel	apporte	les fromages	à ses parents.

2. Indirect objects may be expressed by an **à**-phrase or by an indirect-object pronoun, **lui** for the singular and **leur** for the plural.

		Ind.-Obj. à-phrase		Ind.-Obj. Pronoun	
Singular	Il donne de l'eau	à son père.	Il	**lui**	donne de l'eau.
	Il donne de l'eau	à sa mère.	Il	**lui**	donne de l'eau.
Plural	Il donne de l'eau	à ses amis.	Il	**leur**	donne de l'eau.
	Il donne de l'eau	à ses amies.	Il	**leur**	donne de l'eau.

3. As you have seen, some verbs take an indirect object but no direct object.

Il parle **à sa sœur.**   Il **lui** parle.

Il téléphone **à son ami.**   Il **lui** téléphone.

4. In most cases, indirect-object pronouns immediately precede the verb to which their meaning is tied. However, in the affirmative command, the indirect object immediately follows the verb.

Il	**lui** donne	de l'eau.			
Il ne	**lui** donne	pas d'eau.			
Il va	**lui** donner	de l'eau.	*but,*	Donne-**lui**	de l'eau!
Ne	**lui** donne	pas d'eau!			

38 Jean-Marcel aide sa mère. ⊗

Donne le vin à ton père.
Verse de l'eau à tes cousines.
Donne du pain à ta grand-mère.
Apporte le beurre à ton cousin.

D'accord, je vais lui donner le vin.
D'accord, je vais leur verser de l'eau.
D'accord, je vais lui donner du pain.
D'accord, je vais lui apporter le beurre.

39 Ensuite, elle lui demande... ⊗

de passer les hors-d'œuvre à son cousin.
de donner du melon à ses grands-parents.
de verser du vin à son grand-père.
de passer le sel à son père.
de verser de l'eau à sa cousine.

Et il lui passe les hors-d'œuvre.

Et il leur donne du melon.
Et il lui verse du vin.
Et il lui passe le sel.
Et il lui verse de l'eau.

40 Un mercredi après-midi chez des amis. ⊗

Qu'est-ce qu'il prend, ton ami?   Oh, donne-lui un Coca-Cola.
Et tes cousins? / Et ta cousine? / Et tes amies?
donne-leur / donne-lui / donne-leur

41 EXERCICE DE COMPREHENSION ⊗ For script, see p. T26.

	0	1	2	3	4	5	6	7	8	9	10
Chez le boucher											
Chez le boulanger											
Chez le charcutier											
Chez le crémier	√										

42 EXERCICE ECRIT

Récrivez chaque phrase en utilisant **lui** ou **leur.**
1. Est-ce que tu vas téléphoner à Philippe et à Catherine? Est-ce que tu vas leur téléphoner?
2. Demande à Philippe et à Catherine s'ils sont libres dimanche. Demande-leur s'ils sont libres dimanche.
3. On va acheter des fleurs à Grand-mère. On va lui acheter des fleurs.
4. Elle apporte toujours un bon dessert à ses enfants. Elle leur apporte toujours un bon dessert.
5. Tu ne réponds pas à ta sœur? Tu ne lui réponds pas?
6. Réponds à ta sœur! Réponds-lui!

43 EXERCICE DE CONVERSATION

Des amis viennent pour le déjeuner. Dites ce que vous allez leur donner à manger.

The name "bagnat" comes from the word "baigner," to soak, since the bread is "soaked" in olive oil.
Also Pan-Bagnat.

44 Une spécialité provençale : le pain-bagnat. ⊗

Voici un sandwich délicieux et très facile à faire. Il vous faut :

Many different sorts of lettuce are used in France. Boston lettuce is the most common type.

une laitue   un poivron vert

un oignon   un oeuf dur

une tomate   un anchois

Coupez la tomate et l'œuf dur en tranches. Hachez la laitue, le poivron vert et l'oignon. Mettez dans un petit pain. Ajoutez un peu de sel, un peu de poivre, de l'huile d'olive, du vinaigre et un anchois.

VOCABULAIRE: **facile** _easy;_ **il vous faut** _you need;_ **coupez** _cut;_ **hachez** _mince;_ **ajoutez** _add;_ **huile d'olive** _olive oil;_ **vinaigre** _vinegar;_ **anchois** _anchovy._

WORD LIST

1–16

une course *errand*
faire les courses *to go grocery shopping*
un marchand *salesperson*
une marchande *salesperson*
un marché *market*
un supermarché *supermarket*

un légume *vegetable*
une carotte *carrot*
un champignon *mushroom*
un concombre *cucumber*
un *haricot *bean*
des *haricots verts *green beans*
une pomme de terre *potato*
une tomate *tomato*

une fleur *flower*
le Marché aux Fleurs *the Flower Market*
un fruit *fruit*
un ananas *pineapple*
une banane *banana*
une cerise *cherry*
un melon *melon*
une orange *orange*
un pamplemousse *grapefruit*
une pêche *peach*
une poire *pear*
une pomme *apple*
du raisin *grapes*

un gramme *gram*
un kilo *kilogram*
une livre *pound*

acheter *to buy*
coûter *to cost*
dépenser *to spend*
élever *to rear*
lever *to raise*
vendre *to sell*
avoir l'air *to look (good . . .)*

cher, chère *expensive*
délicieux, –euse *delicious*
juteux, –euse *juicy*
mûr, –e *ripe*

Bon Appétit! *Enjoy your meal!*
Vous en prenez combien de kilos? *How many kilos (of them) do you want?*
1 F la pièce *1 franc each*

17–29

une boucherie *butcher shop*
un boucher, une bouchère *butcher*
l'agneau (m.) *lamb*
un gigot d'agneau *leg of lamb*
un bifteck *steak*
le bœuf *beef*
un rôti de bœuf *roast of beef*
un poulet *chicken*
la viande *meat*

une boulangerie-pâtisserie *bakery-pastry shop*
un boulanger, une boulangère *baker*
un gâteau *pastry*
le pain *bread*

une charcuterie *a meat shop specializing in pork products and prepared dishes*
un charcutier, une charcutière *pork butcher*
le porc *pork*
une côtelette de porc *pork chop*

une crémerie *dairy outlet*
un crémier, une crémière *salesperson in a dairy outlet*
le beurre *butter*
la crème fraîche *heavy soured cream*
le fromage *cheese*
un œuf *egg*
une douzaine d'œufs *a dozen eggs*
un yaourt *yogurt*

une épicerie *grocery store*
un épicier, une épicière *grocer*
le Beaujolais *Beaujolais (wine)*
la moutarde *mustard*
un pot de moutarde *jar of mustard*
le poivre *pepper*
le sel *salt*
le vin *wine*
une bouteille de vin *a bottle of wine*

économiser *to save*
prendre *to take*

une bouteille *bottle*
une douzaine *dozen*
un litre *liter*
un pot *jar, pot*
une tranche *slice*

assez de *enough of*
beaucoup de *much, many*
combien de *how much, how many*
un peu de *a little of*
trop de *too much*

de son côté *his / her own way*

30–44

un assaisonnement *dressing*
une fin *end*
à la fin *at the end*
un plat *dish*
des provisions (f.) *grocery supplies*
un repas *meal*
une table *table*
A table! *Dinner (Lunch) is served!*
une tasse *cup*

le petit déjeuner *breakfast*
une brioche *brioche*
le café au lait *coffee with milk*
la confiture *jam*
un croissant *croissant*

le déjeuner *lunch*
un *hors-d'œuvre *hors d'œuvre*
des *hors-d'œuvre *hors d'œuvres*
des frites (f.) *French fried potatoes*
le poisson *fish*
une salade *salad*
une vinaigrette *oil and vinegar*

le déjeuner (cont.)
un fromage *cheese*
le fromage de chèvre *goat cheese*
un dessert *dessert*
une mousse au chocolat *chocolate mousse*
une tarte *pie, tart*
le café *coffee*

le dîner *dinner, supper*
la soupe *soup*
une omelette *omelet*
des pâtes (f.) *noodles*

aider *to help*
il l'aide *he helps her*
commencer à *to start to*
oublier *to forget*
passer *to pass*
servir (like sortir) *to serve*
il sert *he serves*
verser *to pour*

il boit *he drinks*
il met la table *he sets the table*
vient le plat principal *the main dish comes*

leur *(to, for) them*
il leur passe les fruits *he passes them the fruit*
lui *(to, for) him / her*
lui dit sa mère *his mother says to him*
tout *everything*

léger, –ère *light*
principal, –e *main*
propre *clean*
provençal, –e *from Provence*
râpé, –e *grated*
varié, –e *varied*

à droite *on the right*
à gauche *on the left*
ensuite *then*

In the Word List, **h**'s that behave like consonants will be preceded by *

There are other names for "une surprise-partie," such as "une boum," or "une surboum."

9

La Surprise-Partie

Since Philippe and Catherine are giving the party together, they share in the preparations equally.

1 Tout est prêt! ⊗

Philippe et Catherine donnent une surprise-partie : ils ont invité une dizaine de copains qui vont arriver dans une demi-heure. La surprise-partie va avoir lieu dans le sous-sol où Philippe et Catherine ont une pièce à eux. Ils vérifient que tout est en ordre.

? DOUZAINE

- acheter pâté de campagne ✓
-      "   saucisson ✓
- préparer sandwiches ✓
- descendre disques ✓
- balayer ✓
- ranger ✓
- réparer électrophone ✓

CATHERINE Où est ma liste? J'ai perdu ma liste! En ce moment tout va mal! … Ah, la voilà!… Voyons… On a acheté le pâté et le saucisson… On a préparé les sandwiches… On a descendu les disques… Tu as déjà rangé?

PHILIPPE Non, pas encore; mais j'ai balayé un peu; je vais continuer maintenant.

CATHERINE Papa a réparé l'électrophone?

PHILIPPE Oui, hier soir. Il marche bien maintenant.

CATHERINE Alors on a presque tout fini!

Nous avons balayé et rangé notre pièce.

Papa a réparé l'électrophone.

2 Répondez aux questions.

1. Qu'est-ce que Catherine et Philippe donnent aujourd'hui?
2. Où est-ce que la surprise-partie va avoir lieu?
3. Ils ont invité combien de copains?
4. Qu'est-ce qu'il y a sur leur liste?
5. Qu'est-ce que Philippe a fait?
6. Qui a réparé l'électrophone?

The feminine form of "copain" is "copine," a word felt to be more colloquial than its masculine counterpart.

3 Et vous?

1. Est-ce que vous donnez des surprises-parties?
2. Combien de copains est-ce que vous invitez en général?
3. Qu'est-ce que vous faites avant une surprise-partie?
4. Qu'est-ce que vos parents font pour aider?
5. A quelle heure est-ce que vos surprises-parties commencent et finissent?

4 EXERCICE ORAL ⊗

5

EXPRESSING PAST TIME
The Passé Composé with avoir

Répondez aux questions qui suivent les exemples. ⊗

Tu répares l'électrophone, **en ce moment?**   Non, **j'ai réparé** l'électrophone **hier soir.**
Which sentence refers to present time? Which refers to past time? In the sentence on the right,
how many parts does the verb have? The first part is called the auxiliary; the second is called
the past participle. The auxiliary is a form of what verb?

Je vais **jouer.**	J'ai jou**é.**	Je vais **servir.**	J'ai serv**i.**
Je vais **choisir.**	J'ai chois**i.**	Je vais **attendre.**	J'ai attend**u.**

What is the ending of the past participle of **jouer?** Of **choisir?** Of **servir?** Of **attendre?**

6 Lisez la généralisation suivante.

1. The passé composé is used to refer to past time. It is composed of two parts:
   a. a present-tense form of an auxiliary verb, **avoir** or **être;** b. a past participle.
   Avoir is the auxiliary for most verbs. The past participle of most verbs consists of a stem + a
   participle ending: **jou-é, serv-i, chois-i, attend-u.**

	Auxiliary	Past Participle
j'	**ai**	
tu	**as**	
elle / il	**a**	**jou-é**
nous	**avons**	**serv-i**
vous	**avez**	**chois-i**
elles / ils	**ont**	**attend-u**

2. In negative constructions, **ne** precedes the auxiliary and the second negative word (**pas,
   plus, jamais, rien**) immediately follows it: Ils **n'**ont **pas** descendu les disques. Notice the
   exception, however: Ils **n'**ont descendu **ni** les disques **ni** l'électrophone.

3. Words like **déjà, encore, souvent, toujours, presque, assez, beaucoup, trop, bien,** and
   mal often come between the auxiliary and the past participle.

7 Nous donnons une surprise-partie! ⊗

Il faut inviter les copains.   J'ai déjà invité les copains.
acheter du pâté / ranger la pièce / choisir des disques / descendre ces disques
j'ai . . . acheté / j'ai . . . rangé / j'ai . . . choisi / j'ai . . . descendu

8 Catherine et Philippe ont donné une surprise-partie hier. ⊗

Et vous?   Moi, j'ai travaillé.
Et vos frères? / Et vous deux? / Et votre cousin?
Eux, ils ont travaillé. / Nous, nous avons travaillé. / Lui, il a travaillé.

9 Catherine et Philippe sont au café. ⊗

Je vais choisir.   Tu n'as pas encore choisi?
commander / manger / finir / payer
Tu n'as pas encore commandé? / Tu n'as pas encore mangé? / Tu n'as pas encore fini? / Tu n'as pas encore
payé?

10 Quels vêtements est-ce qu'ils mettent? ⊗

Catherine, elle, a choisi un pull bleu (le bleu lui va très bien) et une jupe longue. Elle a mis des bijoux : une bague, un bracelet et un collier.

Philippe a décidé de mettre un polo rouge et un jean. Il met son polo mais ne trouve pas son jean. « Qu'est-ce que j'ai fait de ce jean?… Quelqu'un a pris mon jean! Rendez-moi mon jean!… Bon, tant pis, je n'ai pas le temps de le chercher partout. Qu'est-ce que je mets? Oh, après tout, je garde ce pantalon! »

11 Répondez aux questions.

1. Quelle est la couleur du pull de Catherine?
2. Est-ce que cette couleur lui va bien?
3. Qu'est-ce qu'elle a mis comme bijoux?
4. Qu'est-ce que Philippe a décidé de mettre?
5. Pourquoi est-ce qu'il ne peut pas mettre son jean?
6. Qu'est-ce qu'il va mettre?

12 EXERCICE ORAL ⊗

13 THE VERB mettre

The following chart includes the present-tense forms of the verb **mettre,** *to put (on).* ⊗

Je	**mets**	un pull.	Nous	**mettons**	un pull.
Tu	**mets**	un pull?	Vous	**mettez**	un pull?
Elle / Il	**met**	un pull.	Elles / Ils	**mettent**	un pull.

14 Qu'est-ce qu'on va mettre? ⊗

Tu ne mets pas de jean? — Je ne mets jamais de jean.
Catherine ne met pas de jean? — Elle ne met jamais de jean.
Vous ne mettez pas de jean, vous deux? — Nous ne mettons jamais de jean.
Tes cousins ne mettent pas de jean? — Ils ne mettent jamais de jean.
Ton père ne met pas de jean? — Il ne met jamais de jean.

15 Et vous, qu'est-ce que vous mettez quand vous sortez? ⊗

une chemise   un Ti-shirt   un chemisier   un blouson

des bottes   des chaussures   des sandales   une robe

16 EXERCICE DE CONVERSATION

Demandez à des camarades de décrire (to describe) ce qu'ils mettent quand ils sortent.

17 EXERCICE ORAL ⊗

18 MORE ON PAST PARTICIPLES

The following chart shows the past participles of the irregular verbs you know which form their passé composé with **avoir.** ⊗

Infinitive	Past Participle	
avoir	**eu**	Je n'ai pas **eu** le temps.
être	**été**	J'ai **été** occupé.
faire	**fait**	J'ai **fait** des sandwiches.
mettre	**mis**	J'ai **mis** un disque.
prendre	**pris**	J'ai **pris** de la limonade.

19 EXERCICE ECRIT For answers, see p. T28.

Récrivez le paragraphe suivant au passé composé :
Philippe et moi, nous donnons une surprise-partie. Nous préparons les sandwiches. Nous rangeons notre pièce. Nous réparons l'électrophone. Nous descendons les disques. Nous choisissons nos vêtements.

20 EXERCICE DE COMPREHENSION ⊗ For script, see p. T27.

	0	1	2	3	4	5	6	7	8	9	10
Hier soir	✓										
Dans une heure											

21 La surprise-partie bat son plein. ⊗

Toute la bande est là. Les copains ont apporté leurs guitares et leurs banjos, des disques et des tas de bonnes choses à boire et à manger.

1 Ils mangent et ils boivent.

BRIGITTE Corine! Tu veux des chips?
CORINE Merci[1], mais j'en ai. Euh… Je veux bien quelque chose à boire.
PHILIPPE Qu'est-ce que tu bois?
CORINE Passe-moi une bouteille de Schweppes… s'il y en a encore.

2 Ils dansent des danses rapides et après, des danses lentes.

PHILIPPE Allez, Sylvie, on danse?
SYLVIE D'accord.
PHILIPPE Attends. Il faut que je change le disque. Qu'est-ce que je mets?
SYLVIE Mets-en un lent. Je suis fatiguée.

CORINE Qu'est-ce qu'on chante?
BERNARD « Les petites billes, les petites billes! »
CORINE C'est le titre d'une chanson, ça?
PHILIPPE Mais oui! Tu ne connais pas? (*Il chante.*) « Let it be, let it be… »

The Beatles' songs are still very well known in France.

4 Ils jouent de la guitare, du banjo, et ils chantent des chansons.

[1] Notice that here **Merci** means **Non, merci.** If Corine had wanted some **chips,** she would have said, **« S'il te plaît! »**

22 Répondez aux questions.

1. Qu'est-ce que les copains de Catherine et Philippe ont apporté à la surprise-partie?
2. Qu'est-ce que Brigitte demande à Corine?
3. Est-ce que Corine en veut? Qu'est-ce qu'elle veut?
4. Avec qui est-ce que Philippe veut danser?
5. Pourquoi est-ce qu'elle demande une danse lente?
6. Qui change le disque?
7. Quelle chanson est-ce que Bernard veut chanter?

23 Et vous?

1. Est-ce que vous invitez souvent des copains chez vous?
2. Qu'est-ce que vous leur donnez à manger?
3. Qu'est-ce que vous leur donnez à boire?
4. Qu'est-ce qu'ils apportent?
5. Qui choisit les disques?
6. Qu'est-ce que vous aimez mieux, les danses lentes ou les danses rapides?
7. Est-ce que vous aimez chanter?
8. Quels sont les titres de vos chansons préférées?

24 EXERCICE ORAL ⊗

25 THE VERB boire

The following chart includes the present-tense forms of the verb **boire,** *to drink.* ⊗

Je	**bois**	de la limonade.	Nous	**buvons**	de la limonade.
Tu	**bois**	de la limonade?	Vous	**buvez**	de la limonade?
Elle / Il	**boit**	de la limonade.	Elles / Ils	**boivent**	de la limonade.

The past participle of **boire** is **bu: J'ai bu de la limonade.**

26 Quelque chose à boire. ⊗

1. Qu'est-ce que tu bois?   Je ne bois rien.
   Et lui? / Et vous deux? / Et vos amis? Il ne boit rien. / Nous ne buvons rien. / Ils ne boivent rien.
2. Qu'est-ce que tu as bu?   J'ai bu du Coca-Cola.
   Et lui? / Et vous deux? / Et vos amis? Il a bu . . . / Nous avons bu . . . / Ils ont bu . . .

27 THE PRONOUN en

Répondez aux questions qui suivent les exemples. ⊗

Il parle **de la surprise-partie.**	Il **en** parle.
Il joue **du banjo.**	Il **en** joue.
Il mange **des chips.**	Il **en** mange.

In each of the sentences on the right, what does **en** stand for? Does **en** show gender and number? Where does it come in relation to the verb?

28 Lisez la généralisation suivante.

1. The object pronoun **en** is used to refer to things. It stands for a phrase beginning with **de, du, de la,** or **des.**

Nous avons	du Coca-Cola.		Nous	en	avons.
Nous avons	de la limonade.		Nous	en	avons.
Nous avons	des chips.		Nous	en	avons.
Nous avons beaucoup	de petits gâteaux.		Nous	en	avons beaucoup.

2. **En** comes immediately before the verb to which its meaning is tied. In an affirmative command, it immediately follows the verb:

Have students change
the sentences in this chart
by replacing the verb boire
with the verbs manger, apporter, faire, prendre,
acheter, préparer.

J'	**en** bois.			
Je n'	**en** bois	pas.		
J'	**en** ai bu.		*but,*	Buvez-**en!**
Je ne veux pas	**en** boire.			
N'	**en** bois	pas!		

3. Liaison is obligatory

a. when **en** follows an affirmative command: **Buvez-en.** Note the liaison in **Achètes-en:** **-er** verbs which normally have no final **-s** in the singular command take one before **en.**

b. when **en** is followed by a verb form beginning with a vowel sound: **J'en ai acheté.**

29 Préparons tout pour la surprise-partie! ⊗

Il faut acheter du pain.   Qui va en acheter?
apporter des disques / préparer du jus d'orange / faire de la limonade
va en apporter / va en préparer / va en faire

30 J'apporte quelque chose? ⊗ Variation: Elicit negative responses, too: Non, n'en apporte pas.

J'apporte du Coca-Cola?   Oui, apportes-en.
J'achète des chips? / Je prends du pâté? / Je prépare du jus d'orange?
achètes-en / prends-en / prépares-en

31 Il y a eu une surprise-partie. ⊗ Variation: Elicit negative responses, too: Non, ils n'en ont pas
mangé.

Ils ont mangé des sandwiches?   Oui, ils en ont mangé.
bu du Coca-Cola / écouté des disques / joué de la guitare / chanté des chansons
en ont bu / en ont écouté / en ont joué / en ont chanté

32 EXERCICE ECRIT

Ecrivez les réponses des exercices No 29, 30 et 31.

33 EXERCICE DE CONVERSATION

Vous avez été invité à une surprise-partie chez des amis. Dites…
1. quels vêtements vous avez mis. 2. ce que vous avez apporté. 3. qui vous avez rencontré.
4. ce que vous avez mangé et bu. 5. ce que vous avez dansé et chanté.

34 LES SECRETS D'UNE BONNE SURPRISE-PARTIE ⊗

—Invitez vos copains trois semaines à l'avance°.
—Invitez le même nombre de garçons et de filles.
—Invitez des amis qui aiment bien danser et d'autres qui sont amusants pour mettre de l'ambiance°.

—Demandez à vos copains d'apporter des disques de styles très différents. Dites-leur de bien marquer leur nom sur chaque° disque ou cassette.
—Alternez les rythmes lents et les rythmes rapides, les danses individuelles et les danses en groupe.

Voici une boisson rafraîchissante après une danse rapide : un cocktail de jus de fruits. Dans une carafe°, mettez ⅓ de jus de citron°, ⅓ de jus d'orange, un verre de sirop de grenadine, des glaçons°, ajoutez 3 rondelles° de citron et 3 rondelles d'orange; mélangez° et servez. N'oubliez pas les pailles°!

—Prenez des tranches de pain et coupez-les en triangle.
—Tartinez° du pâté, du fromage, etc. Décorez avec une rondelle d'olive verte ou de cornichon°.
—Coupez une baguette en tranches et décorez avec des tranches de tomates, de concombres ou d'œufs durs. Ajoutez du persil haché°.
—Utilisez des assiettes en carton°, c'est plus pratique°.

—Les chaises musicales°.
—Les charades.
—Charmante Rencontre° : chaque personne écrit sur une feuille de papier° puis plie° le papier de façon à cacher° ce qui est écrit et passe la feuille à son voisin°. On écrit sur chaque feuille successivement 1) M. X a rencontré... 2) Mme Y... 3) à... (lieu° de rencontre) 4) M. X a dit : « ... » 5) Mme Y a répondu : « ... » 6) Conclusion : ... Chaque personne lit ensuite la feuille qu'elle a en main.

Une fois la surprise-partie terminée°, n'oubliez pas de tout ranger : vos parents vous laisseront recommencer°!

VOCABULAIRE : **à l'avance** *in advance;* **pour mettre de l'ambiance** *to liven things up;* **chaque** *each;* **carafe** *pitcher;* **citron** *lemon;* **glaçons** *ice cubes;* **rondelles** *slices;* **mélangez** *stir;* **pailles** *straws;* **nourriture** *food;* **tartinez** *spread with;* **cornichon** *pickle;* **persil haché** *chopped parsley;* **assiettes en carton** *paper plates;* **pratique** *practical;* **chaises musicales** *musical chairs;* **Charmante Rencontre** *charming encounter;* **feuille de papier** *sheet of paper;* **plie** *folds;* **de façon à cacher** *so as to hide;* **voisin** *neighbor;* **lieu** *place;* **nettoyage** *cleaning up;* **terminée** *finished;* **vous laisseront recommencer** *will let you do it again.*

35

WORD LIST

1–9

un copain   *pal*
une demi-heure   *half hour*
une dizaine   *about ten*
un électrophone   *record-player*
une liste   *list*
une pièce à eux   *their own room*
le sous-sol   *basement*
une surprise-partie   *party*

balayer   *to sweep*
  tu as balayé, j'ai balayé, nous
  avons balayé   *you swept, I
    swept, we swept*
continuer   *to continue*
marcher   *to function, to work*
  il marche bien   *it's working fine*
ranger   *to straighten up*
  nous rangeons   *we straighten up*
  nous avons rangé   *we straightened
    up*
vérifier   *to check*
perdre   *to lose*
  j'ai perdu   *I lost*
avoir lieu   *to take place*
voyons!   *let's see!*

  on a acheté…   *we've bought*
  on a descendu…   *we've taken down*
  on a tout fini…   *we've finished
    everything*
  on a préparé…   *we've gotten ready*
  Papa a réparé…   *Papa fixed*

déjà   *already*
en ce moment   *now*
hier   *yesterday*
  hier soir   *last night*
pas encore   *not yet*
en ordre   *in order*
tout va mal   *everything's going
    wrong*

la voilà   *there it is*

10–20

des vêtements (m.)   *clothes*
  un blouson   *jacket*
  une botte   *boot*
  une chaussure   *shoe*
  une chemise   *shirt*
  un chemisier   *blouse*
  un jean   *jeans*
  une jupe   *skirt*
  un pantalon   *pants*
  un polo   *polo shirt*
  un pull   *pullover*
  une robe   *dress*
  une sandale   *sandal*
  un Ti-shirt   *T-shirt*

  un bijou   *a piece of jewelry*
    des bijoux   *jewelry*
    une bague   *ring*
    un bracelet   *bracelet*
    un collier   *necklace*

aller (à)   *to suit*
chercher   *to look for*
décider (de)   *to decide (to)*
garder   *to keep*
mettre   *to put (on)*
rendre   *to give back*

été, *past part.* **être**
eu, *past part.* **avoir**
fait, *past part.* **faire**
mis, *past part.* **mettre**
pris, *past part.* **prendre**

quelqu'un   *someone*

long, –ue   *long*

partout   *everywhere*
tant pis   *too bad*

Le bleu lui va très bien.   *She / He
    looks very good in blue.*
le chercher   *to look for it*

21–34

la bande   *the gang*
les chips (f.)   *potato chips*
une chose   *thing*

un tas de   *a lot of, lots of*
un titre   *title*
la musique   *music*
  une chanson   *song*
  une danse   *dance*
  un banjo   *banjo*
  une guitare   *guitar*

changer   *to change*
  nous changeons   *we change*
chanter   *to sing*
danser   *to dance*
boire   *to drink*

fatigué, -e   *tired*
lent, -e   *slow*
rapide   *fast*

quelque chose   *something*

les petites billes   *little marbles*
Allez!   *Come on!*

j'en ai   *I have some*
s'il y en a encore   *if there is any
    left*
La surprise-partie bat son plein.
    The party is going full swing.
Tu ne connais pas?   *You don't know
    it?*

These pictures give glimpses of Ville d'Avray:
1. the church;
2. post office;
3. busy intersection; 4. the ponds;
5. the town hall;
6. railroad station;
7. main street

10

A VILLE D'AVRAY

1

2

3

4

5

6

7

1 La banlieue de Paris. ⊗

Ville d'Avray fait partie de la banlieue résidentielle de Paris : il n'y a pas d'industries à Ville d'Avray et par conséquent, ses habitants doivent aller travailler à Paris. Malgré cela, Ville d'Avray a gardé son caractère de petite ville, avec sa vie bien à elle, centrée sur sa mairie, son église, son école, sa poste et sa rue commerçante.

2 A la Résidence Musset. ⊗

Point out that Musset was a 19th c. poet.

The French way of naming streets is discussed on p. 102.

Denis et Christine Pierre habitent depuis peu de temps à Ville d'Avray. Voici leur adresse : Résidence Musset, 8 rue de la Ronce. L'appartement de la famille Pierre est dans un ensemble d'immeubles modernes, appelé Résidence Musset. Au cours d'une promenade dans le parc qui entoure la Résidence, Christine et Denis font la connaissance de Stéphane. Stéphane aussi habite dans la Résidence, mais pas dans le même immeuble que Christine et Denis.

Stéphane, Christine et Denis

STÉPHANE Vous habitez dans quel immeuble?
DENIS Dans l'immeuble qui est derrière les arbres, là-bas. Tu le vois?
STÉPHANE Ah, mais j'ai beaucoup d'amis dans votre immeuble... Les frères Sitbon, par exemple... Vous les connaissez?
CHRISTINE Nous les voyons de temps en temps dans l'ascenseur ou dans l'escalier, mais nous ne les connaissons pas vraiment.
STÉPHANE Et Marie-Paule Lemoine, vous la connaissez?
DENIS C'est une petite blonde qui habite au deuxième étage?[1]
STÉPHANE Oui, c'est ça... Ils sont tous très sympathiques!

---

[1] **Au deuxième étage** means *on the third floor.* In French buildings, the ground floor is called **le rez-de-chaussée.** The floors above are **le premier étage, le deuxième étage,** and so on.

98   NOS AMIS

3 **Répondez aux questions.**

1. Où habitent Denis et Christine?
2. Depuis combien de temps?
3. Est-ce que c'est loin de Paris?
4. Quelle est leur adresse?
5. Ils habitent dans un appartement ou une maison?
6. Qu'est-ce que c'est la Résidence Musset?
7. Où habite Stéphane?
8. Comment s'appellent les amis de Stéphane?

4 **EXERCICE ORAL** ⊗

5 **FROM CARDINAL NUMBERS TO ORDINAL NUMBERS**

1. Cardinal numbers are *one, two, three,* etc. The corresponding ordinal numbers are *first, second, third,* etc. In French, with the exception of **premier/première,** *first,* ordinal numbers are formed by adding **-ième** to the cardinal numbers. ⊗

Cardinal Numbers		Ordinal Numbers							
		Masculine				Feminine			
un / une	1	le	**premier**	étage	1ᵉʳ	la	**première**	rue	1ᵉʳᵉ
deux	2	le	**deuxième**	étage	2ᵉ	la	**deuxième**	rue	2ᵉ
trois	3	le	**troisième**	étage	3ᵉ	la	**troisième**	rue	3ᵉ
quatre	4	le	**quatrième**	étage	4ᵉ	la	**quatrième**	rue	4ᵉ

   a. When the cardinal number ends in **-e,** the **-e** is dropped before adding **-ième:**
      quatre ⟶ quatrième, trente ⟶ trentième.
   b. Note the following spellings: **cinq ⟶ cinquième** and **neuf ⟶ neuvième.**

2. An ordinal number is an adjective and, like any other adjective, agrees in gender and number with the noun it refers to. It always comes before the noun.
   Les premiers immeubles.   **Les premières maisons.**

6 **Chaîne de mots.**

Liaison is obligatory between plural ordinal numbers and nouns beginning with a vowel sound:
les premiers‿immeubles.

Elève 1 : A quel étage est-ce que tu habites?
Elève 2 : Au rez-de-chaussée. A quel étage est-ce que tu habites?
Elève 3 : Au premier étage. A quel étage est-ce que tu habites?
Elève 4 : Au deuxième étage…

7 **Et vous?**

1. Où est-ce que vous habitez, dans un village, une petite ville, une grande ville, dans la banlieue d'une grande ville?
2. Est-ce que vous habitez dans un immeuble ou dans une maison?
3. Combien d'étages a votre immeuble (maison)?
4. Si vous habitez dans un immeuble, à quel étage est votre appartement?

8   THE VERB connaître

The following are the present-tense forms of the verb **connaître,** *to know.* ⊗

Make sure that connaître is used only with names of persons or of places.

Je	**connais**	les voisins.	Nous	**connaissons**	les voisins.
Tu	**connais**	les voisins?	Vous	**connaissez**	les voisins?
Il / Elle	**connaît**	les voisins.	Ils / Elles	**connaissent**	les voisins.

The past participle of **connaître** is **connu: J'ai connu Stéphane au CES.**

9   Marie-Paule habite dans cet immeuble. ⊗

Toi aussi, tu habites là?

Oui, et je connais bien Marie-Paule.
Oui, mais je ne connais pas Marie-Paule.

Christine aussi habite là?
Vous deux aussi, vous habitez là?
Les frères Sitbon aussi habitent là?
Denis aussi habite là?

elle connaît bien / elle ne connaît pas
nous connaissons bien / nous ne connaissons pas
ils connaissent bien / ils ne connaissent pas
il connaît bien / il ne connaît pas

Variation: Use names of places: Tu habites à Ville d'Avray? Non, mais je connais bien Ville d'Avray.

10   THE DIRECT-OBJECT PRONOUNS le, la, les

Répondez aux questions qui suivent les exemples. ⊗

Je regarde **le parc.**   Je **le** regarde.
Je regarde **la résidence.**   Je **la** regarde.
Je regarde **les immeubles.**   Je **les** regarde.

In the sentences on the right, what do **le, la,** and **les** stand for? Are **le parc, la résidence,** and **les immeubles** used as direct or indirect objects? What kinds of pronouns are **le, la, les,** direct- or indirect-object pronouns? Where do they come in relation to the verb? Do they stand for things or for people?

Je regarde **Denis.**   Je **le** regarde.
Je regarde **Christine.**   Je **la** regarde.
Je regarde **Denis et Christine.**   Je **les** regarde.

What do the pronouns **le, la, les** stand for in these sentences? Do they stand for things or for people?

11   Lisez la généralisation suivante.

1. The pronouns **le, la,** and **les** are used as the direct object of the verb and may stand for either people or things.

Singular	Je regarde Je regarde	**mon voisin.** **son plan.**	Je	**le**	regarde.
	Je regarde Je regarde	**ma voisine.** **sa photo.**	Je	**la**	regarde.
Plural	Je regarde Je regarde	**mes voisins.** **leurs dessins.**	Je	**les**	regarde.

Replace the verb regarder in these charts with the verbs chercher, finir, attendre, sortir, mettre, etc.

2. In most cases, a direct-object pronoun comes immediately before the verb to whose meaning it is most closely related:

Je	**les** regarde.	
Je vais	**les** regarder.	
Je ne	**les** regarde	pas.
Ne	**les** regarde	pas!

3. In an affirmative command, the direct-object pronoun immediately follows the verb. In writing, it is linked to the verb by a hyphen:

Regarde-**le!**
Regarde-**la!**
Regarde-**les!**

4. Liaison and élision occur with **le, la, les.**

Je l'écoute.   Je les écoute.

Use a simple directed drill, like: Dites à (Alain) d'attendre (Sylvie). Attends-la . . .

12 Je n'habite plus à la Résidence Musset.

Tu vois encore Stéphane?   Oui, je le vois de temps en temps.
Et Marie-Paule? / Et Christine et Denis? / Et les frères Sitbon?

je la vois / je les vois / je les vois   Variation: Elicit negative responses.

13 J'ai tout ça chez moi! ⊗

Tu as l'adresse de Stéphane?   Oui, je vais la chercher.
Tu as son numéro de téléphone? / Tu as ses photos? / Tu as son album?

je vais le chercher / je vais les chercher / je vais le chercher

14 Qui est-ce qu'on invite? ⊗

Stéphane?   D'accord, invitons-le!
Son cousin? / Les Sitbon? / Marie-Paule?

invitons-le / invitons-les / invitons-la

15 EXERCICE ECRIT

Ecrivez les réponses des exercices No 12, 13 et 14.

16 Allons en ville! ⊗

STÉPHANE   Allez donc à la Maison des Jeunes. C'est là qu'on rencontre des gens!
CHRISTINE   Tu peux nous expliquer comment y aller?
STÉPHANE   Je n'ai rien à faire; je vais vous montrer le chemin. Suivez le guide!
DENIS   On te suit! On te suit!

17 Répondez aux questions.

1. Pourquoi est-ce que Stéphane dit à Christine et à Denis d'aller à la Maison des Jeunes?
2. Qu'est-ce que Christine demande à Stéphane?
3. Pourquoi est-ce que Stéphane propose de faire le guide?

As shown on the map, Ville d'Avray is surrounded by woods and forests (le bois de Chaville, la forêt de St-Cloud, etc.). Although they are dwindling, they still provide, along with the ponds, a bucolic setting which the painter Corot loved to paint. You might want to show some reproductions of Corot's pictures of Ville d'Avray.

18 Suivons sur le plan! ⊛

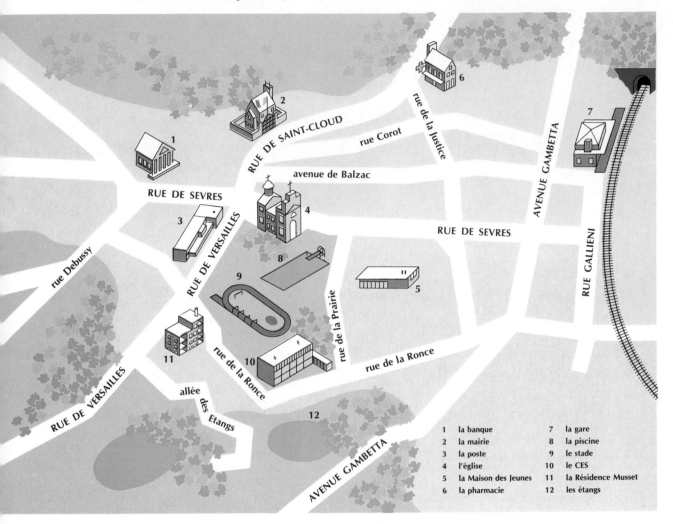

1	la banque	7	la gare
2	la mairie	8	la piscine
3	la poste	9	le stade
4	l'église	10	le CES
5	la Maison des Jeunes	11	la Résidence Musset
6	la pharmacie	12	les étangs

A la sortie de la Résidence, Stéphane, Christine et Denis tournent à gauche. Au croisement de la rue de la Ronce et de la rue de Versailles, ils tournent à droite et suivent la rue de Versailles. Ils passent devant la poste et ils arrivent à l'église. Là, ils tournent à droite, puis ils prennent la première rue à droite, la rue de la Prairie. Stéphane a bien guidé ses nouveaux amis : la Maison des Jeunes est juste devant eux.

19

The streets of Ville d'Avray are named as they usually are in French towns and cities. Some streets take their names from nearby towns, like Versailles, Saint-Cloud, and Sèvres. Some have been named for areas of the town that used to exist, like la Prairie *(the meadow) or* la Ronce *(the blackberry bush). Others have been given the names of famous people, like Gambetta (a statesman), Gallieni (a general), Balzac (a writer), Debussy (a composer), or Corot (an artist who painted scenes of Ville d'Avray).*

20 EXERCICE ORAL ⊗

21 THE VERB suivre

The following are the present-tense forms of the verb **suivre,** *to follow.* ⊗

Je	**suis**	le guide.	Nous	**suivons**	le guide.
Tu	**suis**	le guide?	Vous	**suivez**	le guide?
Il / Elle	**suit**	le guide.	Ils / Elles	**suivent**	le guide.

The past participle of **suivre** is **suivi: Ils ont suivi Stéphane.**

22 Qui passe le premier? ⊗

Vous me suivez tous les deux?   Oui, nous te suivons!
Et toi? / Et Christine? / Et les Sitbon?
je te suis / elle te suit / ils te suivent

23 Ce n'est pas facile à expliquer! ⊗

Tu as compris, toi?   Oui, j'ai suivi.
Et vous deux? / Et Denis? / Et Christine et Stéphane?
nous avons suivi / il a suivi / ils ont suivi

24 C'est vous le guide!   Utilisez *(use)* le plan de la page 102. For answers, see p. T29.

1. Comment est-ce qu'on va de la Résidence Musset à la mairie?
2. Quel chemin est-ce qu'on prend pour aller de la mairie à la gare?
3. Comment est-ce qu'on va de la gare aux étangs de Corot?
4. Quand on est aux étangs de Corot, comment est-ce qu'on va au stade?
5. Quel chemin est-ce qu'on prend pour aller du stade à la poste?
6. Comment est-ce qu'on va de la poste à la Résidence Musset?

25 THE OBJECT PRONOUNS me, te, nous, vous

Répondez aux questions qui suivent les exemples. ⊗

Il **lui** montre le chemin.   Il **me** montre le chemin.
Il **leur** montre le chemin.   Il **te** montre le chemin.
                                          Il **nous** montre le chemin.
                                          Il **vous** montre le chemin.

In the sentences on the left, are the object pronouns **lui** and **leur** direct or indirect? And the object pronouns in the sentences on the right?

Il **le** guide.   Il **me** guide.
Il **la** guide.   Il **te** guide.
Il **les** guide.   Il **nous** guide.
                              Il **vous** guide.

In the sentences on the left, are the object pronouns **le, la, les** direct or indirect? And the object pronouns in the sentences on the right?

Ne **me** montrez pas le chemin!   Montrez-**moi** le chemin!
          Ne **me** guidez pas!   Guidez-**moi!**
Is **me** used in an affirmative command? What is used instead?

26 Lisez la généralisation suivante.

1. The object pronouns **me, te, nous,** and **vous** can be used either as direct or indirect objects. Here is a list of the object pronouns.

Object Pronouns	Direct	Indirect
Singular	**me** **te** **le / la**	**me** **te** **lui**
Plural	**nous** **vous** **les**	**nous** **vous** **leur**

2. The object pronouns **me, te, nous,** and **vous** come before the verb to whose meaning they are most closely related. In the affirmative command, the pronoun follows the verb.

Replace "nous" in the sentences in this chart with "me, le, les, etc.," for drilling.

Elle	**nous** suit.			
Elle ne	**nous** suit	pas.	*but,*	Suivez-**nous!**
Elle ne veut pas	**nous** suivre.			
Ne	**nous** suivez	pas!		

3. In an affirmative command, **moi** is used instead of **me.**

Ne **me** suivez pas! *but,* Suivez-**moi!**

4. Elision occurs with **me, te, le/la,** and liaison occurs with **nous, vous, les.**

Elle m'écoute.   **Elle t'écoute.**   **Elle l'écoute.**

Elle nous écoute.   **Elle vous écoute.**   **Elle les écoute.**

27 Nous ne sommes plus amis avec Stéphane. ⊗

Il vous parle encore?   Non, il ne nous parle plus.
écoute encore / répond encore / invite encore
il ne nous écoute plus / il ne nous répond plus / il ne nous invite plus

28 Dites à des camarades… ⊗

que vous allez les inviter.   Je vais vous inviter.
leur faire un plan / leur montrer le chemin / les guider
Je vais vous faire un plan. / Je vais vous montrer le chemin. / Je vais vous guider.

29 Denis veut aller à la mairie. ⊗

Il faut lui faire un plan.   —Je te fais un plan?
                                              —Oui, fais-moi un plan, s'il te plaît.

Il faut lui montrer le chemin. / Il faut le guider.
Je te montre le chemin? Oui, montre-moi le chemin . . . / Je te guide? Oui, guide-moi . . .

30 EXERCICE ECRIT

Ecrivez les réponses des exercices No 27, 28 et 29.

31 L'appartement de la famille Pierre. ⊗

Stéphane a emmené Christine et Denis à la Maison des Jeunes. Il les a présentés à ses copains. Maintenant les trois amis rentrent à la Résidence, et Christine et Denis invitent Stéphane à monter chez eux. Les Pierre ont un appartement de cinq pièces, cuisine et salle de bains.[1] Christine et Denis ont chacun leur chambre.[2] Ils habitent au 4e étage du bâtiment B de la Résidence Musset.

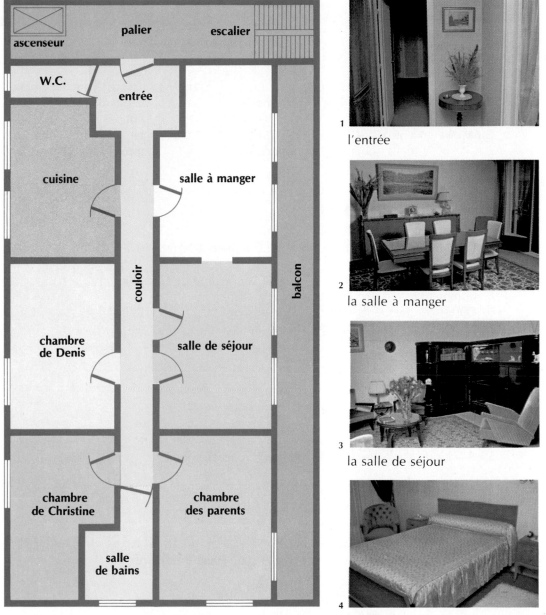

1 l'entrée

2 la salle à manger

3 la salle de séjour

4 la chambre des parents

[1] This is the standard way of describing an apartment. The kitchen and bathroom are not counted in the number of rooms.

[2] Do not confuse **pièce** and **chambre: pièce** refers to any room in general while **chambre** refers only to a bedroom.

La chambre de Christine.

STÉPHANE Ta chambre est très jolie!
DENIS Bien sûr! Elle a pris la plus belle chambre!
CHRISTINE Menteur! Je ne l'ai pas prise! On l'a jouée à pile ou face et j'ai gagné!

La chambre de Denis.

STÉPHANE Tu as l'air passionné de ski! C'est toi qui l'as gagnée, cette coupe?
DENIS Hé oui! Tiens, j'ai une affiche formidable. Regarde!

32 Répondez aux questions.

1. A quel étage est-ce que les Pierre habitent?
2. Combien de pièces est-ce qu'ils ont? Combien de chambres?
3. Décrivez leur appartement.
4. Comment est-ce que Stéphane trouve la chambre de Christine?
5. Comment est-ce que Christine a eu sa chambre?
6. Qu'est-ce que Denis a gagné? En quel sport?
7. Qu'est-ce que Denis montre à Stéphane?

33 Et chez vous?

1. Décrivez votre appartement (maison).
2. A quel étage est votre appartement (chambre)?
3. Est-ce que vous avez une chambre à vous?
4. Est-ce que vous avez déjà gagné une coupe? En quel sport?
5. Est-ce que vous avez des affiches dans votre chambre?

34 EXERCICE ORAL ⊗

35 OBJECT PRONOUNS WITH THE PASSE COMPOSE
Agreement of Past Participle

Répondez aux questions qui suivent les exemples. ⊗

Elle a fait **des affiches.**   Elle **en** a fait.
Elle a donné un disque **à sa cousine.**   Elle **lui** a donné un disque.

In the sentences on the right, what are the object pronouns? What is their position in relation to the auxiliary?

C'est elle qui a fait **ce dessin.**   C'est elle qui **l'**a fai**t.**
C'est elle qui a fait **cette affiche.**   C'est elle qui **l'**a fai**te.**
C'est elle qui a fait **ces dessins.**   C'est elle qui **les** a fai**ts.**
C'est elle qui a fait **ces affiches.**   C'est elle qui **les** a fai**tes.**

The past participle shows gender and number agreement in which of the sentences above?
Are the pronouns used in these sentences direct- or indirect-object pronouns?

36 Lisez la généralisation suivante.

1. In the passé composé, an object pronoun immediately precedes the auxiliary verb.

Nous	**lui** avons	parlé.
Nous	**en** avons	pris.
Nous	**l'** avons	trouvé.

2. The past participle of a verb used with **avoir** agrees in gender and number with a direct-object pronoun: **le, la, les, me, te, nous,** or **vous.** It does not agree with an indirect-object pronoun or with **en.**

Singular	Masc.	**Ce dessin?**	C'est elle qui	**l'**	a	fai**t.**
	Fem.	**Cette affiche?**	C'est elle qui	**l'**	a	fai**te.**
Plural	Masc.	**Ces dessins?**	C'est elle qui	**les**	a	fai**ts.**
	Fem.	**Ces affiches?**	C'est elle qui	**les**	a	fai**tes.**

Replace the verb faire in this chart with the verbs acheter, prendre, choisir.

Notice that past participles behave like adjectives. **Fait, -e** and **mis, -e,** for example, are of the **distrait, -e** type. Most past participles are of the **doué, -e** type.

37 Stéphane est un bon guide.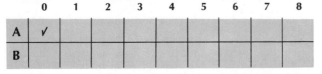

Il t'a bien guidé, Denis?   Oui, il m'a bien guidé.
Et toi, Christine? / Et vous, les frères Sitbon? / Et vous, Christine et Marie-Paule?
il m'a bien guidée / il nous a bien guidés / il nous a bien guidées

38 Ils sont à la Maison des Jeunes.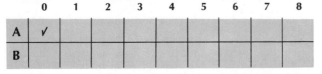

Tu présentes Christine à Marie-Paule?   Je l'ai déjà présentée à Marie-Paule!
Tu présentes Denis à Marie-Paule?   Je l'ai déjà présenté . . .
Tu présentes les Pierre à Marie-Paule?   Je les ai déjà présentés . . .
Tu présentes les frères Sitbon à Christine?   Je les ai déjà présentés . . .

39 Christine demande à son frère :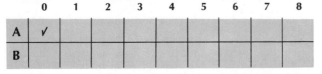

C'est toi qui as fait cette affiche?   Oui, c'est moi qui l'ai faite.
pris ces photos / mis les disques / mangé un peu de pâté / bu de la limonade
les ai prises / les ai mis / en ai mangé / en ai bu   Variation: response: Non, ce n'est pas moi qui l'ai faite.

40 EXERCICE DE COMPREHENSION For script, see p. T28.

	0	1	2	3	4	5	6	7	8
A	√								
B									

41 EXERCICE ECRIT

Récrivez chaque phrase en remplaçant *(replacing)* les mots soulignés par un pronom.

1. Mme Pierre a acheté des affiches <u>pour ses enfants</u>.　Mme Pierre leur a acheté des affiches.
2. Christine et Denis ont joué <u>ces affiches</u> à pile ou face.　Christine et Denis les ont jouées à pile ou face.
3. Denis a gagné <u>l'affiche sur le ski</u>.　Denis l'a gagnée.
4. Christine a pris <u>l'affiche sur la danse</u>.　Christine l'a prise.
5. Christine et Denis ont donné l'affiche sur Paris à <u>Stéphane</u>.　Christine et Denis lui ont donné l'affiche sur Paris.

42 EXERCICE DE CONVERSATION

Un(e) camarade vous invite à venir écouter des disques chez lui (elle). Vous lui demandez où il (elle) habite, si c'est loin de l'école, quel chemin il faut prendre pour aller chez lui (elle), s'il (elle) habite dans un immeuble ou dans une maison, à quel étage…

43 REDACTION

Faites le plan de votre appartement (maison) et décrivez-le (la).

44 WORD LIST

1–15

une **banlieue**　*suburb*
un **arbre**　*tree*
le **caractère**　*character*
une **église**　*church*
un **habitant**　*inhabitant*
une **industrie**　*industry*
une **mairie**　*town hall*
un **parc**　*park*
une **poste**　*post office*
une **rue commerçante**　*shopping street*

un **immeuble**　*apartment building*
une **adresse**　*address*
un **ascenseur**　*elevator*
un **ensemble**　*group*
un **escalier**　*stairway*
un **étage**　*floor*
une **résidence**　*garden apartments*

une **vie**　*life*
　une **vie bien à elle**　*its very own life*
entourer　*to surround*
connaître　*to know (be acquainted with)*
faire la connaissance de　*to make the acquaintance of*
faire partie de　*to be part of*

doivent aller travailler　*have to go to work*
tu **vois**　*you see*
nous **voyons**　*we see*

le　*him, it*
la　*her, it*
les　*them*

appelé, –e　*called*
centré, –e　*centered*
même　*same*
moderne　*modern*
résidentiel, –ielle　*residential*
sympathique　*nice*
premier, –ière　*first*
deuxième　*second*
troisième　*third*

au cours de　*during*
derrière　*behind*
malgré　*in spite of*

de temps en temps　*from time to time*
depuis　*since*
par conséquent　*consequently*

au rez-de-chaussée　*on the ground floor*

16–30

un **chemin**　*way, route*
un **guide**　*guide*
une **sortie**　*exit*
　à la sortie　*on coming out of*
une **banque**　*bank*
un **étang**　*pond*
une **gare**　*railroad station*
une **maison des jeunes**　*youth center*
une **pharmacie**　*drugstore*
un **stade**　*athletic field*

un **plan**　*map*
une **allée**　*lane*
une **avenue**　*avenue*
une **rue**　*street*

expliquer　*to explain*
guider　*to guide*
passer　*to pass by*
tourner　*to turn*
suivre　*to follow*

nouveaux amis　*new friends*
à droite　*on (to) the right*
à gauche　*on (to) the left*
au croisement　*at the intersection*
derrière　*behind*
devant　*in front of*
donc　*so, then*

me　*(to / for) me*
te　*(to / for) you*
nous　*(to / for) us*
vous　*(to / for) you*

31–43

une **pièce**　*room*
　une **chambre**　*bedroom*
　une **cuisine**　*kitchen*
　une **entrée**　*entryway*
　une **salle de bains**　*bathroom (for bathing only)*
　une **salle à manger**　*dining room*
　une **salle de séjour**　*living room*
　des **W.-C.**　*toilet, bathroom*

un **bâtiment**　*building*
　un **balcon**　*balcony*
　un **palier**　*landing*

une **coupe**　*cup, trophy*
menteur, –euse　*liar*

jouer à pile ou face　*to toss a coin*

emmener　*to take (people, animals)*
monter　*to go up*
présenter (à)　*to introduce (to)*

formidable　*terrific*
joli, –e　*pretty*
passionné, –e　*enthusiastic*
la plus belle　*the nicest*

The Eiffel Tower has become symbolic of Paris. At the time it was built in 1889, it was an engineering marvel. For many years it was the tallest structure in the world, 320 meters. Eiffel also built the supporting frame for the Statue of Liberty in New York Harbor.

This painting is by the French artist Robert Delaunay (1885-1941).

11
PARIS

Paris is a little more than 2000 years old. During most of this long period, Paris has held an especially important place in the affairs of France and of the rest of Europe. Taking a walk through Paris is the best way to experience this importance for yourself. If you began on the Ile de la Cité, in front of Notre Dame Cathedral, you would be starting at the beginning. Gauls and Romans lived there. Later, a tribe of Celts, called the Parisii, settled there, and Paris took its name from them. You could go either way from there — to the Left Bank (Rive Gauche) and the Latin Quarter, or to the Right Bank (Rive Droite) and the Louvre. Any direction your exploration takes leads you past landmarks and monuments that bring to mind the people and events that shaped French, and European, history. But you would soon make another discovery. Paris is not like a book that only retells its past, because it is just as alive now with its modern people, its activities, and its history-in-the-making as it ever was.

See map of France for locations of Paris and Dijon. Dijon: 300 km from Paris; has been for centuries the lively cultural and business center of Burgundy; population about 160,000; home of the famous Dijon mustard.

2 Premier jour à Paris. ⊗

Isabelle Sautelet habite à Dijon, en Bourgogne. En ce moment, elle passe quelques jours à Paris, chez son oncle et sa tante. C'est la première fois qu'elle est à Paris, et son jeune cousin, Antoine, lui sert de guide pour visiter la capitale.

Isabelle écrit à ses parents qui sont restés à Dijon : « Le lendemain de mon

Look at the photo of the "bateau-mouche" on p. 113 and the map on the facing page for better understanding of this text.

arrivée, Antoine m'a emmenée faire une promenade en bateau-mouche sur la Seine. Nous sommes partis du pont de l'Alma et nous sommes allés jusqu'à la Cité. Nous sommes passés sous 24 ponts (Antoine les a comptés!) et nous avons vu, entre autres monuments, la Tour Eiffel, l'Obélisque, le Louvre et Notre-Dame...

Notre-Dame, cathédrale de Paris, se dresse depuis le 13e siècle au cœur de la ville, dans l'Ile de la Cité.

La Place de la Concorde (18e siècle) est la plus grande et la plus élégante place de Paris. L'Obélisque, qui est en son milieu, est un cadeau de l'Egypte à la France.

The arrows in the river on the map show the route taken by the "bateaux-mouches." Monuments shown are those one can see from the boats.

« Après notre promenade en bateau-mouche, nous sommes allés au musée du Louvre. Malheureusement, nous sommes arrivés une demi-heure avant la fermeture! Alors, nous sommes allés chacun de notre côté : Antoine est allé voir les antiquités égyptiennes, et moi, je suis allée voir *la Joconde*. Ma visite a eu l'air de lui faire plaisir : elle m'a souri! »

Le Louvre (16ᵉ siècle) est un ancien palais royal qui abrite maintenant un immense musée d'une extraordinaire richesse.

La Joconde, peinte par Léonard de Vinci au 15ᵉ siècle, est célèbre par son sourire.

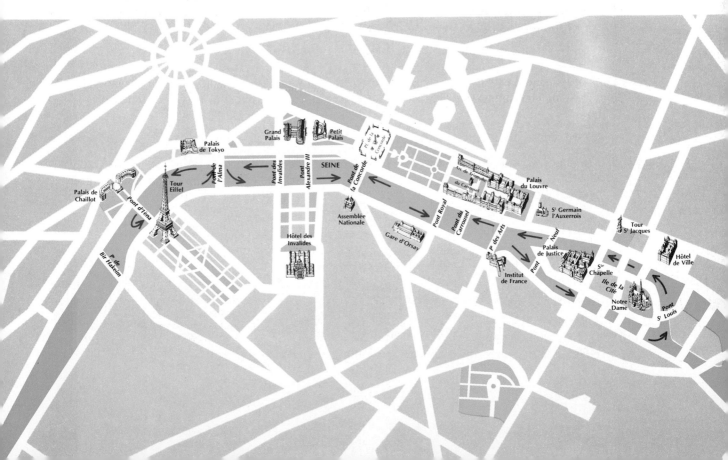

3 Répondez aux questions.

1. Où habite Isabelle Sautelet?
2. Qu'est-ce qu'elle fait en ce moment?
3. Qui est-ce qui lui sert de guide pour visiter la capitale?
4. Où est-ce qu'Antoine l'a emmenée, le lendemain de son arrivée?
5. Ils sont partis de quel pont?
6. Jusqu'où est-ce qu'ils sont allés?
7. Qu'est-ce qu'ils ont vu comme monuments?
8. Où est-ce qu'ils sont allés après la promenade en bateau-mouche?
9. Qu'est-ce qu'Antoine est allé voir? Et Isabelle?

4 Et vous?

1. Est-ce que vous avez déjà pris un bateau pour visiter une ville? Où ça?
2. Quelle grande ville est-ce que vous avez déjà visitée?
3. Qu'est-ce qu'il y a comme monuments dans cette ville?
4. Quel musée est-ce que vous avez déjà visité?
5. Est-ce que vous aimez visiter les musées?

5 EXERCICE ORAL ⊗

6 THE PASSE COMPOSE WITH être

Répondez aux questions qui suivent les exemples. ⊗

Je **suis allé** à Paris hier.
Tu **es allé** à Paris hier?
Il **est allé** à Paris hier.

Nous **sommes allés** à Paris hier.
Vous **êtes allés** à Paris hier?
Ils **sont allés** à Paris hier.

Do the above sentences refer to present time or past time? Is the auxiliary verb in each sentence a form of **avoir** or of **être?**

Antoine est allé au Louvre hier.
Isabelle est allée au Louvre hier.

Les garçons sont allés au Louvre hier.
Les filles sont allées au Louvre hier.

Look at the past participles used in these sentences. Are they spelled alike? What does the past participle agree with in each sentence, the subject or a direct-object pronoun?

7 Lisez la généralisation suivante.

1. The passé composé of some verbs is formed with the auxiliary verb **être** instead of **avoir.**
2. For some verbs that form the passé composé with **être,** the past participle agrees in gender and number with the subject.

Remind students that agreement has to be made with all subject pronouns, not only 3rd person pronouns.

Masculine Subject			Feminine Subject		
je	suis	rentré	**je**	suis	rentrée
tu	es	rentré	**tu**	es	rentrée
il	est	rentré	**elle**	est	rentrée
nous	sommes	rentrés	**nous**	sommes	rentrées
vous	êtes	rentré(s)	**vous**	êtes	rentrée(s)
ils	sont	rentrés	**elles**	sont	rentrées

Notice that this agreement appears in writing only.

3. Liaison is often made between the forms of **être** and the past participle, especially with **est** and **sont**.

Il **est** allé à Dijon.   Ils **sont** allés à Dijon.

4. The following is a list of verbs you already know that form the passé composé with **être**: **aller/allé, arriver/arrivé, partir/parti, rester/resté.**

5. Some verbs, like **passer, monter, descendre, sortir, rentrer,** form the passé composé with either **être** or **avoir**. **Avoir** is used when the verb has a direct object.

Aux.: **être**		Aux.: **avoir**	Dir. Obj.	
Elle **est passée**	par Paris.	Elle **a passé**	**une semaine**	à Paris.
Elle **est montée**	dans sa chambre.	Elle **a monté**	**les livres**	dans sa chambre.
Elle **est descendue**	au sous-sol.	Elle **a descendu**	**les disques**	au sous-sol.
Elle **est sortie**	de la maison.	Elle **a sorti**	**son vélo**	de la maison.
Elle **est rentrée**	dans la maison.	Elle **a rentré**	**son vélo**	dans la maison.

8 Une promenade en bateau-mouche. ⊗

Antoine est sorti?

Oui, il est allé faire une promenade en bateau-mouche.

Et Isabelle? / Et les garçons? / Et les filles?
elle est allée / ils sont allés / elles sont allées

9 « Visite de 10 h à 17 h. » ⊗

Isabelle a visité le Louvre?
Antoine a visité le Louvre?
Catherine et Sylvie ont visité le Louvre?
Stéphane et Denis ont visité le Louvre?
Variation: Tu as visité le Louvre, Antoine? / Vous avez visité le Louvre, les filles?

Non, elle est arrivée après la fermeture.
Non, il est arrivé . . .
Non, elles sont arrivées . . .
Non, ils sont arrivés . . .

10 Les Sautelet ont visité la France. ⊗

For answers, see p. T30.

Tu es passé(e) par Paris?
Et vous deux, vous êtes passé(e)s par Nice?
Et Isabelle, elle est passée par Dieppe?
Et M. et Mme Sautelet, ils sont passés par Montargis?

Oui, j'ai passé une semaine à Paris.

11 EXERCICE ECRIT

Ecrivez les réponses de l'exercice No 8 et des exercices No 9 et 10.

This is a typical "bateau-mouche" on the Seine. The Eiffel Tower and the Pont Alexandre III are in the background.

The map on p. 117 shows all the sights described here except Montmartre and the Sacré-Cœur.

12 En haut de la Tour Eiffel. ⊗

Cela fait trois jours qu'Isabelle est à Paris, et la visite continue...

L'Arc de Triomphe (19e siècle) a été construit en l'honneur des armées de Napoléon. Il domine une place en forme d'étoile et une avenue monumentale appelée Les Champs-Elysées.

ISABELLE   C'est formidable! Quelle vue on a d'ici! On peut voir tout Paris!

ANTOINE   Avec le télescope, on voit encore mieux... Tiens, regarde... l'Arc de Triomphe... le Palais de Chaillot... le Sacré-Cœur... les Invalides...

ISABELLE   Tu as déjà visité les Invalides?

ANTOINE   Oui, j'y suis allé une fois, il y a longtemps, voir le tombeau de Napoléon.

ISABELLE   Tu n'as pas envie d'y retourner avec moi, demain?

ANTOINE   Oh non! J'aime bien Napoléon, mais vraiment j'ai vu assez de monuments comme ça!

Le Palais de Chaillot (20e siècle) abrite quatre musées différents et deux théâtres.

L'Hôtel des Invalides (17e siècle) abrite le Musée de l'Armée et le tombeau de Napoléon.

Le Sacré-Cœur (19e siècle) domine un des quartiers les plus pittoresques de Paris : Montmartre.

13 **Répondez aux questions.**

1. Où est-ce qu'Antoine emmène Isabelle, le troisième jour après son arrivée?
2. Quelle vue est-ce qu'on a du haut de la Tour Eiffel?
3. Dans quoi est-ce qu'Antoine regarde pour mieux voir Paris?
4. Quels monuments est-ce qu'il voit?
5. Est-ce qu'il a déjà visité les Invalides? Quand?
6. Qu'est-ce qu'il y a à voir dans l'Hôtel des Invalides?
7. Pourquoi est-ce qu'Antoine ne veut pas retourner aux Invalides?

14 **EXERCICE ORAL** ⊗

15 **Devinettes.** *Riddles.* ⊗

1. Notre-Dame se dresse dans cette île.   l'Ile de la Cité
2. Paris est sur ce fleuve.   la Seine
3. Cet ancien palais royal est maintenant un très grand musée.   le Louvre
4. L'Obélisque est au milieu de cette place.   la Place de la Concorde
5. L'Arc de Triomphe domine cette avenue monumentale.   l'Avenue des Champs-Elysées
6. Le Sacré-Cœur est dans ce quartier.   Montmartre
7. On peut y voir le tombeau de Napoléon.   l'Hôtel des Invalides
8. Elle est célèbre par son sourire.   la Joconde

16 ## THE VERB voir

The following are the present-tense forms of the verb **voir,** *to see.* ⊗

Je	**vois**	la Tour Eiffel.	Nous	**voyons**	les Invalides.
Tu	**vois**	le Palais de Chaillot?	Vous	**voyez**	les Champs-Elysées?
Il / Elle	**voit**	le Sacré-Cœur.	Ils / Elles	**voient**	l'Arc de Triomphe.

The past participle of **voir** is **vu: Antoine a vu le tombeau de Napoléon.**

17 **Le télescope ne marche pas.** ⊗

Tu vois le Palais de Chaillot?   Non, je ne vois rien!
Vous voyez l'Arc de Triomphe, vous deux?   Non, nous ne voyons rien!
Antoine voit l'Obélisque?   Non, il ne voit rien!
Antoine et Isabelle voient le Sacré-Cœur?   Non, ils ne voient rien!

18 **D'un bateau-mouche.** ⊗

Tu connais le Louvre?   Je l'ai vu d'un bateau-mouche.
Vous connaissez la Tour Eiffel, vous deux?   Nous l'avons vue . . .
Antoine connaît Notre-Dame?   Il l'a vue . . .
Antoine et Isabelle connaissent l'Ile de la   Ils l'ont vue . . .
Cité?

19   THE PRONOUN y

Répondez aux questions qui suivent les exemples. ⊗

Quand est-ce qu'ils vont **à la Tour Eiffel?**   Ils y vont cet après-midi.
On peut monter **en haut de l'Arc de Triomphe?**   Bien sûr qu'on peut y monter.
Tu vas souvent **dans l'Ile de la Cité?**   Oui, j'y vais tous les jours.

In the sentences on the left, what do the phrases **à la Tour Eiffel, en haut de l'Arc de Triomphe, dans l'Ile de la Cité** describe? In the sentences on the right, what word stands for each of these phrases? Where does this word come in relation to the verb?

20   Lisez la généralisation suivante.

1. The pronoun **y** frequently refers to locations. It stands for phrases beginning with **à, en, sur, en haut de, dans, chez.**

Il va souvent	**à Paris?**	Oui, il	**y**	va tous les jours.
Il est souvent	**chez lui?**	Oui, il	**y**	est tous les soirs.
Il va souvent	**dans le parc?**	Oui, il	**y**	va tous les matins.

2. **Y** comes immediately before the verb to which its meaning is tied. In an affirmative command, however, **y** immediately follows the verb:

Il	**y**	reste.			
Il n'	**y**	reste	pas.		
Il veut	**y**	rester.		*but,*	Restez-y!
Il	**y**	est resté.			
N'	**y**	restez	pas.		

3. Liaison is obligatory when **y** immediately follows a command form.

     Allons‿y!   Vas‿y!   Restez‿y!   Restes‿y!

Notice that the familiar command form of **aller** and verbs ending in **-er,** like **rester,** takes a final **-s** when followed by **y.**

Remind students that "en" works in the same way. Refer to p. 94, if necessary.

21   Antoine parle à Isabelle : ⊗

Tu es allée aux Champs-Elysées?   Non, je n'y suis pas allée.
Tu es montée en haut de l'Arc de Triomphe?   Non, je n'y suis pas montée.
Tu es passée par la Place de la Concorde?   Non, je n'y suis pas passée.
Tu es retournée dans l'Ile de la Cité?   Non, je n'y suis pas retournée.

Variation: Elicit affirmative responses for more practice.

22   M. Sautelet parle à Isabelle : ⊗

J'ai envie de retourner à Paris.   Eh bien, retournes-y!
de passer par Montargis / d'aller au Louvre / de monter en haut de la Tour Eiffel
passes-y / vas-y / montes-y

23   EXERCICE ECRIT

Ecrivez les réponses des exercices No 21 et 22.

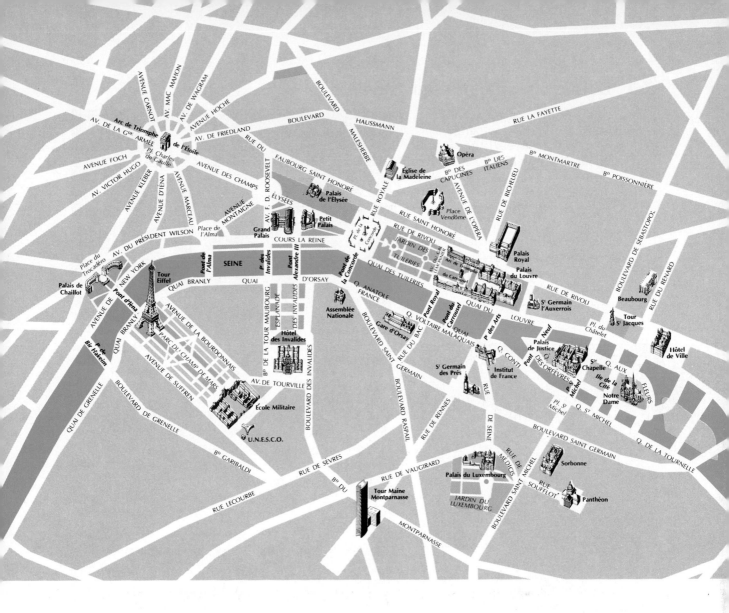

24 **Suivez la piste!** ⊗ For answers, see p. T31.

Votre classe visite Paris. Comme vous êtes nombreux, vous formez plusieurs groupes. Tous les groupes suivent le même itinéraire : Palais de Chaillot–Arc de Triomphe–Place de la Concorde–Madeleine–Opéra–Louvre. Dites comment vous allez...

du Palais de Chaillot à l'Arc de Triomphe,   Nous prenons l'Avenue Kléber.
de l'Arc de Triomphe à la Concorde,
de la Concorde à la Madeleine,
de la Madeleine à l'Opéra,
de l'Opéra au Louvre.

Quand chaque groupe a décidé du chemin à prendre, le chef du groupe donne les réponses. C'est le groupe qui a fait le moins d'erreurs qui arrive le premier. Maintenant, recommencez avec l'itinéraire suivant : Tour Eiffel–Invalides–Jardin du Luxembourg–Ile de la Cité. Quel groupe arrive le premier?

VOCABULAIRE : **la piste** the path; **nombreux** a lot of people; **plusieurs** several; **itinéraire** route; **le chef** the leader; **le moins** the fewest.

This game might be better used after the text accompanying pictures of No. 25 has been studied. Accept different answers from those given on p. T31, if they appear to be reasonable alternatives. **Chapitre 11 Paris 117**

25 Dernier° coup d'œil° sur Paris. ⊗

Pendant son séjour° à Paris, Isabelle tient un journal°. Voici ce qu'elle écrit vers la fin de son séjour : « Ce matin, je suis allée faire des courses° dans les grands magasins°. C'est facile, car ils sont presque tous groupés dans le quartier° de l'Opéra et de la Madeleine. J'ai acheté des cadeaux° pour la famille et pour les amis, mais je n'ai rien acheté pour moi parce que les choses que j'aime ici ne sont pas à vendre°.

1

La Madeleine (19ᵉ siècle) est une église construite sur le modèle d'un temple grec.

« Par exemple : le Quartier Latin, avec ses étudiants°, ses librairies°, ses cinémas, ses vieilles° églises. Et les quais de la Seine, avec leur calme, leurs grands arbres, leurs pêcheurs à la ligne° et les bateaux qui passent. Et Beaubourg avec son atmosphère de fête populaire° dans un décor° futuriste. Enfin°, j'emporte° tout de même° un peu de tout ça avec moi, puisqu'°en bonne touriste° j'ai pris des tas de photos… Espérons° qu'elles seront réussies°. »

2   3

Beaubourg, appelé officiellement le Centre National d'Art et de Culture Georges Pompidou, présente de nombreuses expositions d'art moderne.

Jongleur amusant les badauds devant Beaubourg.

VOCABULAIRE : **dernier** *last;* **coup d'œil** *glimpse;* **séjour** *stay;* **tient un journal** *keeps a journal;* **faire des courses** *to shop;* **dans les grands magasins** *in the department stores;* **le quartier** *the district;* **des cadeaux** *some gifts;* **à vendre** *for sale;* **étudiants** *university students;* **librairies** *bookstores;* **vieilles** *old;* **pêcheurs à la ligne** *anglers;* **fête populaire** *street fair;* **décor** *setting;* **enfin** *anyway;* **j'emporte** *I am taking back;* **tout de même** *all the same;* **puisque** *since;* **en bonne touriste** *like a good tourist;* **espérons** *let's hope;* **elles seront réussies** *they'll turn out.*

4

5

Le Jardin du Luxembourg est le lieu de promenade préféré des étudiants du Quartier Latin.

Les quais de la Seine...

26 REDACTION

Décrivez votre visite d'une grande ville :
1. Comment s'appelle la ville que vous avez visitée?
2. Combien de temps est-ce que vous y êtes resté(e)?
3. Avec qui est-ce que vous avez visité cette ville?
4. Quels monuments est-ce que vous avez vus?
5. Dans quels musées est-ce que vous êtes allé(e)?
6. Qu'est-ce que vous avez aimé le plus dans cette ville?
7. Est-ce que vous avez pris des photos pendant votre séjour? De quoi?

27 EXERCICE DE COMPREHENSION ⊗ For script, see p. T30.

	0	1	2	3	4	5	6	7	8
Le Louvre									
Notre-Dame									
L'Arc de Triomphe									
L'Obélisque									
Beaubourg									
Le Sacré-Cœur									
Les Invalides	✓								

You might want to end this unit with a photo quiz: Show familiar pictures of Paris from the unit and ask for identification. You might also have students point them out on the map.

28

FOR REFERENCE

2.2. The Place de la Concorde (18th cent.) is the largest and most elegant square in Paris. The obelisk in the center was a gift to France from Egypt.
2.3. Notre Dame, the cathedral of Paris, has stood since the 13th century at the heart of the city, on the Ile de la Cité.
2.4. The Louvre (16th cent.) is a former royal palace which now houses an immense museum of extraordinary wealth.
2.5. La Joconde (Mona Lisa), painted by Leonardo da Vinci in the 15th century, is famous for her smile.

12.2. The Arc de Triomphe (19th cent.) was built in honor of Napoleon's armies. It stands in the center of a star-shaped plaza and at the head of a majestic avenue called the Champs-Elysées.
12.3. The Palais de Chaillot (20th cent.) houses four different museums and two theatres.

12.4. The Sacré-Cœur (Sacred Heart) (19th cent.) looks down on one of the most picturesque quarters of Paris: Montmartre.
12.5. The Hôtel des Invalides (17th cent.) houses the Museum of the Army and Napoleon's tomb.

25.1. The Madeleine (19th cent.) is a church modeled on a Greek temple.
25.2. Beaubourg, whose official name is the Georges Pompidou National Center of Art and Culture, offers a great many modern-art shows.
25.3. Juggler entertaining passers-by in front of Beaubourg.
25.4. The Luxembourg Gardens, in the Latin Quarter, is the park where students like to go for walks.
25.5. The embankments of the Seine...

29

WORD LIST

2–11

une antiquité *antique item*
une arrivée *arrival*
un bateau-mouche *excursion boat*
la fermeture *closing*
la fois *time*
le lendemain *following day, on the following day*
un monument *monument, landmark*
un musée *museum*
un pont *bridge*
une visite *visit*

faire plaisir à *to please (someone)*
faire une promenade *to take a jaunt*
servir de *to act as*
visiter *to visit*
voir *to see*
  vu, past part. **voir** *seen*

Elle m'a souri. *She smiled at me.*

égyptien, –ienne *Egyptian*

entre *among*
jusqu'à *as far as, until*
sous *under*

y *there*

malheureusement *unfortunately*

7

Elle est passée par Paris.
Elle a passé une semaine à Paris.
Elle est montée dans sa chambre.
Elle a monté les livres dans sa chambre.
Elle est descendue au sous-sol.
Elle a descendu les disques au sous-sol.
Elle est sortie de la maison.
Elle a sorti son vélo de la maison.
Elle est rentrée dans la maison.
Elle a rentré son vélo dans la maison.

She went through Paris.
She spent a week in Paris.
She went up to her room.
She took the books up to her room.
She went down to the basement.
She took the records down to the basement.
She went out of the house.
She took her bike out of the house.
She went back into the house.
She took her bike back into the house.

12–27

un télescope *telescope*
un tombeau *tomb*
une vue *view*

un boulevard *boulevard*
un cours *mall*
un jardin *garden*
une place *square*
un quai *bank*
une tour *tower*

retourner *to return*

demain *tomorrow*

en haut de *at the top of*

il y a longtemps *a long time ago*
une fois *once*

Jean-Marcel Giuliani appeared in Unit 8. The map of France will give locations of Nice and Monaco. Monaco is 18 km from Nice, about a half hour by train. For those who know Jacques Cousteau from television, you will want to emphasize that the Calypso has her home port in Monaco.

12
LA LETTRE
chapitre de révision

Stamp 1: reproduction of "La Tapisserie de l'Apocalypse," housed at the tapestry museum in Angers. Stamp 2: reproduction of a painting by Georges Braque (1882-1963). Stamp 3: reproduction of a stained-glass window (un vitrail) from the cathedral at Sens.

Nice, le 3 juillet

Ma chère Aline,
Mon cher Christian,

Vous n'allez pas me croire, mais hier je suis allé pour la première fois à Monaco. Je sais, c'est tout près de Nice, mais je n'ai jamais eu l'occasion d'y aller avant! Et j'y suis allé tout seul!! Le Musée Océanographique est formidable. Il y a un aquarium avec des poissons de toutes les formes et de toutes les couleurs. Vous n'avez jamais vu une chose pareille! Ça doit être vraiment bien de faire de l'exploration sous-marine. J'ai vu deux soucoupes plongeantes de Cousteau. Il y en a une qui peut descendre jusqu'à 3.000 mètres! Je suis aussi monté sur la terrasse où je suis bien resté un quart d'heure, l'œil collé au télescope. Ça m'a coûté une fortune en pièces de 1 F. Savez-vous qu'en un quart d'heure, il y a eu 23 bateaux qui sont entrés dans le port et 18 qui en sont sortis! Ensuite je suis allé visiter le Palais du Prince. Sur la place, il y a des canons énormes. Il paraît que c'est Louis XIV qui les a offerts au Prince de Monaco. Je crois que je vous ai tout raconté. J'ai hâte de recevoir de vos nouvelles.

Je vous embrasse.
Votre cousin,
Jean-Marcel

2 *Monaco is a small territory on the Côte d'Azur. It is governed by the Prince of Monaco and is independent of France. The language spoken there, however, is French. Monaco has its own franc, equal in value to the French franc which is also used there. It has its own postage stamps, too, which have to be used to mail cards and letters from Monaco. One of Monaco's outstanding contributions to science is the Oceanographic Institute and Museum. The Museum has on display one of the most extensive collections of marine life to be found anywhere as well as a wide variety of equipment for underwater explorations. It also houses oceanographic laboratories and a research library.*

3 ## Répondez aux questions.

1. Qui sont Aline et Christian?
2. Où est-ce que Jean-Marcel est allé pour la première fois?
3. Est-ce que c'est loin de Nice?
4. Qu'est-ce qu'il y a au Musée Océanographique?
5. Qu'est-ce que Jean-Marcel a fait sur la terrasse?
6. Que fait le Commandant Cousteau?
7. Combien de bateaux sont entrés dans le port? Combien en sont sortis?
8. Qu'est-ce que Jean-Marcel a visité ensuite?
9. Qu'est-ce qu'il y a sur la place?
10. Qui les a offerts au Prince de Monaco?

4 ## EXERCICE ORAL ⊗

5 ## Comment écrire une lettre. ⊗

a. le lieu et la date

Paris, le 1ᵉʳ mai
Nice, le 2 septembre

b. la formule de début

à un ami
à une amie
à un adulte
à une adulte

(Mon) cher Christian
(Ma) chère Aline
cher Monsieur
Chère Madame

c. la formule finale

à un ami ou à une amie

{ Je t'embrasse
  Amitiés

à un adulte ou à une adulte

{ Meilleurs souvenirs
  Meilleures pensées

6 *Even though Jean-Marcel was writing only an informal letter to his cousins, he still made a rough draft of it before copying it neatly onto his own stationery. Generally speaking, French people care a great deal about the appearance of the letters they send and receive. The style they use when they write is often much more formal than the style they use when they talk: they feel that a clear distinction has to be made between the two. Personal letters are almost always handwritten. Typewritten letters are not sent to anyone other than business associates.*

7 THE VERB écrire

The following are the present-tense forms of the verb **écrire,** *to write.* ⊗

J'	**écris**	à mon cousin.	Nous	**écrivons**	à notre cousin.
Tu	**écris**	à ton cousin?	Vous	**écrivez**	à votre cousin?
Il / Elle	**écrit**	à son cousin.	Ils / Elles	**écrivent**	à leur cousin.

The past participle of **écrire** is **écrit: Jean-Marcel a écrit à ses cousins.**
Décrire, *to describe,* follows the same pattern as **écrire.**

8 Ils n'écrivent jamais! ⊗

J'ai hâte de recevoir de vos nouvelles.   Ça tombe mal, nous n'écrivons jamais.
de tes nouvelles / des nouvelles de Jean-Marcel / des nouvelles de Christian et Aline
je n'écris jamais / il n'écrit jamais / ils n'écrivent jamais

9 Un coup de téléphone ou une lettre. ⊗

Tu as téléphoné?   Non, j'ai écrit.
Et vous deux, vous avez téléphoné? / Et Jean-Marcel? / Et ses parents?
nous avons écrit / il a écrit / ils ont écrit

10 Quels sont les mois de l'année? ⊗

janvier	mars	mai	juillet	septembre	novembre
février	avril	juin	août	octobre	décembre

11 Quelle est la date aujourd'hui? ⊗

       C'est aujourd'hui le premier janvier.   C'est aujourd'hui le quatre juillet.
Notice that in giving the date in French, cardinal numbers are always used except in the case
of the first of the month, **le premier.**

12 Lisez les dates suivantes : ⊗   For answers, see p. T32.

8/1/1904   Le huit janvier mille neuf cent quatre.
4/7/1976; 29/2/1982; 14/5/1960; 24/9/1999; 1/1/1980; 12/10/1492

13 Au Musée Océanographique.

This type of shell is called "un bénitier" (font for holy water) because it is often used for that purpose in churches.

Heures d'ouverture

1er octobre-15 juin: de 9 h 30 à 19 h
16 juin-30 septembre: de 9 h à 19 h

A giant sea turtle swimming in the aquarium

PRONOUNS—SUMMARY

The following charts include all the pronouns you have been learning.

Independent Pronouns	Subject Pronouns	Direct-Object Pronouns	Indirect-Object Pronouns
moi	je (j')	me (m') *or* moi	me (m') *or* moi
toi	tu	te (t')	te (t')
lui	il	le (l')	lui
elle	elle	la (l')	lui
nous	nous (nous^z)	nous (nous^z)	nous (nous^z)
vous	vous (vous^z)	vous (vous^z)	vous (vous^z)
eux	ils (ils^z)	les (les^z)	leur
elles	elles (elles^z)	les (les^z)	leur

Pronoun replacing de + *noun phrase*	Pronoun replacing à (en, sur, dans, chez) + *noun phrase*
en (en^n)	y

15 Qu'est-ce que Jean-Marcel va faire? ⊗

Il va aller au Musée Océanographique?	Oui, il va y aller.
Il va visiter l'Aquarium?	Oui, il va le visiter.
Il va voir beaucoup de poissons?	Oui, il va en voir beaucoup.
Il va voir les soucoupes plongeantes?	Oui, il va les voir.
Il va monter sur la terrasse?	Oui, il va y monter.

16 Allons au Musée Océanographique! ⊗

On y va avec Jean-Marcel?   D'accord, allons-y avec lui.
Avec Aline? / Avec les garçons? / Avec les filles?
allons-y avec elle / allons-y avec eux / allons-y avec elles

17 Jean-Marcel n'a plus d'argent. ⊗

Il a tout dépensé?	Oui, donne-lui 1 franc.
Toi aussi, tu as tout dépensé?	Oui, donne-moi 1 franc.
Les garçons aussi, ils ont tout dépensé?	Oui, donne-leur 1 franc.

18 Jean-Marcel est rentré chez lui. Sa mère lui demande : ⊗

Tu es allé au Musée Océanographique?	Oui, j'y suis allé.
Tu as vu les soucoupes plongeantes?	Oui, je les ai vues.
Tu es monté à la terrasse?	Oui, j'y suis monté.
Tu as vu les canons?	Oui, je les ai vus.

Variation: Elicit negative responses.

19 EXERCICE ECRIT

Ecrivez les réponses des exercices No 15, 16, 17 et 18.

EXPRESSING TIME
Present, Future, and Past

1. Present time is expressed by the present tense.

	jouer	sortir	choisir	attendre
EN CE MOMENT	je **joue** tu **joues** il elle } **joue** nous **jouons** vous **jouez** ils elles } **jouent**	je **sors** tu **sors** il elle } **sort** nous **sortons** vous **sortez** ils elles } **sortent**	je **choisis** tu **choisis** il elle } **choisit** nous **choisissons** vous **choisissez** ils elles } **choisissent**	j' **attends** tu **attends** il elle } **attend** nous **attendons** vous **attendez** ils elles } **attendent**

2. Future time can be expressed
a. by the present tense + a time expression: **Je pars à Dieppe dans une heure.**
b. by a present-tense form of **aller** followed by the infinitive form.

		aller	*Infinitive*
DANS UNE HEURE	je tu il nous vous ils	**vais** **vas** **va** **allons** **allez** **vont**	**jouer** **sortir** **descendre** **choisir** **servir** **rentrer**

3. Past time can be expressed by the passé composé: a present-tense form of **avoir** or **être** + a past participle.

		avoir	*Past Part.*		être	*Past Part.*
HIER SOIR	j' tu il/elle nous vous ils/elles	**ai** **as** **a** **avons** **avez** **ont**	**joué** **fini** **attendu** **choisi** **servi** **entendu**	je tu il/elle nous vous ils/elles	**suis** **es** **est** **sommes** **êtes** **sont**	**allé(e)** **rentré(e)** **arrivé(e)** **parti(e)s** **resté(e)(s)** **sorti(e)s**

a. Most verbs form the passé composé with **avoir.** The past participle of these verbs agrees in gender and number with a direct-object pronoun: **Il a vu les canons,** but **Il les a vus.** It does not agree with an indirect-object pronoun or with **en** or **y: Ça leur a coûté 1 F. Il en a vu beaucoup. Il y est monté, à la terrasse.**
b. The passé composé of some verbs is formed only with **être.** You have seen **aller, arriver, partir,** and **rester.** The past participle of these verbs agrees in gender and number with the subject: **Elles sont arrivées à Monaco. Ils sont partis.**
c. The passé composé of some verbs is formed with either **avoir** or **être: passer, monter, descendre, sortir, rentrer. Avoir** is used when the verb has a direct object and **être** when it does not: **Il a sorti de l'argent,** but **Il est sorti.**

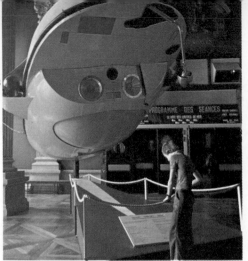

1. Cousteau's diving saucer
2. A poisonous fish, "une rascasse volante"
3. Coral and some "poissons-clowns"

21 Comment visiter le Musée Océanographique. ⊗

1. Entrez dans le hall. Achetez un billet.
2. Descendez voir l'aquarium au sous-sol.
3. Remontez au rez-de-chaussée et regardez les soucoupes plongeantes.
4. Visitez la salle de zoologie.
5. Montez au premier étage.
6. Admirez les maquettes des bateaux.
7. Faites un tour dans les deux salles.
8. Prenez l'ascenseur. Montez à la terrasse.
9. Mettez une pièce d'un franc dans le télescope.
10. Et regardez la vue!

22 Et vous?

1. Vous racontez à des amis comment vous avez visité le musée : « D'abord, je suis entré(e)… »
2. Vous dites à un(e) ami(e) comment visiter le musée : « D'abord, entre… »
3. Pour montrer qu'il (elle) a bien compris, il (elle) dit ce qu'il (elle) va faire : « D'abord, je vais entrer… »

23 EXERCICE DE COMPREHENSION ⊗ For script, see p. T31.

	0	1	2	3	4	5	6	7	8	9
En ce moment										
Dans une heure										
Hier soir	✓									

24 EXERCICE DE CONVERSATION

Votre ami Christian vous a écrit. Vous racontez à vos camarades ce qu'il vous dit dans sa lettre. Voici ce qu'il écrit :

1. Christian est allé passer une semaine à Nice chez son cousin Jean-Marcel et ses parents. Il vous décrit la famille.
2. Christian vous décrit leur maison.
3. Christian et les Giuliani sont allés au Marché aux Fleurs. Christian vous le décrit.
4. Un après-midi, Jean-Marcel a invité des amis. Christian vous raconte ce qu'ils ont fait.

25 EXERCICE ECRIT For answers, see p. T32.

Vous écrivez à un(e) ami(e) pour l'inviter chez vous.

1. Dites que vous allez donner une surprise-partie et que vous l'invitez.
2. Donnez-lui la date et l'heure.
3. Dites quels amis vous avez invités.
4. Dites-lui quels vêtements il faut mettre.
5. Demandez-lui quels disques il (elle) peut apporter.
6. Dites-lui que vous attendez sa réponse avec impatience.
7. Donnez-lui votre numéro de téléphone.

26 Comment adresser une enveloppe. ⊗

l'adresse du destinataire

le nom ——→ *Mademoiselle Aline Leroux*
       → *Monsieur Christian Leroux*

la rue ——→
le numéro ——→ *12, rue Montalembert*

le code postal ——→ *87000 Limoges*
la ville ——→

l'adresse de l'expéditeur

Jean-Marcel Giuliani
2, rue des Meuniers
06000 Nice

"L'adresse de l'expéditeur" can also be written on one line at the very top of the back flap. Point out that it is always on the back flap.

27 Il va mettre sa lettre à la poste.

1

Jean-Marcel goes into the post office to buy stamps.

2

He drops his letter into the outside letter box.

Chapitre 12 La Lettre 127

This brochure page is similar to a page from a booklet distributed by the French Post Office to help foreign tourists in France.

28 A la Poste.

POSTE POST POSTE
Où est le bureau de poste le plus proche? *Where is the nearest Post Office?* Wo ist das nächste Postamt?
Est-ce que le courrier est arrivé? *Did the mail come?* Ist die Post eingetroffen?
Avez-vous des lettres adressées à... ? *Do you have any letters addressed to . . . ?* Haben Sie Briefe für . . . ?
Combien coûte cette lettre, cette carte postale par avion pour... ? *How much does this letter, this postcard, cost by air mail for . . . ?* Was kostet dieser Brief, diese Postkarte, per Luftpost nach . . . ?
Je voudrais... timbres-postes à... Francs. *I want . . . Franc stamps.* Ich möchte . . . Briefmarken zu . . . Francs.
Je voudrais des timbres de collection. *I want some collectors' stamps.* Ich möchte Sammlermarken.

29   WORD LIST

1–4
un aquarium *aquarium*
un bateau *boat*
  des bateaux *boats*
un canon *cannon*
une exploration *exploration*
une forme *shape*
une fortune *fortune*
une lettre *letter*
un mètre *meter*
des nouvelles (f.) *news*
une occasion *opportunity*
un œil *eye*
  des yeux *eyes*

un palais *palace*
une pièce *coin*
une soucoupe *saucer*
une terrasse *terrace*

croire *to believe*
raconter *to tell*
recevoir *to receive*
avoir *hâte (de) *to look*
    forward to
je sais *I know*
savez-vous *do you know*
il les a offerts... *he offered*
    them...

cher, chère *dear*
collé, –e *glued*
énorme *huge*
plongeant, –e *diving*
seul, –e *alone, by oneself*
sous-marin, –e *underwater*

une chose pareille *such a thing*

5–20
une année *year*
une date *date*
un lieu *place*
un mois *month*
  janvier (m.) *January*
  février (m.) *February*
  mars (m.) *March*
  avril (m.) *April*
  mai (m.) *May*
  juin (m.) *June*
  juillet (m.) *July*

août (m.) *August*
septembre (m.) *September*
octobre (m.) *October*
novembre (m.) *November*
décembre (m.) *December*

admirer *to admire*
décrire *to describe*
écrire *to write*

un(e) adulte *adult*

une formule de début *salutation*
une formule finale *closing*
  amitiés *love*
  je t'embrasse (lit.) *I kiss you*
  meilleurs souvenirs *regards*
  meilleures pensées (lit.) *best*
    thoughts

21–28
un billet *ticket*
un *hall *entrance hall*

un code postal *zip code*
un(e) destinataire *addressee*
une enveloppe *envelope*
un(e) expéditeur (-trice) *sender*
un timbre *stamp*

remonter *to go back up*

City Life

In the last 100 years, the population of the world has doubled, and the concentration in cities has often increased tenfold. The same trend has been present in the cities of French-speaking countries of Europe and America where 70% to 80% of the population live. The old cities are very different in looks, not only from one country to the next, but also often within one country. The different styles in architecture were often dictated by climate needs and local resources. The newer cities, however, are built in very similar styles. Such styles became popular in several countries at one time and since cities are cosmopolitan and open to outside influence, they incorporated them.

(1) Old Quebec City. The roofs are steeply inclined so that the snow will slide off them.
(2) Old Menton. Red-tiled roofs are very common in the South of France.
(3) Colmar in Alsace. Many-colored tiles on roofs are also found in Switzerland and Germany.
(4) Lyon, located where the Saône and the Rhône rivers meet, is France's third largest city.
(5) Place Stanislas in Nancy, in Lorraine.
(6) Old and new buildings in Liège, Belgium.
(7) Market day in Neuchâtel, Switzerland.
(8) Skyscraper and a Calder "stabile" in the new district of Paris called "La Défense."
(9) Nice, on the Côte d'Azur.

5

6

7

8   9

Plate 11

The hearts of cities are slowly becoming business centers. Their residents are moving to the suburban areas, which are being built all around the cities. From these suburbs people commute to work. Many regret this trend which segregates areas either as business or as residential. In an attempt to reverse this process, a new district called La Défense was built just outside Paris. It combines office and residential buildings. However, businesses are reluctant to leave their quarters in the center of Paris and move to La Défense. The development of an efficient public transportation system is tied to business expansion. In cities, subways are an especially convenient way of traveling at peak hours when streets are paralyzed by traffic jams.

(1) A printer's shop in Liège, Belgium.
(2) New subway stations are often combined with underground shopping malls (this one in Paris).
(3) Aux Trois Quartiers is one of the big department stores in Paris.
(4) La Défense district outside Paris.
(5) Subway route map in Montreal, Canada.
(6) Street sign in Paris.
(7) French hairdresser at work.
(8) Engineer monitoring French TV broadcasting.
(9) Subway sign in Montreal.
(10) Parisian bus.

5 6

7 8

9   10

Plate 13

Sipping a drink on the terrace of an outdoor café and watching people go by is a favorite pastime in many French-speaking cities. Cafés are often chosen as meeting places since people do not usually call on each other at their homes. Flea markets, antique shows, or shows of any kind attract many people who are not necessarily shopping for anything special but who often treat themselves to a small gift. Young people often go to flea markets to buy jeans or other American-inspired clothing.

1

2  3

4

Plate 16

5

13

La Journée de Viviane

To make up, one needs rouge — du fard à joues; eye shadow — du fard à paupières; liquid make-up — du fond de teint; mascara — du mascara; lipstick — du rouge à lèvres.

1 Tôt le matin. ⊗

La journée de Viviane commence à 7 h du matin. Son réveil sonne… Viviane se réveille et se lève d'un bond. Si elle ne se lève pas immédiatement, elle perd courage et elle met une demi-heure à se lever! Elle commence par faire sa toilette.

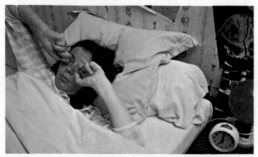

1 Elle se lève.

2 Elle se lave les dents.

3 Elle se brosse les cheveux.

4 Elle se fait du chocolat.

Ensuite, elle prend son petit déjeuner : un bol de chocolat et une tartine de pain beurré. Puis, elle s'habille, elle se maquille un peu et elle se donne un coup de peigne. A 8 h, elle est prête à partir au travail.

2

Bagneux is south of Paris and is on maps of Paris suburbs. Point out location of Ville d'Avray and the contrast between the residential (Ville d'Avray) and industrial (Bagneux) suburbs.

Viviane Simorre is sixteen. She lives in Bagneux, an industrial suburb of Paris, where she and her parents have an apartment in a lower-income housing development — an HLM (Habitation à Loyer Modéré). Since French students may leave school if they wish at the age of sixteen, Viviane chose this year to work rather than continue in school. She found a job in Paris selling clothes in a fashionable boutique for men. Now, with the money she makes, she can help her family, with whom she will probably live for another few years.

3 Répondez aux questions.

1. A quelle heure commence la journée de Viviane?
2. Est-ce que Viviane se lève immédiatement? Pourquoi?
3. Qu'est-ce qu'elle fait avant de prendre son petit déjeuner?
4. Qu'est-ce qu'elle prend au petit déjeuner?
5. Qu'est-ce qu'elle fait après son petit déjeuner?
6. A quelle heure est-ce qu'elle est prête à partir au travail?

4 EXERCICE ORAL ⊗

5

REFLEXIVE CONSTRUCTIONS

Répondez aux questions qui suivent les exemples. ⊗

Viviane réveille **sa mère** à 7 h.   Viviane **se** réveille à 7 h.

What is the object of the verb in the sentence on the left? What is the object of the verb in the sentence on the right? To whom does **se** refer?

Elle **se** réveille à 7 h.   Elles **se** réveillent à 7 h.
Tu **te** réveilles à 7 h.   Vous **vous** réveillez à 7 h.
Je **me** réveille à 7 h.   Nous **nous** réveillons à 7 h.

Se is an example of a reflexive pronoun. In the sentences above, what are the other reflexive pronouns?

6 **Lisez la généralisation suivante.**

1. A reflexive construction is one in which the subject and the object of the verb refer to the same person.

Nonreflexive Construction	Reflexive Construction	
Tu lèves ton verre.	**Tu te lèves.**	
Il lave son bol.	**Il se lave**	les dents.
Nous brossons notre chien.	**Nous nous brossons**	les cheveux.

2. The following are the forms of the reflexive pronouns:

Je	**me**	lave.	Nous	**nous**	lavons.
Tu	**te**	laves?	Vous	**vous**	lavez?
Il / Elle	**se**	lave.	Ils / Elles	**se**	lavent.

3. Like object pronouns, reflexive pronouns are placed before the verb to whose meaning they are most closely related. In the affirmative command, the pronoun follows the verb.

Vous	**vous** levez.				
Vous ne	**vous** levez	pas.	*but,*	Levez-**vous!**
Vous allez	**vous** lever.				
Ne	**vous** levez	pas!			

4. In an affirmative command, **te** is replaced by **toi : Ne te lève pas!** *but,* **Lève-toi!**
5. Elision occurs with **me, te,** and **se.** Liaison occurs with **nous** and **vous.**
6. The English equivalent of a French reflexive construction sometimes includes a reflexive pronoun : **Je me fais du chocolat.** *I am making myself some hot chocolate.* However, most of the time it does not:

      Je me lève.   *I get up.*
      Il se lave les mains.   *He is washing his hands.*
      Elle se maquille.   *She is putting on her makeup.*

7. In a reference list, the infinitive of a reflexive verb includes the reflexive pronoun **se : se réveiller,** *to wake up,* **s'habiller,** *to get dressed.*
8. In a sentence with a reflexive infinitive, the reflexive pronoun corresponds to the subject of the verb. **Nous allons nous lever à 8 h. A quelle heure est-ce que tu veux te lever?**

7 Viviane a un petit frère. ⊗

Elle le réveille le matin?	Non, il se réveille tout seul.
Elle le lave?	Non, il se lave tout seul.
Elle l'habille?	Non, il s'habille tout seul.
Elle lui brosse les cheveux?	Non, il se brosse les cheveux tout seul.
Elle lui fait du chocolat?	Non, il se fait du chocolat tout seul.

8 Il est l'heure de partir. ⊗

Viviane est prête?	Pas encore. Elle s'habille.
Et ses parents, ils sont prêts?	Pas encore. Ils s'habillent.
Et toi, tu es prêt?	Pas encore. Je m'habille.
Et vous deux, vous êtes prêtes?	Pas encore. Nous nous habillons.

9 Viviane parle à sa mère : ⊗   Variation: Response: Alors ne te lève pas!

Je n'ai pas envie de me lever.   Courage! Lève-toi!
de me laver / de m'habiller / de me maquiller / de me donner un coup de peigne
   lave-toi / habille-toi / maquille-toi / donne-toi un coup de peigne

10 EXERCICE ECRIT

Ecrivez les réponses de l'exercice No 9.

11 Qu'est-ce que Viviane utilise comme objets de toilette? ⊗

The typical French wash-cloth is in the shape of a mitt.

The word "trousse" is also used to refer to a toilet kit: "une trousse (de toilette)."

une brosse à dents   du dentifrice

un gant de toilette

une brosse à cheveux   un peigne   du savon   du shampooing

A chaîne de mots similar to the one in Unit 4 (p. 40) is easily adapted to these items:

12 Devinettes. ⊗   Elève 1: Dans la trousse de Viviane, il y a un peigne . . .

1. Il en faut un pour se laver.   un gant
2. Il en faut pour se laver.   du savon
3. Il en faut une pour se brosser les cheveux.   une brosse à cheveux
4. Il en faut un pour se donner un coup de peigne.   un peigne
5. Il en faut pour se laver les cheveux.   du shampooing
6. Il en faut pour se brosser les dents.   du dentifrice
7. Il en faut une pour se brosser les dents.   une brosse à dents

Photo 1: Viviane has her ticket(s) stamped in a special machine as she boards the bus. Photo 2: Viviane coming out of the Concorde subway station. Point out that the same tickets are used for both buses and subways. Buses charge one or two tickets depending on zones traveled; the subway requires only one. It is possible to buy a book of 10 tickets (un carnet). The subway has two classes, first and second. First class tickets, of course, cost more.

13 Et vous?

1. Vous vous réveillez tout(e) seul(e) ou ce sont vos parents qui vous réveillent?
2. A quelle heure vous vous levez pendant la semaine?
3. Vous mettez du temps à vous lever? Combien de temps?
4. Qu'est-ce que vous faites pour commencer? Vous vous lavez? Vous vous habillez?
5. Qui fait votre petit déjeuner?
6. A quelle heure est-ce que vous partez de chez vous?

14 REDACTION

Décrivez ce que vous faites le matin chez vous, du moment où vous vous réveillez jusqu'au moment où vous partez pour l'école. Utilisez les questions de l'exercice No 13 comme modèle.

15 La matinée°. ⊗

Viviane a un long trajet° à faire pour se rendre° à son travail, et elle met une heure environ° pour y arriver. Elle prend d'abord l'autobus° pour aller de Bagneux à Paris. Puis dans Paris, elle prend le métro°. Elle sort du métro Place de la Concorde, et de là, elle va à pied° jusqu'à la rue du Faubourg-Saint-Honoré, où se trouve° la boutique où elle travaille. Cette boutique s'appelle « Saint-Laurent, Rive Gauche » et elle vend des vêtements pour hommes.

Quand Viviane arrive le matin, il n'y a encore personne° dans le magasin°. Viviane se change°, puis elle met de l'ordre dans le magasin, et elle s'assure° que rien ne manque°. Quand son patron° arrive, tout est en place°. Le magasin est maintenant ouvert° et les clients° commencent à entrer. Viviane s'occupe° d'eux. Et elle est d'une telle gentillesse° que personne ne° quitte le magasin sans avoir acheté° au moins° une chemise et une cravate°!

VOCABULAIRE : **la matinée** *morning;* **trajet** *trip;* **se rendre** *to get to;* **environ** *about;* **autobus** *bus;* **métro** *subway;* **à pied** *on foot;* **se trouve** *is located;* **il n'y a encore personne** *nobody is there yet;* **magasin** *store;* **se change** *changes her clothes;* **s'assure** *makes sure;* **rien ne manque** *nothing is missing;* **patron** *boss;* **en place** *in place, neat;* **ouvert** *open;* **clients** *customers;* **s'occupe** *takes care of, waits on;* **d'une telle gentillesse** *so nice;* **personne ne...** *nobody . . .;* **sans avoir acheté** *without buying;* **au moins** *at least;* **cravate** *tie.*

16 Répondez aux questions.

1. Combien de temps met Viviane pour aller de chez elle à son travail?
2. Comment est-ce qu'elle va de Bagneux à Paris?
3. Que vend la boutique où elle travaille?
4. Que fait Viviane quand elle arrive au magasin?
5. Qu'est-ce qu'elle fait quand les clients commencent à entrer?

17 Et vous?

1. Vous avez un long trajet à faire pour vous rendre à l'école?
2. Combien de temps est-ce que vous mettez pour faire ce trajet?
3. Vous allez à l'école à pied, en autobus, en métro, en voiture, en vélo?

18 EXERCICE ORAL ⊗

If students work after school, ask them to talk about it. Ask also about older brothers and sisters who are working.

19 MORE ON REFLEXIVE VERBS

A verb used nonreflexively often has a different equivalent from the same verb used reflexively.

Nonreflexive		Reflexive	
lever *to raise*	Elle **lève** la main.	**se lever** *to get up*	Elle **se lève** à 8 h.
rendre *to give back*	Le client **rend** deux chemises.	**se rendre** *to get to*	Elle **se rend** à son travail.
trouver *to find*	Il ne **trouve** pas son jean.	**se trouver** *to be (located)*	L'Obélisque **se trouve** Place de la Concorde.

20 EXERCICE ECRIT   For answers, see p. T34.

Faites des phrases en utilisant les mots donnés dans l'ordre donné.
Ex. : frère et moi / nous / se lever / tôt   Mon frère et moi, nous nous levons tôt.
1. nous / se laver / et / nous / s'habiller / vingt / minute
2. pour / petit déjeuner / nous / se faire / chocolat
3. huit / heure / nous / être / prêt / partir / école
4. nous / avoir / trajet / une / heure / pour / se rendre / école
5. nous / prendre / d'abord / autobus / puis / nous / y / aller / pied

21 Dans le métro. ⊗   For answers, see p. T34. Accept alternative routes.

Chaque° matin, Viviane prend le métro entre la station° Porte d'Orléans et la station Concorde. Elle prend d'abord la ligne° No 4, direction Porte de Clignancourt; elle change à la station Montparnasse; puis elle prend la ligne No 12, direction Porte de la Chapelle, jusqu'à la station Concorde. Trouvez la façon d'°aller : 1) de la station Odéon à la station Trocadéro; 2) de la station Trocadéro à la station Père-Lachaise.

VOCABULAIRE : **chaque**   *each;* **station**   *stop, station;* **ligne**   *line;* **la façon de**   *the way to.*
This game can, of course, be expanded.

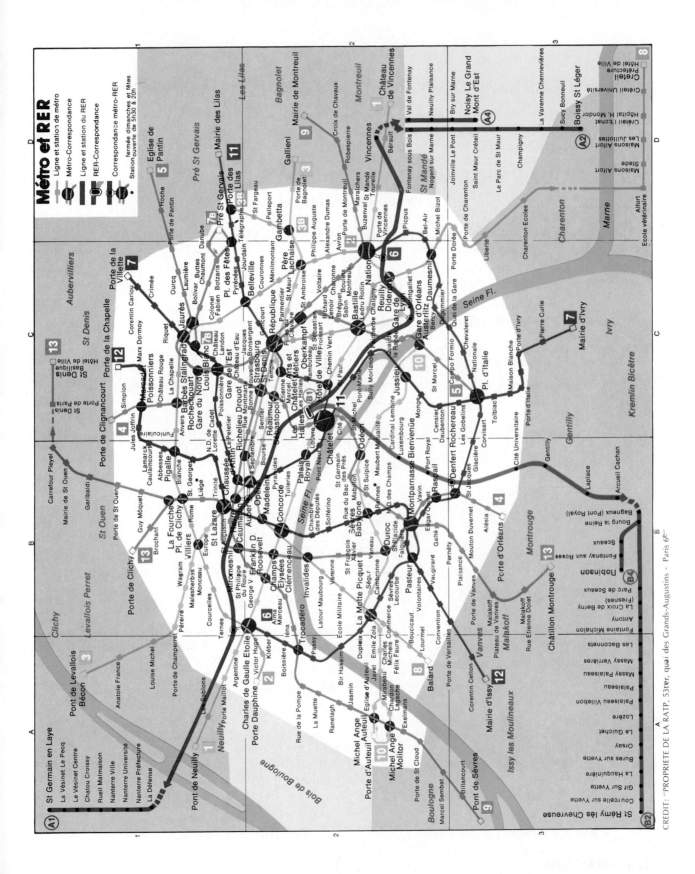

22   rien AND personne

Répondez aux questions qui suivent les exemples. ⊗

Vous voyez **quelque chose?**	Non, je **ne** vois **rien.**
Vous voyez **quelqu'un?**	Non, je **ne** vois **personne.**

Is **quelque chose** used in a negative sentence? What is used instead? Is **quelqu'un** used in a negative sentence? What is used instead? Where are **rien** and **personne** placed in relation to the verb? Where is **ne** placed?

Ils **ne** voient **rien.**	**Rien ne** manque.
Ils **ne** voient **personne.**	**Personne n'**est sorti.

What are **rien** and **personne** in the sentences on the left, direct objects or subjects? And in the sentences on the right?

Je **n'**ai **rien** vu.	Je **n'**ai vu **personne.**
Je **ne** peux **rien** voir.	Je **ne** veux voir **personne.**

Where is **rien** placed when it is used with a verb in the passé composé? In an infinitive construction? Where is **personne** placed in both cases?

23   Lisez la généralisation suivante.

1. **Rien** and **personne** are negatives and, like other negatives, they are used with **ne.**

Affirmative		Negative			
Elle voit	**quelque chose.**	Elle	**ne**	voit	**rien.**
Elle voit	**quelqu'un.**	Elle	**ne**	voit	**personne.**

2. **Rien** and **personne** can be used as subjects as well as objects (direct or indirect).

Subject		Object	
Rien	**ne** manque.	Elle **ne** voit	**rien.**
		Elle **ne** pense	**à rien.**
Personne	**ne** sort.	Elle **ne** voit	**personne.**
		Elle **ne** parle	**à personne.**

3. When it is used as a direct object, **rien** behaves like other negative words. It comes before the past participle in the passé composé and before the infinitive in an infinitive construction. **Personne,** however, comes last in each case.

rien			personne	
Elle **n'**a	**rien**	vu.	Elle **n'**a vu	**personne.**
Elle **ne** veut	**rien**	voir.	Elle **ne** veut voir	**personne.**

24   Il n'y a rien dans cette boutique! ⊗

Viviane a acheté quelque chose?	Non, elle n'a rien acheté.

a trouvé / a choisi / a pris

elle n'a rien trouvé / elle n'a rien choisi / elle n'a rien pris

25 Personne! ⊗

Les garçons ont rencontré quelqu'un?   Non, ils n'ont rencontré personne.
ont vu / ont entendu / ont suivi

ils n'ont vu personne / ils n'ont entendu personne / ils n'ont suivi personne

26 Le patron de Viviane lui demande : ⊗

Quelqu'un a téléphoné?   Non, personne n'a téléphoné.
a appelé / est entré / a payé   personne n'a appelé / personne n'est entré / personne n'a payé
Quelque chose manque?   Non, rien ne manque.

27 L'heure du déjeuner. ⊗

A midi, Viviane sort du magasin. Elle a deux heures pour déjeuner, et souvent elle déjeune avec Isabelle, une amie qui travaille dans le quartier. Quand il fait beau, comme aujourd'hui, les deux amies déjeunent en plein air.

1

Elles ont rendez-vous dans les Jardins des Champs-Elysées. Elles mangent un sandwich et partagent avec les pigeons.

2

Elles parlent de leur travail, de leurs amis communs. Elles rient beaucoup et s'amusent bien.

3

Elles font un tour dans les Jardins et regardent l'exposition de sculptures modernes qui vient de commencer.

4

Elles se promènent dans la rue du Faubourg-Saint-Honoré et elles s'arrêtent devant toutes les vitrines.

A deux heures, les deux amies se dépêchent de retourner à leur travail.

Photo 4: The renowned "rue du Faubourg-Saint-Honoré" is lined with "chic" boutiques (St-Laurent, Lanvin, Cardin, Hermès), beauty salons (Carita, Helena Rubinstein), antique shops, and art galleries. It's also the street where the President of the French Republic has his residence, the Elysée Palace.

Chapitre 13   La Journée de Viviane   137

28   Répondez aux questions.

1. Combien de temps a Viviane pour déjeuner?
2. A quelle heure est-ce qu'elle sort déjeuner?
3. Avec qui est-ce qu'elle déjeune souvent?
4. Que font les deux amies quand il fait beau?
5. Où est-ce qu'elles ont rendez-vous?
6. Qu'est-ce qu'elles mangent?
7. Avec qui est-ce qu'elles partagent?
8. De quoi est-ce qu'elles parlent?
9. Où est-ce qu'elles vont se promener?
10. Qu'est-ce que les deux amies font à deux heures?

29   Et vous?

1. Combien de temps est-ce que vous avez pour déjeuner?
2. Vous déjeunez chez vous ou à l'école?
3. Quand vous déjeunez à l'école, qu'est-ce que vous apportez ou qu'est-ce que vous achetez à manger? Vous partagez avec quelqu'un?
4. Avec qui est-ce que vous déjeunez en général?

30   EXERCICE ORAL ⊗

31   MORE REFLEXIVE VERBS

The following chart includes the reflexive verbs you have seen in **La matinée** and **L'heure du déjeuner.** ⊗

se rendre	to get to (a place)	**s'occuper**	to take care of
s'appeler	to be named	**s'amuser**	to have fun
se trouver	to be (located)	**se promener**	to walk
se changer	to change clothes	**s'arrêter**	to stop
s'assurer	to make sure	**se dépêcher**	to hurry

32   Dans les Jardins des Champs-Elysées. ⊗

Qu'est-ce que tu fais ici?   Je me promène.
Et vous deux? / Et Viviane? / Et Viviane et Isabelle?
Nous nous promenons. / Elle se promène. / Elles se promènent.

33   Rue du Faubourg-Saint-Honoré. ⊗

Tu passes voir Viviane?   Oui, je vais m'arrêter à la boutique.
Et vous deux? / Et Philippe? / Et Bernard et Dominique?
nous allons nous arrêter / il va s'arrêter / ils vont s'arrêter

34   Vous parlez...   ... à un ami :   ... à deux amis : ⊗

Dites-lui / leur...	... à un ami :	... à deux amis :
de s'arrêter.	Arrête-toi!	Arrêtez-vous!
de se dépêcher.	Dépêche-toi!	Dépêchez-vous!
de se changer.	Change-toi!	Changez-vous!
de s'amuser.	Amuse-toi!	Amusez-vous!

35 L'après-midi et le soir. ⊗

L'après-midi de Viviane n'est pas très différent de sa matinée : elle s'occupe des nombreux clients qui entrent dans le magasin.

A six heures et demie, le magasin ferme°, et Viviane reprend le chemin° de Bagneux. C'est l'heure d'affluence°, et après avoir passé° toute la journée debout° dans le magasin, Viviane doit rester debout° pendant tout le trajet de retour°. Quand elle arrive chez elle à sept heures et demie, elle s'écroule° dans un fauteuil°, épuisée°. Elle se repose° un peu, elle se change, et à huit heures elle dîne avec ses parents et son frère. Ils mangent et ils parlent de leur journée en même temps°. Après le dîner, elle aide sa mère à faire la vaisselle°, puis elle dit bonsoir° à ses parents et elle va dans sa chambre.

Maintenant, elle peut vraiment se détendre° : elle met un disque, elle se déshabille°, elle se couche° et elle lit un bon roman°. A dix heures et demie, elle ferme son livre, elle remonte° son réveil, elle éteint° et elle s'endort°... Fin d'une journée bien remplie°! Bonne nuit°, Viviane! Fais de beaux rêves°!

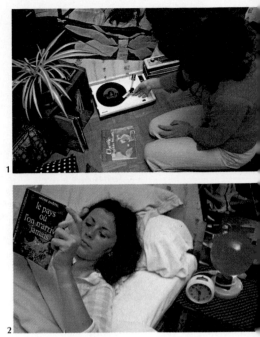

VOCABULAIRE : **ferme** *closes;* **reprend le chemin** *starts back;* **l'heure d'affluence** *rush hour;* **après avoir passé** *after spending;* **debout** *standing;* **doit rester debout** *has to stand;* **trajet de retour** *trip home;* **s'écroule** *collapses;* **un fauteuil** *armchair;* **épuisée** *exhausted;* **se repose** *rests;* **en même temps** *at the same time;* **faire la vaisselle** *to do the dishes;* **dit bonsoir** *says good night;* **se détendre** *to relax;* **se déshabille** *gets undressed;* **se couche** *goes to bed;* **lit un bon roman** *reads a good novel;* **remonte** *sets;* **éteint** *turns out the light;* **s'endort** *goes to sleep;* **bien remplie** *very full;* **Bonne nuit!** *Good night! (used only when you are about to go to sleep);* **Fais de beaux rêves!** *Sweet dreams!*

36 EXERCICE DE COMPREHENSION ⊗ For script, see p. T33.

	0	1	2	3	4	5	6
A							
B	✓						

37 EXERCICE DE CONVERSATION

Racontez une de vos journées. Dites...
- à quelle heure vous vous levez.
- ce que vous faites avant de partir.
- comment vous allez à l'école.
- à quelle heure vous déjeunez et combien de temps vous avez.

- à quelle heure vous rentrez chez vous.
- à quelle heure vous dînez et avec qui.
- ce que vous faites après le dîner.
- à quelle heure vous vous couchez.

38 REDACTION

Racontez une de vos journées, en utilisant l'exercice No 37 comme modèle.

1–14

un bol *bowl*
un bond *a leap*
un cheveu *a hair*
   les cheveux *hair*
le chocolat *hot chocolate*
une dent *tooth*
un réveil *alarm clock*
une tartine *slice of bread*
   (with butter and/or jam on it)
un objet de toilette *toilet article*
   une brosse à cheveux *hairbrush*
   une brosse à dents *toothbrush*
   le dentifrice *toothpaste*
   un gant de toilette *wash mitt*
   un peigne *comb*
   le savon *soap*
   le shampooing *shampoo*

se brosser *to brush*
se faire *to do for oneself*
s'habiller *to get dressed*
se laver *to get washed*
se lever *to get up*
se maquiller *to put on makeup*
se réveiller *to wake up*
utiliser *to use*

se donner un coup de peigne
   to comb one's hair
faire sa toilette *to get washed*
mettre une demi-heure *to take*
   a half hour
perdre courage *to get lazy*

immédiatement *right away*
tôt *early*

beurré, –e *buttered*

me *myself*
te *yourself*
se *himself, herself, itself, oneself*
nous *ourselves*
vous *yourself, yourselves*
se *themselves*

15–26

un autobus *bus*
le métro *subway*
   prendre le métro *to take the subway*
un trajet *trip*

un magasin *store*
un(e) client(e) *customer*
une cravate *necktie*
un patron, une patronne *boss*

la gentillesse *niceness*
une matinée *morning*

manquer *to lack*
   rien ne manque *nothing is*
   missing
s'assurer *to make sure*
se changer *to change one's*
   clothes
s'occuper (de) *to take care of,*
   to wait on
se rendre *to get to*
se trouver *to be located*

sans avoir acheté *without*
   buying

à pied *on foot*
   aller à pied *to walk*
au moins *at least*
en place *in place, neat*
environ *about*
ouvert, –e *open*
tel, telle *so much*
   d'une telle gentillesse
   so nice
ne... personne *nobody,*
   not . . . anybody
ne... rien *nothing, not . . .*
   anything
personne ne... *nobody . . .*
rien ne... *nothing . . .*

27–34

une exposition *exhibition*
un pigeon *pigeon*
un rendez-vous *meeting, date*
une sculpture *sculpture*
une vitrine *store window*

partager *to share*
   nous partageons *we share*
s'amuser *to have fun*

s'appeler *to be named*
   nous nous appelons, vous vous
   appelez, ils/elles s'appellent
s'arrêter *to stop*
se dépêcher *to hurry*
se promener (like **acheter**)
   to walk

commun, –e *mutual*
en plein air *outside*

il fait beau *it's nice (weather)*
qui vient de commencer *which*
   just started
elles rient *they laugh*

35–38

un fauteuil *armchair*
un roman *novel*
la vaisselle *dishes*
   faire la vaisselle *to do the dishes*
l'heure d'affluence *rush hour*
un trajet de retour *trip home*

fermer *to close*
remonter son réveil *to set*
   (his, her) alarm
reprendre (le chemin) *to start*
   back
se coucher *to go to bed*
se déshabiller *to get undressed*
se détendre *to relax*
s'écrouler *to collapse*
s'endormir (like **sortir**) *to go to*
   sleep
se reposer *to rest*
éteint *turns out the light*

debout *standing up*
en même temps *at the same*
   time

épuisé, –e *exhausted*
rempli, –e *full*

Bonne nuit! *Good night!*
bonsoir *good night*
Fais de beaux rêves! *Sweet*
   dreams!
après avoir passé *after spending*
doit rester debout *has to stand*

14
JAZZ
à Luneray

The emblem of the "Canards" is the "duck" design shown below.

1 Les Canards à l'Orange. ⊗

Nos amis de Luneray, Catherine et Philippe Lardan, font partie d'un petit groupe de musiciens amateurs, Les Canards à l'Orange. Les voici, avec leurs instruments :

1

Bernard joue de la clarinette.

Olivier joue du piano. Il joue aussi du saxo.

3

Jean-Marie joue de la contrebasse.

4

Didier joue de la trompette.

5

Philippe joue de la batterie.

6

Catherine joue du banjo.

7

Bruno joue du trombone.

Tous les membres du groupe sont de Luneray, sauf Didier qui vient de Dieppe. Les Canards jouent un peu de tout : du jazz, du rock, de la musique pop. Et ils jouent un peu partout dans la région : à des kermesses, à des bals, à des mariages, etc.

L'été est leur grande saison. Ce sont les vacances, et ils sont libres d'aller et venir entre une kermesse et un mariage, un bal et une surprise-partie… Ça ne leur rapporte pas beaucoup d'argent, mais ils s'amusent bien.

En ce moment, ils jouent surtout à des kermesses. Ils viennent de jouer à celle de Luneray, et dimanche, ils vont jouer à celle d'un village voisin, Ouville.

2 *The Canards à l'Orange play the kind of music that most young French people like to listen to: American music in all its forms (jazz, rock, folk, pop, country, etc.). Of course, many French composers, musicians, and singers are just as important to France's young people as their equivalents are to Americans in the United States. Maxime Le Forestier and Marie-Paule Belle are just two examples of very popular French singer-musicians.*

3 **Répondez aux questions.**

1. De quel groupe font partie Catherine et Philippe Lardan?
2. De quel instrument joue Catherine? Et Philippe?
3. Qui sont les autres Canards? Et de quoi jouent-ils?
4. Qu'est-ce qu'ils jouent comme musique?
5. Où est-ce qu'ils jouent?
6. Pourquoi est-ce que l'été est leur grande saison?
7. Ça leur rapporte beaucoup d'argent? Pourquoi est-ce qu'ils jouent?
8. Qu'est-ce qu'ils font en ce moment?
9. Où est-ce qu'ils viennent de jouer?
10. Où est-ce qu'ils vont jouer, dimanche?

4 **Et vous, de quels instruments est-ce que vous jouez?** ⊗

Du violon?

De la guitare électrique?

Du tuba?

De la flûte?

Du violoncelle?

Du xylophone?

Du tam-tam?

De l'orgue?

De l'harmonica?

5 **EXERCICE ORAL** ⊗

6 **EXERCICE DE CONVERSATION**

Demandez à vos camarades…
1. s'ils jouent d'un instrument.[1]
2. s'ils en jouent bien.
3. s'ils font partie d'un groupe.
4. comment s'appelle ce groupe.
5. qui est dans ce groupe.
6. de quel instrument ils jouent.
7. quels sont les groupes et la musique qu'ils aiment le mieux.

[1] The usual negative responses are: **« Je ne joue d'aucun** (any) **instrument »** and **« Je n'en joue pas »** (one in particular).

7 THE VERB venir

The following chart includes the present-tense forms of the verb **venir,** *to come.* ⊗

Je	**viens**	de la kermesse.	Nous	**venons**	de la kermesse.
Tu	**viens**	de la kermesse?	Vous	**venez**	de la kermesse?
Il	**vient**	de la kermesse.	Ils	**viennent**	de la kermesse.

The past participle of **venir** is **venu : Ils sont venus hier.** Notice that **venir** forms its passé composé with **être.**

8 Didier vient de Dieppe.

1. Et toi, d'où est-ce que tu viens? Moi, je viens de...
   Et vous deux? / Et lui? / Et eux? Nous, nous venons de . . . / Lui, il vient de . . . / Eux, ils viennent de . . .
2. Quand est-ce que tu es venu(e) ici? Je suis venu(e) ici en 19...
   Et lui? / Et vous deux? / Et eux? Il est venu ici en 19 . . . / Nous sommes venu(e)s ici en 19 . . . / Ils sont venus ici en 19 . . .

9 EXPRESSING PAST TIME: venir de + infinitive

Répondez aux questions qui suivent les exemples. ⊗

Bernard est là? Oui, il **vient d'arriver.**
Bernard a déjà joué? Oui, il **vient de jouer.**

Do the sentences on the right refer to present time or past time? What follows **vient** in each of these sentences? What form of the verb follows **de?**

10 Lisez la généralisation suivante.

The English expression *to have just* is expressed in French by a present-tense form of **venir + de** followed by an infinitive.

Il vient d'arriver. *He has just arrived.*
Il vient de jouer. *He just played.*

11 Bernard est le dernier! Il dit aux autres : ⊗

Tiens, tu es déjà là? Oui, je viens d'arriver.
Vous deux aussi? / Et eux aussi? / Et lui aussi?
nous venons d'arriver / ils viennent d'arriver / il vient d'arriver

12 Bernard demande à la mère de Bruno : ⊗

Il est sorti? Oui, il vient de sortir.
Il est parti? / Il a téléphoné? / Il est descendu? / Il a déjeuné?
il vient de partir / il vient de téléphoner / il vient de descendre / il vient de déjeuner

13 EXERCICE ECRIT For answers, see p. T35.

Récrivez les phrases suivantes, en utilisant **venir de + infinitif.**
1. Je suis entré dans un groupe.
2. Nous avons joué dans toute la région.
3. Mon groupe est allé à Luneray.
4. Nous avons rencontré les Canards.
5. J'ai entendu leur dernier disque.

The "Canards" rehearse in an old toolshed which they have set up for that purpose.

14 La répétition. ⊗

OLIVIER	Qu'est-ce qu'on va jouer à la kermesse, dimanche?
BERNARD	Je ne sais pas. Quels morceaux est-ce que vous préférez?
JEAN-MARIE	On peut jouer une de tes compositions...
BERNARD	Je crois qu'il vaut mieux choisir des airs que tout le monde connaît, comme « Oh, when the Saints ».
DIDIER	Moi, je préfère « Petite Fleur ».[1] Ça plaît toujours.
JEAN-MARIE	Qu'est-ce qu'il y a d'autre au programme?
BERNARD	Oh, un chanteur de rock, un illusionniste et un autre groupe.
JEAN-MARIE	Quel genre de groupe?
BERNARD	Je ne sais pas exactement. Un groupe de musique folk, je crois.
DIDIER	Alors, on répète ou quoi?
BERNARD	D'accord, répétons d'abord « Oh, when the Saints ».

15 Répondez aux questions.

1. Pourquoi est-ce que Bernard ne veut pas jouer une de ses compositions?
2. Qu'est-ce qu'il propose? Et Didier?
3. Qu'est-ce qu'il y a d'autre au programme?
4. Qu'est-ce que les Canards vont répéter d'abord?

16 Et vous?

1. Quel genre de musique est-ce que vous préférez?
2. Est-ce que vous aimez chanter? Est-ce que vous chantez bien?
3. Quel est votre chanteur préféré? Votre chanteuse préférée?
4. Quelle est votre chanson préférée? Qui la chante?

17 EXERCICE ORAL ⊗

18 EXERCICE DE COMPREHENSION (MUSICALE!) ⊗ For script, see p. T35.

0		1	2	3	4	5	
batterie	√	saxophone	tuba	banjo	guitare	flûte	
trombone		violoncelle	orgue	piano	trompette	violon	

[1] "Petite Fleur" was composed by the late Sydney Bechet, a New Orleans clarinetist who went to France early in his life, became very popular and famous there, and had a long career.

19

INTERROGATIVE ADJECTIVES
quel, quelle, quels, quelles

Répondez aux questions qui suivent les exemples. ⊗

Quel chanteur est-ce que tu aimes?   **Quels** chanteurs est-ce que tu aimes?
Quelle chanteuse est-ce que tu aimes?   **Quelles** chanteuses est-ce que tu aimes?

In each of the sentences above, what interrogative word precedes the noun? With what does this interrogative word agree?

20   Lisez la généralisation suivante.

1. The interrogative adjectives **quel, quelle, quels, quelles,** *which, what,* agree in gender and number with the noun to which they refer.

	Singular		Plural	
Masc.	**Quel**	chanteur?	**Quels**	chanteurs?
Fem.	**Quelle**	chanteuse?	**Quelles**	chanteuses?

2. With a form of **être,** the order is usually **quel + être +** noun: **Quel est cet air?**

21   Parlons de musique! ⊗

J'aime beaucoup ce groupe.   Quel groupe?
cette chanson / ces disques / ces chanteuses
Quelle chanson? / Quels disques? / Quelles chanteuses?

22

THE VERB préférer

The verb **préférer,** *to prefer,* follows the same pattern as other verbs ending in **-er,** but it shows a change in the vowel sound of the **je, tu, il,** and **ils** forms. ⊗

Je	**préfère**	ça.	Nous	**préférons**	ça.
Tu	**préfères**	ça?	Vous	**préférez**	ça?
Elle / Il	**préfère**	ça.	Elles / Ils	**préfèrent**	ça.

The verbs **répéter,** *to rehearse,* and **espérer,** *to hope,* follow the same pattern as **préférer.**
Practice the verbs with item substitution drills.

23   Qu'est-ce qu'on met comme disques? ⊗

Tu aimes le rock?   Non, je préfère le jazz.
Et Bruno et Didier? / Et Catherine? / Et vous deux?
ils préfèrent / elle préfère / nous préférons

24

MORE ON AGREEMENT OF THE PAST PARTICIPLE

You already know that in the passé composé the past participle of **"avoir"** verbs agrees with a direct-object pronoun which comes before it. This is the case with any direct object which comes before the verb, whether it be a pronoun or a noun.

Tu **l'**as aim**ée, cette chanson?**   **Quelle chanson** est-ce que tu as préfér**ée?**

Photo 1: General view of the "kermesse."
Photo 2: A lottery or raffle where the prizes are live animals, such as geese or hens.

25 EXERCICE ECRIT   For answers, see p. T35.

Ecrivez la question qui se rapporte *(refers)* aux mots soulignés.
Ex. : Il a joué plusieurs morceaux.   Quels morceaux est-ce qu'il a joués?
1. Il a écouté un groupe de jazz.   3. Ils ont répété un air de jazz.
2. Ils ont chanté des chansons françaises.   4. Ils ont choisi plusieurs morceaux.

26 A la kermesse.

27 « Et voici les Canards à l'Orange! » ⊗

Dans quelques minutes, ça va être le tour des Canards à l'Orange. Olivier, le pianiste, n'a pas pu venir; c'est Bernard qui le remplace au piano. Et aujourd'hui, comme souvent d'ailleurs, les Canards ont des « invités » qui jouent avec eux. Philippe a installé son magnétophone et il a branché ses écouteurs. Catherine va faire l'ingénieur du son et va enregistrer le concert.

BERNARD   Tu as vérifié la sono?
PHILIPPE   Oui, pourquoi, le micro ne marche pas?
BERNARD   Si, si. Mais tourne un peu ce haut-parleur vers l'estrade.
PHILIPPE   Lequel? Celui-là?
BERNARD   Non, celui de droite. Voilà. Tu as installé ton magnéto?
PHILIPPE   Oui. J'ai apporté deux bandes. Laquelle est-ce qu'on met?
BERNARD   Mettons celle qui est la plus longue. C'est plus sûr. Attention, c'est à nous! Allons-y!

« Et maintenant, Mesdames, Mesdemoiselles, Messieurs, j'ai le plaisir de vous présenter, les Canards à l'Orange!! On les applaudit bien fort! »

28 Répondez aux questions.

1. Où sont les Canards à l'Orange?
2. Qui remplace Olivier au piano?
3. Qui joue avec le groupe?
4. Qu'est-ce que Philippe a fait?
5. Qu'est-ce que Catherine va faire?
6. Qu'est-ce que Philippe a vérifié?
7. Combien de bandes est-ce qu'il a apportées? Laquelle est-ce qu'il va mettre?
8. Que font les gens quand les Canards montent sur l'estrade?

29 Et vous?

1. Est-ce que vous avez un magnétophone?
2. Qu'est-ce que vous enregistrez comme musique?
3. Qu'est-ce que vous préférez, les cassettes ou les disques?
4. A quel genre de concert est-ce que vous allez?

30 EXERCICE ORAL ⊗

31 Comment se servir d'un magnétophone. ⊗

Avant l'enregistrement :
   Branchez le magnétophone; mettez la bande; branchez le micro.
   Faites un essai : appuyez sur le bouton d'enregistrement; parlez; arrêtez; rembobinez;
   appuyez sur le bouton d'écoute.
   Vérifiez le volume : s'il est trop fort, baissez; s'il est trop bas, mettez plus fort.

Après l'enregistrement :
   Rembobinez; retirez la bande; débranchez le micro; débranchez le magnétophone.

32 EXERCICE DE CONVERSATION

1. Un(e) camarade se sert du magnétophone pour la première fois. Dites-lui comment faire :
   Branche le magnétophone…
2. Vous vérifiez si votre camarade a bien suivi vos instructions :
   Tu as branché le magnétophone?…

33

THE INTERROGATIVE PRONOUNS
lequel, laquelle, lesquels, lesquelles

Répondez aux questions qui suivent les exemples. ⊗

J'ai entendu **un groupe formidable!**	Ah oui? **Lequel?**
J'ai entendu **une chanteuse formidable!**	Ah oui? **Laquelle?**
J'ai entendu **des disques formidables!**	Ah oui? **Lesquels?**
J'ai entendu **des chansons formidables!**	Ah oui? **Lesquelles?**

In the responses on the right, what are the question words? What does each stand for? Notice that **lequel** is a combination of the article **le** and the masculine singular interrogative adjective **quel.** What is **laquelle** composed of? And the plural forms?

34 Lisez la généralisation suivante.

The interrogative pronouns **lequel, laquelle, lesquels, lesquelles,** *which one(s),* agree in gender and number with the noun they stand for.

Singular	Masc.	**Quel chanteur**	préfères-tu?	**Lequel**	préfères-tu?
	Fem.	**Quelle chanteuse**	préfères-tu?	**Laquelle**	préfères-tu?
Plural	Masc.	**Quels chanteurs**	préfères-tu?	**Lesquels**	préfères-tu?
	Fem.	**Quelles chanteuses**	préfères-tu?	**Lesquelles**	préfères-tu?

35 **Philippe n'a pas tout vérifié.** ☺

Il y a un micro qui ne marche pas!   Lequel?
un haut-parleur / deux haut-parleurs / une guitare électrique
Lequel? / Lesquels? / Laquelle?

36 **Dans le magasin « Etoile Musique ».** ☺

C'est combien, ce magnétophone?   Lequel?
cette radio / ce micro / ces cassettes / ces écouteurs
Laquelle? / Lequel? / Lesquelles? / Lesquels?

37

THE DEMONSTRATIVE PRONOUNS
celui, celle, ceux, celles

Répondez aux questions qui suivent les exemples. ☺

Quel banjo est-ce qu'on prend?	**Celui** de Catherine.
Quelle guitare est-ce qu'on prend?	**Celle** de Bernard.
Quels haut-parleurs est-ce qu'on prend?	**Ceux** de Philippe.
Quelles cassettes est-ce qu'on prend?	**Celles** de Didier.

In each of the responses on the right, what does the pronoun stand for?

> You may want to add a step to the discovery: C'est celui qui est sur la table? Non, c'est celui-là. Etc. And ask what follows the pronouns celui / celle / ceux / celles when used without de or qui / que.

38 **Lisez la généralisation suivante.**

The demonstrative pronouns **celui, celle, ceux, celles,** *this/that one, the one(s), these, those,* agree in gender and number with the noun they stand for. When they appear alone, **-là** follows.

	Singular		Plural	
Masc.	**Quel banjo?**	**Celui-là?**	**Quels banjos?**	**Ceux-là?**
Fem.	**Quelle guitare?**	**Celle-là?**	**Quelles guitares?**	**Celles-là?**

39 **Préparons tout pour le concert.** ☺

Laquelle de ces bandes est-ce que tu veux?   Celle-là.
lequel de ces magnétophones / laquelle de ces clarinettes / lesquels de ces écouteurs
Celui-là. / Celle-là. / Ceux-là.

40 **Chez un ami.** ☺

C'est à toi, cette cassette?   Laquelle? Celle-là?
cette trompette / ces écouteurs / ce disque / ces bandes
Laquelle? Celle-là? / Lesquels? Ceux-là? / Lequel? Celui-là? / Lesquelles? Celles-là?

41 **EXERCICE DE CONVERSATION**

Vous allez donner un concert dans votre école. Vous décidez quels morceaux vous allez jouer, qui va les jouer, quels instruments vous allez utiliser, etc.

42 **REDACTION**

Vous faites partie d'un groupe de musiciens amateurs. Votre groupe vient de donner un concert. Décrivez ce que vous avez fait, en utilisant l'exercice No 41 comme modèle.

Variation: Vous venez d'aller à un concert donné par votre groupe préféré. Décrivez ce qu'ils ont fait.

43 Chanson : L'Orchestre.

ICI, DANS CETTE GRANDE SALLE

I - ci, dans cett' grand' sal - le Il y-a un orchestr'
I - ci, dans cett' grand' sal - le On joue du piano Pi - a, pi - a,
pi - a - no, Pi - a, pi - a, pi - a - no, Pi - a, pi - a, pi - a - no, Pi - a, pi - a - no!

2. ... du Violon. Vio, vio, violon.   4. ... des Timbales. Doumba doumbaba.
3. ... d'la Trompette. Tara tara tatata.   5. ... du Tambour. Rata rata rataplan.

44 WORD LIST

1–13 **Les Canards à l'Orange** *"Ducks in Orange Sauce"*
un instrument *instrument*
  un banjo *banjo*
  une batterie *drums*
  une clarinette *clarinet*
  une contrebasse *double bass*
  une flûte *flute*
  une guitare *guitar*
  un harmonica *harmonica*
  un orgue *organ*
  un piano *piano*
  un saxo(phone) *saxophone*
  un tam-tam *drums*
  un trombone *trombone*
  une trompette *trumpet*

  un tuba *tuba*
  un violon *violin*
  un violoncelle *cello*
  un xylophone *xylophone*
un groupe *group*
  un membre *member*
  un(e) musicien (-ienne) *musician*
la musique *music*
  le jazz *jazz*
  la musique pop *pop music*
  le rock *rock*
une région *area*
un bal *dance*
une kermesse *fair*
un mariage *wedding*

l'été (m.) *summer*
une saison *season*
les vacances (f.) *vacation*

jouer de *to play (an instrument)*
rapporter *to bring in*
venir *to come*
venir de *to have just*

électrique *electric*
voisin, –e *neighbor*

celle *the one*
aller et venir *to come and go*
de quels instruments *which instruments*

14–25 **la musique** *music*
  un air *tune*
  un(e) chanteur (-euse) *singer*
  une composition *composition*
  un genre *a kind*
  un morceau *piece, number*
  des morceaux *pieces*
  la musique folk *folk music*
un illusionniste *magician*
un programme *program*
une répétition *rehearsal*

enregistrer *to record*
espérer *to hope*
préférer *to prefer*
répéter *to rehearse*

je crois *I think*

préféré, –e *favorite*
quel, quelle *which, what*
quels, quelles *which, what*

exactement *exactly*
plus fort *louder*
plus sûr *safer*

Allons-y! *Come on, let's go!*
Attention! *Watch out!*
Ça plaît toujours. *That always goes over.*
il vaut mieux *it's better to*
Qu'est-ce qu'il y a d'autre? *What else is there?*

26–43 **un concert** *concert*
  une estrade *platform*
  un(e) invité(e) *guest*
  le tour *turn*
  un(e) pianiste *pianist*
  le son *sound*
  une bande *tape*
  un bouton d'écoute *playback button*
  un bouton d'enregistrement *record button*
  un écouteur *earphone*
  un enregistrement *recording*
  un essai *test*
  un *haut-parleur *loudspeaker*
  un magnéto(phone) *tape recorder*
  un micro(phone) *microphone*
  la sono(risation) *sound*
  le volume *volume*

applaudir (like **choisir**) *to clap*
appuyer *to press*
  j'appuie, tu appuies, il appuie, ils appuient
arrêter *to stop*
baisser *to lower*
brancher *to plug in*
débrancher *to unplug*
installer *to set up*
rembobiner *to rewind*
remplacer *to replace*
  nous remplaçons *we replace*
retirer *to take off*
se servir (de) *to make use (of)*
mettre la bande *put the tape on*
il n'a pas pu *he couldn't*

d'ailleurs *as a matter of fact*
bas *low, soft*
fort *loud*
vers *toward*
quelques *a few, some*
la plus longue, le plus long *the longest*
lequel, laquelle *which one(s)*
lesquels, lesquelles *which one(s)*
celui (–là), celle (–là) *that one, this one, the one*
ceux (–là), celles (–là) *these, those, the ones*
J'ai le plaisir de vous présenter... *I am pleased to present to you . . .*
On les applaudit bien fort. *Let's give them a nice hand.*
va faire l'ingénieur du son *is going to be the sound engineer*

This map, showing part of the Laurentian Mountains north of Montreal, will be used in connection with the game "Le jeu des stations," No. 27, p. 158.

15
SKI AU QUEBEC

MONT TREMBLANT

Lac Manitou

Ivry

Rivière du Nord

89

86

Ste-Agathe
H Le Chalet Suisse

80

AUTOROUTE DES LAURENTIDES

76

St-Adolphe d'Howard
H La Légende

Ste-Lucie
A Les Lacs
A Ste-Lucie

Val David
M Les Pays d'en haut

Val Morin
H Belle-Neige

Ste-Marguerite
A Alpine

Estérel
H L'Estérel

370

69

Ste-Adèle
H Montclair
H La Liberté

Lac l'Achigan

67

M Le Totem
M Le Nomade

60

Piedmont

St-Hippolyte
H La Source

Morin Heights
H Bellevue

Point out the mixture of French, English and Indian names, which reflects the history of Quebec Province.

St-Sauveur
H Mont Habitant
M Les Pentes
A Les Monts

58

55

Shawbridge
H Mocassin

MONTRÉAL

N

LÉGENDE
A une auberge
H un hôtel
M un motel

329

Lafontaine
M Rose

45

St-Colomban

117

364

1 Le ski avant tout! ⊗

1

3

Nous sommes au Québec, dans la banlieue de Montréal. C'est l'hiver. C'est la saison préférée de nos amies canadiennes, Denise et Louise Goulet : c'est la saison du ski, et elles adorent ce sport. Tous les samedis, sauf quand il fait trop mauvais, leur père les emmène faire du ski à Saint-Sauveur. C'est une station de ski dans les Laurentides, les montagnes au nord de Montréal. Avant de partir, M. Goulet taquine un peu ses filles.

M. GOULET   Il ne fait pas très beau aujourd'hui... Vous voulez quand même aller à Saint-Sauveur?

LOUISE   Bien sûr, Papa! D'après la météo, la neige est parfaite aujourd'hui!

DENISE   Et il ne fait pas si froid que ça... Je viens de regarder le thermomètre : il fait moins cinq.[1]

M. GOULET   Alors, dans ces conditions, on y va!

2 Répondez aux questions.

1. Où habitent Denise et Louise?
2. C'est quelle saison?
3. Pourquoi est-ce que l'hiver est la saison préférée des sœurs Goulet?
4. Où est-ce qu'elles vont faire du ski?
5. Qu'est-ce que c'est, les Laurentides?
6. Qui emmène Denise et Louise à Saint-Sauveur?
7. Quand est-ce que Denise et Louise y vont?
8. Qu'est-ce que leur père fait avant de partir?
9. D'après la météo, comment est la neige?
10. D'après Denise, est-ce qu'il fait froid aujourd'hui? Il fait combien?

3 EXERCICE ORAL ⊗

[1] This refers to the Celsius system of measuring temperature, not to the Fahrenheit. −5° (**moins cinq degrés**) Celsius corresponds to 23° Fahrenheit. The word **degrés** is usually omitted in everyday conversation.

4 Quelle saison est-ce? Quel temps fait-il?

C'est l'hiver.
En hiver :
il fait froid et il
neige.

C'est le printemps.
Au printemps :
il fait bon et il
fait frais.

C'est l'été.
En été :
il y a du soleil et
il fait chaud.

C'est l'automne.
En automne :
il pleut et il fait
du vent.

5 Ça fait combien en Fahrenheit?

$$\frac{9}{5}C + 32 = F \qquad \text{Ex.}^1 : \left(\frac{9}{5} \times 20°C\right) + 32 = 68°F$$

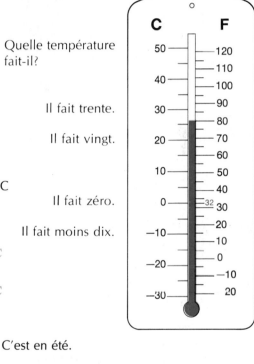

Quelle température
fait-il?

6 A vous maintenant!

1. 14°C... 57°F   3. 25°C... 77°F   5. −2°C... 29°F
2. 17°C... 62°F   4. 31°C... 88°F   6. −15°C... 5°F

Il fait trente.

Il fait vingt.

7 Ça fait combien en Celsius?

$$(F - 32) \times \frac{5}{9} = C \qquad \text{Ex.}^2 : (95°F - 32) \times \frac{5}{9} = 35°C$$

Il fait zéro.

Il fait moins dix.

8 A vous maintenant!

1. 41°F... 5°C   3. 77°F... 25°C   5. 68°F... 20°C
2. 104°F... 40°C   4. −20°F... −29°C   6. 32°F... 0°C

9 En quelle saison est-ce?

Le mois de juillet?   C'est en été.
de janvier / d'août / de mai / d'octobre
C'est en hiver. / C'est en été. / C'est au printemps. / C'est en automne.

10 Et vous?

1. Qu'est-ce que vous faites comme sports en hiver?
2. Et au printemps? En été? En automne?
3. Quelle saison est-ce que vous aimez le mieux? Pourquoi?
4. Quel temps fait-il en hiver là où vous habitez? Quelle température fait-il?
5. Et au printemps? Et en été? Et en automne?
6. Quel temps fait-il aujourd'hui? Quelle température fait-il?

¹ 20°C multiplié par 9 égale (*equals*) 180, divisé par 5 égale 36; plus 32 égalent 68°F.
² 95°F moins 32 égale 63; 63 multiplié par 5 égale 315; divise par 9 égale 35°C.

11 Sur les pistes. ⊗

Arrivées à Saint-Sauveur, Louise et Denise achètent leurs billets et vont au chalet pour se préparer. Elles ont leurs propres skis, chaussures et bâtons. Heureusement, car il faut faire la queue longtemps quand on loue son équipement.

LOUISE   Brr… J'ai toujours froid sur le télésiège. Pas toi?

DENISE   Oh, une fois sur les pistes, on se réchauffe vite.

LOUISE   Quelle piste est-ce que tu veux prendre, « novice » ou « intermédiaire »?

DENISE   « Intermédiaire » bien sûr! Je ne suis plus une novice!

En haut des pistes, les deux filles s'élancent… Pour Louise, tout va bien. Mais Denise, elle, est partie trop vite et elle est tombée. Louise remonte la pente pour voir si sa sœur a besoin d'aide.

LOUISE   Tu t'es fait mal?

DENISE   Oui, à la jambe… Aïe! J'espère que je ne me suis pas cassé la jambe!

LOUISE   Attends, je vais t'aider à te relever.

12 Répondez aux questions.

1. Que font Louise et Denise après leur arrivée à Saint-Sauveur?
2. Est-ce qu'elles louent leur équipement? Pourquoi?
3. Qu'est-ce qu'elles prennent pour monter en haut des pistes?
4. Quelle piste est-ce que Denise veut prendre? Pourquoi?
5. Qu'est-ce qu'elles font, une fois arrivées en haut des pistes?
6. Comment est-ce que les deux filles descendent la pente?
7. Pourquoi est-ce que Louise remonte la pente?
8. Est-ce que Denise s'est fait mal? Où ça?
9. Qu'est-ce que Louise va faire?

13 EXERCICE ORAL ⊗

The "équipement" is of course just as suitable for "un bon skieur."

14 L'équipement d'une bonne skieuse. ⊗

1   un bonnet

2   des lunettes

3   un anorak

4   des gants

5   un pantalon de ski

6   des chaussures de ski

7   des skis

8   des bâtons

15 Et vous?

1. Vous faites du ski?
2. Dans quelle station est-ce que vous allez? C'est loin de chez vous?
3. Il faut faire la queue pour prendre les télésièges? Pendant combien de temps?
4. Avec qui est-ce que vous allez faire du ski?
5. Vous avez votre propre équipement ou vous le louez?
6. Vous êtes un bon skieur (une bonne skieuse)?
7. Qu'est-ce que vous mettez comme vêtements pour faire du ski?
8. Est-ce que vous avez un anorak? Il est de quelle couleur?

16 Chaîne de mots.

ELÈVE 1 : Quand je vais faire du ski, j'emporte des skis.
ELÈVE 2 : Quand je vais faire du ski, j'emporte des skis et des bâtons.
ELÈVE 3 : Quand je vais faire du ski, j'emporte des skis, des bâtons et un anorak.
ELÈVE 4 : Quand...

17 Quelle température fait-il? ⊗

Il fait −3°...   Voilà pourquoi j'ai froid!
Il fait −12°...   Voilà pourquoi j'ai très froid!
Il fait 25°...   Voilà pourquoi j'ai chaud!
Il fait 37°...   Voilà pourquoi j'ai très chaud!

EXPRESSING PAST TIME
REFLEXIVE CONSTRUCTIONS

Répondez aux questions qui suivent les exemples. ⊗

> **Louise s'est réchauffée.**　　Louise **s'est réchauffé** les mains.
> **M. Goulet s'est réchauffé.**　　M. Goulet **s'est réchauffé** les mains.

Do reflexive verbs form the passé composé with **avoir** or **être**? In the sentences on the left, is the reflexive pronoun **se** a direct or an indirect object? Does the past participle show agreement? In the sentences on the right, is **se** a direct or an indirect object? Does the past participle show any agreement?

19 **Lisez la généralisation suivante.**

1. Reflexive pronouns can either be direct or indirect objects.

	D.O.			I.O.	
M. Goulet	**s'**	est réchauffé.	M. Goulet	**s'**	est réchauffé **les mains.**
M. Goulet	**s'**	est lavé.	M. Goulet	**s'**	est lavé **les mains.**

2. The passé composé of reflexive verbs is always formed with **être,** but agreement of the past participle follows the pattern used when **avoir** is the auxiliary. Therefore, if the reflexive pronoun is the direct object of the verb, the past participle agrees with it. If the reflexive pronoun is the indirect object, there is no agreement.

	D.O.		Agreement			I.O.		No Agreement	
Papa	**l'**	a	**relevée**	(Louise).	Louise	**lui**	a	**acheté**	du chocolat.
Denise	**s'**	est	**relevée**	seule.	Denise	**s'**	est	**acheté**	du chocolat.

20 **Denise et Louise sont allées faire du ski.** ⊗

A quelle heure est-ce qu'elles se sont levées?　　Elles se sont levées à 6 h.
Et vous, M. Goulet? / Et vous, Mme Goulet? / Et vous, les garçons? / Et vos parents?

Je me suis levé . . . / Je me suis levée . . . / Nous nous sommes levés . . . / Ils se sont levés . . .

21 **Denise s'est fait mal à la main.** ⊗

Louise l'a aidée à se lever?　　　　　　　　Non, elle s'est levée toute seule.
à se laver les mains / à se changer / à se déshabiller / à se faire du chocolat

elle s'est lavé les mains / elle s'est changée / elle s'est déshabillée / elle s'est fait du chocolat

22 **EXERCICE ECRIT**

Complétez chaque phrase selon (*according to*) le modèle.
Denise et Louise se réveillent tous les samedis à 6 h, mais hier elles <u>se sont réveillées</u> à 7 h.
1. Elles se lèvent toujours tout de suite, mais hier elles _____ une heure après. se sont levées
2. Leur père se lave toujours en dix minutes, mais hier il _____ en une demi-heure. s'est lavé
3. Elles se préparent toujours du chocolat, mais hier elles _____ du café. se sont préparé
4. En général, les Goulet se couchent tôt le samedi, mais hier ils _____ tard. se sont couchés

23 Au chalet. ⊗

Denise a trop mal à la jambe pour continuer à skier. Elle s'appuie sur le bras de Louise, et elle descend au chalet pour se reposer. Là, autour du feu de bois, les deux sœurs retrouvent leurs amis, Raymond et Jocelyne. Ils boivent un chocolat chaud ensemble, et Louise leur dit ce qui est arrivé à Denise. Jocelyne trouve que Denise devrait aller à l'infirmerie, mais Denise ne veut pas. Raymond est allé chercher Paul Dufresne, un de ses amis qui est moniteur.

1

2

PAUL   Où est-ce que tu as mal?
DENISE Euh… au genou.
PAUL   Auquel? A celui-là?
DENISE Oui.
PAUL   Marche un peu pour voir…
        Ça va?
DENISE Ça va mieux.
PAUL   Alors, tu vois, ce n'est
        pas grave!

24 Répondez aux questions.

1. Où est-ce que les deux sœurs vont se reposer?
2. Qui est-ce qu'elles retrouvent là-bas?
3. Que font les quatre amis ensemble?
4. Que trouve Jocelyne?
5. Est-ce que Denise veut y aller?
6. Qui est-ce que Raymond est allé chercher?
7. Où est-ce que Denise a mal?
8. Qu'est-ce que le moniteur lui dit de faire?
9. D'après lui, est-ce que c'est grave?

25 EXERCICE ORAL ⊗

26 Et vous?

1. Est-ce que vous skiez bien?
2. Est-ce que vous tombez souvent?
3. Est-ce que vous vous êtes déjà fait très mal?
4. Est-ce que quelqu'un vous a aidé à vous relever? Qui?
5. Où est-ce que vous êtes allé(e), au chalet, à l'infirmerie?
6. Où est-ce que vous allez vous reposer quand vous êtes fatigué(e) de faire du ski?
7. Qu'est-ce que vous y faites?

27   Le jeu des stations. ⊗

Vous êtes allé(e) faire du ski. Vous dites à vos camarades quel chemin vous prenez. Ils doivent° suivre sur la carte° p. 151 et vous dire où vous allez. Par exemple :

VOUS	Je suis l'autoroute° des Laurentides jusqu'à la sortie No 60. Je prends la route No 364. J'arrive à une station. Laquelle?
VOTRE CAMARADE	St-Sauveur.
VOUS	Il y a un hôtel / un motel / une auberge°. Lequel / lequel / laquelle?
VOTRE CAMARADE	Le Mont Habitant / le Motel des Pentes / l'Auberge des Monts.

VOCABULAIRE : **doivent** *have to;* **la carte** *map;* **une autoroute** *highway;* **une auberge** *inn.*

28   MORE ON INTERROGATIVE PRONOUNS
Contractions with à and de

The interrogative pronouns **lequel, lesquels,** and **lesquelles** contract with the prepositions **à** and **de** in the same way as the articles **le** and **les.** ⊗

Contraction					
à + lequel	**Auquel**	as-tu parlé?	de + lequel	**Duquel**	as-tu parlé?
à + lesquels	**Auxquels**	as-tu parlé?	de + lesquels	**Desquels**	as-tu parlé?
à + lesquelles	**Auxquelles**	as-tu parlé?	de + lesquelles	**Desquelles**	as-tu parlé?
No Contraction					
à + laquelle	**A laquelle**	as-tu parlé?	de + laquelle	**De laquelle**	as-tu parlé?

29   A qui est-ce que Raymond a parlé? ⊗

Raymond a parlé à un moniteur.	Auquel est-ce qu'il a parlé?
Raymond a parlé à une monitrice.	A laquelle est-ce qu'il a parlé?
Raymond a parlé à des moniteurs.	Auxquels est-ce qu'il a parlé?
Raymond a parlé à des monitrices.	Auxquelles est-ce qu'il a parlé?

30   Louise a perdu son bonnet. ⊗

Je l'ai donné à un de ses amis.	Auquel?
Je l'ai donné à une de ses amies.	A laquelle?
Je l'ai donné à un de ses camarades.	Auquel?
Je l'ai donné à une de ses camarades.	A laquelle?
Je l'ai donné à deux de ses amis.	Auxquels?
Je l'ai donné à deux de ses amies.	Auxquelles?

31   Autour d'un feu de bois. ⊗

Ils parlent d'une station de ski.	De laquelle?
Ils parlent d'un chalet.	Duquel?
Ils parlent des moniteurs.	Desquels?
Ils parlent des monitrices.	Desquelles?

32 EXERCICE DE COMPREHENSION ⊗ For script, see T36.

	0	1	2	3	4	5	6
A							
B	✓						
C							

33 EXERCICE DE CONVERSATION

Racontez une journée que vous avez passée à faire du ski. Dites…
1. à quelle station vous êtes allé(e).
2. quand, avec qui, comment.
3. ce que vous avez mis comme vêtements.
4. si vous avez loué votre équipement.
5. si vous avez fait la queue.
6. quelle piste vous avez choisie.
7. si vous avez bien skié ou si vous êtes tombé(e).
8. si vous êtes allé(e) au chalet après le ski et ce que vous y avez fait.

34 REDACTION

Décrivez une journée sur les pistes de ski. Utilisez l'exercice No 33 comme modèle.

35 Skier. ⊗

Choisissez les pistes les plus faciles°. Prenez des leçons avec un moniteur.
Soyez solidaire°. Arrêtez-vous pour porter secours° à un skieur en difficulté.
Couchez-vous de bonne heure°. La fatigue° peut causer une jambe cassée le lendemain.
Oubliez un peu le ski. Il y a d'autres choses à faire en montagne : marche°, raquettes°, luge°, patinage°.
Faites-vous des amis. Les sports d'hiver, c'est l'occasion de rencontrer des gens, de se faire de nouveaux amis. C'est l'occasion de se mêler° à des activités collectives, de bien s'entendre° avec les autres.

N'essayez pas d'être élégant. Habillez-vous chaudement°. Mettez collants°, bonnet, mouffles° ou gants, grosses chaussettes°, pantalon et anorak chauds.
Ne sous-estimez° pas les consignes de sécurité°. Si une piste est fermée, c'est qu'il y a une raison°.
Ne jouez pas les guides. Ne vous lancez pas seul dans un itinéraire°, même si vous le connaissez. Seuls les professionnels de la montagne peuvent sentir° le danger.
Ne skiez pas pour la galerie°. Ne slalomez° pas entre les débutants°. Ne vous arrêtez pas pile° devant les files d'attente°.

VOCABULAIRE : **les plus faciles** the easiest; **soyez solidaire** be of help to others; **porter secours** to bring help; **de bonne heure** early; **la fatigue** being tired; **marche** hiking; **raquettes** snow-shoeing; **luge** sledding; **patinage** ice-skating; **se mêler** to get involved; **s'entendre** to get along with; **chaudement** warmly; **collants** long underwear; **mouffles** mittens; **grosses chaussettes** heavy socks; **sous-estimez** underestimate; **consignes de sécurité** safety signs; **raison** reason; **itinéraire** route; **sentir** sense; **pour la galerie** to show off; **slalomez** ski in and out; **débutants** beginners; **ne vous arrêtez pas pile** don't stop short; **files d'attente** waiting lines.

The sign at the bottom of the page can be seen along the road by tourists who leave St-Sauveur. The other side of the sign (facing those who enter) reads "Bienvenue" (Welcome). "Paroisse" means parish, used here as another designation for the community. The full name of this ski resort is St-Sauveur-des-Monts.

36

WORD LIST

1–10

le ski *skiing*
les Laurentides *Laurentian Mountains*
une montagne *mountain*
une station de ski *ski area or resort*

le temps *weather*
Quel temps fait-il? *What's the weather like?*
un degré *degree*
la météo *weather report*
la neige *snow*
la température *temperature*
Quelle température fait-il? *What's the temperature?*
le thermomètre *thermometer*

le Québec *Quebec (Province)*
au Québec *in Quebec*

une saison *season*
Quelle saison est-ce? *What season is it?*
l'automne (m.) *fall*
en automne *in the fall*
l'été (m.) *summer*
en été *in the summer*
l'hiver (m.) *winter*
en hiver *in the winter*
le printemps *spring*
au printemps *in the spring*

adorer *to like very much*
taquiner *to tease*

canadien, –ienne *Canadian*
parfait, –e *perfect*

au nord (de) *north (of)*
avant tout *before anything*
d'après *according to*
On y va! *Let's go!*
quand même *anyway*

il fait beau *the weather is nice*
il fait bon *it's nice*
il fait chaud *it's hot*
il fait cinq *it's five degrees*
il fait frais *it's cool*
il fait froid *it's cold*
il fait mauvais *the weather is bad*
il fait du vent *it's windy*
il neige *it's snowing*
il va neiger *it's going to snow*
il pleut *it's raining*
il va pleuvoir *it's going to rain*
il y a de la neige *there's snow*
il y a du soleil *it's sunny*

il fait (cinq) *it is (five) degrees*
moins (cinq) *(five) degrees below*
zéro *zero*

11–22

un chalet *chalet*
une pente *slope*
une piste *ski trail*
une queue *line*
un(e) skieur (-euse) *skier*
un télésiège *chairlift*

une jambe *leg*

l'équipement (m.) *equipment*
un anorak *ski jacket*
un bâton *ski pole*
un bonnet *ski cap*
une chaussure de ski *ski boot*
un gant *glove*
des lunettes (f.) *goggles*
un pantalon de ski *ski pants*
un ski *ski*

aider à *to help*
se casser *to break*
s'élancer *to push off*
se faire mal (à) *to hurt*
Tu t'es fait mal? *Did you hurt yourself?*
louer *to rent*
se préparer *to get ready*
se réchauffer *to warm up*
se relever (like **acheter**) *to get up again*
tomber *to fall*

avoir froid *to be cold*
faire la queue *to stand in line*

intermédiaire *intermediate*
novice *beginning*
propre *one's own*

heureusement *luckily*
vite *fast*

23–35

un bras *arm*
un feu de bois *wood fire*
un genou *knee*
des genoux *knees*
une infirmerie *infirmary*
un moniteur, une monitrice *(ski) instructor*

s'appuyer *to lean on*
arriver (à) *to happen (to)*
avoir mal (à) *to hurt*
Elle a mal à la jambe. *Her leg hurts.*
devrait aller *should go*
skier *to ski*

autour de *around*

16

UN VILLAGE
DANS LES PYRÉNÉES

Souvenirs d'Ore

1 Ore. ⊗

Monique Fort habite à Paris depuis cinq ans. Avant, elle et ses parents habitaient à Ore, un petit village dans les Pyrénées. Monique a encore des cousins là-bas : Louis Fort, sa femme Georgette et leurs enfants Angel, Jean-François et Alain.

Note that the basic text of No. 1 continues on the facing page, below the message side of the postcard.

2

Ore is a small village of about 250 people who are mostly farmers. They grow their own vegetables and fruit and keep farm animals. Most of what they eat comes from their own farms. There are no stores in the village. Every day the butcher's and the baker's trucks make a stop at Ore. For more important purchases, the people of Ore go to Luchon or other nearby towns.

3 Répondez aux questions.

1. Où habite Monique maintenant? Depuis combien de temps?
2. Où est-ce qu'elle et ses parents habitaient avant?
3. Où se trouve Ore?
4. Qui est-ce qui habite encore à Ore, dans la famille de Monique?
5. Qu'est-ce que Louis et Georgette Fort ont fait cet été?
6. Pourquoi est-ce que les cousins de Monique sont très occupés?
7. Comment est la ferme maintenant?
8. Qu'est-ce que Monique a planté jadis? Qu'est-ce qu'il est devenu?

Les Pyrénées et les champs de blé
La Vieille Église
La Grand-rue
Les Bois, les prés et les moutons

Mes parents chéris,

Juste un petit mot pour vous dire qu'ici tout va bien. Les cousins vous envoient leur bonjour. Ils sont très occupés en ce moment: ils font la moisson. J'ai à peine reconnu la ferme tant elle a changé: il y a maintenant une nouvelle étable sous le grenier à foin et un nouveau hangar qui abrite un beau tracteur rouge. Il y a aussi une belle grange à la place du vieux mur. Le noyer que j'ai planté jadis est devenu un très bel arbre. Maintenant je vous quitte. Je vous écrirai une longue lettre bientôt. Je vous embrasse. Monique

Monsieur et Madame Michel Fort

13, rue de la Plaine

75020 Paris

Cet été, Louis et Georgette Fort ont invité Monique à passer ses vacances dans leur ferme. C'est la première fois que Monique retourne à Ore. Peu après son arrivée, elle écrit à ses parents pour leur donner de ses nouvelles. Voilà sa carte postale.

4 **Et vous?**

Décrivez une ferme où vous êtes allé(e). Dites…
1. quand vous y êtes allé(e) la dernière fois.
2. qui y habite.
3. si vous y allez souvent.
4. si c'est une grande ou une petite ferme.
5. s'il y a un grenier à foin, une grange, un hangar.
6. s'il y a un tracteur, et de quelle couleur il est.
7. dans quel village se trouve cette ferme.
8. si ce village est loin de chez vous.
9. s'il y a une église, une grand-rue, etc.
10. s'il y a des bois, des champs, des prés.
11. si vous allez retourner dans cette ferme bientôt.

5 **EXERCICE ORAL** ⊗

6   THE ADJECTIVES beau, nouveau, vieux

1. The adjectives **beau, nouveau,** and **vieux** usually precede the noun they refer to. ⊗

2. The following chart includes all the forms of these adjectives.

	Before consonant sound		Before vowel sound	
	Singular	Plural	Singular	Plural
M	un **beau** mur	de **beaux** murs	un **bel** arbre	de **beaux** arbres
	un **nouveau** mur	de **nouveaux** murs	un **nouvel** arbre	de **nouveaux** arbres
	un **vieux** mur	de **vieux** murs	un **vieil** arbre	de **vieux** arbres
F	une **belle** rue	de **belles** rues	une **belle** étable	de **belles** étables
	une **nouvelle** rue	de **nouvelles** rues	une **nouvelle** étable	de **nouvelles** étables
	une **vieille** rue	de **vieilles** rues	une **vieille** étable	de **vieilles** étables

3. Notice the special forms **bel, nouvel,** and **vieil,** which are used before a masculine singular noun beginning with a vowel sound. Liaison is obligatory when one of the plural adjectives is followed by a noun beginning with a vowel sound.

Notice that **de** instead of **des** is used before an adjective preceding a plural noun.

7   Les parents de Monique lui parlent au téléphone : ⊗

Il y a une grange, maintenant?   Oui, une belle grange.
Ils ont acheté un tracteur?   Oui, un beau tracteur.
Ils ont planté un arbre?   Oui, un bel arbre.
Il y a un hangar, maintenant?   Oui, un beau hangar.

8   Monique dit à ses cousins : ⊗

Je n'ai jamais vu ce tracteur.   Bien sûr, c'est un nouveau tracteur.
ce hangar / cette étable / cette voiture / cet abri
un nouveau hangar / une nouvelle étable / une nouvelle voiture / un nouvel abri

9   Monique demande à ses cousins : ⊗

Vous ne vous servez plus de ce hangar?   Non, c'est un vieux hangar!
cette grange / cet abri / cette étable / ce tracteur
une vieille grange / un vieil abri / une vieille étable / un vieux tracteur

10   EXERCICE ECRIT   For answers, see p. T38.

Récrivez les phrases suivantes en utilisant l'adjectif entre parenthèses.
1. Ils ont une ferme. (nouveau)   4. Ils ont gardé la grange. (vieux)
2. Il y a un hangar. (beau)   5. Il y a des arbres à Ore. (beau)
3. Ils ont acheté un tracteur. (nouveau)   6. Le grenier n'a pas changé. (vieux)

Jean-François, who is 12, appeared in Unit 1. During the year he and his brother Alain go to Ore's "école primaire." Angel, their older brother, is 15 and goes to the CES in a neighboring town. Angel is a Spanish name. The influence of Spain is evident in the Ore region since it is close to the Spanish border. As a matter of fact, many people of the region speak Spanish as well as French.

11 A la ferme. ⊗

1 Louis Fort fait les foins avec Angel.

2 Jean-François se sert souvent du tracteur maintenant qu'il sait le conduire.

3 Angel vient d'aller chercher de la paille pour la litière du cochon.

4 Georgette Fort cultive son jardin potager.

5 Le matin, Alain emmène les vaches au pré et il les ramène le soir.

6 Ce sont les parents qui se chargent de traire les vaches.

The pictures and captions on this page continue on the next.

Jean-François garde les moutons avec l'aide de son chien César.

Monique donne à manger et à boire aux poules et aux lapins.

12 Répondez aux questions.

1. Que font Louis Fort et Angel?
2. Pourquoi est-ce que Jean-François se sert souvent du tracteur?
3. Qu'est-ce qu'Angel vient d'aller chercher? Où est-ce qu'il va en mettre?
4. Que fait Georgette Fort?

5. Où est-ce qu'Alain emmène les vaches le matin?
6. Qu'est-ce qu'il fait le soir?
7. Que fait Jean-François avec l'aide de son chien César?
8. Que fait Monique pour aider?

13 EXERCICE ORAL ⊗

14 THE VERB savoir

The following are the present-tense forms of the verb **savoir,** *to know, to know how to.* ⊗

Je	**sais**	conduire.	Nous	**savons**	conduire.
Tu	**sais**	conduire.	Vous	**savez**	conduire.
Elle / Il	**sait**	conduire.	Elles / Ils	**savent**	conduire.

The past participle of **savoir** is **su : Je n'ai jamais su ça.** *I never knew that.*

15 Monique demande à Jean-François : ⊗

Tu te charges de traire les vaches?
Et vous deux? / Et Angel? / Et les garçons?

Non, je ne sais pas le faire.

nous ne savons pas / il ne sait pas / ils ne savent pas

16 Et vous?

1. Est-ce que vous savez traire les vaches?
2. Est-ce que vous savez conduire un tracteur? Une voiture?
3. Est-ce que vous savez cultiver un jardin potager?
4. Est-ce que vous savez faire les foins?
5. Qu'est-ce que vous savez faire comme travail dans une ferme?

17

connaître OR savoir

Connaître and **savoir** both mean *to know,* but they are not interchangeable:

- **connaître** indicates familiarity with a person, a place, or a thing;
- **savoir** indicates knowledge acquired through experience or learning.

Il connaît	Monique. Ore. la montagne.	Il sait	l'espagnol. pourquoi. conduire.

Note that when **savoir** is followed by an infinitive, it means *to know how to:*

Il sait conduire.   *He knows how to drive.*

18 ## Monique vient d'arriver à Ore. ⊗

On va te présenter aux voisins.   Je connais déjà les voisins.
On va t'expliquer comment y aller.   Je sais déjà comment y aller.
On va te montrer Ore.   Je connais déjà Ore.
On va te raconter ce qui est arrivé.   Je sais déjà ce qui est arrivé.
On va te présenter à Cousin Georges.   Je connais déjà Cousin Georges.

19 ## Savez-vous ce que ces animaux mangent? ⊗

le canard

la poule

de l'herbe

le cheval

le mouton

du maïs

de l'avoine

le lapin

la vache

du blé

le cochon

SOLUTION : le mouton, la vache et le lapin mangent de l'herbe; le cheval mange de l'herbe et de l'avoine; le cochon mange du maïs; la poule et le canard mangent du maïs ou du blé.

20 Devinettes. ⊗

1. Il nous réveille le matin.   le coq
2. Elle nous donne des œufs.   la poule
3. Il adore les carottes.   le lapin

4. Elle nous donne du lait.   la vache
5. Ils suivent toujours le premier.   les moutons

21 EXERCICE DE COMPREHENSION ⊗   For script, see p. T38.

un mouton ___**1**___
un canard _____
une poule _____
une vache _____

un cochon _____
un chien _____
un pigeon _____
un chat _____

22 Les cris des animaux… en français! ⊗

Les vaches font « Meuh ».
Les poules font « Cot, cot, cot, codèt ».
Les coqs font « Cocorico ».
Les chiens font « Ouah, Ouah ».
Les oiseaux font « Cui, cui ».

Les moutons font « Bêê ».
Les chats font « Miaou ».
Les canards font « Coin, coin ».
Les ânes font « Hi, han ».

VOCABULAIRE : **les cris des animaux**   *animal sounds;* **les coqs**   *roosters;* **les ânes**   *donkeys.*

23 EXERCICE DE CONVERSATION

Vous êtes dans une ferme. Racontez une de vos journées. Dites…
1. à quelle heure vous vous levez.
2. si vous allez travailler dans les champs.
3. si vous vous servez d'un tracteur et comment est ce tracteur.
4. de quels animaux vous vous occupez et comment.
5. si vous avez un jardin potager et ce que vous y avez planté.
6. ce que vous faites le soir, et à quelle heure vous vous couchez.

24 C'était le bon temps! ⊗

Monique a rencontré un de ses amis d'enfance, Pierre Bise. Ils parlent du temps où ils étaient plus jeunes.

PIERRE   Je viens de passer devant la ferme du Père Janin. Tu te souviens de lui?

MONIQUE   Je pense bien! Il nous laissait monter son cheval, Eclair.

PIERRE   Tu te souviens quand on faisait les foins avec les fils Gaillard?

MONIQUE   Oui, et Madame Gaillard nous donnait toujours un pot de sa confiture de mûres.

PIERRE   Et quand on allait dans le pré de Madame Blanc, sous prétexte d'aller chercher de l'herbe pour les lapins?

MONIQUE   Oui, en fait on allait plutôt cueillir ses figues et ses noisettes!

25 **Répondez aux questions.**

1. Qui est-ce que Monique a rencontré?
2. De quoi est-ce qu'ils parlent?
3. De qui est-ce qu'ils parlent d'abord?
4. Qu'est-ce que le Père Janin laissait Monique et Pierre faire?
5. Qu'est-ce qu'ils faisaient avec les fils Gaillard?
6. Qu'est-ce que Madame Gaillard leur donnait?
7. Dans quel pré est-ce qu'ils allaient?
8. Sous quel prétexte est-ce qu'ils allaient dans le pré de Madame Blanc?
9. Pourquoi est-ce qu'ils y allaient en fait?

26 **EXERCICE ORAL** ⊗

27 **EXPRESSING PAST TIME**
The Imparfait

Répondez aux questions qui suivent les exemples. ⊗

Quand Monique et Pierre étaient plus jeunes...
      ils **montaient** le cheval du Père Janin.
      ils **faisaient** les foins avec les Gaillard.
      ils **allaient** dans le pré de Mme Blanc.
Do the above sentences refer to present or past time?

Nous **faisons** les foins.	On **faisait** les foins.
Nous **allons** dans le pré.	On **allait** dans le pré.

Are the verbs in the left-hand column in the present or in the past? What form of the verb is used in each of these sentences, the **vous** form, the **nous** form . . . ? Look at the verbs in the right-hand column. Compare the stems of these verbs with those in the left-hand column. Are they the same or different?

J'all**ais** dans le pré.	Nous all**ions** dans le pré.
Tu all**ais** dans le pré.	Vous all**iez** dans le pré.
Il all**ait** dans le pré.	Ils all**aient** dans le pré.

What are the endings of the verb forms? Which verb forms sound alike? Are these verb forms spelled alike or differently?

28 **Lisez la généralisation suivante.**

1. The imparfait and the passé composé are two ways of expressing past time. As seen in most examples in this unit, the imparfait expresses what used to take place repeatedly:

Tous les ans, ils aidaient les Gaillard à faire les foins.	*Every year, they helped the Gaillards with the haying.*
Mme Gaillard leur **donnait toujours** un pot de confiture.	*Mme Gaillard always gave them a jar of jam.*
Le Père Janin les **laissait** monter son cheval.	*Père Janin used to let them ride his horse.*

The imparfait has other uses. Its uses will be contrasted with those of the passé composé in the next unit.

2. With the exception of **être,** the imparfait stem of all verbs is the same as the stem of the present-tense **nous** form. The imparfait endings are the same for all verbs.

Present-tense **nous** form			Imparfait		
nous	jou		je	jou	-ais
			tu		-ais
	sort	-ons	il	sort	-ait
	choisiss		nous	choisiss	-ions
			vous		-iez
	all		ils	all	-aient

Notice that there are only three different spoken endings, one for the **nous** form, one for the **vous** form, and a third for all the other forms.

3. The imparfait stem of **être** is **ét-** : **j'étais, tu étais,** etc.

4. Note the following spelling changes:
   commencer : nous **commençons**
   je **commençais,** tu **commençais,** il **commençait,** ils **commençaient,**
   but nous commencions, vous commenciez.
   manger : nous **mangeons**
   je **mangeais,** tu **mangeais,** il **mangeait,** ils **mangeaient,**
   but nous mangions, vous mangiez.
   Changer, corriger, and **ranger** show the same spelling changes as **manger.**

5. Here are the imparfait forms of two verbs that are used only in the **il** form:
   il va pleuvoir : **il pleuvait**   il va neiger : **il neigeait**

29 Jean-François parle au Père Janin : ⊗

Je garde les moutons.	Moi aussi, je gardais les moutons.
Je m'occupe des lapins.	Moi aussi, je m'occupais des lapins.
Je donne à manger aux poules.	Moi aussi, je donnais à manger aux poules.
J'emmène les vaches au pré.	Moi aussi, j'emmenais les vaches au pré.
Je fais les foins avec mon père.	Moi aussi, je faisais les foins avec mon père.
J'aide ma mère à cultiver son jardin.	Moi aussi, j'aidais ma mère à cultiver son jardin.

Variation: Responses: Nous aussi, nous . . . / Eux aussi,
ils . . . / Elles aussi, elles . . . / Elle aussi, elle . . . / Lui aussi, il . . .

30 Pierre et Monique parlent de Mme Blanc : ⊗

Elle ne t'aimait pas beaucoup.	Bien sûr! Je mangeais toutes ses figues.
Elle ne nous aimait pas beaucoup.	Bien sûr! Nous mangions . . .
Elle n'aimait pas beaucoup Angel.	Bien sûr! Il mangeait . . .
Elle n'aimait pas beaucoup les garçons.	Bien sûr! Ils mangeaient . . .

31 Pierre parle à Monique : ⊗

Comment est-ce qu'il était, le Père Janin?	Il était toujours très gentil avec moi.

Et Mme Gaillard? / Et les fils Gaillard? / Et moi? / Et mon frère et moi?
elle était / ils étaient / tu étais / vous étiez

32 EXERCICE DE COMPREHENSION ⊗ For script, see p. T38.

	o	1	2	3	4	5	6	7	8	9	10
Maintenant											
Avant	✓										

33 EXERCICE ECRIT For answers, see p. T38.

Récrivez le paragraphe suivant à l'imparfait. Commencez : Il y a six ans…

Mes parents et moi, nous habitons Ore. Nous avons une grande ferme. Mon père cultive nos champs de blé et de maïs. Ma mère s'occupe du jardin potager. Moi, je garde nos moutons avec l'aide de mon chien César. Mon frère s'occupe des vaches. Nous aidons aussi nos parents à faire les foins. En général, c'est moi qui fais la litière du cochon. J'aime beaucoup les travaux de la ferme.

34 EXERCICE DE CONVERSATION

For more on country life in the French-speaking world, see Photo Essay: Country Life, Plates 17-24.

Vous rencontrez un(e) ami(e) d'enfance. Vous parlez de ce que vous faisiez quand vous passiez vos vacances ensemble dans le même petit village. Dites…

1. comment vous aidiez les fermiers.
2. s'il y avait un tracteur.
3. si on vous laissait le conduire.
4. quels genres d'animaux il y avait.
5. de quels animaux vous vous occupiez.
6. si vous alliez cueillir des noisettes, des mûres, des fruits.
7. ce que sont devenus vos amis de jadis.

35 REDACTION

Racontez ce que vous faisiez quand vous passiez vos vacances dans un petit village. Utilisez l'exercice No 34 comme modèle.

36 Le jeu de la ferme.

Il y a six erreurs dans ce dessin. Trouvez-les. Solution p. 172.

De replaces un, une, du, de la, des in a negative sentence which conveys the idea of "not any." (Je ne mange pas de pain. Je ne vois pas de tracteur. Je n'ai pas de chien.) In negative sentences which do not convey this idea, de can be followed by an article as in the sentences below.

SOLUTION : 1. On ne met pas un tracteur dans une étable; on le met dans un hangar. 2. On ne met pas des tomates dans un grenier à foin; on y met du foin. 3. On ne se sert pas de fleurs pour faire la litière du cochon; on se sert de paille. 4. On ne donne pas de la confiture aux lapins; on leur donne de l'herbe. 5. On ne donne pas des haricots verts aux poules; on leur donne du maïs. 6. Les moutons ne font pas « Meuh! »; ils font « Bêê! »

37 La météo du fermier. ⊗

Quand les cochons éparpillent leur litière, il va faire mauvais.
Quand les vaches se groupent au milieu des prés, il va pleuvoir.
Quand les chèvres cabriolent, il va faire du vent.

VOCABULAIRE : **éparpillent** *scatter;* **chèvres** *goats;* **cabriolent** *frolic.*

38 WORD LIST

1–10

le blé *wheat*	**abriter** *to protect*	**beau, bel, belle, beaux, belles**
un bois *woods*	**envoyer** *to send*	*pretty*
une carte postale *postcard*	**j'envoie, tu envoies,**	**chéri, –e** *dear, darling*
un champ (de blé) *(wheat) field*	**il envoie, ils envoient**	**nouveau, nouvel, nouvelle,**
une étable *cowshed*	**devenir** (like **venir**) *to become*	**nouveaux, nouvelles** *new*
une femme *wife*	**planter** *to plant*	**vieux, vieil, vieille, vieux,**
une ferme *farm*	**reconnaître** (like **connaître**)	**vieilles** *old*
le foin *hay*	*to recognize*	
la grand-rue *main street*	**donner de ses nouvelles** *to tell*	**juste un petit mot…** *just a line…*
une grange *barn*	*how one's doing*	**tant elle a changé** *it has changed*
un grenier à foin *hayloft*	**faire la moisson** *to harvest*	*so much*
un *hangar *shed*	**ils habitaient** *they used to live*	
la moisson *harvest*	**j'écrirai** *I will write*	
un mouton *sheep*		
un mur *wall*	**à la place de** *in place of*	
un noyer *walnut tree*	**à peine** *hardly*	
un pré *meadow*	**bientôt** *soon*	
un tracteur *tractor*	**jadis** *in the old days*	

11–23

un animal *animal*	**l'avoine** (f.) *oats*	**se charger (de)** *to take charge (of)*
des animaux *animals*	**l'herbe** (f.) *grass*	**nous nous chargeons** *we take*
un canard *duck*	**un jardin potager** *vegetable*	*charge*
un cheval *horse*	*garden*	**ils se chargent de traire les vaches**
des chevaux *horses*	**une litière** *litter*	*they take charge of milking*
un cochon *pig*	**le maïs** *corn*	*the cows*
un lapin *rabbit*	**la paille** *straw*	**conduire** *to drive*
une poule *hen*		**cultiver** *to grow, to tend*
une vache *cow*	**donner à boire** *to give water to*	**ramener** (like **acheter**) *to lead back*
	donner à manger *to feed*	**savoir** *to know, to know how to*
	faire les foins *to hay, to do*	**savez-vous** *do you know*
	the haying	
		avec l'aide de *with the help of*

24–37

un(e) ami(e) d'enfance *childhood*	**se souvenir de** (like **venir**) *to*	**en fait** *in fact*
friend	*remember*	**plutôt** *rather, instead*
un éclair *lightning*		**sous prétexte** *with the excuse*
une figue *fig*	**on allait** *we used to go*	
une mûre *blackberry*	**elle donnait** *she used to give*	**C'était le bon temps!**
une noisette *hazelnut*	**ils étaient** *they were*	*Those were the days!*
	on faisait *we used to do*	
aller chercher *to go get*	**on allait cueillir** *we used to*	
laisser *to let*	*go pick*	
Il nous laissait monter son cheval.		
He used to let us ride his horse.	**jeune** *young*	

Photo 1: "des bananes vertes," which are fried and used as vegetables. The pear-shaped vegetables next to them are called "chayottes."

The opening four pages of this unit (173-176) take the form of a travel brochure on Martinique. They should be worked on as a whole.

17

PENSEZ A...

La Martinique

Photo 2:
Le
François

si vous voulez partir à l'aventure
aux Tropiques, dans le sillage
des corsaires d'autrefois...

si vous voulez découvrir une île, à
la fois douce et sauvage, baignée
par une mer bleue et calme...

si vous voulez vous bronzer au soleil
sur une plage de sable fin, ou rêver
à l'ombre des cocotiers...

si vous voulez plonger
et nager dans le monde enchanté
des poissons exotiques...

si vous voulez explorer des forêts
tropicales, pleines de fleurs, de fruits
et d'oiseaux multicolores.

Photo 3: The mountains in background are the island of Dominique.

iquemartiniquemartinique

This map gives only major Caribbean Islands. Point out that some of the names here are used with the feminine articles (la Floride, etc.) and that others are used without any article at all (Cuba, Haïti, Porto-Rico, Trinidad)

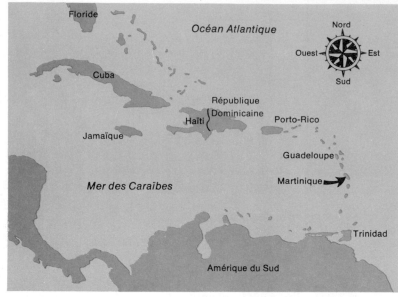

Floride

Océan Atlantique

Nord
Ouest — Est
Sud

Cuba

République
Dominicaine
Haïti
Porto-Rico

Jamaïque

Guadeloupe

Mer des Caraïbes

Martinique

Trinidad

Amérique du Sud

Photo 4: Le Morne Rouge

4

Photo 5: Flower called "fleur de balisier"

5

The Word List includes only the names of islands used with an article. Point out also the French spelling of Puerto Rico.

A quatre heures de New York par avion, baignée par la mer des Caraïbes, « la perle des Antilles » , la Martinique vous attend…

Photo 7: Flower market in Fort-de-France

7

6

Photo 6: Fond-Lahaye: small fishing village

Photo 8: Banana plantation

8

Photo 9: Fort-de-France bay

martiniquemartin

quemarti

174

9

Photo 10: Bellefontaine: coastline near Case Pilote

Photo 11: Commercial harbor of Fort-de-France

Photo 12: Le Rocher du Diamant

Photo 13: Marina at Fort-de-France

Photo 14: Traditional costume, worn once or twice a year for festivals. Head-dress is called "un madras."

Photo 15: Sunset at Anse Mitan, near Les Trois-Ilets

10

Vous pouvez y aller quand vous voulez, car la Martinique est l'île du perpétuel été. Et les Martiniquais sont très accueillants :

"En Martinique" could be used also.

"Soyez les bienvenus à la Martinique!"

11

13

12

14

15

16

Photo 16: Waterfall in the Rain Forest

The numbers on the map indicate the distance between two towns—e.g., between Basse-Pointe and Marigot there are 16 km, and between Basse-Pointe and le Morne Rouge, 17 km.

1 km (un kilomètre) = 0,62 mi.
1 mi. (un mile) = 1,6 km

17

Voici deux circuits qui peuvent vous aider à explorer les plus beaux sites de la Martinique.

NORD DE L'ILE : CIRCUIT ROUGE

Fort-de-France La capitale—baie magnifique entourée de collines.
La Trinité Presqu'île de la Caravelle—belles plages—côte pittoresque.
Grand'Rivière Un des sites les plus sauvages de l'île.
Le Morne Rouge Point de départ des excursions à la Montagne Pelée, le célèbre volcan de la Martinique.
St-Pierre Ville détruite en 1902 par l'éruption de la Montagne Pelée.
Le Carbet Lieu de débarquement de Christophe Colomb en 1502.

SUD DE L'ILE : CIRCUIT VERT

Fort-de-France La capitale.
Le Lamentin Vaste plaine où on cultive la canne à sucre.
Les Trois-Ilets Lieu de naissance, en 1763, de Joséphine, femme de Napoléon Ier.
Le Rocher du Diamant Le plus beau site de l'île—plage de 4 km.
Le Marin Vue splendide sur la baie.
Ste-Anne Joli village de pêcheurs.
Le Vauclin Belle plage bordée de cocotiers.

18

Photo 17:
Fond-Lahaye

Photo 18: Fort-de-France Town Hall
Photo 19: Le Rocher du Diamant
For other photos of Fort-de-France and Le Diamant, see Unit 1, p. 5.

martiniquemartiniq

martiniqu

176

19

2 Répondez aux questions.

1. Dans quelle mer se trouve la Martinique?
2. Qu'est-ce qu'on peut faire sur les plages de la Martinique?
3. Comment sont les forêts de la Martinique?
4. Est-ce qu'il y a une saison pour aller à la Martinique? Pourquoi?
5. Combien de temps est-ce qu'on met pour aller en avion de New York à la Martinique?
6. Comment s'appelle la capitale de la Martinique?
7. La Montagne Pelée, qu'est-ce que c'est?
8. Qui a visité la Martinique en 1502?
9. Qu'est-ce qu'on cultive près du Lamentin?
10. Le Diamant, qu'est-ce que c'est?

3 EXERCICE ORAL ⊗

4 Combien de kilomètres et de miles est-ce qu'il y a entre… ⊗

Fort-de-France et la Trinité?	Il y a 30 kilomètres. Ça fait 18 miles.
la Trinité et Grand'Rivière?	Il y a 44 kilomètres. Ça fait 27 miles.
Grand'Rivière et St-Pierre?	Il y a 55 kilomètres. Ça fait 34 miles.
St-Pierre et Fort-de-France?	Il y a 28 kilomètres. Ça fait 17 miles.
Fort-de-France et les Trois-Ilets?	Il y a 30 kilomètres. Ça fait 18 miles.
les Trois-Ilets et le Diamant?	Il y a 24 kilomètres. Ça fait 15 miles.
le Diamant et Ste-Anne?	Il y a 47 kilomètres. Ça fait 29 miles.
Ste-Anne et le Vauclin?	Il y a 16 kilomètres. Ça fait 10 miles.
le Vauclin et Fort-de-France?	Il y a 35 kilomètres. Ça fait 22 miles.

5 Au nord, au sud, à l'est ou à l'ouest de Fort-de-France? ⊗

Où se trouve St-Pierre?	Au nord-ouest de Fort-de-France.
Et la Trinité?	Au nord-est de Fort-de-France.
Et le Diamant?	Au sud de Fort-de-France.
Et Ste-Anne?	Au sud-est de Fort-de-France.
Et le François?	A l'est de Fort-de-France.

6 Regardez la carte des Antilles, p. 174. ⊗ For answers, see p. T40.

Où se trouve la Martinique?	Au sud de la Guadeloupe et au nord de Trinidad.

Et Haïti? / Et Cuba? / Et la Guadeloupe? / Et la Jamaïque? / Et Porto-Rico?

7 Et vous?

1. Est-ce que vous avez déjà visité une des Antilles? Laquelle?
2. Qu'est-ce que vous avez fait pendant votre séjour sur cette île?
3. Si vous rêvez d'aller aux Tropiques, quelle île est-ce que vous rêvez de découvrir?
4. Pourquoi?
5. Dans vos rêves, qu'est-ce que vous faites sur cette île?

8 THE VERBS pouvoir AND vouloir

1. The following are the present-tense forms of the verbs **pouvoir,** *to be able, can,* and **vouloir,**
to want. ⊗

Je	**peux**		je	**veux.**
Tu	**peux**		tu	**veux.**
Il	**peut**	y aller, quand	il	**veut.**
Nous	**pouvons**		nous	**voulons.**
Vous	**pouvez**		vous	**voulez.**
Ils	**peuvent**		ils	**veulent.**

2. The past participle of **pouvoir** is **pu : Je n'ai pas pu y aller.**
   The past participle of **vouloir** is **voulu : Je n'ai pas voulu y aller.**

3. **Je veux,** *I want,* is often replaced by the more polite **Je voudrais,** *I would like.*
   Je voudrais vous parler.   *I would like to speak to you.*

9 C'est bientôt les vacances. ⊗

Variation: Tu es resté à la maison?
Oui, je n'ai pas voulu explorer la région.

Tu restes ici?   Oui, je veux explorer la région.
Et ton frère? / Et tes parents? / Et vous deux?

il veut explorer / ils veulent explorer / nous voulons explorer

10 Nous allons à la plage. ⊗

Tu viens avec nous?   Je ne peux pas, j'ai du travail.
Et vous deux? / Et Denise? / Et Monique et Pierre?

nous ne pouvons pas, nous avons / elle ne peut pas, elle a / ils ne peuvent pas, ils ont

11 Ça coûte trop cher. ⊗

Tu n'es pas allé(e) à la Martinique?   Non, je n'ai pas pu.
Et Monique? / Et Louise et Denise? / Et vous deux?

elle n'a pas pu / elles n'ont pas pu / nous n'avons pas pu

12 Chansons. ⊗   These are rounds or canons. The first will be familiar.

HO ET HISSE ET HO!

Ho et hisse et ho! Vogue mon ba- teau! Saute la vague, la vague, la vague Dans le bleu des flots!

LA PLAGE CALME

La   pla - ge cal - me   Dort   sous les pal - mes   La   lune est pâ - le.

VOCABULAIRE : **vogue** *sail;* **saute la vague** *riding the waves;* **des flots** *waves;* **dort** *sleeps;* **la lune** *moon.*

Doris and Danou Dubois appear in Units 1 and 3. Use the map on p. 176 to locate Fort-de-France, la Trinité, and la Caravelle. Photo 3: David eating a "bitter" orange. Photo 4: Mme Dubois preparing "un féroce"—marinated salt cod

avo-
cado,

manioc flour
mashed tò-
gether with
peanut oil.

13 Une famille martiniquaise. ⊗

Doris Dubois · 1

leur mère · 4

2 · Danou Dubois

3 · leur petit frère, David

5 · leur père

Les Dubois habitent à Fort-de-France. M. Dubois est professeur de mathématiques dans un CES, et Mme Dubois est assistante sociale. Doris et Danou sont élèves dans un CES, et David va encore à l'école primaire. En plus de leur maison de Fort-de-France, les Dubois ont une « case » au bord de la mer, près de la Trinité. Ils y vont tous les week-ends pour se reposer, se baigner et faire du bateau.

14 Une sortie en mer. ⊗

Ce week-end, Doris et Danou vont à la pêche avec Daquin, un vieux pêcheur qu'ils connaissent depuis toujours. Ils vont pêcher la langouste du côté de la Pointe du Diable, à l'extrémité de la presqu'île de la Caravelle.

DANOU   La dernière fois qu'on est allé par là avec Papa, on a fait un peu d'exploration sous-marine dans les récifs de coraux.

DORIS   C'était vraiment fantastique, tous ces poissons multicolores…

DAQUIN   Vous en avez attrapé pour votre aquarium?

DORIS   Danou était en train d'essayer, quand il a eu un accident…

DANOU   Oui, je poursuivais un beau poisson-clown avec mon épuisette, quand une énorme vague m'a jeté contre un rocher plein d'oursins!

"Enorme" can either
follow or precede the
noun it
modifies.

DAQUIN   Ça peut être dangereux, ça…

DANOU   Oh, je m'en suis tiré avec quelques piquants dans la main, et pas de poisson-clown!

1

2

The colorful fishing boats of Martinique are called "gommiers" after the trees they are made from. Each "gommier" is given a special poetic name (see p. 25, photo 2).

15 Répondez aux questions.

1. Où habitent les Dubois?
2. Que font M. et Mme Dubois? Et Doris, Danou et David?
3. Où est-ce qu'ils passent leurs week-ends?
4. Qu'est-ce qu'ils font là-bas?
5. Avec qui est-ce que Doris et Danou vont à la pêche ce week-end?
6. Qu'est-ce qu'ils vont pêcher? Où ça?
7. Qu'est-ce qu'ils ont fait la dernière fois qu'ils sont allés à la Pointe du Diable?
8. Est-ce qu'ils ont attrapé des poissons pour leur aquarium? Pourquoi?
9. Décrivez l'accident de Danou.
10. Comment est-ce qu'il s'en est tiré?

16 EXERCICE ORAL ⊗

17 Dans la mer des Caraïbes. ⊗

1. une langouste	6. un requin	11. une méduse
2. une pieuvre	7. un poisson volant	12. un poisson-ange
3. un crabe	8. une murène	13. un baracuda
4. un oursin	9. un lambi	14. une tortue
5. une étoile de mer	10. un poisson-clown	15. un hippocampe

Est-ce que ça peut être dangereux?

SOLUTION : Peuvent être dangereux :
un crabe, un oursin, un requin, une murène, une méduse, une tortue, un baracuda.

This is standard equipment for scuba diving for men and women alike.

18 Danou va plonger. ⊗

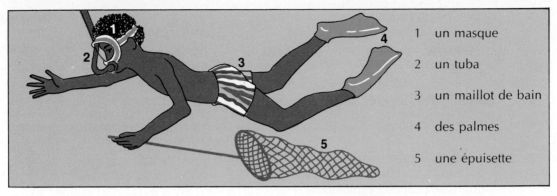

1 un masque

2 un tuba

3 un maillot de bain

4 des palmes

5 une épuisette

19 Et vous?

1. Est-ce que vous avez déjà fait de l'exploration sous-marine? Où ça?
2. Qu'est-ce que vous portiez?
3. Quels poissons est-ce que vous avez vus?

4. Vous en avez attrapé? Lesquels?
5. Est-ce que vous avez un aquarium?
6. Qu'est-ce que vous avez comme poissons?

20 IMPARFAIT OR PASSE COMPOSE

The imparfait and the passé composé are two ways of expressing past time in French. The use of the imparfait or the passé composé does not depend on when the action took place but on how the speaker chooses to describe what happened.

1. The imparfait is used if the speaker wants to describe:

   a. **an action in progress** when something else happened.
   Danou **était** en train de nager quand il a eu un accident.
   Danou was swimming when he had an accident.

   Il **poursuivait** un poisson-clown quand une vague l'a jeté contre un rocher.
   He was chasing a clown fish when a wave threw him against a rock.

   b. **a repeated action.**
   Ils **allaient** à la plage tous les week-ends.
   They used to go to the beach every weekend.

   Ils **faisaient** du bateau tous les dimanches.
   They used to go sailing every Sunday.

   c. **conditions** at the time of the action.
   Il **faisait** beau.
   The weather was nice.
   C'**était** fantastique.
   It was fantastic.

2. The passé composé is used if the speaker wants to describe a **completed action.**
   Danou s'en **est tiré.**
   Danou pulled through.
   Il n'**a** rien **attrapé.**
   He didn't catch anything.

21 Qu'est-ce que les Dubois ont fait ce week-end? ⊗

Ils ont fait du bateau?

Oui, ils faisaient du bateau quand nous les avons rencontrés.

Ils sont allés à la pêche? / Ils ont exploré la côte? / Ils ont visité l'île? / Ils ont fait une excursion?

ils allaient à la pêche / ils exploraient la côte / ils visitaient l'île / ils faisaient une excursion

22 Nous, l'été dernier, nous faisions ça tous les jours! ⊗

Hier, nous sommes allés à la plage.

Nous, l'été dernier, nous allions à la plage tous les jours!

Nous nous sommes baignés.

. . . nous nous baignions . . .

Nous nous sommes bronzés au soleil.

. . . nous nous bronzions au soleil . . .

Nous avons fait de l'exploration.

. . . nous faisions de l'exploration . . .

Nous avons attrapé des poissons exotiques.

. . . nous attrapions des poissons exotiques . . .

Variation: Responses: Eux, l'été dernier, ils . . . / Elles, l'été dernier, elles . . . / Lui, l'été dernier, il . . . / Elle, l'été dernier, elle . . . / Moi, l'été dernier, j' . . .

23 EXERCICE ECRIT For answers, see p. T41.

Récrivez le paragraphe suivant au passé. Commencez : Samedi dernier, comme il...
C'est samedi aujourd'hui. Comme il fait beau et chaud, mon père décide de nous emmener faire de l'exploration sous-marine. Nous prenons notre équipement, nous allons au port, nous montons sur notre bateau et nous partons. Mais, comme nous arrivons près des récifs de coraux, le temps commence à changer et la mer devient mauvaise. Les vagues jettent notre bateau vers les rochers... C'est très dangereux. Nous partons le plus vite possible vers une petite baie qui n'est pas loin de là, pour attendre le beau temps.

24 EXERCICE DE COMPREHENSION ⊗ For script, see p. T39.

	0	1	2	3	4	5
A	✓					
B						

We have printed the choices of this Listening Exercise to give students some extra help.

Exemple : A. Doris essayait d'attraper un poisson pour son aquarium.
B. Doris a attrapé un poisson pour son aquarium.

1. A. Danou a fait de l'exploration sous-marine le week-end dernier.
   B. Danou faisait de l'exploration sous-marine avant son accident.

2. A. Daquin n'est jamais allé à la pêche.
   B. Daquin allait à la pêche tous les jours quand il était plus jeune.

3. A. Danou poursuivait un poisson-clown quand il a eu un accident.
   B. Danou a attrapé un poisson-clown et des oursins.

4. A. Doris, Danou et Daquin sont allés pêcher la langouste du côté de la Pointe du Diable.
   B. Doris est allée pêcher avec son père du côté de la Pointe du Diable.

5. A. Avant, il y avait des récifs de coraux du côté de la Pointe du Diable, mais maintenant il n'y en a plus.
   B. Le week-end dernier, les Dubois ont exploré les récifs de coraux de la Pointe du Diable.

25 EXERCICE DE CONVERSATION

Racontez à un(e) ami(e) ce que vous avez fait pendant vos dernières vacances. Dites que vous êtes allé(e) au bord de la mer, qu'il faisait très beau, que vous vous baigniez tous les jours, que vous faisiez souvent du bateau, qu'une fois vous êtes allé(e) à la pêche avec un vieux pêcheur, etc.

Use the map on p. 176 to locate St-Pierre and the Montagne Pelée.

26 Une excursion à St-Pierre. ⊗

Photo 1: Ruins of the church of St-Pierre

Quand ils ne sortent pas en mer avec Daquin, Doris et Danou aiment explorer leur île en compagnie de leur père°. Aujourd'hui, ils visitent les ruines° de St-Pierre, ville qui a été détruite° en 1902 par l'éruption volcanique de la Montagne Pelée.

Au début du siècle°, St-Pierre était une ville de 26,000 habitants, riche et brillante°, qu'on appelait « le Petit Paris » des Antilles. Au nord de la ville, la Montagne Pelée était un volcan inactif° depuis longtemps. Un lac° occupait son cratère°, et les gens de St-Pierre y allaient en excursion le dimanche. Jusqu'au 8 mai 1902… Ce jour-là, à 8 h du matin, alors que° les habitants de St-Pierre dormaient° encore, la Montagne Pelée a explosé°. Un nuage brûlant° a recouvert° la ville et l'a détruite en quelques minutes. Il n'y a eu qu'un seul survivant° : un prisonnier° que les murs de son cachot° avaient protégé!°

Photo 2: Engraving made shortly after the eruption

VOCABULAIRE : **en compagnie de leur père** *in the company of their father;* **les ruines** *the ruins;* **qui a été détruite** *which was destroyed;* **au début du siècle** *at the beginning of the century;* **brillante** *glamorous;* **inactif** *dormant;* **un lac** *lake;* **son cratère** *its crater;* **alors que** *while;* **dormaient** *were sleeping;* **a explosé** *exploded;* **un nuage brûlant** *a burning cloud;* **a recouvert** *covered;* **il n'y a eu qu'un seul survivant** *there was only one survivor;* **un prisonnier** *a prisoner;* **son cachot** *his cell;* **avaient protégé** *had protected.*

27 PROJET *Project*

Faites un dépliant touristique (*travel folder*) sur une région où vous aimeriez (*would like*) passer vos vacances. Prenez comme modèle le dépliant sur la Martinique (pp. 173–176). Illustrez avec des cartes, des photos, des cartes postales ou des dessins. Votre dépliant doit pouvoir répondre à des questions comme :

• Où se trouve cette région, au sud, au nord, à l'est ou à l'ouest de notre ville?
• C'est à combien de kilomètres de notre ville?
• Comment est-ce qu'on peut y aller?
• Quelle est la bonne saison pour y aller?
• Est-ce que les gens de cette région sont accueillants?
• Qu'est-ce qu'il y a d'intéressant à voir? Et à faire?

28 WORD LIST

1–12
l'Amérique (f.) *America*
les Antilles (f.) *West Indies*
la Floride *Florida*
la Guadeloupe *Guadeloupe*
la Jamaïque *Jamaica*
la République Dominicaine
  Dominican Republic

l'aventure (f.) *adventure*
un avion *airplane*
une baie *bay*
la canne à sucre *sugar cane*
un circuit *route*
un cocotier *coconut tree*
une colline *hill*
un corsaire *pirate*
une côte *coastline*
un débarquement *landing*
une éruption *eruption*
une excursion *excursion*
une forêt *forest*
un kilomètre *kilometer*
un lieu *place*
un(e) Martiniquais(e) *person from*
  Martinique
le monde *world*
une naissance *birth*
l'ombre (f.) *shade*
un pêcheur *fisherman*
une perle *pearl*
une plaine *plain*

un point de départ *starting point*
une presqu'île *peninsula*
un rocher *rock*
le sable *sand*
le sillage *wake*
un site *site*
les Tropiques *tropics*
une vague *wave*
un volcan *volcano*

se bronzer *to sunbathe*
découvrir *to discover*
explorer *to explore*
nager *to swim*
  nous nageons *we swim*
plonger *to dive*
  nous plongeons *we dive*
pouvoir *to be able, can*
  vous pouvez, ils peuvent *can*
rêver *to dream*
vouloir *to want*

le nord *north*
l'est (m.) *east*
le sud *south*
l'ouest (m.) *west*

accueillant, – e *hospitable*
baigné, –e *bathed*
bordé, –e de *edged with*
célèbre *famous*
détruit, –e *destroyed*
doux, douce *gentle*
enchanté, –e *enchanted*
entouré, –e de *surrounded by*
exotique *exotic*
fin, –e *fine*
magnifique *magnificent*
multicolore *many-colored*
perpétuel, –elle *constant*
pittoresque *picturesque*
plein, –e *full*
le plus beau *the most beautiful*
sauvage *wild*
  le plus sauvage *the wildest*
splendide *splendid*
transparent, –e *transparent*
tropical, –e *tropical*
vaste *enormous*

autrefois *the old days*
à la fois *at the same time*

soyez les bienvenus! *welcome!*

13–27
un accident *accident*
une assistante sociale *social*
  worker
un professeur de mathématiques
  math teacher
une case *cabana*
du corail, des coraux *coral*
une école primaire *elementary*
  school
une épuisette *landing net*
une extrémité *tip*
une langouste *spiny lobster*
un oursin *sea urchin*
un piquant *spine*
un poisson-clown *clown fish*
un récif *reef*
une sortie en mer *boat trip*
un week-end *weekend*

un baracuda *barracuda*
un crabe *crab*
une étoile de mer *starfish*
un hippocampe *sea horse*
un lambi *conch*
une méduse *jelly fish*
une murène *moray eel*
une pieuvre *octopus*
un poisson-ange *angelfish*
un poisson volant *flying fish*
un requin *shark*
une tortue *turtle*

un maillot de bain *bathing suit*
un masque *mask*
une palme *flipper*
un tuba *snorkel*

attraper *to catch*
se baigner *to go swimming*
jeter *to throw*
  je jette, tu jettes, il jette,
  ils jettent
pêcher *to fish*
poursuivre (like **suivre**) *to go*
  after
se tirer de *to get oneself out of*
aller à la pêche *to go fishing*
faire du bateau *to go boating*

fantastique *fantastic*

contre *against*
en plus de *in addition to*
par là *over there*
au bord de la mer *at the shore*

Hourtin is 60 km north of Bordeaux. The map of France on p. 8 gives the location of Bordeaux.

François and his friends are wearing life jackets (un gilet de sauvetage), which are compulsory whenever they are on the water.

18
François à l'école de voile
chapitre de révision

François Le Sève is spending the summer learning how to sail at a camp called "La Gracieuse." This camp is located on a lake, l'Etang d'Hourtin, near Bordeaux. Just like François, many campers come back summer after summer so that they can reach a high level of proficiency in sailing. The camp has boys' sessions and girls' sessions. The campers live in tents in the dense pine forest that covers the entire region. They are assigned to a crew when they arrive, and they do everything with their crew until the end of their two-week session. Among other things, they learn how to handle a sailboat, how to row, and how to keep watch from the camp's observation tower. Crews also take turns cooking for the whole camp and doing the dishes after meals.

1

2

3

4

Comment s'est passée mon arrivée.

Nous sommes arrivés à « La Gracieuse » en fin d'après-midi, samedi. Le camp se trouve dans les dunes, sous les pins. (Comme ça sent bon!) Le lac est très grand et très beau. Tout est parfait sauf une chose: on nous a dit de ne jamais nous promener pieds-nus à cause des vipères !!! On nous a divisés en équipes et chaque équipe a fait la connaissance de son chef. Le nôtre s'appelle Alain Plon. Il vient de Toulouse.

Ce que nous avons fait.

Alain nous a conduits à notre tente. Nous nous sommes installés: nous avons étalé nos sacs de couchage par terre, nous avons sorti nos affaires de nos sacs à dos. Puis nous sommes allés nous laver un peu à la pompe. (L'eau n'est pas chaude!) Nous avons dîné. Puis nous nous sommes réunis pour parler du programme du lendemain. Nous nous sommes lavé les dents et nous nous sommes couchés. Nous avons dormi à poings fermés jusqu'à six heures le lendemain.

3 **Répondez aux questions.**

1. Quand est-ce que François et ses camarades sont arrivés à « La Gracieuse »?
2. Où se trouve « La Gracieuse »?
3. Pourquoi est-ce qu'il ne faut pas marcher pieds-nus?
4. Comment s'appelle le chef d'équipe de François?
5. Qu'est-ce que l'équipe de François a fait avant le dîner?
6. Qu'est-ce qu'elle a fait après?

4 # REFLEXIVE CONSTRUCTIONS

1. A reflexive construction is one in which the subject and the object of the verb refer to the same person : **Je me réveille. Elle s'habille.**

2. Like object pronouns, reflexive pronouns are placed before the verb to whose meaning they are most closely related.

Affirmative	Negative
Tu te promènes?	Tu ne te promènes pas?
Tu vas te promener?	Tu ne vas pas te promener?
Tu t' es promené?	Tu ne t' es pas promené?
Promène-toi!	Ne te promène pas!

Notice that in an affirmative command **toi** is used instead of **te.**

3. The passé composé of reflexive verbs is always formed with **être.** The past participle agrees in gender and number with a direct object when it comes before the verb:
Les garçons se sont réchauffés, but **Les garçons se sont réchauffé les mains.**

5 **Le chef d'équipe dit :** ⊗

Va dire à François de se lever. —Il ne s'est pas encore levé?
—Mais si, il vient de se lever.

Va lui dire de se laver. —Il ne s'est pas encore lavé?— . . . de se laver.
Va lui dire de s'habiller. —Il ne s'est pas encore habillé?— . . . de s'habiller.
Va lui dire de se changer. —Il ne s'est pas encore changé?— . . . de se changer.

6 ## EXERCICE DE CONVERSATION

1. Vous passez l'été dans un camp de vacances. Racontez comment vous passez votre journée. Commencez : Tous les jours, je me lève à huit heures...

2. Vous revenez d'un camp de vacances. Vous racontez comment vous avez passé votre temps. Commencez : Tous les jours, je me levais à huit heures...

7 ## EXERCICE ECRIT

Vous avez passé l'été dans un camp de vacances. Vous écrivez à un(e) ami(e) pour lui raconter comment tout s'est passé.

8 Le jeu des messages. ⊗

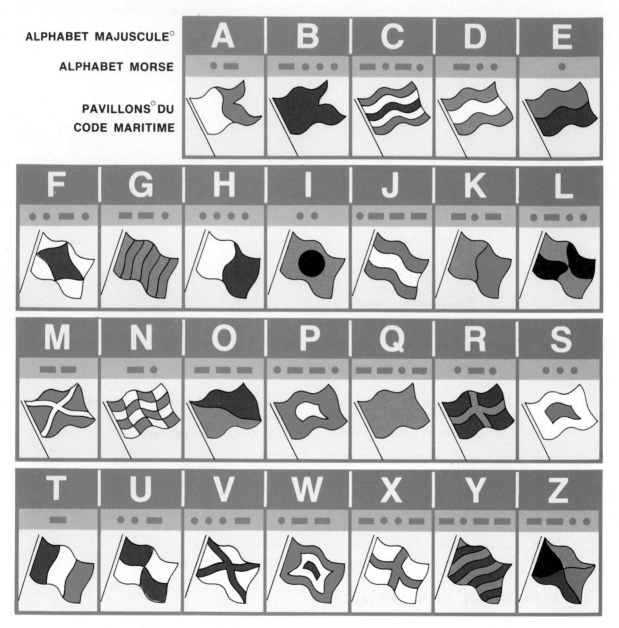

ALPHABET MAJUSCULE°

ALPHABET MORSE

PAVILLONS° DU CODE MARITIME

A	B	C	D	E
F	G	H	I	J	K	L
M	N	O	P	Q	R	S
T	U	V	W	X	Y	Z

Jadis, et quelquefois encore de nos jours°, les bateaux communiquaient à l'aide de° pavillons ou de signes lumineux°. Voyez si vous pouvez déchiffrer° le message suivant et si vous pouvez envoyer vos propres messages. (Annoncez° la lettre D, par exemple, de la façon suivante : un tiret°, deux points°.)

• — • — • •• • — — • • / • • • — — — — — — • — • • /
— • — — — — — / • — • / — — — — — • — • • • • •

VOCABULAIRE : **l'alphabet majuscule** *alphabet in capital letters;* **pavillons** *flags;* **de nos jours** *nowadays;* **à l'aide de** *with the help of;* **signes lumineux** *light signals;* **déchiffrer** *decipher;* **annoncez** *give;* **tiret** *dash;* **point** *dot.*

MON JOURNAL DE BORD   3ᵉ jour

Ce que nous avons fait aujourd'hui.

Quand nous nous sommes levés ce matin, il ne faisait pas beau. La météo annonçait une tempête sur le lac. Nous devions prendre les bateaux et aller sur une plage voisine pour faire un pique-nique et nous baigner. Malheureusement notre chef nous a dit qu'il fallait renoncer à notre sortie à cause du temps. Dommage ! Nous étions déjà tout contents à l'idée de ne pas avoir à faire la cuisine et la vaisselle !

Ce que j'ai appris.

C'est moi qui ai fait la première partie de la veille de nuit dans le sémaphore. La nuit était très claire. Les étoiles m'ont semblé beaucoup plus brillantes qu'à Montargis. J'ai noté le passage de deux bateaux qui traversaient le lac. C'était assez impressionnant d'être seul la nuit, perché dans les arbres !

Photo 3: François in the watchtower
Photo 4: The watchtower

10 **Répondez aux questions.**

1. Quel temps faisait-il quand les garçons se sont levés?
2. Qu'est-ce que la météo annonçait?
3. Qu'est-ce que François et son équipe devaient faire ce jour-là?
4. Qu'est-ce que leur chef leur a dit?
5. Pourquoi est-ce qu'ils étaient déjà tout contents?
6. Qui a fait la première partie de la veille de nuit?
7. Quel temps faisait-il?
8. Comment est-ce que François a trouvé les étoiles?
9. Qu'est-ce qu'il a noté?
10. Que faisaient ces bateaux?

11 **Histoire en chaîne.**

Vous avez passé une journée dans les bois tous ensemble. Vous racontez ce que vous avez fait.
ELÈVE 1 : Nous sommes partis très tôt.
ELÈVE 2 : Il faisait très beau.
ELÈVE 3 : Nous étions vingt garçons et quinze filles.
ELÈVE 4 : Dans nos sacs à dos, nous avions...

12 **PASSE COMPOSE OR IMPARFAIT**

The passé composé and the imparfait both express past time. The passé composé is used to indicate that the action has been completed. The imparfait is used to indicate that the action was in progress at a certain time. The following chart reviews the uses of the passé composé and the imparfait.

PASSE COMPOSE	IMPARFAIT
Completed Nous **avons parlé** de nos vacances.	Repetition Nous **allions** tous les ans à « La Gracieuse ».
Completed J'**ai noté** le passage de deux bateaux.	In Progress Ils **traversaient** le lac.
Completed J'**ai fini** ma veille à 10 h. Nous **sommes rentrés** à 2 h.	Existing Condition Il **faisait** très beau. Nous **avions** très faim.

13 **François raconte à un ami :** ⊗

Ce jour-là, nous avons attrapé des poissons.
Ce jour-là, nous nous sommes baignés.
Ce jour-là, Alain est venu avec nous.
Ce jour-là, j'ai traversé le lac.
Ce jour-là, je suis revenu seul.
Ce jour-là, des garçons sont partis sans leur chef.

Mais en général, nous n'attrapions jamais de poissons.
...nous ne nous baignions jamais.
...il ne venait jamais avec nous.
...je ne traversais jamais le lac.
...je ne revenais jamais seul.
...ils ne partaient jamais sans leur chef.

14 Quand François était à « La Gracieuse ». ⊗

Il allait souvent à la plage.
Il se baignait souvent.
Il faisait souvent la veille de nuit.
Il traversait souvent le lac en bateau.

Moi, je suis allé(e) à la plage hier.
Moi, je me suis baigné(e) hier.
Moi, j'ai fait la veille de nuit hier.
Moi, j'ai traversé le lac en bateau hier.

15 Le père de François allait dans un camp de vacances. ⊗

Hier, nous avons fait une excursion.

De mon temps, on ne faisait jamais d'excursion.

Hier, nous sommes allés à la pêche.
Hier, nous avons exploré l'île.
Hier, nous avons joué au volley-ball.
Hier, nous avons passé la nuit dans le sémaphore.

. . . on n'allait jamais à la pêche.
. . . on n'explorait jamais l'île.
. . . on ne jouait jamais au volley-ball.
. . . on ne passait jamais la nuit dans le sémaphore.

16 EXERCICE ECRIT For answers to 2 and 3, see p. T42.

1. Lisez ce que François a écrit dans son journal de bord et étudiez l'emploi du passé composé et de l'imparfait.

2. Récrivez le paragraphe suivant en mettant les verbes au passé composé ou à l'imparfait : Je me lève tôt. Tout le monde dort encore. Je sors de la tente. Il fait beau. Ça sent bon les pins. Les oiseaux chantent. Je ne sais pas où aller. Je décide de me promener au bord du lac. Il y a déjà beaucoup de bateaux sur le lac. Je suis tout content à l'idée de faire un pique-nique l'après-midi.

3. Récrivez le même paragraphe au passé comme si François parlait de lui et d'un de ses amis. Commencez : Nous nous sommes levés tôt…

17 EXERCICE DE COMPREHENSION ⊗ For script, see p. T41.

	0	1	2	3	4	5	6	7	8
Un bateau	✓								
Un lac									
Une plage									
Une tente									

18 EXERCICE DE CONVERSATION

Vous rencontrez un(e) camarade de classe que vous n'avez pas vu(e) depuis trois ans. Ensemble vous vous souvenez…
1. de quand vous étiez en classe ensemble : des amis que vous aviez, du genre de musique que vous aimiez, des sports que vous faisiez, etc.
2. d'une excursion que vous avez faite ensemble.
3. d'une sortie que vous avez faite en mer.
4. d'un été que vous avez passé dans une ferme.

19 Quatre nœuds. ⊗

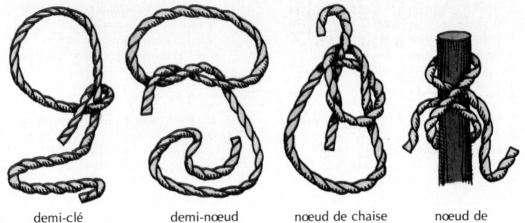

demi-clé demi-nœud nœud de chaise nœud de cabestan

Si vous voulez faire de la voile, il est très utile de savoir faire ces quatre nœuds. Exercez-vous à les faire avec de la ficelle.

VOCABULAIRE : **nœuds** *knots;* **demi-clé** *half hitch;* **demi-nœud** *half knot;* **nœud de chaise** *bowline;* **nœud de cabestan** *clove hitch;* **faire de la voile** *to sail;* **utile** *useful;* **exercez-vous** *practice;* **ficelle** *string.*

20 WORD LIST

1–8
des affaires (f.) *belongings*
un camp *camp*
 un camp de vacances *summer camp*
un chef *leader*
une dune *dune*
un journal de bord *"log," diary*
un lac *lake*
le **nôtre** *ours*
un pin *pine tree*
une pompe *pump*
un sac à dos *backpack*
un sac de couchage *sleeping bag*
une tente *tent*
une vipère *poisonous snake*
une voile *sail*
 une école de voile *sailing school*

diviser en *divide into*
dormir (like **sortir**) *to sleep*
 dormir à poings fermés *to sleep like a log*
étaler *to spread out*
s'installer *to settle in*
se réunir (like **choisir**) *to get together*
sentir (like **sortir**) *to smell*

pieds-nus *barefoot*

en fin d'après-midi *at the end of the afternoon*
finalement *at last, finally*
par terre *on the ground*

on nous a conduits *they took us*

9–19
une étoile *star*
la nuit *night*
un passage *passing*
un pique-nique *picnic*
un sémaphore *watchtower*
une tempête *storm*
une veille *watch*

annoncer *to announce*
 nous annonçons *we announce*
noter *to write down*
renoncer à *to give up*
 nous renonçons *we give up*
sembler *to seem*
traverser *to cross*

brillant, –e *bright*
clair, –e *clear*
content, –e *pleased*
impressionant, –e *impressive*
noué, –e *knotted*
perché, –e *perched*

dommage *too bad*

tout(e) *very*

The photographs on the next page give an aerial view of the new Charles-de-Gaulle Airport in Roissy, near Paris. The round building is the main air terminal, and the buildings surrounding it are the "Satellites" where planes depart and arrive. That is why at Roissy passengers depart from "Satellites" rather than the more usual "porte."

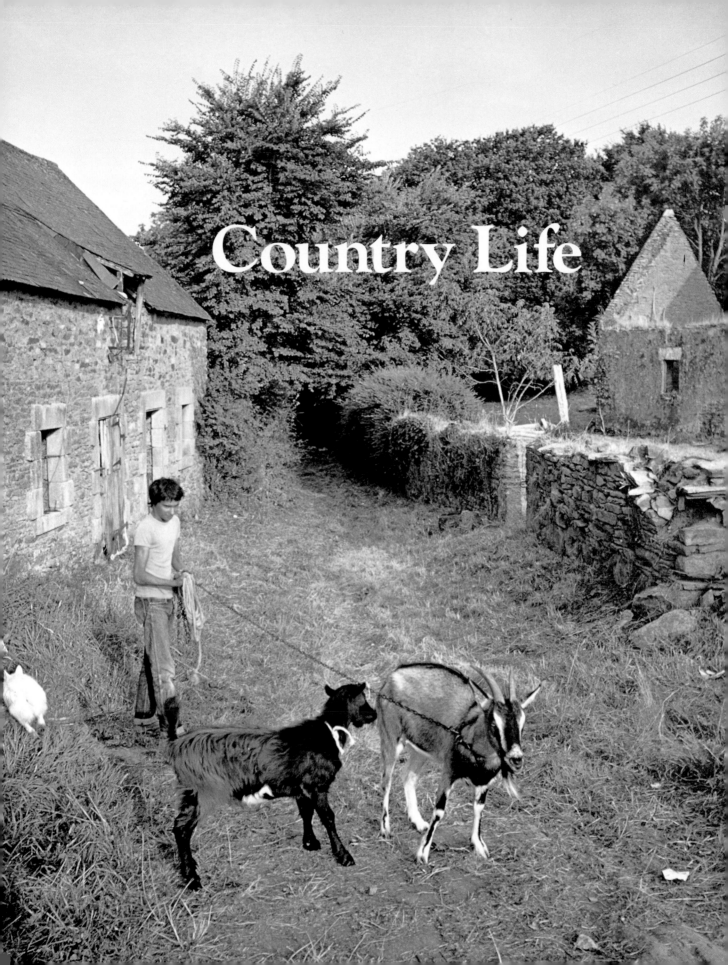

Country Life

1　2　3　4　5

French-speaking people have a very strong feeling for the land, its culture, and its products. They enjoy food, and they know that the secret of good cuisine lies in quality farming and husbandry. Farms in France, Switzerland, and Quebec are mechanized to some extent, but on the whole they are still small family farms cultivating a variety of products on a small scale. Whatever the farmers grow or raise, their work is very hard, tied as it is to the cycle of the seasons and the demands of the livestock. However, the satisfaction of living a life close to nature is very strong, and most of these farmers would not think of a life away from the land.

Here are a few glimpses of farm life in French-speaking countries.

(1) Field lying fallow in Quebec Province.
(2) Barn in the Pyrenees.
(3) Vineyard in Alsace.
(4) Picking squash in Brittany.
(5) Herding cows in the Swiss Jura.
(6) Sheep grazing in the Pyrenees.
(7) Tending apple trees in orchard in Brittany.
(8) Farm on the Ile d'Orléans, Quebec.
(9) Feeding calves on a farm in Normandy.

Plate 19

Each village is built in one style which is the style of its region, and each region has its distinctive style. These "country" styles evolved a long time ago, when regions were fairly isolated from one another and had a life of their own. Each style reflects the kind of building materials available in the region and the demands of its climate. Here are some examples.

(1) Aquitaine style: yellow stones, tiled roof.
(2) Brittany style: gray stone walls and roof.
(3) Corsica style: pastel-colored walls.
(4) Quebec style: wooden walls, double windows.
(5) Alsace style: white walls with wood designs.

1

2 3

4 5

At weddings, fairs, or festivals, country people, young and old, love to wear the traditional dress of their region. Just like architectural styles, and for much the same reasons, traditional "country" dress styles vary widely from region to region. Here are a few examples of them worn by: (1) lady from Brittany, (2) "gardian" from Camargue, (3) little girls from Alsace, (4) young women from Aquitaine. It should be noted, though, that nowadays these beautiful country costumes are worn only on special occasions, and that in everyday life country people are more likely to be found wearing jeans and T-shirts!

Plate 23

Villages and small towns come alive regularly on market and fair days. Markets take place once a week, with farmers coming from the surrounding countryside to sell milk products, vegetables, poultry, etc., and to buy what they need and do not produce themselves. Once a month, some small towns hold country fairs devoted to the selling and buying of livestock: cattle, horses, sheep, etc. These fairs are for business, but they are also occasions to meet friends and have a good time after all the hard work on the farm.

Plate 24

19
A L' AEROPORT

A l'aéroport Charles-de-Gaulle. ⊗

Richard et Arnaud Aché sont allés chercher le correspondant anglais de Richard à l'aéroport de Roissy.[1] Nigel Barns vient passer un mois avec les Aché pour apprendre à parler français. C'est la première fois que Nigel et Richard vont se rencontrer : en effet, les deux garçons ne se connaissent que par correspondance. Ils ont échangé leur photo pour pouvoir se reconnaître à l'aéroport. Nigel a écrit à Richard qu'il prenait le vol Air France 849 arrivant à 16 h à Roissy. Richard et Arnaud sont un peu en avance. Les deux frères vont au comptoir de la compagnie Air France pour demander des renseignements.

RICHARD	Pardon, Mademoiselle. Le vol 849 est à l'heure?
L'HÔTESSE	Voyons, le vol 849 en provenance de Londres... Tous les vols en provenance de Londres ont été retardés d'une heure.
RICHARD	Une heure de retard!
L'HÔTESSE	Hé oui! A cause du brouillard!
ARNAUD	Qu'est-ce qu'on va faire pendant une heure?
L'HÔTESSE	Allez donc à la terrasse.
ARNAUD	Bonne idée! Allons-y!

2   De la terrasse, ils regardent les avions décoller et atterrir.

2 Répondez aux questions.

1. Où sont allés Richard et Arnaud? Pourquoi?
2. Est-ce que Nigel et Richard se sont déjà rencontrés?
3. Comment est-ce qu'ils vont se reconnaître à l'aéroport?
4. Quel vol est-ce que Nigel doit prendre?
5. Qu'est-ce que Richard demande à l'hôtesse?
6. Pourquoi est-ce que le vol 849 a une heure de retard?
7. Qu'est-ce que les deux frères vont faire pendant une heure?
8. Qu'est-ce qu'ils vont faire sur la terrasse?

3 Et vous?

1. Vous avez déjà pris l'avion?
2. Vous avez pris quelle compagnie?
3. Vous êtes parti(e) de quel aéroport?
4. Où est-ce que vous êtes arrivé(e)?
5. Avec qui est-ce que vous étiez?
6. C'était un petit ou un grand avion?
7. On vous a servi un repas?
8. Vous avez regardé un film? Lequel?
9. Vous êtes arrivé(e) à l'heure?
10. Qui vous attendait à l'aéroport?

4 EXERCICE ORAL ⊗

[1] Paris has two airports open for passenger service. The newest is the Charles-de-Gaulle Airport, located at Roissy-en-France, about fifteen miles north of Paris. The other one is Orly, which is divided into several terminals.

5 MORE ON REFLEXIVE CONSTRUCTIONS

1. The plural reflexive pronouns **nous, vous,** and **se** may mean *each other:*

Nous **nous** téléphonons souvent.	*We call each other often.*
Vous **vous** connaissez?	*Do you know each other?*
Ils ne **se** sont jamais vus.	*They have never seen each other.*

2. In the passé composé, remember that when the reflexive pronoun is the direct object of the verb, the past participle agrees with it: **Ils se sont rencontrés il y a trois ans.** There is no agreement when the reflexive pronoun is the indirect object: **Ils ne se sont jamais parlé.**

6 Nigel est le correspondant de Richard. ⊗

Richard écrit souvent à Nigel. Nigel écrit souvent à Richard.	Richard et Nigel s'écrivent souvent.
Richard n'a jamais vu Nigel. Nigel n'a jamais vu Richard.	Richard et Nigel ne se sont jamais vus.
Richard ne connaît pas Nigel. Nigel ne connaît pas Richard.	Richard et Nigel ne se connaissent pas.
Richard a téléphoné à Nigel. Nigel a téléphoné à Richard.	Richard et Nigel se sont téléphoné.

7 Devant le tableau des arrivées. ⊗

Richard et Arnaud sont redescendus regarder le tableau des arrivées. Le vol de Nigel est peut-être affiché maintenant! Eh non, toujours rien, malheureusement!

Indicatif musical suivi d'une annonce : ♩♩♪ « Arrivée en provenance de Dakar, vol Air France 304, sortie porte No 11. *Arrival from Dakar, Air France flight 304, exit gate No 11.* »

ARRIVEES			
Vol	**Provenance**	**Horaire**	**Porte**
AF 849	LONDRES	16:00	
AF 914	AMSTERDAM	16:15	14
AF 636	ROME	16:45	16
AF 600	ATHENES	16:50	15
AA 18	ALGER	17:00	17
AF 304	DAKAR	17:05	11
TW 801	NEW-YORK	17:15	
AF 138	TEL-AVIV	17:35	
AF 606	ANKARA	18:00	

RICHARD Tiens, je vais te poser des colles… C'est où Dakar?

ARNAUD Au Sénégal, bien sûr!

RICHARD Et Tel-Aviv?

ARNAUD En Israël!

RICHARD Je parie que tu ne sais pas où est Ankara.

ARNAUD C'est vrai. Aucune idée.

RICHARD En Turquie! C'est la capitale de la Turquie.

ARNAUD A toi, maintenant. Quelle est la capitale du Maroc?

RICHARD Rabat, bien sûr!

8 Répondez aux questions.

1. Où se trouvent Richard et Arnaud?
2. Est-ce que le vol de Nigel est affiché?
3. Qu'est-ce qu'on entend?
4. D'où vient le vol Air France 304?
5. Où se trouve Dakar?
6. Et Tel-Aviv?
7. Quelle est la capitale de la Turquie?
8. Et la capitale du Maroc?

There is no gate number for the London flight, because gate numbers are posted only when planes are about to land or have already landed.

9 Et vous, êtes-vous bon (bonne) en géographie? ⊗

I. Où se trouvent ces pays? Trouvez-les sur la carte p. 197.

l'Algérie   l'Angleterre   la Belgique   l'Espagne   l'Italie
le Maroc   le Portugal   la Russie (l'U.R.S.S.)   la Tunisie

II. Ce sont les capitales de quels pays? Trouvez-les sur la carte p. 197.

Moscou   Lisbonne   Tunis   Bruxelles   Londres   Alger   Madrid   Rome   Rabat

A game you might play: Ça commence par un A et ça finit par un E. Response: C'est l'Algérie . . .

10 EXERCICE ORAL ⊗

11 NAMES OF COUNTRIES

Répondez aux questions qui suivent les exemples. ⊗

Paris est **en France.**   C'est la capitale de **la France.**
Ottawa est **au Canada.**   C'est la capitale **du Canada.**

In the sentences on the right, what is the gender of **France,** masculine or feminine? And of **Canada?** In the sentences on the left, what preposition is used with **France, en** or **à?** And with **Canada?** Is an article also used with **France?** And with **Canada?**

12 Lisez la généralisation suivante.

1. Names of countries, like other nouns, are either masculine or feminine. The articles **le, la,** or **les** normally precede them: **La France est un beau pays.** Note, however, that no article is used with **Israël : Israël est un beau pays.**

2. With names of countries that are feminine singular and with those that are masculine singular beginning with a vowel sound, **en** is used to express "to" or "in" and **de** to express "from." In both cases no article follows **en** or **de.** With all other names of countries, **au/aux** is used to express "to" or "in" and **du/des** to express "from."

	• Feminine names of countries • Masculine names of countries beginning with a vowel sound.		• Masculine names of countries beginning with a consonant sound. • Plural names of countries.	
IN	J'habite J'habite	en en	France. Israël.	J'habite J'habite	au aux	Canada. Etats-Unis.
TO	Je vais Je vais	en en	France. Israël.	Je vais Je vais	au aux	Canada. Etats-Unis.
FROM	Je viens je viens	de d'	France. Israël.	Je viens Je viens	du des	Canada. Etats-Unis.

13 Richard et Arnaud se posent des colles. ⊗

Où se trouve Ottawa?   Au Canada, bien sûr! C'est la capitale du Canada.

Et Londres? / Et Rome? / Et Dakar? / Et Paris? / Et Washington? / Et Tunis? / Et Bruxelles? / Et Rabat? / Et Moscou? / Et Madrid? / Et Lisbonne? En Angleterre . . . de l'Angleterre. / En Italie . . . de l'Italie. / Au Sénégal . . . du Sénégal. / En France . . . de la France. / Aux Etats-Unis . . . des Etats-Unis. / En Tunisie . . . de la Tunisie. / En Belgique . . . de la Belgique. / Au Maroc . . . du Maroc. / En U.R.S.S. . . . de l'U.R.S.S. / En Espagne . . . de l'Espagne. / Au Portugal . . . du Portugal.

14 Bon Voyage! ⊗

Choisissez un vol. Par exemple, le vol Paris-Bucarest avec escales à Milan et Zagreb. Dites…

1. de quel pays vous partez. De France.
2. quels pays vous allez survoler. L'Italie et la Yougoslavie.
3. dans quel pays vous allez arriver. En Roumanie.

Variation: Have students make up routes with stops.

VOCABULAIRE : **Bon Voyage!** *Have a good trip!;* **une escale** *stop-over;* **survoler** *to fly over.*

On this map, we have deliberately used the names by which the countries are known in ordinary French conversation. We have also indicated the gender of the name **Chapitre 19**   **A l'Aéroport**   **197** of each country to help students play the game.

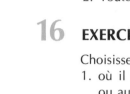

15 Demandez à un(e) camarade :

1. De quels pays est-ce qu'on vient dans ta famille?
2. Toute ta famille habite ici?
3. Est-ce que tu connais des gens qui viennent d'autres pays? Desquels?
4. Est-ce qu'ils sont en visite?

16 EXERCICE DE CONVERSATION

Choisissez un pays et dites tout ce que vous savez sur ce pays. Dites...

1. où il se trouve : à l'est, à l'ouest, au nord ou au sud de quel pays.
2. si c'est un grand ou un petit pays.
3. quelle en est la capitale.
4. comment est le climat : chaud en été, etc.
5. quels en sont les fleuves, les montagnes, les grandes villes, etc.

17 A l'arrivée. ⊗

Finalement l'avion de Nigel a atterri. Richard a la photo de Nigel en mains, et il essaie de le reconnaître parmi les passagers qui arrivent.

ARNAUD	Tiens, le grand blond qui parle avec la dame brune!
RICHARD	Mais non, ce n'est pas lui. Ce n'est pas un Anglais de toute façon. Je te parie que c'est un Américain.
ARNAUD	A quoi est-ce que tu vois ça?
RICHARD	A sa façon décontractée de marcher.
ARNAUD	Moi, je trouve qu'il a plutôt l'air allemand.
RICHARD	Approchons-nous un peu pour voir quelle langue ils parlent.
ARNAUD	Tu comprends ce qu'ils disent?
RICHARD	Je pense bien! Ce sont des Français!

18 Epilogue. ⊗

Malheureusement, Nigel n'était pas dans cet avion. Il avait raté celui qu'il devait prendre, et il avait pris le vol suivant qui allait atterrir... une heure plus tard!

19 Répondez aux questions.

1. Qu'est-ce que Richard a en mains?
2. Qu'est-ce qu'il essaie de faire?
3. Est-ce que Richard trouve que le grand blond a l'air anglais?
4. D'après Arnaud, est-ce que le grand blond est américain? Qu'est-ce qu'il est?
5. Pourquoi est-ce que Richard et Arnaud s'approchent du grand blond et de la dame brune?
6. Est-ce que ce sont des Allemands?
7. Est-ce que Richard et Arnaud ont finalement trouvé Nigel? Pourquoi?

20 EXERCICE ORAL ⊗

21

THE VERB dire

The following chart includes the present-tense forms of the verb **dire,** *to say, to tell.* ⊗

Qu'est-ce que je	**dis?**	Qu'est-ce que nous	**disons?**
Qu'est-ce que tu	**dis?**	Qu'est-ce que vous	**dites?**
Qu'est-ce qu'il	**dit?**	Qu'est-ce qu'ils	**disent?**

The past participle of **dire** is **dit : Il n'a rien dit.**

22 ### Tout le monde parle français. ⊗

Tu comprends ce qu'ils disent?　　　　　Pas tout ce qu'ils disent.
ce que je dis / ce qu'il dit / ce que nous disons

Pas tout ce que tu dis. / Pas tout ce qu'il dit. / Pas tout ce que vous dites.

23 ### On n'entend rien à l'aéroport. ⊗

Qu'est-ce que tu as dit?　　　　　Je n'ai rien dit.
elle a dit / ils ont dit / vous avez dit, vous deux

Elle n'a rien dit. / Ils n'ont rien dit. / Nous n'avons rien dit.

24 # NATIONALITIES AND LANGUAGES

1. Nationality may be expressed by an adjective: **Je suis américain(e). Ils/Elles sont américain(e)s.** These adjectives can also be used as nouns: **C'est un(e) Américain(e). Ce sont des Américain(e)s.** With a noun, **ce** is used to express "he," "she," or "they."

2. Names of languages are masculine. They usually take the form of a masculine adjective of nationality. They are usually preceded by the article **le,** except when they immediately follow **parler. Je comprends le français,** but **Je parle français.**

Make clear: nouns of nationality are capitalized; adjectives of nationality and names of languages are not.

25 ### Pays, nationalités et langues. ⊗

Il / Elle vient...	Il / Elle est...	Il / Elle parle...
d'Allemagne.	allemand, -e.	allemand.
d'Angleterre.	anglais, -e.	anglais.
de Belgique.	belge.	français et néerlandais.
du Canada.	canadien, -ienne.	français et anglais.
d'Espagne.	espagnol, -e.	espagnol.
des Etats-Unis.	américain, -e.	anglais.
de France.	français, -e.	français.
d'Israël.	israélien, -ienne.	hébreu.
d'Italie.	italien, -ienne.	italien.
du Maroc.	marocain, -e.	arabe et français.
du Portugal.	portugais, -e.	portugais.
de Russie (d'U.R.S.S.).	russe.	russe.
du Sénégal.	sénégalais, -e.	ouolof et français.
de Tunisie.	tunisien, -ienne.	arabe et français.

The expression "avoir l'air" + adjective was manipulated extensively in Unit 8, pp. 76-77, and should give no trouble here.

26 Richard et Arnaud parlent des passagers : ⊗

Celui-là, il a l'air anglais.	Oui, c'est sûrement un Anglais.
Ceux-là, ils ont l'air espagnols.	Oui, ce sont sûrement des Espagnols.
Celle-là, elle a l'air italienne.	Oui, c'est sûrement une Italienne.
Celles-là, elles ont l'air françaises.	Oui, ce sont sûrement des Françaises.
Ceux-là, ils ont l'air américains.	Oui, ce sont sûrement des Américains.
Ceux-là, ils ont l'air allemands.	Oui, ce sont sûrement des Allemands.
Ceux-là, ils ont l'air russes.	Oui, ce sont sûrement des Russes.

27 De quelle nationalité étaient-ils? ⊗

Louis Pasteur?   Il était français.

Elizabeth I d'Angleterre? / Don Quichotte de la Manche? / Ludwig Van Beethoven? / William Shakespeare? / Benjamin Franklin? / Betsy Ross? Elle était anglaise. / Il était espagnol. / Il était allemand. / Il était anglais. / Il était américain. / Elle était américaine.

28 Un passager dit à un autre : ⊗

Je vais à Rome.   Vous parlez italien?

à Mexico / à New York / à Moscou / à Bonn

Vous parlez espagnol? / Vous parlez anglais? / Vous parlez russe? / Vous parlez allemand?

29 Et vous?

1. Le français c'est facile ou difficile, d'après vous?
2. Est-ce que vous apprenez une autre langue?
3. Quelles langues est-ce que vous parlez chez vous?
4. Quelles langues est-ce que vos parents ou grands-parents parlent?
5. Est-ce que vous comprenez tout ce que votre professeur de français dit?

30 EXERCICE DE COMPREHENSION ⊗ For script, see p. T43.

				4	5	6	7	8
Un garçon								
Une fille	✓							

31 EXERCICE ECRIT

Récrivez le paragraphe suivant en utilisant des noms de pays, de villes, etc.

En août, je vais en _____ . Je vais chez des amis qui habitent à _____ . Tout le monde dit que les _____ sont très sympathiques. Ensuite, je vais au _____ pendant deux jours. Malheureusement, je ne parle pas bien _____ . Je vais seulement acheter quelques disques _____ parce que j'aime beaucoup les chansons _____ , et ensuite je vais rentrer.

32 EXERCICE DE CONVERSATION

Dites d'où viennent les membres de votre famille. Par exemple : « Le grand-père de ma mère était italien. Il habitait dans un petit village dans le sud de l'Italie. Il est venu aux Etats-Unis en 18—. Il ne parlait pas l'anglais quand il est arrivé, seulement l'italien, mais il a appris l'anglais très vite. »

33 REDACTION

Imaginez que vous avez un(e) correspondant(e). Dites…
1. de quelle nationalité il/elle est.
2. en quelle langue il/elle vous écrit.
3. si vous vous écrivez souvent.
4. si son anglais est bon ou mauvais.
5. si vous avez une photo de lui/d'elle (si oui, décrivez-le/la).
6. si vous vous êtes rencontré(e)s, si vous allez bientôt vous rencontrer, et où.

34 Si vous allez dans un pays étranger°. ⊗

VOCABULAIRE : **étranger** *foreign;* **une valise** *suitcase;* **les bagages** *luggage;* **avoir droit à** *to be allowed;* **un siège** *seat;* **côté fenêtre** *window side;* **côté allée** *aisle side;* **un endroit** *place, section;* **vous asseoir** *to sit;* **attachez vos ceintures** *fasten seatbelts;* **défense de fumer** *no smoking;* **consignes de sécurité** *safety rules;* **ennuyez** *bother;* **hôtesse** *stewardess;* **rien à déclarer** *nothing to declare;* **Qu'est-ce que ça peut vous faire!** *What business is it of yours?;* **la douane** *customs;* **soyez poli** *be polite;* **un douanier** *customs official.*

Photographs on facing page, from left to right, top to bottom: 1) Modern hotel in Tunis (Hôtel du Lac). 2) Old ramparts in Sousse. 3) Resort near Sousse. 4) Modern mosque and minaret in Tunis. 5) Typical market scene in Sousse. 6) Nadia, Aziz, and Imed Slim on beach near Sousse. 7) Tunisia produces many beautiful handcrafted items; for example, these copper trays. 8) Olive trees are one of the principal agricultural resources of Tunisia. 9) Typical Tunisian house: whitewashed walls, blue painted doors and shutters, flat roof with cupola. 10) Donkeys and camels are the principal beasts of burden in Tunisia. 11) Example of the new Tunisian (continued below)

35   WORD LIST

1–6

un aéroport *airport*	**l'Angleterre** (f.) *England*	**anglais, –e** *English*
un avion *airplane*	**la Belgique** *Belgium*	
le brouillard *fog*	**l'Espagne** (f.) *Spain*	**arrivant** *arriving*
une compagnie *airline*	**le Maroc** *Morocco*	
un comptoir *counter*	**la Turquie** *Turkey*	**à l'heure** *on time*
un(e) correspondant(e) *pen pal*		**1 h de retard** *an hour late*
une hôtesse *hostess*	**apprendre à** (like **prendre**)	**en avance** *early*
une idée *idea*	*to learn*	**en provenance de** *from, coming*
des renseignements (m.)	**atterrir** (like **choisir**) *to land*	*from*
information	**se connaître** *to know each other*	
une terrasse *observation deck*	**décoller** *to take off*	**en effet** *the fact is*
un vol *flight*	**échanger** *to exchange*	**par correspondance** *in writing*
Bruxelles *Brussels*	**se reconnaître** *to recognize*	**pardon** *excuse me*
Londres *London*	*each other*	
	se rencontrer *to meet each*	**ils ont été retardés d'une heure**
	other	*they were delayed an hour*

7–16

l'Allemagne *Germany*	**afficher** *to post*	**aucun, –e** *no*
une annonce *announcement*	**parier** *to bet*	**fort, –e** *strong*
une capitale *capital*	**redescendre** *to go down again*	**suivi, –e (de)** *followed (by)*
un indicatif musical *chimes (to*		
indicate an announcement)	**poser des colles** *to quiz*	
une porte *gate*		
le tableau des arrivées *arrivals*		
board		

17–34

une dame *lady*	**s'approcher (de)** *to get closer*	**allemand, –e** *German*
une façon *way, manner*	**comprendre** (like **prendre**) *to*	**décontracté, –e** *loose, easy-going*
un(e) passager (-ère) *passenger*	*understand*	**de toute façon** *anyway*
un Américain *an American*	**dire** *to say, to tell*	**en mains** *in hand*
un Anglais *an Englishman*	**marcher** *to walk*	**parmi** *among*
un Français *a Frenchman*	**rater** *to miss*	
		A quoi est-ce que tu vois ça?
	il avait pris *he had taken*	*How can you tell?*
	il avait raté *he had missed*	**je pense bien** *of course*
	il devait prendre *he was*	
	supposed to take	

25

un pays *country*	**une nationalité** *nationality*	**une langue** *language*
l'Allemagne (f.) *Germany*	**allemand, –e** *German*	**l'allemand** (m.) *German*
l'Angleterre (f.) *England*	**anglais, –e** *English*	**l'anglais** (m.) *English*
la Belgique *Belgium*	**belge** *Belgian*	**le français, le néerlandais** *French,*
		Dutch
le Canada *Canada*	**canadien, –ienne** *Canadian*	**le français, l'anglais** (m.) *French,*
		English
l'Espagne (f.) *Spain*	**espagnol, –e** *Spanish*	**l'espagnol** (m.) *Spanish*
les Etats-Unis (m.) *the United*	**américain, –e** *American*	**l'anglais** (m.) *English*
States		
la France *France*	**français, –e** *French*	**le français** *French*
Israël (m.) *Israel*	**israélien, –ienne** *Israeli*	**l'hébreu** (m.) *Hebrew*
l'Italie (f.) *Italy*	**italien, –ienne** *Italian*	**l'italien** (m.) *Italian*
le Maroc *Morocco*	**marocain, –e** *Moroccan*	**l'arabe** (m.), **le français** *Arabic,*
		French
le Portugal *Portugal*	**portugais, –e** *Portuguese*	**le portugais** *Portuguese*
la Russie (l'U.R.S.S.) *Russia*	**russe** *Russian*	**le russe** *Russian*
(U.S.S.R.)		
le Sénégal *Senegal*	**sénégalais, –e** *Senegalese*	**le ouolof, le français** *Wolof,*
		French
la Tunisie *Tunisia*	**tunisien, –ienne** *Tunisian*	**l'arabe** (m.), **le français** *Arabic,*
		French

20
EN TUNISIE

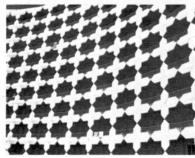

Photo 2: general view of Sousse, with the "ville moderne" in the foreground and the Mediterranean behind. Sousse's population: 100,000, second to Tunis, 700,000.

1 A Sousse, en Tunisie. ⊗

Photo 1: Samir, 14, is on the left, and Aziz, 16, on the right. Both are high-school students.

Aziz Slim et son frère Samir vivent à Sousse, en Tunisie. La Tunisie est en Afrique du Nord. (Regardez la carte p. 197.) C'est un pays à peu près grand comme la Floride, avec une population d'environ six millions d'habitants.

Photo 3: Mixture of Arabic features (design of upper windows) and European features (design of shop windows). French culture and language have been part of Tunisian life since 1881 when France imposed a "protectorate" which lasted until 1956. Tunisia then became independent.

Comme toutes les villes d'Afrique du Nord, Sousse se compose de deux villes : la vieille ville ou « médina », entourée de remparts, et la ville moderne à l'extérieur des remparts.

Comme tous les Tunisiens, les gens de Sousse parlent aussi bien le français que l'arabe et vivent à la fois à l'européenne et à l'orientale.

Dans les rues, on voit un mélange de vêtements européens et de vêtements traditionnels tels que des saris rouges ou blancs pour les femmes, des djellabas (longues robes) et des chéchias (calottes rouges) pour les hommes.

Photo 4: The red costume of these women is typical of Sousse and its region. Traditional women's dress varies from region to region: on the island of Djerba women wear long dark-blue robes and veils and little straw hats; in the desert to the south, women wear black robes and veils adorned with heavy silver jewelry.

2 Dans la médina. ⊗

"Medina" means "Arabic city" and "souk" means "market." Artisans and merchants tend to set up shop with others dealing in the same craft or trade. Each of these groups is a small "market," for example "le souk des orfèvres," or "le souk des potiers." Collectively, the large marketplace is therefore called "les souks."

Aziz et Samir vont souvent flâner dans les souks de la médina. Ici, ils regardent un artisan au travail. Là, ils discutent avec un marchand. Plus loin, ils admirent des tapis, des poteries, des plateaux en cuivre, des bijoux en argent ou des poufs en cuir.

Aziz parle à Omar, un orfèvre :

AZIZ Qui est-ce qui t'a appris ton métier?
OMAR Mon père. Mais lui, c'est un artiste!
AZIZ Qu'est-ce qui t'empêche d'être un artiste, toi aussi?
OMAR Ça ne rapporte pas!

Pour faire des achats dans les souks, il faut savoir marchander...

SAMIR C'est combien ce portefeuille?
ABDEL Cinq dinars.[1]
SAMIR Tu me prends pour un touriste! Deux dinars!
ABDEL Pour qui est-ce que tu achètes ça?
SAMIR Pour mon père.
ABDEL Alors, dans ce cas, je te fais un prix d'ami : trois dinars!

3 Répondez aux questions.

1. Où habitent Aziz et Samir Slim?
2. Où est-ce qu'ils vont souvent flâner?
3. Qui est-ce qui travaille dans les souks?
4. Qu'est-ce qu'on vend dans les souks?
5. Qui est-ce qui a appris le métier d'orfèvre à Omar?
6. Pour qui est-ce que Samir veut acheter un portefeuille? Qu'est-ce qu'il fait?

[1] Tunisian currency: one dinar is roughly equivalent to two dollars.

Many Arabic first names have lexical meanings in Arabic: Aziz means "darling" or "beloved"; Hassan, "good"; Ali, "high"; Imed, "pillar"; Rachid, "wiseman"; Samir, "faithful companion"; and Monia, "hope."

1 Rachid, le potier, fait des poteries. 2 Hassan, le tailleur, fait des burnous.

Point out that this exercise, No. 4, is based on captions and photos 1, 2, 3, 4, and continues on facing page.

4 Qu'est-ce qu'ils font, ces artisans? ⊗

Qu'est-ce qu'il fait, Rachid?	Des poteries.
Qui est-ce qui fait des poteries?	Rachid, le potier.
Qu'est-ce qu'il fait, Hassan?	Des burnous.
Qui est-ce qui fait des burnous?	Hassan, le tailleur.

5 EXERCICE ORAL ⊗

6 INTERROGATIVE PRONOUNS

Répondez aux questions qui suivent les exemples. ⊗

Qui est-ce qui travaille ici? **Les artisans?**
Qu'est-ce qui rapporte? **Les bijoux?**

What is the subject of **travaille?** And of **rapporte?** Does **qui est-ce qui** refer to people or to things? And **qu'est-ce qui?**

Qui est-ce que tu cherches? **Les frères Slim?**
Qu'est-ce que vous voulez? **Des poufs?**

Is **qui est-ce que** the subject or the object of **cherches?** Is **qu'est-ce que** the subject or the object of **voulez?** Does **qui est-ce que** refer to people or does it refer to things? And **qu'est-ce que?**

De qui est-ce que tu parles? **De ton père?**
De quoi est-ce que vous parlez? **De votre métier?**

Is it a person or a thing that is being discussed in the first question? What question word follows the preposition **de?** Is it a person or a thing that is being discussed in the second question? What question word follows the preposition **de?**

3

Ali, le cordonnier, fait des sandales.

4

Lamia, la tapissière, fait des tapis.

Qu'est-ce qu'il fait, Ali?	Des sandales.
Qui est-ce qui fait des sandales?	Ali, le cordonnier.
Qu'est-ce qu'elle fait, Lamia?	Des tapis.
Qui est-ce qui fait des tapis?	Lamia, la tapissière.

7 Lisez la généralisation suivante.

Interrogative pronouns are used to ask questions. Their form depends on whether they are subjects or objects of the verb and on whether they follow a preposition. Their form also changes depending on whether they refer to people or to things.

1. As subjects, interrogative pronouns end with **qui : qui est-ce qui / qu'est-ce qui.**

People	**Qui**	est-ce qui	travaille ici?	*Who works here?*
Things	**Qu'**		rapporte bien?	*What pays well?*

Qui est-ce qui can be used interchangeably with **qui.** For example: **Qui travaille ici?**

2. As objects, interrogative pronouns end with **que : qui est-ce que / qu'est-ce que.**

People	**Qui**	est-ce que	tu cherches?	*Whom are you looking for?*
Things	**Qu'**		vous voulez?	*What do you want?*

3. After prepositions (such as **de, à, chez**), the following interrogative pronouns are used: **qui est-ce que / quoi est-ce que.**

People	**De qui**	est-ce que	tu parles?	*Whom are you talking about?*
Things	**De quoi**		vous parlez?	*What are you talking about?*

8 Aziz dit à Samir qu'il va dans les souks :

Je vais voir Rachid, le potier.　　　　　Qui est-ce que tu vas voir?
Je vais acheter un burnous.　　　　　　Qu'est-ce que tu vas acheter?
Je vais acheter des sandales.　　　　　Qu'est-ce que tu vas acheter?
Je vais voir le tailleur.　　　　　　　　Qui est-ce que tu vas voir?
Je vais acheter un pouf.　　　　　　　　Qu'est-ce que tu vas acheter?

9 Aziz connaît bien les artisans.

Hassan est un bon tailleur.　　　　　　Qui est-ce qui est un bon tailleur?
Mais ses burnous sont trop chers.　　　Qu'est-ce qui est trop cher?
Ali est un bon cordonnier.　　　　　　　Qui est-ce qui est un bon cordonnier?
Mais ses sandales sont trop chères.　　Qu'est-ce qui est trop cher?
Omar est un bon orfèvre.　　　　　　　　Qui est-ce qui est un bon orfèvre?
Mais ses plateaux sont trop chers.　　　Qu'est-ce qui est trop cher?

10 Aziz parle de Rachid, le potier, à Samir :

Rachid travaille pour son oncle.　　　　Pour qui est-ce qu'il travaille?
Il travaille avec ses cousins.　　　　　　Avec qui est-ce qu'il travaille?
Il parle toujours de son métier.　　　　De quoi est-ce qu'il parle toujours?
Il habite chez son oncle.　　　　　　　　Chez qui est-ce qu'il habite?
Il écrit souvent à ses parents.　　　　　A qui est-ce qu'il écrit souvent?
Il rêve d'avoir une boutique à lui.　　　De quoi est-ce qu'il rêve?

11 EXERCICE ECRIT

Ecrivez les questions qui correspondent aux mots soulignés :
Ex. : C'est Ali qui a fait ces sandales.　　　Qui est-ce qui a fait ces sandales?
　　　　　　　　　　　　　　　　　　　　　　　　Qu'est-ce qu'Ali a fait?

1. C'est Samir qui a fait ce plateau en cuivre.　1. Qui est-ce qui a fait ce plateau en cuivre?
2. Il fait aussi des bijoux en argent.　　　　　　　Qu'est-ce que Samir a fait?
3. Il travaille pour un marchand des souks.　2. Qu'est-ce qu'il fait aussi?
4. Il parle toujours de son métier.　　　　　　　　En quoi est-ce qu'ils sont?
　　　　　　　　　　　　　　　　　　　　　　　　3. Pour qui est-ce qu'il travaille?
12 EXERCICE DE COMPREHENSION　　　4. De quoi est-ce qu'il parle toujours.

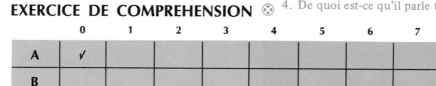

	0	1	2	3	4	5	6	7	8
A	✓								
B									

For script, see p. T45.

13 Et vous?

1. Est-ce qu'on parle plusieurs langues dans votre région? Lesquelles?
2. Est-ce que vous connaissez des gens qui parlent arabe? D'où viennent-ils?
3. Est-ce que vous connaissez des artisans? Qu'est-ce qu'ils font?
4. Est-ce que vous avez déjà marchandé? Où ça?
5. Qu'est-ce que vous avez acheté? Est-ce que vous avez bien marchandé?

Nadia is 19 and in her first year at the University of Tunis. She is studying for a degree in English. Leïla is 17 and is a high-school student. Monia is 10 and goes to "l'école primaire." Imed is 12 and goes to a secondary school.

14 Chez les Slim. ⊗

Aziz et Samir Slim ont trois sœurs—Nadia, Leïla, Monia—et un frère, Imed. Les Slim habitent dans la ville nouvelle où ils ont une grande maison blanche et moderne, entourée d'un jardin plein de bougainvilliers. La plage n'est pas loin de chez eux, et ils y vont souvent tous ensemble pour pique-niquer et s'amuser.

De gauche à droite : Imed, Leïla, Nadia, Monia et Mme Slim. Ils attendent M. Slim. Il est en train de sortir la voiture du garage.

Point out traditional Tunisian colors (white and blue) and Arabic designs (windows, door, gate) used for this modern house.

Nadia, Samir, Imed et Aziz jouent aux boules.

"Les boules" is a very popular game, especially in southern France. It is usually played with heavy metallic balls (each player has two) which are thrown as close as possible to a small wooden ball called "le cochonnet." The game is usually played between two teams of two players each. Here the Slims play the game with tennis balls—not at all orthodox, but great fun!

15 Répondez aux questions.

1. Combien de frères et sœurs ont Aziz et Samir?
2. Comment s'appellent leurs sœurs? Et leur frère?
3. Où habitent les Slim : dans la médina ou dans la ville nouvelle?
4. Comment est leur maison? Et leur jardin?
5. Où est-ce qu'ils vont souvent tous ensemble? Pour quoi faire?

Couscous is not an exclusively Tunisian dish but more generally North African, since it can be found anywhere in North Africa.

16 La cuisine tunisienne. ⊗

Nadia, Leïla et Monia aident leur mère à préparer le repas du soir. Madame Slim a décidé de faire des briks, une salade méchouia et un couscous.

Les briks sont des crêpes de pâte feuilletée, dans lesquelles on met un œuf et une farce; elles sont frites à l'huile et servies chaudes, avec des rondelles de citron.

La salade méchouia est un mélange de tomates, d'oignons et de poivrons grillés, coupés et arrosés d'huile d'olive; on la décore avec des tranches d'œuf dur.

Le couscous est un plat qui consiste en de la semoule de blé dur servie chaude avec un mélange de légumes et de viande (poulet ou mouton).

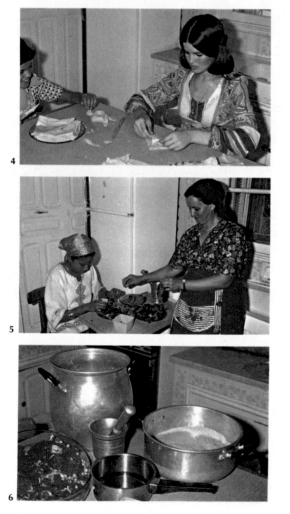

C'est Nadia qui se charge de faire les briks. Elle demande à sa petite sœur Monia de l'aider.

Leïla a commencé à préparer la salade méchouia. Elle a grillé des poivrons doux et maintenant elle les pèle. Leïla apprend à faire la cuisine, et elle suit les conseils de sa mère.

Madame Slim, elle, prépare le couscous. Elle épluche les légumes, elle assaisonne le mouton, et elle fait cuire le tout dans une grande marmite. La semoule qu'on appelle aussi « couscous » est cuite à la vapeur dans un panier placé au-dessus des légumes et de la viande.

17 **Répondez aux questions.**

1. Qui est-ce qui prépare le repas du soir?
2. Qu'est-ce que Madame Slim a décidé de faire?
3. Qui est-ce qui fait les briks?
4. A qui est-ce qu'elle demande de l'aider?
5. Qui apprend à faire la cuisine?

6. Et qu'est-ce qu'elle prépare?
7. Qui est-ce qui prépare le couscous?
8. Dans quoi est-ce qu'elle fait cuire les légumes et la viande?
9. Comment est cuite la semoule?

18 **EXERCICE ORAL** ⊗

19 **VERB + INFINITIVE**

Répondez aux questions qui suivent les exemples. ⊗

> Nadia **apprend à préparer** le couscous.
> Nadia **commence à préparer** le couscous.

What preposition connects the verb with the infinitive in the two sentences above?

> Nadia **décide de préparer** le couscous.
> Nadia **finit de préparer** le couscous.

What preposition connects the verb with the infinitive in the two sentences above?

> Nadia **veut préparer** le couscous.
> Nadia **aime préparer** le couscous.

Does a preposition connect the verb with the infinitive in the two sentences above?

20 **Lisez la généralisation suivante.**

When the meaning of a verb is completed by an infinitive, the infinitive is connected with the verb in one of the following ways:

verb + infinitive	Il **veut faire** la cuisine.
verb + **à** + infinitive	Il **apprend à faire** la cuisine.
verb + **de** + infinitive	Il **décide de faire** la cuisine.

You will see from the following lists that some verbs can be connected directly with an infinitive that completes their meaning. Others use **à** as the connector. Still others use **de** as the connector. There is no way to tell, other than by learning them individually, which verb uses which preposition or goes without a preposition.

1. Verbs directly connected with an infinitive.

aimer	Ils **aiment flâner** dans les souks.
penser	Ils **pensent aller** chez Omar.
pouvoir	Ils **peuvent aller** dans la médina.
préférer	Ils **préfèrent sortir** ensemble.
savoir	Ils **savent marchander**.
vouloir	Ils **veulent acheter** un pouf.

Verbs of movement, like **aller, descendre, monter, partir, passer, sortir,** and **venir,** are in this category also. For example: **Ils passent voir leur ami Omar.**

2. Verbs commonly connected with an infinitive by **à.**

aider à	Elle m'**aide à faire** la salade.
s'amuser à	Il **s'amuse à éplucher** les légumes.
apprendre à	Il **apprend à faire** la cuisine.
commencer à	Je **commence à parler** français.
continuer à	Nous **continuons à travailler** ensemble.
donner à	Elle **donne à manger** au chat.
inviter à	Ils m'**invitent à dîner.**
se préparer à	Je **me prépare à sortir.**
réussir à	Je **réussis à me lever** à l'heure.

3. Verbs commonly connected with an infinitive by **de.**

s'arrêter de	Nous **nous arrêtons de travailler.**
se charger de	Il **se charge de faire** les courses.
décider de	Nous **décidons de préparer** un couscous.
demander de	Je lui **demande d'acheter** la viande.
se dépêcher de	Il **se dépêche de mettre** la table.
dire de	Je lui **dis de faire** un gâteau.
empêcher de	Ils m'**empêchent d'écouter** la radio.
finir de	Nous **finissons de nous habiller.**
oublier de	J'**ai oublié de servir** le gâteau.
parler de	Ils **parlent de jouer** aux cartes.
proposer de	Je **propose de regarder** la télévision.

Notice that most verbs of communication, like **demander, dire,** and **proposer,** require **de** before the infinitive.

4. Some verbal expressions can also be connected with an infinitive. You have seen three that use **de** as the connector:

avoir l'air de	Ils **ont l'air de s'amuser.**
avoir envie de	Ils **ont envie de sortir.**
avoir hâte de	Ils **ont hâte de partir.**

21 M. Slim va en ville faire les courses. Il demande : ⊗

Quelqu'un vient avec moi?   Oui, je viens faire les courses avec toi.
Quelqu'un descend avec moi? / Quelqu'un sort avec moi? / Quelqu'un part avec moi?
je descends avec toi / je sors avec toi / je pars avec toi

22 Nadia demande à Aziz : ⊗

Tu voulais préparer le dîner.
Tu as commencé?   Oui, j'ai commencé à préparer le dîner.
Tu voulais faire des briks.
Tu as réussi?   Oui, j'ai réussi à faire des briks.
Tu voulais préparer le couscous.
Tu as appris?   Oui, j'ai appris à préparer le couscous.
Tu voulais éplucher les légumes.
Tu as commencé?   Oui, j'ai commencé à éplucher les légumes.

23 Mme Slim demande à Nadia : ⊗

C'est toi qui vas préparer le couscous?
Tu t'en charges?   Oui, je me charge de préparer le couscous.
C'est Aziz qui va acheter la viande?
Tu lui as demandé?   Oui, je lui ai demandé d'acheter la viande.
C'est Leïla qui va faire les briks?
Tu lui as dit?   Oui, je lui ai dit de faire les briks.
C'est Samir qui va éplucher les légumes?
Tu lui as demandé?   Oui, je lui ai demandé d'éplucher les légumes.
C'est Monia qui va faire la salade?
Tu lui as dit?   Oui, je lui ai dit de faire la salade.

24 EXERCICE ECRIT   For answers, see p. T45.

Faites des phrases en utilisant les mots donnés dans l'ordre donné.
Ex. : Samir / décider / aller / dans / médina   Samir décide d'aller dans la médina.
  1. Samir / aimer / flâner / dans / souk
  2. il / vouloir / acheter / quelque chose / pour / mère
  3. il / décider / acheter / plateau / cuivre
  4. Samir / s'amuser / marchander
  5. marchand / lui / demander / payer / dix / dinar
  6. Samir / lui / dire / garder / plateau / cuivre
  7. marchand / commencer / baisser / prix
  8. Samir / continuer / marchander
  9. A / fin / il / réussir / acheter / plateau / cuivre / pour / cinq / dinar
 10. Samir / avoir hâte / montrer / achat / Aziz

25 Thé° à la tunisienne°. ⊗

Ce soir, les Slim ont des invités, et pour la circonstance°, ils se sont tous habillés à l'orientale°. Nadia, par exemple, porte un très joli caftan turquoise° brodé d'argent°, et Aziz, un caftan de laine blanche°. Après le dîner, les Slim et leurs invités passent au salon° pour prendre le thé. Ils s'installent° sur des divans° ou par terre, sur des coussins°. Mme Slim et Nadia font le thé sur une petite table basse°, avec une théière° qui chauffe° sur un brasero°. Le thé tunisien est un thé rouge, très fort, que l'on sert dans de petits verres décorés°. On boit le thé en croquant des pignons° et en savourant° des loukoums° ou des baklavas°.

VOCABULAIRE : **le thé** tea; **à la tunisienne** as it is served in Tunisia; **circonstance** occasion; **à l'orientale** in Eastern (Arab) clothes; **un caftan turquoise** turquoise caftan; **brodé d'argent** with silver embroidery; **de laine blanche** of white wool; **passent au salon** go into the living room; **ils s'installent** they take places (seats); **sur des divans** on sofas; **sur des coussins** on cushions; **une petite table basse** a little, low table; **une théière** a teapot; **chauffe** heats up; **un brasero** a brazier; **décorés** painted; **en croquant des pignons** munching on pine nuts; **en savourant** enjoying; **loukoums** Turkish delight (jelly candies); **baklavas** baklava (honey and nut pastries).

The difference between a "burnous," a "djellaba," and a "caftan" is the following: a burnous is a heavy wool cloak with a hood, worn draped around the shoulders to go out during the winter; a "djellaba" is a robe of fine cotton or wool with sleeves and a hood, which in Tunisia is worn only by men; a "caftan" is a dressy lounge robe with sleeves, but usually no hood, worn by either men or women.

26 EXERCICE DE CONVERSATION

Imaginez que vous êtes en Tunisie. Vous allez dans les souks pour faire des achats. Vous parlez aux artisans et vous marchandez avec eux.

27 DISCUSSION ET REDACTION

Dites ce que vous savez maintenant de la famille Slim, de la Tunisie, des Tunisiens et de la vie en Tunisie. Faites ensuite une petite rédaction.

28 Le jeu des photos.

You can use this game to review vocabulary and structure and also to stimulate discussion of Tunisian culture.

Regardez toutes les photos de ce chapitre. Choisissez une de ces photos et décrivez-la. Vos camarades doivent trouver la photo que vous avez décrite.

29 FOR REFERENCE

1.1. *Aziz Slim and his brother Samir live in Sousse, in Tunisia. Tunisia is in North Africa. (See the map, page 197.) It is a country roughly the size of Florida, with a population of about six million inhabitants.*

1.2. *Like all cities in North Africa, Sousse is made up of two cities, the old city or medina, surrounded by ramparts, and the modern city, located outside the ramparts.*

1.3,4. *Like all Tunisians the people of Sousse speak French as well as Arabic. Their way of life is a combination of Western and Middle Eastern styles. On the streets, a mixture of European and traditional clothes is evident: red or white saris on women, djellabas (long robes) and chéchias (red skullcaps) on men.*

16.1. *"Briks" are flaky-dough thin pancakes stuffed with seasonings and a raw egg. They are fried in some oil and served hot with slices of lemon.*

16.2. *"Salade méchouia" is a mixture of tomatoes, onions, and green peppers which have been grilled, cut up, and sprinkled with olive oil. It is decorated with slices of hard-cooked eggs.*

16.3. *"Couscous" is a dish made from semolina, a fine cereal-like hard wheat, which is served hot with a spicy sauce, mixed vegetables and meat (chicken or lamb).*

30 WORD LIST

1–13

un achat *purchase*
faire des achats *to shop*
un burnous *long Arab cloak*
un plateau *platter*
des plateaux *platters*
un portefeuille *wallet*
une poterie *piece of pottery*
un pouf *hassock*
un tapis *rug*
l'argent (m.) *silver*
le cuir *leather*
le cuivre *brass, copper*

un artisan *craftsperson*
un artiste *artist*
 C'est un artiste! *He's a real artist!*
un métier *craft, trade*
 un cordonnier *shoemaker*
 un orfèvre *craftsperson in metals*
 un potier *potter*
 un tailleur *tailor*
 un(e) tapissier (-ière) *rug-maker*
une médina *medina (old part of an Arab city)*
un souk *market*
 un dinar *dinar (Tunisian currency)*
un(e) touriste *tourist*

empêcher de *to keep from*
flâner *to browse*
marchander *to bargain*
rapporter *to bring in (money)*
 Ça ne rapporte pas! *It doesn't pay enough!*

qui est-ce qui *who?*
qu'est-ce qui *what?*
qui est-ce que *whom?*
qu'est-ce que *what?*

dans ce cas *in that case*
là *there*
plus loin *further on*

14–28

un bougainvillier *bougainvillea*
un conseil *advice*
le couscous *couscous*
un garage *garage*
une marmite *pot*
le mouton *lamb*
un panier *colander, basket*
un poivron doux *green pepper*
la semoule *semolina*
le tout *the whole thing*

assaisonner *to season*
éplucher *to peel, clean*
griller *to grill*
peler (like **acheter**) *to peel, to pull the skin away*
pique-niquer *to have a picnic*

faire cuire *to cook*
faire la cuisine *to cook*
jouer aux boules *to play boule (a bowling-type game)*

cuit, –e *cooked*
 cuit à la vapeur *steamed*

au-dessus *on top of, over*

Another game "Le jeu des artisans" might go like this: Vous dites ce que vous faites. Vos camarades doivent deviner votre métier. You could add a few occupations, like "un maroquinier" (maker of leather goods) or "un luthier" (maker of musical instruments).

21
LA FÊTE
FORAINE

Traveling fairs make stops once a year in most villages, towns, and cities in France. They may stay in one place for only a few days or as long as a few weeks. The size of the town or city very often determines how elaborate the fair will be: the more people there are to come to the fair, the larger it will be and the longer it will stay. The "Fête des Loges" is one good example of one of the larger French fairs. This fair spends six weeks every year in the Forest of St. Germain, near Paris, and by the end of its stay some three million people will have been entertained there. Its location in the middle of a beautiful forest helps its popularity, but the variety of amusements it offers — rides of all sorts, shooting galleries, penny arcades, and so on—promises some kind of fun for everyone.

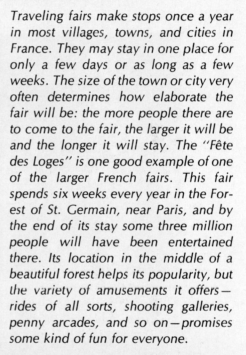

No. 2 continues on the facing page and should be read following the order of photographs.

2   Anna et Sylvie à la fête. ⊗

Anna, 15, is the brunette and Sylvie, 16, the blond.

Sur le grand huit.

Anna is not really calling her mother, but expressing mock fear.

A.   <u>Maman</u>! J'ai le vertige!

S.   Ferme les yeux et agrippe-toi!

Dans la maison magique,
où elles jouent à cache-cache.

S.   Anna, où es-tu? J'ai peur!

A.   Derrière toi, <u>froussarde</u>!!

Au stand de la loterie.

S.   Tu veux tenter ta chance?

A.   Non, moi à la loterie, je ne gagne jamais… Allons plutôt au tir, faire un carton.

Au stand de tir.

S.   Regarde, ça! J'ai mis en plein dans le mille!

A.   Une vraie championne! On va t'envoyer dans le Far-West!

3   Répondez aux questions.

1. Pourquoi est-ce que Sylvie dit à Anna de fermer les yeux sur le grand huit?
2. Qu'est-ce qu'Anna et Sylvie font dans la maison magique?
3. Est-ce qu'Anna veut tenter sa chance à la loterie? Pourquoi?
4. Qu'est-ce qu'elle veut faire?
5. Qui est-ce qui est une vraie championne de tir? Pourquoi?
6. Comment est-ce qu'Anna trouve le Bobsleigh? Et Sylvie?
7. Qu'est-ce que Sylvie fait pour se reposer?
8. Pourquoi est-ce que dans les autos tamponneuses Anna dit, « Pas de panique! »?
9. Qui est-ce qui a le mal de mer sur la grande roue?
10. Pourquoi est-ce qu'elle a le mal de mer?

Expressions underlined on this page and the next are colloquial expressions commonly used by French teenagers.

Sur le Bobsleigh.

A. C'est la dernière fois que je monte sur ce truc... C'est dément!

S. Moi, je trouve ça extra!

Sur le manège.

S. Un petit tour de manège... rien de tel pour se reposer!

Dans les autos tamponneuses.

S. Attention à droite... De grosses brutes foncent sur nous!

A. Pas de panique! On vire à gauche... et on les sème!

Sur la grande roue.

A. Tu es verte... Tu as le mal de mer?

S. Arrête de faire tanguer la nacelle! Tu n'es pas drôle!!

4 Et vous?

1. Est-ce que vous êtes déjà allé(e) à une fête foraine? Où ça?
2. Avec qui est-ce que vous y êtes allé(e)?
3. Est-ce que vous avez tenté votre chance à la loterie?
4. Est-ce que vous avez gagné? Quoi?
5. Est-ce que vous avez fait un carton au stand de tir?
6. Combien de points est-ce que vous avez faits?
7. Sur quoi est-ce que vous êtes monté(e), sur le grand huit, la grande roue, etc.?
8. Qu'est-ce que vous préférez? Pourquoi?
9. Qu'est-ce que vous n'aimez pas? Pourquoi?
10. Est-ce que vous voulez retourner à cette fête foraine? Pourquoi?

"C'est dément" literally means "It's insane." "Extra" is short for "extraordinaire." "Semer" literally means "to sow," but here it means "to shake off."

5 Anna, Sylvie et le fakir. ⊗

S. Anna! Viens voir le fakir qui dévoile l'avenir!

A. Ah, mais c'est une machine! Comment ça marche?

S. Avec les signes du Zodiaque, je crois.

A. Je suis Verseau. Et toi, tu es née sous quel signe, déjà?

S. Sous le signe des Poissons.

S. Alors, qu'est-ce que le fakir te prédit?

A. « Vous ferez de longs voyages; vous gagnerez beaucoup d'argent; vous vous marierez quand vous aurez 28 ans… »

S. Avec un homme qui sera beau et riche, et viendra d'un pays étranger. C'est ça?

A. Exactement! Ma vie sera un vrai conte de fées!… Allez, maintenant, à ton tour!

S. Ah non, j'ai lu mon horoscope dans le journal, ce matin… Ça me suffit! Et puis, moi, de toute façon, je ne crois pas à l'astrologie!!

6 Répondez aux questions.

1. Que fait le fakir?
2. Qu'est-ce que c'est que ce fakir?
3. Comment est-ce que ça marche?
4. Sylvie est née sous quel signe?

5. Et Anna, qu'est-ce qu'elle est?
6. Répétez ce que le fakir prédit à Anna.
7. Comment sera sa vie?
8. Où est-ce que Sylvie a lu son horoscope?

7 EXERCICE ORAL ⊗

8 THE FUTURE TENSE

Répondez aux questions qui suivent les exemples. ⊗

Quand est-ce qu'il **va parler** à Anna?   Il lui **parlera** dans une semaine.
Quand est-ce qu'il **va sortir** avec Anna?   Il **sortira** avec elle dans une semaine.
Quand est-ce qu'il **va répondre** à Anna?   Il lui **répondra** dans une semaine.

Do the verbs in the left-hand column refer to present or future time? And the verbs in the right-hand column? What verb forms are used in the left-hand column? Compare the infinitives with the stems of the future-tense verbs in the right-hand column. Are they the same?

Je finir**ai** bientôt.   Nous finir**ons** bientôt.
Tu finir**as** bientôt.   Vous finir**ez** bientôt.
Il finir**a** bientôt.   Ils finir**ont** bientôt.

What are the endings of the verb forms? Which forms sound the same?

9 Lisez la généralisation suivante.

1. Future time can be expressed by
   a. a present-tense form + time expression.   Je **sors dans une heure.**
   b. **aller** in the present tense + infinitive.   Je **vais sortir.**
   c. a future-tense form.   Je **sortirai.**

2. The future tense of all verbs is formed by adding the endings listed below to the future stem. The future stem of most verbs is the same as the infinitive. When the infinitive ends in **-re,** the final **-e** is dropped: **attendre / j'attendrai, répondre / je répondrai, mettre / je mettrai, connaître / je connaîtrai,** etc.

Infinitive	Future		
	Pronoun	Stem	Ending
jouer	je	**jouer**	-ai
sortir	tu	**sortir**	-as
choisir	il	**choisir**	-a
attendre	nous	**attendr**	-ons
	vous		-ez
	ils		-ont

3. **Acheter,** and other verbs like it, forms the future stem as follows: **achèter- / j'achèterai.**

4. A few common verbs have irregular future stems.

Infinitive	Future		
	Pronoun	Stem	Ending
faire		**fer**	
être	je	**ser**	-ai
avoir	tu	**aur**	-as
aller	il	**ir**	-a
venir	nous	**viendr**	-ons
voir	vous	**verr**	-ez
pouvoir	ils	**pourr**	-ont
vouloir		**voudr**	
savoir		**saur**	

5. The verb in a clause beginning with **quand** is in the future tense when the main verb in the sentence is also in the future tense.
   Nous viendrons quand nous pourrons.   *We'll come when we can.*

10 Fakir, dévoile-nous l'avenir! ⊗

Est-ce que je serai riche?   Oui, tu gagneras beaucoup d'argent.
Est-ce que Sylvie sera riche?   Oui, elle gagnera beaucoup d'argent.
Est-ce que mes frères seront riches?   Oui, ils gagneront beaucoup d'argent.
Et ma sœur et moi, nous serons riches?   Oui, vous gagnerez beaucoup d'argent.

11 Vous jouez les fakirs et vous dites à un(e) camarade qu'il (elle) va... ⊗

avoir toujours beaucoup d'amis.
faire de longs voyages.
habiter dans un pays étranger.
être très riche.
avoir une vie très heureuse.

Tu auras toujours beaucoup d'amis.
Tu feras de longs voyages.
Tu habiteras dans un pays étranger.
Tu seras très riche.
Tu auras une vie très heureuse.

Variation: Address the person as "vous."

12 D'après le fakir, la vie d'Anna va changer. ⊗

Je ne vais jamais en voyage.
Mon ami ne vient jamais me voir.
Je ne peux jamais sortir seule.
Je ne sais pas conduire.
Je ne vois jamais mes cousins.

Tu iras bientôt!
Il viendra bientôt!
Tu pourras bientôt!
Tu sauras bientôt!
Tu les verras bientôt!

13 EXERCICE ECRIT

Ecrivez les réponses des exercices No 10 et 12.

14 EXERCICE DE COMPREHENSION ⊗   For script, see p. T46.

	0	1	2	3	4	5	6	7	8	9	10
Jadis											
A l'avenir	✓										

15 Anna et Sylvie dans les autos tamponneuses. ⊗

Après avoir déjeuné dans une rôtisserie en plein air, Anna et Sylvie remontent, sans attendre, dans les autos tamponneuses.
A. Passe-moi le volant, j'ai envie de conduire!
S. Bon, allons-y. Tiens, voilà les types de tout à l'heure... A notre tour de les poursuivre!
A. (*Vlan!!*) Ça n'a pas eu l'air de leur plaire!
S. Ça y est, ils se retournent contre nous...
A. Essayons de les semer...
S. Ils nous talonnent toujours... Ils sont tenaces! On aurait dû mieux les regarder avant de les attaquer!!
A. Attention, tiens-toi bien! Ils vont nous rentrer dedans... (*Vlan!!!*)
LES GARÇONS Alors, les filles, on rêve?!
S. Espèces de crétins!! Vous ne pouvez pas regarder où vous allez, non?!!

Couvertes de bleus et les jambes un peu molles, Anna et Sylvie s'achètent une barbe à papa pour se réconforter. Et après ça, qui est-ce qu'elles rencontrent au détour d'une allée?... Les garçons des autos tamponneuses! Comme Anna et Sylvie ne sont pas rancunières, elles partagent leur barbe à papa avec eux. Et ils font connaissance...

The underlined words in No. 15 are again familiar expressions. "Espèce(s) de + derogatory word" is a common formula for French name-calling: "espèce d'imbécile" or "espèce de brute" are other examples. Note also that "barbe à papa" is used in the singular because each girl buys one for herself. In Unit 22, the student will encounter other examples of this usage as it applies to parts of the body: "Ils ont tous levé la tête." (see p. 228).

16 **Répondez aux questions.**

1. Où est-ce qu'Anna et Sylvie sont allées déjeuner?
2. Que font-elles après avoir déjeuné?
3. Qui est-ce qui prend le volant? Pourquoi?
4. Qui est-ce qu'Anna et Sylvie décident de poursuivre?
5. Est-ce que les garçons sont contents? Qu'est-ce qu'ils font?
6. Qu'est-ce qu'Anna veut essayer de faire?
7. Est-ce que les garçons se laissent semer? Qu'est-ce qu'ils font finalement?
8. Comment sont Anna et Sylvie quand elles sortent des autos tamponneuses?
9. Qu'est-ce qu'elles s'achètent pour se réconforter?
10. Avec qui est-ce qu'elles partagent leur barbe à papa?

17 **EXERCICE ORAL** ⊗

18 **PREPOSITION + INFINITIVE**

In French, the verb that follows a preposition (other than **en**) is always an infinitive.

Elles s'achètent une barbe à papa	**pour**	**se réconforter.**
Elles ont joué à la loterie	**sans**	**gagner.**
Elles veulent tenter leur chance au tir	**avant de**	**partir.**

The preposition **après** is followed by a past infinitive. The past infinitive of a verb is composed of two parts:
• **être** or **avoir,** depending on which auxiliary the verb takes in the passé composé;
• the past participle of that verb.

Infinitive	Passé Composé	Past Infinitive	
monter	Je **suis monté(e).**	**Après être monté(e),**	j'ai fait un tour.
se reposer	Je **me suis reposé(e).**	**Après m'être reposé(e),**	j'ai fait un tour.
déjeuner	J'**ai déjeuné.**	**Après avoir déjeuné,**	j'ai fait un tour.

Notice that the agreement of the past infinitive follows the same rules as those outlined for the passé composé.

19 **Pourquoi est-ce qu'elles vont à la fête?** ⊗

Elles veulent s'amuser?   Oui, elles y vont pour s'amuser.
tenter leur chance / monter sur le grand huit / faire un carton / manger de la barbe à papa
pour tenter leur chance / pour monter sur le grand huit / pour faire un carton / pour manger de la barbe à papa

20 **Nous avons rencontré les garçons…** ⊗

avant de monter sur le grand huit?   Non, après être montées sur le grand huit.
avant de faire un tour de grande roue?   Non, après avoir fait un tour de grande roue.
avant de déjeuner dans la rôtisserie?   Non, après avoir déjeuné dans la rôtisserie.
avant d'aller au stand de tir?   Non, après être allées au stand de tir.
avant de monter sur le Bobsleigh?   Non, après être montées sur le Bobsleigh.

21 Chaîne de mots.

Décrivez tout ce qu'Anna et Sylvie ont fait à la fête foraine.
ELÈVE 1 : Elles sont montées sur le grand huit.
ELÈVE 2 : Après être montées sur le grand huit, elles sont allées dans la maison magique.
ELÈVE 3 : Après être allées dans la maison magique, elles ont joué à la loterie.
ELÈVE 4 : Après avoir joué à la loterie…

22 EXERCICE DE CONVERSATION

Vous venez d'aller à une fête foraine. Vous racontez à un(e) camarade tout ce que vous avez fait.

23 Que dit votre horoscope?

Regardez l'horoscope de la page suivante. Lisez ce qui correspond à votre signe. Demandez à un(e) camarade de quel signe il (elle) est, et ce que l'horoscope lui prédit pour cet été.

Be sure your students understand that the glossary for the horoscope on p. 223 is at the bottom of this page.

24 Et vous?

1. Quand est-ce que vous êtes né(e)?
2. Quel est votre signe?
3. Est-ce que vous lisez souvent votre horoscope dans le journal?
4. Est-ce que vous croyez (*believe*) à l'astrologie? Pourquoi?

25 REDACTION

Dites ce que l'horoscope vous prédit pour cet été, puis décrivez ce que vous ferez vraiment cet été.

Before playing this game, you might want to have your students read what the horoscope says for signs other than their own.

26 Le jeu de l'horoscope.

Toute la classe fait l'horoscope de vacances d'un(e) camarade X. Une feuille de papier passe d'élève à élève. Chaque élève écrit une phrase et plie le papier pour la cacher. Résultat possible :
ELÈVE 1 : « X passera ses vacances en montagne. »
ELÈVE 2 : « Il / elle deviendra champion(ne) de ski nautique. »
ELÈVE 3 : « Il / elle sera toujours de mauvaise humeur. »
ELÈVE 4 : « Tout le monde le / la trouvera charmant(e). » Etc.

VOCABULAIRE DE L'HOROSCOPE : **BELIER** *ARIES;* **ski nautique** *water skiing;* **TAUREAU** *TAURUS;* **travaux** *work;* **n'en faites pas trop** *don't overdo it;* **GEMEAUX** *GEMINI;* **vous ferez du camping** *you will go camping;* **vous aurez beaucoup de succès** *you will be very popular;* **ne flirtez pas trop** *don't flirt too much;* **CANCER** *CANCER;* **familial** *family;* **surmontez** *get over;* **timidité** *shyness;* **LION** *LEO;* **maison de campagne** *country house;* **autoritaire** *bossy;* **VIERGE** *VIRGO;* **vacances studieuses** *study vacation;* **ne le regretterez pas** *will not be sorry;* **BALANCE** *LIBRA;* **moniteur, monitrice** *counselor;* **colonie de vacances** *summer camp;* **qui vous plaira beaucoup** *whom you'll like a lot;* **gardez les pieds sur terre** *keep your feet on the ground;* **SCORPION** *SCORPIO;* **ne suffiront pas** *will not be enough;* **vous vous sentirez frustré(e) et incompris(e)** *you will feel frustrated and misunderstood;* **mauvaise humeur** *bad mood;* **SAGITTAIRE** *SAGITTARIUS;* **agréables** *pleasant;* **CAPRICORNE** *CAPRICORN;* **vous feront confiance** *will have confidence in you;* **VERSEAU** *AQUARIUS;* **chantier** *work site;* **entrain** *liveliness;* **POISSONS** *PISCES;* **en pleine forme** *in the peak of condition.*

This is a summer or vacation horoscope as it might appear in an end-of-school issue of a young people's magazine.

27

VOTRE HOROSCOPE ⊗

BELIER (21 mars–20 avril).
Vous passerez des vacances sportives. Vous deviendrez un(e) champion(ne) de ski nautique° et vous ferez beaucoup de tennis. Vous vous amuserez beaucoup. Attention aux accidents!

TAUREAU (21 avril–20 mai).
Vous passerez vos vacances à la campagne, dans une ferme. Vous serez heureux (-se) d'être en contact avec la nature et d'aider aux travaux° de la ferme. N'en faites pas trop°!

GEMEAUX (21 mai–20 juin).
Vous partirez en vacances avec des cousins. Vous ferez du camping°. Vous rencontrerez beaucoup de gens intéressants. Vous aurez beaucoup de succès°. Attention… ne flirtez pas trop°!

CANCER (21 juin–22 juillet).
Vous passerez vos vacances en famille, au bord d'un lac. Le climat familial° sera bon. Vos parents vous encourageront à sortir. Surmontez° votre timidité° et vous vous ferez des amis.

LION (23 juillet–22 août).
Vous inviterez des amis à passer les vacances avec vous dans la maison de campagne° de vos parents. Vous organiserez des excursions dans la région. Attention, vous êtes autoritaire°!

VIERGE (23 août–22 sept.).
Vous passerez des vacances studieuses° dans un petit village. Des amis vous écriront pour vous inviter à passer une semaine en montagne avec eux. Acceptez, vous ne le regretterez° pas!

BALANCE (23 sept.–23 oct.).
Vous serez moniteur (monitrice)° dans une colonie de vacances° où tout le monde vous trouvera charmant(e). Vous rencontrerez quelqu'un qui vous plaira beaucoup°. Gardez les pieds sur terre°!

SCORPION (24 oct.–20 nov.).
La mer, le soleil, les amis ne vous suffiront° pas. Vous vous sentirez frustré(e) et incompris(e)°. Vous serez souvent de mauvaise humeur°. Attention, vous risquez de perdre des amis!

SAGITTAIRE (21 nov.–21 déc.).
Vos vacances seront très agréables°. Vous irez dans un pays étranger pour en étudier la langue. Vous ferez aussi beaucoup de sport. Vous apprendrez à faire du cheval.

CAPRICORNE (22 déc.–20 jan.).
Vous travaillerez pendant une partie de vos vacances. Vous aurez envie de partir en montagne. Vos parents vous feront confiance° et vous laisseront partir seul(e).

VERSEAU (21 jan.–18 fév.).
Vous passerez vos vacances sur un chantier°. Vous vous ferez de nombreux amis sympathiques et drôles. On appréciera votre entrain°, mais on vous trouvera trop indépendant(e).

POISSONS (19 fév.–20 mars).
Vous passerez vos vacances au bord de la mer. Vous ferez de la natation, de la voile, de la pêche sous-marine, etc. Dans l'eau et sur l'eau, vous serez dans votre élément, et en pleine forme°.

WORD LIST

1–4

une auto tamponneuse *bumper car*
une brute *bully*
un(e) champion(ne) *champion*
la chance *luck*
une fête *fair*
   une fête foraine *traveling fair*
un(e) froussard(e) *scaredy-cat!*
un grand huit *roller coaster*
une grande roue *Ferris wheel*
la loterie *lottery, raffle*
une maison magique *fun house*
le mal de mer *seasickness*
un manège *a ride*
un stand *stand, booth*
le tir *shooting gallery*
un truc *thing*
le vertige *vertigo, dizziness*

s'agripper *to hold on*
foncer *to rush*
   nous fonçons *we rush*
semer (like **acheter**) *to lose*
virer *to veer, to swerve*
avoir le mal de mer *to be seasick*
avoir le vertige *to be dizzy*
avoir peur *to be afraid*
faire un carton *to go target-shooting*
jouer à cache-cache *to play hide*
   and seek
tenter sa chance *to try one's luck*

J'ai mis en plein dans la mille. *I got*
   it right in the bull's-eye.
Arrête de faire tanguer la nacelle!
   Stop making the car swing!

drôle *funny*
gros, grosse *big*

rien de tel *nothing like it*

C'est dément! *It's too wild!*
C'est extra! *It's really great!*
Maman! *Somebody help me!*
Pas de panique! *Don't panic!*

5–14

l'astrologie (f.) *astrology*
l'avenir (m.) *future*
un conte de fées *fairy tale*
un fakir *fortune-teller, fakir*
un horoscope *horoscope*
une machine *machine*
les Poissons *Pisces*
un signe *sign*
un tour *a turn*
   A (ton) tour! *(Your) turn!*
le Verseau *Aquarius*
la vie *life*
le Zodiaque *Zodiac*

dévoiler *to uncover*
se marier *to get married*
prédire (like **dire**) *to predict*
faire un voyage *to take a trip*

j'ai lu *I have read*
je ne crois pas à *I don't believe in*
qui sera *who will be*
qui viendra *who will come*
vous aurez *you will have*
vous ferez *you will take (make)*
vous gagnerez *you will make*
vous vous marierez *you will get*
   married

étranger, –ère *foreign*
riche *wealthy*

Ça me suffit! *That's enough*
   for me!

Je suis né(e). *I was born.*
Tu es né(e). *You were born.*
Il est né. *He was born.*
Elle est née. *She was born.*
Nous sommes né(e)s. *We were*
   born.
Vous êtes né(e)(s). *You were*
   born.
Ils sont nés. *They were born.*
Elles sont nées. *They were born.*

15–27

une allée *walkway, path*
une barbe à papa *cotton candy*
une rôtisserie *barbecue*
un type *guy*
un volant *steering wheel*

attaquer *to attack*
réconforter *to give comfort*
remonter *to go back on*
rentrer dans *to bump into*
talonner *to tail, to be at one's heels*

Tiens-toi bien! *Hang on!*
On aurait dû… *We should have…*
Ça n'a pas eu l'air de leur plaire!
   They didn't seem to like that
   very much!
Ça y est! *That did it!*

mou, molle *weak, limp*
rancunier –ière *holding a*
   grudge
tenace *persistent*

au détour de *at a turn in*
dedans *inside, into*

couvert(e) de bleus *all black*
   and blue
de tout à l'heure *from before*
Espèces de crétins! *What are*
   you, some kind of idiots!

22
GYMNASTIQUE ET ATHLETISME

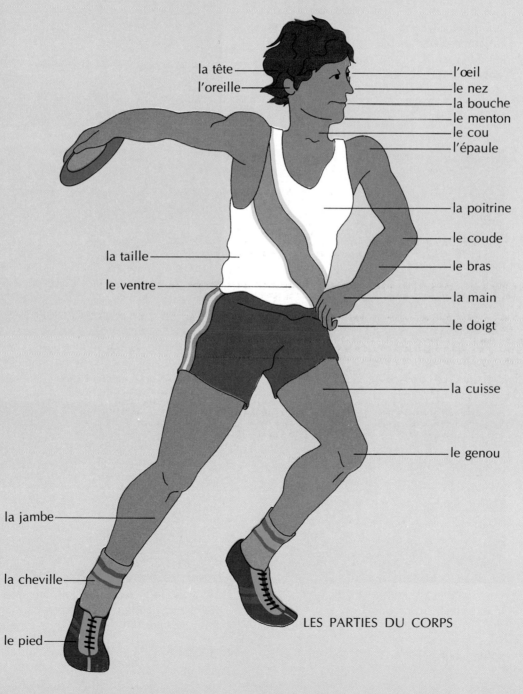

la tête

l'oreille

l'œil

le nez

la bouche

le menton

le cou

l'épaule

la poitrine

le coude

le bras

la main

le doigt

la taille

le ventre

la cuisse

le genou

la jambe

la cheville

le pied

LES PARTIES DU CORPS

2 La mise en train. ⊗

Nous sommes à l'Ecole Secondaire Polyvalente Antoine-Brossard, à Brossard dans la province de Québec. Dans quelques jours aura lieu le championnat d'athlétisme annuel. Ce championnat réunit les quatre écoles secondaires de la région. Yves Lefort, professeur de gymnastique, dirige l'entraînement des « athlètes » (garçons et filles) d'Antoine-Brossard.

Ils commencent par faire des exercices au sol pour se mettre en train. « Sur le dos, appuyés sur les coudes, levez la jambe, puis baissez-la très lentement. Ensuite pliez la jambe, le genou vient toucher le menton. La jambe droite d'abord. Allons-y! 1, 2, 3… J'ai dit la jambe *droite*, pas la jambe gauche! Mais qu'est-ce que vous avez aujourd'hui? Soyez donc un peu plus énergiques que ça! Bon, alors on recommence, d'abord lentement, puis plus rapidement. »

Après les exercices au sol viennent les exercices à la poutre. Voici Ghislaine en train d'essayer de garder l'équilibre.

Puis ce sont les exercices au cheval de voltige. Jean-François prend son élan et… hop! Il fait un saut périlleux!

Les exercices continuent aux barres parallèles. Hélène fait très bien ces exercices, mais elle pourrait être plus gracieuse.

Les voici tous, Jean-François, Suzanne, Jean-Raymond, Hélène, Louis et Ghislaine en train de faire des exercices aux espaliers.

3 Répondez aux questions.

1. Où se trouve l'école Antoine-Brossard?
2. Qu'est-ce qui aura lieu dans quelques jours?
3. Qui est Yves Lefort?
4. Qu'est-ce qu'il fait?
5. Par quel genre d'exercices est-ce que les élèves commencent? Pour quoi faire?
6. Ils font un exercice au sol; décrivez-le.
7. Qu'est-ce qu'il faut essayer de faire à la poutre?
8. Quel exercice fait Jean-François au cheval de voltige?
9. Que fait Hélène?
10. Quels exercices est-ce qu'ils font tous ensemble?

4 Qu'est-ce qu'on peut faire encore comme exercices? ⊗

On peut faire des exercices aux anneaux.

On peut grimper à la corde lisse ou à la corde à nœuds.

On peut aussi faire des exercices à la barre fixe.

5 Et vous?

1. Est-ce que vous êtes bon(ne) en gymnastique?
2. Combien d'heures de gymnastique est-ce que vous avez par semaine?
3. Nos six amis font certains exercices. Lesquels est-ce que vous pouvez faire, vous aussi?
4. Quels exercices de gymnastique est-ce que vous préférez?
5. Est-ce que vous êtes déjà allé(e) à un championnat? De quoi?

6 EXERCICE ORAL ⊗

7 THE ARTICLES le, la, and les
with nouns referring to the body

Nouns referring to the body (face, hair, hands, etc.) are normally preceded by the articles **le, la,** or **les** when it is clear whose face, hair, hands, etc., they are.

Lève **le bras** droit!	*Raise your right arm!*
J'ai mal à **la jambe.**	*My leg hurts.*
Elle se brosse **les cheveux.**	*She brushes her hair.*

Notice in the following example that **tête** is in the singular while its English equivalent, *heads,* is in the plural. The singular is always used in French in this situation.

Ils ont **tous** levé **la tête.**   *They all raised their heads.*

8 Le jeu de « Jacques a dit ». ⊗

Le premier élève dit : « Jacques a dit, Levez le bras droit! » Tout le monde lève le bras droit. Le deuxième élève dit : « Baissez le bras droit! » Personne ne doit baisser le bras droit parce qu'il n'a pas commencé par « Jacques a dit ». Ceux qui le baissent sont éliminés. Le troisième élève dit...

9 FROM ADJECTIVE TO ADVERB

Words like **lentement,** *slowly,* and **rapidement,** *quickly,* are called adverbs.
1. Many adverbs are formed by adding **-ment** to the feminine form of the adjective: **gracieuse–gracieusement.** However, for adjectives whose written masculine form ends in a vowel, **-ment** is added to the masculine form: **joli–joliment.**

Adjectives Masculine Feminine	+ -ment	Adverbs
gracieuse	+ -ment	**gracieusement**
joli	+ -ment	**joliment**

2. Many adverbs are not formed from adjectives: **bien, vite, trop, très** are examples of those you already know.

10 Comment est-ce qu'elle fait ses exercices? ⊗

Elle est très lente.   Elle fait tout très lentement.
sérieuse / énergique / distraite / rapide / gracieuse

sérieusement / énergiquement / distraitement / rapidement / gracieusement

11 Le jeu des adverbes. ⊗

Un(e) de vos camarades sort. Vous choisissez un adverbe; par exemple, « énergiquement ». Votre camarade rentre : il (elle) doit deviner l'adverbe choisi. Pour cela, il (elle) pose à chacun de vous des questions. Vous lui répondez sur un ton énergique et avec des gestes qui indiquent « énergiquement ».

A similar game you might try is "Jacques a dit" using adverbs in the commands: Parle lentement! Marche rapidement! Etc.

VOCABULAIRE : **doit deviner** *has to guess;* **sur un ton** *in a tone of voice;* **avec des gestes** *with gestures;* **qui indiquent** *which give the feeling of.*

12 L'entraînement. ⊗

Suzanne est très bonne à la course, particulièrement au 100 mètres, et Yves Lefort
espère qu'elle battra son record de 13″2[1] lors
du championnat. Elle vient de finir `le
premier essai. Son temps : 13″4. Pas aussi
bon qu'elle ne voudrait. En place pour le deuxième essai. Elle va courir contre Jean-Raymond
et Louis. Yves Lefort donne le départ : « A vos marques, prêts, partez! » Jean-François, Hélène
et Ghislaine chronomètrent leurs camarades et les encouragent. « Vas-y, Suzanne. Plus vite!
Un petit effort! Tu y es presque! » Top, c'est fini. On annonce les temps : 14″2 pour Louis,
13″8 pour Jean-Raymond... et 13″5 pour Suzanne. Le premier essai était meilleur. « Tant pis,
je ferai mieux la prochaine fois, » se dit-elle.

*"Top" in-
dicates the
beginning
or ending
of a race
or some
other
activity.*

Le seul point faible de Suzanne, ce sont les
lancers. Elle n'arrive pas à la cheville du
champion des champions qui est indiscutablement Louis. Il lance le poids à 13 m, le
disque à 35,5 m et le javelot à 38,5 m! Son
secret? Il faut être beau, intelligent... et très
fort, dit-il. Il faut aussi s'entraîner régulièrement.

Au saut en hauteur, Suzanne fait 1,22 m.[2]
Elle est meilleure que Louis, mais pas aussi
bonne que Jean-François : il arrive à sauter
plus haut que sa taille (il mesure 1,70 m et
saute 1,73 m). Au saut en longueur, la
performance de Suzanne n'est pas mauvaise : 3,81 m.

13 Répondez aux questions.

1. Quel est le record de Suzanne au 100 m?
2. Quel est le temps de Suzanne au premier essai? D'après elle, c'est un bon temps?
3. Suzanne va courir contre qui dans le deuxième essai?
4. Qui donne le départ? Qu'est-ce qu'il dit?
5. Que font Jean-François, Hélène et Ghislaine?
6. Le deuxième essai de Suzanne est meilleur que le premier? Qu'est-ce qu'elle se dit?
7. Que fait Jean-François au saut en hauteur?
8. Qui est le champion aux lancers? Quelles sont ses performances? Quel est son secret?

14 EXERCICE ORAL ⊗

[1] Treize (secondes) deux (dixièmes).
[2] Un mètre vingt-deux (centimètres).

15   THE VERB courir

1. The following are the forms of the verb **courir,** *to run,* in the present tense. ⊗

Je	**cours**	vite.	Nous	**courons**	vite.
Tu	**cours**	vite.	Vous	**courez**	vite.
Il / Elle	**court**	vite.	Ils / Elles	**courent**	vite.

2. The past participle of **courir** is **couru: Elle a couru le 100 m en 13″6.**
3. **Courir** has an irregular future stem: **courr-**   **je courrai, tu courras,** etc.

16   Suzanne court très vite! ⊗

Et toi?   Moi aussi, je cours très vite.

Et vous deux? / Et Jean-François? / Et Jean-Raymond et toi? / Et Hélène et Louis?

nous aussi, nous courons / lui aussi, il court / nous aussi, nous courons / eux aussi, ils courent

17   Pas de chance! ⊗

Je me suis cassé la jambe.   Je ne courrai pas le 100 m.

nous / Suzanne / vous / Jean-Raymond et Louis

nous ne courrons pas / elle ne courra pas / vous ne courrez pas / ils ne courront pas

18   Mesurons en mètres et centimètres. ⊗

> 1 pied (*1 foot*) = 30,5 cm
> 1 pouce (*1 inch*) = 2,54 cm
> 100 cm = 1 m

19   Quelles sont vos performances en mètres et centimètres?

1. Au saut en hauteur.   2. Au saut en longueur.   3. Au lancer du poids.   4. Au javelot.

20   Combien est-ce que vous mesurez?

m / cm	1,27	1,29	1,32	1,34	1,37	1,39	1,42	1,44	1,47	1,49
ft. / in.	4′2″	4′3″	4′4″	4′5″	4′6″	4′7″	4′8″	4′9″	4′10″	4′11″

m / cm	1,52	1,54	1,57	1,59	1,62	1,64	1,68	1,70	1,73	1,75
ft. / in.	5′	5′1″	5′2″	5′3″	5′4″	5′5″	5′6″	5′7″	5′8″	5′9″

m / cm	1,78	1,80	1,83	1,85	1,88	1,90	1,93	1,95	1,98	2,00
ft. / in.	5′10″	5′11″	6′	6′1″	6′2″	6′3″	6′4″	6′5″	6′6″	6′7″

21   Demandez à des camarades…

1. combien ils mesurent.
2. s'ils sautent aussi haut que ça.
3. quel sport ils aiment le mieux.
4. quel est leur record.
5. combien d'heures ils s'entraînent par semaine.
6. quels autres sports ils aiment.
7. quelle sont leurs performances.

MAKING COMPARISONS

22

Répondez aux questions qui suivent les exemples. ⊗

Suzanne s'entraîne **plus** sérieusement **que** Louis.   Elle est **plus** sérieuse **que** lui.
Louis s'entraîne **moins** sérieusement **que** Suzanne.   Il est **moins** sérieux **qu'**elle.
Hélène s'entraîne **aussi** sérieusement **que** Suzanne.   Elle est **aussi** sérieuse **qu'**elle.
In these sentences, what words mean *more . . . than?* What words mean *less . . . than?* What words mean *as . . . as?* What word follows the adverb or adjective in each sentence? In the sentences on the right, what kind of pronoun follows **que?**

23 **Lisez la généralisation suivante.**

1. When you compare a person, thing, or group with another, you make either a comparison of equality (as . . . as) or a comparison of inequality (more / less . . . than).

2. In French, comparisons of equality are expressed by **aussi… que:**
   Hélène court **aussi vite que** Louis.   *Hélène runs as fast as Louis.*

3. Comparisons of inequality are expressed by **plus… que** and **moins… que:**
   Suzanne est **plus rapide que** Louis.   *Suzanne is faster than Louis.*
   Suzanne est **moins forte que** Louis.   *Suzanne is less strong than Louis.*

4. The following chart summarizes the ways of expressing comparisons in French.

	plus / moins / aussi	*Adverb or Adjective*	**que**	*Independent Pronoun or Noun*
Suzanne court	**plus** **moins** **aussi**	**vite**	**que**	lui.
Suzanne est	**plus** **moins** **aussi**	**sérieuse**	**que**	Jean-François.

5. There are a few irregular comparatives: **meilleur, -e,** the comparative of the adjective **bon, bonne,** and **mieux,** the comparative of the adverb **bien.**
   Suzanne est **meilleure** que Louis au saut.   *Suzanne is better than Louis in jumping.*
   Il fait **mieux** qu'elle aux lancers.   *He does better than she at throwing.*

6. Adverbs such as **beaucoup** can be used to reinforce comparatives:
   Elle court **beaucoup plus vite que** lui.   *She runs much faster than he does.*
   Il est **beaucoup plus fort que** moi.   *He is much stronger than I am.*

24 **Les performances de nos amis.** ⊗

Suzanne court le 100 m en 13"2 et Hélène en 13"4.   Suzanne court plus vite qu'Hélène.

Jean-François saute 1,73 m et Suzanne 1,22 m.   Jean-François saute plus haut que Suzanne.

Louis lance le poids à 13 m et Jean-Raymond à 10 m.   Louis lance le poids plus loin que Jean-Raymond.

25 Ils sont tous très bons en athlétisme. ⊗

Suzanne court très vite.
—Plus vite que toi?
—Non, mais aussi vite que moi.

Jean-François saute très haut. —Plus haut que toi? —Non, mais aussi haut que moi.
Louis lance le disque très loin. —Plus loin que toi? —Non, mais aussi loin que moi.
Hélène s'entraîne très bien. —Mieux que toi? —Non, mais aussi bien que moi.

26 Jean-Raymond et Hélène. ⊗

Jean-Raymond est fort en gymnastique.
—Plus fort qu'Hélène?
—Non, il est moins fort qu'elle.

rapide à la course / sérieux à l'entraînement / bon en athlétisme
—plus rapide . . . —moins rapide . . . / —plus sérieux . . . —moins sérieux . . . / —meilleur . . . —moins bon

27 Comparons les performances de Jean-François et de Louis. ⊗

ATHLETISME
FICHE PERSONNELLE DE PROGRESSION

NOM: Jean-François PLANTE

SEC.: secondaire 3   AGE: 14

CAT.: B ☐ C ☑ JR ☐ JV ☐

		PERF.1	PERF.2
VITESSE	100 m	12"9	
DEMI-FOND	800 m	2'45"	
HAIES	100 m	17"5	
HAUTEUR		1,73m	
LONGUEUR		4,77 m	
POIDS	4 Kg	10,51m	
DISQUE	1,5 Kg	27,43 m	
JAVELOT	800 g	34,14m	

ATHLETISME
FICHE PERSONNELLE DE PROGRESSION

NOM: Louis LAFERRIERE.

SEC.: secondaire 3   AGE: 14

CAT.: B ☐ C ☑ JR ☐ JV ☐

		PERF.1	PERF.2
VITESSE	100 m	13"8	
DEMI-FOND	800 m	2'53"	
HAIES	100 m	18"	
HAUTEUR		1,59 m	
LONGUEUR		3,78 m	
POIDS	4 Kg	13 m	
DISQUE	1,5 Kg	35,50m	
JAVELOT	800 g	38,50m	

28 EXERCICE DE CONVERSATION

Regardez les fiches de progression de Jean-François et de Louis.
1. Comparez leurs performances. Dites, par exemple : Au 100 m (vitesse), Jean-François est meilleur que Louis. Il court plus vite que Louis.
2. Comparez vos performances à celles de Jean-François et de Louis.

Abbreviations in No. 27: SEC. = Section CAT. = Catégorie B = Benjamin(e) C = Cadet(te)
JR = Junior JV = Juvénile PERF. = Performance

29 EXERCICE ECRIT

1. Comparez les performances de Jean-François et de Louis.
2. Comparez vos performances à celles de vos camarades.

LES VAINQUEURS – Daniel Gauvin, Johanne Gauthier, Michel Normand, Suzanne Côté et Jean-François Plante.

TROPHEES SCOLAIRES

compte rendu de Robert Couronne

Hier a débuté le championnat d'athlétisme de Brossard. Il n'y a pas eu de surprise. Suzanne Côté, la favorite du 100 m, n'a pas déçu. C'est toujours elle la meilleure de sa catégorie. Avec un temps de 13″1 elle bat son record de l'année dernière qui était de 13″2. Elle a également remporté le 80 m haies en 14″1. Johanne Gauthier, la plus courageuse de nos jeunes sportives, a pris la deuxième place mais a remporté le 800 m, une victoire bien méritée.

Du côté garçons, trois vainqueurs mais deux épreuves seulement. Premiers ex aequo au 100 m, Daniel Gauvin et Michel Normand; au 800 m, Jean-François Plante. Aucun concurrent ne s'est présenté au 100 m haies. A noter : c'est encore l'école Antoine-Brossard (AB) qui a remporté le plus grand nombre d'épreuves. Les autres écoles qui participaient à ce championnat étaient : La Magdeleine (MAG), St-Rémi (SR), et St-François-Xavier (SF). Le résultat des courses :

CADETS-FILLES

Vitesse 100 m	1. Côté, Suzanne (AB)	13″1
	2. Gauthier, Johanne (AB)	13″3
	3. Vallée, Diane (SR)	13″4
	4. Desrosiers, Sylvie (MAG)	13″6
Demi-Fond 800 m	1. Gauthier, Johanne (AB)	3′01″7
	2. Benoit, Marie-Josée (AB)	3′04″7
	3. Belhumeur, Nicole (MAG)	3′08″5
Haies 80 m	1. Côté, Suzanne (AB)	14″1
	2. Champagne, Elaine (MAG)	14″2
	3. Oligny, Solange (MAG)	16″8

CADETS-GARÇONS

Vitesse 100 m	1. Gauvin, Daniel (SF)	12″4
	1. Normand, Michel (SR)	12″4
	2. Thibault, François (MAG)	12″6
	3. Ricard, François (AB)	12″7
	4. Bibeau, Yves (SF)	13″1
Demi-Fond 800 m	1. Plante, Jean-François (AB)	2′44″4
	2. Cardinal, Jacques (AB)	2′47″1
	3. Robidoux, Denis (SR)	2′47″3
Haies 100 m	Aucun concurrent	

31 Répondez aux questions.

1. Qu'est-ce qui a débuté hier?
2. Qui a remporté le 100 m chez les filles?
3. De combien de dixièmes de seconde est-ce qu'elle a battu son record?
4. Quelle autre épreuve a remporté Suzanne?
5. Comment est-ce que le journaliste décrit Johanne?
6. Qu'est-ce qu'elle a remporté?
7. Quels ont été les vainqueurs chez les garçons?

32 EXERCICE ORAL ⊗

MAKING COMPARISONS: SUPERLATIVES

Répondez aux questions qui suivent les exemples. ⊗

Johanne est plus **courageuse** que nous.   C'est **la plus courageuse de** la classe.
Louis est plus **fort** que nous.   C'est **le plus fort de** la classe.
Ces filles sont plus **jeunes** que nous.   Ce sont **les plus jeunes de** la classe.

What are the adjectives in the above sentences? In the sentences on the right, what words mean *the most*? Is the same article used with **plus** in each sentence? With what does the article agree? What word follows the adjective?

C'est Suzanne qui court **le plus vite.**
Ce sont les garçons qui s'entraînent **le plus sérieusement.**

What are **vite** and **sérieusement**? What words mean *the most*? Does the article seem to agree with anything in the sentence?

34   Lisez la généralisation suivante.

1. When you compare a person, thing, or group with several others, you use the superlative: *the most* or *least*. To form the superlative in French, you use the appropriate article **le, la,** or **les** followed by **plus** or **moins.**

2. Superlatives of adverbs are always formed with **le.**

	le	plus moins	*Adverb*
C'est Suzanne qui court	**le**	**plus**	**vite.**
C'est Sylvie qui court	**le**	**moins**	**vite.**

3. Superlatives of adjectives are formed with the appropriate article **le, la,** or **les.**

	le/la/les	plus moins	*Adjective*	de	
Suzanne est	**la**	**plus**	**sportive**	**de**	la classe.
Suzanne et Johanne sont	**les**	**plus**	**sportives**	**de**	la classe.
Marc est	**le**	**moins**	**sportif**	**de**	la classe.
Marc et Luc sont	**les**	**moins**	**sportifs**	**de**	la classe.

4. **Ce** (rather than **il, elle, ils,** or **elles**) is normally used before **être** when followed by a superlative:

    Suzanne? C'est la plus courageuse.   *Suzanne? She is the most courageous one.*

35   Leurs performances sont très bonnes. ⊗

Jean-François saute haut.   C'est lui qui saute le plus haut.
Louis lance le poids loin.   C'est lui qui lance le plus loin.
Suzanne court vite.   C'est elle qui court le plus vite.
Suzanne gagne souvent.   C'est elle qui gagne le plus souvent.
Louis s'entraîne bien.   C'est lui qui s'entraîne le mieux.

36 Comment sont ces élèves? ⊗

Suzanne est très courageuse.	C'est la plus courageuse de la classe.
Jean-Raymond n'est pas très rapide.	C'est le moins rapide de la classe.
Hélène est très sportive.	C'est la plus sportive de la classe.
Jean-Raymond est très drôle.	C'est le plus drôle de la classe.
Louis est très fort.	C'est le plus fort de la classe.
Anne et Alain ne sont pas très énergiques.	Ce sont les moins énergiques de la classe.
Hélène est très jeune.	C'est la plus jeune de la classe.

37 EXERCICE ECRIT   For answers, see p. T48.

Faites des phrases en utilisant les mots suivants dans l'ordre donné.
Ex. : Suzanne / être / plus / sportif / classe   Suzanne est la plus sportive de la classe.
1. Hélène / être / plus / courageux / classe
2. ce / être / Jean-François / qui / sauter / plus / haut
3. Louis / être / plus / bon / classe / lancers
4. ce / être / Johanne / qui / courir / plus / vite
5. ce / être / Jean-Raymond / qui / être / moins / bon / course
6. Ghislaine / faire / plus / bien / prochain / fois
7. ce / être / Suzanne / qui / être / plus / rapide / classe
8. ce / être / Louis / qui / lancer / javelot / plus / loin
9. ce / être / Jean-François / qui / faire / moins / bien / exercices
10. Johanne / gagner / plus / souvent

38 EXERCICE DE COMPREHENSION ⊗   For script, see p. T48.

	0	1	2	3	4	5	6	7	8	9	10
Vrai	✓										
Faux											

39 EXERCICE DE CONVERSATION

1. Regardez les résultats des courses du championnat et dites quels sont les meilleurs des garçons, quelles sont les meilleures des filles, etc.
2. Dans votre classe, quels sont les meilleurs?
   • Quels sont les plus rapides au 100 m vitesse. Quelles sont les plus rapides au 80 m haies?
   • Qui lance le poids le plus loin?
   • Qui saute le plus haut?
   • Qui travaille le mieux?
   • Qui est le (la) plus drôle de la classe?

40 REDACTION

1. Vous vous comparez à votre meilleur(e) ami(e). Dites par exemple s'il (elle) est plus petit(e) ou plus grand(e) que vous, plus ou moins intelligent(e), sportif (-ive), etc.
2. Dites quels sont les meilleurs de votre classe en chaque matière, et quels sont les meilleurs dans chaque épreuve sportive.

1–11

un(e) **athlète** *athlete*
l'**athlétisme** (m.) *athletics*
un **championnat** *championship*
l'**entraînement** (m.) *training*
la **mise en train** *warm-up*
la **gymnastique** *gymnastics*
  les **anneaux** (m.) *rings*
  la **barre fixe** *horizontal bar*
  les **barres parallèles** *parallel bars*
  le **cheval de voltige** *vaulting horse*
  la **corde lisse** *rope*
  la **corde à nœuds** *knotted rope*
  les **espaliers** (m.) *stall bars*
  les **exercices** (m.) **au sol** *floor exercises*
  la **poutre** *balance beam*
  un **saut périlleux** *somersault*
les **parties** (f.) **du corps** *parts of the body*
  la **bouche** *mouth*
  le **bras** *arm*
  la **cheville** *ankle*
  le **cou** *neck*
  le **coude** *elbow*
  la **cuisse** *thigh*
  le **doigt** *finger*
  le **dos** *back*

les **parties du corps** (cont.)
  l'**épaule** (f.) *shoulder*
  le **genou** *knee*
  les **genoux** *knees*
  la **jambe** *leg*
  la **main** *hand*
  le **menton** *chin*
  le **nez** *nose*
  l'**œil** (m.) *eye*
  les **yeux** *eyes*
  l'**oreille** (f.) *ear*
  le **pied** *foot*
  la **poitrine** *chest*
  la **taille** *waist*
  la **tête** *head*
  le **ventre** *abdomen*

baisser *to lower*
diriger *to direct*
  nous dirigeons *we direct*
garder l'équilibre *to keep one's balance*
grimper *to climb*
se mettre en train *to warm up*
plier *to bend*
prendre son élan *to take a running start*

recommencer *to start again*
  nous recommençons *we start again*
réunir (like **choisir**) *to bring together*
toucher *to touch*

elle **pourrait** *she could*
Soyez...! *Be . . . !*

annuel, –elle *annual*
appuyé, –e *propped up*
droit, –e *right*
énergique *energetic*
  plus énergique *more energetic*
gauche *left*
gracieux, –euse *graceful*
  plus gracieuse *more graceful*
polyvalent, –e *comprehensive*

lentement *slowly*
rapidement *quickly*
  plus rapidement *more quickly, faster*

Qu'est-ce que vous avez...? *What's the matter with you . . . ?*

12-29

un **effort** *effort*
une **performance** *performance*
  la **course** *race, running*
  le **disque** *discus*
  un **essai** *attempt*
  le **javelot** *javelin*
  un **lancer** *throw*
  le **100 m** *100-meter dash*
  le **poids** *shot*
  un **record** *record*
  le **saut en *hauteur** *high jump*
  le **saut en longueur** *long jump*

un **centimètre** *centimeter*
un **mètre** *meter*
un **pied** *foot*
un **pouce** *inch*
une **seconde** *second*
  un **dixième** *a tenth*
une **fiche de progression** *record card*
la **taille** *size*

le **demi-fond** *middle-distance run*
les ***haies** (f.) *hurdles*
la **vitesse** *sprint*

battre *to break (a record)*
  je bats, tu bats, il bat, nous battons, vous battez, ils battent
chronométrer *to time*
  je chronomètre, tu chronomètres, il chronomètre, ils chronomètrent
comparer *to compare*
courir *to run*
donner le départ *to give the signal to start*
encourager *to encourage*
  nous encourageons *we encourage*
s'entraîner *to train*
lancer *to throw*
  nous lançons *we throw*
mesurer *to measure*
sauter *to jump*

faible *weak*
meilleur, –e *better*
personnel, –elle *personal*
prochain, –e *next*

lors de *at the time of*

indiscutablement *indisputably*
particulièrement *especially*
régulièrement *regularly*

aussi bonne que *as good as*
*haut *high*
  plus *haut que *higher than*
aussi... que *as . . . as*
plus... que *more . . . than*
moins... que *less . . . than*

pas aussi bon qu'elle ne voudrait *not as good as she would have liked*
ne pas arriver à la cheville de *not to be mentioned in the same breath with*
A vos marques, prêts, partez! *On your marks, get set, go!*
Tu y es presque! *You're almost there!*
se dit-elle *she says to herself*
dit-il *he says*

30-40

une **catégorie** *category*
un **compte rendu** *account*
un(e) **concurrent(e)** *competitor*
une **épreuve** *event*
un(e) **favori(te)** *favorite*
un **résultat** *outcome*
un(e) **sportif (-ive)** *sportsperson*
une **surprise** *surprise*
un **trophée scolaire** *school trophy*
un **vainqueur** *winner*
une **victoire** *victory*

débuter *to start*
participer (à) *to take part (in)*
se présenter (à) *to enter*
remporter *to win*

(elle) **a pris la deuxième place** *(she) came in second*
elle **n'a pas déçu** *she didn't disappoint*

à noter *to be noted*
du côté garçons *on the boys' side*
ex aequo *tied*

cadet, –ette *junior*
courageux, –euse *courageous*
dernier, –ière *last*
mérité, –e *deserved*
sportif, –ive *athletic*

également *also*

la plus courageuse *the most courageous*
la meilleure de *the best in*
le plus grand nombre *the largest number*
Aucun concurrent ne s'est présenté au 100 m haies. *No competitor entered the 100-meter hurdles.*

Aujourd'hui
Demain et toujours
Joyeux Anniversaire!

Joie

Bonheur

Espoir

Santé

Photo 1: The main square of Liège. Locate Belgium on map, p. 197. Liège is on the Meuse close to the Netherlands border.

2 L'embarras du choix. ⊗

Liège, en Belgique. C'est là qu'habitent Claude et Monique Dupont et leurs quatre enfants, Françoise, Vincent, Frédérique et Xavier.

C'est bientôt l'anniversaire de Madame Dupont. Françoise et Vincent vont en ville pour lui acheter un cadeau. Ça fait deux mois qu'ils font des économies.

V. Alors, qu'est-ce qu'on lui achète?
F. Je ne sais pas. Tu as une idée?
V. On pourrait lui acheter du parfum.
F. Je crois qu'elle aimerait mieux un foulard.
V. Quoi d'autre? Des boucles d'oreille?
F. Oui, ça lui ferait certainement plaisir. De toute façon, allons à la galerie marchande; il y a des tas de boutiques; on trouvera bien quelque chose.

The Duponts appeared in Unit 7. They are relatives of the Lardans.

3 Et vous, qu'est-ce que vous aimeriez acheter à votre mère? ⊗

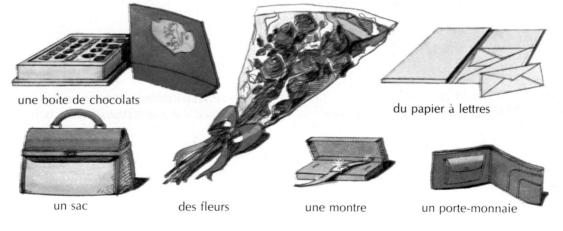

une boîte de chocolats

du papier à lettres

un sac

des fleurs

une montre

un porte-monnaie

4 Répondez aux questions.

1. Où habitent les Dupont?
2. Ils ont combien d'enfants?
3. C'est l'anniversaire de qui?
4. Où vont Françoise et Vincent?
5. Qu'est-ce que Vincent propose de lui acheter?
6. Qu'est-ce qu'elle aimerait mieux, d'après Françoise?
7. Qu'est-ce qui lui ferait plaisir?
8. Où est-ce que Françoise et Vincent décident d'aller?
9. Pourquoi?

5 Et vous?

1. Qu'est-ce que vous avez acheté à votre mère (à votre tante, à votre grand-mère) pour son anniversaire? Est-ce qu'elle a aimé votre cadeau?
2. Qu'est-ce que votre père lui a acheté?
3. Et les autres membres de votre famille?
4. Qu'est-ce qui vous ferait plaisir pour votre anniversaire? Vous l'aurez, d'après vous?
5. Qu'est-ce que vous avez eu à votre dernier anniversaire?
6. Quelle est la date de votre anniversaire? Quel âge avez-vous?

6 EXERCICE ORAL ⊗

7 THE CONDITIONAL

Répondez aux questions qui suivent les exemples. ⊗

> On **pourrait** lui acheter du parfum.
> Elle **aimerait** mieux un foulard.
> Ça lui **ferait** certainement très plaisir.

Do the above sentences refer to what has happened, what will happen, or what might happen?

J'**aimerais** mieux du parfum.	Nous **aimerions** mieux du parfum.
Tu **aimerais** mieux du parfum?	Vous **aimeriez** mieux du parfum?
Elle **aimerait** mieux du parfum.	Elles **aimeraient** mieux du parfum.

What is the stem of the verb in these sentences? The stem of what tense that you have already learned is the same as this stem? What are the endings? The endings of what tense that you have already learned are the same as these endings?

8 Lisez la généralisation suivante.

1. The conditional is used to express what one might do or what might happen under certain circumstances:

> On **pourrait** lui acheter des fleurs.   *We could buy her some flowers.*
> Elle **aimerait** beaucoup ça.   *She would like that very much.*

2. The conditional of all French verbs is composed of
   • the future stem of the verb, plus
   • the imparfait endings.

	Stem	Ending	
Je	**voudr**	-ais	un sac.
Tu	**aimer**	-ais	un sac de quelle couleur?
Ça me	**fer**	-ait	plaisir.
Nous	**achèter**	-ions	bien un sac.
Vous	**pourr**	-iez	inviter des amis.
Ils	**ser**	-aient	très contents de venir.

Notice that just like the imparfait, the conditional has only three spoken endings: one for the **nous** form, one for the **vous** form, and a third for all the other forms.

9 Françoise doit acheter un cadeau. ⊗

Tu veux venir?
Tu veux sortir?
Tu veux aller au cinéma?
Tu veux jouer aux cartes?

Je viendrais bien, mais je ne peux pas.
Je sortirais bien, mais je ne peux pas.
J'irais bien au cinéma, mais je ne peux pas.
Je jouerais bien aux cartes, mais je ne peux pas.

10 Françoise demande à Vincent :

Qu'est-ce que je pourrais lui acheter?
Qu'est-ce que papa pourrait lui acheter?
Qu'est-ce que Frédérique et moi, nous pourrions lui acheter?
Qu'est-ce que Frédérique et Xavier pourraient lui acheter?

Tu pourrais lui acheter…
Il pourrait lui acheter…
Vous pourriez lui acheter…

Ils pourraient lui acheter…

11 EXERCICE DE CONVERSATION

Un(e) ami(e) veut donner une surprise-partie pour son anniversaire. Il (Elle) vous demande conseil. Vous lui dites…
1. quel jour de la semaine vous donneriez cette surprise-partie.
2. qui vous inviteriez et ce qu'il y aurait à manger et à boire.
3. quel genre de musique et quels jeux il y aurait.
4. à quelle heure ça commencerait et à quelle heure ça finirait.

12 REDACTION

Vous donnez ces conseils par écrit (*in writing*). Utilisez l'exercice No 11 comme modèle.

13 A la galerie marchande. ⊗

1

Devant une maroquinerie.

V. Si on empruntait de l'argent à Papa, on pourrait acheter un sac…
F. Ah non, moi, quand je fais un cadeau, c'est avec mon argent!
V. Bien sûr, avec tout l'argent de poche que Papa te donne!

2

Dans un magasin de vêtements.

V. On lui achète des gants?
F. On ne connaît pas sa taille.
V. Elle pourra toujours les échanger s'ils ne lui vont pas.
F. Dans ce cas, il faut garder le reçu… et ça devient très compliqué.

3 Devant une parfumerie.

V. Ça coûte cher le parfum?
F. Ça dépend.
V. Si je n'ai pas assez d'argent, tu pourras m'en prêter un peu?
F. Mais on a dit qu'on n'achetait pas de parfum!

4 Dans une librairie-papeterie.*

V. Tu aimes cette carte?
F. Elle n'est pas très originale.
V. Et celle-là?
F. Tu sais, les cartes humoristiques, Maman n'aime pas beaucoup ça!
V. Oui, je crois que tu as raison.

5 Finalement, Vincent et Françoise sont allés dans une boutique appelée Pic Pus qui vend des cadeaux.

6 Françoise a acheté un foulard en soie et Vincent, deux bracelets fantaisie.

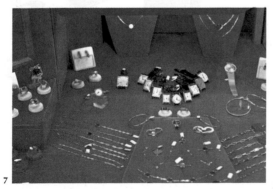

7 Dans une bijouterie.

Le même jour, M. Dupont a acheté une montre en or pour sa femme.

8 Chez un fleuriste.

Xavier et Frédérique ont acheté des fleurs pour leur mère.

*Stores which sell only books are "librairies," and stores which sell only cards and stationery, etc., are "papeteries." They are not necessarily combined.

1–12   **un anniversaire** *birthday*
Bon Anniversaire! *Happy Birthday!*
un baiser *kiss*
le bonheur *happiness*
l'espoir (m.) *hope*
la joie *joy*
la santé *health*
un souhait *wish*
une galerie marchande *shopping arcade*
un cadeau *gift*
   des cadeaux *gifts*
   une boîte de chocolats *box of chocolates*
   une boucle d'oreille *earring*
   des boucles d'oreille *earrings*
   un foulard *scarf*
   une montre *watch*
   du papier à lettres *writing paper*
   du parfum *perfume*
   un porte-monnaie *change purse*
   des porte-monnaie *change purses*
   un sac *handbag*

on pourrait lui acheter... *we could buy her . . .*
elle aimerait mieux... *she would like better . . .*
ça lui ferait plaisir *that would make her happy*
... vous aimeriez acheter... *. . . you would like to buy . . .*

faire des économies *to save*

quoi d'autre *what else*

joyeux, –euse *joyous*

c'est là que *it's where*
l'embarras du choix *embarrassment of riches*

13–26   **l'argent de poche** *allowance*
une carte *greeting card*
un reçu *receipt*

l'or (m.) *gold*
   en or *made of gold*
la soie *silk*
   en soie *made of silk*
un magasin *store*
   une bijouterie *jewelry shop*
   un(e) fleuriste *florist*
   une librairie-papeterie *book and stationery store*
   une maroquinerie *leather-goods store*
   une parfumerie *perfume shop*

un cadeau *gift*
   un bouton de manchette *cufflink*
   des boutons de manchette *cufflinks*
   un bracelet fantaisie *bracelet (costume jewelry)*
   une ceinture *belt*
   une écharpe *(long) scarf*
   un mouchoir *handkerchief*
   un porte-clés *key ring*
   des porte-clés *key rings*
   un porte-documents *portfolio*
   des porte-documents *portfolios*
   un rasoir électrique *electric razor*

aller à *to fit*
emprunter (à) *to borrow (from)*
   si on empruntait *how about borrowing*
prêter (à) *to lend (to)*

ça dépend *it depends*

avoir raison *to be right*
faire un cadeau *to give a gift*

compliqué, –e *complicated*
curieux, –euse *curious*
humoristique *funny, humorous*
original, –e *new, original*
   originaux (m. pl.) *original*

27–39   **une hésitation** *hesitation*
l'inspiration (f.) *inspiration*
des préparatifs (m.) *preparations*
un souhait *wish*

simplement *simply*
juste comme *just like*

plaire (à) *to please*
en faire autant *to do the same thing*
c'est bien pour ça... *that's exactly why . . .*
écrire un petit mot *to write a little something*

le mien, la mienne, les miens, les miennes *mine*
le tien, la tienne, les tiens, les tiennes *yours*
le sien, la sienne, les siens, les siennes *his / hers*
le nôtre, la nôtre, les nôtres *ours*
le vôtre, la vôtre, les vôtres *yours*
le leur, la leur, les leurs *theirs*

bien des *many*
de retour à la maison *back home*

Identification of photographs for Unit 24 opener (facing page) are as follows: Photo 1: Street scene, Abidjan, Ivory Coast. Photo 2: Sun collector. Photo 3: Scene from Police Woman. Photo 4: Scene from Star Trek. The young people in Unit 24 have all appeared before: Suzanne in Unit 22, Aziz in Unit 20, Sylvie in Unit 21, and Danou in Unit 17.

24
LA TELEVISION
chapitre de révision

Le genre d'émissions que nos amis aiment. ⊗

SUZANNE : Moi, ce que j'aime le mieux ce sont les documentaires sur la nature, sur la vie des animaux ou sur des pays lointains… Et puis, j'aime bien regarder le journal télévisé.

AZIZ : Moi, je trouve que les émissions les plus intéressantes sont celles où l'on parle de problèmes actuels, comme la conservation de l'énergie. J'aime aussi les émissions scientifiques.

SYLVIE : Moi, je regarde la télévision pour me distraire, pas pour m'instruire. J'aime les feuilletons ou les séries américaines. J'aime aussi regarder les émissions de variétés.

DANOU : Moi, ce que j'aime le mieux, ce sont les films de science-fiction. Malheureusement, mon père ne me laisse pas toujours les regarder car lui, il préfère les émissions sportives!

French television programs are carried on three channels, all publicly owned. Advertising does not interrupt programs, but between programs there may be five minutes of commercials at a time. A great deal of special programming is scheduled for Wednesday, the day during the week when most young people do not have to go to school. General programming in France includes many exchanges and simultaneous broadcasts among European countries through a system called "Eurovision."

3 Répondez aux questions.

1. Qu'est-ce que Suzanne aime regarder à la télévision? Pourquoi?
2. D'après Aziz, quelles sont les émissions les plus intéressantes? Par exemple?
3. Est-ce que Sylvie regarde la télévision pour s'instruire ou pour se distraire?
4. Qu'est-ce qu'elle aime regarder? Pourquoi?
5. Qu'est-ce que Danou aime le mieux? Qu'est-ce que son père préfère?

4 Demandez à vos camarades…

1. quelles émissions ils regardent à la télévision.
2. s'ils regardent la télévision pour se distraire ou pour s'instruire.
3. ce qu'ils aiment le mieux.
4. si leurs parents les laissent regarder tout ce qu'ils veulent.
5. s'ils ont la télévision en couleurs ou en noir et blanc.

5 Suzanne veut regarder la télévision. ⊗

1. Elle demande la permission de mettre la télévision.
2. Elle s'assure que le poste est branché.
3. Elle l'allume.
4. Elle règle le son s'il est trop bas ou trop fort.
5. Elle règle l'image, si elle est floue, trop sombre, trop claire, si elle saute ou si les couleurs sont mauvaises.
6. Quand elle arrête de regarder la télévision, elle n'oublie pas d'éteindre le poste avant de quitter la pièce.

6 EXERCICE DE CONVERSATION

Dites ce que vous faites quand vous voulez regarder la télévision.

Variation: Un(e) ami(e) met la télévision. L'image et le son ne sont pas bons. Dites-lui ce qu'il faut faire.

7 Documentaire sur le Sénégal. ⊗

SUZANNE Tu veux regarder *Fenêtre sur l'Afrique?*
RAYMOND C'est sur quel pays, aujourd'hui?
SUZANNE C'est sur le Sénégal.
RAYMOND Ah, formidable! C'est un des pays où j'aimerais aller.
SUZANNE Moi aussi. D'ailleurs voyager, c'est mon rêve. Si je pouvais, je ferais le tour du monde!
RAYMOND Qui sait? Peut-être qu'un jour tu le feras, le tour du monde.

La République du Sénégal est située sur la côte occidentale de l'Afrique. C'est un petit pays, mais il présente une grande variété de paysages : savanes, forêts tropicales, déserts, plaines fertiles. Le climat est doux et les gens sont très accueillants. La population se compose de différents groupes éthniques qui ont chacun leur langue. Le français est la langue officielle. Le Sénégal est un pays en pleine expansion, aussi bien agricole qu'industrielle.

PHOTOS p. 251 : **1.** Usine de fabrication d'engrais dans la région de Thiès. **2.** Younousse Seye, peintre célèbre, et ses tableaux. **3.** Jeune Sénégalaise portant ses affaires sur la tête à la façon traditionnelle. **4.** Pêcheurs à Cayar. **5.** Une plage près de Dakar. **6–7.** Dakar, la capitale du Sénégal, est non seulement un centre administratif, mais aussi un centre culturel et artistique. **8.** Dans le parc national de Niokolo-Koba, éléphants, lions, hippopotames, crocodiles, singes et panthères vivent en liberté.

Locate Senegal on the map from the Photo Essay "French Throughout the World," Plates 2-3. If you have a map of Senegal available, point out Dakar, Cayar, le parc de Niokolo-Koba.

1

2

3

4

5

6

7

8

8 THE FUTURE AND THE CONDITIONAL

1. The future / conditional stem of most verbs is the infinitive. If the infinitive ends in **-re,** the **e** is dropped. The conditional endings are the same as those of the imparfait.

Infinitive	Future			Conditional		
	je		-ai	je		-ais
jouer	tu	**jouer**	-as	tu	**jouer**	-ais
sortir	il	**sortir**	-a	il	**sortir**	-ait
choisir	nous	**choisir**	-ons	nous	**choisir**	-ions
attendre	vous	**attendr**	-ez	vous	**attendr**	-iez
	ils		-ont	ils		-aient

2. **Acheter,** and verbs like it, has the following future / conditional stem: j'**achèter**-ai.

3. The following verbs have irregular future / conditional stems:

aller : ir-	**courir : courr-**	**faire : fer-**	**savoir : saur-**	**voir : verr-**
avoir : aur-	**être : ser-**	**pouvoir : pourr-**	**venir : viendr-**	**vouloir : voudr-**

4. The following chart shows the uses of the future and the conditional in the patterns you have learned.

Quand + *Future*	*Future / Imperative*
Quand nous aurons le temps,	⎰ **nous irons** à Paris. ⎱ **allons** à Paris.
Si + *Present*	*Future / Imperative*
Si nous avons le temps,	⎰ **nous irons** à Paris. ⎱ **allons** à Paris.
Si + *Imparfait*	*Conditional*
Si nous avions le temps,	**nous irions** à Paris.

9 Tout est possible! ⊗

J'aimerais voyager.   Peut-être qu'un jour tu voyageras.
faire le tour du monde / aller en Afrique / avoir un bateau à voiles / jouer dans un western
tu feras le tour du monde / tu iras en Afrique / tu auras un bateau à voiles / tu joueras dans un western

10 Demandez à des camarades :

Qu'est-ce que tu ferais si...
1. tu avais un grand bateau à voiles?
2. tu n'avais pas besoin d'aller à l'école?
3. tu pouvais voyager pendant un an?
4. tu gagnais beaucoup d'argent à la loterie?

11 EXERCICE DE CONVERSATION

1. Racontez à vos camarades ce que vous rêvez de faire un jour. Dites par exemple : Un jour, j'achèterai un grand bateau à voiles avec des copains, et nous irons au Sénégal...
2. Racontez la même chose, mais commencez : Si je pouvais...

12 EXERCICE DE COMPREHENSION ⊗ For script, see p. T51.

	0	1	2	3	4	5	6	7	8	9	10
C'est sûr											
Si ça arrivait	✓										

These products and commercials are fictional.

13 Quelques publicités. ⊗

Bronzez de la façon la plus naturelle du monde avec la crème Bronzosol.

Vos cheveux sont ternes et difficiles à peigner?... Avec Ecladou, vos cheveux seront plus brillants, plus souples, plus... doux!

Fruita, c'est plus frais, c'est plus pétillant, c'est plus délicieux, en un mot c'est meilleur!

Le plus pratique des cyclomoteurs, le plus économique, c'est Amycycle.

14 Répondez aux questions.

1. D'après la publicité, quand est-ce qu'on doit se servir d'Ecladou?
2. Qu'est-ce que Bronzosol? Fruita? Amycycle?
3. Quelles sont les qualités de l'Amycycle?

15 COMPARATIVES AND SUPERLATIVES OF ADJECTIVES

1. The comparatives and superlatives of adjectives agree in gender and number with the nouns they refer to.

Comparative			Superlative		
Ce savon est	**plus** cher **moins** cher **aussi** cher	que celui-là.	C'est	**le plus** cher **le moins** cher	de tous.
Cette crème est	**plus** chère **moins** chère **aussi** chère	que celle-là.	C'est	**la plus** chère **la moins** chère	de toutes.
Ces savons sont	**plus** chers **moins** chers **aussi** chers	que ceux-là.	Ce sont	**les plus** chers **les moins** chers	de tous.
Ces crèmes sont	**plus** chères **moins** chères **aussi** chères	que celles-là.	Ce sont	**les plus** chères **les moins** chères	de toutes.

2. In a construction including a noun, the placement of the superlative is as follows:
   - if the adjective normally follows the noun, the order is noun + adjective:
     C'est **un appareil très cher.**   C'est **l'appareil le plus cher.**
   - if the adjective normally precedes the noun, the superlative may either precede or follow: C'est **le plus petit appareil,** or C'est **l'appareil le plus petit.**
     Note: the article is always retained before the noun when the superlative follows it.

3. The possessive article is also used in superlative constructions
   - with an adjective that follows the noun: C'est **ma photo la plus extraordinaire.**
   - with an adjective that precedes the noun:
     C'est **ma meilleure photo,** or C'est **ma photo la meilleure.**

16 Jouons aux publicités. ⊗ For answers, see p. T51.

Ce savon est très doux.

—Il est moins doux que celui-là.
—Oui, celui-là est plus doux.
—C'est le plus doux de tous.

Cet appareil est très simple.
Cette eau minérale est très bonne.
Ce jeu est très amusant.
Cette moto est très rapide.
Cette voiture est très chère.
Ces haut-parleurs sont très bons.

17 REDACTION

Ecrivez vos propres publicités. Vous pouvez choisir un shampooing, une crème, une eau minérale, un jus de fruit, des vêtements, un appareil-photo, un vélo, etc.

This is a composite program taken from an actual French TV listing for this particular day. All of the programs have been telecast in France. The three channels are called "chaînes": —C'est sur quelle chaîne? —Sur la première chaîne.

SAMEDI 19 FEVRIER

1

11.55 PHILATELIE CLUB
Le Sénégal à travers° ses timbres.

12.30 MIDI PREMIERE
Danièle Gilbert reçoit° une vedette° de la chanson.

12.45 JEUNES PRATIQUE°
Les métiers du tourisme.

13.00 ACTUALITES°

13.35 LA FRANCE DEFIGUREE°

14.05 COSMOS 1999
Violente tempête sur la lune°...

15.05 EN PISTE°
Trois couples sont en compétition pour le titre de champions de France de danse.

15.50 RUGBY : TOURNOI° DES CINQ NATIONS
Angleterre-France.

18.05 DES ANIMAUX ET DES HOMMES
Les chiens de traîneaux.°

18.40 MAGAZINE AUTO-MOTO

19.00 VINGT MINUTES POUR VOUS DEFENDRE
Actualités de la consommation.°

19.20 ACTUALITES REGIONALES

20.00 ACTUALITES

20.30 RALLYE MONTE-CARLO
Emission de variétés avec Pétula Clark et Julien Clerc.

21.45 CHAPEAU MELON ET BOTTES DE CUIR°
Steed et Emma Peel essaient d'empêcher° le plus grand hold-up du siècle°...

22.40 CATCH° A DRANCY

23.10 ACTUALITES ET FIN°

2

11.45 JOURNAL DES SOURDS ET DES MAL ENTENDANTS°

12.00 RADIO TELE SCOLAIRE
Un jeu éducatif.°

12.30 JOURNAL

13.30 HEBDO° MUSIQUES
Magazine de l'actualité du disque : chansons, pop, folk, classique etc.

14.10 LES JEUX DU STADE
Emission sportive. Aujourd'hui : les arts martiaux.°

15.50 RUGBY : TOURNOI DES CINQ NATIONS
Angleterre-France.

17.30 TRENTE MILLIONS D'AMIS
Le magazine des animaux familiers. Aujourd'hui : *Kim l'inconsolable.* Kim est un vieux cocker qui chaque jour traverse° Le Havre pour se rendre sur la tombe° de son maître.°

18.00 LA COURSE AUTOUR DU MONDE

18.55 LE MOT LE PLUS LONG
Jeu : Avec huit lettres tirées au sort,° deux joueurs doivent former des mots aussi longs que possible.

19.20 ACTUALITES REGIONALES

20.00 JOURNAL

20.30 NUIT DES CESARS 1979
Récompense° les meilleurs acteurs et les meilleurs films de l'année.

22.30 SWITCH
Série policière. Aujourd'hui : *L'Affaire de l'Emeraude.*

23.10 JUKE-BOX : STEVIE WONDER

23.30 JOURNAL ET FIN

3

12.15 REPONSE A TOUT
Des concurrents doivent répondre à des questions posées par les téléspectateurs.°

12.30 ACTUALITES A DAKAR

13.40 LA PETITE SCIENCE
Les planètes.

15.00 LES VIKINGS
Les aventuriers de l'an 1000.

15.50 VIVE° LE SPORT

16.45 LA PARADE DES DESSINS ANIMES

18.00 A LA BONNE HEURE°
Deux équipes de jeunes présentent leurs reportages.°

18.40 L'ILE AUX ENFANTS
Marionnettes, chansons.

19.00 JEAN PINOT, MEDECIN D'AUJOURD'HUI
Feuilleton de Michel Fermaud (13e épisode).

19.20 EH BIEN RACONTE
Des histoires drôles.

20.00 ACTUALITES

20.30 L'AMERICAIN
Film français de Marcel Bozzuffi (1969). Bruno revient à Rouen, sa ville natale,° après un séjour de onze ans aux Etats-Unis. Il retrouve° de vieux amis, mais il se sent un peu étranger° dans ce qui était autrefois son monde.
Avec :
J.-L. Trintignant......... Bruno
Simone Signoret........ Léone
Bernard Fresson........ Raymond
Marcel Bozzuffi......... Jacky
Jacques Perrin......... Patrick

23.10 ACTUALITES ET FIN

VOCABULAIRE : **à travers** *through;* **reçoit** *welcomes;* **une vedette** *star;* **Jeunes Pratique** *Tips for the Young;* **actualités** *news;* **défigurée** *defaced;* **la lune** *the moon;* **en piste** *take your places;* **un tournoi** *tournament;* **les chiens de traîneaux** *sled dogs;* **actualités de la consommation** *consumer news;* **Chapeau melon et bottes de cuir** *The Avengers (lit.: bowler hat and leather boots);* **empêcher** *to prevent;* **siècle** *century;* **catch** *wrestling;* **fin** *sign-off;* **Journal des sourds et des mal entendants** *News for the deaf and hard of hearing;* **éducatif** *educational;* **hebdo** *weekly;* **les arts martiaux** *martial arts;* **traverse** *goes through;* **la tombe** *grave;* **maître** *master;* **tirées au sort** *drawn at random;* **récompense** *rewards;* **téléspectateurs** *viewers;* **vive** *long live;* **à la bonne heure** *well done;* **reportage** *reporting;* **la ville natale** *city of birth;* **retrouve** *sees again;* **se sent étranger** *feels strange*

19 EXERCICE DE CONVERSATION

Regardez le programme de télévision à la page 255 et dites...
1. ce que vous regarderiez si vos parents vous laissaient regarder tout ce que vous voulez.
2. quelle est, d'après vous, l'émission la plus intéressante et pourquoi.
3. quelle est l'émission la plus ennuyeuse et pourquoi.
4. quelle est l'émission la plus amusante et pourquoi?

20 WORD LIST

1–4

la conservation *conservation*
une émission *program*
  un documentaire *documentary*
  une émission de variétés *variety show*
  un feuilleton *serial*
  le journal télévisé *TV news*
  une série *series*
l'énergie (f.) *energy*
la nature *nature*
un problème *problem*

se distraire *to be entertained*
s'instruire *to learn*

actuel, –elle *current*
lointain, –e *far away*
scientifique *scientific*

5–6

une image *picture*
la permission *permission*
un poste *television set*

allumer le poste *to turn on the TV set*
éteindre le poste *to turn off the TV set*
mettre la télévision *to turn on the TV set*
oublier *to forget*
régler *to adjust*
  je règle, tu règles
  il règle, ils règlent
l'image saute *the picture flips*

clair, –e *bright*
flou, –e *fuzzy, out of focus*
sombre *dark*

où l'on = où on

7–12

une fenêtre *window*
un rêve *dream*

l'Afrique (f.) *Africa*
un centre *center*
un climat *climate*
un engrais *fertilizer*
la fabrication *manufacturing*
un paysage *landscape*
  un désert *desert*
  une savane *savannah*
un peintre *painter*
la population *population*
une république *republic*
un tableau *painting*
  des tableaux *paintings*
une variété *variety*

faire le tour du monde *to go around the world*

un animal *animal*
  des animaux *animals*
  un crocodile *crocodile*
  un éléphant *elephant*
  un hippopotame *hippopotamus*
  un lion *lion*
  une panthère *panther*
  un singe *monkey*

se composer *to be made up of*
vivent en liberté *live in their natural environment*

portant *carrying*

peut-être que... *maybe. . .*

administratif, –ive *administrative*
agricole *agricultural*
artistique *artistic*
célèbre *famous*
culturel, –elle *cultural*
doux, douce *mild*
éthnique *ethnic*
fertile *fertile*
industriel, –ielle *industrial*
national, –e *national*
occidental, –e *western*
officiel, –ielle *official*
situé, –e *located*

à la façon traditionnelle *in the traditional way*
en pleine expansion *booming*

13–19

une pub(licité) *commercial*

bronzer *to sunbathe, to tan*
peigner *to comb*

brillant, –e *shiny*
doux, douce *soft*
économique *economical*
naturel, –elle *natural*
pétillant, –e *bubbly, sparkling*
pratique *practical*
souple *manageable*
terne *dull*

Festivals

French-speaking people love a good festival. It gives them a feeling of community, of being part of a greater whole. The 14th of July (Bastille Day) is the French "Fête Nationale." It commemorates the beginning of the Revolution of 1789, which saw the birth of democracy in France. In Paris, the festivities start in the morning with a huge military parade that goes down the Champs-Elysées. They continue late into the night with spectacular fireworks set off from the Tour Eiffel and with thousands of people dancing in the streets.

1

2

3

5

4

The "Fête de l'Indépendance" of Ivory Coast (December 7) commemorates the birth, in 1960, of this modern, independent state. The main celebration takes place in a different city or town each year. This encourages the chosen city or town to modernize and beautify itself so that it can stand proudly in the spotlight turned on it during the celebration. The festivities usually include an impressive parade of different organized groups and numerous floats depicting the economic progress of the country.

Plate 27

The great majority of French-speaking people in Europe and the Americas are Roman Catholic, and several of their festivals relate to special days in the Catholic calendar. One of these festivals is the "Fête-Dieu" (Corpus Christi), shown here as celebrated every year in Fribourg, Switzerland. The high point of the festival is a mass celebrated by the Bishop of Fribourg. It is followed by a procession accompanied by the music of school bands and hymns sung by young children. The route followed by the procession is decorated with many colorful flags. Hundreds of people dressed up in their Sunday best come from all over the region to attend the festival.

1

2 3

4 5

Plate 28

The "Fête de Jeanne d'Arc" (May 8) is the great festival of the town of Orléans, on the Loire River, in France. It commemorates an event in the Hundred Years' War: on May 8, 1429, the French troops, led by Joan of Arc, liberated Orléans from English occupation. Joan of Arc was later declared a saint by the Catholic Church, and the "Fête de Jeanne d'Arc" is celebrated with a combination of religious and historic pageantry. After a solemn mass celebrated in the Orléans cathedral, a massive parade of representatives of all the French provinces in traditional costumes winds its way through the town. The parade is led by a young woman on horseback, dressed as Jeanne.

Besides patriotic and religious festivals which celebrate historical or religious events, there are regional festivals to celebrate local products and the people who produce them. The "Fête pastorale de la St-Roch" is a festival of the people who live in the region of Bigorre (the Bigourdans) in the Pyrenees. They raise cattle and sheep, and the festival is given to honor the shepherds and their way of life.

1

2

3

Plate 30

Festivals celebrate any product important to a region. It might be sauerkraut, as in (2) these "Journées de la Choucroute" in Colmar, Alsace; or flowers, as in (3) this "Fête des Fleurs" in Luchon, Pyrenees. However, because France is a great wine-producing country, the product most often celebrated in these festivals in France is wine, as in (4) this "Fête du Vin" in Eguisheim, Alsace.

Plate 31

"Carnaval" is a traditional festival that lasts for about two weeks at the end of winter. It is a time for fireworks and parades, for costumes and masks, for games and competitions, for dancing and singing, and for forgetting the hardships of winter. "Carnaval" is celebrated all over, but some carnival festivities are more spectacular than others: the "Carnaval de Nice," for instance, or the one shown here, "Le Carnaval du ben bon monde" (The Good Folks Carnival) in Quebec City.

1

2 3

4

Plate 32

5

Grammar Summary

Articles

Singular		Plural
Masculine	Feminine	
un frère **un** [n] ami	**une** sœur	**des** frères / sœurs **des** [z] amis / amies
le frère **l'**ami	**la** sœur **l'**amie	**les** frères / sœurs **les** [z] amis / amies
ce frère **cet** [t] ami	**cette** sœur	**ces** frères / sœurs **ces** [z] amis / amies
mon frère **mon** [n] ami	**ma** sœur **mon** [n] amie	**mes** frères / sœurs **mes** [z] amis / amies
ton frère **ton** [n] ami	**ta** sœur **ton** [n] amie	**tes** frères / sœurs **tes** [z] amis / amies
son frère **son** [n] ami	**sa** sœur **son** [n] amie	**ses** frères / sœurs **ses** [z] amis / amies
notre frère	**notre** sœur	**nos** frères / sœurs **nos** [z] amis / amies
votre frère	**votre** sœur	**vos** frères / sœurs **vos** [z] amis / amies
leur frère	**leur** sœur	**leurs** frères / sœurs **leurs** [z] amis / amies

Adjectives — Agreement

	Singular		Plural	
	Masculine	Feminine	Masculine	Feminine
	un garçon…	une fille…	des garçons…	des filles…
Different sound / *Different spelling*	distrait sérieux	distraite sérieuse	distraits sérieux	distraites sérieuses
Same sound / *Different spelling*	doué	douée	doués	douées
Same sound / *Same spelling*	timide	timide	timides	timides

Regular Verbs

INFINITIVE

Stem	Ending	Stem	Ending	Stem	Ending	Stem	Ending
jou	**–er**	sort	**–ir**	chois	**–ir**	attend	**–re**

PRESENT

Stem	Ending	Stem	Ending	Stem	Ending	Stem	Ending
jou	**–e** **–es** **–e**	sor	**–s** **–s** **–t**	chois	**–is** **–is** **–it**	attend	**–s** **–s** **—**
jou	**–ons** **–ez** **–ent**	sort	**–ons** **–ez** **–ent**	choisiss	**–ons** **–ez** **–ent**	attend	**–ons** **–ez** **–ent**

COMMANDS

Stem	Ending	Stem	Ending	Stem	Ending	Stem	Ending
jou	**–e** **–ons** **–ez**	sor / sort	**–s** **–ons** **–ez**	chois / choisiss	**–is** **–ons** **–ez**	attend	**–s** **–ons** **–ez**

Regular Verbs

PASSE COMPOSE with **avoir**			PASSE COMPOSE with **être**			IMPARFAIT	
	Stem	Ending		Stem	Ending	Stem	Ending
ai as a	jou sort	**–é** **–i**	suis es est	rentr	**–é(e)**	jou sort	**–ais** **–ais** **–ait**
avons avez ont	chois attend	**–i** **–u**	sommes êtes sont	rentr	**–é(e)s**	choisiss attend	**–ions** **–iez** **–aient**

Regular Verbs

FUTURE		CONDITIONAL	
Stem	Ending	Stem	Ending
jouer sortir choisir attendr	**–ai** **–as** **–a** **–ons** **–ez** **–ont**	jouer sortir choisir attendr	**–ais** **–ais** **–ait** **–ions** **–iez** **–aient**

Pronouns

Independent Pronouns	Subject Pronouns	Direct-Object Pronouns	Indirect-Object Pronouns	Reflexive Pronouns
moi	je (j')	me (m') or moi	me (m') or moi	me (m')
toi	tu	te (t')	te (t')	te (t') or toi
lui	il	le (l')	lui	se (s')
elle	elle	la (l')	lui	se (s')
nous	nous (nous z)	nous (nous z)	nous (nous z)	nous (nous z)
vous	vous (vous z)	vous (vous z)	vous (vous z)	vous (vous z)
eux	ils (ils z)	les (les z)	leur	se (s')
elles	elles (elles z)	les (les z)	leur	se (s')

Pronouns

Pronoun replacing **de** + *noun phrase*	Pronoun replacing **à, dans, sur**... + *noun phrase*
en (en n)	y

Verb Index

Following is an alphabetical list of verbs with stem changes, spelling changes, or irregular forms. This list will guide you to the appropriate entries in the following pages for the verb whose pattern it follows. Verbs like **sortir** have also been included in the list. All verbs in **–ir** which have not been included are like **choisir.**

Verbs with Stem and Spelling Changes

Verbs listed in this section are not irregular, but they do show some stem and spelling changes. The only sets of forms listed are those in which stem and spelling changes occur, and the forms in which the changes occur are printed in boldface type.

ACHETER

Present	**achète, achètes, achète,** achetons, achetez, **achètent**
Commands	**achète,** achetons, achetez
Future	**achèterai, achèteras, achètera, achèterons, achèterez, achèteront**
Conditional	**achèterais, achèterais, achèterait, achèterions, achèteriez, achèteraient**

APPELER

Present	**appelle, appelles, appelle,** appelons, appelez, **appellent**
Commands	**appelle,** appelons, appelez
Future	**appellerai, appelleras, appellera, appellerons, appellerez, appelleront**
Conditional	**appellerais, appellerais, appellerait, appellerions, appelleriez, appelleraient**

APPUYER

Present	**appuie, appuies, appuie,** appuyons, appuyez, **appuient**
Commands	**appuie,** appuyons, appuyez
Future	**appuierai, appuieras, appuiera, appuierons, appuierez, appuieront**
Conditional	**appuierais, appuierais, appuierait, appuierions, appuieriez, appuieraient**

COMMENCER

Present	commence, commences, commence, **commençons,** commencez, commencent
Commands	commence, **commençons,** commencez
Imparfait	**commençais, commençais, commençait,** commencions, commenciez, **commençaient**

ESSAYER

Present	**essaie, essaies, essaie,** essayons, essayez, **essaient**
Commands	**essaie,** essayons, essayez
Future	**essaierai, essaieras, essaiera, essaierons, essaierez, essaieront**
Conditional	**essaierais, essaierais, essaierait, essaierions, essaieriez, essaieraient**

MANGER

Present	mange, manges, mange, **mangeons,** mangez, mangent
Commands	mange, **mangeons,** mangez
Imparfait	**mangeais, mangeais, mangeait,** mangions, mangiez, **mangeaient**

PREFERER

Present	**préfère, préfères, préfère,** préférons, préférez, **préfèrent**
Commands	**préfère,** préférons, préférez

Verbs with Irregular Forms

Verbs listed in this section are those that do not follow the pattern of verbs like **jouer,** verbs like **choisir,** verbs like **sortir,** or verbs like **attendre.**

ALLER

Present	vais, vas, va, allons, allez, vont
Commands	va, allons, allez
Passé Composé	*Auxiliary:* être *Past Participle:* allé
Imparfait	allais, allais, allait, allions, alliez, allaient
Future	irai, iras, ira, irons, irez, iront
Conditional	irais, irais, irait, irions, iriez, iraient

AVOIR

Present	ai, as, a, avons, avez, ont
Passé Composé	*Auxiliary:* avoir *Past Participle:* eu
Imparfait	avais, avais, avait, avions, aviez, avaient
Future	aurai, auras, aura, aurons, aurez, auront
Conditional	aurais, aurais, aurait, aurions, auriez, auraient

BATTRE

Present	bats, bats, bat, battons, battez, battent
Commands	bats, battons, battez
Passé Composé	*Auxiliary:* avoir *Past Participle:* battu
Imparfait	battais, battais, battait, battions, battiez, battaient
Future	battrai, battras, battra, battrons, battrez, battront
Conditional	battrais, battrais, battrait, battrions, battriez, battraient

BOIRE

Present	bois, bois, boit, buvons, buvez, boivent
Commands	bois, buvons, buvez
Passé Composé	*Auxiliary:* avoir *Past Participle:* bu
Imparfait	buvais, buvais, buvait, buvions, buviez, buvaient
Future	boirai, boiras, boira, boirons, boirez, boiront
Conditional	boirais, boirais, boirait, boirions, boiriez, boiraient

CONNAITRE

Present	connais, connais, connaît, connaissons, connaissez, connaissent
Commands	connais, connaissons, connaissez
Passé Composé	*Auxiliary:* avoir *Past Participle:* connu
Imparfait	connaissais, connaissais, connaissait, connaissions, connaissiez, connaissaient
Future	connaîtrai, connaîtras, connaîtra, connaîtrons, connaîtrez, connaîtront
Conditional	connaîtrais, connaîtrais, connaîtrait, connaîtrions, connaîtriez, connaîtraient

COURIR

Present	cours, cours, court, courons, courez, courent
Commands	cours, courons, courez
Passé Composé	*Auxiliary:* avoir *Past Participle:* couru
Imparfait	courais, courais, courait, courions, couriez, couraient
Future	courrai, courras, courra, courrons, courrez, courront
Conditional	courrais, courrais, courrait, courrions, courriez, courraient

DIRE

Present	dis, dis, dit, disons, dites, disent
Commands	dis, disons, dites
Passé Composé	*Auxiliary:* avoir *Past Participle:* dit
Imparfait	disais, disais, disait, disions, disiez, disaient
Future	dirai, diras, dira, dirons, direz, diront
Conditional	dirais, dirais, dirait, dirions, diriez, diraient

ECRIRE

Present	écris, écris, écrit, écrivons, écrivez, écrivent
Commands	écris, écrivons, écrivez
Passé Composé	*Auxiliary:* avoir *Past Participle:* écrit
Imparfait	écrivais, écrivais, écrivait, écrivions, écriviez, écrivaient
Future	écrirai, écriras, écrira, écrirons, écrirez, écriront
Conditional	écrirais, écrirais, écrirait, écririons, écririez, écriraient

ENVOYER

Present	envoie, envoies, envoie, envoyons, envoyez, envoient
Commands	envoie, envoyons, envoyez
Passé Composé	*Auxiliary:* avoir *Past Participle:* envoyé
Imparfait	envoyais, envoyais, envoyait, envoyions, envoyiez, envoyaient
Future	enverrai, enverras, enverra, enverrons, enverrez, enverront
Conditional	enverrais, enverrais, enverrait, enverrions, enverriez, enverraient

ETRE

Present	suis, es, est, sommes, êtes, sont
Passé Composé	*Auxiliary:* avoir *Past Participle:* été
Imparfait	étais, étais, était, étions, étiez, étaient
Future	serai, seras, sera, serons, serez, seront
Conditional	serais, serais, serait, serions, seriez, seraient

FAIRE

Present	fais, fais, fait, faisons, faites, font
Commands	fais, faisons, faites
Passé Composé	*Auxiliary:* avoir *Past Participle:* fait
Imparfait	faisais, faisais, faisait, faisions, faisiez, faisaient
Future	ferai, feras, fera, ferons, ferez, feront
Conditional	ferais, ferais, ferait, ferions, feriez, feraient

LIRE

Present	lis, lis, lit, lisons, lisez, lisent
Commands	lis, lisons, lisez
Passé Composé	*Auxiliary:* avoir *Past Participle:* lu
Imparfait	lisais, lisais, lisait, lisions, lisiez, lisaient
Future	lirai, liras, lira, lirons, lirez, liront
Conditional	lirais, lirais, lirait, lirions, liriez, liraient

METTRE

Present	mets, mets, met, mettons, mettez, mettent
Commands	mets, mettons, mettez
Passé Composé	*Auxiliary:* avoir *Past Participle:* mis
Imparfait	mettais, mettais, mettait, mettions, mettiez, mettaient
Future	mettrai, mettras, mettra, mettrons, mettrez, mettront
Conditional	mettrais, mettrais, mettrait, mettrions, mettriez, mettraient

PLEUVOIR

Present	il pleut
Passé Composé	il a plu
Imparfait	il pleuvait
Future	il pleuvra
Conditional	il pleuvrait

POUVOIR

Present	peux, peux, peut, pouvons, pouvez, peuvent
Passé Composé	*Auxiliary:* avoir *Past Participle:* pu
Imparfait	pouvais, pouvais, pouvait, pouvions, pouviez, pouvaient
Future	pourrai, pourras, pourra, pourrons, pourrez, pourront
Conditional	pourrais, pourrais, pourrait, pourrions, pourriez, pourraient

PRENDRE

Present	prends, prends, prend, prenons, prenez, prennent
Commands	prends, prenons, prenez
Passé Composé	*Auxiliary:* avoir *Past Participle:* pris
Imparfait	prenais, prenais, prenait, prenions, preniez, prenaient
Future	prendrai, prendras, prendra, prendrons, prendrez, prendront
Conditional	prendrais, prendrais, prendrait, prendrions, prendriez, prendraient

SAVOIR

Present	sais, sais, sait, savons, savez, savent
Passé Composé	*Auxiliary:* avoir *Past Participle:* su
Imparfait	savais, savais, savait, savions, saviez, savaient
Future	saurai, sauras, saura, saurons, saurez, sauront
Conditional	saurais, saurais, saurait, saurions, sauriez, sauraient

SUIVRE

Present	suis, suis, suit, suivons, suivez, suivent
Commands	suis, suivons, suivez
Passé Composé	*Auxiliary:* avoir *Past Participle:* suivi
Imparfait	suivais, suivais, suivait, suivions, suiviez, suivaient
Future	suivrai, suivras, suivra, suivrons, suivrez, suivront
Conditional	suivrais, suivrais, suivrait, suivrions, suivriez, suivraient

VENIR

Present	viens, viens, vient, venons, venez, viennent
Commands	viens, venons, venez
Passé Composé	*Auxiliary:* être *Past Participle:* venu
Imparfait	venais, venais, venait, venions, veniez, venaient
Future	viendrai, viendras, viendra, viendrons, viendrez, viendront
Conditional	viendrais, viendrais, viendrait, viendrions, viendriez, viendraient

VOIR

Present	vois, vois, voit, voyons, voyez, voient
Commands	vois, voyons, voyez
Passé Composé	*Auxiliary:* avoir *Past Participle:* vu
Imparfait	voyais, voyais, voyait, voyions, voyiez, voyaient
Future	verrai, verras, verra, verrons, verrez, verront
Conditional	verrais, verrais, verrait, verrions, verriez, verraient

VOULOIR

Present	veux, veux, veut, voulons, voulez, veulent
Passé Composé	*Auxiliary:* avoir *Past Participle:* voulu
Imparfait	voulais, voulais, voulait, voulions, vouliez, voulaient
Future	voudrai, voudras, voudra, voudrons, voudrez, voudront
Conditional	voudrais, voudrais, voudrait, voudrions, voudriez, voudraient

Numbers

Cardinal

0	zéro	14	quatorze	71	soixante et onze
1	un/une	15	quinze	72	soixante-douze
2	deux	16	seize	80	quatre-vingts
3	trois	17	dix-sept	81	quatre-vingt-un/une
4	quatre	18	dix-huit	90	quatre-vingt-dix
5	cinq	19	dix-neuf	91	quatre-vingt-onze
6	six	20	vingt	100	cent
7	sept	21	vingt et un/une	101	cent un/une
8	huit	22	vingt-deux	200	deux cents
9	neuf	30	trente	201	deux cent un/une
10	dix	40	quarante	1 000	mille
11	onze	50	cinquante	1 001	mille un/une
12	douze	60	soixante	1 906	mille neuf cent six
13	treize	70	soixante-dix	2 000	deux mille

Ordinal

1st	premier, première	1er, 1ère	5th	cinquième	5^e	9th	neuvième	9^e
2nd	deuxième	2^e	6th	sixième	6^e	10th	dixième	10^e
3rd	troisième	3^e	7th	septième	7^e	100th	centième	100^e
4th	quatrième	4^e	8th	huitième	8^e	1,000th	millième	1 000^e

French-English Vocabulary

This vocabulary includes most of the words that appear in the 24 units of **Nos Amis.** Those not included are the names of people and words from optional material (color-coded purple). Verbs are given in the infinitive; verb forms are given only for important and frequently used verbs which are presented late in the book.

Nouns are always given with a gender marker. If gender is not apparent, however, it is indicated by *m.* (masculine) or *f.* (feminine) following the noun. Plurals in **-x** and those of compound nouns are also given, abbreviated *pl.* An asterisk (*) before a word beginning with **h** indicates an aspirate **h.**

The number after each definition refers to the unit in which a word or phrase appears. In cases where a single entry is followed by two numbers, the first number indicates the unit in which the word is introduced passively, and the second, the unit in which the word becomes active. The first number may also indicate the unit in which a word is introduced actively, and the second, the unit in which it reappears as part of a category.

A

à *to, in,* 1; *at,* 4; *on,* 10; à + le = au, 4; à + les = aux, 4; à côté (de) *next to,* 4; à deux pas *a few feet from,* 3; à droite *on (to) the right,* 8, 10; à gauche *on (to) the left,* 8, 10; à la fin *at the end,* 8; à la fois *at the same time,* 17; à l'heure *on time,* 19; à la maison *at home,* 5; de retour à la maison *back home,* 23; à la place (de) *in place of,* 16; à noter *to be noted,* 22; à peine *hardly,* 16; à pied *on foot,* 13; A table! *Dinner (lunch) is served!* 8; A (ton) tour! *(Your) turn!* 21; à vendre *for sale,* 11; A vos marques, prêts, partez! *On your marks, get set, go!* 22; c'est à toi (de) *it's your turn (to),* 3; une pièce à eux *their own room,* 9; une vie bien à elle *its very own life,* 10

un **abri** *shed,* 4; un abri pour bicyclettes *bicycle shed,* 4
abriter *to protect,* 16
un **accident** *accident,* 17
accueillant, –e *hospitable,* 17
un **achat** *purchase,* 20; faire des achats *to shop,* 20
acheter *to buy,* 8; sans avoir acheté *without buying,* 13
actuel, -elle *current,* 24
une **addition** *check,* 5
administratif, –ive *administrative,* 24
l' **administration** (f.) *administration,* 4
admirer *to admire,* 12
adorer *to like very much,* 15
une **adresse** *address,* 10
un(e) **adulte** *adult,* 12
un **aéroport** *airport,* 19

des **affaires** (f.) *belongings,* 18
une **affiche** *poster,* 3
afficher *to post,* 19
l' **Afrique** (f.) *Africa,* 24
âge: Quel âge as-tu? *How old are you?* 1
l' **agneau** (m.) *lamb,* 8; un gigot d'agneau *leg of lamb,* 8
agricole *agricultural,* 24
s' **agripper** *to hold on,* 21
aide: avec l'aide de *with the help of,* 16
aider (à) *to help,* 8, 15
ailleurs: d'ailleurs *as a matter of fact,* 14
aimer *to like,* 2; aimer le mieux *to like best,* 4; aimer mieux *to prefer,* 2
un **air** *tune,* 14
air : avoir l'air *to look (good, etc.),* 8; en plein air *outside,* 13; Ça n'a pas eu l'air de leur plaire! *They didn't seem to like that very much!* 21
un **album** *album,* 7
une **allée** *lane,* 10; *walkway, path,* 21
l' **Allemagne** (f.) *Germany,* 19
l' **allemand** (m.) *German,* 4, 19
allemand, –e *German,* 19
aller *to go,* 4; aller à *to suit,* 9; *to fit,* 23; aller à la pêche *to go fishing,* 17; aller à pied *to walk,* 13; aller chercher *to go get,* 16; aller et venir *to come and go,* 14; Allez! *Come on!* Allons-y! *Let's go!* 5, 14; Ça va? *How's everything?* 6; Ça va. *Okay.* 6 Allô. *Hello.* 6
allumer (le poste) *to turn on (the TV set),* 24
alors *then,* 3
amateur *amateur,* 3
un(e) **Américain(e)** *American,* 19

américain, –e *American,* 19; football américain *football,* 2
l' **Amérique** (f.) *America,* 17
un(e) **ami(e)** *friend,* 2; un(e) ami(e) d'enfance *childhood friend,* 16
amis : nos amis *our friends,* 1; nouveaux amis *new friends,* 10 **Amitiés.** *Love.* 12
l' **amour** (m.) *love,* 5; une histoire d'amour *love story,* 5
amusant, –e *fun,* 2, 4
s' **amuser** *to have fun,* 13
un **an** *year,* 1; J'ai 15 ans. *I am 15 years old.* 1; tous les ans *every year,* 7
un **ananas** *pineapple,* 8
l' **anglais** (m.) *English,* 4, 19
un(e) **Anglais(e)** *English person,* 19
anglais, –e *English,* 19
l' **Angleterre** (f.) *England,* 19
un **animal** (pl. : **–aux**) *animal,* 16
animé : un dessin animé *an animated cartoon,* 5
les **anneaux** (m.) *rings,* 22
une **année** *year,* 4, 12; une année scolaire *school year,* 4
un **anniversaire** *birthday,* 23; Bon Anniversaire! *Happy Birthday!* 23
une **annonce** *announcement,* 19
annoncer *to announce,* 18
un **annuaire** *phone book,* 6
annuel, –elle *annual,* 2
un **anorak** *ski jacket,* 15
les **Antilles** (f.) *West Indies,* 17
une **antiquité** *antique item,* 11
août (m.) *August,* 12
un **appareil** *telephone,* 6
un **appareil(-photo)** (pl. : **appareils-photo**) *camera,* 3
un **appartement** *apartment,* 1
appelé, –e *called,* 10
appeler *to call,* 6; s'appeler *to be named,* 13

appelle(s) : Comment t'appelles-tu? *What is your name?* 1; Je m'appelle... *My name is . . .* , 1

appétit : Bon appétit... *Enjoy your meal!* 8

applaudir *to clap,* 14; On les applaudit bien fort. *Let's give them a nice hand.* 14

apporter *to bring,* 5

une **appréciation** *comment,* 4

apprendre à *to learn,* 19

s' **approcher (de)** *to get closer,* 19

appuyé, –e *propped up,* 22

appuyer *to press,* 14; s'appuyer *to lean on,* 15

après *after,* 5; après avoir passé *after spending,* 13; d'après *according to,* 15

l' **après-midi** (m.) *afternoon,* 4; en fin d'après-midi *at the end of the afternoon,* 18

un **aquarium** *aquarium,* 12

l' **arabe** (m.) *Arabic,* 19

un **arbre** *tree,* 10

l' **argent** (m.) *money,* 5; *silver,* 20; l'argent de poche *allowance,* 23

s' **arrêter** *to stop,* 13; arrêter *to stop,* 14

arrière *fullback,* 2

arrivant *arriving,* 19

une **arrivée** *arrival,* 11; le tableau des arrivées *arrivals board,* 19

arriver *to arrive,* 5; arriver (à) *to succeed (in),* 6; *to happen (to),* 15; ne pas arriver à la cheville de *not to be mentioned in the same breath with,* 22

un **artisan** *craftsperson,* 20

un **artiste** *artist,* 20; C'est un artiste. *He's a real artist!* 20

artistique *artistic,* 24

un **ascenseur** *elevator,* 10

un **assaisonnement** *dressing,* 8

assaisonner *to season,* 20

assez *rather,* 4; assez (de) *enough, enough of,* 5, 8; assez de place *enough room,* 5

une **assiette** *a plate,* 8

une **assistante sociale** *social worker,* 17

s' **assurer** *to make sure,* 13

l' **astrologie** (f.) *astrology,* 21

un(e) **athlète** *athlete,* 22

l' **athlétisme** (m.) *athletics,* 22

attaquer *to attack,* 21

Attendez! *Wait a minute!* 5

attendre *to wait for,* 7

attention : faire attention *to be careful,* 4; Attention! *Watch out!* 14

atterrir *to land,* 19

attraper *to catch,* 17

au = à + le, 4

au cours de *during,* 10

aucun, -e *no,* 19.

au-dessus (de) *on top of,* 20

au fond (de) *at the far end (of),* 4

aujourd'hui *today,* 5

au moins *at least,* 13

Au revoir. *Goodbye.* 6

aussi *too, also,* 1

aussi... que *as . . . as,* 22

autant : en faire autant *to do the same thing,* 23

un **autobus** *bus,* 13

l' **automne** (m.) *autumn, fall,* 15; en automne *in the fall,* 15

une **auto tamponneuse** *bumper car,* 21

autour (de) *around,* 15

un(e) **autre** *another (person),* 4; quoi d'autre *what else,* 23

autrefois *(in) the old days,* 17

aux = à + les, 4

avance : en avance *early,* 19

avant *forward,* 2

avant (de) *before,* 5

avec *with,* 2

l' **avenir** (m.) *future,* 21

l' **aventure** (f.) *adventure,* 17

une **avenue** *avenue,* 10

un **avion** *airplane,* 17, 19; une maquette d'avion *model airplane,* 3

un(e) **avocat(e)** *lawyer,* 7

l' **avoine** (f.) *oats,* 16

avoir *to have,* 3; avoir... ans *to be . . . years old,* 1 : J'ai... an. *I am . . . years old,* 1; avoir l'air *to look (good, etc.),* 8; avoir faim *to be hungry,* 5; avoir froid *to be cold,* 15; avoir *hâte (de) *to look forward to,* 12; avoir lieu *to take place,* 9; avoir mal (à) *to hurt,* 15 : Elle a mal à la jambe. *Her leg hurts.* 15; avoir le mal de mer *to be seasick,* 21; avoir peur *to be afraid,* 21; avoir raison *to be right,* 23; avoir soif *to be thirsty,* 5; avoir le vertige *to be dizzy,* 21; Qu'est-ce que vous avez...? *What's the matter with you . . .?* 22

avril (m.) *April,* 12

B

une **bague** *ring,* 9

une **baguette** *long French bread,* 5

une **baie** *bay,* 17

baigné, –e *bathed,* 17

se **baigner** *to go swimming,* 17

bains : une salle de bains *bathroom,* 10

un **baiser** *kiss,* 23

baisser *to lower,* 14, 22

un **bal** *dance,* 14

balayer *to sweep,* 9

un **balcon** *balcony,* 10

une **balle** *ball (baseball, tennis),* 2

un **ballon** *ball* (football, soccer, etc.), 2

une **banane** *banana,* 8

une **bande** *gang,* 9; *tape,* 14

un **banjo** *banjo,* 9, 14

une **banlieue** *suburb,* 10

une **banque** *bank,* 10

un **baracuda** *barracuda,* 17

une **barbe à papa** *cotton candy,* 21

la **barre fixe** *horizontal bar,* 22

les **barres parallèles** *parallel bars,* 22

bas *low, soft,* 14

le **base-ball** *baseball,* 2

le **basket-ball** *basketball,* 2

bat : La surprise-partie bat son plein. *The party is going full swing.* 9

un **bateau** (pl. : –x) *boat,* 12; faire du bateau *to go boating,* 17; un bateau-mouche *excursion boat,* 11

un **bâtiment** *building,* 10

un **bâton** *ski pole,* 15

une **batte** *baseball bat,* 2

une **batterie** *drums,* 14

battre *to break,* 22

bavarder *to talk,* 4

beau, bel, belle, beaux, belles *beautiful,* 16; il fait beau *the weather is nice,* 13, 15

beaucoup (de) *much, many, a lot,* 2, 8

le **Beaujolais** *Beaujolais,* 8

belge *Belgian,* 19

la **Belgique** *Belgium,* 7, 19; en Belgique *in Belgium,* 7

le **beurre** *butter,* 8

beurré, –e *buttered,* 13

une **bibliothèque** *library,* 4

bien *well,* 3; Ça tombe bien! *Terrific!* 5; bien des *many,* 23; bien sûr *of course,* 4; je pense bien *of course,* 19; On les applaudit bien fort. *Let's give them a nice hand.* 14

bientôt *soon,* 16

bienvenus : Soyez les bienvenus! *Welcome!* 17

un **bifteck** *steak,* 8

un **bijou** (pl. : –x) *a piece of jewelry,* 9

une **bijouterie** *jewelry shop,* 23

une **bille** *marble,* 9

un **billet** *bill (money),* 5; *ticket,* 12

le **blanc** *white,* 2

le **blé** *wheat,* 16

le **bleu** *blue,* 2; couvert(e) de bleus *all black and blue,* 21

bleu, –e *blue,* 7

blond, –e *blond,* 7

un **blouson** *jacket,* 9

le **bœuf** *beef,* 8; un rôti de bœuf *roast of beef,* 8

boire *to drink,* 9; donner à boire *to give water to,* 16

un **bois** *woods,* 7, 16
une **boisson** *drink,* 5
une **boîte** *box,* 4; une boîte de chocolats *box of chocolates,* 23; une boîte de couleurs *paintbox,* 4
un **bol** *bowl,* 13
bon, bonne *good,* 4; Bon Anniversaire! *Happy Birthday!* 23; Bon Appétit! *Enjoy your meal!* 8; il fait bon *it's nice,* 15
un **bond** *leap,* 13
le **bonheur** *happiness,* 23
Bonne nuit! *Good night!* 13
un **bonnet** *(ski) cap,* 15
bonsoir *good night,* 13
bord : un journal de bord *"log," diary,* 18; au bord de la mer *at the shore,* 17
bordé, –e de *edged with,* 17
une **botte** *boot,* 9
la **bouche** *mouth,* 22
un(e) **boucher (–ère)** *butcher,* 8
une **boucherie** *butcher shop,* 8
une **boucle d'oreille** (pl. : **boucles d'oreille**) *earring,* 23
un **bougainvillier** *bougainvillea,* 20
un(e) **boulanger (–ère)** *baker,* 8
une **boulangerie-pâtisserie** *bakery-pastry shop,* 8
boules : jouer aux boules *to play boule (a bowling-type game),* 20
un **boulevard** *boulevard,* 11
bout : à l'autre bout du fil *at the other end of the line,* 6
une **bouteille** *bottle,* 8
bouton : un bouton d'écoute *playback button,* 14; un bouton d'enregistrement *record button,* 14; un bouton de manchette *cufflink,* 23
un **bowling** *bowling alley,* 5
un **bracelet** *bracelet,* 9; un bracelet (fantaisie) *bracelet (costume jewelry),* 23
brancher *to plug in,* 14
un **bras** *arm,* 15, 22
bricoler *to tinker,* 3
brillant, –e *bright,* 18; *shiny,* 24
une **brioche** *brioche,* 8
se **bronzer** *to sunbathe,* 17; bronzer *to sunbathe, to tan,* 24
une **brosse** *brush,* 13; une brosse à cheveux *hairbrush,* 13; une brosse à dents *toothbrush,* 13
brosser *to brush,* 13; se brosser les cheveux *to brush one's hair,* 13
le **brouillard** *fog,* 19
brun, –e *dark (haired),* 7
une **brute** *bully,* 21
Bruxelles *Brussels,* 19
un **bulletin trimestriel** *report card,* 4
un **bureau** (pl.: **–x**) *office,* 4; employé(e) de bureau *office worker,* 7
un **burnous** *long Arab cloak,* 20

un **but** *goal,* 2

C

ça *that,* 2; ça fait combien *that's how much,* 5, 15; Ça va? *How's everything?* 6; Ça va. *Okay.* 6; Ça y est! *That did it!* 21
une **cabine téléphonique** *phone booth,* 6
cache-cache : jouer à cache-cache *to play hide and seek,* 21
un **cadeau** (pl. : **–x**) *gift,* 23; faire un cadeau *to give a gift,* 23
cadet, –ette *junior,* 22
un **café** *café,* 5
le **café** *coffee (flavor),* 5; *coffee,* 8; le café au lait *coffee with milk,* 8
un **cahier** *notebook,* 4
calculer *to figure out,* 5
un(e) **camarade** *classmate,* 4
le **camembert** *Camembert cheese,* 5
un **camp** *camp,* 18
le **Canada** *Canada,* 19; au Canada *in Canada,* 1
canadien, –ienne *Canadian,* 15, 19
un **canard** *duck,* 16; les Canards à l'Orange *Ducks in Orange Sauce,* 14
la **canne à sucre** *sugar cane,* 17
un **canon** *cannon,* 12
un **capitaine** *captain,* 2
une **capitale** *capital,* 1, 19
car *for,* 7
le **caractère** *character,* 10
Caraïbes : la mer des Caraïbes *Caribbean Sea,* 1
une **carotte** *carrot,* 8
un **cartable** *schoolbag,* 4
une **carte** *playing card,* 3; *map,* 15; *greeting card,* 23
une **carte postale** *post card,* 16
carton : faire un carton *to go target-shooting,* 21
cas: dans ce cas *in that case,* 20
une **case** *cabana,* 17
se **casser** *to break,* 15
une **cassette** *cassette,* 3
une **catégorie** *category,* 22
ce *this, that,* 1
une **ceinture** *belt,* 23
célèbre *famous,* 17, 24
celle (–là) *the one, that one, this one,* 14
celles (–là) *the ones, these, those,* 14
celui (–là) *the one, that one, this one,* 14
un **centime** *centime,* 5
un **centimètre** *centimeter,* 22
un **100 m(ètres)** *100-meter dash,* 22
un **centre** *center,* 24

centré, –e *centered,* 10
ce que *what,* 2
une **cerise** *cherry,* 8
certainement *certainly, of course,* 3
ces *these, those* 3
un **CES** *secondary school,* 4
c'est *it is,* 1; c'est à toi (de) *it's your turn (to),* 3; c'est bien pour ça... *that's exactly why . . . ,* 23; C'est dément! *It's too wild!* 21; C'est extra! *It's really great!* 21; c'est là que *it's where,* 23
cet *this, that,* 2
cette *this, that,* 1
ceux (–là) *the ones, these, those,* 14
chacun, –e *each one,* 7
un **chalet** *chalet,* 15
une **chambre** *bedroom,* 10
un **champ** *field,* 16; un champ de blé *wheat field,* 16
un **champignon** *mushroom,* 8
un(e) **champion(ne)** *champion,* 21
un **championnat** *championship,* 22
la **chance** *luck,* 21; pas de chance *no luck,* 6
changer *to change,* 9; se changer *to change one's clothes,* 13
une **chanson** *song,* 9
un **chant** *a song,* 7; le chant des oiseaux *birdcalls,* 7
chanter *to sing,* 9
un(e) **chanteur (–euse)** *singer,* 14
un **chapitre** *unit,* 1; un chapitre de révision *review unit,* 6
chaque *each,* 7, 13
une **charade** *charade,* 8
une **charcuterie** *a meat shop specializing in pork products and prepared dishes,* 8
un(e) **charcutier (–ière)** *pork butcher,* 8
se **charger (de)** *to take charge (of),* 16
un **chat** *cat,* 7
chaud : il fait chaud *it's hot (weather),* 15
une **chaussure** *shoe,* 9; une chaussure de ski *ski boot,* 15
un **chef** *leader,* 18
le **chemin** *way, route,* 10
une **chemise** *shirt,* 9
un **chemisier** *blouse,* 9
cher, chère *expensive,* 8; *dear,* 12
chercher *to look up,* 6; *to look for,* 9; aller chercher *to go get,* 16
chéri, –e *dear, darling,* 16
un **cheval** (pl. **–aux**) *horse,* 16; le cheval *horseback-riding,* 2; faire du cheval *to go horseback-riding,* 2; monter un cheval *to ride a horse,* 16
le **cheval de voltige** *vaulting horse,* 22
les **cheveux** (m.) *hair,* 13; une brosse à cheveux *hairbrush,* 13

la **cheville** *ankle*, 22; ne pas arriver à la cheville de *not to be mentioned in the same breath with*, 22
chez *at (to) someone's house*, 5; chez eux *at their house*, 5
un **chien** *dog*, 7
les **chips** (f.) *potato chips*, 9
le **chocolat** *chocolate (flavor)*, 5; *hot chocolate*, 13
choisir *to choose*, 5
choix : l'embarras du choix *embarrassment of riches*, 23
une **chose** *thing*, 9
chronométrer *to time*, 22
le **cinéma** *movies*, 5
un **circuit** *route*, 17
clair, –e *clear*, 18; *bright*, 24
une **clarinette** *clarinet*, 14
une **classe** *a class*, 4; en classe *in class*, 4; une salle de classe *classroom*, 4
un(e) **client(e)** *customer*, 13
un **climat** *climate*, 24
un **cochon** *pig*, 16
un **cocotier** *coconut tree*, 17
un **code postal** *zip code*, 12
un **cœur** *heart*, 3
une **colle** *question*, 19; poser des colles *to quiz*, 19
collé, –e *glued*, 12
collectionner *to collect*, 3
un(e) **collectionneur (–euse)** *collector*, 3
un **collier** *necklace*, 9
une **colline** *hill*, 17
combien (de) *how much, how many*, 3, 8; ça fait combien *how much*, 5
un **combiné** *receiver*, 6
comique : un film comique *a comedy*, 5
commander *to order*, 5
comme *like, as*, 1; *for*, 2
commencer *to start*, 4; commencer (à) *to start (to)*, 8; commencer (par) *to start (with)*, 4
comment *what, how*, 1; Comment t'appelles-tu? *What is your name?* 1
un(e) **commerçant(e)** *merchant*, 7; une rue commerçante *a shopping street*, 10
commun, –e *mutual*, 13
une **communication** *call*, 6
une **compagnie** *airline*, 19
comparer *to compare*, 22
un **compas** *compass*, 4
compléter *to complete*, 15
compliqué, –e *complicated*, 23
composer · *to dial*, 6; se composer *to be made up of*, 24
une **composition** *composition (musical)*, 14; une composition française *composition*, 4
comprendre *to understand*, 19
compter *to count*, 3

un **compte rendu** *account*, 22
un **comptoir** *counter*, 19
un **concert** *concert*, 14
un **concombre** *cucumber*, 8
un(e) **concurrent(e)** *competitor*, 22
conduire *to drive*, 16
la **confiture** *jam*, 8
connaissance : faire la connaissance de *to make the acquaintance of*, 10
connaître *to know (be acquainted with)*, 10; se connaître *to know each other*, 19
un **conseil** *advice*, 20
conséquent : par conséquent *consequently*, 10
la **conservation** *conservation*, 24
consulter *to read*, 6
un **conte de fées** *fairy tale*, 21
content, –e *pleased*, 18
continuer *to continue*, 9
contre *against*, 17
une **contrebasse** *double bass*, 14
un **copain** *pal*, 9
un **coquillage** *shell*, 3
le **corail** (pl. : **–aux**) *coral*, 17
la **corde à nœuds** *knotted rope*, 22
la **corde lisse** *rope*, 22
un **cordonnier** *shoemaker*, 20
le **corps** *body*, 22
correct, –e *correct*, 6
correspondance : par correspondance *in writing*, 19
un(e) **correspondant(e)** *pen pal*, 19
correspondre *to correspond*, 20
corriger *to correct*, 4
un **corsaire** *pirate*, 17
une **côte** *coastline*, 17
côté : à côté (de) *next to*, 4; du côté garçons *on the boys' side*, 22; du côté de ma mère *on my mother's side*, 7; de son côté *his/her own way*, 8
une **côtelette** *chop*, 8
le **cou** *neck*, 22
couchage : un sac de couchage *sleeping bag*, 18
se **coucher** *to go to bed*, 13
le **coude** *elbow*, 22
une **couleur** *color*, 2
un **couloir** *hallway*, 4
un **coup de peigne** : se donner un coup de peigne *to comb one's hair*, 13
un **coup de téléphone** *phone call*, 6
une **coupe** *cup, trophy*, 10
une **cour** *courtyard, schoolyard*, 4
courageux, –euse *courageous*, 22
courent : ils/elles courent *they run*, 7
courir *to run*, 22
un **cours** *course, class*, 4
cours : au cours de *during*, 10
la **course** *race, running*, 22
une **course** *errand*, 8; faire des courses *to go shopping*, 11; faire

les **courses** *to go grocery shopping*, 8
le **couscous** *couscous*, 20
un(e) **cousin(e)** *cousin*, 7
un **couteau** (pl.: **–x**) *a knife*, 8
coûter *to cost*, 8
un **couvert** *a place setting*, 8
couvert(e) de bleus *all black and blue*, 21
un **crabe** *crab*, 17
une **cravate** *necktie*, 13
un **crayon** *pencil*, 4
la **crème fraîche** *heavy soured cream*, 8
une **crémerie** *dairy outlet*, 8
un(e) **crémier (–ière)** *salesperson in a dairy outlet*, 8
crétins : Espèces de crétins! *What are you, some kind of idiots!* 21
un **crocodile** *crocodile*, 24
croire *to believe*, 12; je crois *I think*, 14; je ne crois pas à *I don't believe in*, 21
un **croisement** *intersection*, 10
un **croissant** *croissant*, 8
une **crosse** *hockey stick*, 2
cueillir *to pick*, 16
cuillère : une petite cuillère *teaspoon*, 8
le **cuir** *leather*, 20
cuire : faire cuire *to cook*, 20
une **cuisine** *kitchen*, 4, 10; faire la cuisine *to cook*, 20
la **cuisse** *thigh*, 22
cuit, –e *cooked*, 20; cuit à la vapeur *steamed*, 20
le **cuivre** *brass, copper*, 20
cultiver *to tend, to grow*, 16
culturel, –elle *cultural*, 24
curieux, –euse *curious*, 23

D

d'abord *first of all*, 4
d'accord *okay*, 5
d'ailleurs *as a matter of fact*, 14
une **dame** *lady*, 19
les **dames** (f.) *checkers*, 3
dangereux, –euse *dangerous*, 2, 4
dans *in*, 1
une **danse** *dance*, 9
danser *to dance*, 9
d'après *according to*, 15
la **date** *date*, 12
de *of, from*, 1; *about*, 4; de temps en temps *from time to time*, 10; de toute façon *anyway*, 19
un **débarquement** *landing*, 17
debout *standing up*, 13
débrancher *to unplug*, 14
début : une formule de début *salutation*, 12
débuter *to start*, 22
décembre (m.) *December*, 12

décider (de) *to decide (to),* 9
décoller *to take off,* 19
décontracté, –e *loose, easy-going,* 19
découvrir *to discover,* 17
décrire *to describe,* 9
décrivez *describe,* 4
décrocher *to pick up the receiver,* 6
déçu : elle n'a pas déçu *she didn't disappoint,* 22
dedans *inside, into,* 21
un **degré** *degree,* 15
déjà *already,* 9
un **déjeuner** *lunch,* 7, 8
déjeuner *to have lunch,* 4
de la *some, any,* 5
délicieux, –euse *delicious,* 8
demain *tomorrow,* 11
demander (à) *to ask,* 4
dément : C'est dément! *It's too wild!* 21
demi *halfback,* 2
demie : et demie *half past (the hour),* 4
le **demi-fond** *middle distance run,* 22
une **demi-heure** *half hour,* 9; mettre une demi-heure *to take a half hour,* 13
une **dent** *tooth,* 13; une brosse à dents *toothbrush,* 13
le **dentifrice** *toothpaste,* 13
un(e) **dentiste** *dentist,* 7
se **dépêcher** *to hurry,* 13
dépend : ça dépend *it depends,* 23
dépenser *to spend,* 8
depuis *since,* 10
dernier, –ière *last,* 22
derrière *behind,* 10
des = de + les, 4
des *some, any,* 3, 5
descendre *to go down,* 7; *to take down,* 9
un **désert** *desert,* 24
se **déshabiller** *to get undressed,* 13
désirer *to want,* 5
un **dessert** *dessert,* 8
le **dessin** *drawing, art,* 4; un dessin animé *animated cartoon,* 5
un(e) **dessinateur (–trice)** *illustrator,* 7
un(e) **destinataire** *addressee,* 12
se **détendre** *to relax,* 13
détour : au détour de *at a turn in,* 21
détruit, –e *destroyed,* 17
devant *in front of,* 10
devenir *to become,* 16
deviner *to guess,* 7
une **devinette** *riddle,* 11
dévoiler *to uncover,* 21
un **devoir** *homework,* 4
différent, –e *different,* 4
une **difficulté** *trouble, difficulty,* 3
dimanche (m.) *Sunday,* 4

un **dinar** *dinar (Tunisian currency),* 20
un **dîner** *dinner (supper),* 7, 8
dîner *to have dinner,* 7
dire *to say, to tell,* 19
diriger *to direct,* 22
une **discussion** *discussion,* 20
discuter *to talk over,* 3
Dis donc! *So listen!* 6
le **disque** *discus,* 22
un **disque** *record,* 3
se **distraire** *to be entertained,* 24
distrait, –e *inattentive,* 4
dit : il/elle dit (à) *he/she says (to),* 4
dites *say, tell,* 4
diviser (en) *to divide (into),* 18
un **dixième** *a tenth,* 22
une **dizaine** *about ten,* 9
un **documentaire** *documentary,* 24
un **doigt** *finger,* 22
dois : je dois *I have to,* 5
doit : il/elle doit *he/she has to,* 13
doivent : ils/elles doivent *they have to,* 10
les **dominos** (m.) *dominoes,* 3
dommage *too bad,* 18
donc *so, then,* 10; Dis donc! *So listen!* 6
donner *to give,* 5; donner à boire *to give water to,* 16; donner à manger *to feed,* 16; donner de ses nouvelles *tell how one's doing,* 16; donner le départ *to give the signal to start,* 22; donner un coup de téléphone *to make a phone call,* 6; se donner un coup de peigne *to comb one's hair,* 13
dormir *to sleep,* 18; dormir à poings fermés *to sleep like a log,* 18
le **dos** *back,* 22; un sac à dos *backpack,* 18
doué, –e *gifted, talented,* 4
doux, douce *gentle,* 17; *mild, soft,* 24
une **douzaine** *dozen,* 8
droit, –e *right,* 22; à droite *on (to) the right,* 8, 10
drôle *funny,* 21
du = de + le, 4
du *some, any,* 5
une **dune** *dune,* 18
durer *to last,* 7

E

l' **eau** (f.) *water,* 5; l'eau minérale *mineral water,* 5
échanger *to exchange,* 19
une **écharpe** *(long) scarf,* 23
les **échecs** (m.) *chess,* 3
un **éclair** *lightning,* 16
une **école** *school,* 4; une école de

voile *sailing school,* 18; une école primaire *elementary school,* 17
économies : faire des économies *to save,* 23
économique *economical,* 24
économiser *to save,* 8
écoute : un bouton d'écoute *playback button,* 14
écouter *to listen (to),* 3
un **écouteur** *earphone,* 14
écrire *to write,* 12
écrit, –e *written,* 4
écrivez *write,* 4
s' **écrouler** *to collapse,* 13
effacer *to erase,* 4
effet : en effet *the fact is,* 19
un **effort** *effort,* 22
également *also,* 22
une **église** *church,* 10
égyptien, –ienne *Egyptian,* 11
élan : prendre son élan *to take a running start,* 22
s' **élancer** *to push off,* 15
électrique *electric,* 14
l' **électronique** (f.) *electronics,* 3
un **électrophone** *record-player,* 9
un **éléphant** *elephant,* 24
un(e) **élève** *pupil, student,* 4
élever *to rear,* 7, 8
elle *her,* 1; *she,* 1, 2; *it,* 8; elles *they,* 2; *them,* 7
l' **embarras du choix** *embarrassment of riches,* 23
embrasser *to kiss,* 12
une **émission** *program,* 24; une émission de variétés *variety show,* 24
emmener *to take (people, animals),* 10
empêcher (de) *to keep from,* 20
un **emploi du temps** *schedule,* 4
un(e) **employé(e) de bureau** *office worker,* 7
emprunter (à) *to borrow (from),* 23; si on empruntait *how about borrowing,* 23
en *in,* 4; en avance *early,* 19; en ce moment *now,* 9; en effet *the fact is,* 19; en face (de) *in front of, facing,* 4; en fait *in fact,* 16; en général *usually,* 7; en *haut de *on top of,* 11; en mains *in hand,* 19; en même temps *at the same time,* 13; en mettant *making,* 6; en place *in place, neat,* 13; en plein : J'ai mis en plein dans le mille. *I got it right in the bull's-eye.* 21; en plein air *outside,* 13; en pleine expansion *booming,* 24; en plus de *in addition to,* 17; en provenance de *from, coming from,* 10; en remplaçant *replacing,* 10; en train de... *in the process of . . . ,* 3; se mettre en train *to warm up,* 22; la mise en train *warm-up,* 22; en utilisant *using,* 6

270   NOS AMIS

en any, 3
enchanté enchanted, 17
encore still, 7; pas encore not yet, 9; s'il y en a encore if there is any left, 9
encourager to encourage, 22
s' **endormir** to go to sleep, 13
l' **énergie** (f.) energy, 24
énergique energetic, 22
enfance : un(e) ami(e) d'enfance childhood friend, 16
un **enfant** child, 4, 7
enfin anyway, 11
un **engrais** fertilizer, 24
ennuyeux, –euse boring, 2, 4
énorme huge, 12
un **enregistrement** recording, 14; un bouton d'enregistrement record button, 14
enregistrer to record, 7, 14
enseigner to teach, 7
un **ensemble** group, 10
ensemble together, 7
ensuite then, 8
entendre to hear, 7
entouré, –e de surrounded by, 17
entourer to surround, 10
l' **entraînement** (m.) training, 22
s' **entraîner** to train, 22
entre between, 7; among, 11
une **entrée** entryway, 10
une **enveloppe** envelope, 12
envie : avoir envie de to want to, 5
environ about, 13
envoyer to send, 16
l' **épaule** (f.) shoulder, 22
une **épicerie** grocery, 8
un(e) **épicier (–ière)** grocer, 8
éplucher to peel, 20
une **épreuve** event, 22
épuisé, –e exhausted, 13
une **épuisette** landing net, 17
l' **équilibre** (m.) balance, 22
une **équipe** team, 2
un **équipement** (m.) equipment, 15
une **erreur** mistake (wrong number), 6
une **éruption** eruption, 17
un **escalier** stairway, 10
l' **Espagne** (f.) Spain, 19
l' **espagnol** (m.) Spanish, 19
espagnol, –e Spanish, 19
les **espaliers** (m.) stall bars, 22
Espèces de crétins! What are you, some kind of idiots! 21
espérer to hope, 14
l' **espoir** (m.) hope, 23
un **essai** test, 14; attempt, 22
essayer (de) to try (to), 7
l' **est** (m.) east, 17
est-ce que...? do (you, they) . . . ? 2
une **estrade** platform, 14
et and, 1
une **étable** cowshed, 16
un **étage** floor, 10

étaler to spread out, 18
un **étang** pond, 10
les **Etats-Unis** (m.) the United States, 19; aux Etats-Unis in the United States, 1, 19
l' **été** (m.) summer, 14, 15; en été in the summer, 15
éteindre (le poste) to turn off (the TV set), 24
éteint turns out the light, 13
éthnique ethnic, 24
une **étoile** star, 18
une **étoile de mer** starfish, 17
étranger, –ère foreign, 21
être to be, 3
étudier to study, 4
eux them, 5; une pièce à eux their own room, 9; chez eux at their house, 5
exactement exactly, 14
ex aequo tied (score), 22
excepté except, 7
une **excursion** excursion, 17
excusez-moi excuse me, 6
un **exemple** example, 4; par exemple for instance, 3
un **exercice** exercise, 4; les exercices au sol floor exercises, 22; un exercice de compréhension listening exercise, 4; un exercice écrit writing exercise, 4
exotique exotic, 17
expansion : en pleine expansion booming, 24
un(e) **expéditeur (-trice)** sender, 12
expliquer to explain, 10
une **exploration** exploration, 12
explorer to explore, 17
une **exposition** exhibition, 13
extra : C'est extra! It's really great! 21
extraordinaire exceptional, 3
une **extrémité** tip, 17

F

la **fabrication** manufacturing, 24
face : en face (de) in front (of), facing, 4; jouer à pile ou face to toss a coin, 10
une **façon** way, manner, 19; de toute façon anyway, 19
faible weak, 22
faim : avoir faim to be hungry, 5
faire to do, 2; to make, 4; faire attention to be careful, 4; faire cuire to cook, 20; faire de la natation to swim, 2; faire de la photo to take pictures, 3; faire de la voile to sail, 18; faire des achats to shop, 20; faire des courses to shop, 11; faire des économies to save, 23; faire du bateau to go boating, 17; faire du

cheval to go horseback-riding, 2; faire du judo to practice judo, 2; faire du ski to ski, 2; faire du vélo to go bike-riding, 2; faire la connaissance de to make the acquaintance of, 10; faire la cuisine to cook, 20; faire la moisson to harvest, 16; faire la queue to stand in line, 15; faire la vaisselle to do the dishes, 13; faire le numéro to dial the number, 6; faire les courses to go grocery shopping, 8; faire les foins to hay, to do the haying, 16; faire l'ingénieur du son to be the sound engineer, 14; faire partie (de) to be part (of), 10; faire plaisir à to please (someone), 11; faire sa toilette to get washed, 13; faire un cadeau to give a gift, 23; faire un carton to go target-shooting, 21; faire une promenade to take a jaunt, 11; faire un tour to take a ride, 2; faire un voyage to take a trip, 21; en faire autant to do the same thing, 23; se faire to do for oneself, 13; se faire mal (à) to hurt, 15; ça fait combien how much, 5; Fais de beaux rêves! Sweet dreams! 13; fait, –e made, 7; il fait beau the weather is nice, 13; il fait bon it's nice, 15; il fait chaud it's hot, 15; il fait du vent it's windy, 15; il fait frais it's cool, 15; il fait froid it's cold, 15; il fait mauvais the weather is bad, 15; il fait (cinq) it's (five) degrees, 15; Quel temps fait-il? What's the weather like? 15; Quelle température fait-il? What's the temperature? 15
fait : en fait in fact, 16
un **fakir** fortune-teller, fakir, 21
une **famille** family, 7
fantaisie : un bracelet fantaisie bracelet (costume jewelry), 23
fantastique fantastic, 17
fatigué, –e tired, 9
faut : il faut (que) must, have to, 4
une **faute d'orthographe** spelling mistake, 4
un **fauteuil** armchair, 13
faux, fausse false, 4
un(e) **favori(te)** favorite, 22
fées : un conte de fées fairy tale, 21
une **femme** wife, 16
une **fenêtre** window, 24
une **ferme** farm, 16
fermer to close, 13
la **fermeture** closing, 11
un(e) **fermier (–ière)** farmer, 7
fertile fertile, 24
une **fête** fair, 21; une fête foraine traveling fair, 21
un **feu de bois** wood fire, 15

un **feuilleton** *serial*, 24

un **feutre** *felt-tip pen*, 4

février (m.) *February*, 12

une **fiche de progression** *record card*, 22

une **figue** *fig*, 16

fil : à l'autre bout du fil *at the other end of the line*, 6

un **filet** *net*, 2

une **fille** *girl*, 1

un **film** *movie, film*, 5; un film comique *comedy*, 5; un film policier *detective film*, 5

la **fin** *end*, 8; en fin d'après-midi *at the end of the afternoon*, 18

fin, –e *fine*, 17

finale : une formule finale *a closing*, 12

finalement *at last, finally*, 18

finir *to end, to finish*, 5

flâner *to browse*, 20

une **fleur** *flower*, 8; le Marché aux Fleurs *the Flower Market*, 8

un(e) **fleuriste** *florist*, 23

la **Floride** *Florida*, 17

flou, –e *fuzzy, out of focus*, 24

une **flûte** *flute*, 14

le **foin** *hay*, 16; faire les foins *to hay, to do the haying*, 16

la **fois** *time*, 11; à la fois *at the same time*, 17

une **fois** *once*, 11; une fois terminé *once finished*, 5

foncer *to rush*, 21

fond : au fond (de) *at the far end (of)*, 4

le **football** *soccer*, 2; le football américain *football*, 2

une **forêt** *forest*, 17

une **forme** *form*, 6; *shape*, 12

formidable *terrific*, 10

formule : une formule de début *salutation*, 12; une formule finale *closing*, 12

fort *loud*, 14

fort, –e *strong*, 19

une **fortune** *fortune*, 12

un **foulard** *scarf*, 23

une **fourchette** *a fork*, 8

frais : il fait frais *it's cool*, 15

la **fraise** *strawberry (flavor)*, 5

un **franc** *franc*, 5

le **français** *French*, 4, 19

français, –e *French*, 19

un(e) **Français(e)** *French person*, 19

la **France** *France*, 1, 19; en France *in France*, 1

un **frère** *brother*, 7

des **frites** (f.) *French fries*, 8

froid, –e *cold*, 5; avoir froid *to be cold*, 15; il fait froid *it's cold*, 15

le **fromage** *cheese*, 8; le fromage de chèvre *goat cheese*, 8

un(e) **froussard(e)** *scaredy-cat!* 21

un **fruit** *fruit*, 8; un jus de fruit *fruit juice*, 5

G

gagner *to win*, 3; *to make (money)*, 7

une **galerie marchande** *shopping arcade*, 23

un **gant** *glove*, 15; un gant de toilette *wash mitt*, 13

un **garage** *garage*, 20

un **garçon** *boy*, 1; *waiter*, 5

garder *to keep*, 9; garder des enfants *to baby-sit*, 7; garder l'équilibre *to keep one's balance*, 22

une **gare** *railroad station*, 10

un **gâteau** (pl. : **–x**) *cake*, 7; *pastry*, 8

gauche *left*, 22; à gauche *on (to) the left*, 8, 10

général : en général *usually*, 7

une **généralisation** *generalization*, 4

un **genou** (pl. : **–x**) *knee*, 15, 22

un **genre** *kind, sort*, 14

les **gens** *people*, 7

la **gentillesse** *niceness*, 13; d'une telle gentillesse *so nice*, 13

la **géographie** *geography*, 4

un **gigot d'agneau** *leg of lamb*, 8

une **glace** *ice cream*, 5

une **gomme** *eraser*, 4

gracieux, –euse *graceful*, 22

la **grammaire** *grammar*, 4

un **gramme** *gram*, 8

grand, –e *big, large*, 1, 4; *tall*, 7

une **grande roue** *Ferris wheel*, 21

un **grand huit** *roller coaster*, 21

une **grand-mère** *grandmother*, 7

un **grand-père** *grandfather*, 7

une **grand-rue** *main street*, 16

des **grands-parents** *grandparents*, 7

une **grange** *barn*, 16

un **grenier à foin** *hayloft*, 16

des **grésillements** (m.) *static*, 6

griller *to grill*, 20

grimper *to climb*, 22

gris, –e *gray*, 7

gros, grosse *big*, 21

un **groupe** *group*, 14

le **gruyère** *Swiss cheese*, 5

la **Guadeloupe** *Guadeloupe*, 17

un **guide** *guide*, 10

guider *to guide*, 10

une **guitare** *guitar*, 9, 14

un **gymnase** *gymnasium*, 4

la **gymnastique** *gym*, 4; *gymnastics*, 22

H

s' **habiller** *to get dressed*, 13; habiller *to dress*, 13

un **habitant** *inhabitant*, 10

habiter *to live*, 1, 2

les ***haies** (f.) *hurdles*, 22

un ***hall** *entrance hall*, 12

un ***hangar** *shed*, 16

un ***haricot** *bean*, 8; des *haricots verts *green beans*, 8

un **harmonica** *harmonica*, 14

*hâte : avoir *hâte (de) *to look forward to*, 12

*haut *high*, 22; en *haut de *on top of*, 11

*hauteur : le saut en *hauteur *high jump*, 22

un ***haut-parleur** (pl. : ***haut-parleurs**) *loudspeaker*, 14

l' **hébreu** (m.) *Hebrew*, 19

l' **herbe** (f.) *grass*, 16

une **hésitation** *hesitation*, 23

une **heure (h)** *hour*, 4; l'heure d'affluence *rush hour*, 13; à l'heure *on time*, 19; de tout à l'heure *from before*, 21; il est (une) heure *it's (one) o'clock*, 4; Quelle heure est-il? *What time is it?* 4; 1 h de retard *an hour late*, 19

heureusement *luckily*, 15

hier *yesterday*, 9; hier soir *last night*, 9

un **hippocampe** *sea horse*, 17

un **hippopotame** *hippopotamus*, 24

l' **histoire** (f.) *history*, 4; une histoire d'amour *love story*, 5

l' **hiver** (m.) *winter*, 15; en hiver *in the winter*, 15

le ***hockey sur glace** *ice hockey*, 2

un **homme** *man*, 6

un **hôpital** (pl. : **–aux**) *hospital*, 7

un **horoscope** *horoscope*, 21

un ***hors-d'œuvre** (pl. : ***hors-d'œuvre**) *hors d'œuvre*, 8

une **hôtesse** *hostess*, 19

huit : un grand huit *roller coaster*, 21

humoristique *funny, humorous*, 23

I

ici *here*, 4; juste ici *right here*, 4

une **idée** *idea*, 19

identifier *to identify*, 7

il *he*, 2; *it*, 8

une **île** *island*, 1

un **illusionniste** *magician*, 14

illustrer *to illustrate*, 17

il paraît (que) *they say (that)*, 5

ils *they*, 2

il y a *there is (are)*, 4; s'il y en a encore *if there is any left*, 9; Qu'est-ce qu'il y a d'autre? *What else is there?* 14; il y a du soleil *it's sunny*, 15; il y a longtemps *a long time ago*, 11

une **image** *picture*, 24

imaginer *to imagine*, 19

immédiatement *right away*, 13

un **immeuble** *apartment building*, 10

impatience : avec impatience *impatiently*, 7

impossible *impossible*, 6
impressionnant, –e *impressive*, 18
un **indicatif (musical)** *chimes*, 19
indiqué, –e *indicated*, 7
indiscutablement *indisputably*, 22
une **industrie** *industry*, 10
industriel, –elle *industrial*, 24
une **infirmerie** *infirmary*, 15
un(e) **infirmier (–ière)** *nurse*, 7
un **ingénieur** *engineer*, 7; un ingénieur du son *sound engineer*,
14; faire l'ingénieur du son *to be
the sound engineer*, 14
l' **inspiration** (f.) *inspiration*, 23
installer *to set up*, 14; s'installer
to settle in, 18
des **instructions** (f.) *directions*, 6
s' **instruire** *to learn*, 24
un **instrument** *instrument*, 14
intelligent, –e *intelligent*, 4
intermédiaire *intermediate*, 15
un(e) **invité(e)** *guest*, 14
inviter *to invite*, 7
Israël (m.) *Israel*, 19
israélien, –ienne *Israeli*, 19
l' **Italie** (f.) *Italy*, 19
l' **italien** (m.) *Italian*, 19
italien, –ienne *Italian*, 19

J

j' = je
jadis *in the old days*, 16
la **Jamaïque** *Jamaica*, 17
jamais *never*, 7; ne… jamais
never, 7
une **jambe** *leg*, 15, 22
le **jambon** *ham*, 5
janvier (m.) *January*, 12
un **jardin** *garden*, 11; un jardin
potager *vegetable garden*, 16
le **jaune** *yellow*, 2
le **javelot** *javelin*, 22
le **jazz** *jazz*, 14
je *I*, 2
un **jean** *jeans*, 9
jeter *to throw*, 17
un **jeu** (pl. : **–x**) *game*, 3
jeudi (m.) *Thursday*, 4
jeune *young*, 16; les jeunes
young people, 3; une maison des
jeunes *youth center*, 10
la **joie** *joy*, 23
joli, –e *pretty*, 10
jouer *to play*, 2; jouer (à) *to play
(a sport)* 2, *(a game)*, 3; jouer à
cache-cache *to play hide and
seek*, 21; jouer à pile ou face *to
toss a coin*, 10; jouer (de) *to play
(an instrument)*, 14
un **jour** *day*, 4; ce jour-là *that day*,
7; tous les jours *every day*, 4; le
jour où *the day when*, 4
un **journal** (pl. : **–aux**) *newspaper*, 5;
un journal de bord *"log," diary*,
18; le journal télévisé *TV news*, 24

un(e) **journaliste** *journalist*, 7
une **journée** *a day*, 5; toute la journée
all day long, 5
joyeux, –euse *joyous*, 23
le **judo** *judo*, 2; faire du judo *to
practice judo*, 2
juillet (m.) *July*, 7, 12
juin (m.) *June*, 12
une **jupe** *skirt*, 9
un **jus de fruit** *fruit juice*, 5
jusqu'à *as far as, until*, 11
juste : juste ici *right here*, 4; juste
un petit mot… *just a line . . .*, 16
juteux, –euse *juicy*, 8

K

une **kermesse** *fair*, 14
un **kilo** *kilogram*, 8
un **kilomètre** *kilometer*, 17

L

l' = le, la
la *the*, 1
la *her, it*, 10
là *there*, 20; c'est là que *it's
where*, 23; par là *over there*, 17;
là-bas *over there*, 4; ce jour-là
that day, 7; celui-là *that one*, 14
un **laboratoire** *laboratory*, 4
un **lac** *lake*, 18
laisser *to leave*, 5; *to let*, 16
le **lait** *milk*, 5
un **lambi** *conch*, 17
lancer *to throw*, 22
une **langouste** *spiny lobster*, 17
une **langue** *language*, 4, 19; une
langue vivante *modern language*,
4
un **lapin** *rabbit*, 16
laquelle *which one*, 14
le **latin** *Latin*, 4
latin, –e *Latin*, 4
les **Laurentides** *the Laurentian Mountains*, 15
se **laver** *to get washed*, 13; laver *to
wash*, 13
le/la *the*, 1
le *him, it*, 10
léger, –ère *light*, 8
un **légume** *vegetable*, 8
lendemain : le lendemain *on the
following day*, 11
lent, –e *slow*, 9
lentement *slowly*, 22
lequel *which one*, 14
les *the*, 3
les *them*, 10
lesquels, lesquelles *which ones*,
14
une **lettre** *letter*, 12; du papier à
lettres *writing paper*, 23
leur *(to, for) them*, 8
leur *their*, 3, 7
le **leur**, la **leur**, les **leurs** *theirs*, 23

leurs *their*, 6, 7
lève : elle lève la main *she raises
her hand*, 4
lever *to raise*, 8; se lever *to get
up*, 13
liberté : vivent en liberté *live in
their natural environment*, 24
une **librairie-papeterie** *book and stationery store*, 23
libre *free*, 5
un **lieu** *place*, 12, 17; avoir lieu *to
take place*, 9
une **ligne** *line (phone connection)*, 6
la **limonade** *lemon soda*, 5
un **lion** *lion*, 24
lire *to read*, 3
lisent : ils/elles lisent *they read*, 7
lisez *read*, 4
lisse : la corde lisse *rope*, 22
une **liste** *list*, 9
lit : il/elle lit *he/she reads*, 3
une **litière** *litter*, 16
un **litre** *liter*, 8
un **livre** *book*, 3
une **livre** *pound*, 8
loin (de) *far (from)*, 1; plus loin
further on, 20
lointain, –e *far away*, 24
Londres *London*, 19
long, longue *long*, 9
longtemps : il y a longtemps *a
long time ago*, 11
longueur : le saut en longueur
long jump, 22
lors de *at the time of*, 22
la **loterie** *lottery, raffle*, 21
louer *to rent*, 15
lui *him*, 1
lui *(to, for) him/her*, 8
lundi (m.) *Monday*, 4; le lundi
on Mondays, 4
les **lunettes** (f.) *eyeglasses*, 7; goggles, 15
un **lycée** *high school*, 7

M

m' = me
M. *Mr.*, 4
une **machine** *machine*, 21
madame (Mme) *Mrs.*, 4
mademoiselle (Mlle) *Miss*, 4
un **magasin** *store*, 13, 23
un **magnéto(phone)** *tape recorder*, 14
magnifique *magnificent*, 17
mai (m.) *May*, 12
un **maillot de bain** *bathing suit*, 17
une **main** *hand*, 4, 22; en mains *in
hand*, 19; lever la main *to raise
one's hand*, 4
maintenant *now*, 4
une **mairie** *town hall*, 10
mais *but*, 3; mais si *of course we
are*, 2
le **maïs** *corn*, 16

une **maison** *house*, 1; à la maison *at home*, 5; de retour à la maison *back home*, 23; une maison des jeunes *youth center*, 10; une maison magique *fun house*, 21

mal *badly*, 3; avoir mal (à) *to hurt*, 15; tout va mal *everything's going wrong*, 9

le **mal de mer** *seasickness*, 21; avoir le mal de mer *to be seasick*, 21

malgré *in spite of*, 10

malheureusement *unfortunately*, 11

maman *mom, mommy*, 7; Maman! *Somebody help me!* 21

manchette : un bouton de manchette (pl.: boutons de manchette) *cufflink*, 23

un **manège** *a ride*, 21

manger *to eat*, 5; donner à manger *to feed*, 16; une salle à manger *dining room*, 10

manquer *to lack*, 13; rien ne manque *nothing is missing*, 13

une **maquette** *model*, 3

se **maquiller** *to put on makeup*, 13

un(e) **marchand(e)** *salesperson*, 8

marchande : une galerie marchande *shopping arcade*, 23

marchander *to bargain*, 20

un **marché** *market*, 8; le Marché aux Fleurs *the Flower Market*, 8

marcher *to work, to function*, 9; *to walk*, 19

mardi (m.) *Tuesday*, 4

un **mariage** *wedding*, 14

se **marier** *to get married*, 21

une **marmite** *pot*, 20

le **Maroc** *Morocco*, 19

marocain, –e *Moroccan*, 19

une **maroquinerie** *leather-goods store*, 23

marquer *to mark down*, 3; marquer les points *to keep score*, 3

marques : A vos marques, prêts, partez! *On your marks, get set, go!* 22

le **marron** *brown*, 2

marron (f. & pl.: **marron**) *brown*, 7

mars (m.) *March*, 12

un(e) **Martiniquais(e)** *person from Martinique*, 17

la **Martinique** *Martinique*, 1; à la Martinique *in Martinique*, 1

un **masque** *mask*, 17

un **match** *game*, 2

les **mathématiques** (m.) *mathematics*, 17

les **maths** (m.) *math*, 4

une **matière** *subject*, 4

le **matin** *morning*, 4

une **matinée** *morning*, 13

mauvais, –e *poor, bad*, 4; il fait mauvais *the weather is bad*, 15

me *(to, for) me*, 10; *myself*, 13

un **médecin** *doctor*, 7

une **médina** *medina (old part of an Arab city)*, 20

une **méduse** *jelly fish*, 17

meilleur, –e *better*, 22; la meilleure de *the best in*, 22; meilleures pensées (lit.) *best thoughts*, 12; meilleurs souvenirs *regards*, 12

un **melon** *melon*, 8

un **membre** *member*, 14

même *same*, 10; en même temps *at the same time*, 13; tout de même *all the same*, 11

menteur, –euse *liar*, 10

le **menton** *chin*, 22

la **mer** *sea*, 1; la mer des Caraïbes *Caribbean Sea*, 1; au bord de la mer *at the shore*, 17; le mal de mer *seasickness*, 21; avoir le mal de mer *to be seasick*, 21

merci *thanks*, 4

mercredi (m.) *Wednesday*, 4

une **mère** *mother*, 7

mérité, –e *deserved*, 22

mes *my*, 7

mesurer *to measure*, 22

la **météo** *weather report*, 15

un **métier** *craft, trade*, 20

un **mètre** *meter*, 12, 22; le 100 m *100-meter dash*, 22

le **métro** *subway*, 13

mettant : en mettant *making*, 6

mettez *make*, 5

mettre *to put (on)*, 9; mettre la table *to set the table*, 8; mettre la télévision *to turn on the TV*, 24; mettre une demi-heure *to take a half hour*, 13; se mettre en train *to warm up*, 22

un **micro(phone)** *microphone*, 14

midi *noon*, 4

le **mien**, la **mienne**, les **miens**, les **miennes** *mine*, 23

mieux *better*, 2; aimer mieux *to prefer*, 2; il vaut mieux *it's better to*, 14; le mieux *best*, 4; aimer le mieux *to like best*, 4

mille : J'ai mis en plein dans le mille. *I got it right in the bull's-eye*, 21

minéral : l'eau minérale (f.) *mineral water*, 5

minuit *midnight*, 4

une **minute** *minute*, 5

la **mise en train** *warm-up*, 22

Mlle *Miss*, 4

Mme *Mrs.*, 4

un **modèle** *model*, 13

moderne *modern*, 10

moi *me*, 1

moins *less*, 4; *below (zero)*, 15; moins (cinq) *(five) degrees below*, 15; moins le quart *quarter to/of (the hour)*, 4; moins... que *less ... than*, 22; au moins *at least*, 13; le/la/les moins... (de) *the least ... (in)*, 22

un **mois** *month*, 7, 12

la **moisson** *harvest*, 16; faire la moisson *to harvest*, 16

molle : mou, molle *weak, limp*, 21

moment : en ce moment *now*, 9

mon *my*, 7

le **monde** *world*, 17; faire le tour du monde *to go around the world*, 24; tout le monde *everybody*, 4

un(e) **moniteur (–trice)** *ski instructor*, 15

monnaie : une pièce de monnaie *coin*, 3

monsieur (M.) *Mr.*, 4

une **montagne** *mountain*, 15

monter *to go up*, 10; *to take up*, 11; monter un cheval *to ride a horse*, 16

une **montre** *watch*, 23

montrer *to show*, 7

un **monument** *monument, landmark*, 11

un **morceau** (pl. : **–x**) *piece, number*, 14

un **mot** *word*, 4; juste un petit mot... *just a line . . .*, 16; écrire un petit mot *to write a little something*, 23

une **moto** *motorcycle*, 3

mou, molle *weak, limp*, 21

un **mouchoir** *handkerchief*, 23

une **mousse au chocolat** *chocolate mousse*, 8

la **moutarde** *mustard*, 8

un **mouton** *sheep*, 16; le mouton *lamb*, 20

moyenne : de taille moyenne *of medium height*, 7

multicolore *many-colored*, 17

un **mur** *wall*, 16

mûr –e *ripe*, 8

une **mûre** *blackberry*, 16

une **murène** *moray eel*, 17

un **musée** *museum*, 11

un(e) **musicien(ne)** *musician*, 14

la **musique** *music*, 4, 14; la musique folk *folk music*, 14; la musique pop *pop music*, 14

N

nacelle : Arrête de faire tanguer la nacelle! *Stop making the car swing!* 21

nager *to swim*, 17

une **naissance** *birth*, 17

la **natation** *swimming*, 2; faire de la natation *to swim*, 2

national, –e *national*, 24

une **nationalité** *nationality*, 19

la **nature** *nature*, 24

naturel, –elle *natural*, 24

ne: ne... jamais *never*, 7; ne... ni... ni... *neither . . . nor . . .*, 5, 7; ne... pas *not*, 3, 7; ne... personne *nobody, not . . . anybody*, 13;

ne... plus *no more, not . . . any more,* 5, 7; ne... rien *nothing, not . . . anything,* 6, 13; personne ne... *nobody . . .,* 13; rien ne... *nothing . . .,* 13

né(e) : je suis né(e). *I was born,* 21

le **néerlandais** *Dutch,* 19

la **neige** *snow,* 15

neiger *to snow,* 15; il neige *it's snowing,* 15

n'est-ce pas? *isn't it?* 1

le **nez** *nose,* 22

ni... ni... *neither . . . nor . . .,* 5, 7; ne... ni... ni... *neither . . . nor . . .,* 5, 7

nœuds : la corde à nœuds *knotted rope,* 22

le **noir** *black,* 2

une **noisette** *hazelnut,* 16; la noisette *hazelnut (flavor),* 5

les **nombres** *numbers,* 1

un **nom** *name,* 1, 4

non *no,* 1

le **nord** *north,* 17; au nord (de) *north (of),* 15

nos *our,* 7; nos amis *our friends,* 1

une **note** *grade,* 4

noter *to write down,* 18; à noter *to be noted,* 22

notre *our,* 7

le **nôtre, la nôtre, les nôtres** *ours,* 18, 23

noué, –e *knotted,* 18

la **nourriture** *food,* 9

nous *we,* 2; *us,* 5; *(to, for) us,* 10; *ourselves,* 13

un **nouveau, une nouvelle** *a new boy, a new girl,* 4

nouveau, nouvel, nouvelle, nouveaux, nouvelles *new,* 16; nouveaux amis *new friends,* 10

des **nouvelles** (f.) *news,* 12; donner de ses nouvelles *to tell how one's doing,* 16

novembre (m.) *November,* 12

un(e) **novice** *beginner,* 15

novice *beginning,* 15

un **noyer** *walnut tree,* 16

la **nuit** *night,* 18; Bonne nuit! *Good night!* 13

un **numéro** *number,* 4; faire le numéro *to dial the number,* 6; refaire le numéro *to dial the number again,* 6; Quel numéro demandez-vous? *What number do you want?* 6

nus : pieds-nus *barefoot,* 18

O

un **objet de toilette** *toilet article,* 13

une **occasion** *opportunity,* 12

occidental, –e *western,* 24

une **occupation** *occupation,* 7

occupé, –e *occupied, busy,* 6

s' **occuper (de)** *to take care of, to wait on,* 13

octobre (m.) *October,* 12

un **œil** (pl. : **yeux**) *eye,* 12, 22

un **œuf** *egg,* 8

officiel, –elle *official,* 24

un **oiseau** (pl. : **–x**) *bird,* 7; le chant des oiseaux *birdcalls,* 7

l' **ombre** (f.) *shade,* 17; à l'ombre *in the shade,* 17

une **omelette** *omelet,* 8

on *one, people, they, we,* 2; où l'on = où on, 24; On y va! *Let's go!* 15

un **oncle** *uncle,* 7

l' **or** (m.) *gold,* 23; en or *made of gold,* 23

l' **orange** (m.) *orange,* 2

une **orange** *an orange,* 8

ordre : en ordre *in order,* 9

une **oreille** *ear,* 22; une boucle d'oreille (pl. : boucles d'oreille) *earring,* 23

un **orfèvre** *craftsperson in precious metals,* 20

un **orgue** *organ,* 14

original, –e (m. pl. : **–aux**) *original,* 23

l' **orthographe** (f.) *spelling,* 4; une faute d'orthographe *spelling mistake,* 4

ou *or,* 1

où *where,* 1; où l'on = où on, 24

oublier *to forget,* 8

l' **ouest** (m.) *west,* 17

oui *yes,* 1

le **ouolof** *Wolof,* 19

un **oursin** *sea urchin,* 17

ouvert, –e *open,* 13

ouvrez *open,* 4

un(e) **ouvrier (–ière)** *factory worker,* 7

ovale *oval,* 2

P

une **page** *page,* 4; à la page 32 *on page 32,* 4

la **paille** *straw,* 16

le **pain** *bread,* 8; une tartine de pain *slice of bread (with butter and/or jam on it),* 13

un **palais** *palace,* 12

un **palier** *landing,* 10

une **palme** *flipper,* 17

un **pamplemousse** *grapefruit,* 8; un jus de pamplemousse *grapefruit juice,* 5

un **panier** *basket (basketball),* 2; *colander, basket,* 20

panique : Pas de panique! *Don't panic!* 21

un **pantalon** *pants,* 9; un pantalon de ski *ski pants,* 15

une **panthère** *panther,* 24

papa *dad, daddy,* 7; une barbe à

papa *cotton candy,* 21

la **papeterie :** une librairie-papeterie *book and stationery store,* 23

du **papier à lettres** *writing paper,* 23

par *by,* 7; par conséquent *consequently,* 10; par correspondance *in writing,* 19; par exemple *for instance,* 3; par là *over there,* 17; par terre *on the ground,* 18

un **paragraphe** *paragraph,* 16

paraît : il paraît (que) *they say (that),* 5

un **parc** *park,* 10

parce que *because,* 2

pardon *excuse me,* 19

pareille : une chose pareille *such a thing,* 12

les **parents** (m.) *parents (mother, father),* 7

paresseux, –euse *lazy,* 4

parfait, –e *perfect,* 15

le **parfum** *perfume,* 23

une **parfumerie** *perfume shop,* 23

parier *to bet,* 19

parler *to talk,* 2

parmi *among,* 19

partager *to share,* 13

participer (à) *to take part (in),* 22

particulièrement *especially,* 22

une **partie** *game,* 7; *part,* 22; faire partie (de) *to be part of,* 10

partir *to leave,* 5

partout *everywhere,* 9

pas : à deux pas de *a few feet from,* 3

pas *not,* 2; pas de chance *no luck,* 6; pas encore *not yet,* 9; ne... pas *not,* 3, 7

un **passage** *passing, passage,* 18

un(e) **passager (–ère)** *passenger,* 19

passer *to spend (time),* 3, 7; *to pass,* 8; *to pass by,* 10

un **passe-temps** (pl.: **passe-temps**) *pastime,* 3

passionné, –e *enthusiastic,* 10

le **pâté** *pâté,* 5

des **pâtes** (f.) *noodles,* 8

une **patinoire** *skating rink,* 5

un(e) **patron(ne)** *boss,* 13

payer *to pay,* 5

un **pays** *country,* 19

un **paysage** *landscape,* 24

une **pêche** *peach,* 8

la **pêche** *fishing,* 17; aller à la pêche *to go fishing,* 17

pêcher *to fish,* 17

un **pêcheur** *fisherman,* 17

un **peigne** *comb,* 13; se donner un coup de peigne *to comb one's hair,* 13

peigner *to comb,* 24

peine : à peine *hardly,* 16

un **peintre** *painter,* 24

peler *to peel, to pull the skin away,* 20

une **pelouse** *lawn,* 7
pendant *during,* 6
pense: je pense bien *of course,* 19
pensées : meilleures pensées *best thoughts,* 12
une **pente** *slope,* 15
perché, –e *perched,* 18
perdre *to lose,* 3, 9; perdre courage *to get lazy,* 13
un **père** *father,* 7
une **performance** *performance,* 22
périlleux : un saut périlleux *somersault,* 22
une **perle** *pearl,* 17
la **permission** *permission,* 24
perpétuel, –elle *constant,* 17
personne *nobody,* 13; personne ne… *nobody,* 13; ne… personne *nobody, not . . . anybody,* 13
personnel, –elle *personal,* 22
pétillant, –e *bubbly, sparkling,* 24
petit, –e *little, small,* 1, 4; *short,* 7
le **petit déjeuner** *breakfast,* 8
une **petite cuillère** *a teaspoon,* 8
un **peu** *a little,* 4
un **peu (de)** *a little (of),* 8
peur : avoir peur *to be afraid,* 21
peut : il/elle peut *he/she can,* 3
peut-être *maybe,* 3; peut-être que… *maybe . . .,* 24
peuvent : ils/elles peuvent *they can,* 7
la **pharmacie** *drugstore,* 10
une **photo** *photograph, picture,* 3; faire de la photo *to take pictures,* 3
un(e) **photographe** *photographer,* 3
une **phrase** *sentence,* 5
un(e) **pianiste** *pianist,* 14
un **piano** *piano,* 7, 14
une **pièce (de monnaie)** *coin,* 3, 5
une **pièce** *room,* 10; une pièce à eux *their own room,* 9
pièce : 1 F la pièce *1 F each,* 8
un **pied** *foot,* 22; à pied *on foot,* 13; aller à pied *to walk,* 13; pieds-nus *barefoot,* 18
une **pieuvre** *octopus,* 17
un **pigeon** *pigeon,* 13
pile : jouer à pile ou face *to toss a coin,* 10
un **pin** *pine tree,* 18
le **ping-pong** *Ping-Pong,* 2
un **piquant** *spine,* 17
un **pique-nique** *picnic,* 18
pique-niquer *to have a picnic,* 20
pis : tant pis *too bad,* 9
une **piscine** *swimming pool,* 5
la **pistache** *pistachio (flavor),* 5
une **piste** *(ski) trail,* 15
pittoresque *picturesque,* 17
une **place** *square,* 11
place : à la place de *in place of,* 16; assez de place *enough room,* 5; en place *in place, neat,* 13;

elle a pris la 2e place *she came in second,* 22
une **plage** *beach,* 3
une **plaine** *plain,* 17
plaire (à) *to please,* 23; Ça n'a pas eu l'air de leur plaire! *They didn't seem to like that very much!* 21; Ça plaît toujours. *That always goes over.* 14; s'il te plaît, s'il vous plaît *please,* 4
plaisir : avoir le plaisir (de) *to be pleased (to),* 14; faire plaisir (à) *to please,* 11
un **plan** *map,* 4, 10
planter *to plant,* 16
un **plat** *dish,* 8
un **plateau** (pl.: **–x**) *platter,* 20
plein, –e *full,* 17; en plein air *outside,* 13; en pleine expansion *booming,* 24; en pleine forme *in the peak of condition,* 21
pleut : il pleut *it's raining,* 15
pleuvoir *to rain,* 15
plier *to bend,* 22
plongeant, –e *diving,* 12
plonger *to dive,* 17
le **pluriel** *plural,* 6
plus : en plus (de) *in addition (to),* 17; le/la/les plus… (de) *the most . . . (in),* 22; ne… plus *no . . . more, not . . . any more,* 5; plus… que *more . . . than,* 22
plutôt *rather, instead,* 16
poche : l'argent de poche *allowance,* 23
le **poids** *shot,* 22
un **point** *a point,* 3
un **point de départ** *starting point,* 17
une **poire** *pear,* 8
le **poisson** *fish,* 8; un poisson-ange *angel fish,* 17; un poisson-clown *clown fish,* 17; un poisson volant *flying fish,* 17
les **Poissons** *Pisces,* 21
la **poitrine** *chest,* 22
le **poivre** *pepper,* 8
un **poivron doux** *green pepper,* 20
policier, –ière *detective,* 5
un **polo** *polo shirt,* 9
polyvalent, –e *comprehensive,* 22
une **pomme** *apple,* 8
une **pomme de terre** *potato,* 8
une **pompe** *pump,* 18
un **pont** *bridge,* 11
la **population** *population,* 24
le **porc** *pork,* 8; une côtelette de porc *pork chop,* 8
un **port** *port,* 1
portant *carrying,* 24
une **porte** *gate,* 19
un **porte-clés** (pl.: **porte-clés**) *key ring,* 23
un **porte-couteau** (pl.: **porte-couteaux**) *a knife-rest,* 8
un **porte-documents** (pl.: , **porte-documents**) *portfolio,* 23

un **portefeuille** *wallet,* 20
un **porte-monnaie** (pl.: **porte-monnaie**) *change purse,* 23
porter *to wear,* 7
le **portugais** *Portuguese,* 19
portugais, –e *Portuguese,* 19
le **Portugal** *Portugal,* 19
poser : poser des questions *ask questions,* 7; poser des colles *to quiz,* 19
postal : le code postal *the zip code,* 12
un **poste** *television set,* 24; allumer le poste *to turn on the TV set,* 24; éteindre le poste *to turn off the TV set,* 24
une **poste** *post office,* 10
un **pot** *jar, pot,* 8; un pot de moutarde *jar of mustard,* 8
potager : un jardin potager *vegetable garden,* 16
une **poterie** *piece of pottery,* 20
un **potier** *potter,* 20
un **pouce** *inch,* 22
un **pouf** *hassock,* 20
une **poule** *hen,* 16
un **poulet** *chicken,* 8
pour *for,* 3
un **pourboire** *tip,* 5
pourquoi *why,* 2
poursuivre *to go after,* 17
la **poutre** *balance beam,* 22
pouvoir *can, to be able,* 17
pratique *practical,* 24
un **pré** *meadow,* 16
prédire *to predict,* 21
préféré, –e *favorite,* 14
préférer *to prefer,* 14
prendre *to take,* 8; prendre son élan *to take a running start,* 22
des **préparatifs** (m.) *preparations,* 23
préparer *to get ready,* 6; se préparer *to get ready,* 15
près (de) *near,* 1
la **présentation** *appearance,* 4
présenter (à) *to introduce (to),* 10; *to present,* 14; se présenter (à) *to enter,* 22
presque *almost,* 1; Tu y es presque! *You're almost there!* 22
une **presqu'île** *peninsula,* 17
pressé, –e *busy, in a hurry,* 6
prêt, –e *ready,* 5
prêter (à) *to lend (to),* 23
prétexte : sous prétexte *with the excuse,* 16
primaire *elementary,* 17
un(e) **prince(sse)** *prince (princess),* 12
principal, –e *main,* 8
le **printemps** *spring,* 15; au printemps *in the spring,* 15
le **prix** *cost,* 6
un **problème** *problem,* 6, 24
prochain, –e *next,* 22
un **prof(esseur)** *teacher,* 4
une **profession** *profession,* 7

un **programme** *listing of films*, 5; *program*, 14

un **projet** *project*, 17

une **promenade** *walk*, 7; faire une promenade *to take a jaunt*, 11

se **promener** *to walk*, 13

proposer *to suggest*, 7

propre *clean*, 8; *one's own*, 15

provenance : en provenance de *from, coming from*, 19

provençal, –e *from Provence*, 8

des **provisions** (f.) *grocery supplies*, 8

une **pub(licité)** *commercial*, 24

puis *then*, 6

un **pull** *pullover*, 9

Q

un **quai** *bank*, 11

quand *when*, 5

quand même *anyway*, 15

un **quart** *quarter*, 4; *1/4 litre*, 5; moins le quart *quarter to/of (the hour)*, 4; et quart *quarter past (the hour)*, 4

la **quatrième** *9th grade*, 4

que *which, that*, 4

le **Québec** *Quebec (Province)*, 15

quel, quelle, quels, quelles *which, what*, 14; Quel âge as-tu? *How old are you?* 1

quelque chose *something*, 9

quelquefois *sometimes*, 7

quelques *a few, some*, 14

quelqu'un *someone*, 9

qu'est-ce que *what*, 2, 20; Qu'est-ce que vous avez? *What's the matter with you?* 22; Qu'est-ce qu'il y a d'autre? *What else is there?* 14

qu'est-ce qui *what*, 20

une **question** *question*, 4

une **queue** *line*, 15; faire la queue *to stand in line*, 15

qui *who*, 1; *whom*, 3

qui est-ce que *whom*, 20

qui est-ce qui *who*, 3, 20

quitter *to leave*, 6; Ne quittez pas! *Hold on!* 6

quoi *what*, 2

quoi d'autre *what else*, 23

R

raccrocher *to hang up (the phone)*, 6

raconter *to tell*, 12

une **radio** *radio*, 3

du **raisin** *grapes*, 8

raison : avoir raison *to be right*, 23

ramener *to lead back*, 16

rancunier, –ière *holding a grudge*, 21

ranger *to straighten up*, 9

râpé, –e *grated*, 8

rapide *fast*, 9

rapidement *quickly*, 22

rappeler *to call back*, 6, 13

rappelle : je te rappelle *I'll call you back*, 6

rapporter *to bring in (money)*, 14, 20; Ça ne rapporte pas! *It doesn't pay enough!* 20

une **raquette** *racket*, 2

un **rasoir** *razor*, 23

rater *to miss*, 19

recevoir *to receive*, 12

se **réchauffer** *to warm up*, 15

un **récif** *reef*, 17

une **récitation** *recitation*, 4

recommencer *to start again*, 22

réconforter *to give comfort*, 21

reconnaître *to recognize*, 16; se reconnaître *to recognize each other*, 19

un **record** *record*, 22

récrivez *rewrite*, 6

un **reçu** *receipt*, 23

une **rédaction** *composition*, 8

redescendre *to go down again*, 19

refaire le numéro *to dial the number again*, 9

un **réfectoire** *lunchroom*, 4

regarder *to watch, to look at*, 2

une **région** *area*, 14

une **règle** *a ruler*, 4

régler *to adjust*, 24

régulièrement *regularly*, 22

se **relever** *to get up again*, 15

rembobiner *to rewind*, 14

remonter *to go back up*, 12; *to go back on*, 21; remonter un réveil *to set an alarm*, 13

remplaçant : en remplaçant *replacing*, 10

remplacer *to replace*, 14

rempli, –e *full*, 13

remporter *to win*, 22

rencontrer *to meet*, 4; se rencontrer *to meet each other*, 19

un **rendez-vous** *meeting, date*, 13

rendre *to give back*, 9; se rendre *to get to*, 13

renoncer (à) *to give up*, 18

des **renseignements** (m.) *information*, 19

rentrer *to come (go) home*, 2; *to take back*, 11; rentrer dans *to bump into*, 21

réparer *to fix*, 3

un **repas** *meal*, 7, 8

répéter *to rehearse*, 14

une **répétition** *rehearsal*, 14

répondez (à) *answer*, 4

répondre *to answer*, 7

une **réponse** *answer*, 4

se **reposer** *to rest*, 13

reprendre (le chemin) *to start back*, 13

une **république** *republic*, 24

la **République Dominicaine** *Dominican Republic*, 17

un **requin** *shark*, 17

une **résidence** *garden apartments*, 10

résidentiel, –ielle *residential*, 10

une **ressemblance** *resemblance*, 7

ressembler (à) *to look like*, 7

rester *to stay*, 5

un **résultat** *outcome*, 22

retard : 1 h de retard *an hour late*, 19

retirer *to take off*, 14

retour : de retour à la maison *back home*, 23

retourner *to return*, 11

retraite : être à la retraite *to be retired*, 7

se **réunir** *to get together*, 18; réunir *to bring together*, 22

un **rêve** *dream*, 24; Fais de beaux rêves! *Sweet dreams!* 13

un **réveil** *alarm clock*, 13; remonter un réveil *to set an alarm*, 13

se **réveiller** *to wake up*, 13

rêver *to dream*, 17

révision : chapitre de révision *review unit*, 6

une **revue** *magazine*, 3

le **rez-de-chaussée** *ground floor*, 1

riche *wealthy*, 21

rien *nothing*, 13; rien de tel *nothing like it*, 21; rien ne... *nothing*, 13; ne... rien *nothing, not . . . anything*, 6, 13

les **rillettes** *potted pork*, 5

une **robe** *dress*, 9

un **rocher** *rock*, 17

le **rock** *rock music*, 14

un **roman** *novel*, 13

un **rond de serviette** *a napkin ring*, 8

rond, –e *round*, 2

une **rondelle** *hockey puck*, 2

un **rôti de bœuf** *roast of beef*, 8

une **rôtisserie** *barbecue*, 21

roue : une grande roue *Ferris wheel*, 21

le **rouge** *red*, 2

roux, rousse *red (headed)*, 7

une **rue** *street*, 10; une rue commerçante *shopping street*, 10

le **rugby** *rugby*, 2

le **russe** *Russian*, 19

russe *Russian*, 19

la **Russie (l'U.R.S.S.)** *Russia (U.S.S.R.)*, 19

S

s' = se

sa *his/her*, 7

le **sable** *sand*, 17

un **sac** *handbag*, 23; un sac à dos *backpack*, 18; un sac de couchage *sleeping bag*, 18 une **saison** *season*, 14, 15

une **salade** *salad*, 8

une **salle** *room*, 4; une salle à manger *dining room*, 10; une salle de bains *bathroom*, 10; une salle de classe *classroom*, 4; une salle de conférences *auditorium*, 4; une salle de séjour *living room*, 10

Salut! *Hi!* 6

samedi (m.) *Saturday*, 4

une **sandale** *sandal*, 9

un **sandwich** *sandwich*, 5

sans *without*, 13

la **santé** *health*, 23

un **saucisson** *salami*, 5

sauf *except*, 4

un **saut** *jump*, 22; le saut en *hauteur *high jump*, 22; le saut en longueur *long jump*, 22; un saut périlleux *somersault*, 22

sauter *to jump*, 22; *to flip*, 24

sauvage *wild*, 17

une **savane** *savannah*, 24

savez-vous *do you know*, 12

savoir *to know, to know how to*, 16

le **savon** *soap*, 13

un **saxo(phone)** *saxophone*, 14

la **science-fiction** *science fiction*, 3

les **sciences** (f.) *science*, 4

scientifique *scientific*, 24

scolaire : une année scolaire *school year*, 4; un trophée scolaire *school trophy*, 22

une **sculpture** *sculpture*, 13

se *himself, herself, itself, oneself, themselves*, 13

secondaire *secondary*, 4

une **seconde** *second*, 22

le **sel** *salt*, 8

une **semaine** *week*, 7

un **sémaphore** *watchtower*, 18

sembler *to seem*, 18

semer *to shake off*, 21

la **semoule** *semolina*, 20

le **Sénégal** *Senegal*, 19

sénégalais, –e *Senegalese*, 19

sentir *to smell*, 18

septembre (m.) *September*, 12

une **série** *series*, 24

sérieux, –euse *serious*, 4

service compris *tip included*, 5

une **serviette** *a napkin*, 8; un rond de serviette *a napkin ring*, 8

servir *to serve*, 8; servir de *to act as*, 11; se servir (de) *to make use of*, 14

ses *her*, 3; *his/her*, 7

seul, –e *alone, by oneself*, 12

seulement *only*, 3

le **shampooing** *shampoo*, 13

si *yes*, 2, 3,; mais si *of course we are*, 2

si *if*, 5; s'il te (vous) plaît *please*, 4

le **sien,** la **sienne,** les **siens,** les **siennes** *his/hers*, 23

un **signe** *sign*, 21

le **sillage** *wake*, 17

simple *simple*, 3

simplement *simply*, 23

un **singe** *monkey*, 24

un **sirop** *flavoring syrup*, 5

un **site** *site*, 17

situé, –e *located*, 24

le **ski** *skiing*, 2, 15; faire du ski *to ski*, 2

un **ski** *ski*, 15

skier *to ski*, 15

un(e) **skieur (–euse)** *skier*, 15

une **soeur** *sister*, 7

la **soie** *silk*, 23; en soie *made of silk*, 23

soif : avoir soif *to be thirsty*, 5

soigner *to take pains with*, 4

le **soir** *evening*, 4; hier soir *last night*, 9

le **sol** *floor*, 22; les exercices au sol *floor exercises*, 22

soleil : il y a du soleil *it's sunny*, 15

une **solution** *solution*, 8

sombre *dark*, 24

son *her*, 3; son, sa, ses *his/her*, 7

le **son** *sound*, 14

sonner *to ring*, 6

la **sono(risation)** *sound*, 14

une **sortie** *outing*, 5; *exit*, 10; une sortie en mer *boat trip*, 17; à la sortie de *on coming out of*, 10

sortir *to go out*, 5; *to take out*, 5

une **soucoupe** *saucer*, 12

un **souhait** *wish*, 23

un **souk** *Arab market*, 20

souligné, –e *underlined*, 6

la **soupe** *soup*, 8

souple *manageable*, 24

souri : elle m'a souri *she smiled at me*, 11

sous *under*, 11

sous-marin, –e *underwater*, 12

le **sous-sol** *basement*, 9

se **souvenir (de)** *to remember*, 16

souvenirs : meilleurs souvenirs *regards*, 12

souvent *often*, 3

Soyez... *Be . . .* 22; Soyez les bienvenus! *Welcome!* 17

splendide *splendid*, 17

un(e) **sportif (–ive)** *sportsperson*, 22

sportif, –ive *athletic*, 22

les **sports** *sports*, 2

un **stade** *athletic field*, 10

un **stand** *stand, booth*, 21

une **station de ski** *ski area, resort*, 15

un **stylo à bille** *ballpoint pen*, 4

le **sud** *south*, 17

suffit : Ça me suffit! *That's enough for me!* 21

suite : tout de suite *right away*, 4

suivant, –e *following*, 4

suivent *follow*, 4

suivi, –e (de) *followed (by)*, 19

suivre *to follow*, 10

un **supermarché** *supermarket*, 8

sur *on*, 1

sûr, –e *sure*, 3, 4; bien sûr *of course*, 4

une **surprise** *surprise*, 22

une **surprise-partie** *party*, 9

sympathique *nice*, 10

T

t' = te

ta *your*, 7

une **table** *table*, 8; A table! *Dinner (Lunch) is served!* 8; mettre la table *to set the table*, 8

un **tableau** (pl. : **–x**) *blackboard*, 4; *painting*, 24; le tableau des arrivées *arrivals board*, 19

la **taille** *size*, 22; *waist*, 22; de taille moyenne *of medium height*, 7

un **tailleur** *tailor*, 20

talonner *to tail, to be at one's heels*, 21

tamponneuse : une auto tamponneuse *bumper car*, 21

un **tam-tam** *bongo drum*, 14

tant *so much*, 16; tant pis *too bad*, 9

une **tante** *aunt*, 7

un **tapis** *rug*, 20

un(e) **tapissier (–ière)** *rug-maker*, 19

taquiner *to tease*, 15

une **tarte** *pie, tart*, 8

une **tartine** *slice of bread (with butter and/or jam on it)*, 13

un **tas (de)** *a lot (of)*, 9

une **tasse** *cup*, 7, 8

te *(to, for) you*, 10; *yourself*, 13

la **technologie** *technology*, 4

tel, telle, tels, telles *so, such*, 13; rien de tel *nothing like it*, 21

la **télé** *TV*, 2

le **téléphone** *phone*, 6; au téléphone *on the phone*, 6; un coup de téléphone *phone call*, 6

téléphoner (à) *to call*, 5

téléphonique : une cabine téléphonique *phone booth*, 6

un **télescope** *telescope*, 11

un **télésiège** *chairlift*, 15

télévisé : le journal télévisé *TV news*, 24

une **télévision** *television*, 3; mettre la télévision *to turn on the TV*, 24

tellement *terribly*, 4

la **température** *temperature*, 15; Quelle température fait–il? *What's the temperature?* 15

une **tempête** *storm*, 18

le **temps** *time*, 3; C'était le bon temps! *Those were the days!* 16; un emploi du temps *a schedule*, 4; de temps en temps *from time* to time, 10; **en même temps** *at the same time,* 13

le **temps** *weather,* 15; **Quel temps fait-il?** *What's the weather like?* 15

tenace *persistent,* 21

le **tennis** *tennis,* 2

une **tente** *tent,* 18

tenter *to try,* 21

terminé : une fois terminé *once finished,* 5

terne *dull,* 24

une **terrasse** *terrace,* 12; *observation deck,* 19

terre : par terre *on the ground,* 18

tes *your,* 7

la **tête** *head,* 22

le **thé** *tea,* 7

un **thème** *translation into a foreign language,* 4

un **thermomètre** *thermometer,* 15

le **tien, la tienne, les tiens, les tiennes** *yours,* 23

tiens *say,* 7

tiens : Tiens-toi bien! *Hang on!* 21

un **timbre** *stamp,* 3, 12

timide *shy,* 4

le **tir** *shooting gallery,* 21

se **tirer (de)** *to get oneself out of.* 17

un **Ti-shirt** *T-shirt,* 9

un **titre** *title,* 9

toi *you,* 1

toilette : faire sa toilette *to get washed,* 13; **un objet de toilette** *toilet article,* 13; **un gant de toilette** *wash mitt,* 13

une **tomate** *tomato,* 8

tomber *to fall,* 15; **Ça tombe bien!** *Terrific!* 5

un **tombeau** *tomb,* 11

ton *your,* 7

tondre *to mow,* 7

une **tortue** *turtle,* 17

tôt *early,* 13

toucher *to touch,* 22

toujours *always,* 5

un **tour** *ride,* 2; *turn,* 14; **A (ton) tour!** *(Your) turn!* 21; **faire le tour du monde** *to go around the world,* 24; **faire un tour** *to take a ride,* 2

une **tour** *tower,* 11; **la Tour Eiffel** *the Eiffel Tower,* 11

un(e) **touriste** *tourist,* 20

tourner *to turn,* 10

tous *all,* 3; *all of them,* 5

tout *everything,* 8; *anything,* 15; **le tout** *the whole thing,* 20; **tout va mal** *everything's going wrong,* 9

tout, toute, tous, toutes *all, the whole,* 7; **toute** *all of,* 2; **tout le monde** *everybody,* 4; **tous les ans** *every year,* 7; **tous les deux, toutes les deux** *both of them,* 6; **tous les**

jours *every day,* 4; **toute la journée** *all day long,* 5

tout *very,* 18; **tout à l'heure** *before,* 21; **tout de suite** *right away,* 4

un **tracteur** *tractor,* 16

traditionnel, –elle *traditional,* 24

train : en train de *in the process of,* 3; **se mettre en train** *to warm up,* 22; **la mise en train** *the warm-up,* 22

traire *to milk,* 16

un **trajet** *trip,* 13; **le trajet de retour** *trip home,* 13

une **tranche** *slice,* 8

transparent, –e *transparent,* 17

le **travail** *work,* 4

travailler *to work,* 7

les **travaux manuels** (m.) *shop,* 4

traverser *to cross,* 18

très *very,* 1

tricoter *to knit,* 3

un **trombone** *trombone,* 14

une **trompette** *trumpet,* 14

trop *too,* 2; **trop de** *too much, too many,* 8

un **trophée** *trophy,* 22

tropical, –e *tropical,* 17

les **Tropiques** (m.) *tropics,* 17

une **trousse** *a pencil case,* 4

trouver *to find, to think,* 2; **se trouver** *to be located,* 13

un **truc** *thing,* 21

tu *you,* 2

un **tuba** *tuba,* 14; *snorkel,* 17

la **Tunisie** *Tunisia,* 10

tunisien, –ienne *Tunisian,* 19

la **Turquie** *Turkey,* 19

un **type** *guy,* 21

U

un, une *a (an),* 1

l' **U.R.S.S.** (f.) *U.S.S.R.,* 19

une **usine** *factory,* 7

utilisant : en utilisant *using,* 6

utiliser *to use,* 10

V

va : Ça va? *How's everything?* 6; **Ça va.** *Okay.* 6; **Le bleu lui va très bien.** *She/He looks very good in blue.* 9; **On y va!** *Let's go!* 15; **tout va mal** *everything's going wrong,* 9

les **vacances** (f.) *vacation,* 14

une **vache** *cow,* 16

une **vague** *wave,* 17

un **vainqueur** *winner,* 22

la **vaisselle** *dishes,* 13; **faire la vaisselle** *to do the dishes,* 13

la **vanille** *vanilla (flavor),* 5

vapeur : cuit à la vapeur *steamed,* 20

varié, –e *varied,* 8

variété : une émission de variétés *variety show,* 24

vaste *enormous,* 17

vaut : il vaut mieux *it's better to,* 14

une **veille** *watch,* 18

un **vélo** *bicycle,* 3

le **vélo** *bike-riding,* 2; **faire du vélo** *to go bike-riding,* 2

un **vélomoteur** *moped,* 3

vendre *to sell,* 8

vendredi (m.) *Friday,* 4

venir *to come,* 14; **aller et venir** *to come and go,* 14; **venir de** *to have just,* 14

le **vent** *wind,* 15; **il fait du vent** *it's windy,* 15

le **ventre** *abdomen,* 22

vérifier *to check,* 9

un **verre** *glass,* 8

vers *about,* 5; *toward,* 14

verser *to pour,* 8

une **version** *translation from a foreign language,* 4

le **vert** *green,* 2

vert, –e *green,* 7

le **vertige** *vertigo, dizziness,* 21; **avoir le vertige** *to be dizzy,* 21

un **vestiaire** *locker room,* 4

des **vêtements** (m.) *clothes,* 9

veulent : ils/elles veulent *they want,* 5

veut : il/elle veut *he/she wants,* 6

veux : tu veux *you want,* 3

la **viande** *meat,* 8

une **victoire** *victory,* 22

la **vie** *life,* 10, 21; **une vie bien à elle** *its very own life,* 10

viens *come on,* 4

vieux, vieil, vieille, vieux, vieilles *old,* 16; **mon vieux, ma vieille** *old friend,* 3

un **village** *village,* 1

une **ville** *city, town,* 1

le **vin** *wine,* 8; **une bouteille de vin** *a bottle of wine,* 8

une **vinaigrette** *oil and vinegar,* 8

un **violon** *violin,* 14

un **violoncelle** *cello,* 14

une **vipère** *poisonous snake,* 18

virer *to veer, to swerve,* 21

une **visite** *visit,* 11

vite *fast,* 15

la **vitesse** *sprint,* 22

une **vitrine** *store window,* 13

vivant, –e *living,* 4

vivent : ils vivent *they live,* 7

voici *here is, here are,* 7

voilà *here is (are), there is (are),* 4

une **voile** *sail,* 18; **une école de voile** *sailing school,* 18; **faire de la voile** *to sail,* 18 voir *to see,* 11

voisin, –e *neighbor,* 14

une voiture *car,* 5; une petite voiture *toy car,* 3

un vol *flight,* 19

un volant *steering wheel,* 21

un volcan *volcano,* 17

le volley-ball *volleyball,* 2

voltige : le cheval de voltige *vaulting horse,* 22

le volume *volume,* 14

vos *your,* 4, 7

votre *your,* 7

le vôtre, la vôtre, les vôtres *yours,* 23

vouloir *to want,* 17

vous *you,* 2, 5; *(to, for) you,* 10; *yourself, yourselves,* 13

un voyage : faire un voyage *to take a trip,* 21

voyons *let's see,* 9

vrai, –e *true,* 3, 4

vraiment *really,* 2

une vue *view,* 11

W

des W.-C. (m.) *toilet, bathroom,* 10

un week-end *weekend,* 17

un western *western,* 5

X

un xylophone *xylophone,* 14

Y

y *there,* 11

un yaourt *yogurt,* 8

les yeux (m.) *eyes,* 7

Z

un zéro *zero,* 15

le Zodiaque *Zodiac,* 21

English–French Vocabulary

This vocabulary is the reverse of the French–English Vocabulary which runs just before it. In this vocabulary, the English equivalents of the French words and phrases used in **Nos Amis** have been listed, followed by the French.

The method of giving the French words and phrases in this vocabulary is exactly the same as that used in the French–English Vocabulary. See page 266 for note.

It is important to use a French word in its correct context. The use of a word can be checked easily by referring back to the unit where it appears.

A

a (an) *un, une,* 1
abdomen *le ventre,* 22
able: to be able *pouvoir,* 17
about *de,* 4; *environ,* 13; *vers,* 5
accident *un accident,* 17
according to *d'après,* 15
account *un compte rendu,* 22
acquaintance: to make the acquaintance of *faire la connaissance de,* 10
to **act as** *servir de,* 11
addition: in addition to *en plus de,* 17
address *une adresse,* 10
addressee *un(e) destinataire,* 12
to **adjust** *régler,* 24
administration *l'administration* (f.), 4; administration office(s) *bureau(x) de l'administration,* 4
administrative *administratif, –ive,* 24
to **admire** *admirer,* 12
adult *un(e) adulte,* 12
adventure *l'aventure* (f.), 17
advice *un conseil,* 20
afraid: to be afraid *avoir peur,* 21
Africa *l'Afrique* (f.), 24
after *après,* 5
afternoon *l'après-midi* (m.), 4; at the end of the afternoon *en fin d'après-midi,* 18
against *contre,* 17
ago: a long time ago *il y a longtemps,* 11
agricultural *agricole,* 24
airline *une compagnie,* 19
airplane *un avion,* 17, 19; model airplane *une maquette d'avion,* 3
airport *un aéroport,* 19
alarm clock *un réveil,* 13; to set an alarm *remonter un réveil,* 13
album *un album,* 7
all *tout, toute, tous, toutes,* 3, 7
allowance *l'argent* (m.) *de poche,* 23
almost *presque,* 1; You're almost there! *Tu y es presque!* 22
alone *seul, –e,* 12
already *déjà,* 9
also *aussi,* 1; *également,* 22

always *toujours,* 5
amateur *amateur,* 3
America *l'Amérique* (f.), 17
American *un(e) Américain(e),* 19
American *américain, –e,* 19
among *entre,* 11; *parmi,* 19
and *et,* 1
animal *un animal* (pl.: –aux), 16
ankle *la cheville,* 22
to **announce** *annoncer,* 18
announcement *une annonce,* 19
annual *annuel, –elle,* 19
another (person) *un(e) autre,* 4
answer *une réponse,* 4
to **answer** *répondre,* 7; answer (someone) *répondre (à),* 7; *(vous) répondez,* 4
antique item *une antiquité,* 11
any *en,* 3; *du, de la, (pas) de,* 5
anybody: not . . . anybody *ne... personne,* 13
anything: before anything *avant tout,* 15; not . . . anything *ne... rien,* 6, 13
anyway *enfin,* 11; *quand même,* 15; *de toute façon,* 19
apartment *un appartement,* 1; apartment building *un immeuble,* 10; garden apartments *une résidence,* 10
appearance *la présentation,* 4
apple *une pomme,* 8
April *avril* (m.), 12
aquarium *un aquarium,* 12
Arabic (language) *l'arabe* (m.), 19
arcade: shopping arcade *une galerie marchande,* 23
area *une région,* 14
arm *un bras,* 15, 22
armchair *un fauteuil,* 13
around *autour de,* 15
arrival *une arrivée,* 11; arrivals board *le tableau des arrivées,* 19
to **arrive** *arriver,* 5
arriving *arrivant,* 19
article: toilet article *un objet de toilette,* 13
artist *un artiste,* 20; He's a real artist! *C'est un artiste!* 20
artistic *artistique,* 24
as *comme,* 1; as . . . as *aussi... que,* 22; as far as *jusqu'à,* 11

to **ask** *demander,* 4, to ask questions *poser des questions,* 7; to ask (someone) *demander (à),* 4
astrology *l'astrologie* (f.), 21
at *à,* 4; *chez,* 5
athlete *un(e) athlète,* 22
athletic *sportif, –ive,* 22
athletics *l'athlétisme* (m.), 22
to **attack** *attaquer,* 21
attempt *un essai,* 22
auditorium *une salle de conférences,* 4
August *août* (m.), 12
aunt *une tante,* 7
autumn *l'automne* (m.), 15
avenue *une avenue,* 10

B

to **baby-sit** *garder des enfants,* 7
back *le dos,* 22
backpack *un sac à dos,* 18
bad *mauvais, –e,* 4; the weather is bad *il fait mauvais,* 15
badly *mal,* 3
baker *un(e) boulanger (–ère),* 8
bakery-pastry shop *une boulangerie-pâtisserie,* 8
balance *l'équilibre* (m.), 22; to keep one's balance *garder l'équilibre,* 22
balance beam *la poutre,* 22
balcony *un balcon,* 10
ball (baseball, tennis) *une balle,* 2; (football, soccer, etc.) *un ballon,* 2
banana *une banane,* 8
banjo *un banjo,* 9, 14
bank *une banque,* 10; *un quai,* 11
barbecue *une rôtisserie,* 21
barefoot *pieds-nus,* 18
to **bargain** *marchander,* 20
barn *une grange,* 16
barracuda *un baracuda,* 17
baseball *le base-ball,* 2; a baseball *une balle,* 2; baseball bat *une batte,* 2
basement *le sous-sol,* 9
basket *un panier,* 2
basketball *le basket-ball,* 2
bathed *baigné, –e,* 17

bathing suit *un maillot de bain,* 17
bathroom (for bathing only) *une salle de bains,* 10; (toilet) *des W.-C.,* 10
bay *une baie,* 17
to **be** *être,* 3; Be . . . *Soyez...,* 22
beach *une plage,* 3
bean *un *haricot,* 8; green beans *des *haricots verts,* 8
Beaujolais *le Beaujolais,* 8
beautiful *beau, bel, belle, beaux, belles,* 16
because *parce que,* 2
to **become** *devenir,* 16
bedroom *une chambre,* 10
beef *le bœuf,* 8; roast of beef *un rôti de bœuf,* 8
before *avant (de),* 5; *tout à l'heure,* 21
beginner *un(e) novice,* 15
beginning *novice,* 15
behind *derrière,* 10
Belgian *belge,* 19
Belgium *la Belgique,* 7; in Belgium *en Belgique,* 19
to **believe** *croire,* 12; I don't believe in *je ne crois pas à,* 21
belongings *des affaires (f.),* 18
below: (five) degrees below *moins (cinq),* 15
belt *une ceinture,* 23
to **bend** *plier,* 22
best *le mieux,* 4; to like best *aimer le mieux,* 4; the best . . . (in) *le/la/les meilleur(e)(s)...(de),* 22
to **bet** *parier,* 19
better *meilleur, –e,* 22
better *mieux,* 2; to like better *aimer mieux,* 2; it's better to *il vaut mieux,* 14
between *entre,* 7
bicycle *un vélo,* 3; bicycle shed *un abri pour bicyclettes,* 4
big *grand, –e,* 1, 4; *gros, grosse,* 21
bike: to go bike-riding *faire du vélo,* 2
bill (money) *un billet,* 5
bird *un oiseau* (pl: –x), 7; birdcalls *le chant des oiseaux,* 7
birth *une naissance,* 17
birthday *un anniversaire,* 23; Happy Birthday! *Bon Anniversaire!* 23
black *le noir,* 2; all black and blue *couvert(e) de bleus,* 21
blackberry *une mûre,* 16
blackboard *un tableau* (pl.: –x), 4
blond *blond, –e,* 7
blouse *un chemisier,* 9
blue *le bleu,* 2
blue *bleu, –e,* 7
board: arrivals board *le tableau des arrivées,* 19
boat *un bateau* (pl.: –x), 12; excursion boat *un bateau-mouche,* 11
boating: to go boating *faire du bateau,* 17
body *le corps,* 22

bongo drum *un tam-tam,* 14
book *un livre,* 3; a science-fiction book *un livre de science-fiction,* 3
book and stationery store *une librairie-papeterie,* 23
booming *en pleine expansion,* 24
boot *une botte,* 9
booth *un stand,* 21
boring *ennuyeux, –euse,* 2, 4
born: I was born *Je suis né(e),* 21
to **borrow (from)** *emprunter (à),* 23; how about borrowing *si on empruntait,* 23
boss *un(e) patron(ne),* 13
both of them *tous les deux, toutes les deux,* 6
bottle *une bouteille,* 8; a bottle of wine *une bouteille de vin,* 8
bougainvillea *un bougainvillier,* 20
boule: to play boule *jouer aux boules,* 20
boulevard *un boulevard,* 11
bowl *un bol,* 13
bowling alley *un bowling,* 5
box *une boîte,* 4; box of chocolates *une boîte de chocolats,* 23; paintbox *une boîte de couleurs,* 4
boy *un garçon,* 1; a new boy, a new girl *un nouveau, une nouvelle,* 4
bracelet *un bracelet,* 9; (costume jewelry) *un bracelet fantaisie,* 23
brass *le cuivre,* 20
bread *le pain,* 8; long French bread *une baguette,* 8
to **break** *se casser,* 15; (a record) *battre,* 22
breakfast *le petit déjeuner,* 8
bridge *un pont,* 11
bright *brillant, –e,* 18; *clair, –e,* 24
to **bring** *apporter,* 5
to **bring in (money)** *rapporter,* 14, 20; It doesn't pay enough! *Ça ne rapporte pas!* 20
to **bring together** *réunir,* 22
brioche *une brioche,* 8
brother *un frère,* 7
brown *marron* (f. and pl. : *marron*), 2, 7
to **browse** *flâner,* 20
brush *une brosse,* 13; hairbrush *une brosse à cheveux,* 13; toothbrush *une brosse à dents,* 13
to **brush** *brosser,* 13; to brush one's hair *se brosser les cheveux,* 13
Brussels *Bruxelles,* 19
bubbly *pétillant, –e,* 24
building *un bâtiment,* 10; apartment building *un immeuble,* 10
bully *une brute,* 21
to **bump into** *rentrer dans,* 21
bumper car *une auto tamponneuse,* 21
bus *un autobus,* 13
busy *occupé, –e,* 6; *pressé, –e,* 6
but *mais,* 3
butcher *un(e) boucher (–ère),* 8

butter *le beurre,* 8
buttered *beurré, –e,* 13
button: playback button *un bouton d'écoute,* 14; record button *un bouton d'enregistrement,* 14
to **buy** *acheter,* 8; without buying *sans avoir acheté,* 13
by *par,* 7

C

cabana *une case,* 17
café *un café,* 5
cake *un gâteau* (pl.: –x), 7
to **call** *téléphoner (à),* 5; to call back *rappeler,* 6, 13; I'll call you back. *Je te rappelle.* 6
to **call** *appeler,* 6
call *une communication,* 6; phone call *un coup de téléphone,* 6
called *appelé, –e,* 10
Camembert cheese *le camembert,* 5; Camembert sandwich *un sandwich au camembert,* 5
camera *un appareil(–photo)* (pl.: *appareils–photo*), 3
camp *un camp,* 18; summer camp *un camp de vacances,* 18
can *pouvoir,* 17; he/she can *il/elle peut,* 3; they can *ils/elles peuvent,* 7
Canada *le Canada,* 19; in Canada *au Canada,* 1
Canadian *canadien, –ienne,* 15, 19
candy: cotton candy *une barbe à papa,* 21
cannon *un canon,* 12
capital *une capitale,* 1, 19
captain *un capitaine,* 2
car *une voiture,* 5; toy car *une petite voiture,* 3
card: greeting card *une carte,* 23; playing card *une carte,* 3; post card *une carte postale,* 16
care: to take care of *s'occuper (de),* 13
careful: to be careful *faire attention,* 4
Caribbean Sea *la mer des Caraïbes,* 1
carrot *une carotte,* 8
carrying *portant,* 24
cartoon: animated cartoon *un dessin animé,* 5
case: pencil case *une trousse,* 4
case: in that case *dans ce cas,* 20
cassette *une cassette,* 3
cat *un chat,* 7
to **catch** *attraper,* 17
category *une catégorie,* 22
cello *un violoncelle,* 14
center *un centre,* 24; youth center *une maison des jeunes,* 10
centered *centré, –e,* 10
centime *un centime,* 5
centimeter *un centimètre,* 22
certainly *certainement,* 3

chairlift *un télésiège*, 15
chalet *un chalet*, 15
champion *un(e) champion(ne)*, 21
championship *un championnat*, 22
to **change** *changer*, 9; to change one's clothes *se changer*, 13
character *le caractère*, 10
charade *une charade*, 8
check *une addition*, 5
to **check** *vérifier*, 9
checkers *les dames* (f.), 3
cheese *le fromage*, 8; Camembert cheese *le camembert*, 5; goat cheese *le fromage de chèvre*, 8; Swiss cheese *le gruyère*, 5
cherry *une cerise*, 8
chess *les échecs* (m.), 3
chest *la poitrine*, 22
chicken *un poulet*, 8
child *un enfant*, 4, 7
chimes *un indicatif (musical)*, 19
chin *le menton*, 22
chocolate (flavor) *le chocolat*, 5; hot chocolate *le chocolat*, 13; chocolate ice cream *une glace au chocolat*, 5
to **choose** *choisir*, 5
chop *une côtelette*, 8; pork chop *une côtelette de porc*, 8
church *une église*, 10
city *une ville*, 1
to **clap** *applaudir*, 14
clarinet *une clarinette*, 14
class *une classe*, 4; in class *en classe*, 4
classmate *un(e) camarade*, 4
classroom *une salle de classe*, 4
clean *propre*, 8
clear *clair, –e*, 18
climate *un climat*, 24
to **climb** *grimper*, 22
cloak: long Arab cloak *un burnous*, 20
to **close** *fermer*, 13
closing *la fermeture*, 11; *une formule finale*, 12
clothes *des vêtements* (m.), 9
coastline *une côte*, 17
coconut tree *un cocotier*, 17
coffee (flavor) *le café*, 5; (drink) *le café*, 8; coffee with milk *le café au lait*, 8; coffee ice cream *une glace au café*, 5
coin *une pièce (de monnaie)*, 3, 5
colander *un panier*, 20
cold *froid, –e*, 5; it's cold (weather) *il fait froid*, 15; to be cold *avoir froid*, 15
to **collapse** *s'écrouler*, 13
to **collect** *collectionner*, 3
collector *un(e) collectionneur (–euse)*, 3
color *une couleur*, 2
to **comb** *peigner*, 24; to comb one's hair *se donner un coup de peigne*, 13
to **come** *venir*, 14; to come home *rentrer*, 2; come on *viens*, 4; *Allez!* 9;

Come on, let's go! *Allons-y!* 14; to come and go *aller et venir*, 14
comedy *un film comique*, 5
comfort: to give comfort *réconforter*, 21
coming: coming from *en provenance de*, 19; on coming out of *à la sortie de*, 10
comment *une appréciation*, 4
commercial *une pub(licité)*, 24
to **compare** *comparer*, 22
compass *un compas*, 4
competitor *un(e) concurrent(e)*, 22
to **complete** *compléter*, 15
complicated *compliqué, –e*, 23
composition *une rédaction*, 8; (musical) composition *une composition*, 14; (written) composition *une composition française*, 4
comprehensive *polyvalent, –e*, 22
concert *un concert*, 14
conch *un lambi*, 17
consequently *par conséquent*, 10
conservation *la conservation*, 24
constant *perpétuel, –elle*, 17
to **continue** *continuer*, 9
to **cook** *faire cuire*, 20; *faire la cuisine*, 20
cooked *cuit, –e*, 20
cool: it's cool (weather) *il fait frais*, 15
copper *le cuivre*, 20
coral *le corail* (pl.: *–aux*), 17
corn *le maïs*, 16
correct *correct, –e*, 6
to **correct** *corriger*, 4
to **correspond** *correspondre*, 20
cost *le prix*, 6
to **cost** *coûter*, 8
to **count** *compter*, 3
counter *un comptoir*, 19
country *un pays*, 19
courageous *courageux, –euse*, 22
course *un cours*, 4
course: of course *certainement*, 3; *bien sûr*, 4; *je pense bien*, 19; of course we are *mais si*, 2
courtyard *une cour*, 4
couscous *le couscous*, 20
cousin *un(e) cousin(e)*, 7
cow *une vache*, 16
cowshed *une étable*, 16
crab *un crabe*, 17
craft *un métier*, 20
craftsperson *un artisan*, 20; craftsperson in precious metals *un orfèvre*, 20
cream: heavy soured cream *la crème fraîche*, 8
crocodile *un crocodile*, 24
croissant *un croissant*, 8
to **cross** *traverser*, 18
cucumber *un concombre*, 8
cufflink *un bouton de manchette* (pl.: *boutons de manchette*), 23
cultural *culturel, –elle*, 24

cup *une tasse*, 7, 8; (trophy) *une coupe*, 10
curious *curieux, –euse*, 23
current *actuel, –elle*, 24
customer *un(e) client(e)*, 13

D

dad, daddy *papa*, 7
dairy outlet *une crémerie*, 8
dairy outlet salesperson *un(e) crémier (–ière)*, 8
dance *une danse*, 9; *un bal*, 14
to **dance** *danser*, 9
dangerous *dangereux, –euse*, 2, 4
dark: dark (haired) *brun, –e*, 7; *sombre*, 24
darling *chéri, –e*, 16
dash: 100-meter dash *un 100 (cent) m (mètres)*, 22
date *la date*, 12; (appointment) *un rendez-vous*, 13
day *un jour*, 4; *une journée*, 5; all day long *toute la journée*, 5; every day *tous les jours*, 4; the day when *le jour où*, 4; (on) the following day *le lendemain*, 11; (in) the old days *autrefois*, 17; in the old days *jadis*, 16; that day *ce jour-là*, 7; Those were the days! *C'était le bon temps!* 16
dear *cher, –ère*, 12; *chéri, –e*, 16
December *décembre* (m.), 12
to **decide (to)** *décider (de)*, 9
deck: observation deck *une terrasse*, 19
degree *un degré*, 15; it's (five) degrees *il fait (cinq)*, 15; (five) degrees below *moins (cinq)*, 15
delicious *délicieux, –euse*, 8
dentist *un(e) dentiste*, 7
depend: it depends *ça dépend*, 23
to **describe** *décrire*, 12; describe *décrivez*, 4
desert *un désert*, 24
deserved *mérité, –e*, 22
dessert *un dessert*, 8
destroyed *détruit, –e*, 17
detective *policier, –ière*, 5
to **dial** *composer*, 6; to dial the number *faire le numéro*, 6; to dial the number again *refaire le numéro*, 6
diary *un journal (de bord)*, 18
different *différent, –e*, 4
difficulty *une difficulté*, 3
dinar *un dinar*, 20
dining room *une salle à manger*, 10
dinner (supper) *un dîner*, 7, 8; Dinner is served! *A table!* 8; to have dinner *dîner*, 7
to **direct** *diriger*, 22
directions *des instructions* (f.), 6
directory: telephone directory *un annuaire*, 6
disappoint: she didn't disappoint *elle n'a pas déçu*, 22

to **discover** *découvrir*, 17
  discus *le disque*, 22
  discussion *une discussion*, 20
  dish *un plat*, 8
  dishes *la vaisselle*, 13; to do the dishes *faire la vaisselle*, 13
to **dive** *plonger*, 17
to **divide (into)** *diviser (en)*, 18
  diving *plongeant*, –e, 12
  dizziness *le vertige*, 21
  dizzy: to be dizzy *avoir le vertige*, 21
to **do** *faire*, 2; to do the dishes *faire la vaisselle*, 13; to do for oneself *se faire*, 13; to do the haying *faire les foins*, 16; to do the same thing *en faire autant*, 23; That did it! *Ça y est!* 21
  doctor *un médecin*, 7
  documentary *un documentaire*, 24
  dog *un chien*, 7
  dominoes *les dominos* (m.), 3
  double bass *une contrebasse*, 14
  dozen *une douzaine*, 8
  drawing *le dessin*, 4
  dream *un rêve*, 24; Sweet dreams! *Fais de beaux rêves!* 13
to **dream** *rêver*, 17
  dress *une robe*, 9
to **dress** *habiller*, 13; to get dressed *s'habiller*, 13
  dressing *un assaisonnement*, 8
  drink *une boisson*, 5
to **drink** *boire*, 9
to **drive** *conduire*, 16
  drugstore *la pharmacie*, 10
  drums *une batterie*, 14
  duck *un canard*, 16; Ducks in Orange Sauce *les Canards à l'Orange*, 14
  dull *terne*, 24
  dune *une dune*, 18
  during *pendant*, 6; *au cours de*, 10
  Dutch (language) *le néerlandais*, 19

E

  each *chaque*, 9, 13
  each one *chacun*, –e, 7
  ear *une oreille*, 22
  early *tôt*, 13; *en avance*, 19
  earphone *un écouteur*, 14
  earring *une boucle d'oreille* (pl.: *boucles d'oreille*), 23
  east *l'est* (m.), 17
  easygoing *décontracté*, –e, 19
to **eat** *manger*, 5
  economical *économique*, 24
  edged with *bordé*, –e de, 17
  effort *un effort*, 22
  egg *un œuf*, 8
  Egyptian *égyptien*, –ienne, 11
  elbow *le coude*, 22
  electric *électrique*, 14
  electronics *l'électronique* (f.), 3;

  electronics magazine *une revue d'électronique*, 3
  elephant *un éléphant*, 24
  elevator *un ascenseur*, 10
  else: what else *quoi d'autre*, 23; What else is there? *Qu'est-ce qu'il y a d'autre?* 14
  embarrassment of riches *l'embarras du choix*, 23
  enchanted *enchanté*, –e, 17
to **encourage** *encourager*, 22
  end *la fin*, 8; at the end *à la fin*, 8; at the end of the afternoon *en fin d'après-midi*, 18; at the other end of the line *à l'autre bout du fil*, 6; at the far end (of) *au fond (de)*, 4
to **end** *finir*, 5
  energetic *énergique*, 22
  energy *l'énergie* (f.), 24
  engineer *un ingénieur*, 7; sound engineer *un ingénieur du son*, 14; to be the sound engineer *faire l'ingénieur du son*, 14
  England *l'Angleterre* (f.), 19
  English (language) *l'anglais* (m.), 4, 19
  English *anglais*, –e, 19
  English person *un(e) Anglais(e)*, 19
  enjoy: Enjoy your meal! *Bon Appétit!* 8
  enormous *vaste*, 17
  enough *assez (de)*, 5, 8; enough room *assez de place*, 5; That's enough for me! *Ça me suffit!* 21
to **enter** *se présenter (à)*, 22
  entertained: to be entertained *se distraire*, 24
  enthusiastic *passionné*, –e, 10
  entryway *une entrée*, 10
  envelope *une enveloppe*, 12
  equipment *un équipement* (m.), 15
to **erase** *effacer*, 4
  eraser *une gomme*, 4
  errand *une course*, 8
  eruption *une éruption*, 17
  especially *particulièrement*, 22
  ethnic *éthnique*, 24
  evening *le soir*, 4
  event *une épreuve*, 22
  everybody *tout le monde*, 4
  everything *tout*, 8
  everywhere *partout*, 9
  exactly *exactement*, 14
  example *un exemple*, 4
  except *sauf*, 4; *excepté*, 7
  exceptional *extraordinaire*, 3
to **exchange** *échanger*, 19
  excursion *une excursion*, 17
  excuse: with the excuse *sous prétexte*, 16
  excuse me *excuse(z)-moi*, 6; *pardon*, 6
  exercise *un exercice*, 4, 22; floor exercises *les exercices au sol* (m.), 22; listening exercise *un exercice de compréhension*, 4; writing exercise

  un exercice écrit, 4
  exhausted *épuisé*, –e, 13
  exhibition *une exposition*, 13
  exit *une sortie*, 10; on coming out of *à la sortie*, 10
  exotic *exotique*, 17
  expensive *cher*, –ère, 8
to **explain** *expliquer*, 10
  exploration *une exploration*, 12
to **explore** *explorer*, 17
  eye *un œil* (pl. : *yeux*), 6, 12, 22
  eyeglasses *les lunettes* (f.), 7

F

  facing *en face (de)*, 4
  fact: in fact *en fait*, 16; the fact is *en effet*, 19; as a matter of fact *d'ailleurs*, 14
  factory *une usine*, 7; factory worker *un(e) ouvrier (–ière)*, 7
  fair *une kermesse*, 14; *une fête*, 21; traveling fair *une fête foraine*, 21
  fairy tale *un conte de fées*, 21
  fakir *un fakir*, 21
  fall *l'automne* (m.), 15; in the fall *en automne*, 15
to **fall** *tomber*, 15
  false *faux, fausse*, 4
  family *une famille*, 7
  famous *célèbre*, 17, 24
  fantastic *fantastique*, 17
  far (from) *loin (de)*, 1; far away *lointain*, –e, 24
  farm *une ferme*, 16
  farmer *un(e) fermier (–ière)*, 7
  fast *rapide*, 9
  fast *vite*, 15
  father *un père*, 7
  favorite *préféré*, –e, 14; *un(e) favori(te)*, 22
  February *février* (m.), 12
to **feed** *donner à manger*, 16
  feet: a few feet from *à deux pas de*, 3
  felt-tip pen *un feutre*, 4
  Ferris wheel *une grande roue*, 21
  fertile *fertile*, 24
  fertilizer *un engrais*, 24
  few: a few *quelques*, 14
  field *un champ*, 16; athletic field *un stade*, 10; wheat field *un champ de blé*, 16
  fig *une figue*, 16
to **figure out** *calculer*, 5
  film *un film*, 5; detective film *un film policier*, 5
  finally *finalement*, 18
to **find** *trouver*, 2
  fine *fin*, –e, 17
  finger *un doigt*, 22
to **finish** *finir*, 5; once finished *une fois terminé*, 5
  fire: wood fire *un feu de bois*, 15
  first of all *d'abord*, 4

fish *le poisson*, 8; angel fish *un poisson-ange*, 17; clown fish *un poisson-clown*, 17; flying fish *un poisson volant*, 17; jelly fish *une méduse*, 17
to **fish** *pêcher*, 17; to go fishing *aller à la pêche*, 17
fisherman *un pêcheur*, 17
fishing *la pêche*, 17
to **fit** *aller (à)*, 23
to **fix** *réparer*, 3
flight *un vol*, 19
to **flip** *sauter*, 24
flipper *une palme*, 17
floor *un étage*, 10; floor exercises *les exercices* (m.) *au sol*, 22; the ground floor *le rez-de-chaussée*, 10; on the ground floor *au rez-de-chaussée*, 10
Florida *la Floride*, 17
florist *un(e) fleuriste*, 23
flower *une fleur*, 8; the Flower Market *le Marché aux Fleurs*, 8
flute *une flûte*, 14
fog *le brouillard*, 19
to **follow** *suivre*, 10
followed (by) *suivi, –e (de)*, 19
food *la nourriture*, 9
foot *un pied*, 22; on foot *à pied*, 13
football *le football américain*, 2
for *comme*, 2; *pour*, 3; *car*, 7
foreign *étranger, –ère*, 21
forest *une forêt*, 17
to **forget** *oublier*, 8, 24
fork *une fourchette*, 8
form *une forme*, 6
fortune *une fortune*, 12
fortune-teller *un fakir*, 21
forward *avant*, 2
franc *un franc*, 5; 1 F each *1 F la pièce*, 8
France *la France*, 1; in France *en France*, 1
free *libre*, 5
French (language) *le français*, 4, 19
French *français, –e*, 19
French fries *des frites* (f.), 8
French person *un(e) Français(e)*, 19
Friday *vendredi* (m.), 4
friend *un(e) ami(e)*, 2; old friend *mon vieux, ma vieille*, 3; childhood friend *un(e) ami(e) d'enfance*, 16; our friends *nos amis*, 1; new friends *nouveaux amis*, 10
from *de*, 1; *en provenance de*, 19
front: in front (of) *en face (de)*, 4; *devant*, 10
fruit *un fruit*, 8
full *rempli, –e*, 13; *plein, –e*, 17
fullback *arrière*, 2
fun *amusant, –e*, 2, 4
fun: to have fun *s'amuser*, 13
to **function** *marcher*, 9
funny *drôle*, 21; *humoristique*, 23
further on *plus loin*, 20

future *l'avenir* (m.), 21
fuzzy *flou, –e*, 24

G

game *un match*, 2; *un jeu*, 3; card game *une partie de cartes*, 7
gang *une bande*, 9
garage *un garage*, 20
garden *un jardin*, 11; vegetable garden *un jardin potager*, 16; garden apartments *une résidence*, 10
gate *une porte*, 19
generalization *une généralisation*, 4
gentle *doux, douce*, 17
geography *la géographie*, 4
German (language) *l'allemand* (m.), 4, 19
German *allemand, –e*, 19
Germany *l'Allemagne* (f.), 19
get: to get closer *s'approcher (de)*, 19; to get dressed *s'habiller*, 13; to get oneself out of *se tirer (de)*, 17; to get to *se rendre*, 13; to get together *se réunir*, 18; to get up *se lever*, 13; to get up again *se relever*, 15; to get washed *se laver*, 13; to go get *aller chercher*, 16
gift *un cadeau* (pl.: –x), 23; to give a gift *faire un cadeau*, 23
gifted *doué, –e (pour)*, 4
girl *une fille*, 1
to **give** *donner*, 5; to give a gift *faire un cadeau*, 23; to give up *renoncer à*, 18; to give back *rendre*, 9; to give water to *donner à boire*, 16
glass *un verre*, 8
glove *un gant*, 15
glued *collé, –e*, 12
to **go** *aller*, 4; to go after *poursuivre*, 17; to go around the world *faire le tour du monde*, 24; to go back on *remonter*, 21; to go back up *remonter*, 12; to go bike-riding *faire du vélo*, 2; to go down *descendre*, 7; to go down again *redescendre*, 19; to go get *aller chercher*, 16; to go out *sortir*, 5; That always goes over. *Ça plaît toujours.* 14; to go shopping *faire des courses*, 11; to go grocery shopping *faire les courses*, 8; to go to bed *se coucher*, 13; to go to sleep *s'endormir*, 13; to go up *monter*, 10; everything's going wrong *tout va mal*, 9; Let's go! *Allons-y!* 5; Let's go! *On y va!* 15
goal *un but*, 2
goalkeeper *un(e) gardien(ne) de but*, 2
goggles *des lunettes* (f.), 15
gold *l'or* (m.), 23; made of gold *en or*, 23
good *bon, bonne*, 4
Goodbye. *Au revoir.* 6

Good Night! *Bonne nuit!* 13; *bonsoir*, 13
graceful *gracieux, –euse*, 22
grade *une note*, 4; 9th grade *la quatrième*, 4
gram *un gramme*, 8
grammar *la grammaire*, 4
grandfather *un grand-père*, 7
grandmother *une grand-mère*, 7
grandparents *des grands-parents* (m.), 7
grapefruit *un pamplemousse*, 8
grapes *du raisin*, 8
grass *l'herbe* (f.), 16
grated *râpé, –e*, 8
gray *gris, –e*, 7
great: It's really great! *C'est extra!* 21
green *le vert*, 2
green *vert, –e*, 7
green pepper *un poivron doux*, 20
to **grill** *griller*, 20
grocer *un(e) épicier (–ière)*, 8
grocery: grocery store *une épicerie*, 8; groceries *des provisions* (f.), 8; to go grocery shopping *faire les courses*, 8
ground: ground floor *le rez-de-chaussée*, 10; on the ground floor *au rez-de-chaussée*, 10; on the ground *par terre*, 18
group *un ensemble*, 10; *un groupe*, 14
to **grow** *cultiver*, 16
grudge: holding a grudge *rancunier, –ière*, 21
Guadeloupe *la Guadeloupe*, 17
to **guess** *deviner*, 7
guest *un(e) invité(e)*, 14
guide *un guide*, 10
to **guide** *guider*, 10
guitar *une guitare*, 9, 14
guy *un type*, 21
gym(nasium) *un gym(nase)*, 4
gym(nastics) *la gym(nastique)*, 4, 22

H

hair *les cheveux* (m.), 13
hairbrush *une brosse à cheveux*, 13
halfback *demi*, 2
half hour *une demi-heure*, 9; half past (the hour) *et demie*, 4
hall: entrance hall *un *hall*, 12
hallway *un couloir*, 4
ham *le jambon*, 5
hand *une main*, 4, 22; in hand *en mains*, 19; Let's give them a nice hand. *On les applaudit bien fort.* 14; to raise one's hand *lever la main*, 8
handbag *un sac*, 23
handkerchief *un mouchoir*, 23
Hang on! *Tiens-toi bien!* 21

to **hang up** (the phone) *raccrocher,* 6
to **happen (to)** *arriver (à),* 15
happiness *le bonheur,* 23
hardly *à peine,* 16
harmonica *un harmonica,* 14
harvest *la moisson,* 16
to **harvest** *faire la moisson,* 16
hassock *un pouf,* 20
to **have** *avoir,* 3; he/she has to *il/elle doit,* 13; I have to *je dois,* 5; they have to *ils/elles doivent,* 10; to have just *venir de,* 14; to have to *il faut,* 4
hay *le foin,* 16; hayloft *un grenier à foin,* 16
to **hay** *faire les foins,* 16
hazelnut (flavor) *la noisette,* 5; (fruit) *une noisette,* 16; hazelnut ice cream *une glace à la noisette,* 5
he *il,* 2
head *la tête,* 22
health *la santé,* 23
to **hear** *entendre,* 7
heart *un cœur,* 3
Hebrew (language) *l'hébreu* (m.), 19
height: of medium height *de taille moyenne,* 7
Hello! *Allô!* 6
help: with the help of *avec l'aide de,* 16
to **help** *aider (à),* 8, 15; Somebody help me! *Maman!* 21
hen *une poule,* 16
her *elle,* 1; *son, ses,* 3; *son, sa, ses,* 7; (to, for) her *lui,* 8; *la,* 10
here *ici,* 4; here is (are) *voilà,* 4; *voici,* 7; right here *juste ici,* 4
hers *le sien, la sienne, les siens, les siennes,* 23
herself *se,* 13
hesitation *une hésitation,* 23
Hi! *Salut!* 6
hide and seek: to play hide and seek *jouer à cache-cache,* 21
high **haut,* 22
high jump *le saut en *hauteur,* 22
high school *un lycée,* 7
hill *une colline,* 17
him *lui,* 1; (to, for) him *lui,* 8; *le,* 10
himself *se,* 13
hippopotamus *un hippopotame,* 24
his *sa, son, ses,* 7; *le sien, la sienne, les siens, les siennes,* 23
history *l'histoire* (f.), 4
hockey: ice hockey *le *hockey sur glace,* 2; hockey puck *une rondelle,* 2; hockey stick *une crosse,* 2
to **hold on** *s'agripper,* 21
home: at home, at the home of *chez, à la maison,* 5; back home *de retour à la maison,* 23
homework *un devoir,* 4
hope *l'espoir* (m.), 23
to **hope** *espérer,* 14
horizontal bar *la barre fixe,* 22
horoscope *un horoscope,* 21

hors d'œuvre *un *hors-d'œuvre* (pl. : **hors-d'œuvre),* 8
horse *un cheval* (pl. : *–aux),* 16; to ride a horse *monter un cheval,* 16; vaulting horse *le cheval de voltige,* 22
horseback-riding *le cheval,* 2; to go horseback-riding *faire du cheval,* 2
hospitable *accueillant, –e,* 17
hospital *un hôpital* (pl. : *–aux),* 7
hostess *une hôtesse,* 19
hot: it's hot (weather) *il fait chaud,* 15
hour *une heure,* 4; rush hour *l'heure d'affluence,* 13; an hour late *1 h de retard,* 19
house *une maison,* 1; fun house *une maison magique,* 21; at their house *chez eux,* 5
how *comment,* 1; how much, how many *combien (de),* 3, 8; How's everything? *Ça va?* 6; how much *ça fait combien,* 5; How old are you? *Quel âge as-tu?* 1
huge *énorme,* 12
humorous *humoristique,* 23
hungry: to be hungry *avoir faim,* 5
hurdles *les *haies* (f.), 22
to **hurry** *se dépêcher,* 13
hurry: in a hurry *pressé, –e,* 6
to **hurt** *se faire mal (à),* 15; *avoir mal (à),* 15

I

I *j',* 1; *je,* 2
ice cream *une glace,* 5
idea *un idée,* 19
to **identify** *identifier,* 7
idiots: What are you, some kind of idiots! *Espèces de crétins!* 21
if *si,* 5
to **illustrate** *illustrer,* 17
illustrator *un(e) dessinateur (–trice),* 7
to **imagine** *imaginer,* 19
impatiently *avec impatience,* 7
impossible *impossible,* 6
impressive *impressionnant, –e,* 18
in *à,* 1; *dans,* 1; *en,* 4
inattentive *distrait, –e,* 4
inch *un pouce,* 22
indicated *indiqué, –e,* 7
indisputably *indiscutablement,* 22
industrial *industriel, –elle,* 24
industry *une industrie,* 10
infirmary *une infirmerie,* 15
information *des renseignements* (m.), 19
inhabitant *un habitant,* 10
inside *dedans,* 21
inspiration *l'inspiration* (f.), 23
instance: for instance *par exemple,* 3
instead *plutôt,* 16
instrument *un instrument,* 14

intelligent *intelligent, –e,* 4
intermediate *intermédiaire,* 15
intersection *un croisement,* 10
to **introduce (to)** *présenter (à),* 10
to **invite** *inviter,* 7
is: it is *c'est,* 1; isn't it? *n'est-ce pas?* 1
island *une île,* 1
Israel *Israël* (m.), 19
Israeli *israélien, –ienne,* 19
it *il, elle,* 8; *le, la,* 10
Italian *italien, –ienne,* 19
Italian (language) *l'italien* (m.), 19
Italy *l'Italie* (f.), 19
its *son, sa, ses,* 7
itself *se,* 13

J

jacket *un blouson,* 9
jam *la confiture,* 8
Jamaica *la Jamaïque,* 17
January *janvier* (m.), 12
jar *un pot,* 8; jar of mustard *un pot de moutarde,* 8
jaunt: to take a jaunt *faire une promenade,* 11
javelin *le javelot,* 22
jazz *le jazz,* 14
jeans *un jean,* 9
jewelry: a piece of jewelry *un bijou* (pl. : *–x),* 9; jewelry shop *une bijouterie,* 23
journalist *un(e) journaliste,* 7
joy *la joie,* 23
joyous *joyeux, –euse,* 23
judo *le judo,* 2; to practice judo *faire du judo,* 2
juice: fruit juice *un jus de fruit,* 5; grapefruit juice *un jus de pamplemousse,* 5
juicy *juteux, –euse,* 8
July *juillet* (m.), 7, 12
jump *un saut,* 22; high jump *le saut en *hauteur,* 22; long jump *le saut en longueur,* 22
to **jump** *sauter,* 22
June *juin* (m.), 12
junior *cadet, –ette,* 22
just *juste,* 16

K

to **keep** *garder,* 9; to keep from *empêcher (de),* 20; to keep one's balance *garder l'équilibre,* 22; to keep score *marquer les points,* 3
key ring *un porte-clés* (pl. : *porte-clés),* 23
kilogram *un kilo,* 8
kilometer *un kilomètre,* 17
kind *un genre,* 14
kiss *un baiser,* 23
to **kiss** *embrasser,* 12

kitchen *une cuisine,* 4, 10
knee *un genou* (pl. : ⁻x), 15, 22
knife *un couteau* (pl. : –x), 8; a knife-rest *un porte-couteau* (pl. : *porte-couteaux*), 8
to **knit** *tricoter,* 3
knotted *noué,* –e, 18; knotted rope *une corde à nœuds,* 22
to **know** (to be acquainted with) *connaître,* 10; to know, to know how to *savoir,* 16; to know each other *se connaître,* 19; do you know? *savez-vous?* 12, 16

L

laboratory *un laboratoire,* 4
lack *manquer,* 13
lady *une dame,* 19
lake *un lac,* 18
lamb *l'agneau* (m.), 8; *le mouton,* 20; leg of lamb *un gigot d'agneau,* 8
to **land** *atterrir,* 19
landing *un palier,* 10; *un débarquement,* 17
landmark *un monument,* 11
landscape *un paysage,* 24
language *une langue,* 4, 19; modern language *une langue vivante,* 4
lane *une allée,* 10
large *grand,* –e, 1, 4
last *dernier,* –ière, 22; at last *finalement,* 18; last night *hier soir,* 9
to **last** *durer,* 7
Latin (language) *le latin,* 4
Latin *latin,* –e, 4
Laurentian Mountains *les Laurentides,* 15
lawn *une pelouse,* 7
lawyer *un(e) avocat(e),* 7
lazy *paresseux,* –euse, 4; to get lazy *perdre courage,* 13
to **lead back** *ramener,* 16
leader *un chef,* 18
to **lean (on)** *s'appuyer (sur),* 15
leap *un bond,* 13
to **learn** *apprendre à,* 19; *s'instruire,* 24
least: at least *au moins,* 13; the least . . . (in) *le/la/les moins… (de),* 22
leather *le cuir,* 20; leather-goods store *une maroquinerie,* 23
to **leave** *partir,* 5; *laisser,* 5; *quitter,* 6
left *gauche,* 22; on (to) the left *à gauche,* 8, 10
left: if there is any left *s'il y en a encore,* 9
leg *une jambe,* 15, 22; leg of lamb *un gigot d'agneau,* 8
lemon soda *la limonade,* 5
lend (to) *prêter (à),* 23
less *moins,* 4; less . . . than *moins… que,* 22
to **let** *laisser,* 16

letter *une lettre,* 12
liar *menteur,* –euse, 10
library *une bibliothèque,* 4
life *la vie,* 10, 21
light *léger,* –ère, 8
lightning *un éclair,* 16
like *comme,* 1
to **like** *aimer,* 2; to like better *aimer mieux,* 2; to like best *aimer le mieux,* 4; to like very much *adorer,* 15; They didn't seem to like that very much! *Ça n'a pas eu l'air de leur plaire!* 21
limp *mou, molle,* 21
line (phone connection) *une ligne,* 6; at the other end of the line *à l'autre bout du fil,* 6
line *une queue,* 15; to stand in line *faire la queue,* 15
line: just a line . . . *juste un petit mot…,* 16
liter *un litre,* 8
litter *une litière,* 16
little *petit,* –e, 1; a little (of) *un peu (de),* 4, 8
to **live** *habiter,* 1, 2; they live *ils/elles vivent,* 7; Where do you live? *Où habites-tu?* 1
living *vivant,* –e, 4; living room *une salle de séjour,* 10
lobster: spiny lobster *une langouste,* 17
located *situé,* –e, 24; to be located *se trouver,* 13
locker room *un vestiaire,* 4
log (diary) *un journal de bord,* 18
London *Londres,* 19
long *long, longue,* 9
long jump *le saut en longueur,* 22
to **look:** to look (at) *regarder,* 2; to look for *chercher,* 9; to look forward to *avoir *hâte (de),* 12; to look like *ressembler (à),* 7; to look up *chercher,* 6; to look (good, ripe, etc.) *avoir l'air,* 8
loose *décontracté,* –e, 19
to **lose** *perdre,* 3, 9
lot: a lot (of) *un tas (de),* 9
lottery *la loterie,* 21
loud *fort,* 14
loudspeaker *un *haut-parleur* (pl. : *haut-parleurs*), 14
love *l'amour* (m.), 5; love story *une histoire d'amour,* 5; Love *Amitiés,* 12
low *bas,* 14
to **lower** *baisser,* 14, 22
luck *la chance,* 21; no luck *pas de chance,* 6; to try one's luck *tenter sa chance,* 21
luckily *heureusement,* 15
lunch *un déjeuner,* 7, 8; Lunch is

served! *A table!* 8; to have lunch *déjeuner,* 4
lunchroom *un réfectoire,* 4

M

machine *une machine,* 21
made (by) *fait,* –e *(par),* 7
magazine *une revue,* 3; an electronics magazine *une revue d'électronique,* 3
magician *un(e) illusionniste,* 14
magnificent *magnifique,* 17
main *principal,* –e, 8
main street *la grand-rue,* 16
to **make** *faire,* 4; to make (money) *gagner,* 7; to make sure *s'assurer,* 13; to make the acquaintance of *faire la connaissance de,* 10; to make use of *se servir (de),* 14; to be made up of *se composer de,* 24; (you) make *(vous) mettez,* 5; making *en mettant,* 6
makeup: to put on makeup *se maquiller,* 13
man *un homme,* 6
manageable *souple,* 24
manner *une façon,* 19
manufacturing *la fabrication,* 24
many *beaucoup (de),* 8; *bien des,* 23
many-colored *multicolore,* 17
map *un plan,* 10; *une carte,* 15
marble *une bille,* 9
March *mars* (m.), 12
to **mark down** *marquer,* 3
market *un marché,* 8; the Flower Market *le Marché aux Fleurs,* 8; Arab market *un souk,* 20
marks: On your marks, get set, go! *A vos marques, prêts, partez!* 22
marry: to get married *se marier,* 21
Martinique *la Martinique,* 1; in Martinique *à la Martinique,* 1; person from Martinique *un(e) Martiniquais(e),* 17
mask *un masque,* 17
math *les maths* (m.), 4
mathematics *les mathématiques* (m.), 17
matter: as a matter of fact *d'ailleurs,* 14; What's the matter with you . . . .? *Qu'est-ce que vous avez…?* 22
May *mai* (m.), 12
maybe *peut-être (que),* 3, 24
me *moi,* 1; (to, for) me *me,* 10
meadow *un pré,* 16
meal *un repas,* 7, 8
to **measure** *mesurer,* 22
meat *la viande,* 8
medina *une médina,* 20
medium: of medium height *de taille moyenne,* 7
to **meet** *rencontrer,* 4; to meet each other *se rencontrer,* 19
meeting *un rendez-vous,* 13

melon un melon, 8
member un membre, 14
merchant un(e) commerçant(e), 7
meter un mètre, 12, 22; 100-meter dash le 100 m, 22
microphone un micro(phone), 14
middle distance run le demi-fond, 22
midnight minuit, 4
mild doux, douce, 24
milk le lait, 5
to **milk** traire, 16
mine le mien, la mienne, les miens, les miennes, 23
mineral water l'eau minérale (f.), 5
minute une minute, 5
Miss mademoiselle (Mlle), 4
to **miss** rater, 19
mistake: spelling mistake une faute d'orthographe, 4; (wrong number) une erreur, 6
mitt: wash mitt un gant de toilette, 13
model une maquette, 3; un modèle, 13; model airplane une maquette d'avion, 3
modern moderne, 10
mom, mommy maman, 7
Monday lundi (m.), 4; on Mondays le lundi, 4
money l'argent (m.), 5
monkey un singe, 24
month un mois, 7; the months of the year les mois de l'année, 12
monument un monument, 11
moped un vélomoteur, 3
moray eel une murène, 17
more: more . . . than plus... que, 22; no . . . more ne... plus, 5
morning le matin, 4; une matinée, 13
Moroccan marocain, –e, 19
Morocco le Maroc, 19
most: the most . . . (in) le/la/les plus... (de), 22
mother une mère, 7
motorcycle une moto, 3
mountain une montagne, 15
mousse: chocolate mousse une mousse au chocolat, 8
mouth la bouche, 22
movie un film, 5; movies le cinéma, 5
to **mow** tondre, 7
Mr. monsieur (M.), 4
Mrs. madame (Mme), 4
much beaucoup (de), 2, 8; so much tant, 16; too much trop (de), 8
museum un musée, 11
mushroom un champignon, 8
music la musique, 4, 9, 14; folk music la musique folk, 14; pop music la musique pop, 14
musician un(e) musicien(ne), 14
must il faut (que), 4
mustard la moutarde, 8
mutual commun, –e, 13

my mon, ma, mes, 7
myself me, 13

N

name un nom, 1, 4; What is your name? Comment t'appelles-tu? 1; My name is . . . Je m'appelle..., 1
named: to be named s'appeler, 13
napkin une serviette, 8; napkin ring un rond de serviette, 8
national national, –e, 24
nationality une nationalité, 19
natural naturel, –elle, 24
nature la nature, 24
near près (de), 1
neat en place, 13
neck le cou, 22
necklace un collier, 9
necktie une cravate, 13
neighbor voisin, –e, 14
neither . . . nor . . . (ne...) ni... ni..., 5, 7
net un filet, 2; landing net une épuisette, 17
never (ne...) jamais, 7
new nouveau, nouvel, nouvelle, nouveaux, nouvelles, 16; original, –e (m. pl. : –aux), 23
news des nouvelles (f.), 12; TV news le journal télévisé, 24
newspaper un journal (pl. : –aux), 5
next prochain, –e, 22
next to à côté (de), 4
nice sympathique, 10; it's nice (weather) il fait bon, 15; the weather is nice il fait beau, 13, 15
niceness la gentillesse, 13; so nice d'une telle gentillesse, 13
night la nuit, 18; Good night! Bonne nuit! 13; bonsoir, 13; last night hier soir, 9
no non, 1
no aucun, –e, 19
nobody (ne...) personne, 13; personne (ne)..., 13
no more ne... plus, 5, 7
noodles des pâtes (f.), 8
noon midi, 4
north le nord, 17; north (of) au nord (de), 15
nose le nez, 22
not pas, 2; ne... pas, 3; not . . . anybody ne... personne, 13; not . . . anymore ne... plus, 5, 7; not . . . anything ne... rien, 6, 7, 13
notebook un cahier, 4
noted: to be noted à noter, 22
nothing (ne...) rien, 6, 7, 13; rien (ne)..., 13; nothing like it rien de tel, 21
novel un roman, 13
November novembre (m.), 12
now maintenant, 4; en ce moment, 9

number un numéro, 4; numbers les nombres, 1; (musical) un morceau (pl. : -x), 14; What number do you want? Quel numéro demandez-vous? 6; wrong number une erreur, 6
nurse un(e) infirmier (–ière), 7

O

oats l'avoine (f.), 16
occupation une occupation, 7
occupied occupé, –e, 6
o'clock: it's (one) o'clock il est (une heure) (1 h), 4
October octobre (m.), 12
octopus une pieuvre, 17
of de, 1
office un bureau (pl. : –x), 4; administration office un bureau de l'administration, 4; office worker un(e) employé(e) de bureau, 7
official officiel, –ielle, 24
often souvent, 3
oil and vinegar une vinaigrette, 8
okay d'accord, 5; Everything's okay. Ça va. 6
old vieux, vieil, vieille, vieux, vieilles, 16; old friend mon vieux, ma vieille, 3; How old are you? Quel âge as-tu? 1; I am . . . years old. J'ai... ans. 1
omelet une omelette, 8
on sur, 1; à, 10
once une fois, 11
one (people, they, we) on, 2; the one(s) celui (-là), celle (-là), celles (-là), ceux (-là), 14
oneself se, 13
only seulement, 3
open ouvrez, 4
open ouvert, –e, 13
opportunity une occasion, 12
or ou, 1
orange (color) l'orange (m.), 2; (fruit) une orange, 8
order: in order en ordre, 9
to **order** commander, 5
organ un orgue, 14
original original, –e (m. pl. : –aux), 23
our notre, 7; nos, 7
ours le nôtre, la nôtre, les nôtres, 18, 23
ourselves nous, 13
outcome un résultat, 22
outing une sortie, 5
outside en plein air, 13
oval ovale, 2
over au-dessus (de), 20
own: one's own propre, 15; their own room une pièce à eux, 9; its very own life une vie bien à elle, 10

P

page *une page,* 4
painter *un peintre,* 24
painting *un tableau* (pl. : –x), 24
pal *un copain,* 9
palace *un palais,* 12
panic: Don't panic! *Pas de panique!* 21
panther *une panthère,* 24
pants *un pantalon,* 9
paragraph *un paragraphe,* 16
parallel bars *les barres parallèles,* 22
parents (mother, father) *les parents* (m.), 7
park *un parc,* 10
part *une partie,* 22; to be part (of) *faire partie (de),* 10
party *une surprise-partie,* 9
to **pass** *passer,* 8; to pass by *passer,* 10
passenger *un(e) passager (–ère),* 19
passing *un passage,* 18
pastime *un passe-temps* (pl. : *passe-temps*), 3
pastry *un gâteau* (pl. : -x), 8; bakery-pastry shop *une boulangerie-pâtisserie,* 8
pâté *le pâté,* 5
path *une allée,* 21
to **pay** *payer,* 5; *rapporter,* 14; It doesn't pay enough! *Ça ne rapporte pas!* 20
peach *une pêche,* 8
pear *une poire,* 8
pearl *une perle,* 17
to **peel** *éplucher,* 20; (to pull the skin away) *peler,* 20
pen: ballpoint pen *un stylo à bille,* 4; felt-tip pen *un feutre,* 4
pencil *un crayon,* 4
peninsula *une presqu'île,* 17
pen pal *un(e) correspondant(e),* 19
people *les gens,* 7; young people *les jeunes,* 3; (one, they, we) *on,* 2
pepper *le poivre,* 8; green pepper *un poivron doux,* 20
perched *perché, –e,* 18
perfect *parfait, –e,* 15
performance *une performance,* 22
perfume *le parfum,* 23; perfume shop *une parfumerie,* 23
permission *la permission,* 24
persistent *tenace,* 21
personal *personnel, –elle,* 22
phone *le téléphone,* 6; phone book *un annuaire,* 6; phone booth *une cabine téléphonique,* 6; phone call *un coup de téléphone,* 6; on the phone *au téléphone,* 6
photograph *une photo,* 3
photographer *un(e) photographe,* 3
pianist *un(e) pianiste,* 7
piano *un piano,* 7, 14
to **pick** *cueillir,* 16; to pick up the receiver *décrocher,* 6

picnic *un pique-nique,* 18; to have a picnic *pique-niquer,* 20
picture *une photo,* 3; *une image,* 24; the picture flips *l'image saute,* 24; to take pictures *faire de la photo,* 3
picturesque *pittoresque,* 17
pie *une tarte,* 8
piece *un morceau* (pl. : –x), 14
pig *cochon,* 16
pigeon *un pigeon,* 13
pineapple *un ananas,* 8
pine tree *un pin,* 18
Ping-Pong *le ping-pong,* 2
pirate *un corsaire,* 17
Pisces *les Poissons,* 21
pistachio (flavor) *la pistache,* 5; pistachio ice cream *une glace à la pistache,* 5
place *un lieu,* 12, 17; in place of *à la place (de),* 16; in place *en place,* 13; to take place *avoir lieu,* 9
place setting *un couvert,* 8
plain *une plaine,* 17
to **plant** *planter,* 16
plate *une assiette,* 8
platform *une estrade,* 14
platter *un plateau* (pl. : –x), 20
to **play** (a sport) *jouer à,* 2; (a game) *jouer à,* 3; (an instrument) *jouer de,* 14; to play hide and seek *jouer à cache-cache,* 21
playback button *un bouton d'écoute,* 14
please *s'il te (vous) plaît,* 4
to **please** *faire plaisir à,* 11; *plaire (à),* 23
pleased *content, –e,* 18; to be pleased (to) *avoir le plaisir (de),* 14
to **plug in** *brancher,* 14
plural *le pluriel,* 6
point *un point,* 3
polo shirt *un polo,* 9
pond *un étang,* 10
poor *mauvais, –e,* 4
population *la population,* 24
pork *le porc,* 8; pork butcher *un(e) charcutier (–ière),* 8; pork chop *une côtelette de porc,* 8; potted pork *les rillettes,* 5
port *un port,* 1
portfolio *un porte-documents* (pl. : *porte-documents*), 23
Portugal *le Portugal,* 19
Portuguese (language) *le portugais,* 19
Portuguese *portugais, -e,* 19
to **post** *afficher,* 9
post card *une carte postale,* 16
post office *une poste,* 10
poster *une affiche,* 3
pot *un pot,* 8; *une marmite,* 20
potato *une pomme de terre,* 8; potato chips *les chips* (f.), 9
potter *un potier,* 20
pottery: piece of pottery *une*

poterie, 20
pound *une livre,* 8
to **pour** *verser,* 8
practical *pratique,* 24
to **predict** *prédire,* 21
to **prefer** *aimer mieux,* 2; *préférer,* 14
preparations *des préparatifs* (m.), 23
to **present** *présenter,* 14
to **press** *appuyer,* 14
pretty *beau, bel, belle, beaux, belles,* 16; *joli, –e,* 10
prince *un prince,* 12
princess *une princesse,* 12
problem *un problème,* 6, 24
process: in the process of . . . *en train de…,* 3
profession *une profession,* 7
program *un programme,* 14; *une émission,* 24
project *un projet,* 17
propped up *appuyé, –e,* 22
to **protect** *abriter,* 16
Provence: from Provence *provençal, –e,* 8
to **pull the skin away** *peler,* 20
pullover *un pull,* 9
pump *une pompe,* 18
pupil *un(e) élève,* 4
purchase *un achat,* 20
purse: change purse *un porte-monnaie* (pl. : *porte-monnaie*), 23
to **push off** *s'élancer,* 15
to **put on** *mettre,* 9

Q

quarter *un quart,* 4; ¼ liter *un quart,* 5; quarter past (the hour) *et quart,* 4; quarter to/of (the hour) *moins le quart,* 4
Quebec (Province) *le Québec,* 15
question *une question,* 4; *une colle,* 19; to ask questions *poser des questions,* 7
quickly *rapidement,* 22
to **quiz** *poser des colles,* 19

R

rabbit *un lapin,* 16
race *la course,* 22
racket *une raquette,* 2
radio *une radio,* 3
raffle *la loterie,* 21
railroad station *une gare,* 10
to **rain** *pleuvoir,* 15; it's raining *il pleut,* 15
to **raise** *lever,* 8; to raise one's hand *lever la main,* 4
rather *assez,* 4; *plutôt,* 16
razor *un rasoir,* 23
to **read** *lire,* 3; *consulter,* 6; he reads *il lit,* 3; read *lisez,* 4; they read *ils lisent,* 7

ready *prêt, –e,* 5
ready: to get ready *préparer,* 6; *se préparer,* 15
really *vraiment,* 2
to **rear** *élever,* 7, 8
receipt *un reçu,* 23
to **receive** *recevoir,* 12
receiver *un combiné,* 6
recitation *la récitation,* 4
to **recognize** *reconnaître,* 16; to recognize each other *se reconnaître,* 19
record *disque,* 3; record-player *un électrophone,* 9; record *un record,* 22; record card *une fiche de progression,* 22
to **record** *enregistrer,* 7, 14; record button *un bouton d'enregistrement,* 14
recording *un enregistrement,* 14
red *le rouge,* 2; red (headed) *roux, rousse,* 7
reef *un récif,* 17
Regards! *Meilleurs souvenirs!* 12
regularly *régulièrement,* 22
rehearsal *une répétition,* 14
to **rehearse** *répéter,* 14
to **relax** *se détendre,* 13
to **remember** *se souvenir de,* 16
to **rent** *louer,* 15
to **replace** *remplacer,* 14; replacing *en remplaçant,* 10
report card *un bulletin trimestriel,* 4
republic *une république,* 24
resemblance *une ressemblance,* 7
residential *résidentiel, –ielle,* 10
resort *une station,* 15
to **rest** *se reposer,* 13
retired: to be retired *être à la retraite,* 7
to **return** *retourner,* 11
review unit *chapitre de révision,* 6
to **rewind** *rembobiner,* 14
rewrite *(vous) récrivez,* 6
riches: embarrassment of riches *l'embarras du choix,* 23
riddle *une devinette,* 11
ride *un tour,* 2; a ride *un manège,* 21; to take a ride *faire un tour,* 2
to **ride (a horse)** *monter,* 16
right *droit, –e,* 22; on (to) the right *à droite,* 8, 10
right: right away *tout de suite,* 4; *immédiatement,* 13; right here *juste ici,* 4; to be right *avoir raison,* 23
ring *une bague,* 9
to **ring** *sonner,* 6
rings *les anneaux (m.),* 22
rink: skating rink *une patinoire,* 5
ripe *mûr, –e,* 8
roast of beef *un rôti de bœuf,* 8
rock *un rocher,* 17
rock music *le rock,* 14
roller coaster *un grand huit,* 21
room *une salle,* 4; *une pièce,* 10
room: enough room *assez de place,* 5

rope *la corde lisse,* 22; knotted rope *la corde à nœuds,* 22
round *rond, –e,* 2
route *le chemin,* 10; *un circuit,* 17
rug *un tapis,* 20
rugby *le rugby,* 2
rug-maker *un(e) tapissier (–ière),* 20
ruler *une règle,* 4
to **run** *courir,* 22
running *la course,* 22
to **rush** *foncer,* 21
Russia (U.S.S.R.) *la Russie (l'U.R.S.S.),* 19
Russian (language) *le russe,* 19
Russian *russe,* 19

S

sail *une voile,* 18
to **sail** *faire de la voile,* 18
sailing school *une école de voile,* 18
salad *une salade,* 8
salami *un saucisson,* 5
salesperson *un(e) marchand(e),* 8
salt *le sel,* 8
salutation *une formule de début,* 12
same *même,* 10
sand *le sable,* 17
sandal *une sandale,* 9
sandwich *un sandwich,* 5
Saturday *samedi (m.),* 4
saucer *une soucoupe,* 12
savannah *une savane,* 24
to **save** *économiser,* 8; *faire des économies,* 23
saxophone *un saxo(phone),* 14
to **say (to)** *dire (à),* 19; he/she says *il/elle dit,* 4; Say! *Tiens!* 7; say (vous) *dites,* 4; they say (that) *il paraît (que),* 5
scaredy-cat *un(e) froussard(e),* 21
scarf *un foulard,* 23
schedule *un emploi du temps,* 4
school *une école,* 4; elementary school *une école primaire,* 17; high school *un lycée,* 7; secondary school *un CES,* 4; sailing school *une école de voile,* 18; school trophy *un trophée scolaire,* 22
schoolbag *un cartable,* 4
schoolyard *une cour,* 4
school year *une année scolaire,* 4
science *les sciences (f.),* 4; science fiction *la science-fiction,* 3
scientific *scientifique,* 24
score: to keep score *marquer les points,* 3
sculpture *une sculpture,* 13
sea *une mer,* 1; Caribbean Sea *la mer des Caraïbes,* 1
sea horse *un hippocampe,* 17
seasick: to be seasick *avoir le mal de mer,* 21
seasickness *le mal de mer,* 21
season *une saison,* 14, 15; What

season is it? *Quelle saison est-ce?* 15
to **season** *assaisonner,* 20
sea urchin *un oursin,* 17
second *une seconde,* 22
secondary *secondaire,* 4
to **see** *voir,* 11; Let's see! *Voyons!* 9
to **seem** *sembler,* 18; it seems . . . *il paraît que…,* 5
to **sell** *vendre,* 8
semolina *la semoule,* 20
to **send** *envoyer,* 16
sender *un(e) expéditeur (-trice),* 12
Senegal *le Sénégal,* 19
Senegalese *sénégalais, -e,* 19
sentence *une phrase,* 5
September *septembre (m.),* 12
serial *un feuilleton,* 24
series *une série,* 24
serious *sérieux, –euse,* 4
to **serve** *servir,* 8
set: to set an alarm *remonter un réveil,* 13; to set the table *mettre la table,* 8; to set up *installer,* 14
to **settle in** *s'installer,* 18
shade *l'ombre (f.),* 17; in the shade *à l'ombre,* 17
to **shake off** *semer,* 21
shampoo *le shampooing,* 13
shape *une forme,* 12
to **share** *partager,* 13
shark *un requin,* 17
she *elle,* 2
shed *un abri,* 4; *un *hangar,* 16; bicycle shed *un abri pour bicyclettes,* 4
sheep *un mouton,* 16
shell *un coquillage,* 3
shiny *brillant, –e,* 24
shirt *une chemise,* 9
shoe *une chaussure,* 9
shoemaker *un cordonnier,* 20
shooting gallery *le tir,* 21
shop *les travaux manuels (m.),* 4
to **shop** *faire des courses,* 11; *faire des achats,* 20
shop: bakery-pastry shop *une boulangerie-pâtisserie,* 8; butcher shop *une boucherie,* 8; flower shop *chez un fleuriste,* 23; jewelry shop *une bijouterie,* 23; meat shop specializing in pork products and prepared dishes *une charcuterie,* 8; perfume shop *une parfumerie,* 23
shopping: shopping arcade *une galerie marchande,* 23; shopping street *une rue commerçante,* 10
shore: at the shore *au bord de la mer,* 17
short *petit, –e,* 7
shot *le poids,* 22
shoulder *l'épaule (f.),* 22
to **show** *montrer,* 7
shy *timide,* 4
side: on my mother's side *du côté de ma mère,* 7; on the boys' side *du côté garçons,* 22

sign *une signe*, 21
signal: to give the signal to start *donner le départ*, 22
silk *la soie*, 23; made of silk *en soie*, 23
silver *l'argent* (m.), 20
simple *simple*, 3
simply *simplement*, 23
since *depuis*, 10
to **sing** *chanter*, 9
singer *un(e) chanteur (-euse)*, 14
sister *une sœur*, 7
site *un site*, 17
size *la taille*, 22
ski *un ski*, 15
to **ski** *faire du ski*, 2; *skier*, 15
ski area *une station de ski*, 15
ski boot *une chaussure de ski*, 15
ski cap *un bonnet*, 15
skier *un(e) skieur (-euse)*, 15
skiing *le ski*, 15
ski instructor *un(e) moniteur (-trice)*, 15
ski jacket *un anorak*, 15
ski pants *un pantalon de ski*, 15
ski pole *un bâton*, 15
ski resort *une station de ski*, 15
skirt *une jupe*, 9
ski trail *une piste*, 15
to **sleep** *dormir*, 18; to sleep like a log *dormir à poings fermés*, 18
sleeping bag *un sac de couchage*, 18
slice *une tranche*, 8; slice of bread (with butter and/or jam on it) *une tartine*, 13
slope *une pente*, 15
slow *lent, –e*, 9
slowly *lentement*, 22
small *petit, –e*, 1
to **smell** *sentir*, 18
smiled: she smiled at me *elle m'a souri*, 11
snake: poisonous snake *une vipère*, 18
snorkel *un tuba*, 17
snow *la neige*, 15
to **snow** *neiger*, 15; it's snowing *il neige*, 15
so *donc*, 10; so, such *tel, telle*, 13
soap *le savon*, 13
soccer *le football*, 2
social worker *une assistante sociale*, 17
soft *bas*, 14
soft *doux, douce*, 24
solution *une solution*, 8
some *du, de la, des*, 5
some *quelques*, 14
someone *quelqu'un*, 9
somersault *un saut périlleux*, 22
something *quelque chose*, 9
sometimes *quelquefois*, 7
song *une chanson*, 9; *un chant*, 7
soon *bientôt*, 16
sort *un genre*, 14

sound *le son*, 14; *la sono(risation)*, 14; sound engineer *un ingénieur du son*, 14; to be the sound engineer *faire l'ingénieur du son*, 14
soup *la soupe*, 8
south *le sud*, 17
Spain *l'Espagne* (f.), 19
Spanish (language) *l'espagnol* (m.), 19
Spanish *espagnol, –e*, 19
sparkling *pétillant, –e*, 24
spelling *l'orthographe* (f.), 4; spelling mistake *une faute d'orthographe*, 4
to **spend** (time) *passer*, 3, 7; (money) *dépenser*, 8; after spending *après avoir passé*, 13
spine *un piquant*, 17
spite: in spite of *malgré*, 10
splendid *splendide*, 17
sports *les sports*, 2
sportsperson *un(e) sportif (-ive)*, 22
to **spread out** *étaler*, 18
spring *le printemps*, 15; in the spring *au printemps*, 15
sprint *la vitesse*, 22
square *une place*, 11
stairway *un escalier*, 10
stall bars *les espaliers* (m.), 22
stamp *un timbre*, 3, 12
stand *un stand*, 21
standing up *debout*, 13
to **stand in line** *faire la queue*, 15
star *une étoile*, 18
starfish *une étoile de mer*, 17
to **start** *commencer*, 4; *débuter*, 22; to start again *recommencer*, 22; to start back *reprendre (le chemin)*, 13; to start (to) *commencer (à)*, 8; to start (with) *commencer (par)*, 4
starting point *un point de départ*, 17
static *des grésillements* (m.), 6
station: railroad station *une gare*, 10
to **stay** *rester*, 5
steak *un bifteck*, 8
steamed *cuit(e) à la vapeur*, 20
steering wheel *un volant*, 21
still *encore*, 7
to **stop** *s'arrêter*, 13; *arrêter*, 14
store *un magasin*, 13, 23; book and stationery store *une librairie-papeterie*, 23; clothing store *un magasin de vêtements*, 23; grocery store *une épicerie*, 8; leather-goods store *une maroquinerie*, 23
storm *une tempête*, 18
to **straighten up** *ranger*, 9
straw *la paille*, 16
strawberry (flavor) *la fraise*, 5
street *une rue*, 10; a main street *une grand-rue*, 10; a shopping street *une rue commerçante*, 10
strong *fort, –e*, 19
to **study** *étudier*, 4
subject *une matière*, 4
suburb *une banlieue*, 10

subway *le métro*, 13; to take the subway *prendre le métro*, 13
to **succeed (in)** *arriver (à)*, 6
such *tel, telle*, 13; such a thing *une chose pareille*, 12
sugar cane *la canne à sucre*, 17
to **suggest** *proposer*, 7
to **suit** *aller à*, 9
summer *l'été* (m.), 14, 15; in the summer *en été*, 15; summer camp *un camp de vacances*, 18
to **sunbathe** *se bronzer*, 17; *bronzer*, 24
Sunday *dimanche* (m.), 4
sunny: it's sunny *il y a du soleil*, 15
supermarket *un supermarché*, 8
supper *le dîner*, 8
sure *sûr, –e*, 3, 4
surprise *une surprise*, 22
to **surround** *entourer*, 10; surrounded by *entouré, –e de*, 17
to **sweep** *balayer*, 9
to **swerve** *virer*, 21
to **swim** *faire de la natation*, 2; *nager*, 17; to go swimming *se baigner*, 17
swimming *la natation*, 2
swimming pool *une piscine*, 5
swing: The party is going full swing. *La surprise-partie bat son plein.* 9; Stop making the car swing! *Arrête de faire tanguer la nacelle!* 21
Swiss cheese *le gruyère*, 5; Swiss cheese sandwich *un sandwich au gruyère*, 5
syrup *le sirop*, 5

T

table *une table*, 8; to set the table *mettre la table*, 8
to **tail** (to be at one's heels) *talonner*, 21
tailor *un tailleur*, 20
to **take** *prendre*, 8; (people, animals) *emmener*, 10; to take back *rentrer*, 11; to take care of *s'occuper (de)*, 13; to take down *descendre*, 11; to take a half hour *mettre une demi-heure*, 13; to take a jaunt *faire une promenade*, 11; to take off *retirer*, 14; to take off (airplane) *décoller*, 19; to take out *sortir*, 5; to take pains with *soigner*, 4; to take part (in) *participer (à)*, 22; to take pictures *faire de la photo*, 3; to take place *avoir lieu*, 9; to take a ride *faire un tour*, 2; to take a running start *prendre son élan*, 22; to take the subway *prendre le métro*, 13; to take a trip *faire un voyage*, 21; to take charge (of) *se charger (de)*, 16
tale: fairy tale *un conte de fées*, 21
talented (for) *doué, –e (pour)*, 4
to **talk** *parler*, 2; *bavarder*, 4; to talk over *discuter*, 3
tall *grand, –e*, 7

tape *une bande*, 14; tape recorder *un magnéto(phone)*, 14

target-shooting *le tir*, 21; to go target-shooting *faire un carton*, 21

tart *une tarte*, 8

tea *le thé*, 7

to **teach** *enseigner*, 7

teacher *un professeur*, 4

team *une équipe*, 2

to **tease** *taquiner*, 15

teaspoon *une petite cuillère*, 8

technology *la technologie*, 4

telephone *un appareil*, 6

telescope *un télescope*, 11

television *la télévision*, 3; to watch television *regarder la télévision*, 3

television set *une télévision*, 3; *un poste (de télévision)*, 24

to **tell** *raconter*, 12; *dire*, 19; (you) tell *(vous) dites*, 4; to tell how one's doing *donner de ses nouvelles*, 16

temperature *la température*, 15; What's the temperature? *Quelle température fait-il?* 15

ten: about ten *une dizaine*, 9

to **tend** *cultiver*, 16

tennis *le tennis*, 2

tent *une tente*, 18

tenth *un dixième*, 22

terrace *une terrasse*, 12

terribly *tellement*, 4

terrific *formidable*, 10; Terrific! *Ça tombe bien!* 5

test *un essai*, 14

thanks *merci*, 4

that *ce, cette*, 1; *cet*, 2; *ces*, 3

that *ça*, 2

that *que*, 4

that one *celui (-là), celle (-là)*, 14

the *le, la*, 1; *les*, 3

their *leur*, 3, 7; *leurs*, 6, 7

theirs *le leur, la leur, les leurs*, 23

them *eux, elles*, 7; (to, for) them *leur*, 8; *les*, 10

themselves *se*, 13

then *alors*, 3; *puis*, 6; *ensuite*, 8

there *y*, 11; *là*, 20; over there *là-bas*, 4; *par là*, 17

there is (are) *il y a*, 4

thermometer *un thermomètre*, 15

these *ces*, 3; *ceux (-là)*, 14; *celles (-là)*, 14

they *ils, elles*, 2; *on*, 2

thigh *la cuisse*, 22

thing *une chose*, 9; *un truc*, 21

to **think** *trouver*, 2; I think *je crois*, 14

thirsty: to be thirsty *avoir soif*, 5

this *ce, cet, cette*, 1

this one *celui (-là), celle (-là)*, 14

those *ces*, 3; *ceux (-là)*, 14; *celles (-là)*, 14

thoughts: best thoughts *meilleures pensées*, 12

throw *un lancer*, 22

to **throw** *jeter*, 17; *lancer*, 22

Thursday *jeudi (m.)*, 4

ticket *un billet*, 12

tied (score) *ex aequo*, 22

time *le temps*, 3; *la fois*, 11; a long time ago *il y a longtemps*, 11; at the same time *en même temps*, 13; à la fois, 17; at the time of *lors de*, 22; from time to time *de temps en temps*, 10; on time *à l'heure*, 19; What time is it? *Quelle heure est-il?* 4

to **time** *chronométrer*, 22

to **tinker** *bricoler*, 3

tip *un pourboire*, 5; tip included *service compris*, 5

tip *une extrémité*, 17

tired *fatigué, –e*, 9

title *un titre*, 9

to *à*, 1; *chez*, 5

today *aujourd'hui*, 5

together *ensemble*, 7; to bring together *réunir*, 22; to get together *se réunir*, 18

toilet *des W.-C.*, 10

toilet article *un objet de toilette*, 13

tomato *une tomate*, 8

tomb *un tombeau*, 11

tomorrow *demain*, 11

too *aussi*, 1; *trop*, 2; too much, too many *trop (de)*, 8; too bad *tant pis*, 9; *dommage*, 18

tooth *une dent*, 13; toothbrush *une brosse à dents*, 13; toothpaste *le dentifrice*, 13

top: on top of *en *haut de*, 11; *au-dessus (de)*, 20

to **toss a coin** *jouer à pile ou face*, 10

to **touch** *toucher*, 22

tourist *un(e) touriste*, 20

toward *vers*, 14

tower *une tour*, 11; the Eiffel Tower *la Tour Eiffel*, 11

town *une ville*, 1; town hall *une mairie*, 10

toy: toy car *une petite voiture*, 3

tractor *un tracteur*, 16

trade *un métier*, 20

traditional *traditionnel, –elle*, 24; in the traditional way *à la façon traditionnelle*, 24

to **train** *s'entraîner*, 22

training *l'entraînement (m.)*, 22

translation (into a foreign language) *un thème*, 4; (from a foreign language) *une version*, 4

transparent *transparent, –e*, 17

tree *un arbre*, 10

trip *un trajet*, 13; trip home *un trajet de retour*, 13; boat trip *une sortie en mer*, 13

trombone *un trombone*, 14

trophy *une coupe*, 10

tropical *tropical, –e*, 17

tropics *les Tropiques (m.)*, 17

trouble *une difficulté*, 3

true *vrai, –e*, 3, 4

trumpet *une trompette*, 14

to **try** *essayer*, 7; to try one's luck

tenter sa chance, 21

T-shirt *un Ti-shirt*, 9

tuba *un tuba*, 14

Tuesday *mardi (m.)*, 4

tune *un air*, 14

Tunisia *la Tunisie*, 19

Tunisian *tunisien, –ienne*, 19

Turkey *la Turquie*, 19

turn *un tour*, 14; at a turn in *au détour de*, 21; it's your turn (to) *c'est à toi (de)*, 3; (Your) turn! *A (ton) tour!* 21

to **turn** *tourner*, 10; to turn off the TV set *éteindre le poste*, 24; to turn on the TV *mettre la télévision*, 24; to turn on the TV set *allumer le poste*, 24; he/she turns out the light *il/elle éteint*, 13

turtle *une tortue*, 17

TV *la télé*, 2

U

uncle *un oncle*, 7

to **uncover** *dévoiler*, 21

under *sous*, 11

underlined *souligné, –e*, 6

to **understand** *comprendre;* 19

underwater *sous-marin, –e*, 12

to **undress** *se déshabiller*, 13

unfortunately *malheureusement*, 11

unit *un chapitre*, 1; review unit *un chapitre de révision*, 6

United States *les Etats-Unis (m.)*, 1, 19; in the United States *aux Etats-Unis*, 1

to **unplug** *débrancher*, 14

until *jusqu'à*, 11

us *nous*, 5; (to, for) us *nous*, 10

to **use** *utiliser*, 13; using *en utilisant*, 6

U.S.S.R. *l'U.R.S.S. (f.)*, 19

usually *en général*, 7

V

vacation *les vacances (f.)*, 14

vanilla (flavor) *la vanille*, 5; vanilla ice cream *une glace à la vanille*, 5

varied *varié, –e*, 8

variety: variety show *une émission de variétés*, 24

vaulting horse *le cheval de voltige*, 22

to **veer**, *virer*, 21

vegetable *un légume*, 8; vegetable garden *un jardin potager*, 16

vertigo *le vertige*, 21

very *très*, 1; *tout*, 18

victory *une victoire*, 22

view *une vue*, 11

village *un village*, 1

violin *un violon*, 14

visit *une visite*, 11

to **visit** *visiter*, 11

volcano *un volcan*, 17

volleyball *le volley-ball,* 2
volume *le volume,* 14

W

waist *la taille,* 22
waiter *un garçon,* 5
to **wait for** *attendre,* 7; Wait a minute!
Attendez! 5
to **wait on** *s'occuper de,* 13
wake *le sillage,* 17
to **wake up** *se réveiller,* 13
walk *une promenade,* 7
to **walk** *aller à pied,* 13; *se promener,*
13; *marcher,* 19
walkway *une allée,* 21
wall *un mur,* 16
wallet *un portefeuille,* 20
walnut tree *un noyer,* 16
to **want** *avoir envie de,* 5; *désirer,* 5;
vouloir, 17; he/she wants *il/elle
veut,* 6; they want *ils/elles veulent,*
5; you want *tu veux,* 3
warm-up *la mise en train,* 22
to **warm up** *se réchauffer,* 15; *se mettre
en train,* 22
to **wash** *laver,* 13; to get washed *faire
sa toilette,* 13; *se laver,* 13
wash mitt *un gant de toilette,* 13
watch *une veille,* 18; *une montre,* 23
to **watch** *regarder,* 2; to watch television *regarder la télévision,* 3
Watch out! *Attention!* 14
watchtower *un sémaphore,* 18
water *l'eau* (f.), 5; mineral water
l'eau minérale, 5; to give water to
donner à boire à, 16
wave *une vague,* 17
way (route) *le chemin,* 10; (manner)
une façon, 19; his/her own way *de
son côté,* 8
we *nous,* 2; *on,* 2
weak *mou, molle,* 21; *faible,* 22
wealthy *riche,* 21
to **wear** *porter,* 7
weather *le temps,* 15; the weather
is nice *il fait beau,* 13; the weather
is bad *il fait mauvais,* 15; weather
report *la météo,* 15; What's the
weather like? *Quel temps fait-il?* 15
wedding *un mariage,* 14

Wednesday *mercredi* (m.), 4
week *une semaine,* 7
weekend *un week-end,* 17
Welcome! *Soyez les bienvenus!* 17
well *bien,* 3
west *l'ouest* (m.), 17
western (film) *un western,* 5
western *occidental, –e,* 24
West Indies *les Antilles* (f.), 17
what *comment,* 1
what *ce que,* 2
what *quel, quelle, quels, quelles,* 14
what *qu'est-ce que,* 2, 20; *qu'est-ce
qui,* 20; *quoi,* 2; what else *quoi
d'autre,* 23
wheat *le blé,* 16; wheat field *un
champ de blé,* 16
when *quand,* 5
where *où,* 1; it's where *c'est là que,*
23
which *que,* 4
which *quel, quelle, quels, quelles,* 14
which one(s) *lequel, laquelle, lesquels, lesquelles,* 14
white *le blanc,* 2
who *qui,* 1; *qui est-ce qui,* 3, 20
whole: the whole *tout, toute, tous,
toutes,* 7; the whole thing *le tout,* 20
whom *qui,* 3; *qui est-ce que,* 20
why *pourquoi,* 2
wife *une femme,* 16
wild *sauvage,* 17; It's too wild! *C'est
dément!* 21
win *gagner,* 3; *remporter,* 22
wind *le vent,* 15
window *une fenêtre,* 24; store window *une vitrine,* 13
windy: it's windy *il fait du vent,* 15
wine *le vin,* 8; a bottle of wine *une
bouteille de vin,* 8
winner *un vainqueur,* 22
winter *l'hiver* (m.), 15; in the winter
en hiver, 15
wish *un souhait,* 23
with *avec,* 2
without *sans,* 13; without buying
sans avoir acheté, 13
Wolof *le ouolof,* 19
woods *un bois,* 7, 16; wood fire *un
feu de bois,* 15
word *un mot,* 4
work *le travail,* 4

to **work** *travailler,* 7; (to function)
marcher, 9
worker: factory worker *un(e)
ouvrier (–ière),* 7; office worker
un(e) employé(e) de bureau, 7
world *le monde,* 17; to go around
the world *faire le tour du monde,* 21
to **write** *écrire,* 12; (you) write *écrivez,*
4; to write a little something *écrire un
petit mot,* 23; to write down *noter,*
18; in writing *par correspondance,*
19
writing paper *du papier à lettres,* 23
written *écrit, –e,* 4
wrong: everything's going wrong
tout va mal, 9; wrong number *une
erreur,* 6

X

xylophone *un xylophone,* 14

Y

year *un an,* 1; *une année,* 4; every
year *tous les ans,* 7; school year
l'année scolaire, 4; to be . . . years
old *avoir... ans,* 1
yellow *le jaune,* 2
yes *oui,* 1; *si,* 2, 3
yesterday *hier,* 9
yet: not yet *ne... pas encore,* 9
yogurt *un yaourt,* 8
you *toi,* 1; *tu,* 2; *vous,* 2, 5; (to,
for) you *te, vous,* 10
young *jeune,* 16; young people *les
jeunes,* 3
your *ton, ta, tes,* 7; *votre, vos,* 4, 7
yours *le tien, la tienne, les tiens, les
tiennes,* 23; *le vôtre, la vôtre, les
vôtres,* 23
yourself *te, vous,* 13; yourselves
vous, 13
youth center *une maison des jeunes,*
10

Z

zero *un zéro,* 15; it's zero degrees
il fait zéro, 15
zip code *un code postal,* 12
Zodiac *le Zodiaque,* 21

English-French Vocabulary   293

Grammar Index

à: contractions with **le, les,** 36; contractions with **lequel, lesquels, lesquelles,** 158; used with names of countries, 196; following verbs, 211f

acheter, verbs like: present, 78; passé composé, 89; imparfait, 169f; future, 219; conditional, 239; summary, 260

address: formal and informal, 38

adjectives: gender markers, 6f; like **distrait, sérieux, doué, timide,** 41; agreement with noun: gender, 41; number, 61; review, 61; summary, 257; position, 66; **beau, nouveau, vieux,** 164; comparatives of, 231; superlatives of, 234; review of comparatives and superlatives, 254. See also interrogative adjectives.

adverbs: formation, 228; comparatives of, 231; superlatives of, 234

agreement: of adjectives with noun: gender, 41; number, 61; of past participle with preceding direct-object pronoun, 106f; of past participle with subject, 112f; of past participle with preceding direct object, 146; of past participle with reflexive pronoun, 156

aller: present, 34; passé composé, 112f; imparfait, 169f; future, 219; conditional, 239; summary, 261; **aller** plus infinitive, 54

appeler, verbs like: present **(je, tu, il),** 2; present **(nous, vous, ils),** 140. See summary, 261.

appuyer, verbs like: present, 150. See summary, 261.

articles: gender markers, 6f; **ce, cette,** 6f, **ces,** 23f; **le, la,** 6f, **les,** 23f; **un, une,** 6f, **des,** 23f; **le, la, les** meaning "in general," 50; review, 59f; **le, la, les** with names of countries, 196; **le** with names of languages, 199; **le, la, les** with nouns referring to the body, 228. See also possessive articles. See summary, 257.

attendre, verbs like: present, 72; passé composé, 89; imparfait, 169f; future, 218f; conditional, 239. See summary, 258.

avoir: present, 30; as auxiliary in passé composé, 89; passé composé, 91; imparfait, 169f; future, 219; conditional, 239. See summary, 262.

battre, verbs like: present, 236. See summary, 262.

beau, bel, belle: 164

boire: present, 93; passé composé, 93; imparfait, 169f; future, 218f; conditional, 239. See summary, 262.

cardinal numbers: one to twenty, 3;

twenty to one thousand, 28. See summary, 265.

ce: as subject pronoun before **être,** 199; with a superlative, 234

ce, cette, ces: see articles.

celui, celle, ceux, celles: 149

choisir, verbs like: present, 53; passé composé, 89; imparfait, 169f; future, 218f; conditional, 239. See summary, 258.

commands: forms and uses, 39; in negative constructions, 39; with pronouns: **lui, leur,** 84, **en,** 94, **le, la, les,** 101, **me, te, nous, vous,** 104, **y,** 116; in reflexive constructions, 131

commencer: present, 44; imparfait, 170. See summary, 261.

comparisons: of adjectives and adverbs, 231; irregular forms, 231; superlatives of adjectives and adverbs, 234; review of comparatives and superlatives of adjectives, 254

conditional: use and regular formation, 239; use in conditions, 243; review of formation and uses, 252

connaître: present, 100; passé composé, 100; vs **savoir,** 167; imparfait, 169f; future, 218f; conditional, 239. See summary, 262.

contractions: **à** and **de** with **le, les,** 36; **à** and **de** with **lequel, lesquels, lesquelles,** 158

countries: names of, 196, 199

courir: present, 230; passé composé, 230; imparfait, 169f; future, 230; conditional, 239. See summary, 262.

de: in negative constructions instead of **un, une, des,** 26f; contractions with **le, les,** 36; in negative constructions instead of **du, de la,** 51; in negative constructions, review, 59f; phrases with **de** replaced by **en,** 93f; contractions with **lequel, lesquels, lesquelles,** 158; before plural adjectives, 164; used with names of countries, 196; following verbs, 211f; following verbal expressions, 212

demonstrative pronouns: 149

dire: present, 199; passé composé, 199; imparfait, 169f; future, 218f; conditional, 239. See summary, 262.

direct object: explained, 84

direct-object pronouns: **le, la, les,** 100f; **me, te, nous, vous,** 103f

distrait, –e: adjectives like, 41

doué, –e: adjectives like, 41

du, de la: indicating quantity, 50

écrire, verbs like: present, 123; passé composé, 123; imparfait, 169f; future,

218f; conditional, 239; summary, 262

elision: explained, 17f; with subject pronoun, 17f; with articles, 18, 23f; 50; with **de,** 27; with **ne,** 27; with **est-ce que,** 48; with direct-object pronouns **le, la,** 101; with direct- and indirect-object pronouns **me, te,** 104; with reflexive pronouns, 131

elle: 2. See also independent pronouns.

en (preposition): used with names of countries, 196

en (pronoun): position and uses, 93f

envoyer, verbs like: present, 172. See summary, 263.

essayer, verbs like: present, 74. See summary, 261.

est-ce que: used in question formation, 48

être: present, 25; passé composé, 91; as auxiliary in passé composé, 112f; imparfait, 170; future, 219; conditional, 239. See summary, 263.

faire: present, 13; passé composé, 91; imparfait, 169f; future, 219; conditional, 239. See summary, 263.

feminine: gender, 6f

future tense: of verbs like **jouer, choisir, sortir, attendre,** 218f; for other verbs, see individual listings; after **quand,** 219; review of formation and uses, 252

future time: expressed by present tense, 54; expressed by **aller** plus infinitive, 54; review, 125. See future tense.

gender: explained, 6f; markers, 7

imparfait: of verbs like **jouer, choisir, sortir, attendre,** 169f; for other verbs, see individual listings; vs passé composé, 181; vs passé composé, review, 190

imperative: see commands.

independent pronouns: **moi, toi, lui, elle,** 2; all forms and uses, 73

indirect object: explained, 84

indirect-object pronouns: **lui, leur,** 83f; **me, te, nous, vous,** 103f

infinitive: explained, 16; following **aller,** 54; of reflexive verbs, 131; following **venir de,** 144; following verbs, 211f; after prepositions, 221; past infinitive, 221

interrogative adjectives: **quel, quelle, quels, quelles,** 146

interrogative pronouns: **lequel, laquelle, lesquels, lesquelles,** 148; contractions with **à** and **de,** 158; **qui est-ce qui, qu'est-ce qui, qui est-ce que, qu'est-ce que,** 206f; **qui** and **quoi** after prepositions, 206f

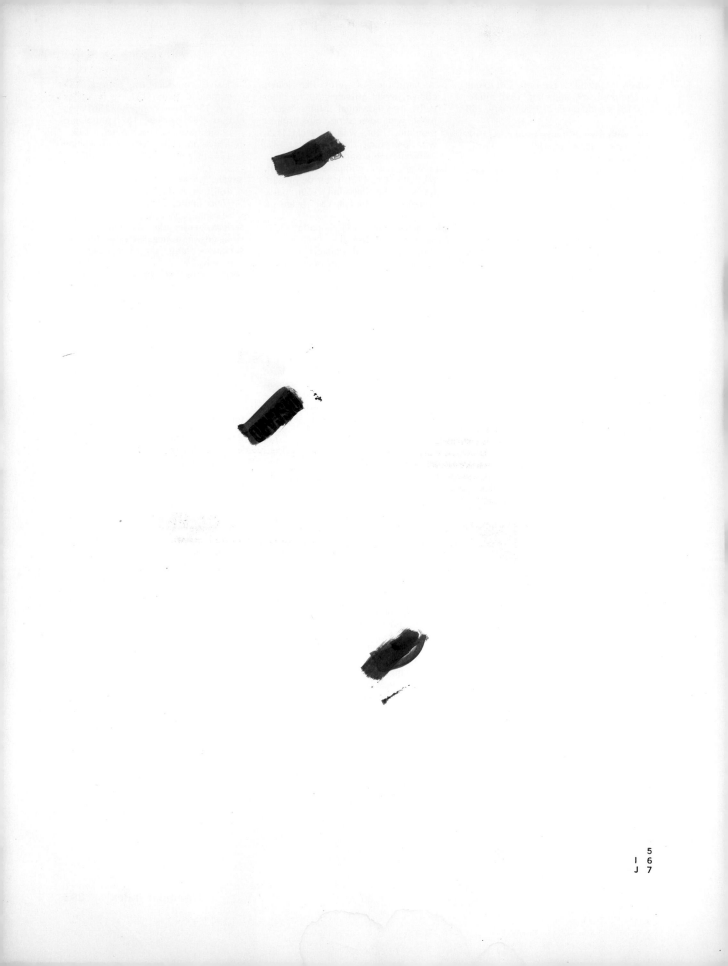